Contents

Foreword by Dr Paul O'Higgins		ix
Table of statutes		xi
Table of cases		xiv
1	**The emergence and definition in English law of the concept of obscenity**	**1**
	I The Hicklin test	5
2	**The Obscene Publications Acts**	**13**
	I Application	14
	II The standard applied	17
	III The jury	34
	IV Rationale of the offence	47
3	**The residual area of the common law**	**51**
	I Inchoate offences	51
	II Substantive common law offences	78

4	Morality, legality and policy	89
	I Legality	89
	II Strict liability	100
	III The enforcement of morality	105
5	Other statutory provisions I	127
	I Protection of children	129
	II Distribution/publication	145
6	Other statutory provisions II	179
	I Displays	179
	II Live shows	201
7	Prior restraint in UK	213
	I Prior restraints	217
	II Prior restriction not constituting a prior restraint	310
8	Enforcement of the law	313
	I The law officers	313
	II The police	315
	III Individuals	318
	IV Practice, policy and censorship	319
9	The constitutional dimension	325
	I Commitments in international law only	328
	II The Treaty of Rome and European Community Act 1972	331
	III A Bill of Rights	333
10	State and federal obscenity controls	345
	I State controls	345
	II Federal obscenity controls	362
11	The *Roth* test	371
	I Applicability	380
	II The standard applied	385
	III Jury decision	404

057
LSD
£21.00

CENSORSHIP AND PUBLIC MORALITY

To Daniel and Elizabeth

Censorship and Public Morality

P. R. MACMILLAN
BA LLB (NATAL),
LLB, Ph.D (Cantab),
formerly lecturer in law,
Bristol University

Gower

© P.R. MacMillan, 1983

All rights reserved. No part of this publication may be reproduced, stored in a retrieval system, or transmitted in any form or by any means, electronic, mechanical, photocopying, recording, or otherwise without the prior permission of Gower Publishing Company Limited.

Published by
Gower Publishing Company Limited,
Gower House,
Croft Road,
Aldershot,
Hants, GU11 3HR.

British Library Cataloguing in Publication Data

MacMillan, P.R.
  Censorship and public morality
  1. Censorship — Social aspects
  I. Title
  363.3'1   Z657   Z657

ISBN 0-566-00376-7

12	**Prior restraint in the USA**	411
	I Procedural standards defined	418
	II Customs controls	423
	III Motion picture censorship	425
	IV Live shows	432
	V Books	435
	VI Broadcasting	436
	VII Procedural problems not involving prior restraints	437
13	*Miller* **and the Burger Court**	441
	I The obscenity test	441
	II Applicability	443
	III The standard applicable	445
	IV Jury decision	453
14	**Obscenity and the First Amendment**	463
	I The *Roth* approach	463
	II Alternative approaches	473
15	**Policy and prohibition**	493
	I Harm to individuals	496
	II Paternalism	513
	III Society	514
Bibliography		521
Index		531

Figures

15.1 Indictable offences recorded by the police (England and Wales) 1946–78   507

15.2 Rape and sexual assault as a proportion of indictable offences recorded by the police   509

Foreword

Peter MacMillan is a very able young South African lawyer who has had experience both of the teaching and the practice of law. His book is concerned to analyse the ways in which British and American law has restricted freedom of expression on the particular ground that the material being communicated is obscene, pornographic or indecent. We already have a number of major contributions in this field. One may mention in particular Norman St John Stevas, *Obscenity and the Law* (Faber and Faber, 1956); Frederick F. Schauer, *The Law of Obscenity* (Bureau of National Affairs, Inc., Washington, 1976); Geoffrey Robertson, *Obscenity* (Weidenfeld and Nicolson, 1979), and the *Report of the Departmental Committee on Obscenity and Film Censorship* (Chairman: Bernard Williams; Cmnd. 7772, 1979). Peter MacMillan's book is an important and significant addition to this literature. Its strength lies only in part in the very detailed and critical analysis of the evolution of the law of obscenity in Great Britain and the United States of America. Despite their quite different constitutional frameworks there is much in common between the two systems' approach to obscenity, notwithstanding their more obvious differences. A vital thread running throughout Peter MacMillan's work is the constant question, why should the law impose criminal penalties upon those who write, produce or disseminate sexually explicit material, whether it be in the form of plays, films, books, periodicals or live shows? What clearly emerges from this book is that to this question there is no certain or secure answer capable of satisfying a liberally minded person as being sufficient to justify sending people to prison, fining them, ruining their livelihood or subjecting them to public obloquy. So far as adults are concerned the restrictions implicit in a law of obscenity can nowadays only possibly be justified on the grounds of the need to protect people against gratuitous offence, or more generally that the toleration of obscene material is damaging to some vague notion of public morality. As regards protecting people from offence there are many more offensive phenomena, poverty, famine, man's inhumanity to man, which the law does not give us protection against our being constantly exposed to them. As regards the public morality justification it rests upon certain assumptions rarely openly disclosed. Some years ago President Nixon was to give expression to this approach when he said 'if an attitude of permissiveness were to be adopted ... this would contribute to an atmosphere condoning anarchy in every other field and would increase the threat to our social order as well as our moral principles.' In the light of this one may legitimately conclude with William Seagle that 'in the last analysis all censorship is political censorship.'

Peter MacMillan writes as a rational libertarian, and having reviewed the evidence of the experience of obscenity laws and their apparent justification, concludes that there is no justification so far as adults are concerned of subjecting them to the law of obscenity. I think he would not disagree with Oscar Wilde, that sensible and sensitive Irishman, that there is no such thing as bad or immoral literature; the only legitimate distinction is between literature which is badly written and literature which is well written. Ultimately one is talking about matters of taste. There is something degrading about a system of legal rules that criminalises not behaviour that damages other humans but conduct which consists merely in the exercise of bad taste in the manner in which an aspect of the human dilemma is portrayed.

Paul O'Higgins
Christ's College
Cambridge

March 1983

Table of statutes

Bail Act 1976
  S 4(1)   255

Children and Young Persons
  (Harmful Publications)
  Act 1955   129
Criminal Law Act 1977
  S 1(1)   69, 76
  S 5(1)   76
  S 5(3)   69, 76
  S 5(6)   68
  S 5(7)   69, 73, 288
  S 53(1)   288
Cinematograph Act 1909
  S 2(1)   273
  S 5(1)(a)(2)   276
  S 5(3)(4)   276
  S 7(2)   276
  S 7(3)   276
Cinematograph Act 1952
  S 3(1)   280, 285
  S 69   284
Customs Consolidation Act
  1876

  S 42a   152, 153,
                                   331–332
Customs and Excise Management Act 1979
  S 49   236
  S 50   152
  S 139   236
  S 170(2)   153
  S 290(2)   153

Disorderly Houses Act 1781
  S 8   85

European Communities Act
  1972   331

Indecency with Children
  Act 1960
  S 1(1)   74, 218
Indecent Advertisements
  Act 1889
  S 3   182
  S 5   182
Independent Broadcasting

Authority Act 1973
S 4(1)(a) 300
S 5(1) 300
S 18(3) 300

Judicial Proceedings (Regulation of Reports) Act 1926
S 1(1) 157, 174

Metropolitan Police Act 1839
S 54(12)

Obscene Publications Act 1959
S 1(1) 13, 29, 53
S 1(2) 13, 14–15
S 1(3) 14, 71, 75, 181, 275, 279–80, 287, 297
S 2(1) 69, 74
S 2(4) 51, 66, 69, 77–78, 297
S 2(4)A 69, 77–78
S 2(5) 16
S 3(1) 240
S 3(2) 241, 243
S 3(3) 246, 247
S 3(5) 251
S 3(7) 249
S 4(1) 30, 53
S 4(2) 34, 53

Obscene Publications Act 1964
S 1(1) 15
S 1(2) 15
S 3 15

Post Office Act 1953
S 8(3) 230
S 11(1) 60, 145, 168, 171, 230
S 16 232

S 66 146
S 58(1) 231
S 66
S 75 147

Post Office Act 1969
S 64 231

Protection of Children Act 1978
S 1 132, 219, 221
S 7(2) 220

Public Order Act 1936
S 5 90, 92, 102–103
S 5A 102
S 9 203

Race Relations Act 1976
S 70 120

Sexual Offences Act 1956
S 30 74

Sunday Entertainment Act 1932
S 4 86

Sunday Observance Act 1780
S 1 86

Sunday Theatres Act 1972
S 1 86

Theatres Act 1968
S 2(1) 204
S 2(4) 203, 204, 207
S 3(1) 205
S 5(1) 204
S 6(1) 204
S 7(1) 69, 74, 81
S 18 203, 206

Town and Country Planning Act 1971
S 29(1) 266
S 22(2)(f) 267

Town Police Clauses Act 1847
S 28 179

Unsolicited Goods and

Services Act 1971
S 4(1) 149, 171

Vagrancy Act 1824
S 4 73, 179
Vagrancy Act 1838
S 2 179

Table of cases

England

Abrahams v *Cavey* [1967]
3 All ER 179   60, 63
American Cyanamid Co v
Ethicon Ltd [1975]
AC 396   261
Attorney-General, ex parte McWhirter v *IBA* [1973]
1 QB 629   60, 147, 260, 300, 302
Attorney-General's Reference (No. 2 1975) [1976]
2 All ER 753   115

Beatty v *Gillbanks*
15 Cox CC 138   104
Bowman v *Secular Society*
[1917] AC 406   96
Brutus v *Cozens* [1973]
AC 854   90, 91, 92, 103, 224
Burge v *DPP* [1962]
1 WLR 265   75

Burke v *Copper* [1962]
2 All ER 14   249, 250, 340
Byrne v *Low* [1972]
Crim L Rev 551   156

Chief Constable v *Woodhall*
[1965] Crim L Rev 660   15
Collymore v *Attorney-General for Trinidad and Tobago*
[1970] AC 538
Commissioners of Customs and Excise v *Sun and Health Ltd* (Unreported)
1973   154, 223
Commissioners of Customs and Excise v *Paul Raymond Publications Ltd*
(Unreported) 1974   153, 154
Conelly v *DPP* [1964]
AC 1254   45
Cox v *Stinton* [1951]
2 KB 1021   246

Derrick v *Commissioners of Customs and Excise* [1972] 1 All ER 993   154, 280
DPP v *A and BC Chewing Gum Ltd* [1968] 1 QB 159   20, 29, 34, 35, 132, 141
DPP v *Beate Utise (UK) Ltd* [1974] 2 WLR 50   150
DPP v *Bhagwan* [1970] 2 WLR 501   52
DPP v *Humphreys* [1977] AC 1   44, 46
DPP v *Jordan* [1977] AC 699   32, 34, 38
DPP v *Whyte* [1972] AC 849   20, 21, 22, 24, 41
DPP v *Withers and Others* [1974] 2 WLR 751   52
Dugdale v *R* (1863) Dears 64   75

Ellis v *Dubowski* [1921] 2 KB 621   274
Entinck v *Carrington* (1765) 19 St Tr 1030   325

Frailey v *Charlton* [1920] 1 KB 147   153

Ghani v *Jones* [1969] 3 All ER 1700   241, 242, 243, 244, 253
GLC v *Langian Ltd* (Unreported) 1977   284
Gouriet v *Union of Post Office Workers* [1978] AC 435   258, 259, 260, 261, 285, 286, 302
Grade v *DPP* [1942] 2 All ER 118   206

Imperial Tobacco Ltd v *Attorney-General* [1979] 2 WLR 805 (CA), [1980] 2 WLR 466 (HL)   45, 46, 258, 261

Jacobs v *Bryor* Law Times Reps July 5, 1851   86
John Calder (Publications) Limited v *Powell* [1965] 1 QB 509   29
Jones v *Randall* (1774) 1 Coup 17; 98 ER 944
Jordan v *Burgoyne* [1963] 2 QB 744   91, 93

Kamara v *DPP* [1974] AC 104
Knuller v *DPP* [1972] 3 WLR 143   19, 52, 53, 54, 55, 56, 57, 58, 59, 60, 64, 65, 67, 70, 71, 83, 86, 99, 147, 236, 319
Kosmos Publications Ltd v *DPP* [1975] Crim L Rev 345   62, 147, 148, 223

Lees v *Parr* [1967] 3 All ER 181   63
LCC v *Bermondsey Bioscope Co Ltd* [1911] 1 KB 445   273
Lord Byron v *Dugdale* (1863) 1 LJ Ch 239

Malone v *Commissioner of Police of the Metropolis (No. 1)* [1979] 1 All ER 256   242, 252
Malone v *Commissioner of Police of the Metropolis (No. 2)* [1979] 2 All ER 620   325
Marks v *Benjamin* (1839)

5 M&W 565	85
Mella v *Monahan* [1961] Crim L Rev 125	181
Mills v *LCC* [1924] 1 KB 213	274, 393
Morgan v *Bowker* [1963] 1 All ER 691	24, 249
Moxom's Case (1841) 2 Townsend's Mod St Trials 356	4
Olympia Press v *Hollis* [1974] 1 All ER 108	249
Paget Publications v *Watson* [1952] 1 All ER 1256	70
Pickin v *British Railways Board* [1974] AC 765	327
R v *Adams* [1980] 1 All ER 473	240
R v *Aldred* (1909) 74 JP 55	101
R v *Allison* (1888) 59 LT 933	7
R v *Anderson* [1972] 1 QB 304	24, 29, 34, 35, 146
R v *Ardalan* [1972] 2 All ER 257	153
R v *Attwood* (1617) Cro Jae 421	3
R v *Bacon* (1664) 1 Lev 146	4, 67
R v *Barker* [1962] 1 All ER 748	25
R v *Barraclough* [1906] 1 KB 201 (CCR)	7
R v *Bensen* [1928] 2 WWR 605	203
R v *Berg and Others* (1927) 20 Cr App Reps 38	85
R v *Boulter* (1908) JP 188	96
R v *Brady and Kam* (1963) Cr App Reps 203	85
R v *Bradlaugh* (1878) 3 QBD 607	8
R v *Brownson* [1971] Crim L Rev 551	206
R v *Burns* (1886) 16 Cox CCI	101
R v *Calder and Boyars Ltd* [1969] 1 QB 151	19, 24, 29, 32, 34, 38, 70, 321
R v *Caunt* (Unreported) 1947	94, 101
R v *Clark* (1963) 47 Cr App Reps 203	75
R v *Clayton* [1962] 3 All ER 500	25
R v *Clifford* [1961] Crim L Rev 486	19
R v *Cinecentre Ltd* (Unreported) Birmingham Crown Court 1976	63, 84, 85
R v *Comptroller General of Patents* [1899] 1 QB 909	44
R v *Curl* (1727) 2 Strange 788	2, 3, 48, 59
R v *Daniel* (1738) Holt KB 344	4, 67, 514
R v *Davies* [1897] 2 QB 199	85
R v *Deleval* (1763) 3 Burr 1438	59, 60
R v *DeMontalk* (1932) 23 Cr App Rep 182	7, 9, 11, 16, 70
R v *Farmer* (1973) 58 Crim App Rep 229	62
R v *Grant* (1848) 7 State Tr Ns 507	101
R v *Greater London Council, ex parte Blackburn (No. 4)* [1976]	

3 All ER 184   48, 61, 258,
   277, 278, 281,
   282, 286, 301,
   318, 321
R v *Greenfield and Others*
  [1973] 3 All ER 1050 69
R v *Harry Key* (1908)
  1 Crim App Reps 135 168
R v *Henn*, R v *Darby* [1978]
  3 All ER 1190 (CA)
R v *Henn*, R v *Darby* [1980]
  2 All ER 166
  (ECJ, HL) 332
R v *Hicklin* (1868) LR 3
  QB 360 4, 5, 7, 11, 17,
  21, 24, 37, 131,
  146, 348, 350,
  351, 352
R v *Higginson* (1962)
  2 Burr 1233 84
R v *Hockhauser* [1964]
  47 WWR 350 203
R v *Holmes* (1953)
  Dears CC 207 203
R v *Inland Revenue*
Commissioners, ex parte
National Federation of
Self-Employed and Small
Businesses Ltd [1980]
  2 All ER 378 286, 301
R v *Jacey (London) Ltd*
and Others, The Times,
  July 6, 1976 73
R v *Jordan* [1976]
  2 All ER 714 32
R v *King* Central Criminal
  Courts Sept 29, 1967
  (Unreported) 74
R v *LCC, ex parte London*
and Provincial Theatres
Ltd [1915] 2 KB 466 273
R v *Lemon* [1979]
  1 All ER 898 87, 96, 101,
  102, 189

R v *Liverpool Corporation,*
ex parte Liverpool Taxi
Fleet Operators
Association [1972]
  2 QB 299 284
R v *Love* (1955)
  39 Cr App Rep 30 7
R v *Mapstone* [1964]
  1 WLR 439 75
R v *Martin Secker, Warburg*
Ltd [1954]
  2 All ER 683 10, 70, 91
R v *Mayling* [1963]
  2 QB 717 52, 203
R v *Metropolitan Police*
Commissioner, ex parte
Blackburn (No. 1) [1968]
  2 QB 118 317, 319
R v *Metropolitan Police*
Commissioner, ex parte
Blackburn (No. 3) [1973]
  2 WLR 43 39, 61, 247,
  258, 285, 317, 320
R v *Metropolitan Police*
Commissioner, ex parte
Blackburn (No. 5) The
Times (Law Report)
  November 30, 1979 318
R v *Payne The Times* (Law
  Report) May 15, 1980 81,
  84, 85
R v *Penguin Books* [1961]
  Crim L Rev 176 7, 29, 32,
  34, 38, 49
R v *Plympton* [1724]
  2 Ld Paym 1377 67
R v *Quinn and Bloom* [1962]
  2 QB 245 83
R v *Ramsay and Foot* (1883)
  48 LT 733 95
R v *Read* (1708) Fortes
  Rep 98 2, 3, 4
R v *Reiter* (1954)
  1 All ER 741

R v *Reynolds*
  (Unreported) 1971 61
R v *Saunders* (1875)
  1 QBD 15 60, 87
R v *Sidley* (1663) 1 Keble
  620 1 Sid 168 2, 59
R v *Stamford* [1972]
  2 WLR 1055 62, 147, 148, 223
R v *Stanley* [1965]
  1 All ER 1035 60, 146, 223
R v *Stannard* (1863)
  Crim Law Cases 405 86
R v *Staniforth* [1976]
  2 All ER 714 32, 39, 197
R v *Straker* [1965]
  Crim L Rev 239 62, 147, 148, 223
R v *Sutton* [1972]
  1 WLR 1086 218
R v *Thomas and Another*:
  Hereford Assizes,
  February 27, 1978
  (Unreported) 74
R v *Tutchin* (1704)
  Ho St Tr 1099 4
R v *Waterfield* [1975]
  2 All ER 40 62
R v *Waterfield (No. 2 1975)* (Unreported) 153
R v *Williams* 26 St Tr
  653 (1797) 3

Scott v *Scott* [1913]
  AC 417
Shaw v *DPP* [1962]
  AC 220 18, 20, 46, 51, 52, 53, 54, 56, 57, 67, 68, 69, 71, 83, 106, 120, 326, 327
Straker v *DPP* [1963]
  1 All ER 697 14, 279

Thomson v *Chain Libraries Ltd* [1954] 2 All ER
  616 248, 250
Thorne v *BBC* [1967]
  1 WLR 1104 302

Weisz v *Monahan* [1962]
  1 WLR 262 75
Wershof v *Metropolitan Police Commissioner*
  [1978] 2 All ER 540 242
Wigan v *Strange* (1965)
  LR 1 CP 175
Wiggins v *Field* (1968)
  Crim L Rev 503 60, 62
Worth v *Terrington* (1845)
  13 M&W 781 63

Youssoupoff v *MGM* (1934)
  50 TLR 581 276

Canada

Re *Nova Scotia Board of Censors et al* (1978)
  84 DLR (3d) 1 (SCC) 56
R v *Cameron* (1966) 4 CCC
  (Ontario Crt App) 273
R v *Praine Schooner News and Powers* (1970) 75
  WWR 585 (Manitoba Ct of App) 196

United States

Adams Newark Theater Co v
  City of Newark 354 US
  931 (1957) 432, 434
Alexander v *Virginia*
  413 US 836 (1973) 415, 443

Bantam Books v *Sullivan*

372 US 58 (1963) 259, 309, 349, 435
Besig v *United States* 208 F 2d 142 (9th Cir 1953) 367, 368
Bethview Amusement Corp v *Cahn* 416 F 2d 410 (2d Cir 1969) 438
Blount v *Rizzi* 400 US 410 (1971) 421
Brandenburg v *Ohio* 395 US 444 (1969) 479
Bridges v *California* 314 US 252 (1941) 476
Burstyn v *Wilson* 343 US 495 (1952) 352, 357, 416
Butler v *Michigan* 352 US 380 (1957) 131, 173, 355, 371, 372, 392, 393, 430, 486

CBS v *Democratic National Committee* 412 US 241 (1974) 304, 305
California v *La Rue* 409 US 109 (1972) 210, 433
Carol Vance v *Universal Amusement Co* 63 L Ed 2d 413 (1980) 413, 426, 427
Chimel v *California* 395 US 752 (1969) 439
Cohen v *California* 403 US 15 (1971) 80, 364, 385–6, 467
Commercial Pictures Corp v *Regents* 346 US 587 (1954) 358, 416
Commonwealth v *Allison* 227 Mass 57, 116 NE (1917) 354
Commonwealth v *Buckley* 200 Mass 346, 86 NE 910 (1909) 350, 351
Commonwealth v *Friede* 271 Mass 318, 171 NE 472 (1930) 351
Commonwealth v *Gordan* 66 Pa D&C 101 (1949) 354, 359, 360, 361
Commonwealth v *Havens* 6 Pa Co 545 (1889) 351
Commonwealth v *Isenstadt* 318 Mass 543, 62 NE 2d 840 (1945) 349, 350, 352, 354, 360, 368, 390
Commonwealth v *Landis* 8 Phila 453 (1870) 349, 350, 351, 352, 361
Commonwealth v *Magid and Dickstein* 91 Pa Super 573 (1927) 351
Commonwealth v *Sharpless* 2 Sard R 91 (Pa Sup Ct 1815) 346
Cox Broadcasting Corp v *Cohn* 420 US 469 (1970) 167

Dennis v *United States* 341 US 494 (1951) 475, 477
Doubleday v *New York* 335 US 848 (1948) 371

Erznoznik v *City of Jacksonville* 423 US 205 (1975) 187, 425, 428, 433, 446, 452, 460, 483, 487

FCC v *Pacifica Foundation*

428 US 726 (1978) 436, 437, 484, 488
Freedman v *Maryland*
380 US 57 (1965) 216, 234, 235, 237, 240, 245. 259, 261, 264, 272, 289, 294, 295, 418, 435, 439

Ginsberg v *New York*
390 US 629 (1968) 27, 131, 134, 293, 295, 355, 392, 394, 447, 456, 485, 487
Ginzburg v *United States*
383 US 463 (1966) 17, 30, 41, 133, 380, 386–389, 395
Gitlow v *New York*
268 US 652 (1925) 353, 377, 475, 476
Griswold v *Connecticut*
381 US 479 (1965) 161, 365
Grove Press Inc v *Christenberry* 276 F 2d (2 Gr 1960) 233, 423

Halsey v *New York Society for Suppression of Vice* 234 NY Suppl, 136 NE 219 (1922) 360, 361
Hamling v *United States*
418 US 87 (1974) 381, 382, 446, 448, 453
Heller v *New York*
413 US 483 (1973) 239, 244, 254, 287, 311, 427, 438, 439 443
Hicks v *Miranda* 422 US 332 (1975) 244, 427, 439
Hoffman v *Pursue*
420 US 592 (1975) 426
Holmby Productions v *Vaughn* 350 US 870 (1956) 357, 416
Hudgens v *NLRB*
424 US 507 (1976) 304, 305

Interstate Circuit, Inc v *City of Dallas* 390 US 676 (1968) 41, 134, 145, 295, 335, 394, 425, 485

Jacobellis v *Ohio* 378 US 184
(1964) 398, 399, 400, 402, 403, 406, 446, 447, 448, 458
Jenkins v *Georgia* 418 US 153 (1974) 433, 444, 452, 455, 456

Kaplan v *California*
413 US 115 (1973) 198, 443, 445, 454
Kingsley Book Inc v *Brown* 354 US 436 (1957) 414, 427, 435
Kingsley International Pictures Corp v *Regents* 360 US 684 (1959) 259, 358, 416–417
Kois v *Wisconsin*
408 US 229 (1972) 397

Lee Art Theater v *Virginia*
392 US 636 (1968) 437, 538
Lloyd Corp v *Tanner*
407 US 551 (1972) 304

Manual Enterprises v *Day*
370 US 478 (1962) 11, 42, 369, 399–400, 448, 458, 459
Marsh v *Alabama*
329 US 501 (1946) 304

Marcus v *Search Warrant*
    367 US 717 (1961)   239,
        418, 439
Memoirs v *Massachusetts*
    383 US 413 (1966)   43,
        388, 398–399, 401,
        405, 449, 450,
        464, 468
Meyer v *Nebraska*
    262 US 390 (1923)   293
Miami Herald v *Tornillo*
    418 US 241 (1974)   305
Miller v *California*
    413 US 15 (1973)   27, 33,
        36, 42, 43, 109, 131,
        134, 145, 188, 193,
        195, 293, 295, 337,
        356, 434, 436, 443,
        444, 445, 446, 447,
        448, 449, 450, 451,
        452, 453, 454, 455,
        456, 457, 458, 459,
        464, 468, 473, 485
Milwaukee Publishing Co
    v *Burleson* 255 US
    407 (1921)   230, 420, 422
Mishkin v *New York*
    383 US 502 (1966)   27,
        198, 391–392,
        437, 445

Near v *Minnesota*
    283 US 697
    (1931)   216, 352,
        412–413, 426,
        435, 492
New York Times v
    Sullivan 376 US 254
    (1964)   469, 470

Paris Adult Theater v
    Slaton 413 US 49
    (1973)   36, 165, 347,
        356, 427, 442, 443,
            444, 454, 456, 486
People v *Berg* 241 App
    Div 549, 272 NYS
    586 (1934)   360, 361
People v *Brainard*
    192 App Div 816,
    183 NYS 452
    (1920)   349, 350
People v *Doris*
    14 App Div 117, 43
    NYS 571 (1897)
People v *Doubleday*
    17 US Law Week (Supr
    Crt Sec 3118) (1947)   355
People v *Eastman*
    188 NY 478, 81 NE
    459   348, 349
People v *Friede*
    133 Misc 611, 233 NYS
    565 (Mag Ct 1929)   351
People v *Muller*
    96 NY 408, 48 Am Rep
    465 (1884)   348, 349, 350,
        351, 352, 361
People v *Seltzer* 122 Misc
    329, 203 NYS 809
    (1924)   348, 349, 352
People v *Wendling*
    258 NY 451, 180 NE
    169 (1932)   347, 349,
        350, 351
Pierce v *Society of Sisters*
    268 US 501
    (1925)   293, 487
Pinkus v *United States*
    436 US 293
    (1978)   23, 133, 141, 144,
        194, 447
Pittsburgh Press Co v
    Human Relations
    Commission 413 US
    376 (1973)   444
Prince v *Massachusetts*
    321 US 158 (1944)   293, 487

A Quantity of Books v
  Kansas 378 US 205
  (1964)   217, 239, 418

Redrup v *New York*
  386 US 767 (1967)   382,
        392, 406, 409,
          459, 486
Roaden v *Kentucky*
  413 US 496
  (1973)   244, 439, 443
Roe v *Wade*
  440 US 113 (1973)   365
Rosen v *United States*
  161 US 29 (1896) 366, 381
Roth v *United States*
  354 US 476 (1957) 11, 17,
    23, 27, 28, 29, 33,
    41, 43, 79, 80, 99,
          195, 337, 338,
          371–380, 385,
       396, 398, 402, 405,
        423, 443, 449, 450,
          456, 457, 458,
          467, 488
Rowan v *United States Post Office Department*
  397 US 728 (1970)   151,
          163, 235, 423

Shelley v *Kraemer*
  334 US 1 (1948)   304
Shenck v *United States*
  249 US 47 (1919)   216,
          412, 476
Smith v *United States*
  431 US 291 (1977)   56,
          195, 448, 450
Smith v *California*
  361 US 147 (1959)   356,
          381, 404, 454
Southeastern Productions v
  Conrad 420 US 546
  (1975)   425, 433,
          434, 452
Splawn v *California*
  431 US 595
  (1977)   33, 444, 446
Stanley v *Georgia*
  394 US 557 (1968)   163,
          164, 165, 166, 176,
          382, 383, 442, 443,
          486, 518
State v *Becker*
  364 Mo 1079, SW 2d
  283 (1954)   359, 360
State v *Lerner*
  81 NE 2d 282 (Ohio,
  1948)   355, 360, 372
State v *Mac Sales & Co*
  Mo App 263, SW 2d
  860 (1954)   349
State v *Pfenninger*
  76 Mo App 313
  (1883)   349, 350
Swearinger v *United States*
  161 US 446
  (1896)   366, 367

Tallman v *United States*
  465 F 2d 282 (7th Cir
  1972)   436
Teitel Films v *Cusack*
  390 US 139
  (1968)   245, 425
Times Film Corp v *Chicago*
  365 US 43
  (1961)   417, 427, 435

United States v *Bennett*
  24 Red Cas 1093, No. 14,
  571 (SDNY 1879)   348,
          502, 513
United States v *Bennett*
  39F 2d 564 (2d Cir
  1930)
United States v *Gagliardo*
  336 2d 720 (9th Cir

1966) 436
United States v
  Kennerley 209F 119
  (SD NY 1913)   367, 368,
  369, 396, 457, 458
United States v *O'Brien*
  391 US 367
  (1968)   430, 434
United States v *One Book
  Called Ulysses* 72 F 2d
  705 (2d Cir
  1934)   368, 390
United States v *One Reel
  of Film* 481 F 2d 206
  (1st Cir 1973)   33, 450
United States v *Orito*
  413 US 139 (1973)   364,
  442, 443, 448
United States v *Reidel*
  402 US 351
  (1971)   441, 460, 486
United States v *Thirty-
  Seven Photographs*
  402 US 363 (1971)   165,
  245, 424, 442
United States v *12 200ft
  Reels* 413 US
  (1973)   157, 165,
  237, 424, 442,
  443, 448, 453

Valentine v *Chrestensen*
  316 US 52 (1942)   444
*Virginia State Bd of
  Pharmacy* v *Virginia
  Citizens Consumer
  Council, Inc*
  425 US 748 (1979)   444,
  472, 483

Walker v *Popenoe*
  149 F 2d 511 (DC Cir
  1945)   233, 368, 420
Walter v *United States*
  65L Ed 2d 410
  (1980)   244, 439, 632
Ward v *Illinois*
  431 US 767 (1977)   42, 193,
  453, 455
Whitney v *California*
  274 US 357 (1927)   476
Winters v *New York*
  333 US 507 (1948)   325,
  326, 356, 357
Wisconsin v *Yoder*
  406 US 1205 (1972)   293,
  393, 487

Yates v *United States*
  354 US 298 (1957)   479
Young v *American Mini
  Theaters* 427 US 50
  (1976)   187, 188, 200, 227,
  272, 311, 429, 430,
  431, 433, 435, 460,
  481, 487, 490, 491

xxiii

1 The emergence and definition in English law of the concept of obscenity

Control of literature on the grounds of obscenity was virtually unknown in early English law.[1] As in most European countries, English church and state were closely identified; rival theological doctrine was seen as far more of a threat than the treatment of sexual matters. As a result the ecclesiastical courts, which since the first decade of Norman rule had had control of public morality, and which in their heyday could have been used to control licentious works, remained in this regard — even after the invention of the printing press in 1440 — largely inactive.[2] Although printing became more general during the sixteenth century, pressure for censorship[3] in terms of public morality did not materialise until the early eighteenth century, possibly because there was until that stage no reading public as such. By that stage, however, any legal restrictions in terms of obscenity, were they to emerge,

---

1   For the historical background I have drawn on the *Minutes of Evidence taken before the Select Committee on the Obscene Publications Bill*, HC 1958, 91–6. See also N. St John Stevas *Obscenity and the Law* (1954); D. Tribe *Questions of Censorship* (1973); J. Chandos 'My Brother's Keeper' in *To Deprave and Corrupt ... Original Studies in the Nature of Definition of 'Obscenity'* (1962) p.15; Leo Alpert 'Censorship of Obscene Literature' 52 (1938) Harv L Rev 40; Alec Craig *Suppressed Books* (1963).

2   Of the few prosecutions for obscenity in ecclesiastical courts, most involved some element of defamation. N. St John Stevas op.cit. at 12.

3   I use the term 'censorship' here and elsewhere broadly to denote both prior and subsequent restraint. Where a more particular emphasis is required, this will be made clear. On the varieties of censorship possible, see Paul O'Higgins *Censorship in Britain* (1972) chapter 1.

would have to do so from the common law courts: by the eighteenth century the laity had effectively escaped the control of the ecclesiastical courts, whose waning influence in this regard was only formally recognised in 1876. The Court of Star Chamber, which as a prerogative court had been concerned with heresy and sedition rather than public morality, had been abolished in 1640, and the licensing laws in 1695.

The first reported common law prosecution for obscene libel was brought in 1708. Holt CJ's answer was succinct: 'There are ecclesiastical courts, why may not this be punish'd there? If we have no precedent, we cannot punish. Show me any precedent.'[1] The common law courts had already made a foray into the area of public morality: in 1663 Sir Charles Sedley was convicted 'for shewing himself naked on a balcony, and throwing down bottles pist in vi et armis among the people in Covent Garden, contra pacem and to the scandel of the Government'.[2] The court in *Read* distinguished *Sedley* on the basis that it essentially involved riotous personal behaviour. The turning point came in 1727 with the publication by printer and bookseller, Edmund Curl, of a tract entitled *Venus in the Cloister, or The Nun in her Smock*. Curl had run a bookshop in Grub Street for more than forty years. Although he stocked scientific and literary works, his infamy was based on the endless succession of dubious sexual material he turned out.[3] On his indictment for publishing an obscene libel, *Read* was overruled, the court accepting rather the argument of the Attorney-General that there were three broad areas of expression subject to restriction under the common law: the publication in question

> ... is an offence at common law as it tends to corrupt the morals of the King's subjects and is against the peace of the King. Peace includes good government and order and that peace may be broken without actual force, 1. if it be against the constitution of civil government; 2. if it be against religion; and 3. if against morality.[4]

It was not possible to deal with the case in terms of obscenity's established relatives seditious or blasphemous libel. The tract's target was the Roman Catholic Church, and it was thus hardly indictable as blasphemy. However, the court remarked: '... since morality is part of the law of the land as the Christian religion is, an act which is destruc-

---

1   *R v Read* (1708) Fortes Rep 98.

2   *R v Sedley* (1663) 1 Keble 620, 1 Sid 168.

3   G. Robertson *Obscenity* (London 1979) at 22.

4   *R v Curl* (1727) 2 Strange 788.

tive of morality in general, such as obscene libel, ought to be punished in the same way as one against the Christian Religion, such as blasphemous libel'.[1] Mr Justice Fortesque's argument in dissent that a tendency to a breach of the peace should be required before the law imposed restrictions, was not accepted.

The case must surely rank as one of the most significant in Anglo/American jurisprudence; not only did it introduce into the common law the offence of publishing an obscene libel, but also tied the concept of obscenity regulation not to action of some sort, but rather to the maintenance by the courts of public morality. Censorship, which until now had been political and religious[2] in basis, had now found an additional — and not unrelated — justification. Obscenity challenged not only established religious tenets, but had also clear political implications, in that conventional sexual morality was seen very much as an essential in the mortar holding together the structure of society. As Morris Ernst and William Seagal wrote in 1929:

> It is important to understand that sex radicalism in modern life is the best general index of radicalism in other spheres. The man who publicly upholds birth control, the single standard, free love, companionate marriage, easy divorce, and legitimisation, is a man prone to play with subversive ideas on private property, to be attracted to criminal syndicalism, to be dubious about the House of Lords, or about the fitness of the republican party to govern, and to question the general efficacy of prayer. When such an individual is attacked under sex censorships it is assumed that no very great tenderness for his rights need be shown.[3]

In maintaining the *status quo* however, obscenity went further than its specifically religious or political counterparts: despite the three-part definition of 'peace' in *Curl*, obscenity was unusual in not being linked to conduct of some sort. It would appear that obscenity, blasphemous libel, and sedition were all introduced into the common law at roughly the same time — over a period of about 100 years in fact.[4] A primary

---

1 *R v Curl* (1727) 2 Strange 788.

2 The two are inseparable in this context: As Mr Justice Ashurst remarked in 1797, blasphemy was 'not only an offence against God, but against all law and government from its tendency to dissolve all the bonds and obligations of Civil Society'. *R v Williams* (1797) 26 St Tr 653 at 715.

3 Ernst and Seagal op.cit. at 176.

4 Obscenity in 1727; blasphemous libel apparently in *R v Attwood* (1617) Cro Jac 421; sedition was well established by the early eighteenth century: see e.g. *R v Tutchin* (1704) Ho St Tr 1095. On the latter two offences see J.F. Stephen *History of the Criminal Law* vol.2 at 359 and 435 (London 1883).

consideration behind their introduction was probably that a charge of incitement, by this stage clearly established in the common law,[1] required subjective intention, and a relationship to conduct itself criminal.[2] It soon became apparent that subjective intention was not required in the ordinary way with either obscenity,[3] blasphemy, or sedition,[4] nor was there requirement of a relationship to conduct itself criminal. There was with blasphemy however an early requirement of a likelihood of a breach of the peace, whilst sedition, although broadly defined, was tied, even if loosely, to civil disturbance.[5] Such limitation had been specifically rejected in *Curl*; the law was squarely launched on the course of enforcing public morality *per se*. Disagreement over the propriety of this rages on today, some 250 years later.[6]

The new offence does not appear during its first half-century of existence to have been extensively utilised: John Cleland's *Fanny Hill, Memoirs of a Woman of Pleasure* was, for example, not prosecuted as obscene when first published in 1748,[7] one of the few reported prosecutions being that in 1770 of John Wilkes for the publication of his poem 'Essay on Woman'.[8] By the end of the eighteenth century however, the Industrial Revolution, fuelled by the Protestant ethic of sobriety, hard work, and obedience was well launched. Society appeared to have set its face inexorably against any threat to this, or any impropriety. One result was the foundation of the first anti-vice societies: perhaps the best known of these, the Society for the Suppression of Vice, was founded in 1802. Its aims included not only the suppression of obscenity, but also of blasphemy and prostitution. Despite the 159 prosecutions (only five were unsuccessful)[9] brought by the

---

1 Cf. e.g. *R v Bacon* (1664) 1 Lev 146; *R v Plympton* (1724) 2 Ld Raym 1377.

2 Cf. *R v Daniel* (1738) Holt KB 344; Stephen op.cit. at 230; *Russell on Crime* (London 1964) at 196; Glanville Williams *Criminal Law: The General Part* (London 1962) at 609.

3 Certainly by the time *R v Hicklin* (1868) LR 3 QB 360 was decided in 1868, no such requirement had been enunciated and established. The *Hicklin* provision in this regard is discussed later in this chapter.

4 For a discussion of the *mens rea* requirement in relation to these offences, see the section on strict liability, chapter 4.

5 See the discussion on the principle of legality, chapter 4.

6 On the policy question of the law and morality, see particularly chapter 4.

7 See Report of the Committee on Obscenity and Film Censorship, (HMSO 1979), Appendix I, p.168.

8 4 Burr 2527 (KB 1770); the original proceedings were instituted in 1764.

9 Ibid; for an example of a successful prosecution of the time (Shelley's 'Queen Mab' in this instance) see *Moxom's Case* (1841) 2 Townshend's Mod St. Trials 356.

Society between 1802 and 1857, pornography continued to flourish. An obvious point of further attack was to prevent the importation of such material: the first customs prohibition on the importation of obscene or indecent material was enacted without Parliamentary discussion in 1846. It was followed in 1857 by the Obscene Publications Act, introduced by Lord Campbell, the Lord Chief Justice of the day, and generally known as Lord Campbell's Act. The measure was a civil and not a criminal one, providing the police with a power of search and seizure with respect to obscene materials,[1] special powers being necessary because of the narrowness of police powers at common law in this regard.[2] Considerable disquiet was expressed in the House of Lords over the measure: concern centred on its possible application to works of merit, the possibility of vexatious interference with legitimate works by individuals invoking its operation, and the absence of any definition of obscenity.[3] Lord Campbell apparently intended his measure to apply only in the narrowest sense, to works which had been written with the object of corrupting their readers. Although definition was left to the courts, and although the first judicial attempt to define obscenity in *R v Hicklin*[4] left the issue of intention open, it was soon to become clear that not only was intention in this form not required, but intention was not required as to material's obscenity at all. But first, the famous *dictum* in *Hicklin*.

I The Hicklin test

Justices in Wolverhampton had issued a warrant under the 1857 Act under which copies of a pamphlet entitled *The Confessional Unmasked: shewing the depravity of the Romish priesthood, the iniquity of the Confessional and the questions put to females in confession* was seized from the premises of Henry Scott, a member of the Protestant Electoral Union.[5] On being brought before the justices, one of whom was Benjamin Hicklin, they were found obscene, and ordered to be destroyed. Scott appealed to the Quarter Sessions, where the Recorder found that because the material was not kept for publication for gain,

---

1 Its statutory successor in this regard, section 3 of the Obscene Publications Act 1959, is discussed together with other prior restraints in chapter 7.

2 The only provision for a search warrant at common law lay in terms of stolen goods. See L.H. Leigh *Police Powers in England and Wales* (London 1974).

3 For an excellent summary of the debate and the doubts raised as to the definition of 'obscene', see Ernst and Seagal op.cit. at 129–34.

4 (1868) LR 3 QB 360.

5 Which was pledged to the repeal of the Catholic Emancipation Act 1828.

nor to prejudice good morals, that its distribution was, despite its obscenity, not a misdemeanour. The Queen's Bench reversed this on the ground that a publisher's innocent motive or object was irrelevant to obscenity. It is Chief Justice Cockburn's famous *obiter dictum* on the meaning of obscenity for which the case is remembered however; the distinction between the permissible and the obscene is

> ... whether the tendency of the matter charged as obscenity is to deprave and corrupt those whose minds are open to such immoral influences and into whose hands a publication of this sort may fall.[1]

This definition is still in effect applied by the courts today. In order to analyse later developments, it is necessary to attempt to isolate the essentials of Cockburn's pronouncement:

(1) The test is apparently concerned only with publications relating to sexuality: the example the court gave of depravity and corruption is the arousal of 'libidinous thoughts'.[2]

(2) The emphasis in the test is entirely on the effect of the work; the nature thereof is not apparently regarded as being *per se* relevant.

(3) In view of the phrase 'whose minds are open to such immoral influences', the court would appear to regard 'deprave and corrupt' (the effect in question) as signifying 'to make morally bad'. Lord Cockburn, moreover, goes on to remark: 'Now, with regard to this work, it is quite certain that it would suggest to the minds of the young of either sex, or even to persons of more advanced years, thoughts of a most impure and libidinous character.'[3] It would appear that the court regarded thoughts only as a sufficiently immoral influence.

(4) A mere tendency to the effect in question is sufficient.

(5) Because the emphasis in the test is on effect, distribution is important, and may operate in two basic ways: where distribution is general, it is apparently sufficient that anyone whom the material reaches be corrupted. Hence the significance under the test of the so-called 'most susceptible person'. In this sense distribution would tend to operate restrictively. Where distribution is particular, the opposite may well be true; although a work might not pass in general distribution, it might be deemed not to corrupt a particular group. The

---

1   *R v Hicklin* (1868) LR 3 QB 360 at 371.

2   Ibid.

3   Ibid.

nature of the audience may well also be significant in terms of whether or not they had previously been exposed to the material in question.
(6) There is no necessity to assess a work as a whole.
(7) As a result, literary value must be irrelevant; no separate defence of literary merit is provided.
(8) The author's motive is irrelevant;[1] *Hicklin* did not, as has sometimes been supposed,[2] decide that intention is irrelevant. Intention may be relevant in this context in four ways with regard
(a) to the literal act of publication;
(b) to the question of knowledge of the contents of the published article;
(c) to the obscenity of the published article; and
(d) to the legal criteria for obscenity.
The position with respect to (a) and (d) above was fairly clear: intention would be required in respect of (a),[3] but in line with the maxim *ignorantia iuris non excusat*, would not be required in respect of (d). It was made clear in *Bradlaugh's case*[4] in 1878 that intention was required as to (b), but not as to (c). This appears to have been confirmed in subsequent cases: in *R v Barraclough*[5] an allegation of intention was held to be a desirable, but unnecessary part of the indictment. This was later confirmed in *de Montalk*, although only with regard to an intention to deprave and corrupt ((c) above). In *de Montalk*, moreover, author and publisher were the same individual, thus leaving the case a less than satisfactory authority in this respect. In *R v Love*[6] a case concerning a publisher only, knowledge of the contents of the work published ((b) above) was asserted as essential. It would seem clear then that intention in the form of (a) and (b) above, but not (c), was required with respect to publication. This view of the common law would appear to have been confirmed in *R v Penguin*

---

1   *R v Hicklin* (1868) LR 3 QB 360 at 371.

2   See N. St John Stevas 'Obscenity and the Law' [1954] *Crim L Rev* 817 and his book of the same name, op.cit.; J.E. Hall Williams 'Obscenity in Modern English Law' 20 (1955) *L & C Probs* 630 at 634–5.

3   See *R v Thomson* (1900) 64 JP 456 at 457.

4   See St John Stevas op.cit. at 73.

5   [1906] 1 KB 201 (CCR) at 212.

6   (1955) 39 Cr App Rep 30, applying *R v Allison* (1888) 59 LT 933.

Books[1] where Byrne J. confirmed that if the defendant published an obscene article, the inference that he intends to deprave and corrupt is irrefutable, or (in essence) that intention as to (c) is not a constituent of the offence. In *Shaw* v *DPP*[2] however, Ashworth J. said: 'If these proceedings had been brought before the passing of the Obscene Publications Act 1959, in the form of the prosecution at common law for publishing an obscene libel, it would no doubt have been necessary to establish an intention to corrupt'.

(9) Obscenity is a matter for the jury, which was to decide, in effect, three questions: (a) the identity of the audience; (b) the influence the material has on the audience; and (c) whether that influence is immoral. Although the test did not formally refer to community standards, and although corruption of public morality was not specifically required, the latter was clearly the essence of an obscenity charge.[3]

(10) Mere possession of an obscene work is not sufficient; publication is necessary.

Prosecutions during the remainder of the nineteenth century and early twentieth century were regular. In 1877 Charles Bradlaugh and Annie Besant were convicted of publishing an obscene libel — a birth control manual which had been freely available for more than forty years.[4] In 1888 the eminent bookseller Henry Vizetelly was successfully prosecuted for his sale of *La Terre* by Emile Zola, *Madame Bovary* by Gustave Flaubert, *Sappho* by Alphonse Daudet, *Bel-Ami* by Guy de Maupassant, and *Mademoiselle de Maupin* by Theophile Gautier.[5] In 1898 Havelock Ellis' *Sexual Inversion* met a similar fate. The Society for the Suppression of Vice had by this stage expired, only to be succeeded (in 1899) by the National Vigilance Association and the Public Morality Council. Anti-pornography pressure found international expression during this period: in 1889 an international conference on the subject met in Switzerland, but it was only in 1923 that the Geneva Convention for the Suppression of the Circulation of the Traffic in Obscene Publications[6] was drawn up. Forty states, inclu-

---

1 [1961] *Crim L Rev* 176.

2 [1962] AC 220 at 227.

3 See *R* v *Bradlaugh*, St John Stevas op.cit. at 73.

4 Ibid.

5 St John Stevas op.cit. at 82—3.

6 Treaty Series No. 1 (1926) Cmnd 2575.

ding Britain, ratified the convention which was nonetheless not to prove particularly effective in providing a concerted international approach to the censorship of pornography. Article 1 made *possession* of obscene publications an offence: this was never enacted into English law, publication (even if only to one other person[1]) always being essential.

Perhaps the high point of the period was the prosectuion in 1928 of Radclyffe Hall's *The Well of Loneliness*, a novel dealing with lesbianism. On appeal to the Quarter Sessions, the Attorney-General Sir Thomas Inskip argued that 'thoughts of a most impure character' would be aroused in 'the young of either sex' and some 'persons of advanced years' when they read the only sentence in the work to suggest actual sexual behaviour: 'And that night they were not divided'. 'What does this *mean*?' he asked: 'Imagine a poor young woman or young man reading it. What is the picture conjured up at once? The man would ask: "What does this woman mean?" It corrupts him, conjures up a picture which the writer of the book intends ... The book seeks to glorify a vice or to produce a plea of toleration for those who practise it ... It is propaganda.'[2] Following the prosecution[3] in 1932 of the bizarre Count Geoffrey Wladislas Vaile Potocki de Montalk, who claimed to be the uncrowned King of Poland, for his attempt to publish privately, for the benefit of friends, some parodies of Verlaine entitled *Here Lies John Penis*, the censorious weight of the law was less frequently invoked. Even in *de Montalk's* case there had come the first acknowledgement of the relevance of literary merit,[4] whilst the new Attorney-General, Sir Donald Somerville KC in 1936 directed the Director of Public Prosecutions and postal and customs authorities not to act against James Joyce's *Ulysses*.[5] The only major prosecution between the mid-1930s and early 1950s appears to have been that of Dr Eustace Chesser, a psychiatrist and gynaecologist, who after his experience in practice in a Manchester slum during the Depression, had written and published the sex manual *Love without Fear*. The author testified that the book had been written in order to enlighten the ignorant and reassure the anxious. As to its explicitness, he answered: 'If I use Latin words, then you do not even know what part of your

---

1   See e.g. *R v De Montalk* (1932) 23 Cr App Rep 182.

2   Vera Brittain 'Radclyffe Hall — A Case of Obscenity' *Femina*, 1968 p.92 ff: quoted in Robertson op.cit. at 36.

3   *R v de Montalk* (1932) 23 Cr App Rep 182.

4   Ibid. at 183—4.

5   Robertson op.cit. at 38.

anatomy it refers to. You must be given something which describes your sexual organs to you and describes what happens during congress.'[1] The jury, in less than an hour, decided to acquit. Dr Chesser continued his writing, and his acquaintance with obscenity law: in 1972 he was to give evidence in *R* v *Gold* of the psychotherapeutic value of four softcore pornographic magazines. The defendants were acquitted on all four counts.[2]

The early 1950s, however, saw a sudden recrudescence of obscenity prosecutions: during 1953 alone 197 prosecutions were instituted in respect of allegedly obscene publications. The reasons for this are not clear, although the phenomenon has been ascribed to the Home Secretaryship of Sir David Maxwell Fyfe, which began in 1951.[3] What is clear is that widespread dissatisfaction with the law and its application now became evident. The immediate cause of much of the disquiet was the institution in 1954 of five major obscenity prosecutions: Werner Laurie for Margot Bland's *Julia*; Secker & Warburg for Stanley Kaufman's *The Philanderer*;[4] Hutchinson for Vivian Connell's *September in Quinze*; Heinemann for Walter Baxter's *The Image and the Search*; and Arthur Barker for Hugh McGraw's *The Man in Control*.

The second of these prosecutions[5] was presided over by Mr Justice Stable, who in his direction to the jury made the first real judicial attempt since 1868 at evaluation in this area. In his application of the *Hicklin* test he adopted the approach of dividing material charged as obscene into pornography on the one hand, and works for which literary or artistic justification might be advanced, on the other. Pornography should be 'stamped out', and stipulations about into whose hands it is likely to fall become as a result irrelevant. Where, however, the jury feel that a work is a serious one, and that '... the author was pursuing an honest purpose and an honest thread of thought or whether that was all just a bit of camouflage to render the crudity, the sex

---

1   Alec Craig *The Banned Books of England* (London 1962) at 99–105; quoted ibid. at 39.

2   Ibid. at 39–40; as to the psychotherapeutic defence, see chapter 2.

3   See Alec Craig op.cit. at 117.

4   Both these works had already been prosecuted in the Isle of Man under the Obscene Publications and Indecent Advertisements Act 1907 – *The Times* 12 August, 5 and 19 September 1953.

5   *R* v *Martin Secker & Warburg Ltd* [1954] 2 All Er 683. The accused were here acquitted; Werner Laurie pleaded guilty; Heinemann were acquitted after two juries failed to agree; Barker were acquitted after the jury had retired for 15 minutes; Hutchinson were found guilty and heavily fined.

of the book sufficiently wrapped up to pass the critical test of the Director of Public Prosecutions',[1] then they must allow the work to pass. The jury should realise that Victorian prudery was not the standard to be applied, nor was the test whether the works shocked or disgusted. Much serious literature might be permissible even though 'wholly unsuitable reading for the adolescent'.[2] The standard to be adopted is that of 'the average, decent, well-meaning man or woman'.

Mr Justice Stable's approach in the *Secker* case was echoed in the principal recommendations made by the Herbert Committee, set up by the Society of Authors as a result of anxiety over this flood of prosecutions. Although a Bill embodying these recommendations was lost in 1955, the matter was on a second attempt, referred to a Select Committee in 1957. In a subsequent report,[3] although it was considered inadvisable to depart substantially from the *Hicklin* test, the committee approved both the formulation adopted in *Secker* with regard to pornography, and the exception urged in favour of serious literature. The report formed the basis of the Obscene Publications Act 1959.

Much the same formulation had in essence been handed down on the other side of the Atlantic the same year by the American Supreme Court. In *Roth* v *United States*[4] the court had opted to regard obscenity as an exception to the First Amendment guarantee of free speech. This meant in turn a constitutional significance for the court's definition of obscenity, for it was in terms of this that material was excepted from First Amendment protection. The test was roughly in terms of catching pornography: obscenity regulation constitutionally proscribed material which appealed to the prurient interest. In *Roth* terms however, obscenity was an exception to the amendment because of its lack of social value; as a result balancing in respect of such value should be excluded, literary merit or other social value providing an absolute defence. In the absence of such defence, the test nonetheless — in terms of prurient appeal — potentially caught, as one moved into the 'swinging sixties', a vast body of material whose proscription hardly coincided with shifting public morality. The court therefore compromised the test, and introduced the concept of patent offensiveness.[5] This returned

---

1 *R v Martin Secker & Warburg Ltd* [1954] 2 All Er 683.

2 The relevance of literary merit in this respect had been proposed some 22 years earlier by the Recorder of London in *R v de Montalk* (1923) 23 Crim App Reps 182; the *obiter* had not however been followed.

3 *Report from the Select Committee* HC 1958; the first Select Committee did not in fact complete its inquiries, a fresh one being set up late in 1957.

4 354 US 476 (1957).

5 *Manual Enterprises v Day* 370 US 478 (1962); see chapter 14.

discretion to decide in terms of public morality or even taste to the jury; in so doing however it fuelled criticisms of overbreadth in respect of the obscenity test, whilst at the same time compromising the First Amendment rationale. Almost before the shift of emphasis from effect to the nature of the material had been made in the United States then, movement towards offensiveness, with its background in English law of variability in terms of restriction rather than prohibition, had begun.

---

2 The Obscene Publications Acts

The suggestions of the second Parliamentary Select Committee were (in most respects) closely followed in the subsequent Obscene Publications Act 1959,[1] the preamble to which declares the intention to 'provide for the protection of literature; and to strengthen the law concerning pornography'.[2] Section 1(1) provides that

> ... an article shall be deemed to be obscene if its effect or (where the article is two or more distinct items) the effect of any one of its items is, if taken as a whole, such as to tend to deprave and corrupt persons who are likely having regard to all relevant circumstances, to read, see or hear the matter contained or embodied in it.

Allowance is made for matter other than written material in the use of the word 'article', which is statutorily defined as '... any description of article containing or embodying matter to be read or looked at or both, any sound record, and any film or other record of a picture or pictures.'[3]

---

1   This was the fifth attempt at enactment of these proposals; the second, third and fourth failed in 1955, 1957 and 1958 respectively.

2   The strengthening in relation to pornography was purportedly achieved by changes to the search, seizure and destruction provisions of the 1857 Act; see chapter 7.

3   Section 1(2).

I) Application

1) *Publication/possession*

The definition of 'article' clearly extends to most forms of speech, including the written word. One of the few difficulties to arise with regard to this subsection concerned photographic negatives. In *Straker v DPP*[1] the question whether a negative could be said to be 'a film or other record of a picture' was left open: it was held that a negative, even if an 'article' under Section 1(2) of the Act, was not capable of being published under Section 1(3) because it is not shown, played or projected to members of the public.[2] The question of photographic negatives was settled by Section 5(3) of the Obscene Publications Amendment Act 1964:

> The Obscene Publications Act 1959 (as amended by this Act) shall apply in relation to anything which is intended to be used, either alone or as one of a set, for the production or manufacture therefrom of articles containing or embodying matter to be read, looked at or listened to, as if it were an article containing or embodying that matter so far as that matter is to be derived from it or the set.

A further uncertainty in relation to Section 1(2) was whether the definition of 'article' set out there extended to video cassettes. The question came before the Court of Appeal on a reference by the Attorney-General under Section 36 of the Criminal Justice Act 1972.[3] The move into the video cassette market by pornographers had caused increasing concern on both sides of the Atlantic.[4] This move began initially in relation to legitimate material: the film industry was slow to respond to the demand for video cassette versions of films, tending to cling to the 'traditional market place of the cinema'. As a result pirate cassettes appeared in increasing numbers: in 1974 the American authorities seized 2,000 pirate (in contravention of copyright) films, but no cassettes; in 1979 they seized 3,545 cassettes, and only 92 films.[5] From this it was a short move to pornography, which, although perhaps

---

1 [1963] 1 All ER 697.

2 It must be remembered that those who aid in the production of, or promote the publication of, an obscene article, may be liable as aiders and abettors. On this see Robertson *Obscenity* (London 1979) at 77–80.

3 *Re Attorney-General's Reference (no. 5 of 1980) The Times* (Law Report), 1 September 1980.

4 See e.g. *The Times*, 1 May 1980.

5 Ibid.

illegal, does not enjoy copyright protection.[1]

The reservoir of skills and equipment — a complete set necessary for the production of cassettes, made up from master tapes, themselves produced from the originals, may cost up to £250,000 — available in London has made it a natural centre for such operations. On the domestic market the cassettes can be sold for as much as £60, and stakes are therefore high. The attention of the police was first aroused when the film industry approached Interpol in 1977, chiefly over 'white', or non-pornographic films. Since then groups such as the Nationwide Festival of Light had urged the accommodation of the trade in pornography within the criminal law. In this case, police officers had raided two small basement cinemas in London. The shows were derived from video cassettes, the images being displayed on a television screen rather than in the manner of a traditional film show. It was argued for the defendants before the Court of Appeal that video tapes had not passed their experimental stage at the time of the passage of the 1959 Act, and that Parliament could not therefore have had them in mind when passing Section 1(2). Lord Justice Lawton ruled that the words of subsections 1(2) and 1(3) were wide enough to cover video cassettes; leave to appeal to the House of Lords was refused.

Under the 1959 Act the commission of the offence was via publication only; possession was not an offence. Section 1(1) of the 1964 measure amends Section 2(1) of the 1959 Act in this regard: after the words 'any person who, whether for gain or not publishes an obscene article', is added 'or who has an obscene article for publication for gain (whether gain to himself or gain to another)'. Publication for gain is defined in Section 1(2): '... a person shall be deemed to have an article for publication for gain if with a view to such publication he has the article in his ownership, possession or control'. In *Attorney-General's Reference (no. 2 of 1975)*[2] the Court of Appeal confirmed that 'The Act is not concerned with the obscenity of articles which are not published or intended or kept for publication'. Mere possession is, in other words, outside the scope of the Act. The word 'gain' in publication for gain was interpreted in *Chief Constable* v *Woodhall*[3] as not being limited to financial gain; the gain in question could, for example, be that effected by a 'swop'.

The inclusion of possession in this sense posed problems with respect to the publisher's intention. Section 3 of the 1964 Act provides in this

---

[1] See *G. Lynn* v *Western Feature Film* [1916] 1 Ch 261.

[2] [1969] 1 QB at 769.

[3] [1965] *Crim L Rev* 660.

regard that he

> (a) '... shall not be convicted of that offence if he proves that he had not examined that article and had no reasonable cause to suspect that it was such that his having it would make him liable to be convicted of an offence against that section.' and
>
> (b) 'the question whether the article is obscene shall be determined by reference to such publication for gain of the article as in the circumstances it may reasonably be inferred he had in contemplation and to any further publication that could reasonably be expected to follow from it, but not to any other publication.'

2)   *Intention*

Section 2(5) of the 1959 Act appeared to have at last settled the question of intention with regard to publication:

> A person shall not be convicted of an offence against this section if he proves that he had not examined the article in respect of which he is charged, and had no reasonable cause to suspect that it was such that his publication of it would make him liable to be convicted of an offence against this section.

Intention as to publication itself is required. The Act would appear however to apply an objective test with regard to knowledge of the nature of the publication: it is sufficient, in other words, that the publisher ought to have known the contents of the publication. As regards intention to deprave and corrupt, this fairly clearly is not required, for any such requirement would in effect render Section 2(5) superfluous.[1] This approach was confirmed in the first reported prosecution under the Act in 1960, with the indictment of Penguin Books for the publication of *Lady Chatterley's Lover*.[2] The case went some way towards clarifying a number of points raised by the Act;[3] this amongst them. The court followed *de Montalk*,[4] and applying the normal rules of statutory interpretation, concluded that no intention to deprave or corrupt is required under the Act. This was upheld in *Shaw* v *DPP*,[5] despite the courts there taking an opposite view of the common law posi-

---

[1]   See J. Smith and B. Hogan *Criminal Law* (4th ed. London 1978) at 703.

[2]   [1961] *Crim L Rev* 177; see also C.H. Rolph *The Trial of Lady Chatterley* (London 1961). The defendants were acquitted.

[3]   For such procedural points as time limitations, see Robertson op.cit. at 74—80.

[4]   (1932) 23 Crim App Rep 182; see chapter 1.

[5]   [1962] AC 220.

tion to that apparently taken in *de Montalk*. Obscenity then was confirmed as a (partially at least) strict liability offence.

The publisher's motive, or even perhaps object, in the sense perhaps of commercial gain, is not, as *Hicklin* decided, relevant here. It is relevant in terms of possession for publication for gain, but even here gain need not denote commercial gain. The law then is apparently not concerned with the commercial exploitation of pornography as such. This contrasts with the United States position, where the Supreme Court, in an attempt apparently to introduce a further factor allowing variability of obscenity in the constitutionally approved test, has followed the line first advocated by Chief Justice Warren in *Roth* v *United States*,[1] and affirmed the relevance of pandering, or the commercial exploitation of lust.[2] The rationale of the relevance of pandering is not particularly convincing: that the commercial promotion of material may ensure the arousal of prurient interest; more convincing is estoppel.[3]

The author's intention, as distinct from the publisher's, does not appear to be relevant, other than obliquely, in the sense of its relevance to a defence of literary or other prescribed merit.

II) **The standard applied**

This consists, unlike the *Hicklin* test, of two parts: the first is concerned with the effect, the second with the nature of the work.

1) *Effect*

(i) *Its nature*. The 1959 Act omitted the reference in the *Hicklin* test to those 'whose minds are open to such immoral influences'. The central aspect of the statutory test of obscenity, the question of the depraving and corrupting effect of the material, apparently remained an open one. Was the phrase 'deprave and corrupt' to be left for the jury, or were the courts to attempt some definition? The latter clearly felt themselves under some pressure to provide the jury with some guidance here. The first attempt at definition, by the court in the *Lady Chatterley* case, did little more than furnish the jury with *The Oxford English Dictionary*'s definitions of the two words. 'Deprave' is 'to make

---

1   354 US 476 (1957) at 496.

2   See *Ginzburg* v *United States* 383 US 463 (1966) at 467; *Splawn* v *United States* 431 US 595 (1977) at 598.

3   See chapter 14.

morally bad, to pervert, to debase, or corrupt morally'; 'corrupt' is 'to render unsound or rotten, to destory the moral purity or chastity, to pervert or ruin a good quality, to debase or defile'.

A major question remained unanswered however: was obscenity to be linked in any way to action? In other words, was action, something which the common law had decisively rejected as an essential in this regard, required here in order that the immorality in question be such as to be classifiable as corrupting? This was squarely before the court in the first major case to go on appeal under the Act, in September 1960. Subsequent to the Wolfenden Report,[1] the Street Offences Act 1959 had introduced severer penalties for soliciting. A result was *The Ladies Directory*, a handbook of prostitutes' addresses and services offered. Frederick Charles Shaw, its publisher, was charged with *inter alia* contravening Section 2(1) of the Obscene Publications Act. Ashworth J remarked in this regard:

> On this third count [of publishing an obscene article], it was further submitted that in the course of his summing-up the learned judge wrongly directed the jury to have regard to what persons did after reading the article, in considering whether it was obscene ... in our view [his words] should not be regarded as a direction to the jury to consider what happened afterwards as a test of the article's obscenity.[2]

It was argued that persons in an area of prostitution came there to engage the services of prostitutes, and were already depraved and corrupt. This argument was rejected: 'The fallacy in this argument is that it assumes that a man cannot be corrupted more than once, and there is no warrant for this'.[3] The court thus clearly rejected any definition of deprave and corrupt in terms of action; beyond asserting the possibility of recorruption, however, it did not specify whether it regarded thoughts as sufficient for moral turpitude. This ruling clearly removed one of the possible varieties of variable obscenity: if it were open to a jury to decide that a man already inured to pornography could be corrupted no further, then such material, when distributed to him, would be permissible; the same material, when published to the uninitiated, would be proscribed. One aspect of distribution's significance had, in other words, been rendered inoperative.

The courts continued to avoid assigning a clear meaning to the

---

1 *Report of the Committee on Homosexual Offences and Prostitution* 1957, Cmnd 247.

2 *R v Shaw* [1961] 1 All ER 330 at 334.

3 Ibid.

phrase 'deprave and corrupt', although they occasionally stressed the strength of the words 'deprave' and 'corrupt':[1] one was not concerned here with shock or outrage; one's concern was not with an affront to public morality, but corruption of it; obscenity under the Act is more than mere vulgarity.[2] One may set against this the elevation into a point of law of the fact that one may be corrupted more than once: if the corruption is relatively profound, the possibility of such recorruption seems a little illogical. There is also the fact that thoughts may well have been sufficient for depravity and corruption; action certainly was not required. The courts' inclination was to leave matters at this, and to leave the jury to decide whether thought arousal was sufficient for depravity and corruption. As Lord Justice Salmon was to remark some eight years after the coming into force of the Act: 'When, as here, a statute lays down the definition of a word or phrase in plain English, it is rarely necessary and often unwise for the judge to attempt to improve upon or re-define the definition.'[3] And yet later in the same judgement the court felt impelled to do just this: the guidance given by the trial judge to the jury was felt to be inadequate: they had in fact 'been thrown in at the deep end'. Lord Justice Salmon attempted to outline the jury's task and more particularly the nature of depravity and corruption; it was the first attempt by a judge to be explicit in this regard:

> The tendency to deprave and corrupt may also take various forms. It may be to induce desires of a heterosexual kind or to promote homosexuality or other sexual perversions or drug-taking or brutal violence.[4]

It is clear from this that the jury have in effect to ask two questions here: the first is what the immediate effect of the material is; the second is whether this effect is depraving and corrupting, or morally debasing. This separation was made quite clear by Lord Chief Justice Parker in *DPP v A and BC Chewing Gum Ltd*, a case involving the obscenity of cards inserted into bubble gum packets:

> There were two matters for consideration. What sort of effect would these cards singly or together have upon children, and no doubt children of different ages; what would it lead them to do? Secondly, was what they were led to do a sign of corruption or

---

1   For example, Lord Reid in *Knuller v DPP* [1972] 3 WLR 143.

2   *R v Clifford* [1961] *Crim L Rev* 486.

3   *R v Calder and Boyars Ltd* [1968] 1 QB 151 at 168.

4   Ibid. at 170.

depravity?[1]

With regard to the first, thought arousal is apparently enough; with regard to the second, assessment is in terms of morality. Although the statutory language does not refer in terms to public morality,[2] deprave and corrupt were confirmed in *Penguin Books* as referring to moral debasement. That such morality is public morality is clear: the jury is to reflect contemporary community standards,[3] or public sexual morality in other words, their concern being with, it would seem, flagrant violations of such morality.[4]

The sufficiency of thought arousal, and the possibility of recorruption, was affirmed some four years after the *Boyars* case by the House of Lords in *DPP* v *Whyte*.[5] The case involved a general bookseller's shop run by the respondents (who were husband and wife); in a distinct part of the shop there was kept and sold a stock of articles described by the justices as including

> ... written descriptions or pictorial representations of sexual activity, ranging from normal sexual intercourse between male and female to such deviant sexual behaviour as intercourse *per oram*, intercourse *per anum*, acts between males, acts between females, and sexual play between or within groups of persons; and some instances of sadistic and violent behaviour.[6]

The justices found the majority of customers entering the shop had been men of middle age and upwards. These men, they concluded, were the most likely purchasers of the articles; they saw the customers as 'inadequate, pathetic, dirty-minded men, seeking cheap thrills — addicts to this type of material, whose morals were already in a state of depravity and corruption. The approach adopted by the justices is significant. They concentrated (a) on the question of who was likely to read the articles; having decided this, they then determined, (b) the question of whether these people were likely to be depraved and corrupted. In assessing this latter point they employed a consequential action type of analysis, and their finding was that the men in question were likely to: '... find the articles fascinating, enabling them to engage in private

---

1 [1968] 1 QB 159 at 164.

2 See Robertson op.cit. at 155–6.

3 See e.g. *Shaw* v *DPP* [1962] AC 220 at 292.

4 See also the discussion of the corruption requirement in the context of conspiracy to corrupt public morals, chapter 3.

5 [1972] AC 849.

6 Ibid. at 853.

fantasies of their own, but not involving overt sexual activity of any kind'.[1] This approach was rejected by the House of Lords on appeal by a majority of 3:2.[2] Their principal consideration was whether depravity and corruption was to be viewed in terms of consequential action only, or whether the promotion of thoughts and mental images was sufficient. They ruled firmly in favour of the latter:

> In my opinion, the words 'deprave and corrupt' in the statutory definition, as in the judgement of Cockburn CJ in *R* v *Hicklin*, refer to the effect of pornographic articles on the mind, including the emotions, and it is not essential that any physical sexual activity (or overt sexual activity, if that phrase has a different meaning) should result. According to the findings the articles did not leave the customers unmoved. On the contrary, they fascinated them and enabled them to engage in fantasies. Fantasies in this context must, I think, mean fantasies of normal or abnormal sexual activities. In the words of Cockburn CJ the pornographic books in the respondents' shop suggested to the minds of the regular customers thoughts of a most impure and libidinous character.[3]

If one's state of mind is the concern of the law, and if the persons considered in *Whyte* for example, purchased the articles they did because of the effect those articles had on their state of mind, then ruling out any law of diminishing corruption — the court certainly does not seem to see this as a possibility[4] — one must inevitably conclude that each time a customer reads one of these articles, he is depraved and corrupted, or rather, re-depraved and re-corrupted. And this (as in *Shaw*) is exactly the conclusion the House of Lords came to — a person may be corrupted more than once: 'The Act is not merely concerned with the once and for all corruption of the wholly innocent; it equally protects the less innocent from further corruption, the addict from

---

1   [1972] AC 849 at 853.

2   Per Lords Wilberforce, Cross of Chelsea and Pearson.

3   *DPP* v *Whyte* [1972] AC 849 at 867, per Lord Pearson.

4   Given their own ruling that erotic thoughts constitute depravity and corruption and the apparently reasonable assumption that customers would not purchase to satiation, their attitude is predictable. That a point of satiation is likely: see *The Report of the Commission on Obscenity and Pornography* (Bantam Books 1971) at page 28, where it is observed that 'The only experimental study to date found that continued or repeated exposure to erotic stimuli over 15 days resulted in satiation (marked diminution of sexual arousal and interest in such material). There was also a partial recovery of interest after two months of non-exposure.'

feeding or increasing his addiction'.[1] The emphasis in the law is thus clearly on the arousal of erotic fantasies as being sufficient to constitute depravity and corruption. The court in *Whyte* did not say that the arousal of such fantasies is *ipso facto* depraved and corrupt; what it did say though is that such depravity does not *necessarily* denote more than such an arousal. This, coupled with the strictures on recorruption, inevitably places the emphasis on thought arousal: it would not be unreasonable to regard the law in this form as being concerned principally with the control of masturbatory fantasies. This emphasis receives further weight when one considers the operation of the 1959 Act: material, although obscene, may escape proscription because of literary or other merit. If the depravity requirement is pitched very high, is it not absurd to excuse material with so profoundly damaging an effect because of literary merit? The entire construction of the Act tends towards a lowering in this sense of the primary requirement.

The jury has ostensible authority to pass, but may perhaps feel constrained to avoid passing, any and all pornography. That the exercise of this authority would countermand the prevailing emphasis in the law was recognised by at least one Law Lord in *Whyte*: Lord Cross of Chelsea remarked:

> ... counsel submitted that 'depravity' and 'corruption' are strong words and that in this day and age ordinary decent people though they may be disgusted at the thought of elderly men buying books of this sort in order to arouse sexual fantasies ... would nevertheless hesitate to say that such men were 'depraved' or 'corrupted'. As to this I would only say that the view taken by the justices [that erotic fantasies corrupted the individuals concerned] appears to me to be one which can reasonably be taken. Whether it is the only view, which can reasonably be taken does not arise for decision in this appeal.[2]

Juries have apparently resisted being boxed-in in terms of thought arousal however: they have since *R v Gold*[3] in the early 1970s, been passing soft-core pornography. Such material generally has no literary or scientific merit which might be pleaded to justify its publication as being for the public good. They are rather written specifically to titillate. It may be that juries in such cases were influenced by the so-called psychotherapeutic defence, that the publications were for the public

---

1   *DPP* v *Whyte* [1972] AC 849 at 863; this was first asserted by Ashworth J. in *Shaw* v *DPP* [1962] AC 220 at 228.

2   *DPP* v *Whyte* [1972] AC 849 at 871.

3   Unreported; see Robertson op.cit. at 4.

good in terms of aiding the psychological health of their readers. It may equally be that such juries were not prepared to find that thought arousal was such as to qualify in terms of depravity and corruption. This trend has manifested itself more recently in cases involving so-called hard-core pornography also. The Williams Committee were, for example, told of 'a succession of cases which had left the prosecuting authorities wondering where the boundary of the legal lay or even sometimes, whether any boundary would soon be left'.[1] In April and September of 1975 juries at the Central Criminal Court could not agree that American magazines depicting bondage and sado-masochism were obscene. In October of the same year Danish pornography ('of a kind described to us by the defendant in that case as the "Rolls-Royce" of pornography')[2] was found by a Portsmouth Crown Court jury not to be obscene, at least insofar as 'photographs of straightforward sexual activity between adults, whether heterosexual or homosexual and however explicit', were concerned. In these cases the juries may have based their decisions on the aversion defence that if the ordinary reader was repelled by the material, it is not obscene. What seems more likely though is that again, thought arousal was not found sufficient.

The American Supreme Court found itself in exactly this dilemma: the *Roth* test (as interpreted) referred, aside from questions of social value, to an appeal to the prurient interest, or thought arousal. The test for obscenity was a very much more specific one than the English one; jury discretion was much narrower, in the sense that the immoral effect in question was a prescribed one. The court very soon found that this was, in terms of public morality, too stringent a standard. In *Manual Enterprises* v *Day*,[3] decided only five years after *Roth*, the court introduced the standard of patent offensiveness into the test. Henceforward, and this remains the position today, the cutting-edge of the test was to be in terms of the material's patent offensiveness. It may be argued that patent offensiveness is a question of positive public morality[4]; one is not concerned then with an enquiry into a prescribed effect, but one into contemporary community standards or public morality, apparently exactly the type of inquiry prescribed by the *Roth* test.

It must be acknowledged though that decision in English law in

---

1 Report of the Committee on Obscenity and Film Censorship (HMSO 1979) para 4.4; hereafter referred to as *Williams*.

2 Ibid.

3 370 US 478 (1962),

4 See chapter 4.

terms of offensiveness has been specifically disapproved by the courts in terms of the so-called aversion defence. Hereby it is argued that though an article may include descriptions that are both graphic and shocking, the tone of that article may be 'compassionate and condemnatory'; the reader would then be so outraged that instead of '... encouraging ... him to homosexuality, drug-taking or senseless, brutal violence, it would have precisely the reverse effect'.[1] Thus although the material may be an affront to public morality, and therefore offensive, this does not mean that it depraves and corrupts. This defence represents an attempt by the courts to assert corruption as something very much more damaging to public morality than the standard employed with restrictions in terms of indecency, mere affront to community standards.[2] It also appears to confirm the emphasis in the law on thought arousal, as one is *a priori* not concerned with incitement, or indeed with the promotion of action at all. It may be that should a jury reject thought arousal as depraving, that non-obscenity, in view of aversion, is technically the only alternative open to them. And yet not every jury refuses to find hard-core pornography obscene: Mr James Anderton, Chief Constable of Greater Manchester, told the Williams Committee that in twenty-seven prosecutions under Section 2 brought between January 1977 and April 1978, all had been successful.[3] Whether the disparity between these and those results quoted earlier are the result of differing jury views as to the immorality of thought arousal, is not clear; it is at least possible that juries have on occasion in effect broken away from the present obscenity framework, and reached a decision in terms of offensiveness.

(ii)   *Distribution*. In terms of Section 2 of the Act, the effect and corruption is to be judged in terms of 'those into whose hands' the material may fall. The relevant audience in terms of the *Hicklin* test was the most susceptible person — the so-called fourteen-year-old schoolgirl rule. This apparently remained the case.[4] Lord Justice Salmon in the *Boyars* case amended this: it is necessary that a 'significant but comparatively small number' of the audience be affected. This reduced the significance of distribution in the assessment in the sense that the larger the relevant portion of the audience, the less

---

1   *R v Calder and Boyars Ltd* [1968] 1 QB 151 at 169; this ruling was confirmed four years later in *R v Anderson* [1972] 1 QB 304.

2   On this distinction and its viability, see displays, chapter 6.

3   *Williams* para 4.23.

4   See e.g. *Morgan v Bowker* [1963] 1 All ER 691.

sensitive distribution becomes in an obscenity determination. This was confirmed in *Whyte*, where Lord Cross remarked that a 'significant proportion of a class means a part which is not numerically negligible but which may be much less than half'.[1]

Distribution had in fact become less relevant in another respect also: in terms of the recorruption formula, the initiated are as much the law's concern as are the uninitiated. As the law has become increasingly concerned moreover with pornography, and as pornography is produced and bought for its effect (of thought arousal), one therefore arrives at a position in theory, if not in practice, that amounts probably to virtually constant obscenity for such material, the exceptions being where the material clearly does not affect its audience. With pornography, in other words, where distribution is general, obscenity is probably a virtual constant. Where distribution is particular however, the same may not be true: what may affect the average adult, may have no effect whatever on (say) a scientific observer. *R v Clayton*[2] provides an illustration of this: two policemen who had been sold certain photographs, testified at the trial that these aroused 'no feelings' in them at all. This was held irrelevant. On appeal Lord Parker C.J. remarked:

> This court cannot accept the contention that a photograph may be inherently so obscene that even an experienced or scientific viewer must be susceptible to some corruption from its influence. The degree of obscenity is, of course, very relevant, but it must be related to the susceptibility of the viewer.[3]

Such causal connection might similarly be absent in the distribution to the average adult of material with appeal to deviant groups, or of the distribution to adults of material with appeal only to minors.[4]

Distribution then is less significant in terms of the proportion of the audience relevant, and in terms of the likelihood of pornography, more and more the focus of concern, causing an effect which the law at any rate regards as sufficient for corruption. The rulings on recorruption have in fact removed another facet of variability for obscenity: the fact that the audience has seen the *same* material before is irrelevant. This can produce quite absurd results. In the United States recently for example[5] Eastman Kodak has been refusing to deliver slides they had

---

1   [1972] AC 849 at 870.

2   [1962] 3 All ER 500.

3   Ibid. at 502.

4   See e.g. *R v Barker* [1962] 1 All ER 748.

5   See *Time* 10 March 1980.

developed for the magazine *Penthouse*. In 1979 Kodak refused 239 out of 1,500 slides of model Teresa Mackey, and 285 slides out of 2,000 of Pet of the Year, Cheryl Rixon. The processors claim that they may be criminally liable for distributing pornography, although their legal position in seizing the material is not clear. Certainly in terms of the average person test applicable in the United States, their argument on the former point seems good. The same could be argued in England and Wales in relation for example to a publisher who refused to return to an author a manuscript he considers obscene; even were it to lead to thought re-arousal in the author, the recorruption ruling seems in these terms a little absurd.

Distribution as an instrument of variability has in fact been even further eclipsed by the introduction of the aversion defence. This specifies that material which repels the ordinary reader should not be found obscene, such revulsion breaking the causal chain in terms of effect, and in turn corruption or moral debasement. What this defence amounts to is an application of an average person standard. It is this standard which, as applied in the American obscenity test, has made distribution virtually irrelevant, obscenity — in terms of its audience — remaining a virtual constant. To what extent is this the position under Section 2 of the 1959 Act? One way of answering this is to look at the assessment of effect in terms of the average person. Only three possibilities appear to exist in this regard: first, the material, as with aversion, may repel the average person; second, it may have no effect whatever on him; and third, it may attract him. What one wishes to know is in what circumstances or ways will an inquiry in these terms *not* reflect the Section 2 test, as interpreted. In the first instance, if the material repels the average person, aversion would hold it non-obscene. In the second, if the material leaves the average person unaffected, it would not be obscene. Would the result be any different under the Section 2 approach? In terms of general distribution, it would: the question would be whether it affects a significant proportion of that audience; the audience might well contain a significant proportion of children for example, whom the material might attract. In particular distribution also the result might be different, as the audience again might be one composed, for example, of minors. What of the final instance, where the material attracts the average person? Where the distribution is general, the actual audience might be left unaffected; it is probable though that at least a significant proportion of such an audience would constitute average people, and provided a significant proportion of the audience is affected, this is enough under Section 2. Where the distribution is particular, the material might attract the average person, but leave its particular audience of children or deviants unaffected. The result in terms of Section 2 would here then be different from that arrived at in terms of a general average person test.

The American Supreme Court has had to modify its average person approach: where distribution is particular and to minors[1] or specifically defined groups of deviants,[2] prurient appeal is determined in terms of such groups, and not the average person.[3] On the basis of these amendments, the distinction between the average person approach and that under Section 2 rests on one's view of whether pornography generally appeals to, revolts, or leaves such an average person unaffected. It has been suggested that the aversion defence undermines obscenity control in the sense that most pornography, or at least hard-core pornography, revolts rather than attracts, the average viewer. Two prominent commentators on American obscenity law, Professors Lockhart and McClure, argued strongly after the *Roth* decision for a return to variable obscenity in the distribution sense. Their concern was with the accommodation within the obscenity test of children and deviants; their basic assumption as far as the average reader was concerned was that hard-core pornography would not appeal to 'sexually mature' adults.[4] The courts both in England and the United States have rejected this approach: Section 2 of the 1959 Act is clearly aimed at pornography, and the courts would not have instituted the aversion defence had they believed that it would thwart this. Equally the American Supreme Court has assumed that such material does appeal to the average person's prurient interest. Although they have not discussed this in an adequate way, the court's views here seem to be borne out by empirical investigations: much pornography does appear to appeal to the average reader.[5] This does not mean to say that he would seek it out, but rather that he would be affected sexually — if only cognitively — by it, if and when he should come into contact with it.

The assessment of effect under Section 2 would not appear then to differ very much from that of appeal to the prurient interest under the

---

1   *Ginsberg* v *New York* 390 US 629 (1968); see protection of children, chapter 5 and chapter 14.

2   *Mishkin* v *New York* 383 US 502 (1966); see chapter 11.

3   The uncertainty that exists in relation to the *Ginsberg* exception in terms of minors, as a result of the ruling in *Miller* v *California* 413 US 15 (1973) that only hard-core pornography may be proscribed is considered elsewhere: see chapters 13 and 14.

4   Lockhart and McClure 'Censorship of Obscenity: The Developing Constitutional Standards' 45 (1960) *Minnesota L Rev* 5, esp. at 68—88; see chapter 11.

5   Such conclusions must obviously make allowance for variations between men's and women's reactions, for example — in other words in terms of the vagueness of the term 'average', a problem discussed below. See, as to the effects of material, e.g. *The Report of the Commission on Obscenity and Pornography* (Bantam Books 1970); H.J. Eysenck and D.K.B. Nias *Sex, Violence and the Media* (London 1978). See chapter 15.

American obscenity test. The only real distinction lies in relation to general distribution of material which leaves the average person unaffected, but attracts its actual audience; if one accepts that much pornography attracts the average person this does not seem very significant. The meaning one attaches to the average person standard may well make such differences even less significant. Does it include children; is it a composite standard, or a reasonable man standard? The American approach is in terms of a composite standard, excluding children: a jury may take into account more sensitive adults, but not children.[1] In these terms, the difference between the American average person standard, and the approach under Section 2 becomes even narrower: if material leaves the average person unmoved, but affects a proportion of the audience, it would ostensibly be proscribed under the Section 2 approach, but not the average person test. But, if the average person is a composite of the community, the difference is elided into one virtually in terms of children only.

Paradoxically, however, both the English test and its American counterpart appear to leave children to some extent unprotected. Doubt exists as to whether the latter provides in terms of its proscription of hard-core pornography, any protection in this respect at all. The English test has also a bizarre result in this respect, in that the truly repulsive passes muster.[2] The aversion defence also probably narrows virtually to vanishing point the applicability of obscenity regulation to violence: most depictions of 'brutal violence' would presumably repel the average person, thus rendering such material permissible.

One has been talking above of the variability of effect on the audience in terms of the immediate effect of pornography. Obscenity may be variable in audience terms with respect also to the corruptive or immoral aspect of whatever immediate effect has been assessed to exist; although there is room for variability here in terms of thought arousal being assessed as corruptive of one audience but not another, the strictures on recorruption may have removed much of the manoeuvrability here.

A mere tendency to the effect in question is sufficient. This was omitted by the Supreme Court from the *Roth* definition. It is relevant in terms of any balancing that might seem appropriate in assessing the justification for this type of prohibition.

2) *The nature of the work*
(i) *Human sexuality, violence and drug-taking.* Until the early 1960s

---

1 *Pinkus v United States* 436 US 293 (1978).

2 See chapter 5, protection of children.

it was true to say that 'Obscenity has always been confined to matters related to sex or the excremental functions'.[1] In 1964 the courts broke new ground: in *John Calder (Publications) Limited* v *Powell*[2] the court upheld a forfeiture order (under the 1959 Act) by Sheffield City Justices on a book advocating drug-taking. This was upheld on appeal: '... there is no reason whatever to confine obscenity and depravity to sex, and there was ample evidence on which the justices could hold that this book was obscene'.[3] The court would perhaps have been better advised to adhere to the general understanding that obscenity related to human sexuality; in departing from this the court undoubtedly[4] imported uncertainty into the law. To leave it there is unfair: it is probably more accurate to say that the court hereby introduced a further uncertainty: the court merely demonstrated how open-ended is the test, for without sacrificing logic in its application, it managed to have it encompass an entirely new and unintended type of material. Three years later the test was extended to violence, picture cards depicting battle scenes (and inserted into bubble-gum packets) being hereby ruled obscene.[5] American obscenity law in contrast is concerned solely with human sexuality.

(ii) *A work as a whole.* Section 1(1) of the 1959 Act made it clear that a work was to be assessed as a whole, rather than in terms of isolated purple passages. This requirement was confirmed in the first reported prosecution under the Act, *R* v *Penguin Books*.[6] It in effect paves the way for the inclusion of a public good defence, in the sense of broadening the inquiry in relation to the material in question. The *Roth* test contains the same 'work as a whole' requirement.

It has subsequently been ruled that where magazines and articles comprise a number of distinct items, these items should be considered one by one, unlike the approach with novels for example, where the work is viewed as a whole in determining its obscenity.[7] This approach would clearly seem to be in accordance with S 1(1) of the 1959 Act;

---

1   N. St John Stevas *Obscenity and the Law* at 2.

2   [1965] 1 QB 509.

3   Ibid. at 515.

4   Cf. D.G.T. Williams 'The Control of Obscenity' [1965] *Crim L Rev* 479 at 522 and 530; Graham Zellick 'Violence as Pornography' [1970] *Crim L Rev* 188 at 191.

5   DPP v *A and BC Chewing Gum Ltd* [1968] 1 QB 159; confirmed by the Court of Appeal in *R* v *Calder and Boyars Ltd* [1968] 1 QB 151.

6   [1961] *Crim L Rev* 176.

7   *R* v *Anderson* [1972] 1 QB 304.

the problem is of course the determination of what constitutes a 'distinct item'. Is it reasonable to take the view, as did the court in the *Oz* case, that an advertisement (for *Suck*, a Dutch sex magazine) was a distinct item, even though it occupied a box 4 inches by 1½ inches in size, in an 8 by 11 inch sized page of classified advertisements? Perhaps even more difficult is the question whether magazine articles are themselves separable, in the sense that an article may consist primarily of illustrations or pictures, the intervening text being ill-disguised fill-in. The American approach to this latter problem has been to require some overall theme: if the pictures bear no reasonable relationship to such a theme, then they may be examined as distinct items.[1] The publisher's/author's intention may be relevant here.

Section 4 of the Act, in providing a defence of public good, refers however to 'article' and not 'items'. The question might be asked then, if a reputable newspaper published a classified column of London prostitutes, could it be pleaded that the publication of the newspaper — the 'article' in question — is for the public good? The court in *R v Gold* accepted that the answer, in terms of the Act, must be 'yes'.[2] A magazine whose publication was for the public good, but which included obscene items, would then be permissible.

(iii)   *Literary or other merit.* Section 4(1) of the 1959 Act provides for a defence of public good: no action or order may be made under the Act if '... it is proved that publication of the article in question is justified as being for the public good on the ground that it is in the interest of science, literature, art or learning, or other objects of general concern'.

The first question is as to the ambit of this defence, difficulty in interpretation arising principally in relation to the word 'learning' and the phrase 'or other objects of general concern'. To begin with the latter: defence counsel in the early 1970s sought to establish the psychological health of the community — or sections of it — as an object of 'general concern'. Such a factor could then be weighed by the jury against a work's corrupting influence, in determining its permissibility. Expert evidence, admissible in relation to the defence of public good, could in turn be called to sustain the defence. The defence in fact resulted in regular acquittals,[3] culminating in that of *Inside Linda Lovelace* at the Old Bailey early in 1976. The case sparked off a consider-

---

1   See e.g. *Ginzburg v United States* 383 US 463 (1966); see chapter 11.

2   See Robertson op.cit. at 64.

3   See Robertson op.cit. at 4.

able debate in the national press, and was probably instrumental in sealing the ultimate fate of the defence. Most of the arguments raised against the defence were spurious. *The Times*, in a highly critical leader, gave the following example of evidence (which they denounced as anything but expert, being given by Dr Brian Richards, 'not a specialist in sexual matters, but a genial general practitioner ... well liked by his patients ... [and] only too plausible a witness, in manner if not in matter') given in such cases:[1]

> Counsel then showed witness several pictures in the magazines:-
> 1. This is a picture of a female in chains, tied up and a naked man pointing a sword at the woman's genitals ...
> Dr Richards: This is for the public good because it produces a masturbatory situation. I would certainly prescribe this for a patient.
> 2. Picture of a naked man with cat of ninetails striking a woman on genitals.
> Dr Richards: This can stimulate a man. It has great therapeutic value.
> 3. Woman inserting an instrument into back passage of a man.
> Dr Richards: Yes, this has therapeutic value for that kind of man. I have patients who would be stimulated by this kind of thing.
> 4. Picture of man with rope round neck and rope round genitals. He is being caned.
> Dr Richards: Yes. This is highly therapeutic for masturbation. Making a man or woman masturbate is a highly beneficial process.
> 5. Girl, with distress in her face, arms manacled and has cuts. She is tied up. A man with a bayonet is inflicting cuts.
> Dr Richards: I have known patients who could benefit by masturbating on this.[2]

The leader concluded that 'We now of course have Dr Richards' standard defence that anything which tends to promote masturbation is for the public good. If that is accepted then even the cruellest pornography must be good, and should presumably be actively encouraged'. Yet the law, as interpreted by the courts, already sanctioned by virtue of the aversion defence much of the more extreme material to which the leader referred. The courts were to argue that the defence, once accepted, increased jury discretion: as the Court of Appeal remarked in

---

1 Dr Richards had given evidence in the *Lovelace* case.

2 *The Times* 30 January 1976; see Dr Richards' reply, *The Times* 5 February 1976; see also *The Times* 3 and 4 February 1976.

R v *Staniforth* and R v *Jordan*:

> the point at which the argument for the appellants ultimately breaks down is when it has to be conceded (as it was at an early stage by counsel for Staniforth) that the expert evidence sought to be advanced commends the merits, not of any particular publication, but of virtually all pornographic material ... Evidence advanced in support of such an argument as this cannot conceivably be within the intended scope of the language used by Parliament in S4 of the 1959 Act. To hold otherwise would be to say that Parliament had provided by S4 an opportunity for every jury to decide for itself as a matter of general public policy whether obscene material should or should not be subject to any restraint on publication under the law. This cannot possibly be a proper subject for debate in the jury room. If the argument is well founded and the experts are right in the opinion they would express in support of it, this can only lead to the conclusion that the 1959 Act is self-stultifying and might as well be repealed. The social arguments for and against maintaining a legal restraint on pornography are proper subjects for public and parliamentary debate but while the present law remains in force, the court's duty is to apply it and not allow it to be ingeniously subverted.[1]

It seems perhaps a little strange that the court should have rejected the defence on the ground of increased jury discretion: the courts placed great faith in the ability of the jury to determine first the audience, then the effect, that effect's immorality, and finally to weigh this against merit, a process which surely involves policy decision? The House of Lords in upholding the Court of Appeal, emphasised that although what is of general concern may change as society changes, the phrase is to be taken as referring to those aesthetic and intellectual values described in Section 4. It relates to 'inherent personal values of a less transient character assumed, optimistically perhaps, to be of general concern'.[2] This then excludes an object achieved in terms of a direct impact on the minds of readers or viewers. There can be no doubt of the basic reason for the courts' rejection of the defence: it was seen as something which would, whether through additional discretion, or through the hearing of expert evidence, move juries to abrogate obscenity law altogether. This the courts were not prepared to countenance, and probably correctly, returned the obscenity ball to the court in

---

1 [1976] 2 All ER 714 at 719–20.

2 *DPP* v *Jordan* [1977] AC 699 at 719, per Lord Wilberforce. The extension in *R* v *Penguin Books* [1961] *Crim L Rev* 176 to ethical value stands therefore, as does that in *R* v *Calder and Boyars* [1969] 1 QB 151 at 171 to 'sociological and ethical merit'.

which it properly belongs: the legislature.

The second problem of interpretation to arise in relation to Section 4(1) concerned the meaning of the word 'learning'. The defence submission here amounted to a perhaps even more oblique attempt to enlarge the scope of the Section 4 defence, and was rejected by the courts in *Attorney-General's Reference (No. 3 of 1977)*. It was argued that the word 'learning' was a noun, and that any sexually orientated material with an arguably educational value would fall under its protective umbrella; the Lord Chief Justice remarked that the word 'learning' in Section 4 is '... a noun, [but] counsel's argument for the respondents in this case ... that "learning" means "teaching", so that any form of education (including sex education) would be comprised in "learning" [fails].'[1]

The *Roth* test did not actually enumerate a public good defence in so many words. A work was however to be assessed as a whole, and its dominant effect was to be an appeal to the prurient interest. The entire construction was based moreover on the lack of social worth of obscenity. The latter point led logically to the interpretation of *Roth* given in *Memoirs* v *Massachusetts*, that for material to be proscribed it should be 'utterly without redeeming social value'.[2] This the *Miller* court found too onerous, and applied the standard that 'the work, taken as a whole, lacks serious literary, artistic, political, or scientific merit'.[3] The latter approach clearly allows some balancing, something rigorously excluded by the *Memoirs* test. The question of psychotherapeutic value has never arisen; the promotion of the psychological health of sections of the community is arguably something of social value. Certainly if the promotion of individual development is the type of freedom consideration relevant to the First Amendment, this could be seen as a First Amendment value. This may have been settled however by the more restrictive *Miller* formulation: in *United States* v *One Reel of Film*[4] for example, the plea (in relation to the film *Deep Throat*) that it had a sexually liberating impact was not accepted as falling within the prescribed literary, artistic, political or scientific values.

(iv)   *The author's intention*. Although this is not relevant to the question of publication, the court in the *Lady Chatterley* case admitted its relevance in relation to the assessment of literary value, for example. Mr Justice Byrne directed that 'as far as literary merit or other matters

---

1   [1978] 3 All ER 1166 at 1169.

2   383 US 413 (1966).

3   *Miller* v *California* 413 US 15 (1973) at 24.

4   481 F 2d 206 (1st Cir 1973).

that can be considered under Section 4 are concerned, I think one has to have regard to what the author was trying to do, what his message may have been, and what his general scope was'.[1] The position in terms of the American test is very similar; in fact this factor has probably received added weight because of the 'serious value' formulation.

III) The jury

1) *Expert evidence*

Section 4(2) of the Act specifically provides that expert evidence is admissible 'as to the literary, artistic, scientific or other merits of an article ...'. With regard to literary merit for example, other books in circulation may be referred to in establishing the obscenity — or non-obscenity — of the work in question, but not to attack the propriety of the prosecution, in the sense that other more objectionable works are in circulation. Mr Justice Byrne in *R* v *Penguin Books* agreed that: 'Other books may be considered, for two reasons, firstly, upon the question of the literary merit of the book which is the subject matter of the indictment, ... where it is necessary to compare that book with other books upon the question of literary merit. Secondly, ... other books are relevant to the climate of literature.'[2]

Such evidence is not admissible on the questions of the effect of material on its audience, the corruptive or immoral nature of that effect, or on the question of whether the publication is for the public good. It did briefly seem that the courts were about to lighten this burden with respect to the first stage of a jury's inquiry at any rate — that is, as to the material's effect on its audience — when in *DPP* v *A and BC Chewing Gum*[3] expert evidence was admitted by the court on this point. The scope of this concession was soon circumscribed: in *R* v *Calder and Boyars Ltd*[4] decided the next year, it was made clear that such admission had been possible only because the case involved children, the assessment required therefore being beyond the ken of the average juror. The *Chewing Gum* case ruling was considered in *DPP* v *Jordan*: Lord Wilberforce, who delivered the leading judgement, remarked that '... there may be an exception in a case where the likely readers are a special class, such that a jury cannot be expected to under-

---

1   Rolph op.cit. at 121–2.

2   Rolph op.cit. at 127.

3   [1968] 1 QB 159.

4   [1969] 1 QB 151; reaffirmed in *R* v *Anderson* [1972] 1 QB 304 at 313.

stand the likely impact of the material upon its members without assistance. In such a clear case evidence from persons qualified by study or experience of that class may be admissible'.[1] This special class he defined as including 'sexual abnormals or deviants'. Such evidence was not admissible in the instant case because the shop in question in *Jordan* was a 'normal' newsagency, selling articles that were not 'specialised', to 'ordinary' members of the public. Presumably the exception applies in the case of young children or extreme examples of deviancy; it is a moot point where homosexuals would be seen to stand in this.[2]

The exclusion of expert evidence in this way is based on the 'ultimate issue' rule in English law: no opinion evidence is admissible which relates to the very issue which the court has to decide. The rule has been subject to considerable criticism: Wigmore has rejected it as lacking any justification in principle,[3] whilst Sir Rupert Cross has taken the view that 'The exclusion of opinion evidence can easily become something of a fetish'.[4] The rule 'is nowadays more honoured in the breach than in the observance':[5] as Lord Parker argued in the *Chewing Gum* case:

> I cannot help feeling that with the advance of science more and more in-roads have been made into the old common law principles. Those who practise in the criminal courts see every day cases of experts being called on the question of diminished responsibility, and although technically the final question, 'Do you think he was suffering from dininished responsibility?' is strictly inadmissible, it is allowed time and again without any objection. No doubt when dealing with the effect of certain things on the mind science may still be less exact than evidence as to what effect some particular thing will have on the body, but that, it seems to me, is purely a question of weight.[6]

The Court of Appeal's answer in *Anderson* was brusque: 'We are not oblivious of the fact that some people, perhaps many people, will think a jury, unassisted by experts, a very unsatisfactory tribunal to decide such a matter. Those who feel like that must campaign elsewhere for a

---

1 [1977] AC 699 at 718; *contra* Viscount Dilhorne at 722.

2 See Robertson op.cit. at 155.

3 Wigmore *A Treatise on the Anglo-American System of Evidence in Trials at Common Law* (1940) para 1920.

4 R. Cross *Cross on Evidence* (5th edn, London 1979).

5 Robertson op.cit. at 159.

6 [1968] 1 QB 159 at 164.

change.'[1] The admission of such evidence would not pre-empt jury decision: the jury after all, would remain the final arbiters as to questions of fact. Such admission would however clearly be another mechanism whose operation would tend towards constant obscenity. The courts' reluctance to admit such evidence at this stage is easy to understand: with the emphasis in the law on thought arousal, and with the aversion defence, such evidence, if it tended to establish that thought arousal was not immoral, might render the law virtually inapplicable. Alternatively, such testimony might slant the jury inquiry in terms of community standards as to offensiveness, also something the courts apparently wish to avoid. Certainly it would involve a far more thorough examination of that with which the law is concerned; this the courts at this stage stage seem reluctant to permit.

The American position was a very much more liberal one. Such evidence was permitted as to prurient appeal, patent offensiveness, and social value, but not as to the question of obscenity itself. As the average person standard, assessed nationally, applied, it was argued that national community standards were beyond the ken of the average juror. Such constant obscenity has been eroded to some extent by the *Miller*[2] ruling however: community standards are now to be judged locally. Admissible is evidence as to the effect of material on deviants,[3] and probably young children, although this exception to the average person standard is, in view of the *Miller* hard-core pornography ruling, open to some doubt. Thus expert testimony is admissible on the same issues as are relevant for these purposes in English law. The extent of the tightening as to such admissibility effected by *Miller* and *Paris* must be open to some doubt however: the Supreme Court did not define 'local'; such standards may well be state-wide, something almost as far beyond the ken of the average juror as a mythical national standard. The extent to which such eivdence is constitutionally admissible is not therefore altogether clear.

2)   Jury challenges

In view of the inadmissibility of expert evidence as to contemporary community standards, the composition of the jury is clearly of considerable relevance. In the United States prospective jurors may be questioned at length by both sides, and even be subject to psychiatric or other investigation to gauge possible antagonisms. The Williams

---

1   [1972] 1 QB 304 at 311.

2   *Miller* v *California* 413 US 15 (1973).

3   *Paris Adult Theater* v *Slaton* 413 US 49 (1973) at 56.

Committee reported considerable concern at the use of jury challenges in this country in obscenity trials. 'The law allowed each defendant seven peremptory challenges, so that in a case involving more than one defendant the chances of getting a jury thought to be sympathetic were much increased.'[1] Twenty-six prospective jurors were challenged in the *Oz* trial, and twelve in the *Lovelace* case, before twelve jury members were finally chosen. *The Times*, in disapproving the type of acquittal obtained in *Lovelace*, remarked that 'The defence often uses its right to challenge the jury in order to try to get a number of sympathetic looking jurors, perhaps young men of radical appearance, and to remove unsympathetic jurors such as women'.[2]

Such jury manipulation might clearly result in something quite other than community standards being represented. However Williams found that concern over this had subsided after the introduction of Section 43 of the Criminal Law Act 1977. This measure, not confined to obscenity trials, reduced the number of peremptory challenges from seven to three. Juries tend to be middle-aged, and jury challenging in this limited form may then be seen to be working in favour of greater representativeness:

> Those who have observed obscenity trials at the Old Bailey for several years would tell you that the majority of jurors are generally in the extremity of middle and late-middle age. If a jury is to be a cross-section of the community, and it is vital in such a case, the chances of it so being without defence challenges are small. Despite this, juries tend to be middle-aged and therefore by your facile definition 'unsympathetic' to pornography. Perhaps this is appropriate since the majority of *aficionados* interested in the kind of drivel which is contained inside Linda Lovelace are of the age of Times leader writers or even older.[3]

Nonetheless, can a jury reliably be said to be representative in this so crucial manner, as far as obscenity trials are concerned? The aversion defence is an integral part of the obscenity test; say that the exhibits are so repellent that a juror feels unable to pass impartial judgement. If all such jurors are excused, the operation of the defence is surely threatened. Equally, what of prospective jurors with strong ideas on pornography? The Court of Appeal has emphasised that

> A jury consists of twelve individuals chosen at random from the

---

1   *Williams* para 4.11.

2   *The Times*, leader column, 30 January 1976.

3   Letter from Nicholas de Jongh, a journalist on *The Guardian*, in reply to the editorial of 30 January 1976; *The Times* 3 February 1976.

appropriate panel. A juror should be excused if he is personally concerned in the facts of a particular case ... (but) it is contrary to established practice for jurors to be excused on more general grounds such as race, religion or political beliefs or occupation.[1]

It is quite clear that juries should reflect contemporary community standards of morality: if however jurors are to be excused on the ground that moral beliefs are *sui generis* 'race, religion, political beliefs or occupation', how could juries be representative? Equally if jurors are *not* to be excused on these grounds is this not contrary to the obvious rule that a juror should not serve if he has preconceived ideas as to the facts in the case? This gives one a neat illustration of the difficulties involved in insisting that decisions in terms of depravity or immorality are questions of fact at all. The difficulties inherent in representative jury function in this area surely demand — if one wishes to ensure that something more than subjective prejudice and personal taste is enforced — the admission of expert testimony as to such standards.

3)   *The process of decision*

The 1959 Act did not spell out the precise relationship between obscenity and the defence of public good. Is a work justified on the latter ground not obscene, or is it obscene, but justifiable? Lord Justice Salmon gave, in *R v Calder and Boyars Ltd*,[2] a long overdue[3] explanation in this regard. The jury is first to consider whether the article is obscene or not; only when this has been determined can the defence and expert evidence therewith be considered. It is not only the sequence that is of importance; Lord Justice Salmon laid down also how a jury was to go about assessing the success or failure of such a defence: they are to balance the degree of obscenity of the article against 'the strength of the literary, sociological or ethical merit' which they assess it to possess:

> A book may be worthless; a book may have slight, but real merit; it may be a work of genius. Between these extremes the gradations are almost infinite. A book may tend to deprave and corrupt a significant but comparatively small number of its readers or a large number or indeed a majority of its readers. The tendency to deprave and corrupt may be strong or slight.

The jury has first of all to assess the audience, then the effect on

---

1   Practice Direction [1973] 1 All ER.

2   [1968] 1 QB 151 at 170; this was confirmed in *DPP v Jordan* [1977] AC 699.

3   *Penguin Books* had provided some guidance on this point.

that audience, whether that effect is depraving or immoral, the question of public good, and finally to balance any obscenity against public good. A jury supposedly sits to determine questions of fact; can all of these determinations be seen as factual, or not? The question of the audience, and the effect on it may be analogous to decisions of fact elsewhere in the law; when one reaches the question of depravity or immorality however, one is surely requiring of the jury a quasi-legislative decision. Despite difficulties in terms of representativeness as far as the community is concerned, and without the aid of expert evidence, can a jury seriously be expected to assess something as subjective, and in recent years as mobile as positive sexual morality, as a question of fact?

Standards over the last two decades have changed enormously. If polls are to be believed, most adults in Britain favour the removal of controls on most erotica, provided the sale of such material does not involve gratuitous offence to the public.[1] In 1977 a marketing survey found that soft-core pornography reached 27,000,000 readers each year.[2] The Metropolitan Commissioner of Police, answering criticism of police laxity in respect of Soho pornography dealers, replied that 'The comparative absence of public complaint suggests that pornography causes less public unease than most other breaches of the law'.[3] At the same time, there are many who favour stringent controls: the Williams Committee for example record that 'the most repressive proposals submitted to us were from a group of people who wanted the meaning of obscenity made explicit through a list which included "photographic portrayal of the adult female breast" '.[4] It may be that a general moral consensus in this regard was not a problem in 1868 when the *Hicklin* test was handed down: the general consensus in society probably then was that the artificial arousal of erotic fantasies depraved and corrupted. As standards have changed, one has, via the stage of admitting literary merit, arrived at the present position. With greater freedom, has come greater divergence of view. This divergence has been recognised by the courts: as Lord Justice Bridge pointed out in *Staniforth*:

> The difficulty [for the jury], which becomes ever-increasingly

---

1   A December 1973 poll revealed that 74 per cent of those questioned agreed with the proposition that 'Adults should be allowed to buy whatever indecent or erotic books and magazines they like, as long as they are not on public display'. See 'It's Not Easy to Shock the British' *The Sunday Times* 30 December 1973, reporting the results of a poll conducted by the Opinion Research Centre.

2   'Mintel' Survey, reported in *Campaign* 21 January 1977; quoted in Robertson op.cit. at 8.

3   Affidavit of Sir Robert Mark, quoted in *R v Metropolitan Commissioner of Police, ex parte Blackburn* [1973] 2 WLR 43 at 52.

4   *Williams* para 9.26.

apparent, is to know what is the current view of society. In times past there was probably a general consensus of opinion on the subject, but almost certainly there is none today. Not only in books and magazines on sale at every bookstall and newsagents' shop, but on the stage and the screen as well, society appears to tolerate a degree of sexual candour which has already invaded a large area considered until recently to lie within the forbidden territory of the obscene. The jury's formidable task, with no other guidance than S1 of the 1959 Act gives them (and that is precious little), is to determine where the line should be drawn. However conscientiously juries approach this responsibility, it is doubtful, in the present climate of opinion, whether their verdicts can achieve any reasonable degree of consistency.[1]

The courts have essentially been caught between two stools: on the one hand there has been the recognition of the need to define the phrase 'deprave and corrupt'; in other words to contain jury discretion to some extent, thus countering criticism of the law in terms of its overbreadth and lack of certainty. There had been a shift towards an emphasis on the nature of material with the inclusion in the Act of the public good defence. This the courts continued, placing more emphasis on the nature of material, and less on its variable effect: obscenity came to be virtually equated with pornography,[2] providing something far closer to constant obscenity. Assuming that much pornography affects the average person, one's immediate effect factor came closer to being a constant, whilst variability as to corruption in terms of re-exposure was ruled out. The non-commercial intention of the author or publisher, another possible avenue for variability, is not relevant either, whilst aversion ensures that material repellent to the average person is not covered, and that the law does not operate in terms of an even vaguer offensiveness standard. Although two linked factors tending to provide constancy were excluded — national standards and expert evidence — something close to a constant may have been achieved.

All this was to assume however a reasonably constant positive morality: if obscenity may vary in terms of the audience, the intentions of the publisher and the breadth of locality used for assessment, it may also vary in terms of time. And here the courts found themselves in difficulty: an obscenity test couched in terms of proscribing material without value, and written to titillate — pornography — has probably

---

1   [1976] 2 All ER 714 at 720.

2   'Pornography' is not a precisely defined term, but the gist of most attempted definitions would appear to be material without pretensions to literary, artistic or scientific merit, which is produced with the object of engendering sexual titillation amongst its audience, in other words material which evokes sexual fantasies; see chapter 11.

become an anachronism in terms of today's standards. Hence the courts' reluctance to prescribe thought arousal as *ipso facto* depraving or immoral. The jury then find themselves in an odd position: the test is weighted in favour of thought arousal as sufficient, an aspect of this being the aversion defence, which excludes decision in terms of patent offensiveness. This emphasis may mean that they feel constrained to restrict material they do not rate as corrupting, and sanction material they wish to proscribe; they are on the other hand told that depravity and corruption is a question for their discretion. The courts have in effect achieved the worst of two worlds: they have, in trying to reduce overbreadth, to some extent tied the jury to a particular view of morality, thus making it difficult for them to reflect change; at the same time they assert that discretion remains to the jury, a discretion which is nowadays exercised in terms of a positive sexual morality which is far more disparate than that of twenty years ago. Their efforts have confused juries, without substantially evading difficulties of overbreadth and lack of specificity inherent in the type of discretion still apparently accorded juries in this area. The courts have on occasion openly acknowledged how unsatisfactory the law now is in this regard: as Lord Wilberforce remarked in *Whyte*

> I have serious doubts whether the Act will continue to be workable in this way, or whether it will produce tolerable results. The present is, or in any rational system ought to be a simple case, yet the illogical and unscientific nature of the Act has forced the Justices into untenable positions.[1]

The American Supreme Court has encountered similar difficulty in defining obscenity. The *Roth* test originally defined obscenity in terms of an appeal to the prurient interest. The attractions of this were obvious in that the basic policy decision as to what type of effect merited proscription had already been taken, thereby reducing jury discretion and grounds for challenge to the standard as overbroad. The Court in fact went out of its way to emphasise that while the obscenity standard was not overbroad, virtually any alternative in this area would be.[2] Overbreadth was also to an extent refuted by movement towards constant obscenity, in that appeal was judged in terms of the average person, with the help of expert testimony, and with reference to national standards. A commercial motive, although proposed by Chief Justice Warren in *Roth*, was not approved by the court until *Ginzburg* v *United*

---

1   [1972] AC 849 at 862.

2   See e.g. *Interstate Circuit, Inc* v *Dallas* 390 US 676 (1968); see also chapters 10 and 11.

States.[1] As one reached the 1960s, and a rapidly shifting positive sexual morality, it soon became clear that this was too restrictive. The Court therefore introduced in 1962 in *Manual Enterprises* v *Day*[2] the concept of patent offensiveness. This is quite clearly a broader standard than the original one, with its fairly narrowly defined concern with an appeal to the prurient interest; constant obscenity helped to some extent to contain overbreadth. However by the early 1970s, positive morality had shifted even further in the direction of tolerance; this much is hardly open to dispute. The Court was once again threatened with having obscenity law left high and dry by this receding tide. There is not, and probably in a country as diverse as the United States, never has been, a national standard: experts, in attempting to establish such a standard, would probably tend to be influenced by the more progressive and tolerant areas of the country than the more reactionary. Certainly by the mid-1970s a number of states had abolished their obscenity laws with respect to adults altogether; by applying a supposed national standard as a constant, the Court ran the risk of reducing the ambit of any prohibition to a minimal level.

Hence the return in *Miller* to local standards, and the abandonment of the strict 'utterly without redeeming social value' approach to the First Amendment value section of the test. The ambit of the test, even though the word 'local' in terms of standards has not been defined by the Court, has clearly been broadened. Sensitive to charges of overbreadth, the Court therefore introduced a list-type limitation on what may be regulated by obscenity laws.[3] This limitation has been rendered virtually toothless by a subsequent ruling[4] that these were merely examples, and not an exhaustive list; no limit is therefore placed on the types of sexual conduct which may be listed, as long as listed they are. The Supreme Court has therefore couched obscenity so that the cutting edge of the test is in terms of patent offensiveness, an ill-defined concept subject to overbreadth criticism; the attempt to pre-empt such criticism has not been conspicuously successful. The similarities between the two jurisdictions in terms of this aspect of jury function are striking; the difference lies in the fact that an American jury is not tied to prurient appeal in the same way that an English counterpart, with the law's emphasis on thought arousal, may feel itself to be.

In addition to the process described above, a jury must then proceed

---

1 383 US 463 (1966).

2 370 US 478 (1962).

3 *Miller* v *California* 413 US 15 (1973) at 25; see chapter 13.

4 *Ward* v *Illinois* 431 US 767 (1977); on the difficulties of a list approach in definition, see displays, chapter 6.

to assess, this time with expert help, the defence of public good. Such testimony is not permissible on the question of public good itself; as a result the jury has to proceed itself to weigh, as though one is talking in terms of pounds and ounces, obscenity against public good, to determine whether the material should be proscribed or not: '... they must ask themselves whether more people will be enlightened than will be depraved, which is one of the great imponderables of all time'.[1] This final aspect of the assessment means that jury discretion at this end of the scale is wide. They are in effect here again making a policy decision: although the grounds on which something may be for the public good appear to be fairly circumscribed, once within their ambit, the jury is asked to weigh harm against merit. This amounts to being asked to weigh individual freedom, particularly freedom of speech, as manifested in terms of literary, artistic or intellectual merit, against corruptive effect. Not only does this fuel criticisms of overbreadth; there is also something peculiarly absurd in saying that material is obscene, but permissible. Certainly the harm the material occasions cannot be vital if literary merit can outweigh it. The recognition of literary or other merit perhaps presaged the shift in positive morality away from what may have been a general consensus on thought arousal: if thought arousal is permissible where occasioned by material of recognised literary merit, why should it not be permissible when aroused by less tasteful or significant productions? As Williams remarked

> ... many pointed out to us the assumption embodied in the present law, which they found extraordinary, that there could be a work which tended to deprave and corrupt those who read it, but that, at the same time, it was for the public good that readers be depraved and corrupted, so long as it was by art.[2]

American law managed to avoid this pitfall: the *Roth* test (as interpreted) applied only to material which was 'utterly without redeeming social value'.[3] As a result the jury was not permitted to balance First Amendment value against obscenity. There was thus no question of material being obscene but justifiable. *Miller* has changed this: material with less than 'serious' literary, artistic or other specified value may be proscribed, what value there is presumably being balanced against obscenity. The court, in introducing greater variability into the test in terms of local standards, did the same with 'serious' value. Discretion at

---

1   Graham Zellick 'Obscene or Pornographic? Obscenity and the Public Good' (1969) 27 *Camb LJ* 177 at 178.

2   *Williams* para 2.19.

3   *Memoirs v Massachusetts* 383 US 413 (1966).

this end of the scale is nonetheless considerably narrower than under the English test.

4) *Double jeopardy*

It is an established rule in English criminal law that once acquitted or convicted of an offence, one cannot be re-tried on the same charge. The supposed variability of obscenity provides an exception to this: if the obscenity of a published article depends on its audience, it follows that every publication, dependent on variations in that audience, constitutes a separate offence on which different jury verdicts are possible. Neither pleas of *autrefois acquit* nor *autrefois convict*, as the case may be, will be available.

On what other grounds may the courts control prosecutions, in the sense of being able to stop a prosecution? This is an area which has received scant attention in terms of analysis and comment;[1] it is also something which cannot be entered upon fully here. An attempt will therefore be made to assess possible grounds of judicial action principally in terms of their relationship to obscenity prosecutions. The first such ground would appear to be the entry, in exceptional circumstances, by the Attorney-General of a *nolle prosequi* to stop a trial on indictment. The prosecution ends there; the Attorney-General's decision cannot be questioned.[2] In addition the Director of Public Prosecutions may take over any proceedings, and (in terms of the Prosecution of Offences Act 1908, Section 2(3)) offer no evidence or invite acquittal. Were this to be done in an obscenity prosecution, that would be an end of the matter. The second possibility is *res iudicata* in the sense of issue estoppel, a rule of civil law which precludes one party to litigation from raising an issue which has been conclusively determined in an earlier hearing. The House of Lords in *DPP* v *Humphrys*[3] decided that this doctrine has no place in the criminal law, apart from *autrefois* principles. Because juries do not specify necessarily which facts were found proved, the exclusion of this doctrine from the criminal law may be sensible.[4] What *Humphrys* did not consider was a decision of law by a civil court, and its potential operation in this sense. There would not seem to be

---

1   I drew here on an article by a colleague David Feldman, 'Declarations and the Control of Prosecutions', due to appear in *The Criminal Law Review*; I am grateful to him for a preview of his work. The article has since been published: (1981) *Crim L Rev* 25.

2   See e.g. *R* v *Comptroller General of Patents* [1899] 1 QB 909 at 914.

3   [1977] AC 1.

4   Feldman op.cit.

anything in principle to prevent such estoppel from operating.[1] This is of little relevance to obscenity cases, turning as they usually do on questions of fact.

A third situation in which control may be possible is if the prosecution is considered an abuse of the process of the court, vexatious, or oppressive. The House of Lords appears to have confirmed a residual power in the High Court to halt prosecutions under such circumstances.[2] A prosecution would qualify as vexatious were there for example no possibility of its succeeding; as oppressive if it constitutes harassment of the accused; and an abuse of the court's function if the issue which is being argued could conveniently be decided elsewhere. There are apparently three courses open to a court which feels that one or more of these conditions (as appropriate) has been satisfied: it may grant an injunction restraining the prosecutor; a declaration; or as the trial court, halt the prosecution. It would seem clear that the residual power of the High Court in such instances may be exercised in the form of an injunction where there are concurrent civil and criminal proceedings between the same parties, where the facts are not in dispute, and the point of law is the same.[3] This is of little relevance for obscenity cases which usually turn on questions of fact. Its possible relevance is made even more remote in that no injunction can be granted against a prosecutor who is an officer of the crown, or represents the crown.[4]

What of declarations? To obtain a declaration[5] *locus standi* should adhere to the party seeking the declaration. In matters of public concern, such a party would need to demonstrate a direct and substantial interest in the matter in question. It is unlikely that *locus standi* would in these terms adhere to a third party; someone who might himself be prosecuted in relation to certain conduct might claim such an interest. It would appear though that a declaration will not issue merely to clarify the legal position in relation to prospective conduct. Lord Dilhorne in *Imperial Tobacco Ltd v Attorney General*[6] specifically disapproved *dicta* by Lord Denning MR in the Court of Appeal that it might be open to the person who would be the accused in criminal procee-

---

1 Feldman op.cit.

2 See *Conelly* v *DPP* [1964] AC 1254; *DPP* v *Humphrys* [1977] AC 1.

3 Feldman op.cit.

4 Crown Proceedings Act 1947, Section 21.

5 For a fuller discussion, see declarations as a possible prior restraint in relation to books and magazines, chapter 7.

6 [1980] 1 All ER 866.

dings to seek a declaration. He went on: 'I can well see the advantages of persons being able to obtain rulings on whether or not certain conduct on which they propose to embark will be criminal and it may be a defect in our present system that it does not provide for that'. Although he did not say such a declaration could never be made, the circumstances would have to be exceptional.[1] Lord Lane did remark in *Imperial Tobacco*[2] however that where proceedings are 'vexatious or an abuse of the function of the court', a declaration might issue. This would presumably apply where it was felt that the prosecution should not be continued *per se*, or where it was felt that the issue might more conveniently be determined civilly. Where issued, a declaration would not have the effect of *autrefois acquit*,[3] but any prosecution thereafter would clearly be vexatious. Whether this means that a declaration may be issued in relation to past conduct, in order to prevent a future prosecution, or whether Lord Lane merely meant that where declaration proceedings were already on foot, and a prosecution was instituted, the declaration might, despite the prosecution, be granted provided the latter is vexatious, is not clear. Even if the former is correct such declarations would be very sparingly issued, otherwise 'suits would proliferate and become intolerably confused'.[4] If one adds to this the fact that declarations will generally be granted only as to questions of law and not of fact, their relevance in terms of controlling obscenity prosecutions, or indeed as potential prior restraints, is probably very limited.

The last method of stay is for the trial court to refuse to continue with the proceedings.[5] It would seem most unlikely that the courts would exercise this power in an obscenity case. As Lord Morris remarked in *Knuller* v *DPP*, 'Those who skate on thin ice can hardly expect to find a sign which will denote the precise spot where they may fall in'.[6] The authorities cannot always be relied on to honour the spirit of the double jeopardy rule, and technically each publication over time or space involves a separate offence. It might be argued that with much pornography, one has come close to constant obscenity; discretion however remains with the jury, and the argument is unlikely to succeed. Take the case of film maker John Lindsay: after being acquitted in

---

1 [1980] 1 All ER 866 at 875–6.

2 Ibid. at 884.

3 Ibid. at 875 and 877 per Viscount Dilhorne; at 884 and 887 per Lord Lane.

4 Ibid. at 875.

5 *DPP* v *Humphrys* [1977] AC 1 at 45–6 per Lord Salmon; 52–5 per Lord Edmund-Davies.

6 [1972] 3 WLR 143.

conspiracy to publish obscene material, he was indicted in London eleven months later under the 1959 Act in relation to the same films. Despite a second acquittal, he was indicted the next month, again with the DPP's approval, and again in relation to the same film, *Jolly Hockey Sticks*. This despite a statement by the Director at the time, Sir Norman Skelhorn — made two years earlier — that decisions on obscenity prosecutions would be made on 'our experience of how the courts have reacted in previous cases'.[1]

IV) Rationale of the offence

Obscenity has from the time of *Curl*'s case been a clear extension to the criminal law coverage provided by the law of incitement. It has not in other words related to criminal conduct; more recently the courts have confirmed that it does not necessarily relate to conduct at all. It began as, and has continued to be, a restriction in terms of public, or positive morality. Although the statutory phrase 'deprave or corrupt' does not specify a decision in terms of community standards, the courts have made it clear that this is what is entailed. Even had they not done so, the *Oxford English Dictionary* defines the words in terms of moral debasement. If the jury is not to apply subjective, personal standards, it can be concerned only with contemporary community standards of morality.

The courts have interpreted the statute in such a way however, that the definition of obscenity places a clear emphasis on thought arousal as a sufficient effect for corruption. They have also tended, in terms of asserting the possibility of recorruption and aversion, for example, to channel the application of the definition in the direction of constant obscenity. They had good reasons for so doing: such interpretation reduced jury subjectivity, and directed the law towards that which the courts deemed was Parliament's objective — the suppression of pornography. The difficulty with this was that basic community standards were all the while changing. Juries may therefore have found the emphasis in the law one which they regard as outmoded. The courts, anxious not to render the law inoperative, made it clear that discretion still adhered to the jury: it was therefore up to a jury to reach a decision in terms more demanding than thought arousal. Conduct was *a priori* not necessary: the clear alternative was in terms of what they found patently offensive. The courts however, anxious not to allow decision in terms of mere offensiveness, of a mere affront to, rather

---

1 See *The Sunday Times* 1 February 1976; Robertson op.cit. at 76—7.

than a corruption of public morality, have purported, with their emphasis on corruption and the aversion defence, to rule this out.

Jury discretion then remains, whilst the application of the test is confusing, and results unpredictable. As the Williams Committee, set up late in 1977 to investigate this area of law and its operation found, besides concern now largely assuaged over the psychotherapeutic defence and jury challenges, the main criticism of the Act is of the 'deprave and corrupt' formula and its operation.[1] No one appears to be satisfied with the Act: to libertarians, it is too wide; to those on the other end of the spectrum, its prohibition is too narrow and difficult to apply. The judiciary is clearly unhappy about the law: Lord Wilberforce thinks it illogical and unscientific, Lord Justice Bridge feels the 1959 Act gives precious little guidance as to what is obscene, whilst Lord Denning remarked (in the course of reviewing the standard applied by the GLC in licensing films) that the Act has 'misfired'[2] in his view because it does not provide a sufficiently tight control.

One clearly cannot assess the present law and its alleged failure without considering its aims. Its primary aim is clearly the protection and enforcement of public morality. Insofar as this is the case, obscenity law is clearly an instrument designed to protect the *status quo*. Blasphemy, sedition, and obscenity were seen in *Curl* as offences against 'good government'; the law has not and cannot, in its present form, lose this early association with political management. The trials in the early 1970s — *I.T.* in 1970, *Oz* in 1971, and *Nasty Tales* in 1973 — were aimed largely at the political unorthodoxy of the underground press. The next question is whether such a control is still desirable or necessary. It must be asked whether, bearing in mind the astonishing shifts in public sexual morality and the probable fragmentation of what may, in Victorian times, have been a broad consensus on such issues, the enforcement of such morality is justifiable in policy terms. If it is not, are there any other policy considerations which might justify a prohibition of this type? It must be remembered with regard to the enforcement of morality that as consensus in society on this score has diminished, such enforcement becomes increasingly open, in terms of a jury assessment of standards as a question of fact, to the criticism of overbreadth and lack of certainty. This in turn means a reliance on a form of strict liability in terms of *mens rea*.

Not only should permissible policy aims be assessed, but the relevance of individual freedom, particularly freedom of speech, should be taken into account also. Such policy considerations should then be

---

1   *Williams* paras 4.9 to 4.11.

2   *R v Greater London Council, ex parte Blackburn* [1976] 1 WLR 550.

applied in deciding just what type of legal prohibition, if any, society needs or wants in this area. The courts have assiduously avoided any discussion of this sort: one of the few judicial assessments came — prophetically — from Mr Justice Devlin (as he then was). In *R v Penguin Books*, Mr Justice Byrne, besides defining 'deprave and corrupt' in terms of moral debasement, went on to quote with approval a passage from Mr Justice Devlin's remarks in the 1954 prosecution of Hutchinson:

> Just as loyalty is one of the things which is essential to the well-being of a nation, so some sense of morality is something that is essential to the well-being of a nation, and to the healthy life of the community, and accordingly, anyone who seeks by his writing to corrupt that fundamental sense of morality is guilty of obscene libel ... Of course, there is a right to express oneself, either in pictures or in literature. People who hold strong political views are often anxious to say exactly what they think, irrespective of any restraint, and so too a creative writer or a creative artist, one can well understand, naturally desires complete freedom with which to express his talents or his genius. But he is a member of the community like any other member of the community. He is under the same obligation to other members of the community as any other is, not to do harm, either mentally or physically or spiritually, and if there is a conflict between an artist or writer in his desire for self-expression, and the sense that morality is fundamental to the well-being of the community, if there is such a conflict, then it is morality which must prevail.[1]

The remarks above were made in the context of the common law, and to be fair to the courts, it would probably be neither reasonable nor fair to expect them, in the absence of constitutional provisions enabling or obliging them so to do, to explore and pronounce on the type of policy debate outlined above. The reference of these questions, together with indecency and film controls generally, to a governmental committee such as Williams for full consideration was probably long overdue. Before discussing such policy considerations,[2] it is proposed to examine the common law offences applicable in this area, particu-

---

1   Rolph op.cit. at 229–30.

2   It is proposed to consider the questions of criminal jurisprudence and policy raised above in the course of chapter 4. Although there is no Bill of Rights in the United Kingdom, its possible relevance, and indeed the possible constitutional importance of such policy issues will be examined in chapter 9, together with the possible relevance of any international obligations, such as the European Convention on Human Rights. Whether a prohibition is justified in terms of the emergent policy framework, and the Williams Committee's view on these questions, will be discussed in the final chapter.

larly conspiracy to corrupt public morals, which in policy terms appears to be on all fours with statutory obscenity.

3 The residual area of the common law

Section 2(4) of the 1959 Act probably attempted to do away with the common law offences in this area, particularly obscene libel in all its manifestations:[1] 'a person publishing an article shall not be proceeded against for an offence at common law consisting of the publication of any matter contained or embodied in the article where it is of the essence that the matter is obscene'.

I) Inchoate offences

1) *Conspiracy*

In *Shaw* v *DPP*[2] the House of Lords ruled that Section 2(4) did not abolish the old offence of publishing an obscene libel, but merely prevented a prosecution from being brought.[3] The court did not accept that it was Parliament's intention that in future all proceedings in respect of obscene publications should be brought under the Act; emphasis was rather laid by the Lords on the distinction between the publication of an article, and a conspiracy so to publish. The latter consists in

---

1 Cf. J.C. Smith and Brian Hogan, *The Criminal Law* (4th edn London 1978) at 705.

2 [1962] AC 220.

3 Ibid. at 268, 269, 290, 291.

the agreement to publish and not in the *publication*[1] itself. In *Shaw* the accused had been convicted of publishing an obscene article, of conspiracy to corrupt public morals, and of conspiring to outrage public decency. In terms of the Lords' view of both Section 2(4) of the Act and of the nature of a conspiracy charge, it was possible for them to uphold both conspiracy convictions, thereby recognising — some would argue, creating — the offences of conspiracy to corrupt public morals and conspiracy to outrage public decency.[2]

It is beyond the scope of this investigation to discuss the problems of whether those offences were part of the common law prior to *Shaw* or not, or the related question of whether corruption of public morals and outraging public decency are themselves substantive offences at common law. Suffice it to say that the conspiracy offences became an established part of the law, even though it remains doubtful, especially in the case of corruption of public morals, whether a substantive offence is involved.[3]

(i)   *Conspiracy to corrupt public morals.* If conspiracy to corrupt public morals is part of the law, what varieties of conduct might arguably fall within its ambit? The conspiracy aspect here does not raise particular problems. The outstanding question is, what is meant by, and encompassed by, corruption of public morals? An initial question in this regard is, should the corruption necessarily be effected by a particular act or variety of acts? Need the corruption be occasioned by publication for example, as with the Obscene Publications Act 1959? Case law would not appear to have imposed any such limitation on the operation of this offence, whose ambit appears to extend potentially to any means whatever of effecting corruption. A second question here is, what exactly is meant by 'corrupt' in this context? The Law Lords in

---

1   '... the least systematic, the most irrational branch of English penal law [conspiracy] still rests on the legal fiction that the offence lies not in the overt acts themselves which are injurious to the commonwealth but in an inferred anterior agreement to commit them.' Per Lord Diplock in *DPP* v *Bhagwan* [1970] 3 WLR 501 at 509.

2   *Shaw* also purported to recognise the offence of conspiracy to effect a public mischief. This was upheld in *Knuller* v *DPP* [1972] 3 WLR 143, but was reversed in *DPP* v *Withers and Others* [1974] 3 WLR 751. It has been suggested that the way is now open for the recognition also of conspiracy to publish an obscene libel, and for other inchoate offences such as attempt and incitement. See Graham Zellick 'Films and the Law of Obscenity' [1971] *Crim L Rev* 126 at 140. In this respect, see below p.77.

3   The Court of Appeal in *Shaw* v *DPP* [1962] AC 220 held that corruption of public morals is a substantive offence at common law. The House of Lords (at 283, 285, 289–90) left the matter open, and no statutory or judicial pronouncement since then appears to have taken the matter further. Outraging public decency was declared in *R* v *Mayling* [1963] 2 QB 717 to be a substantive offence. This was upheld (*obiter*) by the House of Lords in *Knuller*.

Shaw approved a direction to the jury in which the trial judge remarked: 'I wonder really whether it means in this case and in this context much more than lead astray morally'.[1] Lord Reid in *Knuller* took a somewhat more rigorous view:

> 'Corrupt' is a strong word and the jury ought to be reminded of that as they were in the present case. The Obscene Publications Act appears to use the words 'deprave' and 'corrupt' as synonymous, as I think they are. We may regret that we live in a permissive society, but I doubt if even the most staunch defender of a better age would maintain that all or even most of those who have been at one time or in some way or another led astray morally have thereby become depraved and corrupted. I think that the jury should be told in one way or another that although in the end the question whether matter is corrupting is for them, they should keep in mind the standards of ordinary decent people.[2]

Lord Simon of Glaisdale remarked that: 'The words "corrupt public morals" suggest conduct which a jury might find to be destructive of the very fabric of society.'[3] This would appear definitely to narrow down the ambit of the word 'corrupt'. One should remember however that Lord Reid did not in his remarks in *Knuller* attach any different meaning to 'corrupt' in this context than that it enjoys in the context of the Obscene Publications Act 1959. In the latter case the arousal of thoughts may clearly be a sufficient effect to constitute depravity and corruption. Certainly in *Shaw*[4] the corruption of public morals in question took place via the publication of an article in relation to which no finding of a tendency to promote subsequent conduct was (under the Obscene Publications Act) required. Considerations of this sort reduce the impact of Lord Simon's pronouncement that corrupt should be destructive of 'the very fabric of society'. Although Lord Reid in his stricture about the standards of ordinary decent people does not spell this out, he presumably meant the jury merely to take corruption as being something contrary to, or perhaps flagrantly contrary to, such standards. The courts, with the aversion defence in relation to statutory obscenity, have attempted to exclude offence, in the sense of a mere affront to, rather than corruption of public morality; such distinction

---

1   *Shaw* v *DPP* [1962] AC 220 at 290.

2   [1972] 3 WLR 143 at 148.

3   Ibid. at 180.

4   *Shaw* v *DPP* [1962] AC 220.

may be rather difficult to draw in practice.

The corruption in question here is of 'public morals'. Are these morals *sexual* morals, or is the field broader than this? Although prosecutions that have been brought would appear to be in terms of sexual morality,[1] such distinction has not been judicially drawn; the offence could apparently at present encompass the corruption of public morality of a non-sexual variety. A second and more difficult question is, what are 'public morals'? Are they the morals of those individuals affected by the conduct in question; the morals of the average person; or merely a vague, abstract standard? Certainly corruption of an individual would appear *a fortiori* — in view of the individual's being a member of the public — to be to some extent a corruption of public morals in the latter sense;[2] this does not however take one much further on the question of the standard of reference. Judicial pronouncement is equivocal: Lord Reid would appear to favour something akin to an average person test, in that in judging whether material is corruptive of public morals, the jury should bear in mind 'the standards of ordinary decent people'.[3] Lord Simon would seem to favour an abstract standard of morality: as far as corruption of public morals is concerned, 'public' refers 'to certain fundamental rules regarded as essential social control which yet lack the force of the law'.[4] Lord Morris appears to regard corruption more in terms of effect, such effect being judged in terms of the particular audience: '... it was for the jury to decide whether they thought that the advertisements induced and encouraged readers to indulge in the several practices referred to and whether there was an intention to debauch and corrupt the morals of such readers'.[5] The weight of judicial authority is probably in terms of judging corruption against an abstract standard, either that of the average person, or of prevailing standards of morality, rather than in terms of effect on a particular audience. The point is not an academic one, as it will to some extent determine whether corruption of public morals is variable or constant. In

---

1 For example, *Shaw* v *DPP* [1962] AC 220; *Knuller* v *DPP* [1973] 3 WLR 143; Statement by the Lord Chancellor in the House of Lords 27 June 1972: *Hansard* HL Deb., 27 July 1972, col. 1569.

2 *Shaw* v *DPP* [1962] AC 220 at 277, 278 and 287, per Lords Reid and Tucker; *contra* Ashworth J at 233 (Court of Criminal Appeal).

3 *Knuller* v *DPP* [1972] 3 WLR 143 at 148. He does earlier remark however that conspiracy to corrupt public morals means 'to corrupt the morals of such members of the public as may be influenced by the matter published by the accused'. In these terms, his views are equivocal, to say the least.

4 Ibid. at 184.

5 Ibid. at 154.

the former case it will be constant, in the latter clearly variable. Even in the former instance however it has been emphasised that standards may change over time;[1] in this sense corruption is inevitably variable.

The potential breadth of this standard may be limited in a number of ways. It is clearly not open to argue that the word 'public' here denotes that the conduct should have taken place literally 'in public'. It has been argued however that the use of the word 'public' means that one is concerned only with the morality of conduct *between* members of the public. In other words, in order to offend public morality, one should engage in action which affects other members of the public in a direct, publicly manifested, and not merely private sense.[2] Publishing material that arouses a particular brand of thoughts would in these terms not be corruptive of public morals, as it would affect members of the public in a private, cognitive sense, and would not necessarily relate to their conduct in relation to other members of the public, whether literally in private or not. Such a 'public' requirement has never been specifically required; whatever the precise standard of morality employed, it is broadly the morality of the public, rather than a morality which is public in the sense meant above.

Had the conduct involved literally to take place in public, one might be dealing with a restriction basically aimed at preventing gratuitous offence; were a direct effect on other members of the public required, the prohibition might relate specifically to action. No such limitations are imposed; the offence has therefore a very wide ambit, one which may well be sufficiently wide to extend (for example) to homosexual counselling services: those running the service might well be argued to be conspiring to corrupt public morals by providing a contact service. A variation on the attempts to limit the ambit of the offence by attaching a particular meaning to the word 'public' has been advanced in this regard. One is concerned, it is argued, with the morality of the public; those with whom one has close personal contact cannot, in relation to oneself, be said to be members of the public, and therefore any effect on their morality is not an effect on public morality.[3] This argument appears fallacious on two grounds: first, the standard of morality is probably a general one, and therefore one is not concerned with the effect of the conduct on the morality of the particular group involved; second, even were one so concerned, there is nothing in any of the cases to lead one to suppose that one's close

---

1   See for example Lord Morris in *Knuller*, ibid.

2   On this distinction see D.G. Price 'The Role of Choice in a Definition of Obscenity' 57 (1979) *Can B Rev* 301 at 304.

3   See A.C.E. Lynch 'Counselling and Assisting Homosexuals' [1979] *Crim L Rev* 630 at 640.

acquaintances are *not* members of the public for these purposes.

Whatever the standard of morality employed, its contemporary nature is not to be decisively assessed in terms of Parliamentary statute and more particularly criminality. The appellants in *Knuller* argued that because homosexual conduct in private between consenting adult males was *legal*, it was not corrupting: that is, it was not flagrantly contrary to moral standards. The court rejected this out of hand; Lord Reid remarked: 'I read the [Sexual Offences] Act [1967] as saying that, even though it may be corrupting, if people choose to corrupt themselves in this way that is their affair and the law will not interfere'.[1] This is very much in line with the approach under the Obscene Publications Act 1959: it is not necessary for liability under the Act that illegal conduct (or thoughts of it) result from the publication in question. Thus a publication dealing with homosexuality for example, could be said to corrupt moral standards, even though the homosexual conduct involved is not unlawful. A similar problem has been encountered in Canadian obscenity jurisprudence: in *Re Nova Scotia Board of Censors et al and McNeil*.[2] The Canadian Supreme Court decided that although provincial film censorship measures dealt in effect with public morals, a field usually taken to be an aspect of the criminal law, this did not render the prohibition involved invalid as an encroachment on the federal jurisdiction over criminal law — morality and criminality are not necessarily co-extensive. It has been argued in the United States in turn that where a state has repealed its obscenity statute, *this* is conclusive in terms of local contemporary community standards (of morality) in relation to federal restrictions on obscenity. The Supreme Court's answer was as unequivocal as that of the House of Lords: the absence of a statute is not conclusive of such standards, which remain for determination by the jury.[3]

Conspiracy to corrupt public morals amounts then, it would seem, to little more than an agreement between two or more persons to do something which is flagrantly contrary to general moral standards. As Lord Diplock remarked, urging reversal in *Knuller*: 'The vice of *Shaw*'s case was that it opened a wide field of uncertainty as to what other conduct was also criminal ... it would seem that any conduct of any kind which conflicts with widely held prejudices as to what is immoral ... at any rate if, at least two persons are in any way concerned with it,

---

1   *Knuller* v *DPP* [1972] 3 WLR 143; see *R* v *Bishop* [1974] 2 All ER 1206, where in ruling in respect of imputation on character for evidential purposes, the Court of Appeal held that an allegation of homosexual conduct, even if not of a criminal offence, carried with it a certain 'stigma'.

2   (1978) 84 DLR (3d) 1 (SCC) at 23.

3   *Smith* v *United States* 431 US 291 (1977).

... at any rate if, at least two persons are in any way concerned with it, may *ex post facto* be held to be a crime'.[1] In view of their obvious similarities, it may be useful to compare this offence more closely with that of publishing an obscene article in terms of the 1959 Act. Such a comparison will become all the more relevant in view of the precise relationship, in prosecutional terms, of these two offences:

(a) Obscenity has been held to relate to human sexuality, violence and drug-taking; this is not necessarily a closed list however. Corruption of public morals apparently covers the corruption of any variety of morality.

(b) Obscenity may be charged only in relation to the publication of an article, as statutorily defined. Corruption here may apparently be effected by any conduct whatever.

(c) The law's concern with obscenity is the material's effect. This is arguably not the case here, where corruption is not judged in terms of an effect on a particular audience, but rather in terms of an abstract standard of community morality.

(d) With obscenity, a sufficient effect is the arousal of thoughts. Although corruption is said to be a strong word, it is not to be taken as being any stronger here than with the 1959 Act: thought arousal would therefore presumably be a sufficient corruption. One is not necessarily concerned with effect however: for conduct and resultant corruption one requires merely *any* act that could be said to be flagrantly contrary to accepted norms. The reason why it is contrary to such norms might be that it arouses thoughts, that it leads to conduct,[2] or anything else felt to be relevant.

(e) Obscenity is said to be variable (and certainly is, in certain instances) in terms of its audience. As there is no clear effect requirement, and as the standard is probably an abstract one, corruption of public morals would presumably be a constant in these terms.

(f) Where one is concerned with publication, there is no requirement here, as there is under the 1959 Act, that the material be taken as a whole.

(g) There is no provision here for any public good defence to a charge of conspiracy to corrupt public morals.

(h) The indictments in both *Shaw* and *Knuller* aver an intention to corrupt public morals. This would appear to

---

[1] *Knuller* v *DPP* [1972] 3 WLR 143 at 170.

[2] *Contra* Robertson *Obscenity* (1979) at 218.

encompass:[1]
  (i) intention to engage in the conduct concerned;
  (ii) intention to corrupt public morals; and
  (iii) knowledge of the law.

The first and third propositions here are in line with obscenity *mens rea* requirements. The second requirement is one not made in relation to obscenity and on the face of it, narrows the ambit of the offence fairly dramatically. Where the corruption is effected by means of a publication however, things are rather more complex than might at first appear: intention will be required in relation to publication, and in relation to knowledge of the contents of the publication. The circumstances of the publication must also be such that it is arguably corruptive of public morals: normally this element will comprise a tendency to induce, for example, homosexual thoughts — that is, to encourage readers or potential readers, to homosexuality. All of these considerations could be said to comprise the conduct in question, and intention will be required here also. The difficulty is this: is intention also required as to whether such conduct, taken as a whole, is corruptive of public morals? *Prima facie*, Lord Morris would appear to be asserting that it does. All his remarks however are in terms of encouraging homosexual practices: once this encouragement is determined to exist, an inference of intention as to depravity and corruption is but a short step. An inference of an intention to corrupt is in any event something of an absurdity, in view of the extraordinary width of definition of this requirement.

(i) Expert evidence is not admissible as to the question of depravity and corruption with obscenity: that is, as to the effect of material, and second, whether that effect is depraving and corrupting. The same may not apply here: in view of the fact that the effect of a publication may be an integral part of the conduct in question, it may be dealt with separately from the question of whether that conduct corrupts public morals. If the same reasoning is followed here as is employed in obscenity trials, expert evidence would definitely not be admissible on the latter; the situation as to the former remains open.[2]

(j) The question of corruption of public morals is a question of

---

1 Only one judgement in these two cases would appear to deal with this issue: see *Knuller* v *DPP* [1972] 3 WLR 143 at 152, per Lord Morris.

2 See *Knuller* v *DPP* [1973] AC 435 at 446 (*arguando*; argument not quoted in Weekly Reports).

fact, and a question for the jury. When one is concerned with a publication, the task for the jury here is similar to that which it would face in deciding a question of obscenity: having determined publication, the jury would be likely to direct themselves as to the audience, the effect on them, and the question of corruption. The difference is that with this offence, no such structural inquiry is *prescribed*: the offence covers *any* conduct corruptive of public morals, including publication. Thus an inquiry into effect on a particular audience for example is not required, but would probably follow. As far as the decision on corruption is concerned, the standards employed would appear to be precisely the same: that of community morality in general, as represented by the jury. With obscenity, the emphasis in the law tends to be on thought arousal as being sufficient to constitute moral debasement, and community standards of morality may have tended to ossify at this point, as far as the legal emphasis (if not jury decision) is concerned. With corruption of public morals, discretion as to what is, or is not, contrary to such standards is absolute.

Essentially the two offences, as censorship mechanisms, involve precisely the same inquiry: is the conduct (or the effect involved) flagrantly contrary to generally accepted norms of morality? This view of corruption of public morals lends strong support to the view that it is no more than a generic term for a number of separate and established offences, obscene libel being one of them. In these terms such corruption is not itself a substantive offence, whilst to allow conspiracy in relation to it would be self-defeating.[1] Neither the courts nor Parliament have so far been willing to take this line.

(ii) *Conspiracy to outrage public decency.* Unlike corruption of public morals, the outraging of public decency has been confirmed by the House of Lords as a substantive offence.[2] In so affirming its status, the House made it clear that a number of offences previously recognised — particularly keeping a disorderly house, mounting an indecent exhibition, and indecent exposure — were merely particular applications of a general rule.[3] Lord Simon in reviewing the particular applications of this generalised offence felt that it in fact subsumed not only

---

1   See e.g. Robert Hazell *Conspiracy and Civil Liberties* (A Cobden Trust Memorandum 1974).

2   *Knuller* v *DPP* [1972] 3 WLR 143.

3   Smith and Hogan op.cit. at 235; see also e.g. Lord Reid in *Knuller* at 150.

further offences such as the procuration of the debauchment of an individual, but also the offence of obscene libel itself.[1] It was not in fact necessarily limited to applications involving a sexual element, but might extend to '... indecent words (*Reg* v *Saunders* (1875) 1 QBD 15), selling a wife (cited in *Rex* v *Delaval* (1763) 3 Burr 1434, 1438), exhibiting deformed children (*Herring* v *Walround* (1681) 2 Chan. cas. 110), exhibiting a picture of sores *Reg* v *Grey* (1864) 4 F&F 73) ...'.[2]

The conduct involved need not be of any particular or prescribed nature. It is to be judged in terms of 'public decency'. Attempts have been made at common law to define indecency (or what is contrary to standards of decency): Lord Reid remarked in *Knuller* that: 'Indecency is not confined to sexual indecency; indeed it is difficult to find any limit short of saying that it includes anything which an ordinary decent man or woman would find to be shocking, disgusting or revolting'.[3]

'Indecent' has been defined in a statutory context: such definitions are of at least persuasive relevance here. In *R* v *Stanley*, Lord Parker remarked in the context of the Post Office Act 1953, Section 11, that indecency is something 'that offends against the modesty of the average man ... offending against recognised standards of propriety at the lower end of the scale'.[4] The Court of Appeal felt for example that certain scenes in a television documentary on the American artist, Andy Warhol, were indecent. These included: 'A fat girl, stripping to the waist, daubing her breasts with paint and then painting a canvas with them. She also throws paint down a lavatory pan to form weird patterns. This one she calls Flush Hot' and 'a discussion between a young girl and a man dressed as a Hell's Angel on how they can have sex. She says she will only do it at 60 m.p.h. on his motor cycle'.[5]

In *Abrahams* v *Cavey* anti-Vietnam demonstrators interrupted a televised Labour Party Conference church service; this was determined as falling within the ambit of indecency in terms of an ecclesiastical statute.[6] The DPP in 1973 launched a prosecution against a questionnaire which was sent by an eminent sociologist to volunteer readers of

---

1   *Knuller* at 182; the authority cited for the first proposition: *R* v *Delaval* (1763) 3 Burr 1434; for the second: *R* v *Sidley* 1 Sid 168; *R* v *Curl* (1727) 2 Str 788.

2   *Knuller* at 182.

3   Ibid. at 150.

4   [1965] 1 All ER 1035 at 1038.

5   *Attorney-General, ex parte McWhirter* v *IBA* [1973] 1 QB 629 at 634 and 637.

6   [1967] 3 All ER 179; under Ecclesiastical Courts Jurisdiction Act 1860. *Contra Wiggins* v *Field* [1968] *Crim L Rev* 503.

Forum magazine. The questionnaire was to further research into sexual behaviour, and was allegedly indecent in that it inquired *inter alia* of interviewees whether they had experienced bestiality or anal intercourse.[1]

In terms of the definitions offered of indecency, such holdings or allegations are unexceptionable: the term is so vague as to cover almost anything at all. This, to Lord Denning for example, is a positive recommendation: in reviewing the standard applicable by local authorities to films, he remarked that

> The proof of the pudding is in the eating. The Customs authorities and Post Office apply the simple test: 'Is this indecent?' They have no difficulty in condemning millions of magazines on that account, without their decisions being questioned. But when jurors are asked to apply the test: 'Does this deprave or corrupt?', they have been known to allow the most indecent articles to get into circulation.[2]

Not all judges are this sanguine as to the merits of indecency as a standard of proscription: Lord Justice Bridges remarked in the *GLC* case: 'I don't know how many people today would accept as an appropriate test of criminality what is "shocking, disgusting and revolting" '.[3] Yet another prominent member of the judiciary has warned that in a statute which 'contains a word as subjective and emotional in content as "indecency" there can be little of that precision which is so desirable in criminal law.'[4] There is in fact very little to which the term could not extend: it might include violence,[5] drug-taking, and indeed might even extend as far as the expression of extreme political, religious or social views. Although it might be argued that morality is not concerned with questions of mere taste, there would seem little doubt that the moral standards peculiar to any particular community may be based on feelings of revulsion or disgust. What is at issue then in terms of decency, or recognised standards of propriety, are recognised community standards or positive morality. The courts have on occasion been quite explicit about this:

---

1   Quoted in Robertson op.cit. at 177.

2   *R v GLC exp. Blackburn* [1976] 1 WLR 550 at 556; see also Lord Denning's remarks on this issue in *R v MPC exp. Blackburn* [1973] 2 WLR 43 at 50.

3   Ibid. at 567.

4   Sir Robert Megarry *A Second Miscellany-at-Law* at 316.

5   Where coupled with eroticism, such as sado-masochism and flagellation, it is clearly within the definition: *R v Reynolds*, 8 December 1971; quoted in the Home Office Working Paper on Vagrancy and Street Offences (HMSO 1974) at 42.

> There must be some scaling-down where the allegation is not of obscene articles but of indecent articles ... If what was alleged against this appellant was merely an affront to morality he ought not to be dealt with as severely as if he had been charged with evading the prohibition against articles which deprave and corrupt ...[1]

It follows from this that the law's concern is not here necessarily with effect: the conduct in question is to be assessed in terms of positive morality, and not in terms of any particular audience. There is oblique authority for this in terms of judicial interpretation of the term indecency and its application under the Post Office Act 1953: indecency does not there relate to the people to whom it is published.[2] All the circumstances surrounding mailing are in fact irrelevant; indecency is to be determined with reference to the article, and nothing else.[3] Thus love letters between spouses for example might well be found indecent, and it might still be an offence to mail *Lady Chatterley's Lover*.[4] It has been argued that because the courts have not permitted account to be taken of the nature of the audience when assessing indecency — in terms of the Post Office Act for example — then indecency is in these terms no longer a relative concept.[5] This is to misread the standard of indecency: it is not concerned with effect on a particular audience; it is rather concerned with affront to morality in terms of context. Such context remains relevant with the Post Office Act: a jury is asked whether the presence of such material *in the mail* is indecent.

The relevance of context here would seem to be in accordance with the approach the courts have employed on several occasions in interpreting statutory prohibitions on indecency. In *Wiggins* v *Field* for example, the reader at a public reading of Allen Ginsberg's poem 'America' was charged with using 'indecent language' — in particular in relation to the line 'Go fuck yourself with your atom bomb' — in contravention of a local bye-law. The Divisional Court was of the view that the prosecution ought never to have been brought:

> Whether a word or phrase was capable of being treated as indecent language depended on the circumstances of the case, the

---

1 *R* v *Waterfield* (no. 2) 17 February 1975 (CA) transcript p.6, quoted in Robertson op.cit. at 182; also *R* v *Farmer* (1973) 58 Crim App Rep 229.

2 *R* v *Straker* [1965] *Crim L Rev* 239; *R* v *Stamford* [1972] 2 WLR 1055 at 1058.

3 *Kosmos Publications Ltd* v *DPP* [1975] *Crim L Rev* 345.

4 See Robertson op.cit. at 184.

5 See e.g. Robertson op.cit. at 182–5.

occasion, when, how and in the course of what it was spoken and perhaps to a certain extent what the intention was.[1]

A similar attitude was taken by a court in relation to the use by a doctor of the words 'a pair of stupid bastards' in describing workmen making a noise outside his surgery: 'It is quite impossible to say that the word in this context was indecent.'[2] Account of the setting may equally work the opposite way: in *Abrahams* the defence argued that the standard of indecency was in fact an absolute. The words 'Oh you hypocrite, how can you use the words of God to justify your policies?' were therefore not indecent under an ecclesiastical statute. Not so, however: the court held that 'an act done in a church during divine service might be highly indecent and improper, which would not be so at another time.'[3] The courts have on occasion found this type of distinction difficult to assimilate: in a recent case involving a charge, with respect to a film club, of keeping a disorderly house, Mr Justice Bush directed the jury to ask themselves

> ... having regard to (1) the place in and the circumstances under which the films were shown, and (2) the quality of people who were likely to attend the performances, was there an outrage of public decency? In respect of (2) that is an outrage to those who are likely to go to see the performances ... a film shown in one place — for example a church fete — might outrage public decency, whereas shown in another place it might not.[4]

An obvious way in which the breadth of indecency provisions might be limited would be to prescribe not only the relevance of context, but that the only relevant context is a public one. This is in fact the only context in which an average person assessment of standards of propriety makes sense: an average or reasonable person finds himself in public places, and may be offended by what he sees there; is it sensible though to ask whether he would be offended by a cinema show which he had entered voluntarily, and the nature of which was made clear to him before he entered the cinema? A requirement of a public dimension to the context appears, originally at least, to have been a major limitation

---

1   (1968) 112 *Sol J* 656; [1968] *Crim L Rev* 503.

2   *Lees v Parr* [1967] 3 All ER 181.

3   *Abrahams* v *Cavey* [1967] 3 All ER 179, quoting Baron Parke in *Worth* v *Terrington* (1845) 13 M & W 781.

4   *R* v *Cinecentre Ltd*, Birmingham Crown Court, 15 March 1976, transcript pp.3–4; quoted in Robertson op.cit. at 226.

on the ambit of indecency offences. Thus, however the term may have been subsequently interpreted, most of those statutes originally employing the term 'indecent' involve (primarily at least) *public* display (the Vagrancy Acts, Indecent Advertisements Act, and Metropolitan Police Act) or the use of offensive words in *public* (the Town Police Clauses Act).[1] This is not really surprising, as an important distinction drawn in terms of positive morality, in this society at any rate, is one in terms of public/private conduct. It would appear that outraging public decency carried a very similar emphasis: the word 'public' was not mere surplusage; rather, as Lord Simon remarked in *Knuller*,

> The authorities establish that the word 'public' has a different connotation in the respective offences of conspiracy to corrupt public morals and conduct calculated to, or conspiracy to, outrage public decency. In the first it refers to certain fundamental rules regarded as essential social control which yet lack the force of law: when applicable to individuals in other words 'public' refers to persons in society. In the latter offences, however, 'public' refers to the place in which the offence is committed.[2]

It may be that such assessments even where limited in terms of this distinction are becoming, with changing standards, increasingly difficult to make; this must particularly be the case where the law demands a mere affront to such morality — as with indecency — rather than something more substantial.[3] Where the standard departs from a strict public requirement with concern centring on offence felt at material or conduct gratuitously thrust upon one in public, the assessment of whether standards of propriety have been offended becomes, if anything, even more dubious. And yet it is just this which appears to have been done in relation to the application of many decency standards. To begin with, no such offence would appear to be involved in terms of the Post Office or Customs Statutes.[4] In relation to outraging public decency, Lord Simon qualified his remarks in *Knuller* in relation to the public requirement: he first remarked that: '... the circumstances must be such that the matter ... could have been seen by more than one person, even though in fact no more than one did see it. If it is capable of being seen by one person only, no offence is

---

1   These statutes have all been repealed by the Indecent Displays (Control) Act 1981; see displays, chapter 6.

2   [1972] 3 WLR 143 at 184.

3   For a discussion of the apparent lack of community consensus in terms of the standard of indecency, see displays, chapter 6.

4   See chapter 5.

committed'.[1] He then went on to add that

> ... notwithstanding that 'public' in the offence is used in a location sense, public decency must be viewed as a whole; and I think the jury should be invited, where appropriate, to remember that they live in a plural society, with a tradition of tolerance towards minorities, and that this atmosphere of toleration is itself part of public decency.[2]

A majority of the House in *Knuller* took the view that even though the contents of a book or magazine are concealed behind an innocuous cover, this 'would not necessarily negative the offence ... if the public is expressly or impliedly invited to penetrate the cover'.[3] Indecency need not be clear on the face of it, but may be discoverable on investigation. If the offence was aimed originally at the prevention of gratuitous offence, it no longer appears to be limited to this, and may extend to the inside of a cinema for example. It is true that the word 'public' is defined in the Public Order Act 1936 (for example) to mean any place to which the public have access on payment or otherwise; policy considerations may well dictate differently here.[4] It may be that not only has a broad definition of 'public' made the standard applied dangerously overbroad, but that it has also undermined the very *raison d'être* of this offence. Where choice is involved in viewing there may be less consensus on the immorality of such viewing; such extension provides control that is closer to a prohibition than a restriction. This may in turn, if weighed against individual freedom, render the offence in its present form unsustainable.

A second possible limitation on the ambit of the offence may be found in the requirement of 'outrage'. It has been emphasised judicially that outrage is a very strong word, and that outraging public decency goes considerably beyond offending the susceptibilities of, or even shocking, reasonable people.[5] It should also be borne in mind that the outrage is in relation to recognised minimum standards of decency, 'which are likely to vary from time to time'.[6] *The Shorter Oxford English Dictionary* defines 'outrage' in terms of 'law, right, authority,

---

1   *Knuller* v *DPP* [1972] 3 WLR 143 at 184.

2   *Knuller* v *DPP* [1972] 3 WLR 143 at 184.

3   Ibid. at 159; also 184 and 187. *Contra* Lord Reid at 150.

4   For the relevance of public order considerations in this context, see live shows, chapter 6.

5   *Knuller* v *DPP* [1972] 3 WLR 143 at 184, per Lord Simon; see also Lord Reid at 150.

6   Ibid.

morality, or any principle' as 'to infringe flagrantly'. Outrage then means that the conduct should at least be contrary to standards of decency, or be in other words, indecent. How much more does it require than this? It must be remembered that certain varieties of outraging public decency — for example, indecent exposure — are *a fortiori* outrageous of such decency; the element of outrage would appear to be predetermined in such cases: outrage would in such cases appear to encompass no more than public indecency. Although the publication of indecent matter to the public has not been recognised as a separate offence, now that it has been held to be outrageous of public decency, the emphasis perhaps rests on publicity and decency, and not on the particular demands of the term 'outrage'? Although one cannot perhaps go so far as to say that all conduct constituting public indecency is outrageous of public decency, and that the term 'outrage' is therefore superfluous, what one can probably claim is that in this context it carries no more than its dictionary meaning of conduct 'flagrantly contrary to' positive morality.

A limitation on most indecency regulations is that they do not generally attract heavy sentences. Most can be tried in magistrates' courts only, although if tried on indictment, postal offences carry a twelve months' maximum sentence, whilst more serious smuggling offences may involve up to two years' imprisonment. Such limitation does not of course apply with conspiracy charges.

The ambit of outraging public decency (and of conspiracy so to do) is thus ill-defined; not surprisingly as with obscenity and corruption of public morals, the offence involves strict liability: the conduct must be intentional, and in the case of publication, the publisher must have been aware of the nature of the material in question. It is not required that he should have realised its offensiveness, or even that it was reasonably likely to be regarded as outrageously indecent.[1] The intention of the material's author is quite irrelevant, as no defence of public good is provided. There is no requirement that the material concerned be judged as a whole. The offence invites examination on much the same grounds as do obscenity and conspiracy to corrupt public morals: it involves the enforcement of public or positive morality, whilst jury decision is in terms of an affront to generally held standards of positive morality. The principle of legality surely demands greater precision? A further consideration in this respect is the question of strict liability; as long however as restriction is in terms of the enforcement of morality, the fiction that such morality is determinable as a question of fact, makes modification of the *mens rea* requirement unlikely.

---

1   *Knuller* at 173 per Lord Morris.

(iii) *Other conspiracy charges.* If conspiracy to corrupt public morals or outrage public decency is an admissible charge despite S2(4) of the 1959 Act, there would not seem to be any reason why conspiracy as to a number of other common law offences, otherwise excluded by S2(4) would not be equally permissible. An example is conspiracy to publish an obscene libel, as obscene libel was not, in terms, abolished as a common law offence.[1] There is also conspiracy to contravene the Act itself: such a charge would similarly not be precluded by the provision in S2(4); the following are the figures for the number of persons proceeded against in England and Wales, 1969—78, for conspiracy to publish an obscene article:[2]

1969	∅	1974	—
1970	∅	1975	10
1971	∅	1976	3
1972	∅	1977	—
1973	1	1978	—

(iv) *Conspiracy prosecution and law reform.* It has been strongly argued, in relation to both conspiracy to outrage public decency and conspiracy to corrupt public morals (and their possible substantive equivalents), that such offences should be limited to the breadth of definition of the various substantive offences clearly recognised as falling within their ambit. Such offences would in these terms, become nothing more than generic descriptions.[3] If one examines the possible reasons for the ready recognition and broad definition of the offence, such limitation by the courts may seem somewhat unlikely. The problem facing the court in *Shaw* (for example) was in essence not dissimilar to that which had faced the courts at the time of the introduction of the offence of obscene libel into the common law. At that time the courts were able to deal with the encouragement of unlawful conduct by an incitement charge.[4] Where the conduct involved was not unlawful, but felt to be merely immoral, the courts were faced with a possible lacuna, for an incitement charge was (and is) only proper in respect of conduct that is itself

---

1   Smith and Hogan op.cit. at 705.

2   Table 5, Appendix 7, Report of the Committee on Obscenity and Film Censorship (HMSO November 1979); chaired by Professor Bernard Williams, and hereafter referred to as *Williams*. ∅ indicates figures not available.

3   See e.g. Robert Hazell op.cit.; Graham Zellick 'Films and the Law of Obscenity' [1971] Crim L Rev 126 at 141; also Lord Reid in Knuller v DPP [1972] 3 WLR 143 at 202.

4   Cf. *R v Bacon* (1664) 1 Lev 146; *R v Plympton* (1724) 2 Ld Raym 1377; *R v Vaughan* (1769) 4 Burr 2494; *R v Johnson* (1794) 2 Shaw; *R v Higgins* (1801) 2 East 5.

unlawful,[1] whilst blasphemy and sedition were hardly apposite with anti-Popish tracts. This may well have been one of the factors behind the introduction into the common law of obscene libel. The court in *Shaw* faced a similar potential gap: prostitution was not itself a crime, whilst one had also the prospect of the enactment into law of the Wolfenden Report proposals, thereby legalising homosexual conduct in private between consenting male adults. An incitement charge was not suitable, whilst it was (and is) always open to doubt whether obscenity can be proved within the meaning of the Act. As Viscount Simonds remarked:

> Let it be supposed that at some future, perhaps, early, date homosexual practices between adult consenting males is no longer a crime; would it not be an offence *if even without obscenity*, such practices were publicly advocated and encouraged by pamphlet and advertisement?[2]

When seen in these terms, a limitation by the court of corruption of public morals to specific criminal offences would be self-defeating; the reasoning would be of equal application to outraging public decency. If limitation of this sort of offence by the courts appears unlikely, and if Section 2(4) of the 1959 Act does not preclude their application, have any other limitations been placed on such prosecution? This may be answered by examining their relationship in this regard to statutory obscenity; this may perhaps conveniently be dealt with in there parts.

(a) Either conspiracy may be charged in addition to a charge under

---

1 Cf. *R* v *Daniel* (1738) Holt KB 344; Stephen, *A History of the Criminal Law of England* (London 1883) at 230; *Russell on Crime* (London 1964) at 196; Glanville Williams, *Criminal Law: The General Part* at 609 (London 1962); J.C. Smith and Brian Hogan *Criminal Law* (4th edn London 1978) at 212.

2 *Shaw* v *DPP* [1962] AC 220 at 268 (emphasis added).

the 1959 Act;[1] the result may be conviction on both counts; however, as Viscount Simonds remarked: 'It may be thought superfluous where the 1959 Act can be involved, to bring a charge of conspiring to corrupt public morals, but I can well understand the desirability of doing so where a doubt exists whether obscenity within the meaning of the Act can be proved'.[2] A further reason for including a conspiracy charge is that unlike the 1959 Act, under which a maximum punishment is prescribed,[3] the common law lays down no maximum in this regard; punishment is therefore at the court's discretion, and may be more severe than that which could have been imposed under the Act.[4] The Court of Appeal in 1977 issued a Practice Direction which requires prosecutors to justify the inclusion of a conspiracy charge where the latter overlaps substantive charges; such practice might be justified 'where the interests of justice demand it'.[5] The interests of justice would presumably demand an additional conspiracy charge were 'charges of substantive offences ... not adequately [to] express the overall criminality'.[6] Quite how strong an inhibition this is on

---

1 Subsection 5(6) of the Criminal Law Act 1977 would not appear to be relevant here. The subsection states that 'The rules laid down by Section 1 and 2 above shall apply for determining whether a person is guilty of an offence of conspiracy under any enactment other than Section 1 above, but conduct which is an offence under any other enactment shall not be an offence under Section 1 above'. This provides merely that other statutory *conspiracy* charges must be charged as such, although such charges will be subject to the rules laid down by Section 1 and 2 of the 1977 Act. The subsection clearly cannot mean that conspiracy charges in relation to conduct forming a substantive statutory offence should be charged in relation to that offence only; such an approach would mean, in terms of the latter part of subsection 5(6), that conspiracy under Section 1 cannot generally be charged in relation to statutory offences; this is clearly untenable. The latter part of subsection 5(6) may possibly mean that where conduct may be charged as a substantive statutory offence (say contravening Section 2 of the 1959 Act) then *that* offence *only* should be charged, any additional or alternative conspiracy being incompetent. Such an interpretation is probably incorrect for two reasons: (a) the limitation imposed on the use of conspiracy charges would apply only where statutory offences were involved, and not in relation to substantive common law offences; this seems illogical; (b) the first part of the subsection refers to 'any enactment other than Section 1 above'. It seems a reasonable inference that the words 'any other enactment' in the latter half of the subsection should be similarly interpreted as referring to offences of *conspiracy* under any enactment other than Section 1? See E. Griew *The Criminal Law Act 1977* (London 1978) at 45.5; Smith and Hogan op.cit. at 230, footnote 10.

2 *Shaw* v *DPP* [1962] AC 220 at 268–9.

3 By Section 2(1).

4 Counsel in *Shaw* admitted that this was one reason for including conspiracy in the indictment [1962] AC 220 at 254; The Law Commission Working Paper No. 57 (1974): Conspiracies Relating to Morals and Decency, para 38.

5 Practice Direction [1977] 2 All ER 540.

6 *R* v *Greenfield and Others* [1973] 3 All ER 1050.

additional conspiracy charges in this area, remains to be tested.

There are statutory exceptions to this additional or alternative role for conspiracy: by Section 2(4A) of the Obscene Publications Act (as amended by the Criminal Law Act 1977) no proceedings may be brought for an offence at common law (including conspiracy) in respect of a cinematograph exhibition alleged to be obscene, indecent, offensive, disgusting or injurious to morality. An indictment for statutory conspiracy (contrary to S1 of the Criminal Law Act 1977) would be, provided that the conspiracy related to a substantive offence. Thus provided corruption of public morals is a substantive offence, statutory conspiracy might yet lie here, as it may with regard to outraging public decency.[1] A further exception exists in relation to the theatre: the 1968 Theatres Act precludes[2] proceedings at common law — including conspiracy — where the alleged obscenity of the performance of a play is concerned. Again, statutory conspiracy might presumably lie.

(b) As in *Knuller*, a charge of conspiracy may be laid *instead* of a charge under the Act, even though the latter might appear more apt. Considerable disquiet arose after *Shaw* at this possibility, for it was felt that this circumstance might be used to avoid the safeguards of the Act.[3] These include the defence of public good,[4] the right to call expert witnesses,[5] having the work judged as a whole,[6] and the prescription of maximum penalties. There is some authority for the proposition that it is not legitimate to use the conspiracy charge in order to evade statutory requirements; it is not conclusive.[7] As a result of the disquiet,

---

1   See S53(3). If the intention was to abolish these offences altogether in relation to the cinema, then there would appear to have been a drafting oversight: see Griew op.cit., notes on S5(3) and S53.

2   S2(4); the Act does not apply to performances of plays in private dwellings (S7(1)); as a result the common law is not excluded in relation to such performances.

3   Cf. Graham Zellick [1971] *Crim L Rev* 126 at 140–1; also the Law Commission Report (No. 76, March 1976) on Conspiracy and Law Reform, para 3.16.

4   Obscene Publications Act S4(1). This may have been provided for at common law: *R v de Montalk* (1932) 23 Cr App R 182; it is implicit in the judgement of Stable J. in *R v Martin Secker & Warburg Ltd* [1954] 2 All ER 683; cf. Stephen *Digest of the Criminal Law* (9th edn London 1950) art. 228; St John Stevas op.cit. at 150–2; *Russell on Crime* vol. 2 at 1426.

5   S4(2). Some have argued that this was assured under common law: see Minutes of Evidence taken before the Select Committee on the Obscene Publications Bill HC 1958 at 104, 105–6, 113, 114–15; St John Stevas, op.cit. at 153–5.

6   S1(1). The position at common law was not clear: cf. *Paget Publications Ltd v Watson* [1952] 1 All ER 1256; *R v Calder and Boyars Ltd* [1969] 1 QB 151 at 167; St John Stevas op.cit. at 134–6; Harry Street, *Freedom, The Individual and the Law* (2nd edn London 1967) at 150.

7   Cf. Glanville Williams, op.cit. at 687–8 and 706, note 24.

the Law Officers gave assurances in the House of Commons that a conspiracy charge would not be used in this manner: the latest of these was given in the House of Lords by the then Solicitor-General, Sir Peter Rawlinson, on 7 July 1964.[1] The question is whether the decision to prosecute in *Knuller* for conspiracy to corrupt public morals rather than for the publication of an obscene article can be said to have breached these assurances or not, and if not, just how meaningful, in any case, are such assurances. The assurances were mentioned by several Law Lords in *Knuller*.[2] This does not necessarily assure their efficacy; Lord Reid for example, remarked that 'It is not for me to comment on the undesirability of seeking to alter the law by undertakings or otherwise than by legislation'.[3] As far as the actual prosecution in *Knuller* was concerned, it has been argued that it did not breach the undertakings because of their exclusion of 'incitement to homosexual acts'.[4] This would appear to indicate an acceptance of the assurances as a valid guarantee; a more realistic appraisal would be that they are not worth the paper they are written on?

(c) Certain published articles may, though similar in nature to material that has been prosecuted under the Act, escape prosecution thereunder owing to the existence of technical loopholes, particularly in the definition of 'article' and 'publish'. The principal example here was films, which could be prosecuted for obscenity only if they were shown in a private house; showings in cinemas, factories or clubs were not covered.[5] It was admitted by the Attorney-General in the House of Commons in June 1972 that besides *Shaw* and *Knuller*, there had been thirty-one other *successful* (and unreported) prosecutions[6] for conspiracy to corrupt public morals. Of these cases, *Knuller* appears to be the only case since *Shaw* where such a charge was successful against purely written material. The conduct involved in the rest of these cases ranged from making obscene films, taking obscene photographs in which children participated, and selling sado-masochistic accoutrements.

---

1 *Hansard* HC Deb. vol. 698, cols 315–16; see also vol. 695, col. 1212, 3 June 1964. Also C.J. Miller [1973] *Crim L Rev* 467–8.

2 *Knuller* v *DPP* [1972] 3 WLR 143 at 157 per Lord Morris, at 170 per Lord Diplock, and at 148 per Lord Reid.

3 Ibid. at 150.

4 *Knuller* at 185; also C.J. Miller [1973] *Crim L Rev* 467 at 478.

5 See Hazel, op.cit. at 32; Zellick was of the opinion that films escaped the Act altogether: [1971] *Crim L Rev* 126 at 143. This latter view was supported by the remarks of Lord Diplock in this respect in *Knuller* v *DPP* [1972] 3 WLR 141 at 171.

6 Answer by Attorney-General to a question: *Hansard* HC Deb. 30 June 1971, col. 427.

S1(3) of the 1959 Act (as amended by the Criminal Law Act 1977) now covers all film shows. The only remaining specific exceptions relate to television or sound broadcasting. The authorities have moreover in recent years, even before the change as to films, made less and less use of these two offences. These fluctuations[1] in prosecutional policy probably reflect public disquiet.

	Conspiracy to corrupt public morals	Conspiracy to outrage public decency
1969	0	—
1970	0	—
1971	0	—
1972	—	1
1973	4	—
1974	9	1
1975	—	—
1976	—	—
1977	—	—
1978	—	—

Even though prosecutions may have fallen off in relation to these two offences, they nonetheless still exist as additions or alternatives to, an obscenity charge. They have been the subject of strong criticism. The Law Commission,[2] in reviewing these two offences, emphasised the lack of precision and uncertainty of scope involved:

> It seems to us not merely desirable, but obligatory, that legal rules imposing serious criminal sanctions should be stated with the maximum clarity which the imperfect medium of language can attain. ... It is often said that the jury is the best safeguard against oppressive prosecution, and can be relied upon to reflect public feeling at any given time. We consider, on the contrary, that the role of the jury in some areas of conspiracy is one of the most unsatisfactory aspects of the law ... We ... regard it as a matter of regret that it leads to the

---

1 Figures obtained from the Statistical Division, the Home Office. The figures quoted in Williams, Appendix 7, Table 4, differ from these in that they showed no proceedings for conspiracy to corrupt public morals in 1974 at all, and that one person was proceeded against in 1975 for this offence. The Home Office have confirmed their own figures. *Williams* does not quote figures for conspiracy to outrage public decency. 0 indicates figures not available.

2 The Law Commission Report on Conspiracy and Criminal Law Reform (1976) paras 3.8 to 4.1 (cited hereafter as *Report*), also Law Commission Working Paper No. 50 (1973) on Inchoate Offences; Law Commission Working Paper No. 57 (1974) on Conspiracies Relating to Morals and Decency.

substitution of the judgement of the jury for a clear and satisfactory statement of a rule of law. The jury is traditionally regarded as a guardian of individual freedom, but this is because it is a tribunal of fact, not because it is a law-giving agency, the role it assumes in many conspiracy cases. To ask the jury not only whether the accused did the acts alleged, but whether he ought to be punished, seems to confuse two roles, fact-finding and legislative.[1]

The report comes down heavily against these offences in terms of the principle of legality. The application of a form of strict liability, together with the avoidance of statutory safeguards, and the possibility of increased penalties are all mentioned.[2] Perhaps the conclusive factor in the assessment was however the conclusion that 'the two wide conspiracy offences under consideration have been used either as alternative charges where other charges have been successfully brought, or, alternatively, to fill only minor and easily identifiable lacunae in the armoury of the law'.[3] In view of this, it was clearly considered unsatisfactory to recommend a replacement of the broad common law offences with statutory equivalents. It was therefore a matter of identifying the supposed lacunae, and possibly recommending some specific offences to cover them. In these terms, the conspiracies would clearly be superfluous. The most obvious of the former was the exhibition of films on unlicensed premises: here the 1959 Act did not apply, other than in the case of such showings taking place in a private dwelling, to which the public were not admitted, whether on payment or otherwise. Other than the conspiracy offences (and their possible substantive equivalents), the only other offence apparently applicable to such films was a specific variety of outraging public decency: keeping a disorderly house.[4] The standard here however raised problems: indecency is such that a licensing authority might well approve a film only to find that this amounted to approval of a criminal offence.[5] The report therefore recommended the extension of statutory obscenity to cover all film showings.[6] This has been embodied in the Criminal Law Act

---

1 Working Paper No. 50, paras 9—10, quoted in part in *Report* para 1.8.

2 *Report*, para 3.16.

3 *Report*, para 3.20.

4 On the inapplicability of the Vagrancy Act 1824, Section 4, see films (subsequent restraints), chapter 7.

5 See films (current prior restraints) chapter 7; in particular see *R v Jacey (London) Ltd and Others*, *The Times*, 6 July 1976; *Report*, para 3.28 and 3.47.

6 With a few minor exceptions: see chapter 7.

1977.[1]

A second gap in the law was felt to exist in relation to live shows. This term covers live entertainment not covered by the Theatres Act 1968: in other words, not a play, ballet or opera[2] — in effect, most variety shows, stand-up comedians, tribal dancing, strip shows and live sex shows. Besides the conspiracy offences and their possible substantive equivalents, there are two other possible charges here: mounting an indecent exhibition,[3] and keeping a disorderly house.[4] Conspiracy to corrupt has also been charged in relation to the taking of obscene or indecent photographs in which children participated. The making of such films would appear to be covered by conspiracy or aiding and abetting offences under S2(1) of the 1959 Act.[5] In all of these cases the conspiracy charge was unnecessary, as the defendants were found guilty of alternative statutory offences, such as contravening the Sexual Offences Act 1956 or Section 1(1) of the Indecency with Chil-Children Act 1960.[6] There were certain problem areas: the 1960 Act did not extend to those of fourteen years of age and over, whilst the term 'with or towards' in the Act may not have covered situations where there was no physical contact with the child. Whatever such possible defects, this type of situation is now specifically covered by the Protection of Children Act 1978.[7]

Because the term 'article' in the 1959 Act is limited to matter to be read or looked at, sound records or films, sado-masochistic accoutrements such as whips, rubber and leather garments, straps, etc., would not appear to be covered by the statute. The only possible charge would be conspiracy to corrupt or outrage, or their substantive equivalents. Any specific offence to cover such sales would, the Law Commission felt, be difficult to define, as many of the objects in question are 'the subject of everyday commercial transactions'.[8] The report therefore recommends that this particular lacuna in the criminal law be ignored,

---

1   S53, see chapter 7.

2   See live shows, chapter 6.

3   See *Report* para 3.28; also below, substantive common law offences.

4   See *Report* para 3.29; also below, substantive common law offences.

5   See *R* v *King*: Central Criminal Court 29 September 1967 (unreported).

6   *R* v *Thomas and Another*: Hereford Assizes, 27 February 1968 (unreported); quoted in *Report* para 3.117.

7   See production of pornography, chapter 7.

8   *Report* para 3.129.

pointing out that displays of such items are governed by existing legislation. In particular, the recommendations of the Home Office Working Party on Vagrancy and Street Offences as to indecent displays[1] were felt such as to be sufficient here. It was not thought necessary for these conspiracy offences or any other specific offence, to cover touting (for live shows, for example), as such conduct would in any event be criminal because of the complicity element in relation to any offences applicable to the performances in question.[2] A minor lacuna would exist as to the Theatres Act 1968: this does not apply to performances in private dwellings; if conspiracy charges (and their substantive equivalents) were abolished, it is possible that no criminal offences would apply. It was recommended that the exception provided by S7(1) of the Theatres Act 1968 for such performances should only apply if no one under the age of sixteen was present, and no charge was made for the performances.[3]

The only other possible gap was considered to be the control of advertisements by prostitutes. Aside from conspiracy (and related substantive offences), the only[4] applicable offence would be S30 of the Sexual Offences Act 1956, relating to living off the earnings of prostitution; the prohibition applies only to males however. The commission felt nonetheless, that unless such advertisements were indecent (in which case they would in any event be covered), no prohibition was necessary.[5]

One area of application for these conspiracy offences (and their possible substantive counterparts) which the commission did not consider was that of television and sound broadcasts. These are specifically excepted from the ambit of the 1959 Act,[6] and thus all relevant common law offences are applicable: even were the offences at issue here to be abolished, other common law offences such as publishing an obscene libel,[7] mounting an indecent exhibition, or perhaps keeping a disorderly house might be applicable. The public element in relation to

---

1 See displays, chapter 6.

2 *Report* paras 3.131 and 3.132.

3 *Report* para 3.99; see Theatres Act 1968, chapter 6.

4 This is not an offence under present law: see *Weisz* v *Monahan* [1962] 1 WLR 262 and *Burge* v *DPP* [1962] 1 WLR 265.

5 *Report* paras 3.120 to 3.127.

6 Obscene Publications Act 1959 S1(3).

7 It would seem that libel covers a film: permanence is of the essence here. See *Russell on Crime* vol. 2 at 1424; also *Dugdale* v *R* (1853) Dears 64.

the latter offences would presumably be satisfied as television is shown in public places: for example public houses, which have been held to be public places.[1] Here also then other coverage is available.

The recommendation of the commission therefore was that these varieties of conspiracy (and their potential substantive counterparts) be abolished. This recommendation was based largely on the quite reasonable view that not only were the offences overbroad, but that the necessary coverage already existed in the criminal law. In this respect of course their approach differs dramatically from that of the courts, which appear to have regarded saturation coverage as desirable. The question of the enforcement of morality, and, more broadly, whether one needs coverage by the criminal law of many of these areas at all, was not fundamental to the recommendations. It was just this question which was in essence before the Committee on Obscenity and Film Censorship, set up on 13 July 1977. Although its recommendation in respect of the offences at issue here endorsed that of the Law Commission, this was the result of a much broader policy assessment of offences over the whole obscenity area; those offences that in addition to obscenity, and aside from the common law, provide coverage in this area, will be examined, together with questions of policy in succeeding chapters. Despite the commission's view that the cover they provide essentially duplicates that afforded by other criminal provisions operable in this area, the recommendations of the commission with regard to these two offences have yet to be implemented; this reticence probably reflected a deference to, and a desire not to anticipate the Williams Committee which reported late in 1979. The major recommendation of the commission as to conspiracy — that it be limited to agreements to commit criminal offences only[2] — has however been implemented by the Criminal Law Act 1977, which deals with conspiracy in the following terms:

> Subject to the following provisions of this Part of this Act, if a person agrees with any other person or persons that a course of conduct shall be pursued which will *necessarily* amount to or involve the commission of any offence or offences by one or more of the parties to the agreement if the agreement is carried out in accordance with their intentions, he is guilty of conspiracy to commit the offence or offences in question.[3]

---

1   See *R v Mapstone* [1964] 1 WLR 439; *R v Clark* (1963) 47 Cr App Reps 203.

2   *Report* paras 1.9.

3   Section 1(1); emphasis added.

Section 5(1) provides moreover that 'Subject to the following provisions of this section, the offence of conspiracy at common law is hereby abolished'.

Statutory conspiracy appears to replace common law conspiracy; the former may apparently be charged only in relation to substantive offences. The operation of conspiracy to corrupt public morals or to outrage public decency is thus open to some doubt, unless their status as substantive offences could clearly be established. Such limitation however was in fact clearly not Parliament's intention: Section 5(3) provides that

> Subsection [5] (1) above shall not affect the offence of conspiracy at common law if and insofar as it may be committed by entering into an agreement to engage in conduct which —
> (a) Tends to corrupt public morals or outrages public decency; but
> (b) Would not amount to or involve the commission of an offence if carried out by a single person otherwise than in pursuance of an agreement.

Thus the common law offence of conspiracy continues to exist with regard to corruption of public morals or the outraging of public decency, *provided* that the latter do *not* constitute substantive offences. The prosecution has a choice where such conspiracy charges are involved of charging the accused in the alternative (with either statutory or common law conspiracy); the charge actually upheld would depend on the court's view of the substantive (or otherwise) nature of corruption of public morals or outraging of public decency. The 1977 Act thus leaves the position in this regard essentially very much as it was.

2) *Incitement*

Although there is no authority on this point, the reasoning as to conspiracy and S2(4) of the 1959 Act would appear to apply *mutatis mutandis* to incitement. There is however a general limitation as far as incitement is concerned, in that it may only be charged as to substantive criminal offences. Thus, provided corruption of public morals and outraging of public decency are substantive offences, incitement may lie as to them, or equally as to obscene libel, any other substantive common law offence, or the Act itself. There are some specific limitations as to incitement. Incitement to conspire is not any longer an admissible charge, having been abolished by the Criminal Law Act 1977.[1] The Act appears to make the assumption that an incitement to attempt

---

1   S5(7).

is not an offence,[1] whilst as a common law offence incitement would moreover clearly be excluded as to film exhibitions or the theatre.

3) *Attempt*

The reasoning above would arguably apply also to attempt. As with incitement, attempt is only an offence in relation to criminal conduct, although, unlike incitement, such conduct here should apparently constitute an indictable offence only.[2] Attempt to conspire has been excluded by S5(7) of the Criminal Law Act 1977.

II) Substantive common law offences

The starting point here must be S2(4) and 2(4A) of the 1959 Act. These purport to exclude the common law where the essence of the publication in question is obscenity (S2(4)), or where (S2(4A)), in relation to films, the exhibition is allegedly obscene, indecent, offensive, disgusting or injurious to morality. S2(4) of the Act has always been taken as excluding substantive common law offences, even if not inchoate ones.

Assuming that where the 1959 and 1964 Acts apply, common law offences have no application, the outstanding question here is, when do the obscenity provisions *not* apply? Two areas specifically excepted from the purview of the Acts are sound and television broadcasting. Although such broadcasts are subject to prior restraint, this does not exclude the common law. Broadcasting has however been specifically excluded from the ambit of the only two statutory measures potentially applicable here, the 1959 Act and the Indecent Displays (Control) Act 1981. To abolish such common law offences as might be applicable here would merely be consistent in policy terms with respect to the applicability of criminal restraints to such broadcasts.[3]

The production of films involving indecency with children is now specifically covered by statute. The Law Commission did not feel that touting, advertising in shop windows by prostitutes, or the sale of sado-masochistic accoutrements, probably not covered by the 1959 and 1964 Acts, merited attention. The abolition of common law offences in regard to these areas would leave potential gaps in the criminal law, but they were not thought of particular moment by the Law Commis-

---

1   Smith and Hogan op.cit. at 214.

2   Ibid. at 246.

3   See television and sound broadcasting, chapter 7, on this.

sion, nor were they apparently specifically considered by the Williams Committee.

An area of importance outside the obscenity umbrella, and subject to common law regulation considered by both the Law Commission and the Home Office Working Party on Vagrancy and Street Offences, is that of indecent exposure. The principal criminal offence here is in fact a specific example of outraging public decency. It is not proposed to deal with this question. A line has to be drawn somewhere with regard to freedom of expression; it is proposed to follow that drawn by the United States Supreme Court in relation to the First Amendment: that is, between speech and conduct.[1] Those favouring a more absolute status for the First Amendment would argue that only speech which is so closely associated with proscribable conduct (which falls beyond the Amendment) as to be indistinguishable from it may be regulated.[2] Even those in favour of the present American obscenity regime are now attempting to tie-in hard-core pornography with action in this way.[3] Quite apart from the question whether one can tie pornography in so closely with sexual conduct that it may be seen 'as sex',[4] this raises one of the most difficult questions in this area: what are the philosophical and/or constitutional bases of distinction between 'speech' and 'conduct'. The Williams Committee adroitly sidestep this question: because the word 'speech' does not have a definitive constitutional status in Britain, they express relief at not having to consider the distinction between speech and conduct.[5] They nonetheless proceed with regard to live shows[6] for example, to recommend a prohibition in relation to actual sexual conduct taking place in the course of such a show. This they base largely on the argument that such conduct may lead to a public disturbance; also that it cannot be argued to be necessary in a literary or artistic sense, as simulation would serve such latter purposes just as well. This last argument amounts in essence to saying that the staging of such actual sexual conduct is not concerned with the transmission of ideas, and may therefore be seen in a different light from simulated conduct (for example) which is distinguishable in this respect.

---

1   See the section on live shows, chapter 6; also chapters 12 and 14.

2   See T.I. Emerson *The System of Freedom of Expression* (1970).

3   See Schauer 'Reflections on "Contemporary Community Standards" ' 57 (1978) *N Car L Rev* 1.

4   As proposed by Professor Schauer: see the *Roth* approach, chapter 14.

5   *Williams* para 5.18.

6   See live shows, chapter 6.

The committee draws its own distinction, in other words, between speech and conduct.

That such a distinction has been drawn in English law is clear: those measures considered in the course of this essay are aimed largely at speech in a factual or literal sense: articles to be seen, read or looked at or heard, in other words. Williams therefore managed very largely, in view of their terms of reference, to avoid this issue. The First Amendment to the United States Constitution is couched however in terms of speech; anyone wishing to distinguish conduct from speech in the constitutional sense must presumably motivate this distinction. Rationales for freedom, including freedom of speech, are rehearsed in the next chapter in the course of discussing the policy issues raised by English obscenity law. As will be argued later,[1] none of these approaches appear to constitute a potentially exclusive rationale: the propagation of ideas is probably too narrow, whilst individual freedom in the sense of self-development (for example) could extend to any variety of expression or conduct. Even if one broadens the propagation of ideas concept to the communication of mental stimulus generally, this could still take in many forms of conduct, such as indecent exposure. The situation with regard to a philosophical basis for the constitutional concept of speech appears to be similar to that in relation to privacy: there does not appear to be a single philosophical rationale or principle on the basis of which the term privacy may be clearly delimited.[2] Common sense, if nothing else, would appear to demand some delimitation. A possible basis of distinction is a constitutional one: speech in the literal or factual sense may be argued to have a special constitutional status in a democratic society: the entire political and social structure rests on the basis of informed political participation. This may be seen as philosophically deficient; in the absence of any clearer basis of distinction in the latter sense, it is proposed to follow this approach both in relation to English law, and in relation to 'speech' under the First Amendment.[3] It is by no means a complete answer, as it may well be desired to include within 'speech' expression consisting largely of conduct; in the absence of a clear and exclusive rationale for the First Amendment and freedom of speech generally, this must suffice for the purposes of this essay. It is proposed then to consider theatre, ballet, opera, and live shows, in respect of which speech may well predominate conduct, particularly if one adopts the Williams approach in relation to actual sexual conduct; indecent exposure, indecency in massage parlours, etc.

---

1   See the *Roth* approach, chapter 14.

2   See privacy, chapter 5.

3   The *Roth* approach, chapter 14.

do not in these terms lie for consideration here.

Another area of speech not covered by the 1959 Act is vulgar language. This clearly is speech in terms of the American First Amendment, the obscenity exception, which appears exclusively to cover censorship on the grounds of sexual morality, does not extend to such speech. In *Cohen* v *California*[1] the Supreme Court ruled such restrictions unconstitutional, although they in fact might have taken a different view, and based a validation of the prohibition in terms of offensiveness. Although obscenity in English law does not extend to such speech, indecency, dependent on context, may well do so; such coverage would not, other perhaps than in the case of outraging public decency, appear to extend to the spoken word. The question of this variety of speech will be examined in the context of such statutory offences.[2]

The Obscene Publications Acts would not appear[3] to cover displays. Although the substantive common law (for example, mounting an indecent exhibition) extends to the latter, this coverage is by no means exclusive. Public displays are subject, in terms of an indecency standard, to statutory cover; the abolition of the substantive common law in their regard would not create a lacuna in the law. The Law Commission in fact concluded that the only potential speech area subject to exclusive substantive common law control was that of live entertainment — that is generally any live entertainment not classifiable as theatre, ballet or opera: effectively then strip shows and live sex shows. Assuming the abolition of conspiracy to corrupt or outrage or their substantive equivalents, the only offence applicable to such shows are the substantive common law offences of keeping a disorderly house and mounting an indecent exhibition. The Law Commission, in following through its scheme of rationalisation, had two difficulties in recommending the abolition of such offences: was the area of live shows to be left unrestricted, and second, what else did these offences cover?

To answer the second of these questions first: besides those areas of application already mentioned, keeping a disorderly house applies to brothel keeping, public houses, performances of plays in private dwellings, and was applicable to gaming houses, which are now governed by statute.[4] Brothel keeping is now governed by statute also; the application of the common law has in fact been expressly disapproved by

---

1 403 US 15 (1971); see chapter 12.

2 See displays, chapter 6.

3 For further discussion on this point, see displays, chapter 6.

4 Betting, Gaming and Lotteries Act 1963 and Gaming Act 1968; *Report* para 3.30.

the Court of Appeal.[1] Public houses are similarly governed by statute.[2] The commission recommended the amendment of S7(1) of the Theatres Act 1968, to extend coverage by the Act; the exception in relation to private dwellings would then only apply if no one under sixteen years of age was present, and no charge was made for admission.[3] As far as mounting an indecent exhibition is concerned, its principal use was in relation to indecent displays, already statutorily covered, and in relation to unlicensed film exhibitions, an area from which it is now excluded.

The commission did not feel that it was part of their brief to de-regulate areas: the question of the need for, and rationale of criminal regulation was something best left to a later and more comprehensive survey. Hence their recommendation of an obscenity standard in relation to films. As far as live shows were concerned, although they recognised that audiences with such shows were generally small, and willing, the possibility of performances involving (for example) bestiality, led them, as with films, to leave the question of de-regulation to another body. They therefore recommended a new offence,[4] couched in terms of obscenity, and couched in terms very similar to that of the Theatres Act 1968, to cover 'live performances or displays'. Performances would be taken as a whole, and a defence of public good would be provided. The offence would apply to all such performances, other than those in private dwellings where no person under the age of sixteen is present, and no admission charge was made.[5] There seems considerable logic in this recommendation in that it, together with the Theatres Act 1968 and changes as to film exhibitions, brings one closer to the application of a uniform standard: obscenity. This is one of the principal differences that the First Amendment has made in this area in the United States: controls that regulate speech may apparently be couched in terms of obscenity, and nothing else. It also has merit in the sense of leaving the final review of criminal regulation here, as with films, for the consideration of a body appointed for this purpose. The Williams Committee was appointed with just this brief slightly over a year later.

The commission in the light of all this recommended the abolition of both keeping a disorderly house, and mounting an indecent exhibi-

---

1   Unless there are exceptional circumstances: *R v Payne, The Times* (Law Report), 15 May 1980.

2   *Report* para 3.30.

3   *Report* para 3.99; see Theatres Act 1968, chapter 6.

4   *Report* para 3.90.

5   Ibid. paras 3.92–3.96.

tion, together with obscene libel, which it did not consider served any useful purpose. Such recommendation would mean the abolition, with statutory conspiracy, of conspiracy charges in relation to such offences also; this is in accordance with the general rationalisation approach the commission had adopted. The Williams Committee has in fact endorsed all of the Law Commission's recommendations as to abolitions.[1] It recommended, in line with its general de-regulation conclusion however, that live shows be governed by an offence based on offensiveness to the reasonable person, rather than obscenity.[2] The policy considerations involved will be examined later; the standard recommended for live shows is the same as that recommended to replace indecency generally, and will be examined in detail in the context of statutory controls on displays.[3]

As far as present law in this area is concerned however, the substantive common law offences operative in the specific areas detailed above are:

1) *Corruption of public morals*

The essentials have been considered in detail above. The principal question here is whether there is, or is not, such an offence. The Law Commission felt that there is;[4] the Williams Committee was more cautious.[5] The issue remains for judicial determination, particularly in view of the change in conspiracy law.

2) *Outraging public decency*

This is clearly established as an offence. Its essentials have been considered in detail above.

3) *Keeping a disorderly house*

This is supposedly a specific example of outraging decency. Its elements have been defined by the Court of Appeal as:

> ... a house conducted contrary to law and good order in that matters are performed or exhibited of such a character that their performance or exhibition in a place of common resort

---

1 *Williams* para 13.4, for example.

2 Ibid. para 11.15.

3 See displays and live shows, chapter 6.

4 *Report*.

5 *Williams* Appendix I, para 62.

(a) amounts to an outrage of public decency or (b) tends to corrupt or deprave or (c) is otherwise calculated to injure the public interest so as to call for condemnation and punishment.[1]

Subsection (c) of this was a clear reflection of the court's reliance on the 'residual power' theory propounded by the House of Lords in *Shaw*, but expressly disapproved a decade later in *Knuller*. Of the two subsections applicable, subsection (a) is from a prosecutional point of view, the less demanding. In confirming (in *Knuller*) keeping a disorderly house as a species of outraging public decency, Lord Simon specified that the jury should in both offences be admonished that 'outrage' is a very strong word, going beyond offending the susceptibilities of, or even shocking, reasonable people; 'outrage' would nonetheless not appear to denote much more than flagrancy in relation to the public indecency involved.

The offence, as a species of outraging public decency, is judged in terms of abstract standards of decency, and not in terms of any effect on a particular audience; such standards are however relative in the sense of varying with context. Although the courts have on occasion found difficulty in distinguishing an emphasis on context from an assessment made subjectively in terms of the particular audience,[2] the relevance of context here was clear, as was the emphasis on that context necessarily, in terms of restricting affront to positive morality, being a public one. An early case of keeping a disorderly house concerned, for example, premises where 'certain evil and ill-disposed persons ... came ... to be and remain ... fighting of cocks, boxing, playing at cudgels and misbehaving themselves ... to the great damage and common nuisance of all'.[3] Today the prosecution is not required to show any element of unruly behaviour, or any encouragement towards it, despite the earlier emphasis on public nuisance or gratuitous offence. Take the recent conviction of Mrs Cynthia Payne, a West London brothel-keeper, for keeping a disorderly house. The case raised considerable interest in the national press,[4] both because of the severity of the sentence imposed (eighteen months, later reduced to six by the Court of Appeal) and because of apparently unfounded 'disclosures' by the police officer in charge of the case that the clientele included business men, accountants, barristers, solicitors, several vicars, an Irish

---

1   *R v Quinn and Bloom* [1962] 2 QB 245.

2   See e.g. *R v Cinecentre Ltd* (unreported); quoted in Robertson op.cit. at 225.

3   *R v Higginson* (1762) 2 Burr 1233.

4   See e.g. *The Times* 22 April 1980.

Member of Parliament, and a member of the House of Lords. Whether or not such publicity, or possible relief at its apparent lack of foundation, aided the unfortunate Mrs Payne in having her sentence reduced, is not clear; certainly though the Court of Appeal found no difficulty with the question of outrage. It was not suggested that the house was not 'open', in the sense of access not being restricted to members of a club, or particular group; however it could hardly be argued that customers were offended by the activities inside. Offence had then to be sought in relation to those outside the brothel. The Court of Appeal found no difficulty in finding outrage or public offence: those living in Ambleside Avenue, Streatham must have known about it 'since there were cars parked outside the house and much coming and going of men and women'.[1]

The same description could be given of a neighbourhood veterinary or medical surgery. Arguably — particularly as no formal complaint was made by neighbours in this case — no gratuitous public offence was involved. It was rather the mere knowledge of what was going on, rather than any external manifestations, with which the charge was concerned. As with outraging public decency generally, there may well have been here an erosion of the public offence aspect. Although the Court of Appeal in *Payne* concentrated on offence to those outside the premises, it would appear that the public aspect may here extend *inside*. All that is required is that there be 'an element of keeping open house':[2] in prosecutions of cinema clubs prior to the Criminal Law Act 1977, membership regulations that accorded virtually immediate entrance were no bar to prosecution, nor would it seem, was the payment of an entrance fee.[3] Where choice is disregarded in this way, the offence clearly moves away from considerations of gratuitous offence or public nuisance: provided those inside enter in full knowledge of the nature of conduct within, there seems little room for them to plead offence; as the ambit of the offence is extended, it hovers rather uneasily between restriction and prohibition.

These rather vague basics are augmented by a number of additional requirements: there should, for example, be an element of continuity. In the *Cinecentre* case, Mr Justice Bush directed the jury to 'look at the films as a whole. You look for an element of persistency. You do not condemn the defendants if there is only one film or only one isolated incident which you regard as outraging public

---

1   Ibid.

2   *R v Berg and Others* (1927) 20 Cr Apps Reps 38.

3   Robertson op.cit. at 225.

decency'.[1] There is thus something vaguely akin to the 'work as a whole' requirement under the 1959 Act: outrageous routines on only one or two nights of a long-running variety show will not be enough.[2] The prosecution must in addition prove that each defendant 'kept' the premises involved, this being determined in terms of S8 of the Disorderly Houses Act 1781:

> Whereas, by reason of the many subtle and crafty contrivances of persons keeping bawdy-houses, gaming-houses, or other disorderly houses, it is difficult to prove who is the real owner or keeper thereof, by which means many notorious offenders have escaped punishment: be it enacted by the authority aforesaid, that any person who shall at any time hereafter appear, act, or behave him or herself as master or mistress, or as the person having the care, government, or management of any bawdy-house, gaming house or other disorderly house, shall be deemed and taken to be the keeper thereof, and shall be liable to be prosecuted and punished as such, notwithstanding he or she shall not in fact be the real owner or keeper thereof.

It would seem that neither performers nor spectators are subsumed here; nor would it appear are landlords of premises used as brothels.[3] The jury should in fact be satisfied that 'The defendants appeared, not only as managers of their respective departments (choreography and musical direction of a dance hall), but as masters or managers of the house'.[4] Employees, performers or touts cannot then be liable, but could of course be charged with outraging public decency, or complicity therein. As this is a variety of outraging public decency, intention would presumably not be required as to the offensiveness involved; knowledge as to the conduct itself would apparently be sufficient. Finally, in certain instances, the status of a disorderly house is statutorily predetermined: under S1 of the Sunday Observance Act 1780: 'any house, room or other place which shall be opened or used for public entertainment or amusement ... [on a Sunday, and] to which persons shall be admitted by payment of money or by tickets sold for money ...' is deemed a disorderly house, and the keeper is liable for the common

---

[1] *R v Cinecentre Ltd* (unreported); quoted in Robertson op.cit. at 225.

[2] *R v Brady and Kam* 47 (1963) Cr App Reps 196; also *Marks v Benjamin* (1839) 5 M & W 565; *R v Davies* (1897) 2 QB 199.

[3] *R v Stannard* [1863] Crim Law Cases 405.

[4] *Jacobs v Bryor* 1851 LT 203.

law penalty.[1] Section 1 of the Act also imposes penalties on the keeper and others, such as those managing areas of such establishments, to be forfeit 'to such persons who shall sue for the same'. S1(3) of the Common Informers Act 1951 abolishes the latter penalties, and imposes a £100 fine on those other than the keeper, whose common law penalties remain unchanged.

4)   *Mounting an indecent exhibition*

Although this was recognised in *Knuller*[2] as constituting a seaprate offence, the reported cases are very old indeed. Aside from two such cases involving respectively[3] the exhibition of deformed children and a picture of particularly repulsive sores, the only reported case appears to be of an exhibition, for which an admission charge was made, of indecent material in a booth on the Epsom Downs.[4] The offence has not been the subject of the particularisation and definition accorded indecent exposure or even keeping a disorderly house. One must presume that the rules follow closely those of outraging public decency. The essentials of the offence are then flagrant indecency in public. The offence is probably not limited to gratuitous offence only; the relevant audience in *Saunders* was presumably that which saw the exhibition, and they would probably have done so willingly. *Saunders* did involve the use of crude language by touts outside the booth; it was the material on display however, rather than the touting, which was the essence of the offence. Not even the particular conduct involved has been subject to clear definition: it presumably includes the setting up of any sort of exhibition whatever, and would include material to be seen, heard, read, used, or a combination of all of these.

5)   *Obscene libel*

This has been discussed above.[5]

6)   *Blasphemous libel*

Blasphemy and obscenity are clearly closely connected in origin. Today

---

1   See *Report* para 3.145. Certain exceptions are made: in relation to certain licensed premises where entertainment is provided (Licensing Act 1964, S88); in regard to Sunday opening of museums, cinemas, etc. (Sunday Entertainment Act 1932, S4); in regard to theatrical performances in theatres licensed under the Theatres Act 1968 (Sunday Theatres Act 1972, S1).

2   [1972] 3 WLR 143 at 150.

3   *Herring v Walround* (1681) 2 Chan cas 110; *R v Grey* (1864) 4 F & F 73.

4   *R v Saunders* (1875) 1 QBD 15.

5   See chapter 1.

they are however separate offences, and although the same conduct may fall foul of both offences,[1] the range of such conduct is very limited. The essence of the offence is moreover no longer public order, but the prevention of offence on the grounds of religious belief.[2] This arguably is sufficiently distinct from censorship on the grounds of positive sexual morality to justify not considering blasphemy in detail here.[3] The Williams Committee did not feel that obscenity with religious connotations needed any special obscenity law dispensation, other than that provided in terms of their general recommendations. If such material was caught principally for other reasons by the offence of blasphemous libel, that was beyond their terms of reference. As they point out, blasphemy, along with other crimes against religion, is at present the subject of separate review by the Law Commission.[4]

---

1   For example, the subject of the recent *Gay News* prosecution, a poem about a homosexual's conversion to Christianity, in attributing homosexual acts to Christ, referred explicitly to acts of sodomy and fellatio. See *Williams* para 9.38.

2   A tendency to lead to a breach of the peace is not required: per Lords Edmund-Davies and Scarman, *R v Lemon, R v Gay News Ltd* [1979] 1 All ER 898, at 920 and 925.

3   See generally Robertson op.cit. at 236–43.

4   *Williams* para 9.38.

4 Morality, legality and policy

Both obscenity and the common law offences examined in the last chapter exhibit a number of similar traits in relation to criminal jurisprudence: all would appear for example to involve, at least partially, strict liability. All involve the enforcement of public or positive morality, and all involve the determination of criminal liability in terms of that morality. It is not possible to examine and analyse further these traits in relation to all of these offences; it is proposed therefore to select the two most swingeing of these offences, obscenity and conspiracy to corrupt public morals, as examples in this regard.

I) Legality

With both of these offences, it may be asked whether the question put to the jury is a similar one to those questions of fact faced by juries in other areas of the criminal law. Professor Glanville Williams has suggested a four-part categorisation of jury questions:[1] (i) questions of primary fact: did a witness actually see what he says he saw; (ii) questions of inferential fact: factual inferences to be drawn from the primary facts; (iii) questions of evaluative fact: this involves the assessment of whether a fact situation constitutes negligence (for example) or not;

---

1   Glanville Williams *Textbook of Criminal Law* (London 1978) 126; also [1976] *Crim L Rev* 472 and 532.

(iv) denotative fact: the application of ordinary words in legal circles. The latter classification has received confirmation by the House of Lords in *Brutus* v *Cozens*.[1] Here Lord Reid, in interpreting the phrase 'insulting behaviour' in Section 5 of the Public Order Act 1936 said:

> The meaning of an ordinary word of the English language is not a question of law. The proper construction of a statute is a question of law. If the context shows that a word is used in an unusual sense the court will determine in other words what that unusual sense is. But here there is in my opinion no question of the word 'insulting' being used in any unusual sense — it is for the tribunal which decides the case to consider, not as law but as fact, whether in the whole circumstances the words of the statute do or do not as a matter of ordinary usage of the English language cover or apply to facts which have been proven.[2]

It remains open to doubt to what extent *Brutus* has or will be, followed in this regard.[3] Certainly many statutory phrases, having already been judicially interpreted, are established as questions of legal art; definitions of deprave and corrupt are perhaps good examples of the latter.

As far as an obscenity inquiry is concerned, any question of publication is a question of primary fact. An assessment of the likely audience could be regarded as a question of inferential fact, the inference being made from evidence as to the type of person frequenting, for example, the shop involved. What of the question as to the effect of the material in question? This is not attested by empirical fact or expert evidence, other than in the case of children. It is therefore not a question of primary fact. Is it a question of inferential fact? Arguably yes: if one were to have evidence that the pornographic material had been both written and purchased for its titillation value, it might be a fair inference of fact that erotic thoughts had as a result been aroused. However, one does not always have primary evidence of this kind; one may be required to judge effect in terms of a standard external to oneself: for example, the average person, as with the aversion defence. Here one's operation is presumably closer to an assessment of evaluative fact. The assessment of effect does not appear to fit obviously into either category, and clearly has nothing to do with denotative fact.

What of the question whether the effect involved is corrupting? This

---

1   [1973] AC 854.

2   Ibid. at 861.

3   Glanville Williams *Textbook of Criminal Law* at 129. *Contra* J.A. Andrews 'Uses and Misuses of the Jury' in P.R. Glazebrook (ed.) *Reshaping the Criminal Law* at 42, footnote 31.

is not a matter of primary or inferential fact. Is it a matter of denotative fact? It clearly is not a matter solely for the jury in the sense that 'deprave' and 'corruptive' have been judicially defined. It is true that 'insulting' had been judicially defined prior to *Cozens*.[1] The court in *Cozens* did not specifically overrule this; in fact only one of the Law Lords referred to the previous decision. In effect *Jordan* has been overruled however. Is there any likelihood of the House of Lords reverting to pre-*Martin, Secker Warburg* days in referring 'deprave' and 'corrupt' without explanation to the jury? This would seem most unlikely; *Cozens* has not in any event been scrupulously followed on this point.[2] It would seem therefore that it is rather for the jury to apply the judicial definition of moral debasement, thoughts being sufficient for such debasement. Is the assessment here then an evaluative one? The standard employed is an external one — probably general community standards of morality; is this similar to the type of evaluative decision embodied in the reasonable man standard? There is an essential difference: the application of the reasonable man standard is essentially a question of degree. The question of degree is judged in relation to established primary, or inferred facts. Absolute care could be judged in relation to this, and the level of negligence may then be set in terms of an absolute standard, the reasonable man taking perhaps less than absolute care, but sufficient care not to be culpable. A question of corruption however, is judged in relation to a standard that exists merely in the abstract: community morality is not related in a direct way to primary or inferred fact. The result of all this is that the jury's function in this area becomes more quasi-legislative than fact-determinative: the standard involved provides the jury with the scope to decide unlawfulness. Admittedly this is what they do in relation to questions of reasonableness; in this regard however, the outside parameters of unlawfulness have been determined: it is (for example) potentially unlawful to drive a motor vehicle in such a way as to injure another. The parameters of unlawfulness have been determined, and the jury may decide merely within them (and in relation to them) whether particular conduct was unlawful (negligent) or not. With corruption, however, the outside parameters of unlawfulness are the bounds of morality itself, which cannot be said to be a finite quantity; unlawfulness therefore lies to the jury in a very real sense. This would reflect the situation with corruption of public morals; discretion with obscenity is narrower in two regards: first, obscenity relates only to publications of a specified sort; second, the scope for decision as to corruption (and therefore unlawfulness) is

---

1 *Jordan* v *Burgoyne* [1963] 2 QB 744.

2 Glanville Williams *Textbook of Criminal Law* at 129.

possibly narrower because of the emphasis in the law being on thought arousal as sufficient for such corruption. This is an emphasis however, and not an absolute limit on jury discretion.

As far as a decision in terms of the reasonable man test is concerned, it must be remembered also that negligence as a standard is employed less and less in criminal law today. One is therefore using a standard for comparison which is itself something that is no longer of wide application in the criminal law. Jury discretion may be so wide in other areas however, as to amount to a power to determine unlawfulness. Take the type of denotative fact decision involved in *Cozens*. The House of Lords decided that the term 'insulting'[1] was an ordinary word, and was therefore for the jury to determine as a question of fact. The jury thus, it is true, has a wide discretion. But is this discretion to determine supposedly factual questions quite unfettered? It may be that the term 'insulting' is to be judged objectively;[2] certainly this approach is supported by Lord Dilhorne, who remarked in *Cozens* that,

> The reaction of those who saw the behaviour may be relevant to the question whether a breach of the peace was likely to be occasioned but it is not, in my opinion, relevant to the question, was the behaviour threatening, abusive or insulting.[3]

This view was not shared by Lords Morris,[4] Reid,[5] and Kilbrandon,[6] all of whom apparently felt that the term was one to be assessed in relation to the particular audience. A difficulty which arises here is whether the audience should (subjectively) have *themselves* felt insulted, or whether it is sufficient that the audience (subjectively) felt that others (not present) had been insulted. Lord Morris is less than clear here, but both Lords Reid and Kilbrandon would judge this in terms of the audience having themselves felt insulted. In practice of course, where the insult is to someone (or a group) not present, the likelihood of insult

---

1 In Section 5 of the Public Order Act 1936, which provides that: any person who in any public place or at any public meeting:-
(a) uses threatening, abusive or insulting words or behaviour, or;
(b) distributes or displays any writing, sign or visible representation which is threatening, abusive or insulting, with intent to provoke a breach of the peace or whereby a breach of the peace is likely to be occasioned, is guilty of an offence.

2 See Ian Brownlie *The Law Relating to Public Order* (London 1968) at 13.

3 [1973] AC 854 at 865.

4 Ibid. at 864.

5 Ibid. at 863.

6 Ibid. at 866.

being felt is lower, as would be the likelihood of a breach of the peace. The court in *Jordan* v *Burgoyne* neatly avoided the issue above by pointing out that people in the audience who were not Jews or Communists would be insulted by the assertion that they were merely the tools of the latter. In addition to the audience having themselves (it would seem) felt insulted there must have been a likelihood of a breach of the peace. As Lord Reid pointed out in this regard,

> It would be going much too far to prohibit all speech or conduct likely to occasion a breach of the peace because determined opponents may not shrink from organising or at least threatening a breach of the peace in order to silence a speaker whose views they detest. Therefore vigorous and it may be distasteful or unmannerly speech or behaviour is permitted so long as it does not go beyond any one of three limits. It must not be threatening. It must not be abusive. It must not be insulting.[1]

It is therefore for the jury to decide whether 'the vanishing-point of insult has been reached',[2] in addition to a decision as to breach of the peace. Both are judged in relation to the audience, and therefore must to a large extent be linked: the 'controlling factor' here may well then be the likelihood of a breach of the peace.[3] Certainly in the case of breach of the peace — and this would presumably apply to 'insult' as well — the speaker takes the audience as he finds them.[4]

The result of all this is that jury discretion is not unfettered: the term 'insulting' (or 'abusive' or 'threatening') is for them to determine. It is to be determined in relation to the audience however, and must logically in turn take into account breach of the peace considerations. The question is one of effect on a particular audience: was the language found to be insulting; was it found to be so insulting as to be likely to provoke a breach of the peace? Although the term breach of the peace has not been authoritatively defined, and although its meaning may vary according 'to functional context',[5] it would seem here to comprehend anything that threatens peace and order, this probably taking the form of an act involving danger to the person.[6] The effect in question

---

1   [1973] AC 854.

2   Glanville Williams 'Law and Fact' [1976] *Crim L Rev* 472 at 478.

3   Ibid.

4   *Jordan* v *Burgoyne* [1963] 2 QB 744; D.G.T. Williams 26 (1963) *MLR* 425.

5   Brownlie op.cit. at 4—5 and 6.

6   Ibid.

is incitement to the use of force or violence, or possibly a threat of such. This is all ultimately (probably) an evaluative decision taken in relation to facts, similar to that taken on the effect of material on an audience in an obscenity inquiry. It may also, being a question of degree taken in relation to fact, be in principle similar to decisions under the reasonable man test. For our purposes here the crucial point is, decision as to denotative fact and evaluative fact or no, it does not lie to the jury to determine whether in the circumstances, the likelihood of insult and of a breach of the peace is unlawful or not; this decision has been taken (legislatively) for them. The decision is distinct in principle then from one as to corruption or depravity.

Two common law offences which are perhaps also culpable here are sedition and blasphemy. Sedition was originally very widely defined:

> It embraces all those practices, whether by word, deed, or writing which fall short of high treason (1 Hale 77), but directly tend or have for their object to excite discontent or dissatisfaction; to excite ill-will between different classes of the Sovereign's subjects; to create public disturbance, or to lead to civil war; to bring into hatred or contempt the Sovereign or the government, the laws or constitution of the realm, and generally all endeavours to promote public disorder ... ; or to incite people to unlawful associations, or assemblies, insurrections, breaches of the peace, or forcible obstruction of the execution of the law, or to use any form of physical force in any public matter connected with the State ...[1]

This breadth of definition is no longer accepted: the most recent decisions on sedition[2] require as a result of such discussion a likelihood of 'public disorder, tumult, insurrections, or matters of that kind'.[3] Smith and Hogan describe the *actus reus* of the offence as the tendency in the words to incite public disorder;[4] presumably publication is required.[5] The question as to whether one takes one's audience as one finds them or not has been resolved in favour of an objective test: if the language was likely to incite the average person to violence, that is

---

1   Brownlie op.cit. at 86–7, citing Archbold *Criminal Pleading, Evidence and Practice* (London 1966) para 3147.

2   *R v Aldred* (1909) 74 JP 55; *R v Caunt* see Wade 64 (1948) *LQR* 203.

3   Birkett J in *R v Caunt*.

4   Op.cit. at 805.

5   See Brownlie op.cit. at 88.

sufficient. However, even if the language did not have this tendency, it is sufficient for liability that it is likely to incite the particular audience.[1] Although something in the way of public discussion is required, this would appear to be so vague as once again to leave determination to be made essentially in terms of a likelihood of a breach of the peace. One is concerned here then in essence with the generic version of the statutory offence discussed above. The offence (were it to be revived)[2] amounts to a little, but not much more, than incitement to breach of the peace. Once again, for our purposes, one is concerned with effect, again a prompting to violence or threat of violence. Once this effect is assessed to exist, unlawfulness adheres.

Blasphemous libel[3] is an offence which until the *Gay News* trial in 1977, was thought also to have fallen into desuetude. Lord Denning remarked in 1949 that

> We have attained to as high, if not a higher degree of religious freedom than any other country — the reason for this [blasphemy] law was because it was thought that a denial of christianity was liable to shake the fabric of society, which was itself founded on the Christian religion. There is no such danger to society now and the offence of blasphemy is a dead letter.[4]

Lord Denning was in this instance mistaken: the conviction of the newspaper *Gay News* for the publication of a poem concerning a Roman centurion's homosexual fantasies about Christ was upheld first by the Court of Appeal[5] and finally by the House of Lords.[6] The ambit of the offence was in the process substantially altered. The earlier shift away from the penalisation of mere discussion of religion[7] was confirmed: what the law is concerned with rather is intemperate speech on religion; provided the decencies of controversy are observed, criminal blasphemy is not committed. The essence is not so much an attack, but offensiveness, insult, ridicule or general intemperance in style and presentation. Once again, this requirement would appear to be one to be judged in

---

1 Smith and Hogan op.cit. at 806.

2 See Brownlie op.cit. at 86.

3 See here in particular G. Robertson *Obscenity* (London 1979) at 236–43.

4 *Freedom Under the Law* Hamlyn Lectures (London 1949) at 46.

5 [1978] 3 All ER 175.

6 [1979] 1 All ER 898.

7 See e.g. *R v Ramsay and Foot* (1883) 48 LT 733.

terms of an audience, and is apparently judged subjectively in terms of the actual or likely audience;[1] the concern of the jury here is whether the intemperance of the publication (in relation to the Christian religion) is such that resentment is caused amongst Christians.[2] The Court of Appeal in the process eschewed the requirement, earlier established in *Bowman* v *Secular Society*[3] of a likelihood of a breach of the peace. The offence has then moved away from strict public order considerations towards the protection of deeply held feeling *per se*. How does the jury assessment in terms of the law as it now stands, compare with corruption? Discretion is very broad, and with the abandonment of the breach of the peace requirement, and the possible use of an abstract standard of what Christians find offensive, one is no longer, it would appear, necessarily concerned with a question of effect on an audience. This can serve only to increase jury discretion, decision being made apparently in terms of affront to recognised Christian morality. This offence in its present form appears then to parallel the latitude allowed juries in terms of corruption.[4]

Besides blasphemy, the only other clear example of a decision in terms of morality would appear to be that of dishonesty as required by Section 1(1) of the Theft Act 1968.[5] This requirement is both as to intent and to morality: the jury can in other words determine unlawfulness in terms of morality. Even here though the question of morality is perhaps not likely to be seriously at issue in very many cases. Where it is, standards of morality are possibly — despite the modern prevalence of 'fiddling'[6] — more easily discernible than are those of sexual morality for example? If discretion lies in this area to a jury to determine unlawfulness, the latter's role can fairly be described as quasi-legislative, and therefore discernible from the usual determination of fact required of a jury.

There are those who would argue that public morality *is* a question of fact, and that a jury is thus doing no more than determining fact in the usual way. With corruption the offence is adequately defined: conduct flagrantly contrary to public morality is unlawful; as ignorance of

---

1 See e.g. *R* v *Boulter* (1908) JP 188; also the transcript of summing-up by Mr Justice King-Hamilton in *R* v *Lemon*, Central Criminal Court, July 1977, at 15, cited in Robertson op.cit. at 241, footnote 104.

2 For example [1979] 1 All ER 858 at 925, per Lord Scarman.

3 [1917] AC 406.

4 Glanville Williams *Criminal Law: The General Part* (London 1962) at 502ff.

5 See Glanville Williams op.cit. at 660–2.

6 Ibid. at 667.

the law is no excuse, those convicted cannot complain. This assumes that public morality is an ascertainable question of fact, more particularly ascertainable by both the jury and the miscreant. The jury do not have the help of expert evidence in this respect, whilst any assumptions on the general prevalence of particular standards of sexual morality are today constantly open to question:[1] in reality a jury is determining in terms of *its* idea of morality. The maxim applicable is then not so much *ignorantia iuris non excusat*, but rather *ignorantia moris non excusat*. Determination of unlawfulness in this way accords ill with the principle of legality central to the criminal law: *nullum crimen sine lege, nulla poena sine lege*. Dicey wrote: 'A man may with us be punished for a breach of the law, but he can be punished for nothing else'.[2] This principle is at once both a fundamental political, philosophical and constitutional tenet,[3] the rule of law, which requires that '(1) people should be ruled by the law and obey it, and (2) the law should be such that people will be able to be guided by it'.[4] It is the second aspect with which we are concerned here: the criminal law must *a priori* be clear to the ordinary citizen; any punishment imposed in contravention of this is unjust. As Professor Williams has remarked:

> Observe that the principle is not satisfied merely by the fact that the punishment inflicted is technically legal. The Star Chamber was a legal tribunal, but it did not exemplify the rule of law in Dicey's philosophy. 'Law' for this purpose means a body of fixed rules; and it excludes wide discretion even though that discretion be exercised by independent judges. The principle of legality involves rejecting 'criminal equity' as a mode of extending the law.[5]

The maxim is in this sense a dual injunction: to the legislature not to draw offences so broadly as to provide undue discretion in their enforcement; second, to the judiciary not to mould the common law in similar vein. Where laws are not open and clear, their operation may in

---

1 As to community consensus on the standard of indecency, see displays, chapter 6. See also chapter 15 for further discussion of the question of moral consensus in this area generally.

2 The *Law of the Constitution* 10th edn (London) at 202.

3 See, for example, J. Raz *The Rule of Law and its Virtue* 93 (1977) *LQR* 195; Glanville Williams *Criminal Law* chapter 12; Jennings *The Law of the Constitution*, 5th edn, at 51; L. Fuller *The Morality of Law* (2nd edn, Yale 1969) especially at 197ff. For a summary of Dicey's formulation see A.W. Bradley *Constitutional and Administrative Law* (9th edn, London, 1978) chapter 6.

4 Raz op.cit. at 198.

5 Glanville Williams *Criminal Law* at 576.

fact exhibit the vice of retro-activity. Some conformity to the rule of law has accordingly been put forward as a necessity for any legal system: from this claim Professor Fuller has concluded that there is an essential link between law and morality; law must needs be moral in some respects.[1] Although this latter claim has been vigorously repudiated,[2] there would seem to be general agreement that clarity and prospectivity (amongst other things)[3] are essential in a legal system. In these terms offences such as obscenity and corruption of public morals, in their present form, require the most careful examination and justification.

The courts have not been unmindful of such criticism: in *Knuller* for example, three of the Law Lords dealt with this issue. Lord Diplock in his dissent felt that conspiracy to corrupt morals in particular opened up wide uncertainty as to what is criminal and what is not.[4] This, Lord Morris declared (perhaps a little cryptically), he was not prepared to accept: 'Nor do I know of any procedure under which someone could be told with precision just how far he may go before he may incur some civil or some criminal liability. Those who skate on thin ice can hardly expect a sign which will denote the precise spot where they may fall in'.[5] Lord Simon of Glaisdale dealt at length with the question of uncertainty:

> Certainty is a desirable feature of any system of law. But there are some types of conduct desirably the subject matter of legal rule which cannot be satisfactorily regulated by specific statutory enactment, but are better left to the practice of juries and other tribunals of fact. They depend finally for their juridical classification not upon proof of the existence of some particular fact, but upon proof of the attainment of some degree. The law cannot always say that if fact X and fact Y are proved (both of which will generally be known not only to the tribunal of adjudication, but also, in advance, to the persons involved) legal result Z will ensue. Often the law can only say that if conduct of a stipulated standard is attained (or more often, is not attained) legal result Z will ensue; and whether that standard has been

---

1   Fuller op.cit.

2   See Raz op.cit. at 206–7 for example.

3   Ibid. 199–202 and 206.

4   *Knuller* v *DPP* [1972] 3 WLR 143 at 170.

5   Ibid. at 155.

attained cannot be with certainty known in advance by the persons involved, but has to await the evaluation of the tribunal of fact.[1]

He then went on to list (the list extending over one and a half pages of the law reports)[2] examples of such standards. These consist of the reasonable man standard, dishonesty, and depravity and corruption under the Theatres Act 1968 and the Obscene Publications Act 1959. The only example beyond these was of conspiracy to effect a public mischief, which is now no longer part of the criminal law. As has been pointed out, even though corruption assessments are not alone in offending legality, offend it they do, and this needs careful justification. The reasonable man standard is arguably distinguishable, and is in any case not a widely used measure of criminal culpability. Unless one is prepared to accept that positive (sexual) morality is for a jury a readily ascertainable question of fact, judicial refutation of criticism has so far not answered the case.

Presumably the only justification here would be that the enforcement of public morality, even if not generally held, was absolutely essential, and that the only means of such enforcement, in view of the fluctuating state of morality, was to leave this determination to the jury. We are concerned here only with the second aspect of this, although the two questions are in these terms not entirely separable. It is possible, as the United States Supreme Court did in *Roth*, to permit the legal enforcement of public morality, whilst at the same time drawing the offence in question sufficiently narrowly to exclude the jury's reaching a decision in terms of public morality. If positive sexual morality is in a state of flux, the latter is perhaps best viewed as a closed option. It may be though that in certain areas, or in regard to the implementation of certain policies, clear prohibitions are impossible to formulate. This has been a reason for bureaucratic expansion in recent years: it is often not possible to draw a clear prohibition, and policy implementation is therefore handed over to a body or individual for administrative ruling (the question whether this transgresses the rule of law or not is something which cannot be discussed here).[3] Obscenity and corruption of public morals may well be prohibitions of this sort, in that the state of flux of positive morality may be such that more pre-

---

1   *Knuller* v *DPP* [1972] 3 WLR 143 at 176.

2   Ibid. at 177–8.

3   See e.g. O.D. Schreiner *The Contribution of English Law to South African Law; the Rule of Law in South Africa* Hamlyn Lectures (London 1967); A.S. Mathews *Law, Order and Liberty in South Africa* (Cape Town 1971); J. Dugard *Human Rights and the South African Legal Order* (Princeton 1978) chapter 3.

cise definition results only in legal ossification. It has been suggested[1] that obscenity prohibition and/or restriction aimed at protecting children or preventing public offence be handled administratively. This presupposes an acceptable policy basis for such prohibitions and/or restrictions. This question is discussed in relation to restrictions later in this chapter, and particularly in chapters 5 and 6; there is a discussion of an administrative basis for such restrictions in chapter 7.[2] The viability in policy terms of prohibitions in this ares is considered later in this, and in the final chapter of this book.

II) Strict liability

A further possible point of differentiation between these offences and much of the criminal law is the question of strict liability. Neither obscenity nor corruption of public morals involve strict liability *per se*: it would seem that intention is required with the latter as to the conduct involved and its results (if any), whilst negligence (at least) is required as to the contents or nature of a publication with the former. Intention as to corruption is not required with obscenity; with corruption of public morals, the position is somewhat obscure: intention is required at least as to the totality of conduct involved, but probably not as to the question of corruption of morals itself. *Mens rea* is thus almost certainly not required as to all the elements of these offences. Once again, these two offences are not alone in this regard. Strict liability is something which has been applied to *malum prohibitum* rather than *malum in se*;[3] to so called quasi-criminal offences, in other words, such as 'public welfare offences', 'regulatory offences', or offences which are 'not criminal in any real sense, but acts which in the public interest are prohibited under penalty'.[4] The distinction here would seem to be one of degree: that is between technical offences and those involving some odium. All are offences however, and all are in some sense public welfare contraventions. In fact strict liability has not been limited to such 'technical' offences; aside from obscenity it has been read into a number of offences which can be regarded as *mala in se*:[5] it is proposed to

---

1 Robertson op.cit., chapter 11.

2 See in particular administrative restraints in relation to books and magazines.

3 See generally Williams *Textbook of Criminal Law* chapter 42; Smith and Hogan op.cit., chapter 6.

4 Per Wright J, quoted in e.g. *Alphaced Ltd v Woodward* [1972] AC at 839.

5 Williams *Textbook of Criminal Law* at 912 for further examples.

examine seditious, criminal and blasphemous libel in this respect.

As far as the last of these is concerned, the House of Lords has ruled that 'the law requires no more than an intention to publish words found by the jury to be blasphemous';[1] such *mens rea* requirement mirrors exactly that required under the Obscene Publications Acts.[2] What of seditious libel? The position here is to say the least, obscure. There is authority for the view that an objective test is to be applied.[3] Lord Cockburn (dissenting) in one such authority, *R v Grant*,[4] was of the view that intention or recklessness as to the consequences should, in accordance with principle, be proven. This was followed by Cane J in *R v Burns*, where he remarked that,

> ... although it is a good working rule to say that a man must be taken to intend the natural consequences of his acts, and it is very proper to ask a jury to infer, if there is nothing to show the contrary, that he did intend the natural consequences of his acts, yet, if it is shown from other circumstances, that he did not actually intend them I do not see how you can ask a jury to act upon what has then become a legal fiction.[5]

The ruling in *Burns* was followed in 1947 in *R v Caunt*.[6] This approach is at variance with that adopted in *R v Aldred*, where Mr Justice Coleridge held the test to be whether 'the language used [was] calculated, or was it not, to promote public disorder',[7] and that innocence of motive was no defence. The language would appear to exclude any relevance for intention as to consequences.[8] Lord Scarman, in pointing out this discrepancy in the cases, lent his weight to the *Aldred* approach;[9] although this is admittedly an *obiter dictum*, and although the question remains open, there is then considerable authority for the view that intention is not required with regard to the consequences of the conduct involved.

---

1   Per Lord Scarman *R v Lemon* [1979] 1 All ER 898 at 926.

2   Ibid. at 927.

3   Smith and Hogan op.cit. at 803, footnote 4.

4   (1848) 7 State Tr NS 507.

5   (1886) 16 Cox CC 355 at 364.

6   (1947) unreported.

7   (1909) 22 Cox CC 1.

8   Smith and Hogan op.cit. at 805.

9   *R v Lemon* [1979] 1 All ER 898 at 927.

The requirement of *mens rea* with criminal libel is even more obscure.[1] The position in tort appears to be that negligence is required in practice, even though it is not necessary to prove that the defendant was aware of all the relevant facts.[2] As to the criminal offence, it would seem probable though by no means clear, that the position is the same as that of obscenity: negligence is probably the standard in relation to the facts, but strict liability applies to the question of defamation itself.

The probable congruence of the four libels (and corruption of public morals) on this point has been judicially approved.[3] Two other offences which beg consideration here are those committed in terms of Sections 5 and 5A of the Public Order Act 1936. Section 5A has dropped the Race Relations Act 1965, Section 6, requirement of an intention to stir up racial hatred. Considerable disquiet was expressed in the House of Commons at this: Mr Ronald Bell, moving an amendment in this regard, argued that:

> There is no doubt that for the ordinary citizen the question of what is right or wrong in a criminal sense revolves around what was, or was not, in the mind of the person committing the act. Guilt in a criminal sense, without intention, is also a contradiction in terms. For the man in the street to say that somebody has committed a frightful crime which he did not intend to do, or that it was unintentional, is either a contradiction in terms or also it means that that man was somehow subnormal or subhuman. The criminal act must be one which is intended to be done with malice. It is not unreasonable, and quite understandable, that the criminal law does, in fact, provide that there is no criminal act unless the mind that goes with it is criminal.[4]

The Home Secretary at the time, Mr Roy Jenkins, relied heavily in sustaining the section in its original form, on the fact that precedent for such formulation existed in the form of Section 5 of the Public Order Act 1936. Section 5A(3) in fact provides a defence of non-negligence with regard to written matter, in relation to its effect of being insulting, etc. As this defence is not provided for the spoken word, the implication is that the defendant's unawareness of the insulting, etc. nature and effect of the words, whether spoken or written, would not be a

---

1 See generally J.R. Spencer 'Criminal Libel — A Skeleton in the Cupboard' [1977] *Crim L Rev* 383 and 465.

2 Smith and Hogan op.cit. at 795.

3 Per Lord Scarman in *Lemon* at 927.

4 HC Debates, 9 July 1976, vol. 914, cols 1944—5.

defence. As far as Section 5 is concerned, the position would seem to be similar. It has been argued that intention, or at least negligence, should be required as to the question whether the words are insulting, etc. or not.[1] In *Brutus v Cozens* Viscount Dilhorne remarked that the 'justices may well have concluded that the appellant's behaviour did not evince any intention to insult either players or spectators, and so could not properly be regarded as insulting'.[2] As far as the breach of the peace requirement is concerned, although intention is not essential, negligence is, in that a breach of the peace or, with Section 5A, incitement to racial hatred, must at least be 'likely' to occur.

Thus a number of these censorship measures exhibit similarities in respect of *mens rea*. The outstanding difference is that with the Public Order Act offences, and with sedition, negligence at least is required as to the effect in question; this is not the case with blasphemy — where effect is no longer required — nor with obscenity, although intention would appear to be required as to the conduct involved with corruption of public morals, a consideration that would, where publication is involved, cover effect. Intention as to corruption is of course not required either with obscenity or corruption of public morals, nor, as to affront to Christian morality, with blasphemy. The question of strict liability and such offences may be seen in various lights. It might be argued from a philosophical point of view that retributive punishment demands responsibility. Alternatively, leaving aside questions of wickedness, the principle of responsibility might rest 'on the simple idea that unless a man has the capacity and a fair opportunity or chance to adjust his behaviour to the law its penalties ought not to be applied to him'.[3] An alternative approach would be to limit such liability to offences supposedly *malum in se*. The present position is perhaps a little odd in this regard: offences are regarded as *malum in se* because they attract odium or are contrary to moral standards. Because of this aspect, corresponding to some extent perhaps with the Roman law concept of *infamia*,[4] *mens rea* is required. Yet in relation to those offences *prima facie* most intimately involved with morality, such requirement is dropped.

Perhaps the most interesting aspect of the (varying degrees of) strict liability applied by means of the censorship measures examined above is their relationship to the problem of so-called rival assemblies. Many of these measures were originally, and most still are, public order based,

---

[1] Smith and Hogan op.cit. at 762.

[2] [1973] AC 854.

[3] H.L.A. Hart *Punishment and Responsibility* (London 1968) at 181.

[4] See e.g. A.H.J. Greenidge *Infamia in Roman Law* (Oxford 1894).

in the sense of requiring (amongst other things) a likelihood of a breach of the peace. Insofar as strict liability is applied here, these offences deny any defence based on the plea that others, as opposed to the defendant and/or supporters, caused the disorder or threatened disorder. There is some authority to the contrary, principally (as far as unlawful assembly is concerned) *Beatty* v *Gillbanks*.[1] The decision in this case, that the binding over order on the Salvation Army should be quashed, as foresight of a probable disturbance on their march was not sufficient *mens rea* for unlawful assembly, is on the face of it, difficult to square with the requirements of unlawful assembly, which seem to involve an objective element, in much the same way as do the offences above: the *actus reus* requires 'an assembling of three or more persons in such a manner as to induce persons of ordinary firmness reasonable grounds to fear a breach of the peace'.[2] One might presume then that intention is not required as to the breach of the peace aspect. In fact *mens rea* is required in the sense that one should foresee that the acts in question are likely to cause a breach of the peace. This the Salvationists in *Beatty* should undoubtedly have done; they were nonetheless not liable. A suggested explanation is that their activity did not *cause* the disturbance;[3] arguably though their conduct would satisfy a test of causation. The case is perhaps best seen as applying the (judicial) requirement that the defendants should, for liability, have as their object or purpose the creation, or threat thereof, of disorder. Where their object, and this can be distinguished from motive,[4] is to propound their viewpoint, then, even though they foresee disorder as probable, (and this they probably did) they will not be liable. Not only is negligence not sufficient, but intention in the form not of foresight of a possibility or even a probability, but of having the result as one's object,[5] is required.

The application of strict liability has been, and still is then a result of the balancing process in regard to public order offences: the restriction side of the balance has clearly been felt to be sufficiently weighty to justify such application, despite precedents such as *Beatty*. Whether

---

1 15 Cox CC 138; see Brownlie op.cit. at 42—6 for a discussion of this case and other authorities.

2 Brownlie ibid.

3 Ibid. at 41.

4 See P.R. MacMillan 'Animus Iniuriandi and Privilege' 92 (1975) *SALJ* 144 at 156.

5 This distinction is recognised in English law: see e.g. Smith and Hogan op.cit. at 48. It is classified as *dolus directus* and *dolus* indirectus in South African law; the former arguably corresponds to the requirement for the defeat of the defence of privilege in the law of defamation, at least in South African law: MacMillan loc.cit.

this is a proper result is a question beyond the scope of this inquiry. Such application with morals offences is another matter: if a balancing of interests is appropriate in this area, such balancing will demand an even higher showing in favour of restriction, for strict liability to be justified, for such liability clearly enlarges the scope of the restrictions involved. If such restrictions, in order to avoid the difficulties of overbreadth and vagueness, were to be couched in terms of defined effects, there would seem little reason why negligence at least should not be required. Such couching is perhaps unlikely when one considers the difficulties that often ensue as a result of rapidly changing standards of sexual morality. Take the *Roth* test (as interpreted) in the United States: the breadth of the prurient interest test was such that the addition of a requirement such as patent offensiveness was perhaps difficult to avoid. It may be that such offences and overbreadth are inseparable; as long as one has an offence couched in terms of morality, any requirement of intention as to corruption is most unlikely. Although standards of morality are supposedly questions of fact, and therefore discernible by the jury, jury decision in reality on this question, amounting as it does to a determination of unlawfulness, is not one on which courts or legislatures are likely to welcome the imposition of a requirement of *mens rea*. The crucial question is, should the enforcement of morality — even where the effect is defined — be continued?

III) The enforcement of morality

Whether juries assess unlawfulness or not, what is quite clear is that the law is enforcing, or is synonymous with positive morality of one brand or another. This raises the somewhat daunting question of whether this is a proper function for law. This is a very old question indeed, but one which was re-examined and refurbished as a result particularly of the adoption in England in 1957 of the Wolfenden Report.[1] This recommended the de-criminalisation of both prostitution and homosexual acts between consenting adults in private:

> In this field, [the criminal law's] function, as we see it, is to preserve public order and decency, to protect the citizen from what is offensive or injurious, and to provide sufficient safeguards against exploitation and corruption of others, particularly those who are specially vulnerable because they are young, weak in body or mind, inexperienced, or in a state of special physical, official or economic depen-

---

1   *Report of the Committee on Homosexual Offences and Prostitution* Cmnd 247, 1957.

dence.[1]

Almost contemporaneously, the American Law Institute, in formulating a model penal code, decided to include as criminal only those sex acts involving force or fraud, public indecency, exploitation of minors, or commercialisation.[2] The ensuing debate began with Lord Devlin's famous Maccabæan lecture before the British Academy in 1959. In this lecture he repudiated the Wolfenden approach, favouring the enforcement of positive morality, a view he later amplified[3] in the ensuing debate with Professor H.L.A. Hart.[4] Disagreement was not unnaturally fuelled by the subsequent and far-reaching decision of the House of Lords in *Shaw*. Lord Devlin described the impact of the decision thus:

> The legislators in Whitehall inching forward clause by clause towards their moral objective, topped a rise only to find the flag of their ally, the common law, whom they erroneously believed to be comatose ... , flying over the whole territory, a small part of which they had laboriously occupied.[5]

The scope of this debate[6] has been conducted, it would appear, within broadly utilitarian bounds. Professor Hart, it would seem, does not favour the enforcement of morality by law. He does however admit that every society has necessary a certain basic 'critical' morality, that being concerned with certain universal values: the prevention of harm. He moreover admits that the law may at least complement and mirror such morality.[7] The total separation of law and morality that he appears to favour is subject to further difficulties moreover: accepting that harm prevention is permissible, are *all* harms to be regulated? Clearly they are not, and the basis of selection of harms for regulation

---

1   Ibid. at 23–4.

2   Model Penal Code Section 207.5. The debate leading to the decision is reported in *The Times* 30 May 1955 at 13.

3   See P. Devlin *The Enforcement of Morals* (London 1965). The first chapter here, entitled 'Morals and the Criminal Law' is the Maccabæan Lecture. A number of other chapters are in rebuttal of Professor Hart.

4   See principally H.L.A. Hart *Law, Liberty and Morality* (London 1963).

5   Devlin op.cit. at 98.

6   For an excellent summary see B. Mitchell *Law, Morality and Religion in a Secular Society* (London 1967); see also Report of the Committee on Obscenity and Film Censorship (HMSO 1979), hereafter referred to as *Williams*, at para 5.6. The Committee reported that virtually all the evidence submitted to them accepted the utilitarian harm condition: para 5.1.

7   Ibid. at 15–16.

would appear very often to be positive morality. Such morality, if not enforced in a primary sense, is at least relevant in a secondary sense.[1] Other commentators prefer to admit at least the enforcement of utilitarian, or critical, morality by law.[2] From this point on, they are, in one sense, at one with Hart: their concern is that the law should be enforced only against harms. The countervailing, and apparently now largely abandoned view was that the enforcement of public or positive morality is an end or good in itself, and therefore justified. Although there are a number of variants on this so-called (by Professor Hart) 'extreme' position,[3] perhaps its best exponent was the Victorian judge and jurist James Fitzjames Stephen, who advanced the claim, with comparatively little explanation, that the criminal law should be used not only 'against acts dangerous to society,' but as a 'persecution of the grosser forms of vice'.[4]

The view which has commanded wide support in recent times is that society may act via criminal sanction to prevent harm (a view which may or may not itself entail the enforcement of at least a critical morality). The classic statement of this view is John Stuart Mill's *On Liberty*. He urged this limiting principle thus: 'The only purpose for which power can be rightfully exercised over any member of a civilised community, against his will, is to prevent harm to others. His own good, either physical or moral, is not a sufficient warrant'.[5] One is by no means out of the woods on this basis: the fundamental question still remains: what harm is in question here. A second question, and one which Mill purports to answer, is who or what may legitimately be protected from harm. As far as the latter question is concerned, it would seem unexceptionable to admit (i) harm caused by A to B. What gives rise to difficulty is the question (ii) whether one may prevent A harming himself: is paternalism acceptable? Mill's answer was emphatically, no: 'If society lets any considerable number of its members grow up mere children, incapable of being acted upon by rational consideration of distinct motives, society has itself to blame for the conse-

---

1 The question of harm selection will be dealt with later.

2 See e.g. L. Henkin 'Morals and the Constitution: the Sin of Obscenity' 63 (1963) *Col L Rev* 391; C. Frenkel 'The Moral Environment of the Law' 61 (1977) *Minn L Rev* 920; W. Barnett 'Corruption of Morals — The Underlying Issue of the Pornography Commission Report' (1971) *Law and Soc Order* 189.

3 See Hart op.cit. at 53—69.

4 J.F. Stephen *Liberty, Equality, Fraternity* (London 1873) at 162.

5 *On Liberty* (Everyman edn) at 73.

quences'.[1]

A number of different situations may be at issue here: the first is where A injures himself, for example by committing suicide or wounding himself. Neither of these situations would today involve criminal penalties in Britain; nor does the smoking of tobacco, or the consumption of alcohol. The possession of certain drugs may entail criminal sanctions however, as might in the future, for example, a failure to wear a seat belt when driving a motor car. Besides the question of harm assessment, crucial here is freedom: this is a factor of particular weight where the harm is done by an individual to himself. It is clear *a priori* then that the original model in terms of harm is not comprehensive: when viewed from a libertarian standpoint, freedom is an essential in any assessment of regulation. All agree on this.[2] Mill in fact justified the narrowness of his statement on permissible restriction specifically in terms of freedom: for a society to operate other than on the basis of freedom would be for it to make an assumption of infallibility. Assuming that the truth is knowable, the only way in which society can make progress towards it is by experimentation. For the individual the accepted norm may be inapplicable to his circumstances and character: 'Customs are made for customary circumstances, and customary characters, and his circumstances and character may be uncustomary'.[3] Thus individuality, diversity and self-development should be encouraged from the point of view of the individual and of society, whose interests are interlocking. Freedom has in these terms a primarily instrumental value. The enforcement of paternalism of this sort does not necessarily conflict with the harm model then: what is crucial is the weight attached to individual freedom.

Arguably of course, paternalism fits into the basic harm (caused by A to B) situation: paternalism may in other words be seen as protecting B against himself, even though he consents to harm being caused him by A. It is by adopting this view of paternalism that Hart seeks to fit the concept into the broad harm caused by A to B model advanced by Mill; admittedly he goes further than Mill in admitting this type of paternalism; his main concern appears to be to establish that such admission does not involve the enforcement of positive morality.[4] Consent may be seen here as a manifestation of individual freedom which arguably negates the unlawfulness of the harmful conduct. However it

---

1 Mill op.cit.

2 On freedom, see below.

3 Mill *On Liberty* at 98.

4 See Hart op.cit. at 32–4.

would seem that the harmful conduct is graded in this balancing not only in terms of its rationally assessable effect, but also in terms of the regard in which the conduct is held in terms of positive morality.[1]

All of paternalism can perhaps be fitted into the harm by A to B model, in the sense that where one harms oneself by not wearing a seat belt, one could be seen as harming one's family by perhaps incapacitating oneself physically and therefore economically. Even Mill appeared to recognise this view of paternalism: where individual action was such as to deprive 'assignable individuals' (dependents or creditors) of the performance of specific duties owed by the individual to them, the law might intervene.[2]

A final form of paternalism that most, including Mill, would appear to admit is the protection of children. Again this fits into the general scheme of the prevention of harm: conduct which may not be harmful to adults, may well be such where children are involved, in particular where adults introduce children to such conduct. Thus harms may be differently assessed, whilst the individual freedom involved (that adhering to children) is clearly something which may be properly devalued, in the sense that immaturity may well involve an absence of, or less developed, capacity to select in a judicious manner. This is an approach open to the American Supreme Court to allow obscenity statutes aimed specifically at protecting minors to pass First Amendment constitutional muster.[3] One thus has to assess individual freedom (perhaps in different terms), and one would appear once again to have a role for positive morality: most would agree, even if they do not take the same view with adults, that pornography should not be available to children; at the same time children have access to media materials dealing with violence, religious bigotry, and so on. Presumably the distinction in possible harms is based on positive morality.[4]

The final entity (iii) to which, or manner in which, harm may be occasioned is to society. Mill would appear not to rule such considerations out, in that society may compel its members to play a role in the judicial process, and to perform military service, for example. Hart would not appear to exclude the possibility of such regulation: he appears more concerned with the harm and its rational establishment

---

1 Take for example, the question of sado-masochistic defences: see e.g. L.H. Leigh 'Sado-Masochism, Consent, and the Reform of the Criminal Law' 39 (1976) *MLR* 130.

2 Mill op.cit.

3 But one which has not been adopted; the future of such statutes is in doubt in view of the hard-core pornography approach specifically adopted in *Miller* v *California* 413 US 15 (1973); see the protection of children, chapter 5.

4 See Frenkel op.cit. at 928; *contra* Barnett op.cit. at 194.

than with the view that society may not under any circumstances protect itself. Indeed it would be strange were society not legitimately able to protect itself from espionage say, or to impose restrictions to ensure the proper functioning of the judicial process, or basic public order. One is concerned with individual freedom also, whilst once again one finds that positive morality may be relevant: unemployment almost certainly harms the fabric of society and may lead to social unrest; whether the state acts to institutionalise something close to full employment reflects positive morality.

With all three areas of harm prevention one has, within the broad harm framework, the additional factor of individual freedom, whilst in many cases, the harms regulated, relfect, at least in a secondary sense, some positive morality. Where lies the source of disagreement in this area (besides the question of the enforcement or non-enforcement of morality by harm prevention itself)? This possibly lies in the selection of harms to be regulated: we have already had some hint of this in the discussion above, in the sense that a secondary role at least for positive morality would seem to be inescapable. With this Professor Hart would not agree. Besides the examples of harm selection in relation to children and society, take however those given earlier of harms potentially occasioned by an individual to himself: smoking tobacco, self wounding, and so on. What is the distinguishing factor here? With all of these one has potentially a rationally assessable harm; in some cases such harms are restricted, in others not. A primary distinction must be in terms of the positive morality of the community. It is doubtful whether the smoking of tobacco is regarded as immoral in most Western countries,[1] whereas the taking of certain drugs may well be; equally commercial competition between two businesses may be ruinous of one: it may nonetheless not be thought immoral communally.

Aside however from the question whether harm prevention by the law involves the enforcement of a brand of morality, and aside from disagreement on the secondary role of positive morality, disagreement centres on the identification of what is or is not a harm in the first instance, and particularly on whether *positive* morality should have a *primary* role or not, in the sense that its non-enforcement itself results in harm. One is not arguing here that the enforcement of such morality is a good in itself: rather that a distinct harm results from non-enforcement. This is the essence of Lord Devlin's argument: that some shared positive morality is essential to any society, that it is in fact the cement of society:

> ... an established morality is as necessary as good government to the welfare of society. Societies disintegrate from within

---

[1] Certainly there is a considerable vested economic interest in this not being so.

more frequently than they are broken up by external pressures. There is disintegration when no common morality is observed and history shows that the loosening of moral bonds is often the first stage of disintegration, so that society is justified in taking the same steps to preserve its moral role as it does to preserve its government and other essential institutions.[1]

This 'moderate thesis'[2] (as opposed to the extreme view of enforcement of morality constituting a good in itself) appears to rest not so much on the harm done to individuals as a result of the non-enforcement of positive morality, but on the harm this would occasion society.[3] The content or nature of positive morality is not of critical importance: 'what is important is not the quality of the creeds, but the strength of belief in it. The enemy of society is not error but indifference'.[4] Two separate theses have been detected in this approach: the disintegration and the conservative theses.[5] With the former, the situation is analogous to subversion: anything which subverts common morality, subverts society itself. The latter has not been fully developed as a separate ground of argument; it is similar to the disintegration theory, but rather less dramatic. Society, it argues, has the right to protect itself by protecting existing institutions, positive morality, and the existing social environment. Failure to do so will not necessarily result in the disintegration or destruction of society; what it may result in is a change in the whole tone of the community, with perhaps the most feared of such changes being an undermining of the position of the nuclear family as a fundamental institution. These theses make a number of assumptions which require examination:

(i) Both theories assume that *some* morality is essential to the existence of society. This is an *a priori* assumption rather than an empirically established one. Even though not rationally assessed, this would seem to be an assumption accepted even by Professor Hart, these theses' principal critic.[6] Without some common morality, society will drift

---

1 Devlin op.cit. at 13.

2 Hart op.cit. at 48–52.

3 *Williams* para 5.8.

4 Devlin op.cit. at 114; see also at 94.

5 See H.L.A. Hart 'Social Solidarity and the Enforcement of Morality' 35 (1967) *U Chi L Rev* 1 at 1–2. See also in this regard R. Dworkin 'Lord Devlin and the Enforcement of Morals' 75 (1966) *Yale LJ* 986, and for comprehensive statement of the arguments on both sides, Barnett op.cit. at 203–28.

6 Hart op.cit. at 51.

apart, it is argued;[1] members of society should feel morally as well as legally bound in their relations with their fellows: 'If the whole dead weight of sin were ever to be allowed to fall upon the law, it could not take the strain'.[2] Without moral bonds, one might need one policeman per citizen: there might well in other words be a breakdown in law and order and something approaching anarchy. To the extent that this debate has been conducted within a broad utilitarian framework, both sides would appear to accept that some form of utilitarian morality is what society requires, and that the law may enforce, or at least (*pace* Professor Hart), reflect it. Where the two sides may differ is in relation to the *type* of utilitarian morality they assume permissible and necessary: is it rationalist or not? Insofar as the Devlinites argue that the non-enforcement of positive morality leads to harm, this, if they are to be regarded as rationalists, must be a rationally sustainable assertion. It is to this question we now turn.

(ii) Those supporting the enforcement of positive morality clearly assume that it is ascertainable. There are basically two agencies employed in such ascertainment: the legislature and the jury. Clearly the legislature may employ the means necessary for a rational assessment of such morality. The jury however cannot: expert evidence on the question of community standards is not admissible. The question is one solely for the jury. Lord Devlin is unperturbed: 'If the only question the jury had to decide was whether or not a moral belief was generally held in the community, the jury would, I think, be an excellent tribunal'.[3] In making such assessments a jury is arguably determining unlawfulness rather than fact; in these terms, any claim that community standards have been rationally assessed are unconvincing. It might of course be possible to predetermine legislatively all such questions of morality (by prescribing just what effects — with obscenity — are unlawful, for example). Rationality might thus far be satisfied.

(iii) It is assumed that positive morality is homogeneous: in other words, for enforceability there must be general, if not overwhelming support for the proposition in question.[4] This is subject to qualification: Devlin appears to admit that positive morality may change;[5]

---

1 Devlin op.cit. at 10, 89—90 and 114.

2 Ibid. at 23.

3 Devlin op.cit. at 98. This reflects Lord Devlin's faith in the famous 'man in the Clapham Omnibus', or 'the ordinary man in the jury box, who might be called the reasonable man or the right-minded man': ibid. at 92.

4 Devlin op.cit. at e.g. 17.

5 Ibid. at 13, footnote 1.

when this happens, enforcement should not be dropped until it is quite clear that the old morality has been discarded. The results might otherwise be disturbing for the community.[1] Clearly morality which has nothing like overwhelming support, may, still enforceable, linger on; although general support is necessary for regulation, it is also apparently required for de-regulation. Thus even where positive morality has been legislatively and rationally assessed, changes in standards may mean that the law is being used to enforce something that enjoys little support. This is a factor that should be taken into account in assessing the rationality of claims that de-regulation in such matters would harm society.

(iv) A basic assumption made here is that law has a positive effect on morality: that is, that if the law condemns an act, men will be persuaded of its immorality, but if not, their belief in such immorality may begin to wane. Religion is today too weak a force to support the common morality, and so the state should reinforce it in whatever ways possible: for example, by legal enforcement.[2] There has been little investigation here; however the assertion that the law is capable of sustaining a morality which would otherwise disintegrate, seems a little doubtful. Certainly what little evidence there is, does not support this positive role.[3]

(v) What are the prospects if positive morality is not legally enforced, and permissiveness in relation to sexual morality (or some part of it) is allowed? The disintegration thesis posits here the disappearance of the morality in question. Moral pluralism is ruled out in the sense that the possibility of a new area of morality appearing to complement positive morality as such is not admitted. This assumes not only a positive role for the law, but also that the displacement of one aspect of positive morality opens up a moral vacuum. This is not supported by rational argument, but is an implicit assumption. The conservative thesis is a little less extreme; it poses a perhaps more plausible result: permissiveness would result, it is argued, not in a vacuum, but rather in the replacement in the area of morality concerned, of one brand of morality by another. This again involves the rejection of moral pluralism, in the sense that the possibility of two brands of morality existing together and complementing one another (and the rest of positive morality) is ruled out. Again this is not a rational position, but rather an implicit assertion that this would be the result.

---

1   Mitchell op.cit. at 21.

2   Ibid. at 23 and 25.

3   See e.g. Walker and Argyle 'Does the Law affect Moral Judgments' 4 (1964) *Brit J Criminology* 570.

(vi) What is the result of this destruction or replacement, depending on your view, of an area of positive morality? Both theses take the view that morality (presumably both positive and critical) is indivisible: that it in other words forms, '... a single seamless web, so that those who deviate from any part are likely or perhaps bound to deviate from the whole'.[1] This appears to be what President Nixon had in mind in his public statement rejecting the report of the Commission on Obscenity and Pornography: '... if an attitude of permissiveness were to be adopted ... this would contribute to an atmosphere condoning anarchy in every other field and would increase the threat to our social order as well as our moral principles'.[2]

But is the non-enforcement of sexual morality likely to result in society embracing murder, rape, robbery and fraud? Is this view supported by any rationally assessed evidence? Lord Devlin asserts merely that 'history shows' this to be the case. Counter arguments appear no less convincing: Professor Hart argues that permissiveness in non-essentials (for example sexual morality) may in fact make it easier for many to submit to essential restraints (say on violence). This view has been presented to the English courts in the guise of the so-called psychotherapeutic defence, and has been supported (if not conclusively so) by empirical findings laid before juries in the form of expert evidence.[3] What Lord Devlin appears to be doing here is to lay before one a proposition about a particular brand of morality, attempting in the process to generalise it to cover all situations. He in fact takes the view, looking at this from a different angle, that there is a common moral faith, which includes such virtues as 'justice, unselfishness, benevolence, mercy ... and others of that like'.[4] He includes amongst these others continence. Failure to enforce one of these (continence) must jeopardise the rest. He is setting out the characteristics of a Christian morality, and claiming that they (and critical morality) are indivisible. This does not appear to accord with his stance that the nature of positive morality is not relevant. His argument appears to be based essentially on belief: his belief in a particular brand of morality and the essentials for its continued operation.

On the assumption that morality *is* indivisible, the disintegration thesis poses the destruction of morality as such. The resultant moral vacuum would place intolerable strains on the law, and social disruption

---

1 Hart op.cit. at 51.

2 *New York Times* 25 October 1970.

3 This is of course no longer permissible: see chapter 2.

4 Devlin op.cit. at 120.

or anarchy would result. This sounds plausible, accepting the proposal that society needs some morality; the interceding reasoning is perhaps, from a rationalist point of view less than convincing. Professor Hart is dismissive of the entire theory: 'As a proposition of fact it is entitled to no more respect than the Emperor Justinian's statement that homosexuality was the cause of earthquakes'.[1] Certainly the proponents of this view do not cite a single example of a modern industrial society succumbing in this manner to anarchy. The thesis appears to posit a real harm, but does so on the basis of unsupported assertions. The basis of the thesis seems more than anything else, an emphatic rejection of moral pluralism; there is something of a take it or leave it attitude: what one is to take is the extant Christian sexual morality (for example), a morality which in the process assumes to some extent an aspect of immutability.

The conservative thesis proposes a rather less drastic harm: where an area of positive morality is displaced by a new brand of morality, because morality as such is indivisible, the whole of positive morality will be replaced by a new code. The harm lies in the assertion that this will be a change for the worse. Once again one has the rejection of moral pluralism: *both* the possibility of the new area of morality complementing the old morality in question, or the possibility of the new area displacing the old, but co-existing with the extant general code of positive morality, are ruled out. None of these assertions is supported, and this applies equally to the final assumption in the conservative thesis: that a change in positive morality will be a change for the worse. The thesis does not crudely assert the superiority of this society's extant Judaeo/Christian sexual morality for example; rather it argues that this morality *may* embody the ultimate, eternal good for mankind, and should on this basis be upheld against rivals. This is clearly a question of belief rather than a substantiated assertion: it could be argued that every moral code is an adaptation to circumstances, and that no morality can embody good for mankind at all times and under all circumstances. Homosexuality for example has been regarded in certain societies as moral: a basic practical reason may be that the society's resources could not support further population growth.[2] It may be that our society's exclusive endorsement of heterosexual monogamous marriage was an answer to the requirements of earlier agrarian society:[3] to begin with a large population was perhaps necessary, in military terms, for national survival. To produce children, men and women had,

---

1 Hart op.cit. at 40, quoting Novels 7.1.141.

2 See e.g. A. Honore *Sex Law* (London 1979) at 101 *et seq.*

3 See e.g. Barnett op.cit. at 214.

because of their physical differences, to observe a fairly strict division of labour. Women's need for a breadwinner and protector, especially during child-rearing, may have made marriage an attractive solution, its monogamous nature perhaps being determined to some extent by the ratio of men to women in the society. Such demographic trends may well change, whilst developments in birth control and the fact that children are now economic liabilities rather than assets, has reduced this child-bearing dependence of women. The interchangeability of men and women in the economic sense — with the decline in the importance of physical strength in terms of employment — has further reduced the dependence of women on men. All this is at least potentially relevant to the original marriage model. A further example of change is the fact that children mature earlier, but in economic and career terms cannot afford to undertake familial responsibility for a number of years beyond puberty. Society may presumably be expected to adjust tenets in order to sanction sexual outlets in the interim at least. Morality may then be the product, to some extent at least, of circumstance. When circumstances change, so too may morality. A more fatalistic view of history is to argue that all societies decline eventually, and that changes in the morality characteristic of a society whilst it was flourishing are an inevitable *characteristic*, but not cause, of that decline.[1] In these terms, legal enforcement of a disappearing code would be futile.

The rational establishment of the superiority of a particular moral code for all circumstances is probably not possible. All one has to go on here is an assertion that the extant code in this society *may* be the best for the society; moral pluralism is ruled out on the basis of belief. It is this exclusion of pluralism that is the basic characteristic of both theses: the disintegration thesis excludes pluralism on a take it or leave it basis as far as extant morality is concerned, whilst conservatism recognises the possibility of a new code, but cautions against it as a change for the worse. Pluralism in a developmental sense is excluded, whilst both approaches, with their emphasis on the indivisibility of morality, refuse absolutely to countenance pluralism in the sense of a 'mixed' morality. Just as society was at one time identified with a particular religious belief, so now it is identified with a particular code of morality, itself based on religious belief. Just as religious pluralism was seen as akin to sedition, so do these theses view moral pluralism; in these terms the historical relationship between blasphemy, sedition and obscenity is clear: sexual immorality (or moral pluralism, depending on viewpoint) is an offence; insofar as it offends accepted beliefs as to the nature and management of society, a political offence. Legally enforceable morality is in these terms the positive morality of the community, or quite

---

1   See *Williams* paras 5.11 to 5.14.

literally the morality of the public: no distinction is drawn for these purposes between conduct taking place in private and that taking place in public. The fact that conduct is contrary to public morality is sufficient. This concept of public morality is a very wide one: such morality has no rationally prescribed basis, and might therefore justify the restriction of conduct taking place in private on the basis of the disgust or abhorence with which the community view such conduct:

> ... I do not think one can ignore disgust if it is deeply felt and not manufactured. Its presence is a good indication that the bounds of tolerance are being reached. Not everything is to be tolerated. No society can do without intolerance, indignation, and disgust; they are the forces behind the moral law, and indeed it can be argued that if they or something like them are not present, the feelings of society cannot be weighty enough to deprive the individual of freedom of choice.[1]

Any consideration of offence as a harm, is in these terms unnecessary. A crucial question in this formulation clearly is the assessment of public morality. Lord Devlin, as we have seen, is happy that this be left to 'the man in the Clapham Omnibus'. This clearly creates problems in terms of certainty as far as the relevant offences are concerned. These may be obviated, without affecting the basic enforcement of positive or public morality, by leaving the assessment of such morality to the legislature. Even were one to accept the enforcement of such morality, such an acceptance does not necessarily commit one to accepting the present regime with corruption of public morals, for example.

As is already probably clear, perhaps the central point of disagreement between Lord Devlin and his opponents is then the question whether utilitarianism should be rational only, or not. In other words, are the harms posited by the disintegration and conservative theses, although not empirically established, nonetheless acceptable, or not? The emphatic answer from such opponents is that they are not. Only rationally assessable harms are the proper basis of regulation, such regulation in turn demonstrating a rational connection with the harm in question. This clearly excludes considerations of damage to, or changes in, positive morality as a harm. Two questions remain unanswered however: first, what harms are then permissible; second, does such an approach rule out the enforcement of positive morality altogether?

In dealing with the first of these questions, physical harm is something which is *prima facie* capable of being rationally assessed. Much more difficult is the question of offence. Clearly if one admits offence

---

1   Devlin op.cit. at 17.

in the remotest sense as a harm, one is opening the way for the enforcement of positive morality. Conduct may be felt to be immoral: if the mere *thought* of such conduct taking place were to be admitted as offensive, and therefore a rationally assessed harm, then *all* such conduct would be liable to proscription. On the other hand it has been argued that offence may well constitute a rational harm:[1] that which is deeply offensive to people may stir deep-seated insecurities, which may, because the threats are less palpable, be more acute than those raised by physical aggression. Citizens may, in other words, demand protection of their psychic as well as physical integrity. One approach here would be to exclude secondary offence (as opposed to primary or 'live' offence, where the conduct involved is forced upon one) as a rationally assessed harm. The harm occasioned by the mere knowledge that others are not behaving, in private, in accordance with one's beliefs, is not immediate, nor is it necessarily forced upon one; arguably it does not constitute (rationally) a harm at all. Alternatively, were one to admit secondary offence as a harm, one might well exclude it in terms of balancing freedom (a factor relevant to any decision on regulation)[2] against it. In either case, live offence only would be proscribed,[3] a balance approximating to that struck in the English law of torts in relation to claims for nervous shock.

What of the role of positive morality? Professor Hart claims that it should be excluded completely. As has been pointed out already, positive morality appears to be an inevitable concomitant of the process of harm selection, even taking the view that only rationally assessable harms may be regulated. Not all conduct which may rationally be regarded as harmful, is classified as a proscribable harm. Its role may be more extensive than this: take the question of sedition for example. It is notoriously difficult to determine (*vide* the American Supreme Court's problems here) how far regulation may proceed beyond controls on incitement to crime. Besides the question of freedom involved, a determinant may be whether a proper government objective is involved, in the form of the control of a rationally assessable harm.[4] This latter assessment will certainly be affected by the nature of the society in relation to which it is asked: certain brands of positive political morality may, for example, prescribe a non-democratic frame-

---

1   By Professor Schwartz 'Morals, Offences and the Model Penal Code' 63 (1963) *Col L Rev* 669 at 672.

2   See Hart op.cit. at 46.

3   For further discussion of offence as a rationally assessable harm, see displays, chapter 6.

4   See e.g. Henkin op.cit.

work, within which dissent may be regarded as a rationally assessed harm *per se*. Thus positive morality may affect not only the choice of harms, all rationally assessed, but also the assessment of whether conduct rationally does constitute a harm. Professor Hart perhaps tries to avoid the latter point in regarding the forum as a libertarian one. Even accepting this, the difficulty still remains: take the question of psychic harm. Unless one has access to a value-free concept of mental health, this involves moral judgements about psychological harm: 'Value-soaked definitions and explanations ... leave the scientific, objective status of mental health in a decidedly shakey condition'.[1]

To define mental health in terms of adjustment takes one very little further: the psychotherapeutic argument is for example that moral pluralism (at least as far as sexual morality is concerned) leads to better adjustment. Here however the moral values are merely implicit rather than explicit: it is after all adjustment to a particular society, with given *mores*. Postivie morality is something which apparently cannot be excluded from consideration. What perhaps can be attempted though is, within a libertarian framework, to regulate as far as possible on the basis of rationally assessed harms, and not on the basis of prejudice and/or belief, even though the latter be held by a majority of the population. Any such regulation should, as was remarked earlier, be rationally related to the previously assessed state objective.[2] This is in fact , in the context of the American Constitution, a general requirement of due process, but may be of general application in other systems; there seems little point in arguing for rationally assessable harms only, then to allow regulation which bears no rational relation to the assessed harm, thereby effectively nullifying the exercise.

What meaning would attach, accepting this rationalist approach, to the term public morality? Accepting the enforcement of utilitarian morality, which Professor Hart apparently does not, public morality is enforceable rational, utilitarian morality only. This is not synonymous with the morality of the public, or positive morality, which, although it may influence decisions on rationality and on the classification of conduct as a harm, is not to be enforced as such. The distinction between conduct committed in private and in public is again not vital: the distinction is rather whether the conduct causes a rationally assessable harm or not. Assuming however that offence is a rational harm only when primary, or live — that is only when it is gratuitously foisted

---

1   Lady Wooton *Social Science and Social Pathology* at 210; quoted in Mitchell op.cit. at 59.

2   See Henkin op.cit.

on the public — the distinction between public and private conduct, although is not fundamental to the reasoning here, remains relevant nonetheless. An insistence on a rational relationship between harm and regulation would ensure that offence regulations do no more than prevent public (in the literal sense) offence. This distinction is one which was (perhaps not on the reasoning above) drawn as early as Roman times;[1] the English courts have more recently succeeded in blurring it however:

> It matters little what label is given to the offending act. To one of your Lordships it may appear an affront to public decency, to another considering that it may succeed in its obvious intention of provoking libidinous desires it will seem a corruption of public morals.[2]

It is quite clear that obscenity and corruption of public morals mirror the Devlin approach, and not the rationalist thesis set out above. Were one to adopt exclusively the latter approach, such offences would needs have to be examined in terms of rationally assessable harms. Were they not rationally related to any such harms as might be assessed, they would stand condemned.[3] It is proposed to defer this discussion to the final chapter of this book. Equally, however, it is not proposed to set the scene for that final discussion in such narrow terms. As has been remarked, the law at present straightforwardly enforces positive morality. This is no argument for its continuing so to do; to allow the enforcement of such morality is perhaps to open society and the law to all manner of potential abuse. Having said that however, one cannot help feeling some misgivings about the apparently partisan approach often adopted by those who purport to favour rationalism only. An example is Section 70 of the Race Relations Act 1976, which makes it an offence either to publish threatening, abusive or insulting written matter (including a sign or visible representation) or to use in any public place or at a public meeting similar language, where (in either case), in all the circumstances, hatred is likely to be stirred up against any racial group in Great Britain. When this provision first appeared in the Race Relations Act 1965, the substitution of a likelihood of racial hatred being stirred up for a likelihood of the stirring up of disorder was opposed by

---

1 As pointed out by Professor Hart, the Romans distinguished between the province of censor who was concerned with (positive) morals, from that of aedile, who was concerned with public decency; Hart op.cit. at 44.

2 *Shaw* v *DPP* [1962] AC 220 at 267–8 per Viscount Simmonds. See also e.g. the discussion of conspiracy to outrage public decency: chapter 3.

3 They may be condemned in their present form in terms of vagueness also.

the Opposition[1] in the House of Commons. It was felt that this involved the enforcement of morality; the counter argument was (and is) that the stirring up of racial hatred sows the seeds of future disorder and violence.[2] This is very probably correct; the point here is though that many libertarians, whilst quite happy with this explanation, would no doubt argue for a much closer rational connection between pornography and supposed harm in order to justify suppression. An alternative argument is that such speech may cause offence. Again this is undoubtedly correct; the restriction would appear to apply though to any area to which the public have access. Anyone attending such a gathering voluntarily, despite clear indications of its nature, might well have consented to the offence occasioned.

The rationalist argument, whilst possibly more intellectually satisfying, is not uniformly applied. Certainly both English and American jurisprudence has, and does, allow the enforcement of positive morality; in this respect one can hardly argue that obscenity and corruption of public morals stand alone. The European Convention on Human Rights and Fundamental Freedoms is as a result carefully qualified to allow a public morality exception.[3] Taking this into account, together with the influence positive morality has even within the rationalist approach, it is proposed to examine within the Devlin framework, the position of censorship imposed on the grounds of positive sexual morality. It may well be that such restrictions are unsustainable even in these terms, and the question of any endorsement of the thesis becomes as such academic.

The factor which may well be decisive in this evaluation is freedom. The relevance of freedom is clear from the foregoing discussion: it is assumed by Mill, Hart and Devlin that some justification is required for regulation. This implies that such regulation is *prima facie* objectionable, and this in turn presumably rests on the importance of freedom. It remains to be answered just why freedom is important.[4] It is on this question that considerable jurisprudential debate has centred. As we have seen, Mill regarded freedom as important because of its instrumentality in the search for optimum modes of living. The assumption is that the truth in these matters is knowable, and that freedom in society provides man with the only means of improving that society, even if

---

1   Hansard HC Deb. vol. 711, p.942.

2   See D.G.T. Williams [1966] *Crim L Rev* 320.

3   See chapter 9.

4   See in particular Mitchell op.cit., chapter 6.

truth as such is not ever attained.[1] This argument may not be a complete answer: it may be that truth needs more of a chance than simply being expected to survive the rigours of commercial competition in the market place. It may be that some intervention is required, in, for example, the form of 'state subventions for the arts, or policies of refusing to design television programmes solely on the basis of ratings, or subsidising institutions of critical enquiry'.[2] This does not mean to say that negative intervention is necessarily a good thing, or even permissible. Lord Devlin appears to adopt a similar approach:

> Freedom is not a good in itself. We believe it to be good because out of freedom there comes more good than bad. If a free society is better than a disciplined one, it is because — and this was certainly Mill's view — it is better for a man himself that he should be free to seek his own good in his own way and better too for the society to which he belongs, since thereby a way may be found to a greater good for all.[3]

He argues however that permissiveness and experimentation lead to, at least the replacement of morality by something worse. Thus although 'the freedom that is worth having is freedom to do what you think to be good notwithstanding that others think it bad', Mill did not, he feels, 'grapple with the fact that along the paths that depart from traditional morals, pimps leading the weak astray far outnumber the spiritual explorers at the head of the strong'.[4] The man on the Clapham omnibus may be trusted to determine what morality is, but strong misgivings are held about his ability to decide for the best between competing moralities. Just how much weight is to be attached to freedom in these terms, particularly as the basic assumption is that optimum morality may *already* be known, is doubtful. Lord Devlin's view of the role of freedom is perhaps best seen not in terms of instrumentality, but rather merely in terms of a presumption that freedom is of value; it is not clear just how strong is this presumption.

A competing view of the importance of freedom has been dubbed the new liberalism.[5] The case for the limitation of regulation is not the instrumentality of freedom in promoting the truth; rather it is assumed

---

1   See *Williams* paras 5.15 to 5.21.

2   Ibid. paras 5.19 and 5.20.

3   Devlin op.cit. at 108.

4   Ibid.

5   Mitchell op.cit. at 89—90 especially.

that not only is the truth not known, but it is not knowable. Tolerance or moral pluralism is the optimum condition for society: because there is no right or wrong (other perhaps than in terms of rationally assessable harms) there is no justification for enforcing one ideal as opposed to any other.

An alternative view of the importance of freedom is that the unimpeded exercise of a free choice is in itself a value. This view, endorsed by Professor Hart (for example)[1] does not rest on the premise that the truth is knowable, known, or not knowable; rather it is argued that a man cannot live a moral life unless he is free to make moral choices. This would appear to rest then on a faith in man's rationality: that whatever is best will be chosen. If the truth is knowable, debate will bring one closer to it; if it is not knowable, individual choice is the optimum option; if the truth is known, then society will opt for it. The alternative form of this view agrees that the (Christian) truth is known, but that it is capable of sustaining itself in free debate; it in fact predicates just such freedom.[2]

Professor Hart has proposed a further buttress for freedom, using utilitarian concepts: restrictions on individual freedoms may cause harm to individuals; the state may *a priori* act to prevent harms; it presumably should not in the process however occasion further harms? Restrictions on individual freedoms may well cause such harms: this is particularly the case with sexual morality he feels, 'For both the difficulties involved in the repression of sexual impulses and the consequences of repression are quite different from those involved in the abstention from "ordinary crime" '.[3]

All then agree that the importance of freedom underpins the requirement of a justification for repression. All agree (on the basis of differing views of freedom) that harms only may be repressed: Williams found that there was virtually unanimous agreement on this.[4] Assertions of the importance of freedom are in this sense then absolute: without a harm, no repression; this depends of course on the view taken of a harm, something which may render this supposed absoluteness nugatory. Where one has a harm however, regulation may be permissible. This does not mean that every harm justifies regulation: even where one has a harm, freedom remains relevant in that it should be balanced against

---

1 Hart op.cit. at 21–22.

2 See Mitchell op.cit. especially at 97–98; see also *Williams* para 5.22.

3 Hart op.cit. at 22; a variant of this is that repression of moral pluralism may make it less, and not more likely that a general observance of prohibitions central to critical morality will be attained, in relation for example, to violence. See above, p.114.

4 *Williams* para 5.1.

the harm. All would appear (implicitly at least) to assume this.[1] Thus viewed, freedom cannot be seen as an absolute: 'It is rather that there is a right to free expression, a presumption in favour of it, and weighty considerations in terms of harms have to be advanced by those who seek to curtail it'.[2]

It is this last point that has in recent years given rise to what purports to be a new school of jurisprudence. For implicit in this balancing process it is argued, has been the Benthamite emphasis on the maximisation of the average welfare, or the good of the majority. In weighing a harm against individual freedom, the harm side of the scale may clearly be seen as much weightier (subject to the nature of that harm of course) were the harm to affect many, the specific curtailment of freedom, very few. It has been argued that this approach does not take sufficient account of fundamental rights; in order that that may be done, balancing should be excluded, certain fundamental rights being regarded as absolute.[3] This clearly involves an emphasis on the value of freedom in itself; in this respect it is similar to that view of freedom favoured by Professor Hart. It goes further however in that it attempts to erect this value into a theory of rights (or liberty), rights which apparently take precedence over all else.

An emphasis solely on rights and their protection as a legitimate aim of government would clearly involve a rejection of utilitarianism, rational or otherwise. This is the view put forward by Robert Nozick: he proposes that the state should concern itself only with the promotion of certain basic rights, which he enumerates as the right not to be killed or assaulted, to be free from coercion, to acquire property, to make contracts, and to defend oneself against the violation of these rights. Rawls proposes also certain basic rights which he apparently regards as absolute: political liberty, freedom of speech and of assembly, liberty of conscience and freedom of thought, freedom of the person, and the right to hold property.[4] Professor Dworkin accepts a modified form of utilitarianism, but also proposes to separate out certain basic liberties the restriction of which involve 'an antecedent likelihood' of a failure to treat all as equals with equal concern and respect: free-

---

1   Mitchell loc.cit; *contra* on Mill, T. Morawetz *The Philosophy of Law* (New York 1980) at 141–2.

2   *Williams* para 5.24.

3   For a seminal statement of this view see John Rawls *A Theory of Justice* (Cambridge, Mass. 1971); also e.g. R. Sartorius 'The Enforcement of Morality' 81 (1972) *Yale L J* 891; R. Nozick *Anarchy, the State, and Utopia* (1974); G. Dworkin *Taking Rights Seriously* (London 1977).

4   Rawls opposes theories of liberty, rather than theories of rights, to utilitarianism.

dom of speech, worship, association, and personal and sexual relationships.

A number of reservations have been expressed about these approaches.[1] One is that most proponents appear to admit, albeit with extreme reluctance, that some compromise is possible on the absoluteness of the rights proposed. Nozick proposes that restriction would be permissible where the exercise of rights impinges on the rights of another. Rawls appears to be the most uncompromising, arguing that liberty may be infringed only for the sake of liberty. It has been argued that this involves the same reasoning as that employed by Nozick, but this appears doubtful.[2] Dworkin admits that the only guaranteed rights are institutional rights (as opposed to background rights) and concrete rights (as opposed to abstract rights).[3] This appears to mean that the absoluteness of the right depends on the particular situation in which it is claimed. 'But this is no more of an assurance than the utilitarian was willing and able to give in saying that rights are labels for benefits of supervening weight *prima facie* but that they must be assessed in particular contexts against competing benefits of comparable weight.'[4] Dworkinians might counter by saying that the contrast between rights and other benefits is so great that the utilitarian notion of balancing is inapt. In other words, although policy is a matter for the legislature, both judiciary and legislature must attend to certain principles (propositions which describe rights) as being more important than policies, in that they reflect more important benefits. In hard cases however, how does the legislator distinguish a right from a goal, a principle from a policy? Presumably by application of Dworkin's basic consideration that all should be treated with equal concern and respect. This surely though is hardly an identifying mark for rights? It is in short difficult to see how a legislator can avoid a weighing-up of harms/benefits against liberty.

Such rights theories arguably rest on slender foundations.[5] Why, as opposed to how, it might be asked, should one give priority to rights? The answer: in order that all should be treated with equal concern and respect. Nozick's answer would be in order to respect the separateness of individuals. Whether such assertions are adequate to found a theory

---

1 Morawetz op.cit. especially at 91–117 and 154–63.

2 See H.L.A. Hart 'Rawls on Liberty and its Priority' 40 (1973) *U Chi L Rev* 534, especially footnote 12.

3 Dworkin op.cit. at 93.

4 Morawetz op.cit. at 165.

5 See H.L.A. Hart 'Between Utility and Rights' 79 (1979) *Colum L Rev* 828.

of rights is arguable. Professor Hart, for example, feels that they are not; that jurisprudence has in this sense entered an uncharted sea between utility and some other safe harbour.[1] This is not the place to attempt to take this any further; it is proposed therefore that freedom be seen as a factor entitled to the utmost respect in any legislative (or judicial)[2] assessment. In other words, freedom will be seen as a factor to be balanced against the enforcement of the two differing varieties of harm: the prevention of rationally assessable harms, and the prevention of harm in a less restrictive sense. The weight one attaches to freedom may clearly be a factor in making a choice between these two brands of utilitarianism; one has also to enter a strong *caveat* in relation to the maximisation of the general good at the expense of what may be regarded as basic liberties. There would not seem to be any reason why legislators should not attach at least primary importance to such liberties, even if not regarding them as absolute.[3]

These questions may of course also be viewed from a constitutional angle: is the enforcement of positive sexual morality a constitutionally permissible aim? Even if it is, does freedom of speech (for example) have a particular constitutional significance? The answer to this in the United States is absolutely clear in terms of the First Amendment, which appears to accord speech an absolute priority. Obscenity offences have then, as a matter of constitutional law, to be squared with the First Amendment. Although the underpinnings of the First Amendment clearly involve philosophical considerations, and although First Amendment theory may implicitly be based on such considerations, it is generally treated as a separate consideration. One must therefore examine such theory in its own right, asking in particular whether its strictures on obscenity regulation have maintained their own internal consistency. If they do not, such constitutional considerations may then be added to the linked, but perhaps separable, philosophical demands for a restatement of the *raison d'etre* of obscenity censorship.

---

1   H.L.A. Hart, 'Between Utility and Rights' 79 (1979) *Col L Rev* 828.

2   The question whether it is the proper function of a constitutional court such as the United States Supreme Court to consider questions of policy cannot be investigated here. In reality there is no doubt of the court's role in this respect. See e.g. J. Spaeth *Supreme Court Policy Making: Explanation and Prediction* (San Francisco 1979).

3   *Contra* Sartorius op.cit.; Hart op.cit., chapter 3.

5 Other statutory provisions I

There is a tendency perhaps, when speaking of obscenity in English law, to confine one's attention to the provisions of the Obscene Publications Acts, and in particular to the definition of obscenity provided in the 1959 Act. This is perhaps understandable: Lord Campbell's Act of 1857 was repealed by the 1959 Act,[1] whilst it would seem probable, as has been pointed out, that Parliament intended with the passage of the Obscene Publications Act to end all common law control of obscenity. Such concentration ignores underlying reality: common law control of published expression is not a thing of the past, albeit its present operation under banners other than that of obscenity. Lord Campbell's Act was not the only statute dealing with obscenity prior to the passage of the Obscene Publications Act. There were other measures, all of which continued in existence after the passage of the 1959 Act,[2] and

---

1   In Great Britain, but not in Northern Ireland.

2   It might be argued that such provisions have been impliedly repealed to the extent that they deal with matter covered by the Obscene Publications Act 1959. In this regard see e.g. *Great Central Gas Consumers Co* v *Clarke* (1862) 13 CBNS 838; *Smith* v *Benabo* (1937) 1 KB 518. Some support for this may emerge from the fact that the statutory definition of obscenity has not been applied outside the 1959 and 1964 Acts. This proposition, however, has never been tested judicially, and there would in any case be a grey area in which it would be impossible to assert conclusively that material was obscene, as opposed to being indecent (the standard employed in virtually all of the other statutory provisions operative in this area). Material clearly obscene might, however, if this argument were to be accepted, be excluded from the purview of such other statutory provisions; references in the following pages to such statutes covering the same area as the obscenity provisions should be read in the light of this possibility.

there have since been additions to their number.

Although one cannot limit an investigation of this sort to the Obscene Publications Act and its provisions alone, what one may perhaps do is to regard it as a point of reference, in terms of which one may attempt to assess the impact these additional statutes may have on the volume of expression already potentially proscribed under it. In this respect three factors are important:

(a) whether the scope of this body of statute law extends to the same (and/or other) forms of expression as do the Obscenity Acts;

(b) should they cover the same forms of expression as does the 1959 Act, do they, via their peculiar circumstances of application, apply only to portions thereof (and do they apply to areas thereof left untouched by the latter statute); and finally

(c) in respect of those forms of expression which they do cover, how broad is the potential prohibition which they exercise.[1] Is such breadth of cover justified in terms of their comprising restrictions only, and in particular, restrictions aimed at public nuisance, or are they concerned also with the preservation of public morals?[2] In other words, are these measures concerned with the enforcement of positive morality in a secondary sense only, their essential concern being gratuitous offence or some other (arguably) rationally assessable harm?

It is proposed (over the next two chapters) to assess these controls in terms of those rationally assessable harms as are relevant to restrictions on speech dealing with sexuality and/or violence; in other words, to follow through one's concern here with positive sexual morality, but to limit the latter to a secondary role only. If these restrictions/prohibitions are not felt justified in these terms, then an attempt will be made to assess what is so viable. The enforcement of positive morality in a primary sense will not be considered here; justifications such as this, or any rationally assessable harms which would found a prohibition rather

---

[1] Parliament did not (with one exception) include a definition of obscenity in any of these measures, nor did it extend the definition of obscenity given in the 1959 Act to any other statutory measure: it was rather provided that this definition should be 'for the purpose of this Act' only. As a result, definition was (and is) generally a matter for the courts; cf. Graham Zellick 'Offensive Advertisements in the Mail' [1972] *Crim L Rev* 124 at 125.

[2] In these terms one may perhaps better appreciate just how powerful a weapon the common law still is in this area: offences such as conspiracy to corrupt public morals for example, are not limited to any particular forms of expression; no detailed circumstances of applicability restrict them (such as applying for example only to expression sent through the post), whilst the vagueness of definition of corruption of public morals (or of outraging public decency, as the case may be) is such that their breadth of potential prohibition is very considerable.

than a restriction, will be considered in the final chapter of this work, and any conclusions and/or recommendations made here will, if necessary, be re-assessed then.

The statutes under consideration may conveniently be grouped (principally) in terms of the policy considerations mentioned above. The first of these is the protection of children.

I) Protection of children

The first statute to be considered here, the Children and Young Persons (Harmful Publications) Act 1955, is aimed at controlling the publication of certain brands of material, and might equally be dealt with under the heading of distribution/publication; the second statute relevant here, the Protection of Children Act 1978, is aimed principally at controlling the production of speech. Beyond a brief statement of its relevance to distribution, it is dealt with primarily as a prior restraint.

1) *The Children and Young Persons (Harmful Publications) Act, 1955*

Protection was at common law potentially afforded children from undesirable publications by virtue of the offence of publishing an obscene libel: the *Hicklin* test operated on the basis of the most susceptible person; provided there was a likelihood of the article in question falling into the hands of a child, its effect was to be judged in terms of that child. Obscene libel applied however only to material dealing with human sexuality. During the campaign for the reform of the common law of obscene libel, over the mid-1950s, the Committee of the Society of Authors proposed and had introduced a Bill, one of the clauses of which proposed to extend the meaning of obscenity to include publications 'that exploit horror, crudity or violence'.[1] The government of the day rejected the proposal, and partially in answer to it introduced the enactment in question here. Parliamentary intention clearly was that it should provide protection for children in relation to materials depicting violence, this to be complemented as to materials dealing with sexuality by obscene libel, later to be put into statutory form in the Obscene Publications Act 1959. This dual protection is still effective today, although the efficacy of the 1959 Act has been extended in one sense, by the inclusion of violence and drug-taking, but diminished in another by the dropping of the most susceptible person application of the test in favour of a significant proportion of the audience, in

---

1 See J.P. Eddy 'Obscene Publications: Society of Authors' Draft Bill' [1955] *Crim L Rev* 218.

terms of which children cannot always be assured of protection.

The 1955 Act provides that it is an offence (with a maximum penalty of four months' imprisonment and a £100 fine) to print, publish, sell or let on hire

> any book, magazine or other like work which is of a kind likely to fall into the hands of children or young persons and consists wholly or mainly of stories told in pictures (with or without the addition of written matter), being stories portraying (a) the commission of crimes; or (b) acts of violence or cruelty; or (c) incidents of a repulsive or horrible nature; in such a way that the work as a whole would tend to corrupt a child or young person into whose hands it might fall.

The forms of expression to which the Act applies are covered by the 1959 Obscene Publications Act: written and pictorial matter. The circumstances under which these are covered are also similar: publication, sale, etc. What of the standard applied here? The Director of Public Prosecutions revealed to the Williams Committee that forty cases involving horror comics had been referred to him since 1955. Six of these referrals had resulted in proceedings under either the 1955 Act or the Obscene Publications Act.[1] As yet there are however no reported judicial decisions in terms of the 1955 Act: one can proceed then only by surmise, and/or analogy with the 1959 Act, the definitional provisions of which are in some ways similar. The specifications (a)–(c) of the varieties of published material which fall potentially within the Act, shade from specificity into virtual generality. Although some objectivity and agreement might be expected on whether material portrays an act of violence or the commission of crime, whether an incident is of a 'horrible nature' or not is rather more subjective. Material of this sort dealing with violence is clearly within the ambit of the Act; the Act may well extend in terms of such words as 'horrible', to certain sexual incidents also. It is not all such material dealing with violence (for example) which is proscribed. The material must have an effect: that effect is corruption, and a mere tendency to the effect is sufficient. 'Corrupt' has not been defined in this context: it presumably means the same as under the 1959 Act — to debase morally. Again working by analogy, such debasement might take a number of forms, one of them being thought arousal. It would thus be up to the magistrate[2] to assess the primary effect, and secondly, whether this was

---

1   All six were successful; Report of the Committee on Obscenity and Film Censorship (HMSO 1979) Appendix 1, para 42; hereafter referred to as *Williams*.

2   There is no right to a jury trial, the offence being triable only in a magistrate's court.

debasing. Such effect is determinable however only in terms of the material's readership or audience. The Act does not deal only with distribution to children or young people (a young person being defined as someone under seventeen years of age) although the publication must be of a kind 'likely to fall into the hands of children or young persons'.

It employs as far as general distribution is concerned the most susceptible person test employed by *Hicklin*. As with the 1959 Act, the distribution aspect would not appear to play a vital role, at least when general: assuming that recorruption is possible, this coupled with the most susceptible person approach, would be sufficient to bring virtually any general distribution potentially within the Act. Only where particular, would distribution be potentially decisive.

The Act, in terms of its circumstances of application, variety of expression, and standard employed, appears to cover ground already covered by the 1959 Act with its extension to violence and drug-taking. The only difference is the employment with obscenity of the significant proportion test. The most susceptible person approach, although giving wider coverage, has been severely criticised, its abandonment being proscribed by the American Supreme Court as early as 1957.[1] Although the constitutionality of statutes aimed at the protection of children in the obscenity area, even when covering distribution to minors only, is now open to doubt, following the Supreme Court's hard-core pornography ruling in *Miller* v *California*,[2] some form of narrowing of the statute in this respect would seem sensible. Any such narrowing, though, would apparently render the offence quite superfluous, the 1959 Act providing virtual duplication via its potential application to particular distribution. A further problem accompanying such reform would be a new audience standard: if one were to prohibit sales to minors only, this itself encompasses anyone from three or four years of age, right up to seventeen. Does one set the standard as the average minor? The exception, in favour of minors, to the average person standard permitted by the American Supreme Court in *Ginsberg* v *New York*[3] did not specify a solution, and should the *Ginsberg* exception remain operable, this remains an unsolved problem.

As far as the application of the standard is concerned, there is a specific requirement that the work be taken as a whole. The same approach would presumably be adopted here, as with the 1959 Act in relation to a work which consists of more than one article. No defence of public good is provided, although an accused may plead that he had not

---

1   In *Butler* v *Michigan* 352 US 380 (1957); see chapter 11.

2   413 US 15 (1973).

3   390 US 629 (1968).

examined the work, and had no reasonable cause to suspect that it was something to which the Act applied. This *mens rea* requirement parallels that under the 1959 Act, negligence being enough as to the nature of the work, intention as to its corruptive effect not being required. The intention of the author is presumably irrelevant, particularly as, with no public good defence, it cannot be taken into account in assessing some alleged merit. Although the effect of the material is a question of fact for the magistrate, expert evidence would be admissible, were the reasoning (in terms of the 1959 Act) in this respect in *DPP v A & BC Chewing Gum Ltd*[1] to be followed.

This measure does not appear to have anything to do with the invasion of privacy, as with unsolicited mail, nor does it appear to have to do with offence; rather it is concerned with the fostering of moral discernment amongst the young. Is such protection justified and necessary, and if so, in what form? We turn now to examining these questions and the Williams recommendations as to them.

2) *The Protection of Children Act 1978*

Section 1(b) of the Act makes it an offence to 'distribute or show ... indecent photographs' of a child — 'meaning in this Act a person under the age of sixteen'. For convenience this aspect of the Act is dealt with together with its prior restraint considerations.[2]

3) *The Williams Committee*

There are strong ethical inhibitions against conducting the same sort of research with children as has been used to measure adult reactions to pornography. Not surprisingly, then, one has a range of views on what effect(s) is/are likely. A major collation of work on the effects of pornography, including this area, was undertaken by the American Presidential Commission on Pornography. The commission concluded that sexual precocity was linked to both deviant home backgrounds and peer influences.[3] The commission also concluded that although children did not as a rule buy pornography, the vast majority of them had been exposed to it: roughly 80 per cent of boys and 70 per cent of girls having seen explicit sexual material before the age of eighteen, and most of them much earlier. Their source was generally material purchased by others (parents, brothers) only to be surreptitiously examined by younger

---

1 [1968] 1 QB 159.

2 Chapter 7; see also the section on distribution (law reform), chapter 6.

3 *Report of the United States Commission on Obscenity* (Bantam Books 1970).

members of the family. The conclusion was that no matter how tight were controls, such exposure would nonetheless take place. Although the commission was not able to use social science to test this, its view was that improved sex education would have a major impact in lessening the interest of the young in pornography and in lessening its effect on them. That it did have an effect was clear; despite the conclusion that precocity resulted essentially from other environmental factors, one of the studies did warn that early and repeated exposure to pornography might well lead to delinquency.[1] In terms of the uncertainty as to the effect of such material on children, and quite apart from its availability to adults, a prohibition on dissemination to minors received the commission's support. A strong argument in favour of such restriction was that even though many children may read such material, and may not be damaged by it, such exposure does take place within the context of societal disapproval; were such disapproval to be removed, moral damage might well then result:

> Psychiatrists ... made a distinction between the reading of pornography, as unlikely to be *per se* harmful, and the permitting of the reading of pornography, which was conceived as potentially destructive. The child is protected in his reading of pornography by the knowledge that it is pornographic, i.e. disapproved. It is outside parental standards and not part of his identification process. To openly permit implies parental approval, and even suggests seductive encouragement. If this is so of parental approval, it is equally so of societal approval — another potent influence on the developing ego.[2]

The Supreme Court had already declared itself persuaded by such arguments. The court had rejected the most susceptible person test, replacing it with the standard of the average person. Any attempt to re-introduce the old standard via the back door by means of emphasising children as a part of a composite average person was firmly rejected.[3] This means that with a control on general distribution, no protection can be provided to minors. This may mean that one cannot even control material in favour of minors by imposing a licensing requirement

---

1   *Report* op.cit. at 63 and 467; see also Eysenck and Nias *Sex, Violence and the Media* (London 1978) chapter 5.

2   Gaylin 'Review: The Prickly Problems of Pornography' 77 (1967) *Yale L J* 579, especially at 594.

3   *Ginzburg* v *United States* 383 US 463 (1966) at 466, footnote 5; *Pinkus* v *United States* 436 US 293 (1978).

that prohibits viewing by minors but leaves adults unaffected.[1] Constitutionally speaking, the cupboard — as far as protection for children — seemed bare. The pressure of such arguments as those raised above proved too strong however: in *Ginsberg* v *New York*[2] the Supreme Court accepted a compromise of the average person test: constitutionality was assumed for statutes prohibiting dissemination to minors, provided prohibition was couched in terms of the obscenity test.

A number of uncertainties exist in relation to this ruling:[3] material to be caught under such a statute must appeal to the prurient interest of minors; it is not clear whether one judges this in terms of the 'average minor'. If so, is such a standard not an absurdity, in view of the composite range being from the very young up to sixteen or eighteen years of age (the court has not indicated decisively what is constitutionally permissible in this respect)? Were one to opt for an average minor in the sense of the reasonable person, would he or she be fourteen years of age, or perhaps twelve? A further difficulty is that to make sense, any adjustment in favour of minors in relation to prurient interest must be accompanied by an adjustment in relation to patent offensiveness and First Amendment value, the other two aspects of the *Roth* test (as subsequently interpreted). Judging material in terms of patent offensiveness to adults or value in adult terms might render the entire exercise nugatory; unless of course, this was taken as being what a reasonable person finds it offensive that a child should see.

Such adjustment has had spin-off in relation to the basic First Amendment approach: if obscenity is to constitute an exception to the amendment in that it does not possess redeeming social value, this is a once and for all decision. It is difficult to appreciate the logic, in terms of the exception approach, in saying that material has such merit and is within the First Amendment, only then to except it in terms of its value to minors. What seems implicit in all this is a balancing of interest, something which the Court has in this area desperately tried to avoid. Despite these difficulties, the Court felt that policy considerations dictated such an exception. That exception's viability is now in doubt in terms of the *Miller* ruling that only hard-core pornography may be proscribed;[4] this does not affect the weight clearly attached by the Court to such considerations.

The findings of the Williams Committee in respect of the effects of

---

1 See *Interstate Circuit, Inc* v *City of Dallas* 390 US 676 (1968).

2 390 US 629 (1968).

3 See particularly chapter 14.

4 *Miller* v *California* 413 US 15 (1973); chapter 13.

pornography and violent material reflect to a large extent (at least as far as pornography is concerned) the conclusions reached above. A number of potential ill-influences were canvassed in submissions made to the committee:[1] Dr Hanna Segal argued that although children may learn to overcome their sexual fantasies by looking at the real world, confirmation by that world (by means of pornography) of their fantasies might well lead to fixation. Not only this, but if an essential element of pornography is cruelty, an early link between sexuality and violence may be forged. Exposure to pornography might, Dr Gallwey of the Portman Clinic argued, constitute the proverbial last straw, in the sense of acting, together with other stress factors, to tip a child towards psychological damage. It was also argued that pornography might be used by adults for the purposes of (homosexual, in particular) seduction of the young.

Rather similar considerations were felt to apply to violent material and its effect on the young. Evidence to the committee appeared to suggest two principal concerns here: the real-life quality of some violence portrayals, as opposed to fairy-tale, or even Western-movie type violence. Second, the increased susceptibility in respect of violent material of those 'deprived of a secure background and the normal socialising influences which enable them to develop their own healthy personality'.[2] A closer link appears to have been shown to exist between violent material and harm as far as adults are concerned, than can be demonstrated in the case of pornography, investigation perhaps indicating a lowering of thresholds in relation to the conduct in question.[3] There would seem to be little reason to suppose that such a link may not exist with children also. The committee, despite the feeling that many children are more robust than may sometimes be supposed, concluded that there was a wide feeling that: '... it was right that those still in the process of emotional development should be shielded from some of the very powerful images of violence, particularly material which appeared to exploit and glorify violent behaviour'.[4] This is not the place to attempt further evaluation of the evidence available;[5] in

---

1 *Williams*, para 6.65.

2 *Williams*, para 6.67.

3 See chapter 16.

4 *Williams* para 6.67.

5 See S. Brady *Screen Violence and Film Censorship, A Review of Research* Home Office Research Unit, Research Study No. 40 (1977); G. Comstock and M. Fisher *Television and Human Behaviour: a Guide to Scientific Literature* (New York 1976); H.J. Eysenck *Sex, Violence and the Media* (London 1978) chapter 5. See chapter 16.

view of the weight of opinion in this respect, it would not seem unreasonable to conclude that in view of their immaturity, and consequent susceptibility to exploitation and misorientation, the young deserve special protection from certain materials dealing in violence and sexuality. This is not to conclude that adults need similar protection, nor is it necessarily to pass unfavourable judgements on the conduct portrayed in such material. Although much of such conduct may itself be criminal, much of it — say heterosexual intercourse between consenting adults — may be perfectly lawful. The concern with children is whether despite their probable robustness, they can be expected to cope with an adult world, adult concepts, relationships and problems. There appears to be a clear consensus that they cannot.

One has here moreover strong back-up from other areas of the criminal law: society — and this would appear to apply to most societies besides this one — has long considered that children need to be protected from involvement in certain aspects of sexual conduct. The considerations are again in terms of immaturity of consent,[1] and it would seem reasonable that if children are to be protected from such conduct because of their inability to assimilate or cope with it, that this protection should extend to shielding them from portrayals of such conduct in speech form. Putting this in terms of rationally assessable harms, one cannot say that a single or even several harms emerge clearly from empirical investigation. What one can say is that there is a reasonable weight of evidence on the harm side of the scale, and that crucially, this is to be weighed against immaturity of consent. Even if seen in terms of paternalism, such restraint is arguably justified as freedom of choice in the case of the young must be an altogether less compelling consideration than it is with their elders. Their immaturity, and consequent inability either to consent, in the full sense, to conduct, or to the assimilation of such conduct via speech, is vital both to the assessment of the harms likely, and to the questions of individual freedom involved in imposing restraint in order to avoid these harms.

The question then is, what prohibitions or restraints are appropriate? In terms of the American First Amendment, a Supreme Court ruling balancing policy aims against minors' First Amendment rights would surely provide the best result. The Williams Committee recommended the repeal of both statutes in this area; the 1978 Protection of Children Act, covering the production of pornography, and proposals for its replacement are considered below with prior restraints. The test under the 1955 Harmful Publications measure of 'a tendency to corrupt a child' the committee regarded as neither realistic nor straightforward.[2]

---

1   See the Production of pornography: prior restraints, chapter 7.

2   *Williams* para 9.37.

Nothing specific is recommended to take its place however; the proposal is rather that the requirement of the protection of children be left to the control recommended in relation to displays. This will be discussed in detail later.[1] Restricted matter is defined as matter

> which, not consisting of the written word, is such that its unrestricted availability is offensive to reasonable people by reason of the manner in which it portrays, deals with or relates to violence, cruelty or horror, or sexual, faecal or urinary functions, or genital organs.[2]

Restricted availability is defined as a ban (*inter alia*)

> (i) on the display, sale, hire etc. of restricted material other than by way of postal or other delivery and ... other than in premises ...
> (a) to which persons under the age of eighteen are not admitted.[3]

It is also recommended that it should be an offence to 'send or deliver restricted material, or advertisements for such material, to ... a person who the sender knew or ought reasonably to have known was under the age of eighteen'.[4] In essence such material (other than purely the written word) which a reasonable person would find offensive if thrust upon him, is restricted rather than prohibited: individual choice is crucial in that should one *choose* to have such material sent to one through the mail, or to have it available for sale in shop displays; one has merely to act accordingly by requesting it, or entering restricted sales premises. With children, such consent is irrelevant: such material is not to be sent to them, or be displayed for sale to them, whether they want it or not. The standard to be applied is that the *unrestricted* availability of such matter should be offensive to reasonable people. In other words, 'there may well be material which reasonable people would not find offensive in itself, but which responsible parents would not want to be available to children and young people, and this is properly restricted'.[5] The standard is a deceptive one: it is *not* material the public display of which a resonable adult himself finds offensive entirely in terms of his own susceptibilities; it rather covers material the display or distribution of which to *minors*, a reasonable adult finds offensive.

---

1 See displays, chapter 6.

2 *Williams* para 9.36.

3 Ibid. para 13.4, subpara 8.

4 Ibid. subpara 12.

5 *Williams* para 9.33; generally paras 9.32–9.34.

This means that the entire apparatus of restriction operates in terms of children: what one sees displayed in shop windows, on billboards, and in other clearly public areas would be monitored in terms of what is suitable for children. What one found inside shops on display, or for sale, would be similarly judged. Materials unsuitable for children could be sold, but only in restricted premises. Such premises would not admit children at all, would display a warning notice, and would have blank windows.[1] The committee justifies this blanket provision, rather than having a separate measure to protect children, in the following terms:

> We considered very carefully the idea that a separate restriction test should be introduced to cover this area of concern, but we have finally decided that this is not necessary. Moreover, we believe that to associate the protection of the young with the same provision as has already been introduced for other reasons serves to bring out an important point, that the concern for the young is focused on just the same features of the material as makes its display offensive to adults. ... If someone thinks, *for the kinds of reasons that are our concern*, that a publication should not fall into the hands of the young, then he will find its public availability not merely undesirable in some general sense, but indeed offensive. We conclude, therefore, that the interest in protecting the young is appropriately met by the restriction formula we propose.[2]

The latter claim is hardly open to question: children would see or have distributed to them nothing that was unsuitable for their consumption. What is rather disingenuous is the claim that such protection is merely a convenient off-spin of a general offensiveness standard: it is rather the *basis* of the offensiveness standard. There is nothing after all to prevent a restriction on public displays being couched in terms of what the reasonable adult finds offensive in terms entirely of his own susceptibilities.

The committee argue that in terms of the proposed standard 'restriction will not be imposed on naturist magazines or on pin-up magazines of a more old-fashioned variety, since we do not propose that simple nudity should bring a publication within the prescribed class'.[3] The proposed standard operates, however, not in terms of what the committee feels should fall within the prescribed class, but what the reasonable adult feels is suitable for children. The standard is overbroad,

---

1   *Williams* para 9.15.

2   Ibid. para 9.34 (emphasis in the original).

3   *Williams* para 9.37.

in that one might arrive at a situation where only what was fit for children would be either displayed or available in normal retail outlets; for anything else one would have to take oneself off to a blank-windowed shop, which might, depending on whether there is a general prohibition or not, contain some very offensive material indeed. This merely to purchase, say, a magazine such as *Cosmopolitan*, with its trendy and inevitable articles on female orgasm, and quizzes allowing one to assess one's own sensuality. Fairly tame stuff essentially, but hardly suitable for the very young.

Accepting that gratuitous offence is a rationally assessable harm,[1] and accepting harm to children from such material as rationally assessable, what one is asked by the committee to accept is that the offence a reasonable adult feels at the rationally assessable harm done by the sale of unsuitable material to a minor, is *itself* a rationally assessable harm. This is to stretch the inclusion of offence within the ambit of such harms to breaking point. It is true that the resultant control is a restriction and not a prohibition, but it is a blanket restriction. To allow this brand of offence as a rationally assessable harm lays one open to letting through offence at the private behaviour of others: one would presumably be equally offended at the thought of a child perusing in private material that was harmful to him. Rather than stretch offence as a policy factor in this way, rather than require two rationally assessable harms, would it not be preferable to limit restriction to the protection of children, and motivate it accordingly? The protection of children has nothing to do with a distinction between public and private, or with consent; offensiveness has everything to do with both these distinctions. The committee has attempted to merge two policy factors that are best kept apart. An additional reason that the committee might have added for selecting the standard they did was to avoid providing a second standard in relation to children, and above all, by limiting their definition to offensiveness, to avoid any definitions of material in terms of harm, corruption, etc.; cogent reasons, but not sufficient to tip the scales in favour of their blanket restriction?

An additional difficulty with the committee's proposals is that although overbroad in terms of the standard applied, they are too narrow in terms of the type of speech covered: the blanket restrictions recommended do not extend to the written word. The committee claims general agreement that written material does not have the impact that visual material has in terms of offence; that some activity is in fact involved in order to take in its contents.[2] Not only this, but written material is

---

1 See the section on displays, chapter 6.

2 *Williams* para 7.7.

more likely to contain opinion, and is a medium which is more likely to give rise to questions of artistic merit.[1] The committee felt that the lower likelihood of gratuitous offence, coupled with the other factors mentioned above, outweighed questions of unsuitability for children; hence the recommendation of no restriction at all in relation to such material.

The question of written materials and offensiveness will be considered later;[2] as far specifically as children are concerned, the conclusions above illustrate the difficulties involved in running offensiveness and the protection of children together. There was the practical consideration that had the committee included written material, in terms of their recommendations bookshops would have been able to stock only what was suitable for children. Clearly the prospect of the average bookshop with blank windows, warning notices, and banned to the young was not a prospect the committee found appetising! In terms of protecting children, however, it is unacceptable that written materials be freely available: adolescents might have free access to the most dubious of publications, whilst relatively inoffensive pictorial material — but perhaps unsuitable for children — would be relegated elsewhere. If the essence of protecting the young is their inability to cope with and assimilate all aspects of an adult world, restrictions on written material seem clearly desirable.

How might one achieve a reconciliation of these views within, but not in terms of, a framework of offence restrictions? If a standard for offence in terms of children is overbroad, the starting point would be to modify the basic offence standard to one which operates with regard to what the reasonable person finds offensive (insofar as unrestricted displays are concerned) in terms of his own susceptibilities, not in terms of the susceptibilities of children. This would give us a restriction in terms of shops and distribution that would exclude the young. What of outlets selling material not offensive in such terms? Clearly some of this may be unsuitable for children. The answer here is a compromise between the individual freedom of adults and prospective harm to children. If children are permitted inside such shops, and material may be displayed and sold there, how can compromise be effected? A suggestion, mooted by the Home Office Working Paper on Vagrancy and Street Offences[3] was that materials subject to restriction be segregated in a separate part of the premises. Williams rejected this, as it would have operated in terms of their basic offence restriction; there is no

---

1   *Williams* para 7.22.

2   See displays, chapter 6.

3   HMSO (1974).

general prohibition recommended additionally, and customers would have been aware that in the restricted section there was virtually any sort of material at all. This they reasoned, might be offensive to such customers.[1] Here segregation would not operate in terms of the basic offensiveness restriction, and this reasoning would not apply. The same may be said of their reasoning in relation to separate displays, high shelves, and so on. To require segregated premises in terms of protecting children might be too onerous a burden on retailers. What is suggested, are separate displays of material unsuitable for children in ordinary retail outlets, coupled with a prohibition on the sale of such material to children.

A crucial question is, how is such material to be defined? The concern of the law remains sexuality and violence; as the committee remarked, any restrictions of this sort beyond this ambit were not their,[2] nor are they this essay's, concern. As far as the standard is concerned, in line with the general concern over the inability of the young properly to consent to exposure to such considerations, a test in terms of exploitation would seem sensible, and would harmonise with the committee's recommendations on the protection of children in the production of pornography.[3] Unrestricted availability to children might be curtailed then in the following terms:

> Publications portraying, dealing with, or relating to violence, cruelty or horror, or sexual, faecal or urinary functions or genital organs so as, in the view of a reasonable person, to exploit the young by unnecessarily arousing fear, anxiety or other emotions, would be subject to restriction.[4]

As expert evidence is under present obscenity law admissible on the question of the effect of publications on children,[5] there would not seem to be any insurmountable hurdle to the same being done here. As far as displays in public places outside shop premises are concerned, this restriction might equally be applied. This would admittedly involve a restriction in terms of children but as it would apply to public displays only, its chilling effect on adult freedoms would not perhaps be

---

1 *Williams* para 9.10.

2 *Williams* para 9.34.

3 See prior restraints, chapter 7.

4 This type of restriction might potentially include vulgar or abusive language; there would seem no reason were coverage of such language to be felt necessary and justifiable in these policy terms, why coverage should not extend beyond publications to include the spoken word?

5 *DPP v A and BC Chewing Gum Ltd* [1968] 1 QB 159.

insupportable.

It might well be asked at this junction just how such protection would compare with what children enjoy under present law. The 1955 Act prohibits the dissemination of corruptive comic books (in effect) of a certain variety; the standard is the most susceptible child. Protection under the Obscene Publications Act 1959 has been severely restricted both because the test in general publication is operated in terms of minors forming a significant proportion of the audience, and because of the aversion defence, in terms of which the average person's finding the material repellent is sufficient to ensure its non-obscenity. This must surely let through much material which one might wish to withhold from the young? This may be to presume that the average person is not a composite of the community, or is a composite exclusive of the young. This has been the approach of the American Supreme Court in relation to the average person aspect of the *Roth* test.[1] These two acts between them, then, cover (to an extent) the same circumstances as do the recommended restriction; they cover the same varieties of expression. The standard recommended is, however, a more explicit one than 'corruption', and should not be open to criticism on the grounds of enforcing positive morality or overbreadth. Certainly such a restriction does involve the enforcement of positive morality, but only in a secondary way, in the sense that the ambit of the offence in terms of sexuality and violence can be explained only in terms of such morality. Such a measure would not be inhibited by the consideration that protection for minors in terms of it would mean a general prohibition on the material involved as far as adults were concerned also, as would be the case with the 1959 Act at present. With such specific provision, protection of the young would probably at once be more effective, and less susceptible to criticism. In terms of rationally assessable harms, such a measure would very probably pass muster: such harms would be balanced against minors' immaturity, and therefore less imperative individual freedom claims, coupled with as small an impingement on adult freedom as possible. The Williams proposals certainly do not appear to satisfy the latter criterion.

The only other controls at present operative that might possibly protect minors are those on indecent displays. It is difficult to estimate whether any protection is provided here, however; indecency is concerned not with effect on a particular audience, but with the context of the conduct in question. It may be that the affront to positive morality occasioned is to some extent based on the involvement of children. Any reliance on this in terms of protecting children is probably misplaced, in the sense of demanding the sort of specificity from indecency as a

---

1   *Pinkus* v *United States* 436 US 293 (1978).

standard which it is not capable of supplying. The Indecent Displays (Control) Act 1981 provides that indecent displays are permissible provided they are not in a public place (an area to which the public had gained access on payment or after adequate warning being excepted from the latter) *and* provided that those under eighteen years of age are not admitted.[1] It is not clear however whether suitability for children would play any role in the assessment of such indecency; in the absence of elaboration on so fundamental a point, and in the absence of any such suggestion in relation to the standard of indecency in the past, it would seem reasonably safe to conclude that protection for children in terms of it, and reforms which employ it, would be solely with respect to the exclusion of children from contact with material broadly offensive in the context in question to current standards of propriety.

A number of further problems remain for consideration here: first, would the Williams standard, or that proposed here, restrict newspaper reports of dreadful events or atrocities? The committee's view was that such reports, together with naturist and 'old-fashioned' pin-up magazines, would not be found by a reasonable person to be unsuitable for the young.[2] This may be correct; arguably the standard suggested here is even tighter in this regard, as a result of the inclusion of the words 'unnecessarily' and 'exploit'. Such statutory language, it is suggested, would provide a jury or magistrate with the leeway necessary to avoid covering such publications; certainly it would not be desirable to have such matter segregated as being unsuitable for children. The same could be argued to apply to contraceptives and their advertisement, presuming an adequate sex education programme. The committee felt, in terms of their proposals, that the law should clearly state such matter to be excluded.[3]

A second problem concerns the question of the age to be specified. The American Supreme Court does not appear to have ruled constitutionally on this. It was submitted to Williams, particularly by the British Youth Council, that it was odd that young people who married with their parents' consent at sixteen, and could engage in sexual activity, could not view the portrayal of such activity by others.[4] Equally the committee itself recommended protection as to the production of pornography to apply to those under sixteen years of age, a selection influenced by the age of consent being set at sixteen. Opinion canvassed

---

1   Section 1(3).

2   *Williams* paras 9.34 and 9.37.

3   Ibid. para 9.37.

4   *Williams* para 9.39.

by the committee seemed to indicate sixteen or eighteen years of age, or an age inbetween, but not some other age. The essence here is the age at which people are sufficiently mature to exercise free choice; expert opinion on this differs. Perhaps the principal ground on which the committee chose eighteen as the relevant age was in terms of the 'slippage' problem: 'the adoption of eighteen as the age below which protection is given will in practice mean that far fewer fifteen-year-olds will be put at risk than if the prescribed age were sixteen'.[1] One way in which such slippage might be prevented would be to make it an offence not only for a shopkeeper to sell to those whom he should reasonably have realised were below the relevant age, and for him to fail to segregate material, but also to make it an offence on the part of the minor concerned to attempt to buy such material or gain access to forbidden premises.[2] The committee took the view that such liability should not be imposed on minors. Imposition of such liability might, however, be a convenient way of lowering the relevant age without jeopardising the adequacy of protection for those under sixteen.

Lowering the age to sixteen would have a valuable spin-off in relation to the final problem for consideration here: the question whether material is assessed in terms of the average minor, or whether this is simply left open. In American terms, failure to stipulate some sort of median would probably mean that the restriction would fall foul of Fourteenth Amendment due process in the sense of there not being a rational connection between barring from seventeen-year-olds material suitable for them, in order to protect eight-year-olds. Clearly a sixteen-years-of-age ceiling would be useful. An answer to the problem might be to adopt the approach used with the average person standard in the United States in relation to adults: to assess the average adult in terms of all adults, including the specially sensitive.[3] This would almost certainly satisfy constitutional requirements in the United States in this respect, and would provide a less arbitrary standard. Further uniformity within this jurisdiction might be achieved by making prosecutions dependent on some central authority's authorisation, the obvious example being the Director of Public Prosecutions.

Constitutionality in American terms[4]

Before moving on to the question of distribution, it may be useful

---

1   *Williams* para 9.39.

2   *Williams* para 9.44.

3   See *Pinkus* v *United States* 436 US 293 (1978).

4   See chapter 14.

briefly to assess in terms of the First Amendment, the proposals made above. Would such restrictions as have been proposed pass constitutional muster? It is suggested that they would. Possible authority to the contrary exists in the form of *Interstate Circuit* v *City of Dallas*,[1] in that any restriction on speech in favour of minors which affects general distribution may be unconstitutional. It may be that the decision was one made primarily in terms of overbreadth: that the standard employed was overbroad in the sense of not being couched in terms of obscenity, a standard which is apparently the only constitutionally permissible one. If this interpretation of *Dallas* is acceptable, it may not prevent a general restriction designed to protect children and which does not impose a prohibition in relation to adults. Such restriction would *a priori* however be couched in terms of obscenity. Paradoxically, the constitutionality of any measure designed to protect children, is, as a result of the *Miller*[2] ruling on hard-core pornography, in doubt. There are two alternatives here: the Court might regard such restriction not as a censorship measure, but as something aimed at the protection of minors, and therefore sustainable, imposing as it does a restriction and not a prohibition on adult First Amendment freedoms. Alternatively, the Court might straightforwardly balance First Amendment values against the harms in question. If the Supreme Court has felt able to approve zoning restrictions on 'adult' cinema in terms of promoting better town planning,[3] it is at least possible that it might similarly, or in terms of straight balancing, approve the measure proposed above: that is, in terms of the protection of children, and as small an interference with the First Amendment rights of adults as possible; the impingement on these rights in terms of a tightly-drawn statute would seem minimal.[4]

II) Distribution/publication

1) *The Post Office Act 1953*

Section 11(1) provides:

> A person shall not send or attempt to send or procure to be sent a postal packet which:
> (b) encloses any indecent or obscene print, painting,

---

1 390 US 676 (1968).

2 *Miller* v *California* 413 US 15 (1973).

3 See *Young* v *American Mini Theaters* 427 US 50 (1976).

4 See displays, chapter 6, and chapter 14.

photograph, lithograph, engraving, cinematograph film, book, card or written communication, or any indecent or obscene article whether similar to the above or not; or

(c) has on the packet, or on the cover thereof, any words, marks or designs which are grossly offensive or of an indecent or obscene character.

Section 66 provides that it is an offence to 'send any message by telephone which is grossly offensive or of an indecent, obscene or menacing character'. This measure clearly does not extend to any form of expression not reviewed by the Obscene Publications Act; it applies only to that percentage of such expression detailed as may be distributed through the mail or by telephone. What proportion of this percentage or area of application is liable to censorship under the Act? This can be answered only in terms of the definition assigned the phrase 'indecent or obscene' by the courts. As far as the word 'obscene' is concerned it was widely believed[1] that it here — and in any other enactment in which it was not specifically defined — enjoyed the traditional common law meaning assigned to it by Cockburn CJ in *R v Hicklin*.[2] The 1959 Act, whilst apparently replacing common law control in this area, did not extend its definition of obscenity to any other enactment; the courts in their turn have refused to link obscenity in this context to either the common law or the statutory definition thereof. Lord Parker CJ in *R v Stanley*[3] held that obscenity here conveyed merely the idea of offending against recognised standards of propriety; a tendency to deprave or corrupt is not required. It is nonetheless a stronger term than indecent, indecency 'being at the lower end of the scale and obscene at the upper end of the scale'.[4]

Not only is the distinction between indecency and obscenity in these terms rather tenuous, but the word 'obscene' now has two meanings in law, the one more indeterminate than the other. The ambit of offence against recognised standards of propriety is very wide; besides

---

1   See e.g. *Minutes of Evidence* at 39 and 42; Zellick [1972] *Crim L Rev* 724 and 725.

2   (1868) LR 3 QB 360; this belief may well have been partly based on the fact that there was a proviso in Lord Campbell's Act 1857 that an article to be liable to forfeiture as obscene under the Act, had to be such that it could constitute the subject of a prosecution at common law for obscene libel. The word obscene therefore, although not defined in the Act, was linked to the common law and whatever definition it might place thereon.

3   [1965] 1 All ER 1035 at 1040; also *R v Anderson* [1972] 1 QB 304 at 311. See conspiracy to outrage public decency, chapter 3.

4   Ibid.

drug-taking and violence[1] to which statutory obscenity has been extended, the phrase is so vague as to extend potentially to virtually anything. There is no provision for a defence of public good, nor for the admission of expert evidence; such evidence has specifically been ruled inadmissible on the question of the indecency or obscenity of the articles in question.[2] Intention as to obscenity or indecency would not appear to be required, nor is there any requirement that the articles be considered as a whole. The standard is relative, but only in terms of context, and not effect on a particular audience; as a result the nature of the addressee is immaterial.[3] It is not certain whether relevance for the context extends from the surrounding circumstances to the actual article itself; in other words, besides the general circumstances, are portions of the article other than that which is allegedly obscene or indecent, relevant in an assessment of the latter? No clear answer has been given, but equally no requirement that an article be taken as a whole is evident.[4]

In these terms the Act constitutes, within its area of operation, a simple alternative to a charge under the 1959 Act; the standards employed provide for the potential prohibition of a far greater proportion of expression. The safeguards provided by the former are largely evaded, although the institution of a right to a jury trial, originally not provided here, was recommended by the James Committee on the Distribution of Criminal Business;[5] this has been implemented by the Criminal Law Act 1977.[6] There is a possible remedy to attempts to circumvent the 1959 Act, in that a court is empowered by Section 75 of the 1953 Act to stop proceedings if it appears that the offence is punishable at common law or under some other statute, and that such a charge would be more appropriate. Also, to be fair to the courts, it must be admitted that beyond the confusion consequent upon the introduction of two definitions into the law of obscenity, the interpretation in question

---

1   Cf. J.C. Smith and B. Hogan *Criminal Law* (4th edn London 1978) at 707; *Knuller* v *DPP* [1972] 3 WLR 143 at 150 per Lord Reid.

2   *R* v *Stamford* [1972] 2 WLR 1055.

3   *R* v *Straker* [1965] *Crim L Rev* 239: *Kosmos Publication Ltd* v *DPP* [1975] *Crim L Rev* 345.

4   See however the Court of Appeal's acceptance of the IBA's 'taken as a whole' argument in relation to an allegedly indecent broadcast; *AG ex rel McWhirter* v *IBA* [1973] 1 QB 629 at 659.

5   James Committee on the Distribution of Criminal Business between Crown Courts and Magistrates' Courts (HMSO 1975) Cmnd. 6323, para 162.

6   Such election increases the sentencing maximum from a £1,000 fine to a possible term of twelve months' imprisonment.

has not had much practical effect. The Act speaks after all, of 'indecent or obscene': even had the courts adopted the statutory definition of obscenity here, it would still in any prosecution under the Act be sufficient if the article in question was indecent.[1] Indecency has been very broadly defined: it conveys the idea merely of offence (at the lower end of the scale) against recognised standards of propriety.[2] Context, but not effect on a particular audience is relevant; as a result the nature of the addressee is irrelevant.[3] The offence is therefore committed whether or not the packet reaches its destination, and irrespective of whether it has been solicited or not.

This legislation gives rise to a number of problems: in the case of discreet under-the-counter sales of possibly indecent items, neither conspiracy to outrage public decency nor the Indecent Displays (Control) Act[4] would appear to be relevant, such purchases falling outside the law. Were such purchases to be made by postal order through the mails, they would not. There does not appear to be any logic behind this inconsistency. A second related difficulty is the rationale of the offence: it does not appear to have anything to do with gratuitous offence, as it applies equally to solicited as well as to unsolicited mailings. The protection of children may well be relevant, but would by no means justify on its own the breadth of restriction described above. Restriction would appear in fact to involve justification in much the same terms as would the broad prohibition under the Obscene Publications Act and conspiracy to corrupt public morals; although one is concerned with affront to positive morality within a prescribed context, such context does not necessarily have anything to do with gratuitous offence. To be weighed against such harms as may appear appropriate, one has besides freedom of speech, the question of privacy: do questions of individual freedom weigh particularly heavily when it comes to private communications between friends, for example? It is proposed to leave the question of privacy[5] and of the rationale of this offence for fuller discussion at the end of this section, once the technicalities of any other relevant statutes have been examined.

In the United States a restriction exists on using the mails for the

---

1   Cf. *R v Straker* [1965] *Crim L Rev* 239; *The Guardian*, 17 February 1965.

2   See conspiracy to outrage public decency, chapter 3.

3   See *R v Straker* [1965] *Crim L Rev* 239; *R v Stamford* [1972] 2 WLR 1055 at 1058; and *Kosmos Publications Ltd v DPP* [1975] *Crim L Rev* 345; see the section on conspiracy to outrage public decency; chapter 3, for a full discussion of this.

4   See displays, chapter 6.

5   See privacy, chapter 6 in particular.

distribution of obscene material. This section[1] was used principally to found a number of Post Office prior restraints with respect to the mails, particularly the seizure of such material in the mail. The statutory basis of such latter operations has been found unconstitutional, and in the absence of amendment, such restraints are no longer employed;[2] the constitutionality of the criminal sanction has not been in question, however. As far as justifications are concerned, such measures, aside from prior restraint issues, have been restricted to operation in terms of obscenity only; the question of justification has therefore been evaded, as the latter category of expression is in First Amendment terms regarded as falling outside protected speech. The alternative issue of privacy has not been raised in relation to the constitutionality of the statute.

2) *The Unsolicited Goods and Services Act 1971*

Section 4(1) reads

> A person shall be guilty of an offence, if he sends or causes to be sent to another person any book, magazine, or leaflet (or advertising material for any such publication) which he knows or ought reasonably to know is unsolicited and which describes or illustrates human sexual techniques.

The Act deals with printed material distributed on an unsolicited basis; it does not extend to any forms of expression not already reviewed by the Obscenity Acts, and applies only to that percentage of printed matter as may be distributed on such a basis. The phrase 'describing or illustrating human sexual techniques' is objective in application: it does not refer to the corrupting influence an article may have on the recipient, nor does it require offensiveness in this respect; it rather prohibits *all* articles indulging in such description, whether they are offensive or not. Negligence as to the unsolicited nature of the mailing is sufficient, whilst no defence of literary, scientific or medical merit is provided. In this sense it provides an even broader[3] potential prohibition for the Act within its area of application than would be achieved under the Obscene Publications Acts, or even the Post Office Act. On the other hand, there might equally be material which although not dealing with human sexual techniques, might be felt to be offensive or even corrupting: in this sense the Act provides a narrower prohibition. There is also of course the prohibition on advertisement, a prohibition which would extend beyond the coverage of the 1959 Act or the Post

---

1   18 USC 1461.

2   See chapters 7 and 12 on prior restraints.

3   Perhaps even including the Bible?

Office Act. The extent of coverage may perhaps best be illustrated by breaking down the material dealt with by this Act into three categories:
  (i) articles dealing with human sexual techniques;
  (ii) advertisements for such articles, the advertisements themselves describing the subject matter in question; and
  (iii) advertisements which do not themselves deal with the subject matter advertised.

Category (i) would probably be covered by the 1959 Act or the Post Office Act were there a tendency to corrupt, or indecency, subject to the limitations discussed above. With category (ii) the situation would be similar. Neither the 1959 Act nor the Post Office Act would apply to (iii), however: this was certainly the principal justification for, and motivation behind the introduction of this Act. Section 4 was not in fact part of the original 1971 Unsolicited Goods and Services Bill, but is one result of what appears to have been a panic backbench amendment, prompted in particular by public outrage over the posting of a leaflet advertising *A Manual of Sexual Technique* to nuns and schoolchildren.[1] The leaflet was not itself indecent, and the character of the addressee being irrelevant under Section 11 of the Post Office Act 1953, no action could as a result be taken.

The section is poorly drafted, and has given rise to a number of difficulties: it must be remembered that with this Act there is no defence of public good: as a result medical and scientific works that fall into category (i) or advertisements therefor that fall into (ii), may be censored if distributed on such a basis; even more important, the prohibition extends under (iii) even to circulars or catalogues (whether containing illustrations, or descriptions of listed books or not) from medical and scientific publications to universities, hospitals or doctors, or to material advertising family planning services.[2] Some tightening of Section 4 is clearly necessary, particularly with regard to the advertising provision. A sensible suggestion with regard to the latter is that such material be double enveloped, the outside envelope clearly stating the contents of the inner to be 'unsolicited advertising matter',[3] since the rationale appears to be the gratuitous offence offered the unwilling recipient of such communications. Another view is in terms of privacy; such mailings transgress the privacy rights of the recipients;

---

1   See Robertson *Obscenity* (London 1979) at 190.

2   Cf. *DPP* v *Beate Uhse (UK) Ltd* [1974] 2 WLR 50 at 52.

3   *Report of the Committee on Privacy* (HMSO 1972) Cmnd 5012 paras 423—4; hereafter referred to as the *Younger Committee Report*.

these have to be weighed against freedom of speech for example. On the basis of such considerations, the 1971 Act was referred to the Younger Committee on Privacy. The committee found that the bulk of those interviewed during the course of a survey of public attitudes commissioned on its behalf objected not so much to unsolicited circulars as such, but more particularly to those unsolicited circulars referring to sexual practices.[1] They came to the conclusion that the issue is essentially one of censorship, and thus declined to express a view on the desirability or otherwise of Section 4 of the Act.

Certainly opinion polls would seem further to bear out the Younger conclusions: a 1973 poll showed that 92 per cent of those canvassed agreed that 'there should be a law against indecent or suggestive materials through the post to people who have not asked for it'.[2] In the United States, 1968, the year after the enactment of the Federal Anti-Pandering Act,[3] saw 450,000 complaints from citizens who averred that they had been the subjects of 'erotically arousing or sexually provocative mail'.[4] Public hostility to this type of intrusion would seem both clear and selective. Such selectivity may be based as far as offensiveness is concerned, on the influence, in a secondary sense, of positive morality; it is not necessarily every source of offence which is controlled, but rather in terms of such morality, a select few. What Younger seems to be saying is that privacy *ipso facto* has nothing whatever to do with positive morality in this way. The fact that freedom to be private is asserted selectively, in other words, means one cannot be concerned with a question of privacy at all. The *effect* of such selective assertion may be to impose censorship: the primary justification for such censorship may be offensiveness, or it may perhaps be an invasion of privacy or a combination of the two. The fact that positive morality is relevant in a secondary sense, does not necessarily mean that the question is divorced entirely from privacy considerations. Because a censorship measure is selective does not mean to say that the only justification can, and must be, the basis of that selectivity.

The relevance of privacy to unsolicited mailings has been clearly upheld by the United States Supreme Court: in *Rowan* v *United States Post Office Department*[5] the Federal Anti-Pandering Act was attacked in terms of the First Amendment. The measure permits the department

---

1 *Younger Committee Report* para 9 and Appendix E.

2 *The Sunday Times*, 30 December 1973.

3 39 USC 3008 (1975 Supp); see chapter 10.

4 *Report of the US Commission on Pornography* at 21.

5 397 US 728 (1970).

to allow an addressee to refuse mail which he 'in his sole discretion believes to be erotically arousing or sexually provocative'. On receipt of the proper notice, the department may order the sender to cease sending any mail to the person in question; failure to comply is a criminal offence. The measure is clearly a selective one, but rather than base their ruling on the permissibility of governmental measures aimed at preventing offence, the Supreme Court ruled that an individual's right to privacy in his own home was sufficient to limit the sender's First Amendment rights.[1] In sustaining such measures, privacy, either as philosophical/policy consideration, or a constitutional guarantee, has at least a secondary sustaining role. Privacy and the question of justifications for, and reform of this offence will be considered at the end of this section.

3) *The Customs Consolidation Act 1876 and the Customs and Excise Management Act 1979*

Section 42a of the 1876 measure prohibits the following categories of imports into Britain: 'Indecent or obscene prints, paintings, photographs, books, cards, lithographs or other engravings or any other indecent or obscene articles'. Customs officers who intercept such articles may either seek their forfeiture, or charge their importer with an offence under the 1979 Customs and Excise Management Act; forfeiture will be dealt with as a potential prior restraint.[2] Section 50 of the 1979 Act provides that it is an offence to import goods with the intent to evade this prohibition. The offence covers varieties of expression covered by the Obscene Publications Act 1959; the latter, however, does not cover importation, applying only in England and Wales. As far as the circumstances of application are concerned here, a criminal charge is likely only when evasion is on a large scale,[3] as with the commercial importation of pornography; technically there would not appear to be any bar to the prosecution of an individual who deceitfully attempts the importation of something he suspects is indecent.

Unusually, intention is clearly required here, both as to importation and indecency or obscenity. Section 290(2) provides however in relation to criminal prosecutions or forfeiture proceedings generally under the Act, that

> Where in any proceedings relating to customs and excise
> any question arises ... as to whether or not ...

---

1 See Privacy, p.159ff; also chapter 12.

2 See chapter 7.

3 Robertson op.cit. at 195.

(b) any goods or other things whatsoever are of the description or nature alleged in the information, writ or other process ... then, where those proceedings are brought by or against the Commissioners ... the burden of proof shall be upon the other party to the proceedings.

This is a considerable burden to place on the accused: many of the prohibited categories of items under the Act are quite clear on the face of it: 'silver coin', 'horns', 'hoof of cattle', etc. Indecency can hardly be seen in the same light. This is the only statute employing the indecency test to place such a burden on the accused, a burden which the criminal law is usually loath to impose.[1] The abandonment of strict liability is virtually nullified by this shift, as it means that the accused has himself to lay an evidential foundation for any absence of *mens rea*[2] defence he means to advance, rather than the prosecution having to establish its presence.

The Act covers not only the actual importer, but also any person who 'knowingly and with intent ... to evade any prohibition ... acquires possession of, or is in any way concerned in carrying, depositing, harbouring, keeping or concealing or in any manner dealing with' prohibited articles.[3] Any subsequent handling of such material will found liability, provided there was at that time knowledge that it had been imported in contravention of the prohibition.[4] The prohibition is in fact even wider, Section 170(2) making it an offence to be 'in any way knowingly concerned in any fraudulent evasion or attempt at evasion ...'; one could be liable, therefore, without handling the goods at all. The latter requirements are a little more stringent in that the requirement of fraudulence implies dishonesty or deceit. It may be though, that the term 'knowingly' in Section 170 implies an element of deceitfulness;[5] certainly most importations intentionally undertaken in contravention of a prohibition would involve some such element.

The only difficulty as to the type of article covered by Section 42

---

1   The court, in the only judicial pronouncement on this issue, did not appear particularly concerned with this burden of proof. See *Commissioners of Customs and Excise v Paul Raymond Publications Ltd*, High Court, 6 February 1974, transcript page 304; cited in Robertson, ibid. The case was admittedly not a criminal one, but one of civil forfeiture.

2   It may be that expert evidence is admissible on this issue specifically: Robertson op.cit. at 198.

3   Customs and Excise Management Act 1979, Section 170(1).

4   *R v Ardalan* [1972] 2 All ER 257.

5   *Frailey v Charlton* [1920] 1 KB 147; also *R v Waterfield* (no. 2) op.cit., transcript page 3 – cited by Robertson op.cit. at 196, footnote 61.

arose in relation to films: a doubt existed as to whether the prohibition applied to film transparencies and negatives, as their indecency would become apparent only on processing and projection. The prohibition is, however, according to the Divisional Court, a catch-all; the phrase 'any other indecent or obscene article' means just what it says, and is not to be interpreted *eiusdem generis* as referring to printed matter only.[1] The standard used is the familiar 'indecent or obscene' test. There has not been any reported judicial interpretation of this phrase in this context, nor for that matter, with the exception of the Post Office Act 1953, in the context of any other statutory measure in which it appears. There would seem no reason to presume that it would not be assigned the same meaning it has received under the Post Office Act: that of affront to recognised standards of propriety, indecency at the lower end of this scale being sufficient. Coverage within the area of application is thus potentially very wide. As with the Post Office Act 1953, this measure does not apparently require material to be judged as a whole, expert evidence would probably be inadmissible on the question of indecency or obscenity, nor does it provide any public good defence. The Court of Appeal in an unreported customs and excise case would appear to have asserted the relevance of the compiler/photographer's intention in relation to a book *Boys Are Boys Again*, a compilation consisting of some 122 photographs of naked boys. In considering whether the work was an indecent import, Lord Justice Bridge remarked that

> ... the conclusion that I reach is that if that book is looked at as a whole ... the very essence of the publication, the reason for publishing it, is to focus attention on the male genital organs. It is a series of photographs in the great majority of which the male genitalia, sometimes in close-up, are the focal point of the picture ... they aim to be interesting pictures of boys' penises ...[2]

This approach would seem to be out of step with that adopted by the courts in relation to the application of this standard under the Post Office Act 1953. Not only this, but it accords ill with the absence of a public good defence under the customs provisions. Such a defence has not been provided in any statute employing this standard, nor by the common law; it must seem very doubtful whether the courts would wish to pursue its importation via the back door in terms of this ruling?

---

1   *Derrick* v *Commissioners of Customs and Excise* [1972] 1 All ER 993.

2   *Commissioners of Customs and Excise* v *Sun and Health Ltd*, Royal Courts of Justice, 29 March 1973, transcript at pp. 5 and 6; quoted in Robertson op.cit. at 303–4. For further discussion of this ruling and its possible relation to the Protection of Children Act 1978, see protection of children, chapter 7.

The ruling serves perhaps merely to underline the inappropriateness of the use of an indecency standard in this context. Where the latter is properly concerned with the prevention of public nuisance, the need for a public good defence hardly arises. Its application in other contexts applies the standard of affront to positive morality on a far broader scale, with consequent difficulties in relation to questions of public good.[1] The court may possibly in this case have been influenced by the unusual requirement of intention on the part of the importer as to indecency. The absence of a public good defence is particularly relevant in terms of the clear applicability of these provisions to films. In view of the considerable proportion of the latter — compared to other media forms — imported into this country, it means that probably the bulk of films exhibited have been filtered in terms of a standard of indecency, without enjoying the safeguards prescribed by the 1959 Obscene Publications Act.

It would seem unlikely that customs and excise apply such safeguards as questions of public good in practice: in 1973 the BBC gave notice to customs and excise that it intended importing what was supposedly the most scientifically advanced sex education kit in the world, put out by associates of Kinsey under the auspices of the Unitarian Church. Customs declared that they would still have to act, as the Act made no exceptions for importations justified in the public interest.[2] In 1964, whilst on his way to an overseas conference, Sir Dingle Foot bought a copy of *The Perfumed Garden* at an airport bookstall. On his return the book fell foul of customs regulation.[3] Such incidents are clearly an embarrassment and the Customs Department has determined to ignore the law in a number of circumstances: a June 1978 directive to officers provides:

> *Articles not to be detained*: in no circumstances is a person to be asked if he has any indecent or obscene books, pictures or other articles, or to be questioned about the character of any book which is found in his possession. With the exception of child pornography, officers are not to detain small quantities consisting of single copies of obscene or indecent books or other articles which have been imported in baggage, and which appear to be intended solely for:
> (a) the passenger's or crew member's own personal use;

---

1   For a discussion of the need for a public good defence in relation to proposed offence restrictions, see displays, chapter 6.

2   *Evening Standard*, 18 September 1973; see Robertson op.cit. at 194.

3   Ibid.

or
(b) serious professional work by university staff, artists, students, etc.[1]

Such relaxation does not mean a reversion to the statutory test for obscenity as the going standard. Officers have been roundly reminded that the standards they apply are quite other:

> In view of the wide publicity given to the recent acquittal of the British publication of *Inside Linda Lovelace* which had been prosecuted under the Obscene Publications Act, staff are reminded that departmental policy has not changed and that any commercial importations of this title should be detained and reported to branch GCC4B for appropriate action.[2]

The Act applies[3] to the same forms of expression as does the 1959 Act, but only to that percentage of such expression as is imported into the country. It is doubtful whether, because of the necessity of publication, the Obscene Publication Acts would find much application here, unless of course possession of the articles for gain could be established on the part of the importer. (The same is true of the Post Office Act 1953, which applies only to postings within the United Kingdom.) The Act in particular applies potentially to private possession, without publication, of such articles. The standard applied is clearly a much broader one.

Two further matters remain for discussion here: one is the relationship and effect of the Treaty of Rome, particularly Article 9 guaranteeing free movement of goods amongst member states: this will be considered below[4] in relation to the effect of EEC provisions on this area of law generally. Suffice it here to say that customs legislation in its present form has not been affected, according to the European Court of Justice by these, and other, considerations. A final question is the rationale for this offence. It does not appear to have anything to

---

1   Robertson op.cit. at 194.

2   *The Guardian* 'London Letter', 20 February 1976; quoted ibid.

3   Prosecutions under the 1979 Act may be brought for up to three years after the commission of the offence. The maximum penalty is two years' imprisonment or a fine either of £100 or three times the market value of the goods at the time of importation. It has been successfully argued that pornography has no market value, as black market values are not relevant in such an assessment. This was overruled by the Divisional Court, which held that the relevant price was that which a willing seller would accept from a willing buyer at the port of entry. The original imposition of a £100 fine was overturned then in favour of a valuation of £2,335. *Byrne* v *Low* [1972] *Crim L Rev* 551.

4   Chapter 9.

do with gratuitous offence or the invasion of privacy in the sense of an unsolicited intrusion. It after all seems most unlikely that anyone would import such materials, only on receipt to plead criminal outrage at their nature, unless perhaps he had been misled as to that nature.

It might be argued that this restriction does have something to do with offensiveness or privacy, at least in a secondary sense: by preventing the importation of indecent material, this restriction prevents its ultimate display. This holds no water though, in view of the fact that the discreet sale of indecent articles in England and Wales is apparently not covered at all. What one appears to have is a restriction based on the enforcement of positive morality in a primary rather than a secondary sense. The Williams Committee recommendations on import controls, together with the question of their rationale, will be considered at the end of this section.

In the United States controls on importation are purely civil, and interest has therefore centred on their potential prior restraint aspects.[1] The same basic justification issues are raised by such controls; the customs statute has come under constitutional attack in terms of invasion of privacy. The statute operates in terms of obscenity as the only standard permissible in terms of the First Amendment. The result is that attacks on the statute in First Amendment terms are *prima facie* nonstarters, as the Supreme Court has consistently held obscenity to fall outside the area of protected speech. The Court repudiated the privacy attack,[2] but its logic in so doing is not impressive: this issue will be returned to later in this section in the discussion of privacy and its relevance to this area in general. The broader question of the viability of the obscenity exception to the First Amendment is clearly something that cannot be examined here: it is considered at length in later chapters on the American jurisdiction.

4) *The Judicial Proceedings (Regulation of Reports) Act 1926*

Section 1(1) of the Act provides that

> It shall not be lawful to print or publish, or cause or procure to be printed or published —
> (a) in relation to any judicial proceedings any indecent matter or indecent medical, surgical or physiological details being matter or details the publication of which would be calculated to injure public morals.

The offence, for which a maximum penalty of four months' imprison-

---

1   See chapter 12.

2   *United States* v *12 200ft Reels* 413 US 123 (1973).

ment or a £500 fine (or both) are provided,[1] is committed only by a proprietor, editor, master printer or publisher, and does not apply to pleadings or transcripts of evidence to be used in connection with judicial proceedings, or to any *bona fide* law reports or 'technical publications intended for circulation among members of the legal or medical professions'.[2] No further provision is made for a defence of public good.

There would not appear to be any *mens rea* requirement as to indecency, although it would presumably be required as to the actual conduct of printing or publishing. The intention of the author would not appear to have any relevance here, as questions of fact under the public good defence would be readily ascertainable on the face of it. Expert evidence would appear equally inappropriate in relation to the defence: whether something is a '*bona fide* law report', for example, is unlikely to be the subject of acute controversy. The offence is triable only in a magistrates' court, without any right to a jury trial. There is no requirement that any article containing such matter be taken as a whole: the word 'indecent' and the phrase 'calculated to injure public morals' are in fact used specifically in relation to the detail in question, the context, in the sense of the rest of the published article, not being apparently relevant.

The standard employed is on the face of it a strange one: it couples indecency and the injuring of public morals, injury presumably being synonymous with corruption in this context. Yet the former was generally concerned with public offence and nuisance, the latter with the protection of positive morality unhindered by questions of contextual distinctions; the former's concern is corruption of such morality, rather than a mere affront to it. Nowhere in the law is the erosion of the above — perhaps often rather tenuous distinction — better illustrated: not only has the public aspect of indecency been eroded, but here it is used interchangeably with corruption of morals. The standards as employed here presumably mean no more than affront to recognised standards of propriety or morality. The morality in question is presumably, as with conspiracy to corrupt public morals, the morality of the public at large; questions of distribution or the particular audience involved are in these terms irrelevant: one's concern is the effect on public morality, not on the morality of a particular individual or group of individuals. The offence covers the same varieties of expression as does obscenity, but only where such expression is related to judicial proceedings. The standard not being limited apparently to sexual matters or morality, but covering simply 'indecent matter', and 'public morality',

---

1   Section 1(2).

2   Section 1(4).

coverage extends potentially therefore to virtually anything at all. The rationale of the offence does not appear to involve considerations of gratuitous offence or invasion of privacy, but simply the straightforward enforcement of positive morality. The Williams Committee view of the offence and its rationale will be considered at the end of this section.

5) *Privacy*

It would clearly be inappropriate to attempt here a detailed examination of the concept of privacy and its operation.[1] Discussion is directed at the relevance of the concept to obscenity and indecency controls,[2] leaving certain central questions in this area for more adequate discussion elsewhere.

A first consideration must be the importance of privacy. Some of the formulations offered as to the importance of individual freedom have been rehearsed above.[3] Privacy can be seen as an aspect of such freedom: 'The protection of privacy is essentially an aspect of the protection of individual freedom of choice, of choice of what kind of person to be'.[4] In this sense privacy might be weighed against, for example, statutory controls, in determining their viability; obscenity controls may, or may not, be an example of this. Freedom of choice may, apparently paradoxically however, be used to *sustain* restriction on such materials:

> The paradox is that it appears possible to argue that respect for privacy requires a regime of freedom in relation to the use and enjoyment of obscene materials, or to argue that respect for privacy requires legal controls upon their use and dissemination.[5]

Privacy, when used to sustain, rather than limit controls, may have a sound utilitarian basis, or it may best be seen in terms of rights: this is not an issue that it is proposed to enter upon here; suffice it to accept

---

1   For a statement of the position in a number of jurisdictions, and a fairly full citation of source material see D. McQuoid-Mason *The Law of Privacy in South Africa* (Cape Town 1978); for a recent comment on the United States position: J. Shattuck *Rights of Privacy* (Ann Arbor. Illinois 1977). Also D.N. MacCormick 'A Note on Privacy' 89 (1973) *LQR*; R. Wacks 'The Poverty of Privacy' 96 (1980) *LQR* 73.

2   In this regard see especially D.N. MacCormick 'Privacy and Obscenity', in Rajeev Dhavan and Christie Davis (eds) *Censorship and Obscenity* (London 1978) at 76.

3   See chapter 3, the enforcement of morality.

4   MacCormick 'Privacy and Obscenity' op.cit. at 92.

5   Ibid. at 76.

the possible relevance of the concept in both the former instances. The next question for consideration is with just what is privacy concerned, and what it means. A number of definitions have been offered over time to describe the concerns involved. Perhaps the best known of these was offered by Prosser, who proposed four categories of invasion: intrusions, public disclosures of private facts, placing a person in a false light and appropriation of another's name or likeness.[1] This has been criticised as not including, for example, legislative regulation.[2] Professor MacCormick prefers to regard one's concern here broadly as an intrusion; such intrusion must be as to something specified.

The intrusion aspect is not too daunting: one is concerned here not with any intrusion in the literal sense, but with intrusion in a narrower sense, encompassing not the actions of a burglar, for example, which may be dealt with on other grounds, but invasions which in effect fall beyond already recognised legal reach. An aspect of intrusion that must be emphasised is that it depends on the absence of consent. Privacy is concerned with individual choice, and it is up to each individual whether, or to what extent, he may waive his claim to privacy in some particular matter. Should he consent to what amounts to an invasion of privacy, this can no longer be seen as an intrusion, and falls outside the area of privacy considerations.

It is with the question of the definition of privacy that real difficulty arises: is it to be limited to the tangible, in the sense of one's home, one's personal belongings, one's telephone, or whatever, or is it to extend to the intangible — to invasions of consciousness, of intellectual activity and private thought, of the marriage relationship, and so on. As Professor MacCormick argues, privacy is 'always in some degree "territorial" ': there is some sphere within which an individual is protected from intrusion. The sphere may be geographical, or one of personal activities which are protected from interference. The selection of such spheres may well be 'culturally relative':[3] the definition of privacy varies in other words over time and place: varies in fact in terms of positive morality. Nor is this influence of positive morality necessarily a one-way process: just as it may influence the recognition of spheres of privacy, so too may it influence the utilisation of such privacy. An individual may after all admit others within a recognised sphere of privacy. His reasons for doing so may be a matter of personal taste; equally, they may be a matter of positive morality, as with the confessional,

---

1   See W.L. Prosser 'Privacy' 48 (1960) *Cal L Rev* 383 at 389.

2   See e.g. G.L. Bostwick 'A Taxonomy of Privacy: Reposé, Sanctuary and Intimate Decisions' 64 (1976) *Cal L Rev* 1447 at 1450.

3   MacCormick 'Privacy and Obscenity' op.cit. at 84.

for example. If an individual may be influenced in this way by positive morality, so may society in selection of intrusions to be subject to legal control. This point will be returned to later.

Positive morality may then be relevant in the same way to the selection of spheres of privacy as it is to the selection of utilitarian harms. Going beyond this, it is not perhaps clear on what grounds spheres of privacy are seen as potentially *within the protection of the law*: is it to prevent rationally assessable harms, or is it on the basis of a theory of rights, recognising (for example) 'equal respect and concern'? The particular philosophical basis of privacy, in terms roughly of freedom of choice as to individual development is so vague as to be of little help. The same problem might be encountered with freedom of expression: where it is desired to use this to justify controls, say in terms of a right of reply, the philosophical basis of that control might be open to the same criticism: similar difficulties might be encountered in defining what is subsumed, for protection purposes, within the term expression, and why. The relationship between individual 'rights', and the basis for their legal enforcement, be it utilitarian or a theory of rights, appears to be so ill-defined as to provide little real help with definitional problems of this sort.

This, as has been remarked, is not the place to attempt to establish the philosophical basis of privacy more firmly: what is tentatively suggested is that absence of clarity in this regard is perhaps largely responsible for the difficulties involved in defining spheres of privacy susceptible of legal control. Certainly the line has not been drawn in the United States, for instance, at the point of the invasion of the tangible: in *Griswold* v *Connecticut*[1] (for example) the Supreme Court declared unconstitutional on invasion of privacy grounds — more specifically the marital relationship — a state statute prohibiting the dissemination of contraceptives and birth control information. A 'degree of figurativeness' has then been admitted into the notion of 'intrusion' into a 'sphere' of privacy.[2] How does such a notion relate, if at all, to obscenity and indecency?

First, let us consider the relevance of privacy in terms of justifying controls. There would hardly appear to be any relevance in this respect for privacy as far as obscenity controls are concerned. If the relevant material harms someone by depraving or corrupting them, by morally debasing them, 'the wrong done to an individual who is exposed to such obscene production does not seem in any way more analogous to the wrong of privacy than is the ... case of wronging a person by

---

1   381 US 479 (1965).

2   MacCormick 'Privacy and Obscenity' op.cit. at 88.

stealing his property or assaulting his person'.[1] The only relevance for privacy here might be that one might argue that one was offended at being conscious of other people behaving in private in a way which one regarded as immoral. Presumably though, one would have here a conflict of positive morality, a conflict of spheres of privacy, the privacy of such actions on the part of others presumably being given preference.

As far as offence is concerned, one has regard to intrusive offence in the sense of the public display of obscene or indecent material. Does such offence, such invasion of consciousness, debatably a rationally assessable harm, constitute an intrusion into a sphere of privacy? The answer must depend on one's definition of privacy. Professor MacCormick argues that if such offence is to be regarded as an invasion of privacy, environmental offence in all its aspects would clamour for similar treatment. Can one sensibly, for example, regard the offence occasioned by the replacement of a 'beautiful old Georgian terrace' by a 'brutal concrete tower block' as an invasion of privacy?[2] He argues not, and concludes: '... if we don't include them all, I cannot see the rationale of including one, that of offence provided by publicly displayed obscene articles'.[3] There is a possible rationale for such selectivity, however, and that is positive morality. Such morality may affect first the selection of a particular example of offence as a rationally assessable harm: it may affect the degree of offence felt.[4] Second, such morality may be relevant in determining which examples of such offence are to be subject to control. There would not seem to be any reason why such morality should not be equally relevant to the selection of spheres of privacy, the decision as to which of these should be potentially within the ambit of legal protection, and which intrusions into such spheres should specifically be controlled. In the case of offence, one is concerned with a harm;[5] because positive morality may affect which harms are actually controlled, does not mean one is no longer concerned with a harm. In the same way, offensiveness may be an invasion of consciousness, which may in turn be a sphere potentially subject to protection; positive morality may influence just *which* intrusions into the sphere are subject to control. When assessing whether a control on offensive displays falls within a rational utilitarian model, one is not concerned so much whether the control is selective, but

---

1   MacCormick 'Privacy and Obscenity' op.cit.

2   Ibid. at 88.

3   Ibid.

4   See for example *Williams* chapter 7, especially para 7.3.

5   See displays, chapter 6.

rather whether offensiveness is a rationally assessable harm. Likewise with privacy: the concern must be not whether the controls are selective, but rather whether the sphere invaded is potentially the subject of protection; this must depend on the definition of privacy, and on the principle(s) (if any) which underlie it. At present there would not seem to be any clear principle which clearly excludes the relevance of privacy to offence restrictions.

Another example of possible relevance for privacy in justifying controls lies with unsolicited mail. It is argued[1] that because the present control (the 1971 Unsolicited Goods and Services Act) is selective, in the sense of prohibiting only such mail as is concerned with human sexuality, that the control therefore has nothing to do with privacy. This view was put forward by the Younger Committee, which preferred to regard the 1971 Act as a censorship measure. Its effect may be censorious, but the same arguments advanced above as to selectivity would be applicable. One is after all concerned here primarily with intrusion into the home: no one has proposed that the sale of material dealing with 'human sexual techniques' be prohibited as such. Emphasis therefore is on intrusion, positive morality affecting just *which* such intrusion is in fact controlled. This appears broadly to have been the approach of the American Supreme Court in *Rowan* v *United Post Office Department*,[2] in which the constitutionality of a roughly similar federal statute controlling unsolicited mail was upheld on the grounds of privacy.[3]

The second question for consideration here is whether privacy can be utilised as *limiting* legislative provisions in the obscenity/indecency area. Take the question of the mere possession of obscene materials. In *Stanley* v *Georgia*,[4] the Supreme Court was faced with the question of the constitutionality of a Georgia statute which made it an offence 'knowingly (to have) possession of ... obscene matter'. A search by federal and state agents of Stanley's home under warrant authorising them to search for materials relating to illegal wagering, unearthed obscene films in his desk drawer. The obscenity of the films was not an issue: the question was rather the constitutionality of making mere private possession a criminal act. Mr Justice Marshall used both freedom of speech — as giving a right to receive information — and privacy in striking the statute down:

---

1 MacCormick 'Privacy and Obscenity' op.cit. at 90.

2 397 US 728 (1970).

3 See Unsolicited Goods and Services Act 1971, above.

4 394 US 557 (1968).

> This right to receive information and ideas, regardless of their social worth ... is fundamental to our free society. Moreover, in the context of this case — a prosecution for mere possession of printed or filmed matter in the privacy of one's own home — that right takes on an added dimension. For also fundamental is the right to be free, except in very limited circumstances, from unwanted governmental intrusions into one's privacy.[1]

This ruling created problems in terms of the First Amendment exception approach to obscenity: was the Court saying that obscenity *was* now within the First Amendment, but that restriction on commercially distributed obscenity was justified, or was it saying that obscenity continued to fall outside the First Amendment, except when in private possession?[2] The privacy aspect of the ruling also created difficulties: it is difficult to conceive of any formulation of privacy which would not extend potentially to the situation in *Stanley*: 'Here, surely, we find an uncomplicated instance of John Stuart Mill's exception of self-regarding activities in relation to which public regulation of individual taste would be wholly contrary to quite fundamental rights of freedom and autonomy'.[3] If the ruling is logically and philosophically sound, it creates two potential problems: first, there would not seem to be any principle in the way of extension of such reasoning to customs and post office restrictions. If private possessions in the home are covered, this surely should extend to private possessions in a suitcase being brought through customs? A second and related problem is that if the harm occasioned by the private perusal of pornography may be outweighed by privacy (and First Amendment) considerations, it will surely make the justification of controls on distribution much more difficult to assert. Not only may such a ruling weaken the weight attached to the alleged harms; it must also be remembered that privacy may possibly extend to, besides the marital relationship (for example), intellectual development and private thought, and may therefore itself be a factor to be weighed against the justifications for controls on the distribution of obscenity as such.

It was presumably with just some of these factors in mind that the majority of the court subsequently limited the *Stanley* ruling to possession of such material in the home only. Attacks on the constitutionality of customs controls and those on interstate transportation of such

---

1   394 US 557 (1968).

2   See chapter 14.

3   MacCormick 'Obscenity and Privacy' op.cit. at 93.

materials therefore failed.[1] As Chief Justice Burger remarked:

> ... Stanley does not permit one to go abroad and bring such material into the country, for private purposes. 'Stanley's emphasis was on the freedom of thought and mind in the privacy of the home. But a port of entry is not a traveller's home.'[2]

As far as the extension of privacy considerations to legislative interference with intellectual activity via obscenity restrictions, the Court has been equally firm: in *Paris Adult Theater I* v *Slaton*[3] the majority ruled that privacy considerations did not render unconstitutional a Georgia statute which prohibited the mounting of obscene film shows, even though minors were not admitted, and patrons were adequately warned about the nature of what they were about to see.

In policy terms the ruling on customs restrictions seems quite unsustainable: if privacy considerations are subject to principle, they should at least be relevant here. English law is marginally more consistent. The Obscene Publications Act 1959 does not cover mere possession, unlike its American state counterparts, most of which (prior to *Stanley*) found such possession enough;[4] there is no limitation to the home as far as such possession is concerned: mere possession anywhere at all (unless it is with a view to publication for gain, in terms of the 1964 Act) is not covered. One appears, so far, to have a consistent application of privacy considerations, but as in the United States, authority has baulked at the implications of pursuing such consistency: there has been no question of extending such application to customs controls or Post Office controls over personal possessions.

By emphasising the privacy of the home in particular, moreover, the influence of privacy can be broadened: although the Law Commission has suggested that common law controls in this area be removed, it felt that no new controls would be necessary in regard to theatrical performances in private dwellings, other than where children are involved or an admission charge is made.[5] The principal basis of such recommendation is privacy within the home; were it to be accepted, there would

---

1 See respectively *United States* v *12 200ft Reels* 413 US 123 (1973); *United States* v *Orito* 413 US 139 (1973).

2 *United States* v *12 200ft Reels* 413 US 123 (1973) at 128, quoting *United States* v *Thirty Seven Photographs* 402 US 363.

3 413 US 49 (1973); see note 'Roe and Paris: Does Privacy Have a Principle' 26 (1974) *Stan L Rev* 1161.

4 See note 'Much Ado About Dirty Books' 75 (1966) *Yale L J* 1364, Appendix II.

5 See the section on live shows, chapter 6.

seem little logic in leaving the 1959 Act covering distribution in the home, as it does at present. And if, after all, the harm done by such material is outweighed by privacy considerations when mere possession in the home is involved, there must be a very strong case for the same being said about distribution or publication in the same setting. All this in turn, if correct, further weakens the weight attached to the harm done by such material; if such harm were decisive, privacy could not possibly outweigh it in this way: the Supreme Court in *Stanley*, for example, was careful to add the rider that nothing they had said about the value of privacy was to be taken as indicating that it justified in the same way the possession of 'other items, such as narcotics, firearms or stolen goods', the keeping of which could legitimately be made criminal, no matter where they were kept.[1]

Whether such privacy considerations are equally applicable to the *Paris* situation must depend on one's definition of, or the central principle(s) applicable to privacy. Even if principle does not deny such applicability, common sense may well dictate caution. As the concept stands at present privacy would seem at least tentatively relevant even in these terms. As far as the justification of restriction is concerned, privacy would seem relevant in principle to invasions of the home and private possessions. Its relationship to gratuitous offence must depend on the central principle(s) — if any — behind privacy. Common sense again may dictate the utmost caution as far as such relevance is concerned, but policy considerations would not seem to rule it out. The possible relevance of privacy in this regard has at least been acknowledged by the Supreme Court: as Mr Justice Marshall remarked in *Stanley*: '... public distribution ... is subject to different objections (from private possession). For example, there is always the danger that obscene material ... might intrude upon the sensibilities or privacy of the general public'.[2]

That there is a possible conflict between these two assertions of privacy is clear from the above. This is surely fairly easily reconcilable: where the right to develop one's own thoughts and personality results in the intrusion of the material involved on others, there is a conflict; provided such public intrusions are controlled, conflict is removed. To accept mere consciousness of what others are doing privately within the ambit of privacy is perhaps to take things too far in terms of policy or common sense. Opposing privacy claims would surely in any event outweigh this.

---

1   394 US 557 (1968) at 568, footnote 11.

2   394 US 557 (1968) at 567.

6) *Law reform and Williams*

Even were one to accept a concept or definition of privacy sufficiently narrow to exclude invasion of consciousness, and therefore to exclude both its relevance to the justification of offence restraints, and its relevance in assessing the viability of general obscenity prohibitions, one would still probably find, in core privacy terms, a relevance for it as far as the control of unsolicited mail, as well as customs and post office mailing restrictions are concerned. The protection of privacy would also appear to be the basis for the 1926 Judicial Proceedings (Regulation of Reports) Act: the type of consideration already basic to the law on the publication of private facts, and more particularly breach of confidence, would appear to be equally applicable to the former measure. The intrusion imposed by the publication of the salacious details of divorce proceedings must merit serious consideration, and would seem to have received just that in the form of the 1926 Act. Respect for newsworthiness would appear to have outweighed such considerations in the United States.[1] It is proposed to look again at each of the restrictions discussed above, bearing in mind this potential common thread. Additionally, one must bear in mind that controls on distribution do already exist, and have been recommended above, in terms of the protection of children.

(i) The prohibition on the sending of obscene or indecent articles through the post was first enacted in 1884, twenty-seven years after Lord Campbell's Act. The historical parallel with the United States is striking: the first American legislation of this sort was passed in 1865, the immediate precursor to that celebrated example of American obscenity legislation, the Comstock Act of 1873.[2] An investigation of the social background of this striking congruence in restriction cannot be attempted here: one may speculate, though, that differences in development and outlook — the Civil War had only just ended in the United States — were far outweighed by the growing dominance of Victorian sexual morality. This of course assumes that the intentions of the two legislatures in passing these measures were the same. It may be that the British measure was aimed more at offensiveness than at enforcing a brand of positive morality *per se*. Although there was very little parliamentary discussion of the measure, the title of the Bill — The Post Office (Protection) Bill 1884 — seems to indicate that protection of the Post Office and its employees was the measure's ostensible justification. Certainly, the purpose of that section (of the Post Office Act 1953) at present embodying the obscenity/indecency control, appears

---

1 See e.g. *Cox Broadcasting Corp* v *Cohn* 420 US 469 (1970) at 471, footnote 1.

2 See chapter 10.

to be just that: to protect members of the postal service from exposure to articles which in transit might prove dangerous. Section 11(1) provides that:

> A person shall not send or attempt to send or procure to be sent a postal packet which
> (a) save as the authority [i.e. the Post Office] may either generally or in any particular case allow, encloses any explosive, dangerous, noxious or deleterious substance, any filth, any sharp instrument not properly protected, any noxious living creature, or any creature, article or thing whatsoever which is likely to injure either other postal packets in course of conveyance or a person engaged in the business of the authority; or
> (b) encloses any indecent or obscene print, painting, photograph, lithograph, engraving, cinematograph film, book, and written communication, or any indecent or obscene article whether similar to the above or not; or
> (c) has on the packet, or on the cover thereof, any words, marks or designs which are grossly offensive or of an indecent or obscene character.

Interpretation of the indecency provisions *eiusdem generis* with those aimed at protecting the mails and those handling them has been clearly ruled out by the Court of Appeal: in a ruling handed down in 1908, but still apparently, *mutatis mutandis*, good law, the judicial view was that the purpose of the statutory indecency provision was to prevent the dissemination of obscene or indecent articles, and not specifically to protect Post Office officials and the mails.[1] There may be some support for this interpretation in the fact that Sections 53 and 58 of the Act make it an offence for Post Office employees to open postal packets: it is very difficult to see the point of an indecency provision aimed at protecting workers from material which they are most unlikely — unless they break the law — to see; unless, of course, the measure is aimed at protecting them from offence possibly occasioned by such material should a postal packet containing it somehow be damaged and burst open. If the latter supposition is correct, the law embodies severe overkill.

As of present the Section 11(1) restriction on indecency can safely be taken as having nothing to do with gratuitous offence, not at least as far as Post Office employees are concerned. Is it to do with gratuitous offence to the recipients of mail? This can scarcely be maintained, as the character of the addressee is immaterial; it would as a result require a peculiar logic to establish any connection between the restric-

---

1   *R v Harry Key* (1908) 1 Crim App Reps 135.

tion and offence to the recipients: such recipients are hardly likely to order something, only on receipt to assert its offensiveness, unless of course they were misled as to its nature — in which case one would be dealing in effect with unsolicited mail. The restriction can hardly be argued to be aimed at preventing gratuitous offence on a wider scale, in the sense that by preventing distribution through the posts, the measure prevents such materials' ultimate offensive display. There are other measures to cover such display, whilst discreet sale as such is not generally unlawful.[1] The restriction equally does not necessarily have anything to do with the protection of children. There does not appear to be any other potential harm specifically relevant to a restriction of this sort on the use of the mails, other than the type of consideration which might be advanced to justify prohibitions of a general sort: the enforcement of positive morality, or some rationally assessable harm caused by the material in question quite aside from its transit through the mail.

To be weighed against any potential harms one has not only freedom of speech, but also privacy: if one's possession of such material is immune as such, there seems little reason why this should not extend to its presence in the mail, whilst an extension of privacy beyond this raises questions of marital privacy, in relation say to letters between spouses. The offence as it stands at present is also open to the same criticisms made of obscenity controls and corruption of public morals: it appears to involve, without any apparent consideration of justification, the enforcement of positive morality; the standard of indecency is so vague that the only factor in its favour in the view of the Williams Committee was that those applying it find such application 'reasonably straightforward',[2] whilst the offence apparently involves strict liability as to such indecency. In these terms and in terms of their conclusion that justifications other than offence and the protection of children were not applicable, the committee recommended the abolition of the offence. Accommodation of the need for protecting children could be achieved by a more limited restriction prohibiting the sending or delivery of restricted material, or advertisements for such material, to 'a person who the sender knew or ought reasonably to have known was under the age of eighteen'.[3] The standard of restriction is whether the reasonable person finds it offensive that a child should see or read the material in question. It was recommended above that a suitable alternative to this test might be, insofar as public displays or distribution to

---

1 See displays, chapter 6.

2 *Williams* para 2.12 and 2.13; see displays, chapter 6, for a full discussion of this point.

3 *Williams* para 13.4, subpara 12(a).

minors are concerned, what is, in a reasonable person's view, exploitative of and unnecessarily stimulating to a child:[1] this might well be applied here. A *mens rea* requirement would exist at least in the form of negligence both as to the age of the recipient and the nature of the material. The standard does not appear overbroad, nor does it involve a straightforward assertion of positive morality.

Three further restrictions would appear necessary. The first relates to the sexual exploitation of children, or the infliction — and not simulation thereof — of actual physical harm on the participants, in producing pornographic films or pictures.[2] If one may rationally control such exploitation, it may be argued that one ought also to prohibit the dissemination of the fruits of activity one has decided to make criminal. Controls on distribution in this sense are clearly based on, or are an extension of, the reasoning employed in justifying the primary prohibition. As the mails are a method of distribution, such restriction on distribution ought to apply by means of the Post Office legislation. The Williams Committee has recommended that distribution be controlled in this, and other, respects, to prevent a flouting of the primary prohibition.[3] They recommend that such control be extended to material coming from outside the country. 'We should not be parochial about the prevention of harm to children: if English law is to protect children against offences in this country, it is hypocritical to permit the trade in photographs and films of the same activities taken overseas.'[4] Second, one has the question of mailing material not prohibited here, into a jurisdiction which forbids its importation and circulation. The United Kingdom is obliged in terms of the Universal Postal Convention 1974 to prohibit such use of the post, and the committee, in noting that Denmark at least, despite its absence of domestic restriction on pornography, has fulfilled its international obligations in this regard, recommends that this country does likewise.[5] This seems sensible, and would mean a similar provision in the Post Office legislation.

Beyond this, the only restriction apparently necessary would be in

---

1   See protection of children, above.

2   See chapter 7, the production of pornography.

3   *Williams* para 6.68.

4   See paragraph (v) in this section; as to the question whether this is best operated through customs procedures or Post Office provisions, and the precise powers of detention and their prior restraint implications, see chapter 7.

5   *Williams* para 10.14; as to international treaty obligations specifically and generally, see chapter 9.

terms of the outside of postal packets, as provided by Section 11(1)(c) of the Post Office Act 1953 at present. A similar provision exists in the United States in the form of 18 USC 1463, which prohibits obscene or scurrilous matter on the outside of mail.[1] A suitable standard would again appear to be that recommended above for public displays. Were such restrictions constitutional in the United States, there would seem little reason to suppose that constitutionality would not extend to such application. Whether anything further than these measures is required or justified in respect of the mails (other than in regard to unsolicited mail) will be considered at the end of this essay.[2]

(ii) A further restriction which the committee felt was justified in terms of use of the mails, was in relation to unsolicited mail. Provided mail is unsolicited, a number of considerations must weigh heavily in favour of its restriction: perhaps the most obvious of these is the gratuitous offence caused by such mail. Privacy, as has been argued above, is also relevant,[3] whilst the protection of the young must certainly be a factor in any assessment here. Accepting that such a control, in terms of the limited restriction it places on freedom of speech, is rationally justifiable, the question remains as to just what form it should take. Present coverage is overbroad, particularly insofar as the control of relevant advertisements is concerned. Williams in fact recommended that 'it should be an offence to send or deliver restricted material, or advertisements for such material, to ... a person who the sender knew or ought reasonably to have known, had not solicited the material'.[4] Restricted material is in turn defined as that (other than the printed word) 'whose unrestricted availability is offensive to reasonable people by reason of the manner in which it portrays, deals with or relates to violence, cruelty or horror, or sexual, faecal or urinary functions or genital organs'.[5] It has been argued that the interests of the young could be safeguarded in terms of public displays and shop interiors by a standard related specifically to this aim, without at the same time impinging too far on the freedom of adults, a vice to which the Williams recommendation is debatably prone. A standard in terms of exploitative and unnecessary stimulation was therefore recommended as to public displays, segregation in shops, and sales to minors. Such a standard would, *a priori*, protect adults from offence. It has also been

---

1   See chapter 10.

2   See chapter 15.

3   *Williams* para 9.19.

4   *Williams* para 13.4 subpara 12.

5   Ibid. para 9.36 and 13.4, subpara 7.

recommended in relation to mailings to those reasonably apprehended to be under the age of eighteen. It would seem logical to employ this standard here also: it would protect the young (covering the printed word as well as pictorial matter), safeguard privacy, and obviate offence to adults.

Its constitutionality in American terms would seem assured: if privacy can justify a restriction in terms of what an individual finds sexually offensive, then coupled with the protection of the young, it would surely justify the limited restriction just proposed? The standard certainly would not seem overbroad, nor does it involve the straightforward enforcement of positive morality. Negligence at least is required both as to standard and the unsolicited nature of the mailing. The Williams Committee did not feel that any more protection than this could be given against the vicarious attentions of the hoaxer, who as a practical joke perhaps, arranges for such material to be sent to someone else; it would seem unreasonable to make the publisher strictly liable in such instances. It was not felt that the incidence of unsolicited mail being dispatched in this way was such as to justify a broader restraint on the use of the mail; the practice in other words was not so widespread as to subvert the reasoning sustaining this narrow control. The same was felt to apply to children: although it is easier to keep children out of a shop, and although a publisher would not be liable here if he could not reasonably have been expected to realise that the recipient was under eighteen years of age, the committee concluded that such difficulties are not significant 'in the way the trade has so far been carried on, and we do not think they tell against allowing mail-order trading altogether'.[1]

The only outstanding question is that of unsolicited advertisements for such mail. Williams recommended that advertisements for material falling within the recommended standard, should be covered. This seems unnecessary. If the advertisement itself contravenes the standard applied, it would in any case be covered, and the interests of the young would be adequately protected. If the advertisement is itself innocuous, questions of privacy and offence would be satisfied by double enveloping the advertisement, the outside envelope proclaiming that the inner contains advertising material. If the advertisement is so innocuous as to mislead the recipient into sending for material falling within the standard, such latter mailing could be regarded as unsolicited, whilst the advertisement would in any case fall under the prohibition imposed by the Trades Descriptions Act 1968 on applying false or misleading descriptions as to quantity or composition to advertised goods. As the Younger Committee, despite its general hands-off policy where this type

---

1 *Williams* paras 9.18 and 9.19.

of restriction was concerned, remarked in relation to the present provision on advertising, it would hesitate

> ... to single out for restriction the distribution of material which, in the law's eye, is not obscene or indecent nor describes or depicts human sexual activity itself, but merely draws attention to the existence of something which the recipient believes he would find objectionable if he chose to send for it. It is at least questionable whether the law should interfere in the freedom of communication to this extent ...[1]

It might be thought convenient to group this restriction on unsolicited material together with that on sale or distribution to children: they both, after all, employ the same standard, whilst the provision on unsolicited material does not belong with postal provisions, applying, as would the control on distribution to children, to distribution generally, whether through the mails or not.

(iii) Policy considerations in relation to customs controls would seem very much the same as those argued with regard to Post Office regulation. The offence as constituted at present appears to have little to do with preventing gratuitous offence or protecting the young, involving rather a straightforward enforcement of positive morality. To be set against this are considerations of freedom of speech and privacy. The customs measures are not the only importation provisions: although it operates in this sense only as a civil measure, and therefore lies for consideration as a prior restraint, the Harmful Publications Act 1955 does make provision for the seizure of materials which fall within its standard. It is the standard, and its justifiability, as applied to imports, rather than the prior restraint method of application, which concerns us here.

In terms of the recommendations above as to the protection of the young, the application of such standards to imports appears wholly unjustifiable. The fact that material may be displayed or distributed to the young, or distributed on an unsolicited basis to anyone at all, does not mean that its importation into the country as such should be prohibited. A prohibition in these terms falls foul of the reasoning advanced in *Butler* v *Michigan*:[2] there can be no rational connection between suppressing the availability of material to all, on the grounds that a minority should not have it, particularly when measures can be created specifically protecting that minority. The only import control that appears justified in these terms is one in respect of material the

---

1 *Younger Committee Report* op.cit. para 4.21.

2 352 US 380 (1957).

production of which involved the sexual exploitation of children, or the reasonable appearance of the infliction of actual physical harm on a participant in such production.[1] The prior restraint aspects of enforcing such a prohibition will be considered later,[2] as will the question of justification in terms of enforcing positive morality, or any other harm justifying general prohibition.

(iv) The primary aim of the Judicial Proceedings (Regulation of Reports) Act 1926 seems a perfectly sustainable one: to protect the privacy of those involved in (primarily) divorce cases. Section 1(1)(a) of the Act presents a somewhat different picture however; it does not appear to be concerned with preventing gratuitous offence, and has nothing specifically to do with protecting minors. It appears rather to involve a straightforward enforcement of positive morality. In the absence of justification for the primary enforcement of positive morality,[3] Section 1(1)(a) of the Act should be repealed.

(v) Control of the production of certain types of film and pictures is discussed in relation to prior restraints.[4] The conclusion reached is that such controls are justified to prevent the sexual exploitation of those under sixteen years of age, and the exploitation for sexual purposes of children and/or adults in the sense of the production in question involving — not as the Williams Committee proposes, reasonably appearing to involve — actual physical harm to the participants. The obvious question arising once this decision is taken, is whether the distribution of such material made in contravention of the law should be prohibited. The Williams Committee felt that it should, and that this prohibition should extend to private as well as commercial circulation: 'If we are to narrow down the law to the area where positive harms are plainly to be seen, we believe that it is right for the most rigorous steps to be taken to ensure that those harms are effectively prevented'.[5] To leave uncontrolled the distribution of material of this sort would be to encourage the flouting of the prohibition on its production.[6] If the production of speech involves the commission of a plainly justifiable criminal offence, then, as Williams argues, the arguments in favour of controlling the subsequent distribution of the fruits of such commission

---

1 See *Williams* para 10.13; see also section (v) below.

2 See prior restraints, chapter 7.

3 See chapter 15.

4 See chapter 7.

5 *Williams* para 10.11.

6 Ibid. para 6.68.

must be very powerful indeed. The committee recommends therefore a general prohibition on the distribution of such material,[1] with specific application in terms of postal legislation and customs controls.

A number of problems exist in relation to these proposals, some of which may be illustrated by examining the constitutionality — in American terms — of these proposals. The first question is whether the basis of prohibition on the production of such films would be constitutional or not. This issue does not appear to have come before the Supreme Court, and one can argue only by analogy. If the approach advocated below — in the discussion of such controls as prior restraints[2] — were followed, and such controls were tied in as far as possible to conduct, they would arguably fall outside First Amendment protection. They would, as with certain live show restrictions, be concerned with the control of conduct, with as little impingement on freedom of speech as possible. Accepting this argument as correct, the next question is whether restrictions imposed on the distribution of such material would be constitutionally acceptable. Once again such a question does not appear to have come before the Court. The first requisite for constitutionality would be a due process rational connection between the prohibition and the governmental aim in question. In other words, would there be a real encouragement, in the absence of such prohibition, to flout the primary prohibition? If one can answer this in reverse fashion, it certainly seems absurd to proclaim that the production of such material is illegal, but that the distribution of it is not. Assuming a rational connection to exist, the prohibition would be weighed in First Amendment and privacy terms.[3] The answer to this must depend on the gravity with which the Court viewed the harm occasioned by the production of such material.

Again assuming constitutional viability, one comes to the question whether the prosecution should be uniformly obliged to establish the age of, or actual physical harm to, the participants in question. As Williams remarked, this would be 'a quite unrealistic burden to impose, and it would probably result in the prosecuting authorities being unable to act ...'.[4] This is very probably correct, insofar as material brought in from overseas is concerned. At the same time the harm(s) involved here must be affected by the proposal that if it appears to a court 'that

---

1 *Williams* para 10.11; also para 13.4, subparas 20, 22 and 23.

2 See chapter 7, the production of pornography.

3 The latter is relevant at least in regard to the Customs aspect of this prohibition, for example.

4 *Williams* para 10.7.

material is *prima facie* prohibited, the burden of proof should shift to the defence to show that it is not'. In these circumstances, the prohibition might cover material depicting individuals who in fact *are* over sixteen years of age; one would be concerned in other words not with conduct, but with effect. The committee regards the infliction of actual physical harm in such circumstances as 'more hypothetical' than anything else. In view of this, it would perhaps be best to require proof in the normal way of all the elements of the offence. Certainly such proof would not seem an insuperable difficulty as far as domestically produced films are concerned, and as far as showing a proper concern for such child abuse abroad, a prohibition on imports would seem sufficient, in relation to which a shift in the burden of proof just might pass muster. One is left suspecting that the committee proposed this shift in the burden of proof in order to add just that bit more — in addition to cinema restrictions[1] — by way of control with regard to violent material. If this is so, they would have done better to recommend prohibition dealing with violent material, and based on the quite separate consideration of such material's effect: this question will be considered later.[2]

What would appear acceptable is the offence proposed, without the relaxation as far as the burden of proof is concerned. A strong case exists for such prohibition. Should such prohibition on distribution extend even within the privacy of the home? Privacy is clearly relevant here: it presumably underlies the exclusion of possession under the 1959 Act, and the exception in relation to private dwellings under the Theatres Act 1968. The type of balancing effected in *Stanley* v *Georgia* would be applicable, the outcome depending on the weight attached by the balancer to the protection of the young in this sense, as opposed to the harm involved in, for example, the possession of firearms. Williams recommends that control here should not extend to private possession, an exception in line with that under the 1959 Act, and wider than one in terms of the home.[3]

A related problem is the question of whether any defence should be available. A defence of public good is not recommended in terms of the production of such material, and would not seem apposite to its distribution.[4] A narrower defence is at present provided under the 1978 Act, in terms of having a legitimate reason for the distribution of such

---

1   See prior restraints, chapter 7, the production of pornography.

2   See chapter 15.

3   *Williams* para 10.11.

4   See chapter 7, the production of pornography.

materials.[1] Some doubt exists as to whether this makes provision, in terms of the indecency standard, for legitimate family snapshots; the defence does not in any case apply to the taking of pictures. Such pictures would clearly not be covered by the standard recommended below[2] in this regard, and hence distribution would not (in these terms) be affected. The legitimate reason defence may have related to other considerations, such as the use of such materials by the police and prosecution authorities, or its use in the treatment of paedophilia for example. Williams found that no problems had arisen under the 1978 Act provisions in this regard in terms of the exploitation of the defence, and therefore regarded the retention of such a defence both as to production and distribution as sensible.[3]

A final problem relates to the breadth of the primary and secondary prohibitions: if one is not permitted to film the infliction of actual physical harm (assuming an element of sexual exploitation) on someone else, then should one be permitted to film scenes of bestiality, for example? The committee was careful not to base its recommendations as to controlling the production of speech on existing criminal law. In fact the 1978 Protection of Children Act already covers the protection of the young aspect; whilst the infliction of the type of harm envisaged in the second aspect of the prohibition may well be covered by existing criminal law, subject to difficulties as to the defence of consent. Should such latter coverage exist, anyone involved in such conduct in the sense of filming it might well find themselves liable for complicity in the principal offence. Thus the conduct covered by the recommendations may well in fact fall within the criminal law at present. Why then the distinction between one variety of criminal conduct and another?

The committee felt basically that the criminal law on sexual offences contains at present so many anomalies as to be virtually useless as a basis of calculation.[4] The committee felt about bestiality, for example, that hostility to such conduct was based on 'extreme distaste and disgust amongst members of the population'.[5] The committee was not prepared to accept this as rational; hence the filming of such conduct was not included in their recommendations as to prohibitions. Although consideration of the law on sexual offences was beyond the brief of both the committee and this essay, there is clearly an overlap in

---

1　Section 1(4)(a).

2　See chapter 7, the production of pornography.

3　*Williams* para 10.16.

4　*Williams* paras 10.3, 10.4 and 10.9.

5　Ibid. para 10.9.

this area. The overlap is such that the committee could not truly be in a position to make recommendations as to offences prohibiting the production of pornography without considering the viability of any and all offences involving violence and/or sexuality. This they clearly could not do. It is to make the law absurd to conclude that material depicting bestiality cannot be prohibited in distribution because no rational harm is caused to viewers or production participants, whilst at the same time allowing the offence of bestiality to continue on the basis of enforcing positive morality. Accepting the two categories of conduct proposed by Williams, an accompanying investigation would seem imperative into related areas of conduct before final delineations can be drawn as to the ambit of the offence proposed here.

6 Other statutory provisions II

I   Displays

The passage of the Indecent Displays (Control) Act 1981 saw the repeal of a number of archaic statutory provisions governing indecent displays: principally,[1] that is, the relevant portion of the Vagrancy Act 1824, the Vagrancy Act 1838, the relevant portion of Section 28 of the Town Police Clauses Act 1847, and the Indecent Advertisements Act 1889. The latter provisions employed a number of standards, principally 'indecent' and 'obscene'; 'obscene' in such context can probably be taken to have had the same meaning as it does in terms of the Post Office Act 1953: that is, offence against recognised standards of propriety, 'obscene' being at the top end of the scale, and 'indecent' at the lower end.[2] The 1981 Act sweeps away 'obscene' in this context, employing only the single standard of indecency. The practical effect of this in terms of reform[3] is limited however in that indecency was a common denominator amongst those measures repealed: only inde-

---

1   It should be noted that not all local legislation (or bye-laws) governing indecent displays were repealed by the new Act; an example of such (presumably unintended) survivals are the relevant provisions in this regard of the City of London Police Act 1838.

2   See the Post Office Act 1953, chapter 5.

3   For a survey of earlier measures and recommendations as to reform, see the Home Office Working Paper on Vagrancy and Street Offences (HMSO 1974).

cency needed to be established for liability. Although the standard under the 1981 Act is then a universally lower one, in practical terms, as compared to its predecessors, it remains unaffected.

The Act provides that it shall be an offence publicly to display indecent matter; matter includes anything capable of display, but does not include an actual human body or part thereof.[1] The public aspect is further defined, in that matter which 'is displayed in or so as to be visible from any public place' is deemed to be publicly displayed. 'Public place' is defined as[2]

> ... any place to which the public have or are permitted to have access (whether on payment or otherwise) while that matter is displayed except —
> (a) a place to which the public are permitted to have access only on payment which is or includes payment for that display; or
> (b) a shop or any part of a shop to which the public can only gain access by passing beyond an adequate warning notice.[3]

There is a proviso to the latter two exceptions:

> ... but the exclusions contained in paragraphs (a) and (b) above shall only apply where persons under the age of 18 years are not permitted to enter while the display in question is continuing.

The Act further provides[4] that although account may be taken of 'juxtaposing one thing with another', any part of a displayed article 'not exposed to view' is not to be taken into account in assessing that article's indecency. The Act apparently clears up then two basic uncertainties which existed in respect of, for example, the Vagrancy Act: it was by no means clear whether the measure extended to the inside of a shop, for example, where such interior was not visible from the street, whether payment of an entrance fee affected such considerations, nor whether it was necessary for an item to be indecent on the face of it. Whether displays would, in these terms, be covered by the Obscene Publications Acts is not clear. The 1964 Act covers shop window displays provided that it can be established (or reasonably inferred) that the proprietor of the shop possesses the articles with a view to their

---

1   Section 1(5).

2   Section 1(3).

3   The requirements in respect of such notice are spelt out in some detail: Section 1(6).

4   Section 1(5).

publication for gain. Section 1(3)(a) of the 1959 Act provides that 'offering for sale or letting on hire' constitutes publication, which would appear to cover shop window displays; in *Mella* v *Monahan*[1] however, it was held that such displays, viewed in the light of the law of contract, implied no more than an invitation to treat, and thus could not be held to constitute 'offering for sale'. Publication is further defined in Section 1(3)(b) of the 1959 Act however: there will have been publication if anyone 'in the case of an article containing or embodying matter to be looked at, or a record, shows, plays or projects it'. Although the word 'shows' may be taken as mere display, it would seem likely that something more than this is required in relation to, for example, a book with an innocuous exterior. If an *eiusdem generis* approach were adopted, 'shows' in this context requires the actual publication of the contents; were the material's exterior potentially obscene, such requirement would *prima facie* be satisfied.

The new measure is clearly concerned with the prevention of gratuitous offence and/or the protection of children. In view of this and of the fact that one is concerned here with a restriction and not a prohibition, and that on visible[2] displays only, a public good defence does not seem apposite, and is not provided by the Act. A work is quite clearly not to be taken as a whole: one is concerned, allowing for juxtaposing, only with the visibly displayed portions thereof. *Mens rea* is probably required on the part of the person 'making, causing or permitting' the display, as to such mounting, but not as to the indecency of the material.

The Act is more sustainable than its predecessors, in that it is aimed at the prevention of what are, arguably, rationally assessable harms. Such sustainability is to a large extent dependent however on the standard employed. Provided this is tightly drawn, and reflects a widely held positive morality, the potential proliferation of offence-based restrictions may be limited. Where the standard employed is overbroad, the very basis of the restriction is once again open to question. In these terms, the measure's retention of indecency as a standard is unfortunate.[3] The Act is a piecemeal reform, and this may well explain the attempted refurbishing of indecency as a standard; even were it to have been re-

---

1 [1961] *Crim Law Rev* 125.

2 But not with those in museums or art galleries, which are specifically excluded provided they are visible only from within the museum or gallery; Section 1(4)(b). Various other exceptions are made, namely in respect of theatrical performances (see the Theatres Act 1968, chapter 6); the cinema (see subsequent restraints currently applicable to films, chapter 7); and television and sound broadcasting (see subsequent restraints on such broadcasts, chapter 7).

3 See p.182ff for a fuller discussion of both indecency as a standard, and the basis of offence-based restrictions.

placed here it would, after all, still have applied by virtue of, for example, the Customs and Post Office Acts, and not, in such contexts, in terms of restricting gratuitous offence. The Home Office Working Paper's proposals and this Act stop coyly short of prohibiting actual sale, as this would obtrude on the functions of the Obscene Publications Acts. And yet the effect of their proposals would be to control virtually all transactions in terms of indecency. If the prohibition under the Obscene Publications Acts is very often applied in practice in terms of offensiveness, this coyness is difficult to sustain: in view of the potential elision of the two standards, the continued viability of the obscenity prohibition is open to serious doubt.[1]

Indecency can presumably be taken here to have the same meaning as it does under the Post Office Act: that is, offence against recognised standards of propriety. It is in this sense not limited to sexuality, but may encompass virtually anything at all. Such standard raises obvious problems: its overbreadth is such that it is questionable whether it any longer has, with changing social and moral standards, any real validity. It is not clear moreover whether the standard incorporates the protection of minors or not: is the standard what the reasonable person finds offensive in terms of his own susceptibilities, or is the line drawn at what he would deem it offensive for a child to see. Although it might be argued that in view of the warning notice to adults provision, the standard is not concerned with children, this is by no means clear. If the standard does include children, one runs the risk of displays in virtually all retail outlets, for example, being reduced to the level of what is suitable for children, who may be anything from five to seventeen years of age; if children are not included, the protection afforded them is judged in terms of the susceptibilities of adults and not children themselves. Whatever the position, the interiors of shops throughout England and Wales are now subject to a standard whose meaning is notoriously overbroad and uncertain. Such overbreadth and uncertainty clearly undermines the measure's basic rationales, and should have been sufficient to ensure indecency's consignment to the legislative scrapheap.

Policy considerations

The Williams Committee was in no doubt on this latter issue; they considered initially, however, the question of justifications. The Committee Report devotes a chapter to the question of offensiveness, quite apart from an earlier chapter dealing with harms. Did they then consider offensiveness as something quite unrelated to the central question of rationally assessable harms and their regulation? The committee begins

---

1 See chapters 4 and 15 in particular.

by making the point that what is considered offensive can vary with both place and time, and that there may be disagreement even in given circumstances, as to whether something is offensive or not.[1] What is found offensive, in other words, may vary in terms of either taste or positive morality or both, and there may be disagreement in any given circumstance in terms of taste and/or such morality. Is, then, the question of the offensiveness of pornography merely one of taste? The committee felt strongly that it is not; what lifts the offensiveness occasioned by pornography beyond being a question of mere taste is the strength of the positive morality involved: the tastelessness of pornography is not

> ... enough to explain its offensiveness; we are surrounded by shallow trash of all kinds, but few people, however sensitive their taste, find it as upsetting and disagreeable as many people certainly find pornography. For many people pornography is not only offensive, but deeply offensive ... Pornography essentially involves making public in words, pictures or theatrical performances, the fulfilment of fantasy images of sex and violence. In some cases the images are of forbidden acts: so it is with images of violence. In other cases, the line that is transgressed is only that between private and public; the acts represented in the images would be all right in private, but the same acts would be objectionable in public ... People have strong sentiments attached to these notions of public and private, of what is 'unsuitable' — in its original sense, *indecent* — to show.[2]

One has to exercise some caution when attempting to assess offence as rational harm:[3] if offensiveness is merely to be an affront to strongly-held notions of positive morality, it would cover, on a rational basis, conduct in private. This seems quite unacceptable; if one is to proscribe conduct in private purely on the grounds of positive morality, this would be better done openly, and not in the form of a would-be rational harm. It is difficult to believe that people are so vitally affected by their sense of offence at the private conduct of others, that such offence could be regarded rationally as a harm. It is precisely this distinction which the committee advances to distinguish the enforcement of positive morality from the restriction of offensiveness in this sense: the element of choice is seen as crucial in this regard, the gratuitous

---

1   *Williams* paras 7.4—7.7.

2   *Williams* paras 7.3—7.4; emphasis in the original.

3   See chapter 4, the enforcement of morality.

nature of such offence being sufficient to occasion something one may view as harmful:

> For those who are not disposed, as willing customers are, to make the scenes of pornography into objects of their own fantasy, those scenes have a special and saddening ugliness. In people who are particularly resistant to such fantasy, either in general, or as involving objects such as these, anger, disturbance and oppression will be the reactions. ... The reactions many people experience to publicly displayed pornography are not just a matter of arbitrary taste, but are deep reactions; the offensiveness it displays to them is, in both a psychological and ethical sense, a deep offensiveness.[1]

The committee goes on to argue that the rules against public sexual activity, in the sense that they are aimed at preventing upset, distress, disgust and outrage, 'would generally be thought to be consistent with the harm condition'.[2] Precisely the same considerations, they felt, were involved in the Wolfenden Committee recommendations as to curbs on the public activities of prostitutes, recommendations which became law in the Street Offences Act 1959:

> The offensiveness of publicly displayed pornography seems to us to fall clearly within the sorts of considerations advanced by the Wolfenden Committee, and to be in line with traditionally accepted rules protecting the interest in public decency.[3]

Offence of this type, the committee felt, may legitimately be regarded as a harm; restriction may be justified in terms of a rationally assessable harm. Alternatively,[4] one may justify such restriction in terms of privacy, should one's definition of privacy extend this far, or in terms of the protection of the young. Williams has proposed that offence and the protection of the young be subsumed under one standard: that of offence to the reasonable adult. The young will be protected in the sense that what the reasonable adult finds offensive for them to see, would be restricted: 'What moves people to feel that pornographic and

---

1 *Williams* para 7.8 and 7.10.

2 Ibid. para 7.12.

3 Ibid. para 7.13.

4 If gratuitous offence may be regarded as an invasion of privacy, and if such offence occasions a rationally assessable harm, the assertion of the relevance of privacy in this context may have a credible utilitarian basis. This is not a question that can be examined here — as was pointed out in the discussion of privacy in chapter 5.

similar materials should not be available to the young is just the same sort of thing that makes them find its display offensive'.[1] This would appear to place far too wide a restriction on speech: anything which is unsuitable for children could not be displayed publicly, or indeed in a shop, unless that shop excluded those under eighteen years of age and put up a warning notice. This is perhaps to 'burn down the house to roast the pig', and more specific restrictions in terms of protecting the young would seem more sustainable. This question has already been discussed:[2] accepting the reasoning already advanced, protection of the young would take the form of a prohibition on distribution to the young and a segregation requirement in shops as far as material unsuitable for the young is concerned, together with a restriction on public displays in the same terms. The standard recommended as to what is unsuitable for the young is a tightly drawn one, and would closely depend on expert evidence as to the effects of material on children. Such measures, if acceptable, would to a considerable extent protect the young from harm, and insofar as this is synonymous with causing offence to adults, would obviate such offence. Such protection would not extend to the inside of shops, in the sense that material unsuitable for the young would merely be segregated and not for sale to minors, but would not be excluded from shops. This compromise in the protection of minors seems justified in terms of the freedom of speech interests of adults.

Such restrictions would arguably[3] pass muster in American constitutional terms. Certainly one could cite a number of justifications for such measures: the prohibition on sales to minors would probably be the least difficult here as the protection of the young could be weighed against the First Amendment rights of minors. The segregation requirements and displays restrictions involve the First Amendment rights of adults, and are clearly more difficult to sustain. There are a number of potential justifications, however, the protection of children being the most obvious; one might add the offence caused to adults by such material being thrust upon children, such offence possibly being seen in privacy terms. These factors must be weighed against freedom of speech; here it must be emphasised that one is concerned with a restriction, and not a prohibition. There would thus apparently be two constitutional avenues open: to bypass the First Amendment as the Court has done in upholding zoning restrictions — that is, by arguing that the restriction is concerned with protecting the young, and not

---

1 *Williams* para 9.34.

2 See protection of children, chapter 5.

3 Ibid.

with suppressing the advocacy of opinion, and that the measure impinges (as a restriction) as little as possible on freedom of speech. A second approach would be to take the First Amendment head-on, justifying in terms of balancing or a clear and present danger approach the restrictions suggested. This would of course mean the admission of protection of the young and offensiveness as considerations to be weighed in terms of the First Amendment. The First Amendment may be an absolute, and the assumption of balancing made in the English context may not necessarily apply: one has thus to establish in First Amendment terms the viability of the policy factors in question, and the restrictions proposed, assuming at all times a rational connection between policy and restriction. What does seem most unlikely is that the Supreme Court would ever rule constitutional the type of blanket restriction in terms of children suggested by Williams, even though it would not apply to the written word. These questions will be returned to when the American position is considered in detail.[1]

Returning to the question of offence, is any further restriction justified? Public displays in the sense of displays in public places in the literal sense, would be covered in terms of a tightly drawn restriction in favour of the young. Shops could nonetheless stock, display and sell anything at all, provided that some form of segregation was affected, and material unsuitable for them was not sold to minors. Do adults need protection from the offence occasioned them by what they might see in shops, in the form of material whose display and availability is unrestricted as far as they are concerned? One may put onto the restriction side of the balance, offence, if accepted as a rational harm, together with privacy considerations, if relevant. One may add the protection of the young here also, as any restriction aimed at preventing offence to adults in terms of their own susceptibilities would have the effect of removing such materials from unrestricted shops, thus strengthening the protection provided for children. Such considerations provide a strong case for restriction. What of the freedom side of the scale? The Williams Committee makes a number of points in this regard:[2] first, an offence restriction would not be aimed at the advocacy of any opinion: '... it is not for advocating any opinion that the restriction is proposed, and ... the upset that they cause to the public is not a reaction to opinions which are found unacceptable ... but rather the form of ... advocacy if there is advocacy at all'.[3] If pornography in fact encourages a view of sex as 'trivial amusement or gratification', that at

---

1 See chapter 14.

2 *Williams* paras 7.15 to 7.23.

3 Ibid. para 7.17.

least is an opinion, and they would find difficulty in advising its prohibition. The committee also makes the related point that 'Restricting the publication to a volunteer audience does not defeat its aim'. This relates to the assertion that restriction is not directed against the advocacy of opinion, but the form of the advocacy, if there is any advocacy at all: in other words, the message can reach an audience provided that audience is prepared to countenance the form in which it is couched. One might put this more broadly: controls on unrestricted display in shops for example are only restrictions and not prohibitions; their impact on speech as such is therefore as small as possible. Almost precisely the same approach has been taken by the American Supreme Court in relation to zoning restrictions and freedom of speech: in *Young* v *American Mini Theaters*[1] the Court had to determine the constitutionality of zoning restrictions on cinemas in terms of an 'adult' standard. Such restrictions are imposed basically to avoid offensiveness. The plurality, apparently wishing to avoid the admission of offence as a valid First Amendment policy consideration, took the view that the variety of speech involved enjoyed only a second-class status, and that the restraint involved was, in relation to the legitimate governmental aim of town planning, therefore constitutional. Justice Powell (concurring) emphasised that the restriction was not in fact aimed at speech — or the advocacy of opinion — at all, but was rather concerned with the quite acceptable objective of proper town planning. In the process it had as small an impact on protected speech as possible, and was therefore constitutional.

The Court has elsewhere in effect, if not in so many words, acknowledged offensiveness as a factor of possible constitutional significance in this area. Any direct acknowledgement has, however, been studiously avoided: in *Erznoznik* v *City of Jacksonville*[2] the Court was asked to rule on the constitutionality of a city ordnance prohibiting the public display of depictions of 'human male or female bare buttocks, human female breasts, or human bare pubic areas'. A number of approaches were open to the Court here: one was to simply follow the old exception approach as to obscenity: as the standard here was not couched in terms of obscenity, it was overbroad, and therefore unconstitutional. What the Court opted for was to emphasise the equality principle as far as the First Amendment was concerned: in other words, all speech must be taken on an equal footing. Rather than proceeding from here to assess such state interests as the protection of children and the prevention of offence, and to relate them to First Amendment guarantees,

---

1   427 US 50 (1976).

2   423 US 205 (1975).

the Court refused in effect to reach such questions, declaring rather that in view of equality, regulation of speech by content is unconstitutional. A grudging admission that the Court might perhaps in the future take the matter further in this regard came with the acknowledgement that if an unwilling viewer in public could not escape exposure to the material in question, some regulation might be permissible.[1]

What is of interest or relevance here is not the question of whether balancing is permissible in terms of the First Amendment, or whether a skirting of the amendment as in *Young* is preferable.[2] Rather, it is that the Supreme Court has at least obliquely in *Young*, and more directly, if *obiter*, in *Erznoznik*, acknowledged offence as a viable policy consideration in this area, a consideration which might justify such restriction as opposed to prohibition, either in terms directly of First Amendment guarantees, or indirectly, by arguing such restrictions to be aimed at viable objectives and not the suppression of speech. The Supreme Court has in fact admitted offence as a factor in yet another, if unacknowledged way: in terms of the prevailing *Miller*[3] formulation of obscenity, material may be suppressed if it has marginal First Amendment — say literary — value; this, provided that it appeals to the prurient interest of the average person and is patently offensive. The reasoning behind this is that obscenity as such forms, because of the absence of First Amendment values in it, an exception to free speech guarantees. What the Court is in fact saying here is that material with slight value — material that is therefore logically protected — may be suppressed if it has prurient appeal and is patently offensive. In many instances, then, the Court is, despite the exception approach, in fact allowing a jury to balance offensiveness (which is, after all, the cutting-edge of the test) against literary or other value.[4]

The reluctance of the Court to acknowledge the relevance of offensiveness as far as the First Amendment is concerned is not difficult to understand: if a restriction on a particular source of offence is acknowledged as being constitutional in First Amendment terms, does this not open the way to any number of other possible sources of offence similarly being argued to ground justifiable and constitutional restrictions on speech? One could hardly claim with certainty that the type of restriction in terms of sexuality/violence is and would be, the only source of offence relevant in this sense. Take the offence of blasphemy in

---

1   423 US 205 (1975) at 206—7.

2   See chapter 14.

3   413 US 15 (1973).

4   See chapters 11 and 14.

English law. The House of Lords has determined that this should be separated from the 'jejeune' requirement of a likelihood of a breach of the peace resulting from the publication in question.[1] This may seem quite reasonable, and what one now has is an offence couched in terms of offensiveness, such offensiveness apparently lying in the presentation more than in the advocacy of opinion; unfortunately, such offensiveness appears to form the basis of a prohibition, and not a restriction. For our purposes here, were the offence reformed as a restriction, one could advance much the same arguments brought forward by Williams in relation to material dealing with sexuality/violence, in order to sustain it. One might argue also, for example, that many people in this society might find the sight of anyone riding past them in a very expensive motor car, particularly in a time of economic recession and high unemployment, deeply offensive; therefore owners of such cars should not drive them in public. That such offence may be occasioned is no doubt correct; to argue a restriction based on this misses a fundamental point made when discussing the identification of utilitarian harms: such identification must depend, to one extent or another, on the positive morality of the society in question. To argue that material has caused maladjustment in a group of readers for example, is to judge such maladjustment — the rational harm — to some extent in terms of the positive moral values of the society. Positive morality plays a secondary role, moreover, in the process of selecting which of a range of rationally assessed harms should be subject to legal control. The position with offence is surely much the same: positive morality will to some extent (together with the lack of consent of the audience) determine whether certain manifestations rationally qualify as offensive, and second, which of such examples of offensiveness should be subject to legal control.

In these terms, there would not seem to be any reason why freedom of speech should be any more threatened by offence considerations than by any other harm. If one adds protection of the young as a further justification for the type of restriction involved here, the likelihood of the First Amendment being virtually overwhelmed under a welter of offence restrictions must seem remote. One thing is clear from the above: if positive morality is to influence the identification of rationally assessed harms, including offensiveness, it presumably must be a widely held morality. It is clear both in terms of the harm formulation and a balance being struck in favour of restriction, that a tightly drawn standard is required here, a standard which closely reflects a widely held morality.

---

1   *R v Lemon* [1979] All ER 898.

The standard employed

A logical point at which to start, as far as the standard employed is concerned, is with indecency, which has for so long been applied in relation to displays. Indecency is beset with difficulties and uncertainties; it is, moreover, by no means clear that indecency as a standard involves any real consensus in society. In 1973, for example, a representative sample of 953 adults around Great Britain were asked for their views on the decency of three different pictures:[1] first a photograph of Rodin's *The Kiss*; second a costume sketch for *Scheherazade*, by Leon Bakst, of 'a reclining nude who sported a tuft of pubic hair'; and third the front cover of *Men Only*. The results indicated that recognised standards of propriety, in terms of indecency at least, do not exist, if differences in age, geographical area, and social class are taken into account. The Bakst nude was thought indecent by 30 per cent of those interviewed; the *Men Only* cover was rated indecent by 28 per cent, 'not really indecent' by 27 per cent, and 'not indecent at all' by 37 per cent; only 7 per cent found the Rodin photograph indecent. Of those between the age of 15 and 24, only 11 per cent thought the Bakst nude indecent, with 18 per cent for *Men Only*; of those over 65 years of age, 57 and 51 per cent of the sample (respectively) found these pictures indecent. The same poll found that 71 per cent of the sample had never been seriously upset by an indecent display. A more recent *Sunday Times* poll indicated that 50 per cent of those interviewed did not consider the reading of soft-porn 'girlie' magazines immoral, and thought it acceptable to most people in Britain, whilst a similar verdict was recorded by 54 per cent of those interviewed in relation to the reserving of special beaches for nude bathing.[2]

The Williams Committee quite rightly point out the difficulties involved in surveys of public opinion in this area.[3] They are perhaps overly dismissive of such findings however: as far as the results above are concerned, they conclude that one cannot ascertain what the nation finds indecent by showing people pictures that were unlikely to be found indecent at law. They point also to the apparent contradiction inherent in the findings, in that by a majority of 54 to 31 per cent, respondents claimed to be in favour of a new law against indecent displays. The type of finding made in the poll which clearly is open to criticism is the response elicited to the following question: 'What would you personally regard as indecent if it were on display in a public place?'

---

1   Poll conducted by Opinion Research Centre for *The Sunday Times*, 30 December 1973.

2   Poll conducted by MORI for *The Sunday Times*, 2 March 1980.

3   Such difficulties have been discussed in chapter 2, in relation to obscenity; see *Williams*, paras 1.13 to 1.16 especially.

The following percentages of those polled listed these concerns:

nakedness	24
suggestive nude poses	21
female breasts	6
nipples	6
sex organs	18
pubic hair	9
sexual intercourse	48
scenes of violence	4
cruelty or brutality	2
bad language	1
homosexuality	1

Although the more conclusive of these results probably can validly ground some conclusion, as Williams points out, verbal descriptions in this area are apt to be misleading: if one offered respondents a verbal description in terms of 'material depicting sex organs', one person 'may have a mental picture of putting fig leaves on statues, another a serious sex education manual and another a highly explicit pornographic magazine.[1] Despite the difficulties of interpretation involved, and the fact that one cannot rely conclusively on such findings, the results do seem to indicate two things: first, that the standard at present employed is so broad as to allow too wide a disparity of view as to what it covers: were the standard clear, there might have been more general agreement in the results above. Second, that a majority do wish for a control of this sort.

Parliamentary confidence in the term 'indecency' in this context is probably not overwhelming: although a 1973 Bill, for example, received all-party support in its second reading, many members were to change their minds during committee scrutiny. One member argued that 'to many people of the Catholic faith who hold their faith strongly, a contraceptive is an indecent article'.[2] Questions were raised as to the indecency of *Playboy* pin-ups, whilst there seemed to be some confusion over whether news films of famine victims in Ethiopia would fall foul of the standard. The Labour Government (which had previously supported this type of Bill) refused in 1974 to re-introduce it as 'the term indecency has no meaningful definition and should not be part of any criminal statute'.[3] Despite the lack of confidence in inde-

---

[1] *Williams* para 1.15.

[2] Cinematograph and Indecent Display Bill, Standing Committee B, 3rd sitting, 29 November 1973, col. 351.

[3] Quoted in Robertson op.cit. at 208.

cency as a standard, the Williams Committee reported overwhelming support for restrictions on public displays: '... there was a very broad consensus that the main objective of the law should be to protect members of the public from the nuisance of offensive materials in places to which normal life happens to take them'.[1] The answer is then to marry this consensus to a standard which is such as to be likely to be able to give effect to such general agreement.

The Williams Committee recommended a standard of what is offensive to the reasonable person, such standard taking into account the susceptibilities of children. It has been suggested that to impose this burden on the inside of all unrestricted premises is to overburden the free speech rights of adults; a standard couched in terms of harm to children has been suggested as to public displays, as to segregation in unrestricted premises, and distribution to minors. The standard at issue now is one in terms of which one will determine what is permissible in an unrestricted shop. One's concern here, as Williams points out,[2] is with sexuality/violence: the type of offensiveness with which one is concerned may be characterised as portraying or dealing with 'violence, cruelty or horror, or sexual, faecal or urinary functions, or genital organs'. This specifies the basic parameters involved, and was recommended in respect of the children's standard proposed above. One now has to specify just what material dealing with these matters is to be caught. Williams isolated three ways in which this could be done:[3] first, by means of a general formula such as the law has used up to now, but 'a new and more useful one'. Second, by means of a detailed listing of what may not be shown; and third by means of administrative control of the sort employed already in relation to the cinema. The committee appears to assume that such approaches are mutually exclusive. Any administrative tribunal would, however, proceed according to some standard, specific or general and one would be faced with the choice of a standard. Administrative controls as an alternative to subsequent criminal prosecution will be considered later in conjunction with other prior restraints.[4]

What then of a specific standard? A number of potential difficulties are apparent:[5] the most obvious perhaps of these is that no such list can

---

1   *Williams* para 9.2; also generally 9.1 to 9.7.

2   *Williams* para 9.31.

3   Ibid. para 9.21; the reasoning here would be equally applicable in relation to the selection of the standard for the protection of children, above: see protection of children, chapter 5.

4   See prior restraints, chapter 7, especially administrative controls in relation to books and magazines.

5   *Williams* paras 9.23 to 9.28.

be exhaustive. As Williams remarked: 'We found it was not difficult to pick holes in the various lists presented to us by our witnesses, and concluded that loopholes were inevitable in any list that it was practicable to produce. But it also seemed to us that it was peculiarly unattractive to attempt to set out an exhaustive list of what was forbidden: in trying to forestall the fertile imagination of pornographers, the list would become ridiculous, embarrassing and itself potentially offensive'. The result would be that the legislature would constantly have to update and extend such a list, unless the restriction was to become toothless. A good illustration of the need constantly to expand such rigid listings is the fate of the formulation laid down in *Miller* v *California* by the Supreme Court. The Court listed the following as examples of subjects which might constitutionally be regulated in terms of obscenity laws:

(a) Patently offensive representations of descriptions of ultimate sex acts, normal or perverted, actual or simulated.
(b) Patently offensive representations or descriptions of masturbation, excretory functions, and lewd exhibitions of the genitals.[1]

This list is clearly not exhaustive: are statutes imposing prohibitions in terms other than these, unconstitutional? The Court drew back from this, and has emphasised that these are merely examples of what may be prohibited: as long as statutes are specific, in terms of the sexual conduct involved, this is enough.[2] The original limitation is thus virtually toothless. No list can ever probably be an exhaustive one. The difficulty here operates potentially in reverse also: any compilation of this sort tends to become ossified. In terms of changing sexual morality and its impact on offensiveness, such a list would probably need constant deletions in order to keep pace with change: 'The standard may no longer be valid even when legislation comes to be enacted; and once it is enacted, it will become an extremely inflexible standard which will tend to attract even more ridicule and odium to the law'.[3]

A final problem with a list standard is that it does not allow the drawing of fine distinctions, and this often produces absurd results: an illustration can be taken from the guidelines submitted in this regard to the Williams Committee by the British Adult Publications Association:

Publications intended to conform with the Association's

---

[1] 413 US 15 (1973) at 25.

[2] See *Ward* v *Illinois* 431 US 767 (1977).

[3] *Williams* para 9.24.

guidelines must not contain photographs showing 'actual sexual contact', and to draw the line at this point implies that a photograph is permissible so long as actual contact is avoided; a centimetre of daylight satisfies the guidelines, though it may not in fact alter the offensiveness of the picture in the slightest. The Association then goes on to muddy the water by explaining that illustrations showing near contact may also be prohibited 'if considered to be over-explicit'; uncertainties about what is 'over-explicit' then begin to detract from the value of trying to be specific.[1]

The committee recommends a general standard, couched in terms of offensiveness. In view of the fact that the harm one is concerned with here is offence, a standard in terms of offensiveness itself seems both direct and sensible. Offensiveness to whom and in what terms, however? Here it must be remembered that one is concerned with widely held standards of positive morality in relation to such offence. The committee recommends 'reasonable people' as the standard here, and this certainly gives one the desired breadth of reference. The terms of such offensiveness were set in discussion above, and comprise roughly violence and the sexual functions. This is not enough: one of the crucial aspects of the justification for restricting offence was that the material should be forced on its audience, or that offence should be gratuitous. One must therefore add to the formulation above the qualification that such offensiveness to reasonable people should be in relation to the unrestricted availability of the material in question.

There are a number of difficulties or points which need further elaboration. First, it must be emphasised that the primary objective is to obviate offence to adults; protection for children would be provided separately. Offensiveness is then to be assessed in terms of the reasonable person's *own* susceptibilities, and not in terms of what he might consider suitable for children. This gives one greater clarity as to what is meant by the reasonable person: it means the reasonable adult. Does this hypothetical reasonable adult take into account those adults more susceptible than himself? The standard 'reasonable' is not so tight as to exclude those who are more sensitive; what it does exclude is those who are so sensitive as to appear unreasonable. The standard may approximate to that laid down recently by the American Supreme Court in relation to the obscenity test: in *Pinkus* v *United States*[2] the Court ruled that the average person aspect of the test excluded children, but included the more sensitive of the adult population; this would appear

---

1   *Williams* para 9.25.

2   436 US 293 (1978).

to mean that the average person is a composite of all adults. The reasonable person test would appear tighter than this. A further difficulty in relation to the reasonable person test is the question of whether the reasonable person is to represent national or local standards. *The Sunday Times* opinion poll quoted above showed clear regional variations, with the Scots being rather more inclined to brand things indecent than the Welsh, the English showing the least concern of all with indecency. That there are regional variations within England itself, from London to rural communities, is not seriously at issue. What is the reasonable person to represent in all this? The answer is an important one, because although gratuitous offence may be regarded as a harm, its classification as such must depend on a strong positive morality. In other words, although one is not merely enforcing positive morality in a primary sense, if there is no such strongly held positive morality, the standard is open to the same criticism made of corruption of public morals and obscenity: that the standard is then overbroad and completely subjective.

There is no easy answer to this, as American experience has shown. The Supreme Court elected with the *Roth* test (as amended) to have community standards judged on a national basis. This was strongly criticised, perhaps the most telling objection being that in a country such as the United States there simply is no such thing as a national standard, particularly not in relation to a prohibition. The *Miller* Court has since affirmed that standards are to be judged locally; the court has omitted to say just what 'locally' means in this context, an ambiguity that might well create difficulties in terms of federal statute prosecutions, particularly if the state in question does not have an obscenity statute.[1] If one looks at the results of *The Sunday Times* opinion poll quoted above, they do not seem to indicate a strong prevailing morality, even in relation to restrictions. If one allows local standards to rule, one runs the risk of absurd variations in enforcement, such enforcement in turn not satisfying one's basic policy concern that the criminal law should be sufficiently certain. To put things in terms of a national standard is probably to institutionalise the non-existent; also, one is after all concerned with offensiveness and its avoidance, and to impose will-he, nill-he, on a conservative community, the standards of West End London may be too rigid.

The best one can do is to leave the standard open to local interpretation in England and Wales, but to institute a number of safeguards in an attempt to ensure reasonable uniformity of application. The first is to tighten the standard even further by requiring that material be found patently offensive as opposed to merely offensive. This standard is

---

1   See *Smith v United States* 431 US 291 (1977); chapter 13.

employed in the American obscenity test, and if applied in the opinion poll on indecency mentioned earlier, might well have resulted in a far higher degree of uniformity in the answers given. A second safeguard might be to channel all prosecutions through a central authority, avoiding private or local police prosecutions. The principal objection to this appears to be that it turns such an office into a censorship bureau. It might nonetheless be a very satisfactory compromise, particularly in relation to suggestions for an administrative prior restraint system.[1]

A third possibility would be to provide what in English law has so far been the unthinkable: expert evidence as to such standards. This issue has been argued above in relation to obscenity, in respect of which such evidence is largely excluded;[2] in terms of law reform it is probably more relevant here. Such exclusion is in line with the 'ultimate issue' rule in the English common law: no opinion evidence should be admitted on the very issue which the court has to decide, questions of fact being for the jury. Although this approach has been much criticised, it is perhaps unavoidable as far as obscenity law in its present form is concerned, with its concern with what appear to be highly subjective moral views as to the necessity of prohibition in any one case. When one considers that a primary aim with the restriction recommended here must be to avoid, if possible, the disparities and absurdities inherent in the old law, and to assess a harm rather than a preference or quirk of taste, then if expert testimony would help to avoid convictions other than for real offensiveness, a strong case exists for its admissibility here. It is after all admitted on such issues in a number of other jurisdictions, notably Canada, where even opinion poll evidence may be introduced.[3] Such evidence has been admitted in the United States as to prurient appeal, patent offensiveness, as well as lack of social value, the Court drawing the line at the actual question of the material's obscenity. Although standards are now to be assessed locally, the term 'locally' has not been defined; state-wide standards may be as far beyond a juror's ken as are national ones: unless strict departure is heralded from past practice, such evidence may well still be admissible on such issues. Such evidence in no way binds the jury, who remain the final arbiters on issues of fact. The judicial view seems to be that the jury is the ultimate repository of common sense in relation to such decisions, so long as they are not 'diverted ... by the irrelevant opinions

---

1   Chapter 8; on administrative restraint, see chapter 7.

2   Chapter 2.

3   R v *Prairie Schooner News and Powers* 75 (1970) WWR 585 (Manitoba Crt of Appl) at 599.

of experts'.[1] But 'why should common sense be so precarious a commodity that it is apt to dissolve at the wave of a doctorate? If juries are paragons of good sense they can be trusted, with the help of competent cross-examination, to reject half-baked theorising'.[2]

A fourth way in which the standard might be tightened is to exclude from its application material which consists purely of the written word. This has been recommended by Williams in their composite standard, but has been argued to be inappropriate as far as protecting the young is concerned.[3] The protection of adults from offence may be a different matter: the committee base their exclusion of purely written material on the argument that it is removed from reality in the sense of not displaying real people and events as do photographs for example, and that 'an activity is in any case needed to take in the content'.[4] Additional factors are that the written word is 'the principal medium for the advocacy of opinions', and has 'chiefly given rise to the traditional problems of serious artistic intent in supposedly obscene material'. The question of written material ties in with a general question: is offence to be judged in terms of the outside cover only? On the face of it gratuitous offence is concerned with the external aspect of material only. To extend control to the undisclosed contents is to run the risks of enforcing positive morality *per se*, and abandoning any attempt to limit offence in the sense of tying it to harms as such. On this basis, purely written material only, without an offensive cover, should not be restricted. Having said this, is it reasonable to allow patently offensive pictorial material, gathered between innocuous covers, into any and every shop? Williams argues strongly that the presence of such pictorial material in an unrestricted shop constitutes a sufficient thrusting of it upon customers as to constitute gratuitous offence.[5] One is stretching the rationale here; in terms of advocacy of opinion and literary or other merit, coupled with its relative lack of visual impact, it does not seem justified to comprehend the written word within such stretching. The Supreme Court in the United States appeared to be moving towards just this position with obscenity statutes and their coverage of books: the Court between 1957 and 1973 held books obscene in only one case,

---

1   *R v Staniforth* [1976] 2 All ER 714 at 720.

2   Robertson op.cit. at 158.

3   See protection of children, chapter 5.

4   *Williams* para 7.7; also 7.22.

5   Ibid. para 9.8.

and there most of the materials were illustrated.[1] Although the Court was dealing with a prohibition and not a restriction in terms of gratuitous offence, and although a policy with respect to books was never articulated, the factors underlying this trend may, particularly in view of the requirement of patent offensiveness in the obscenity test, have been to some extent similar to those raised by Williams.

A final question as to the standard employed is whether this should provide a defence of public good. This question was raised in relation to the standard proposed in terms of protecting minors: would the standard proposed cover frank posters concerning venereal disease, displays of contraceptives, or news reports of horrifying incidents? The committee took the view (in terms of their composite standard) that a reasonable adult would not find such things offensive in terms of the young, nonetheless specifically recommending that contraceptives be excluded from legislative cover.[2] The word 'unnecessarily' in relation to the standard proposed above in terms of children, should ensure the exclusion of such material; what of the standard in terms of offence to adults? If the written word is excluded, literary merit is to begin with probably not a concern: one might venture that the amount of other material which is patently offensive, and which has real artistic or other merit, is probably negligible. Quite irrespective of this one is imposing a restriction and not a prohibition: all that art galleries or shops have to do is comply with the requirements of the restriction; artistic or other merit does not seem an adequate reason to justify the forcing of such material on an unwilling audience.

The restriction

Accepting the standard of restriction proposed in respect of gratuitous offence occasioned to adults by public displays, one has still to specify the circumstances of application of such restriction. The standard proposed in relation to the young, although tightly drawn, should cover appreciably more material than would the adult standard: in other words, one is not concerned here with public displays in shop windows, hoardings, and so on. One is concerned solely with the interiors of shops, which the children's standard would not reach other than to prohibit, in its terms, sales to the young, and to provide for segregation. What restriction is appropriate to protect adults in terms of such interior, albeit segregated, displays? Is it enough to require that materials

---

1 *Mishkin* v *New York* 383 US 502 (1966) at 514–5; the Supreme Court has since confirmed that obscenity applies equally to books: *Kaplan* v *California* 413 US 115 (1973) at 118, footnote 3.

2 *Williams* para 9.37.

caught by the adult standard are themselves segregated? Anything short of segregation in a back room would not seem adequate here, and taking offensiveness and the protection of children in balance, a stricter demarcation appears necessary. In this regard the committee recommended separate shops: 'If ... material is available only to those who choose to look for it and if children are automatically excluded, this seems substantially to satisfy the objective'.[1] This means that those under eighteen years of age would not be admitted to such premises, the premises themselves being required to be separate in the sense of having at least a separate access from the street, and displaying an adequate warning notice as to the possible offensiveness of goods within, and to the effect that those under the age of eighteen were not admitted. The committee considered suggestions that such a shop be precluded from selling other goods, in view of the fact that it might offer ordinary goods at considerable reductions, perhaps as 'loss leaders', in order to lure customers inside.[2] It concluded that no ordinary shop would be prepared to exclude the young and put up warning notices, and if a shop was prepared to go to these lengths, this adequately secured protection for the young and those who did not wish to partake of such materials.

A final aspect of restriction is whether prevention of offence should be taken further, in the sense of the zoning of such shops, or at least of the imposition of a requirement that they preserve blank windows. This takes one back to the question of gratuitous offence: can it be said that a shop selling restricted material causes such offence (a) by reason of having window displays; and/or (b) by its siting? As far as window displays are concerned, the committee argues that such premises should 'maintain a discreet existence and not display in their windows similar but slightly less offensive material: the best course, we believe, is for any such shop not to be allowed any window displays at all, but to present a blank exterior, subject only to the display of its name and the nature of its business'.[3] Any public displays, in say a shop window, would be covered by the standard recommended in terms of the protection of children: nothing offensive could legally appear in such a display. One can probably avoid any questions of how far offensiveness may justify restriction in terms of a demand for blank windows, moreover, in that any shop with such windows is, if anything, more conspicuous, and often appears seedier and more subterranean than other-

---

1   *Williams* para 9.11.

2   Ibid. para 9.16.

3   Ibid. para 4.15.

wise. With the greatest respect, this particular suggestion appears a little absurd.

The question of zoning is rather different: one's answer here must depend on just how far one is prepared to take offensiveness as a justification for restriction. The question is much the same as that in relation to offensiveness caused by the presence of offensive material in a shop, albeit that such material is cased between innocuous covers. If one is prepared to justify the segregation of such material in separate shops, then the zoning of such shops must itself be in the balance. What one is asking here is whether the offence caused by the presence of such shops in particular localities justifies this type of restriction. The offensiveness involved is perhaps rather more extensive than might at first be apparent, as has been the case with the Wolfenden Committee recommendations as to prostitution and soliciting. These drew the offence line at public soliciting, and allow prostitutes (aside from considerations of brothel-keeping) to ply their trade indoors without restriction. Such trade often involves offence, and harm to surrounding, particularly residential, areas. To be weighed against such considerations, if relevant to restricted shops, is principally freedom of speech, a factor which assumes particular weight as zoning restrictions almost certainly constitute a prior restraint. The American Supreme Court in *Young* v *American Mini Theaters*, it is true, took the view that such restrictions do not constitute prior restraints, being constitutional in terms of legitimate town planning aims. Such an approach is perhaps a dangerous one for freedom of speech, as it opens the way to a number of restrictions (as opposed to prohibitions) being found — in American terms — constitutional, possibly without a proper weighing or balancing of interests. *Young* is probably best seen in terms of the Court's difficulties over the First Amendment and the exception approach to obscenity. Taking zoning as a prior restraint, both it and the issues mentioned above will be considered later in conjunction with other such restraints.[1]

To sum up, the restraint recommended above appears justified in policy terms: in other words, in terms of the balancing of competing interests. It is not a perfect world, and therefore no interest can be completely satisfied, but this restriction, taken with the restriction in favour of minors, appears to effect a reasonable balance. The restriction would be on the display or holding for sale of material (other than that consisting solely of the written word) whose unrestricted availability is patently offensive to reasonable people in terms of their own susceptibilities by reason of the manner in which it portrays, deals with or relates to violence, cruelty or horror, or sexual faecal or urinary

---

1   Chapter 7.

functions or genital organs, other than in premises (or a part of premises having a separate access from the street):

- (a) to which persons under the age of eighteen are not admitted; and
- (b) to which access is possible only by passing a prominent warning notice in specified terms.

II)   Live shows

1)   *The Theatres Act 1968*

Theatre[1] in England and Wales was until very recently the subject of prior, rather than subsequent restraint: a royal proclamation of 1551 laid down that no play was to be performed without a licence from the Master of Revels, an office held under the Lord Chamberlain. Restraint here paralleled that on written material: licensing was employed as a mechanism of control, its aim being principally to suppress blasphemy and sedition, at this stage intertwined concepts. In 1843 a new Theatres Act consolidated the Lord Chamberlain's powers to prohibit the performance of any stage play (or any scene therefrom) for as long as he deemed necessary 'whenever he shall be of the opinion that it is fitting for the preservation of good manners, decorum or of the public peace so to do'. Control was firmly in terms of public morality, or at least the Lord Chamberlain's view of it. The Lord Chamberlain operated, for example, a broad definition of indecency, involving the excision of all vernacular references to intercourse, genitalia, birth control and venereal disease. The rules for stage dress were fixed in 1930:

- A. Actresses in movement must not wear less than briefs and an opaque controlling brassiere.
- B. Actresses may pose completely nude provided: the pose is motionless and expressionless. The pose is artistic and something rather more than a mere display of nakedness. The lighting must be subdued.[2]

Although little opposition to this stifling burden of censorship was over the years forthcoming from commercial management, the Royal Shakespeare Company, state-subsidised, and with no profits at stake, launched an all-out attack after a licence was refused to *US* on

---

1   For a resumé of the history of theatre censorship, see R. Findlater *Banned! — A Review of Theatrical Censorship in Britain* (London 1967).

2   G. Robertson *Obscenity* (London 1979) at 247.

the ground that it was 'beastly, anti-American, and left-wing'.[1] Theatre clubs regarded themselves as beyond the reach of licensing requirements: in 1966, however, a London theatre was convicted under the 1843 Act for just such a club performance of Edward Bond's *Saved*.[2] 'It followed from this decision that no word could be uttered on any stage without the Lord Chamberlain's prior approval, and even ad-libbing by an actor who had forgotten his lines was technically an offence'.[3] Disquiet resulted eventually in the 1966 Joint Committee on Theatre Censorship. On the issue of prior restraint, the committee was clear in its disapproval:

> Attendance at theatre is a voluntary act, usually decided upon after more conscious thought than going to the cinema or turning on the television ... it is better that an individual should have the right to decide with full knowledge, what sort of play he wishes to see than that some central authority should attempt to lay down what is suitable for the 'average person'.[4]

The standard exercised here by the Lord Chamberlain would appear to have been similar to that applicable in terms of outraging public decency: the restraint of indecency in a public place ('public' including any area to which the public are admitted whether on payment of a fee or not). If there is a distinction between corruption of public morals and outraging public decency in the sense of the latter involving merely an affront to, rather than a corruption of positive morality, it was the lower standard which was being applied here. The committee appear to favour this, in the sense of emphasising the question of gratuitous offence, or the public element, something which has been devalued, at least in the case of outraging public decency. If individual choice is to be emphasised, no controls are necessary beyond the control of such offence.

Not so, however: the committee, besides recommending the abolition of prior restraint, favoured subjecting the theatre to obscenity law control. Such controls would apply, however, only to 'public' performances, defined to include any performance 'which the public or any section thereof are permitted to attend, whether on payment or otherwise', and any performance held in a 'public place', as defined in the

---

1   Robertson op.cit. at 249.

2   Robertson op.cit.

3   Ibid.

4   Report of Joint Committee on Censorship of the Theatre (HMSO 1967) at xiii.

Public Order Act 1936, namely

> ... any highway, public park or garden, any sea beach, and any public bridge, road, lane, footway, square, court, alley or passage, whether a thoroughfare or not; and includes any open space to which, for the time being, the public are permitted to have access, whether on payment or otherwise.[1]

This covers[2] street and open-air theatres, 'end-of-pier' shows, and probably performances in restaurants,[3] public houses,[4] buses and railway carriages,[5] and perhaps boats on public hire.[6] It would not apply to performances 'given solely or primarily' for the purposes of rehearsal, or for the making of a cinema film or to television or sound productions;[7] a performance staged principally for recording, filming or broadcasting is not covered, even though 'a large audience is invited to supply appropriate applause'.[8] As far as previews of plays are concerned, these would not be accepted as rehearsals 'if tickets are issued to the public, albeit at a reduced rate'.[9] Such controls would clearly not apply to performances given in private dwellings, as these would fall outside the definitions of 'public' above, unless members of the public were admitted on payment, for example. Thus the old emphasis in the law on the 'public' nature of performances was to be preserved, even though this had never been of specific concern with obscenity law: the fact that distribution in terms of the 1959 Act takes place in private in no way affects liability. This concession may have been made in terms of privacy,[10] although this is not specifically alluded to. Alternatively, theatre controls were to be somewhat anoma-

---

1 Theatres Act 1968, S18, and Public Order Act 1936, S9.

2 See Robertson op.cit. at 252.

3 *R v Hockhauser* [1964] 47 WWR 350; *R v Bensen* [1928] 3 WWR 605; quoted in Robertson op.cit.

4 *R v Mayling* [1963] 2 All ER 687.

5 *R v Holmes* (1853) Dears CC 207; *Languish v Archer* (1882) 10 QBD 44.

6 Brownlie *The Law Relating to Public Order* (London 1968) at 61.

7 Theatres Act 1968, S7.

8 Robertson op.cit. at 252.

9 Ibid.

10 On privacy considerations, see chapter 5; such private performances are still subject to the common law via Section 7(1), which excludes the Section 2(4) exclusion in relation to them.

alous, at least in this regard. The committee's recommendations were embodied virtually as they stood in the Theatre Act 1968. The 1843 Act was repealed, and with it prior restraint; obscenity became the sole basis of control:

> a performance of a play shall be deemed to be obscene if, taken as a whole, its effect was such as to deprave and corrupt persons who were likely, having regard to all relevant circumstances, to attend it.[1]

Prior restraint may still be exercised in the form of licensing, but the licensing authority may not refuse a licence to a theatre on the basis of the nature of a play or the manner of its performance.[2] It may, however, take into account safety and health considerations,[3] or 'any condition regulating or prohibiting the giving of an exhibition, demonstration or performance of hypnotism within the meaning of the Hypnotism Act 1952'. Obscenity is the sole basis of control: Section 2(4) of the Act specifically excludes the common law, including common law conspiracy; this does not, of course, apply to statutory conspiracy. In addition, Section 1 offences under the Indecent Displays (Control) Act 1981 have been excluded as to the theatre.[4] Although the Section 2(4) exclusion applies to the common law only, and although statute law other than the 1981 Act would therefore be applicable, the committee's recommendations as to the incitement of racial hatred, and provocation of breaches of the peace have been specifically embodied in the Act: Sections 5(1) and 6(1) make provision for liability for anyone who, whether for gain or not, presented or directed any performance either with the intention of inciting racial hatred or provoking a breach of the peace, or where the performance, taken as a whole, was reasonably likely to have such a result. The Act applies of course to stage 'plays', defined as:

> (a) any dramatic piece, whether involving improvisation or not, which is given wholly or in part by one or more persons actually present and performing and in

---

1 Section 2(1).

2 Section 1(2).

3 Ibid.

4 Indecent Displays (Control Act) 1981, Section 1(4)(d). The 1981 Act repeals that portion of Section 4 of the Vagrancy Act 1824 relating to indecent displays, and in turn repeals Section 2(4)(b) of the Theatres Act 1968, which had prevented prosecutions under Section 2(4)(b) of the 1824 Act in relation to the theatre. The 1981 Act, in repealing virtually all existing statutory provisions relating to indecent displays, has ensured the theatre's insulation from indecent displays provisions as such.

which the whole or a major proportion of what is done by the person or persons performing, whether by way of speech, singing or acting, involves the playing of a role; and

(b) any ballet given wholly or in part by one or more persons actually present or performing, whether or not it falls within paragraph (a) of this definition.

The requirement of role–playing would appear to exclude the stand–up comedian, unless his act involves actually playing various characters in sketches for example;[1] in the same way, most variety shows would seem to be excluded. Just what is covered by the term 'ballet' is less than clear: subsection (b) merely excludes the general requirement of role–playing. The closest guidance is the *Oxford English Dictionary* definition of ballet as the 'combined performance of professional dancers on the stage'. Any decision here would at present be one of fact for the jury, and one likely to involve some difficulty. Is tribal dancing, for example, ballet? The Law Commission's view is that tribal dancing could not be classed as ballet, nor could ballroom or discothèque performances, even when staged by professional dancers.[2]

Controls closely parallel those imposed under the 1959 Act; certain distinctions can however be drawn.

1) Section 3(1) of the 1968 Act provides a defence of public good: a performance may be justified as being for the public good 'on the ground that it was in the interest of drama, opera, ballet, or any other art, or of literature or learning'. The defence relates to the 'giving of a performance' of the play, and not to the play itself. Thus 'pedestrian writing may be redeemed by the excellence of acting, direction or choreography'.[3]

2) Expert evidence is provided for by Section 3(2). A practical difficulty posed by the legislation is that the expert may not have seen the performance in question; Section 9 provides that the script shall be admissible 'as evidence of what was performed and of the manner in which the performance ... was given'. Such experts may then testify by reference to the script.

3) The relevant act here — publication, under the 1959 Act — is, whether for gain or not, to have 'presented or directed' an obscene performance. Section 18(2) provides that 'a person shall be taken to

---

1 Robertson *op.cit.* at 251.

2 Report on Conspiracy and Criminal Law Reform (Law Commission Report No. 76, 1976) para 93.

3 Ibid. at 253.

have directed a performance of a play given under his direction notwithstanding that he was not present during the performance'. The essence is that the director should have directed the performance in question, and provided this is the case, he will be liable even though his association with the play may have ended. In some cases liability may be clear: in *R v Brownson*[1] the defendants quite obviously both presented and directed the play, in that they commissioned the script, employed the cast, directed the actors, and managed and promoted the show. In *Grade v DPP*,[2] however, it was at issue whether a promoter had 'presented' a play with unlicensed dialogue; the unlicensed words had been put in without his knowledge, nor was he negligent in relation to their inclusion. He was held liable, a holding which appears to apply strict liability. Thus the standard as far as intention is concerned may well be far more stringent than under the 1959 Act, and may involve strict liability as to the presentation, as well as its obscene nature. Actors are not normally liable at all, but where they depart from the script, they become liable as their own directors as it were, provided the deviation was without reasonable excuse;[3] whether this excuses the director or not, is not clear. It would appear from all this that playwrights are liable only for their publication of obscene scripts. The performance of the play is not an 'article' within the 1959 Act, nor would they normally direct or act in their own productions.

4) The 1959 Act does not penalise possession of prescribed material unless it is with regard to publication for gain. In much the same way, the 1968 Act exempts (although this exemption may be seen more as the removal of a protection than anything else, in that it permits the operation of often draconian common law measures) performances in private dwellings. This exception, together with that under the 1959 Act, appear to be privacy based;[4] such exceptions serve to weaken the rationale for prohibition: if not merely possession, but as here (in effect) distribution, is to be exempted, the law would appear to be acknowledging that the harms justifying prohibition are outweighed by considerations of individual freedom. It is difficult to see that a harm is any more threatening when occasioned to a voluntary audience in a theatre, as opposed to one in a private dwelling. This would certainly not be the case with, say, the possession of firearms.

---

1   [1971] *Crim L Rev* 551.

2   [1942] 2 All ER 118; a case under the 1842 Act.

3   Section 18(2).

4   On privacy and its relevance in this area, see pp.159–166.

The reasoning here is to an extent speculative, as the exception under the 1968 Act may have been made with the intention that the common law should apply, and continue to apply. The Law Commission, in recommending the abolition of the older common law offences in this area, felt constrained to consider the exception of theatrical performances in private dwellings, as Section 7(1) of the 1968 Act specifically provides that the exclusion of the common law should not be effective in relation to such performances. Common law offences in other words, are the sole regulatory provisions in this regard. The commission, although it based its report on such common law offences principally on an assessment of whether alternative controls already existed, in this instance endorsed an absence of control in relation to such performances, provided no one under the age of sixteen was present, and provided no charge was made for admission. The recommendations, which raise problems of policy, have not been implemented, probably in anticipation of Williams.

2) *Law reform*

The Law Commission, in recommending the abolition of common law offences in this area, isolated the control of live shows as a potential lacuna should abolition be carried through. They did not have occasion to examine theatre controls, as there was already control, in terms of the 1968 Act. They felt that some control was required in relation to live shows, principally on the basis of threats to public order resulting from the more extreme manifestations of such entertainment.[1] They therefore, in view of their recommendation of abolition of common law offences, proposed a control over live shows in terms of obscenity. This proposal, again probably in anticipation of Williams, has not been implemented.

The type of control imposed in terms of the Theatres Act and in terms of the obscenity control recommended by the Law Commission, is clearly a prohibition rather than a restriction. Such a prohibition does not appear to have anything to do with gratuitous offence or any invasion of privacy, nor does it necessarily concern the protection of children. Any harms which may justify a general prohibition would therefore be relevant: these will be considered later, together with any relevance they have here.[2] Leaving this aside, are any restrictions viable in terms of the harms discussed in the last two chapters, and are there

---

1   Law Commission Report No. 76 op.cit.; as to the commission's recommendation on the common law, see p.72ff.

2   Chapter 15.

any harm considerations specifically relevant in this area, perhaps in prohibition terms? What is clearly of relevance here in terms of restriction is the protection of the young. Were the standard recommended earlier in this regard to be applied, it would clearly cover any displays outside theatres or places of entertainment; this presumably would include the activity of touts? What is more pertinent though, is whether such considerations have any bearing on activity inside a theatre or premises in question. The reasoning applied in this regard with respect to the interiors of shops would seem equally applicable: segregation is clearly irrelevant here, but just as it was proposed that the distribution of certain material to the young should be prohibited, there would seem no reason why the same should not operate here. Any purveying of entertainment in premises unrestricted as far as the young are concerned of material unsuitable for them, would be an offence. This is in scope much the same as the recommendation made by Williams:[1] the difference lies in the latter's employment of a composite standard of offence to adults, such offence being judged in terms of what a reasonable adult deems suitable for children. As has been argued, this is too restrictive as far as adults are concerned; hence the recommended standard as to children. In these terms it would be an offence to present any live entertainment unsuitable for the young, other than in premises (or a part of premises having a separate access from the street) to which persons under the age of eighteen are not admitted.

Should this protection for the young apply even within the home? As we have seen, possession is not covered under the 1959 Obscene Publications Acts, whilst the Theatre Act 1968 does not extend to private dwellings; privacy considerations have presumably been instrumental in this. The Law Commission in recommending the removal of common law offences, did not recommend that any new coverage was necessary in relation to theatrical performances in private dwellings; this they qualified by adding the proviso that no one under the age of eighteen should be present. Williams has followed this recommendation, in that live entertainment caught in terms of the restriction they propose would not be exempt merely because it took place in a private dwelling. In terms of the protection of children, this seems a sensible result.

The next question is the applicability of the restrictions proposed earlier for the protection of adults from gratuitous offence caused them in terms of their own sensitivities. The standard proposed would appear equally applicable, *mutatis mutandis*, here; thus it would be an offence to present a performance which a reasonable person found

---

[1] *Williams* para 11.8.

patently offensive on the grounds specified, unless that performance took place in premises (or a part of premises having a separate access from the street) and to which access was permitted only by passing a warning notice in specified terms.

Is there any harm consideration of particular relevance here, which justifies control beyond this? The Williams Committee reported a general lack of concern as to live entertainment, a fact which they attributed to its not being a mass medium. Live entertainment concerns mainly adults, and only a few of them, has to be 'created anew for each performance', no performance 'impinging on more than a tiny fraction of the population'; 'even places where performances can be given are more rarely encountered than shops or cinemas'.[1] It was also felt that those presenting such entertainment, because they realised it probably has a greater impact on its audience than a publication might have, tended therefore to be more wary of transgressing the law. It is, in fact, the question of the impact of such entertainment which the committee emphasised: such entertainment involves the audience actually —

> ... *being in the same space as* people actually engaged in sexual conduct ... the live show is a contemporary happening with an unknown future end, which the audience may be capable of influencing or in which they might participate. It is no longer, as with all other pornography, a matter of fantasy.[2]

The possibility of audience participation may raise public order problems, and the committee noted that the Danish authorities had in fact encountered problems of this sort in relation to live sex shows. The committee was therefore decidedly of the view that such shows should be subject to an additional prohibition. A factor backing up the public order dimension is the fact that such shows may well be presented on licensed premises: the drinking of alcohol in such circumstances can reasonably be taken to add to concern about the maintenance of public order.

A further factor which one may adduce in any justification equation here is the distinction between conduct and speech. As was pointed out earlier,[3] this is a distinction drawn by the American Supreme Court, and is one which has been roughly followed in this work: not everyone would necessarily agree with this delineation, but a line has to

---

1   *Williams* para 11.2.

2   Ibid. para 11.4; emphasis in the original.

3   See substantive common law offences, chapter 3.

be drawn somewhere in terms of the ambit of censorship, our concern here. Although some conduct is clearly expression, to widen one's inquiry to cover freedom of expression as opposed to freedom of speech would be to invite an already daunting inquiry to become quite unmanageable. The line is therefore drawn at speech; this is not always an easy demarcation to make: although theatre and ballet, for example, would (probably) generally be accepted as speech, questions have been raised as to, for example, tribal dancing. A case which brought this issue squarely before the United States Supreme Court was *California v La Rue*:[1] at issue here was the state's power to make the grant of a liquor licence dependent upon the type of entertainment offered in bars and night clubs. The state's target was to put an end to 'bottomless' dancing in such resorts. The Court upheld state power on the basis of a distinction between speech and conduct. It is a question of fact which predominates, speech or conduct; provided it is the latter and provided the restriction imposed on speech is the least restrictive alternative available, the control falls outside the reach of the First Amendment. Prior restraint is therefore not an issue, whilst standards other than obscenity may be employed.

Although demarcation lines may often be difficult to draw, the distinction between speech and conduct probably rests on a fundamental consideration in relation to the importance of freedom of speech: conduct does not generally to the same extent involve advocacy of opinion, and its control does not therefore threaten a basic rationale of the First Amendment. Thus, accepting difficulties of demarcation, live shows involving conduct rather than speech not only fall outside this inquiry; they may also be more susceptible to control, in the sense of individual freedom of speech not being so pressing a concern. Williams took the view that any presentation involving actual sex activity could be excluded from 'theatre': 'What artistic or dramatic requirements do not involve is the performance of real sexual activity; it seems to us, in fact, that the presentation of actual sex on the stage immediately introduces a presumption that the motives no longer have any artistic pretention'.[2] This seems very close to the speech/conduct distinction above, although the committee may well have a better basis of distinction than one drawn in terms of 'theatre', 'ballet', and so on. Their view that *actual* conduct moves the presentation effectively into the conduct area seems reasonable: it would of course justify control of what might be argued to be theatre, without any provision of a public good defence. Such a defence would not seem necessary: where

---

1   409 US 109 (1972); see chapter 12.

2   *Williams* para 11.10.

one deals with actual sexual activity, one has to do with conduct and not speech, whilst theatre 'proper' (although no public good defence would be provided in terms of the offence to adults control) would be subject only to a restriction of the type imposed on displays or shops generally.

If such a prohibition is justified, its justification would seem to rest principally on as clear a distinction as possible between speech and conduct, as it is the conduct which raises public order fears, and has less claim to freedom of speech justifications. The committee has suggested a distinction in terms of 'sexual activity'. As they point out however, kissing is a sexual activity. Should one then opt for the list approach rejected earlier in relation to the adult offence restriction, or should some general standard be devised? The committee recommend a general standard: a performance should be prohibited if it 'involves actual sexual activity of a kind which, in the circumstances in which it is given, would be offensive to reasonable adults; and for the avoidance of doubt, sexual activity should include the act of masturbation and forms of genital, anal or oral connection between humans and animals as well as between humans; or ... involves the sexual exploitation of any person under the age of sixteen'.[1] To deal with this in reverse order, the last provision as to children appears unnecessary: existing law covers virtually every exigency, and any shortfall would best be covered by amendment of, or revamping of, existing law on sexual conduct with minors. This would avoid any difficulties as to prior restraints; the recommendations as to prohibiting the use of children in the production of pornography would be equally applicable here.[2] The limited listing of what 'sexual activity' should include seems sensible, although clearly it must be coupled with a general standard. The committee has selected one of offence. This runs contrary to most of the reasoning over the last two chapters. One is not concerned here with gratuitous offence, as the audience is a voluntary one. To base one's prohibition on offence is to extend offence beyond gratuitous offence; this is to enforce positive morality in a primary sense. It seems unrealistic to apply the offence standard of the reasonable person to the type of performance and situation which he or she would be most unlikely ever to witness. The committee argues that their logic here is 'simple': *prohibitions* on sexual activity in public are justified on the basis of offensiveness, as are *restrictions* on the depiction of sexual activity, if such depiction is offensive. They argue that this can be applied here: simulated sexual activity would be *restricted* on the basis of offence, and

---

[1] *Williams* para 11.15.

[2] See chapter 7.

actual sexual activity *prohibited* on the same grounds. The point here is that offence—based sexual activity controls operate generally in terms of public decency, and impose a restriction when such activity takes place in public; the offensiveness line may be drawn in terms of whether the offence is gratuitous or not. The committee wish to regard the interior of such premises as stage such shows as 'public', despite warning notices, for example; this is the very 'vice' from which much of the law at present suffers.

Would it not be far better to stick to the primary concern here: the preservation of public order. It would in these terms be an offence to present the type of sexual activity described above in circumstances in which a reasonable person might apprehend a breach of the peace. This would maintain the existing links between controls in this area and existing public order restrictions; provided the conduct classification recommended above were allowed, constitutionality in First Amendment terms would seem assured. A last point here is whether the prohibition should extend within the home; in terms of privacy considerations, it would perhaps best be excluded, other than in relation to those under eighteen years of age.

A final consideration here is whether a system of prior restraint would be in any way justifiable or preferable. As a censorship mechanism, licensing has been excluded from application to the theatre. It would appear to have a limited application to places of live entertainment, in terms, for example, of the Greater London Council's restricting establishments providing public music and dancing in terms of the admission of the young. These questions will be examined, together with other prior restraints, in the next chapter.[1]

---

1 Pp.296—7.

7 Prior restraint in UK

Freedom of speech is constitutionally protected in the United States, principally by the First Amendment to the Constitution. Is its position in English law in any way equivalent? As was remarked at the beginning of this work, the United Kingdom does not have a written constitution: there is therefore no equivalent constitutional right in this regard. What one may more properly speak of is a civil 'liberty' in this respect. As Professor Glanville Williams has said: 'A liberty means any occasion on which an act of omission is not a breach of duty. ... A right exists where there is positive law on the subject; a liberty where there is no law against it. A right is correlative to a duty in another, which a liberty is not'.[1] As one of these liberties, freedom of speech is of primary importance in philosophical terms;[2] this is not to say that it does not have a constitutional dimension also. This is not the place to explore the early recognition of this: suffice it to say that such recognition had, by the early eighteenth century, been clearly enunciated by influential legal commentators.[3] The philosophical importance of such liberty is widely recognised by Anglo/American writers in jurisprudence, either as a factor to be balanced against one or other harm, or with a

---

1   See 'The Concept of Liberty' in R.S. Summers (ed.) *Essays in Legal Philosophy* (London 1970); Paul O'Higgins *Cases and Materials on Civil Liberties* (London 1980) at 2.

2   See chapter 4.

3   For example, William Blackstone; see *Commentaries*, vol.4, at 151–2.

213

rights theory, as a primary interest which the state may protect from infringement. Although such discussion is not generally related to Bills of Rights or questions of constitutionality, the link is quite obvious: as has been pointed out,[1] a certain framework is necessary for the development and existence of these very philosophies. This is Mill's view, a view which spans the gap between the philosophical and more concrete constitutional spheres. This is the very basis of government in the United Kingdom: the entire constitution rests on the assumption that the people are sufficiently informed to elect representatives to carry forward their wishes in government.

Having said that the constitutional sphere is a more concrete one, one is confronted with the apparent anomaly that nowhere is such liberty to be found in anything like an officially recognised form. The constitution is an unwritten one, and one must therefore look to the pronouncements of commentators and of the courts. Perhaps the most influential of the former, Professor Dicey, although he was strongly opposed to a Bill of Rights, regarding, perhaps correctly at the time, collective residual liberties (as safeguarded by the courts) as being more than adequate, was in no doubt as to the fundamental importance of freedom of speech.[2] Every leading textbook on constitutional law today carries the same emphasis.[3] Nor have the courts been silent: although they cannot, and perhaps might in any event not wish to, assert a right to free speech, its importance has been recognised in a growing number of judicial pronouncements over the years. Lord Wilberforce, delivering the majority opinion in the recent House of Lords decision that journalists do not have a general immunity based on the public interest when ordered by a court of law to disclose their sources in the interests of justice, was nonetheless in no doubt as to the importance of freedom of the press; Lord Justice Salmon (dissenting) remarked that

> a free press was one of the pillars of freedom in this and any other democratic country. A free press reported matters of general public importance and could not, in law, be under any obligation, save in exceptional circumstances, to disclose the identity of the persons who supplied

---

1   See R. McKeon, R. Merton, W. Gelhorn *The Freedom to Read* (New York 1957) chapter 1.

2   A.V. Dicey *An Introduction to the Study of the Constitution* (10th edn, London 1965) at 251.

3   E.C.S. Wade and C.T. Phillips *Constitutional and Administrative Law* (9th edn, A.W. Bradley, London 1977) at 465.

it with information.[1]

Censorship, or restraint of the free interchange of ideas and information,[2] has then a clearly accepted constitutional dimension. Censorship itself was for many years however seen as pre-publication restraint; where there was no such restraint, there was no censorship:

> The liberty of the press is indeed essential to the nature of a free state; but this consists of laying no *previous* restraints upon publications, and not in freedom from censure for criminal matter, published. Every free man has an undoubted right to lay what sentiments he pleases before the public; to forbid this, is to destroy the freedom of the press; but if he publishes what is improper, mischievous or illegal, he must take the consequences of his own temerity.[3]

Although a much broader view is generally taken today of censorship, so as to include restraints both subsequent and prior to publication, the early identification of censorship with prior restraint is probably a reflection of the particular concern which the latter evokes. The reason for this is obvious: in its more extreme forms, such restraint is a mechanism of repression in most totalitarian states. Decisions are taken administratively, are not necessarily open to debate, nor are they necessarily subject to judicial review. As Blackstone remarked, if energetically pressed, their effect would be — operating as they do prior to publication — to destroy the freedom of the press altogether, and to enforce the withering of thought, debate and intellectual activity and criticism generally. This is, of course, to carry prior restraints to extremes: it does not follow that judiciously formulated and applied, such restraints may not provide a sustainable weapon in the lawmaker's armoury. It is clear though that any such restraint would need to be justifiable in policy and constitutional terms; freedom of speech assumes, in the light of the latter, a particular importance, whilst the nature of the restraint can serve only to add further weight to the freedom side of the scale.

The early identification in England of censorship with prior restraint was mirrored in the United States.[4] By the early eighteenth

---

1 *British Steel Corporation* v *Granada Television Ltd*, *The Times* (Law Report) 7 November 1980.

2 See Paul O'Higgins *Censorship in Britain* (London 1972).

3 W. Blackstone op.cit.

4 See chapter 12.

century the licensing laws had broken down,[1] whilst there can be no doubt that the First Amendment, which gives clear constitutional substance to freedom of speech, was aimed at outlawing prior restraints. It was in fact argued that the Amendment (in Blackstonian terms) precluded *only* prior restraints;[2] it was only in 1919 that the Amendment was held to cover subsequent as well as prior restraints.[3] A casual observer might well, in these terms, have presumed that if the Amendment did clearly prohibit anything, that was prior restraints. This was more or less the conclusion that the Supreme Court came to in the first major case on the issue, *Near* v *Minnesota*, in 1931.[4] The 'more or less' here involved what the Court categorised as exceptional cases; in exemplifying such cases the Court listed the conduct of war, incitement to violence, and obscenity. The growth area for prior restraints, both at the time and subsequently, was obscenity: a number of prior restraints — both state and federal — were in operation at the time, such as post office and customs regulation, film censorship and book and magazine regulation; their numbers increased subsequently. In relation to them the Court has since *Near* fashioned a complex prior restraint doctrine, a doctrine which allows as constitutional carefully tailored restraints of this sort on the basis that they are, theoretically at least, not prior restraints at all. The basic obscenity exception approach to the First Amendment has proven particularly useful in this regard: the reasoning runs that because obscenity is an exception to the Amendment, material properly determined to be obscene is not protected, and therefore pre-publication restraint of it is not a prior restraint at all; the latter doctrine has validity after all only in terms of the First Amendment.

Attention has centred on just what, besides due criminal process, constitutes a proper form of assessment as far as obscenity is concerned. It took the Court thirty-four years to reach anything like a comprehensive verdict in this respect: in *Freedman* v *Maryland*[5] the Court determined that a final restraint can only be imposed by judicial process. Progress towards such determination must be speedy, and the burden of initiating judicial review and of proving obscenity lies on the censor,

---

1   Clyde Duriway *The Development of Freedom of the Press in Massachusetts* (1906) chapters 1–5; cited in T. Emerson 'The Doctrine of Prior Restraint' 20 (1955) *Law and Contemp. Probs.* 648 at 651, footnote 12.

2   See Zachariah Chafee *Free Speech in the United States* (New York 1941) pp. 9–12.

3   In *Shenck* v *United States* 249 US 47 (1919).

4   283 US 697 (1931); see chapter 12.

5   380 US 57 (1965).

and not the owner of the materials. Any *temporary* restraint prior to a final decision must be designed only to preserve the *status quo*. This did not appear to affect the requirement already laid down by the Court in relation to search and seizure provisions,[1] that a temporary restraint should be prefaced by a preliminary *adversary*[2] hearing, although the requirement was not included as such.

As will be argued,[3] the exception approach to obscenity is badly flawed. Were it to be abandoned, the entire structure outlined above is suspect, and it must seem doubtful whether the Court would justify prior restraints in terms of the First Amendment rights of adults. Prior restraint measures may well affect children, however, and might well be justified in terms of the rights of minors, for example. These questions will be examined both below and in their American context.[4]

We turn now to the various prior restraint structures in this area in England and Wales, and the standards in terms of which they operate. Their justifiability must depend to a large extent on the justifiability of the type of subsequent restraint they very often complement; it is proposed in this regard to consider just what in the way of prior restraints would seem justified in relation to the restrictions on speech recommended in chapters 5 and 6. The question of the justification of the type of prior restraint that would stand or fall on the same terms as would a general prohibition, will be considered in the final chapter. A number of restraints, such as the production of pornography and customs controls, will be considered individually; for the rest, discussion will be in terms of the varieties of speech to which the various forms of prior restraint relate.

I Prior restraints

1) *The production of pornography*

(i) *Children.* The publication of material which is corruptive of the young is covered by both the 1959 Obscene Publications Act, and the 1955 Harmful Publications measure. The former covers material dealing with sexuality, drug-taking and/or violence, and covers distribution particular to the young, or general distribution, provided the young form a significant proportion of the assessed audience. The latter covers comic

---

1 See e.g. *A Quantity of Books* v *Kansas* 378 US 205 (1964).

2 As opposed to an *ex parte* hearing.

3 Chapter 14.

4 See chapter 14.

book material, dealing with violence, and perhaps sexuality and drug-taking also; it is sufficient if the most susceptible child in the audience, whether distribution is particular or general, is affected.

In addition to these censorship measures on speech, additional coverage is provided, as the Law Commission pointed out,[1] in relation to indecent conduct with children. Section 1(1) of the Indecency with Children Act 1960 provides that 'Any person who commits an act of gross indecency with or towards a child under the age of fourteen, or who incites a child under that age to such an act with him, shall be liable on conviction on indictment to imprisonment...'. In considering the abolition of common law offences such as conspiracy to corrupt public morals, the Law Commission proceeded largely on the basis of whether the conduct in question was already covered by one or other statutory provision. The three areas of importance which the commission felt might not be adequately covered were live shows, films and the protection of children. Films are now statutorily covered by the 1959 Act, and will be examined later in this chapter; live shows have been considered earlier; one is left, therefore, with children. The Law Commission's concern about lack of coverage in the latter regard centred on technical difficulties with Section 1(1) of the Indecency with Children Act 1961, particularly the phrase 'with or towards'. This arguably excludes sessions in which a child is photographed in provocative poses: provided there is no physical contact with, and no indecent action on the part of the photographer and/or procurer, then the taking of photographs may not fall within the definition 'an act of gross indecency with or towards a child'. The Court of Appeal has suggested that the provision would cover 'an act ... which takes place in an indecent situation'.[2] Doubt remains whether the taking of photographs can be seen as an act 'with or towards' a child, and second, whether the indecency of the situation can convert the *prima facie* innocent act of taking pictures into an act of 'gross indecency'.

A further possible loophole exists in Section 1(1) of the 1960 Act, in that it does not apply to children aged fourteen to fifteen. Children of this age cannot consent to indecent assault; provided the photographer does not touch or threaten them in an indecent manner, the photography of such children falls outside Section 1(1). The Law Commission proposed the abolition of conspiracy to corrupt public morals, which would cover such conduct. Some control was felt to be necessary, and the commission therefore proposed a simple amendment to the 1960 Act, substituting 'under sixteen' for 'under fourteen'. This

---

1   Law Commission Report on Conspiracy and Law Reform (1976).

2   *R v Sutton* [1977] 1 WLR 1086 at 1089.

would not cover the first of the loopholes pointed out above. A possibility here might be to follow the lead given by the Court of Appeal in this regard, and provide specifically that the indecency or otherwise of the conduct of the accused person — say in photographing a child — should be judged in terms of its context; most jurors would presumably find the taking of pictures of children in suggestive poses offensive to standards of propriety. Filming might be specifically included as potentially an act 'towards' a child.

The result of this avenue of reform would have been to ensure that the law in this respect concerned itself with conduct, and not speech. Although a child in an indecent pose could at a stretch be argued to be expressing him/herself, an accommodation of such activity as conduct rather than speech might be made without too much difficulty. But once the prohibition is extended to cover the production of some form of speech portraying the conduct in question one is then faced with a censorship provision. One is after all here concerned not with the effect of the photographs, or the viewing, on the cameraman, or indeed anyone else, but rather with the protection of the child who is the subject of such attentions. One wishes to prevent him/her from engaging in such conduct, and any prohibition would best be linked as closely to that conduct as possible, thereby hopefully excluding censorship considerations.

Subsequent to the Law Commission Report in 1976, considerable public disquiet began to mount as to child pornography. Semi-hysteria, to an extent fanned by the national press,[1] produced a major legislative drive. The result was the Protection of Children Act 1978. Unfortunately, possibly as a result of the campaign leading up to its passage, the Act did not follow the avenue suggested by the Law Commission. Rather, Section 1 of the Act makes it an offence, punishable summarily by six months' imprisonment or a fine of £1,000, or on indictment by up to three years' imprisonment and/or an unlimited fine, for anyone

  (a) to take, or permit to be taken, any indecent photograph of a child (meaning in this Act a person under the age of 16); or
  (b) to distribute or show such indecent photographs; or
  (c) to have in his possession such indecent photographs, with a view to their being distributed or shown by himself or others; or
  (d) to publish or cause to be published any advertisement likely to be understood as conveying that the advertiser

---

1 See e.g. *The Times*, 6 February 1976.

>   distributes or shows such indecent photographs, or
>   intends to do so.

The provision as to the taking of such photographs is arguably a prior restraint: it is as much a prior restraint to make the production of a film an offence, as it is to require a licence for either its production and/or publication. Freedom of speech considerations must weigh very heavily against the acceptance of prior restraints of any sort, particularly where this variety of restraint might have been avoided by a difference of emphasis in the drafting of the offence. It is true that one might wish, even had one couched the offence to avoid any prior restraint, to prohibit the distribution of such materials: censorship considerations would not be altogether evaded in other words. One would, however, as with the present section, distribution prohibition,[1] be dealing with a subsequent, and not a prior restraint; the measure would be an adjunct to the control of conduct and not speech, and in terms of protection of children considerations, such censorship effects might more easily be justified.

Taking the restraint in its present form, just what does it cover? As far as forms of speech are concerned, photographs are clearly the law's principal concern. Section 7(2) of the Act defines an 'indecent photograph' as including 'an indecent photograph comprised in a film', as well as film negative and video recordings; Section 7(3) adds confirmation: 'Photographs (including those comprised in a film) shall, if they show children and are indecent, be treated for all purposes of this Act as indecent photographs of children'. The circumstances in which such articles are covered extends to their production as well as distribution; there is no requirement of a view to gain as far as distribution is concerned. The standard applied is the by now familiar one of indecency. This has not been limited to human sexuality only, and the ambit of this Act is presumably correspondingly as wide. If indecency is assessed here as elsewhere,[2] it will be judged not in terms of effect on an audience, but in terms of the context in which the conduct concerned takes place. The context is here largely predetermined, in the sense that one is concerned with the taking of photographs of children. One's concern is whether the taking of such photographs is an affront to positive morality. It may be that films will contravene the Act if they show children in indecent scenes, even though the indecency may be quite extraneous to the child concerned, who may not even be aware of it. The indecency, in other words, does not have even loosely speaking to be 'with or towards a child'. This means that where children

---

1 See p.175ff above.

2 See e.g. outraging public decency, chapter 3.

are involved in a film, the standard to be applied is indecency; there is, moreover, no defence of public good. This Act constitutes in this respect another exception, in addition principally to conspiracy to corrupt public morals, to the Obscene Publications Act defence of literary or artistic merit.

There are a number of obvious defences to a charge under Section 1: that the photographs are not indecent, that the accused had no part in their production, or that no one under sixteen years of age was photographed. Section 1(d) does not require even that the material advertised be indecent: it is enough that the advertisement is such as to be 'likely to be understood as conveying' a willingness to sell prohibited material. The distributor or exhibitor has an additional defence if charged under Section 1(b) or (c): Section 1(4) provides that it is a defence, if established on a balance of probabilities, that he (the distributor or exhibitor) '(a) ... had a legitimate reason for distributing or showing the photographs or (as the case may be) having them in his possession; or (b) ... had not himself seen the photographs and did not know nor had any cause to suspect, them to be indecent'.

With a charge under Section 1(a) then, intention would be required as to the taking of the pictures; intention would not appear to be required as to their indecency. Under Sections 1(b) and 1(c), whilst intention is required as to distribution, exhibition or possession with a view to exhibition, negligence as to the nature of the pictures is sufficient; again, intention as to indecency would not appear to be required. With Section 1(d) intention is required as to advertising, and negligence would appear to be required as to the nature of the advertisement. There is no requirement that the material be indecent. The photographer or film-maker's intention is in any event irrelevant as there is no defence of public good. There is, however, the Section 1(4)(b) defence of having a 'legitimate reason' for distribution, exhibition or possession in terms of Section 1(b) or (c). The defence is similar to that of public good in the sense that satisfaction of it negates unlawfulness. Its novelty lies in the, for the criminal law, pristine phrase 'legitimate reason'. As Lord Scarman, 'the only judge to participate in the Parliamentary debates on the Bill',[1] explained

> the phrase 'a legitimate reason' has a certain originality about it, and it is the originality about it which commends it to my mind ... There will be parents and others who have no lawful authority — if that phrase means anything in that context — to have in their possession indecent photographs, and yet they do have a legitimate reason — one need not speculate what it

---

[1] Robertson *Obscenity* (London 1979) at 304.

> is — for having them ... when it is available it is a highly respectable and dignified defence, the sort of defence one would wish to take if one had in one's possession for legitimate reasons an indecent photograph.
>
> Do not be frightened of introducing new and original, but simple and understandable language into our statute law. Welcome the opportunity. Get away from the old, hackneyed phrases and use a phrase which means something to ordinary people, and bear in mind that this phrase 'a legitimate reason' really embraces a question of fact on which courts and juries are well able to reach a sensible decision in determining the meaning.[1]

Accepting that novel statutory constructions are not, merely as such, to be rejected out of hand, the phrase 'legitimate reason' is distinguishable from public good defences in that a determination by a jury in terms of this defence is not tied to considerations such as literary or artistic merit. The jury has a free hand in effect to legislate *ad hoc*. Accepting Lord Scarman's strictures on originality, this looseness in drafting can hardly, in terms of certainty, be recommended in the preparation of criminal law statutes.

It is noteworthy that the 'legitimate reason' defence does not extend to the *taking* of such films or pictures. Apparently there can be no legitimate reason for such filming. If family album shots of naked children are to be excluded, the entire weight of this exclusion falls on the term 'indecency' and its precision of definition. Yet indecency is a wonderfully imprecise standard. Fears on this score were dismissed as groundless in the House of Lords debates, particular reference being made to, and store being placed in this respect on, an unreported decision of the Court of Appeal in a Customs and Excise case. The work in question was a book, *Boys are Boys Again*, consisting of some 122 photographs of naked boys, and the question to be decided was whether the book was an indecent import. Lord Justice Bridge approached the question of indecency primarily in terms of the photographer/compiler's intentions:

> ... there is a photograph which has been published upside-down and the boys are standing on their hands, and it has been published in such a way as to suggest, at a casual glance at all events, that those two boys' penises are certainly erect ... it seems to me that (two other photographs) are about as provocative poses of the young body as could be imagined ... the conclusion that I reach is that if the book is looked at as a whole ... the very essence of the publication, the reason

---

1 *Hansard*, H Lords Deb, vol.392, no.81, col. 545–6.

> for publishing it, is to focus attention on the male genital organs. It is a series of photographs in the great majority of which the male genitalia, sometimes in close-up, are the focal point of the picture ... they aim to be interesting pictures of boys' penises ...[1]

This approach was enthusiastically endorsed by the Secretary of State for the Home Office: 'That is exactly how I would expect the issue under the Bill to be decided, ... I think, frankly, that there is no danger that ordinary family snapshots, or legitimate sex education material, would be caught in terms of the Bill'.[2] This view of the law was reiterated during the Third Reading debate on the Bill: '... the test of indecency already exists to separate photographs which are offensive from those which are innocent or which have been taken with a clinical rather than a prurient approach'.[3] Not only is this approach in conflict with decided cases on indecency (admittedly all in terms of the Post Office Act 1953,[4] but nonetheless of strongly persuasive force), but it accords ill with the absence of a public good defence as such in terms of Section 1(a) of the 1978 Act. Lord Justice Bridge, it is implied, might have taken a different view of the pictures had he felt that they aimed not at being 'interesting pictures of boys' penises', but rather at some artistic attainment; yet were he so to do in the context of this enactment, he would in fact be importing via the backdoor a defence of public good which the statute specifically excluded. Whether the statute does clearly exclude the type of domestic snapshot which gave rise to concern is not clear; if indecency is relative in terms of context, and if the latter is largely concerned with the involvement of children, additional contextual factors such as the precise setting, or the intention with which the pictures are taken, may well not be relevant. One is here in essence relying for such distinctions on positive morality. If it can be said that this is a reliable guide to criminal liability, well and good; if not, the offence hardly satisfies demands for certainty.

If Lord Scarman's view of the 'legitimate reason' defence is taken, and it is viewed as an assessment well within the ken of the average

---

1 *Commissioners of Customs and Excise* v *Sun and Health Ltd*, Royal Courts of Justice, 29 March 1973, transcript at pp. 5 and 6; quoted in Robertson op.cit. at 303–4.

2 Lord Harris of Greenwich; *Hansard*, H Lords Deb, 18 May 1978, vol.394, no.103, cols 330–1.

3 *Hansard*, H Lords Deb, vol.394, no.103, col.334.

4 See *R* v *Stamford* [1972] 2 WLR 1055; *R* v *Stanley* [1965] 1 All ER 1035; *R* v *Straker* [1965] *Crim L Rev* 239; *Kosmos Publications Ltd* v *DPP* [1975] *Crim L Rev* 345; chapter 5.

juror, then following *Brutus* v *Cozens*,[1] this will be a question of fact solely for the jury: expert evidence is unlikely to be admitted. There is no requirement that a film or composition of photographs be taken as a whole. The prior restraint involved operates through prosecution, rather than injunction or licence. There is some control over its operation in that all criminal proceedings under Section 1 require the consent of the Director of Public Prosecutions, whilst its assertion additionally involves a judicial hearing.

Although restriction on the taking of pictures of this sort may be justified on the grounds of the protection of children, a number of features of this legislation are open to question. Perhaps the primary concern is its prior restraint form, as opposed to an emphasis on the control of conduct. As Lord Gardiner remarked in the House of Lords Debates:

> there is good law reform and bad law reform. Bad law reform takes place when there is some article in a newspaper ... or some scare, as a result of which there is a demand for instantaneous legislation — and instantaneous legislation is almost invariably bad. I approach this Bill on the footing ... first that there was no evidence whatever that there had been any current increase in pornographic photographs of children. And secondly, that if there were, then, with one small exception, the police had ample power to deal with them. There was really only one small exception which needed to be covered.[2]

The coverage of films would appear to be far too broad: producers of films involving children have now a perhaps unreasonable burden placed upon them, whilst distributors of productions imported from jurisdictions without this coverage, may have, to be safe, to cut into the very vitals of a film. The standard as applied to films suffers from the same vice as does restriction under the Children and Young Persons (Harmful Publications) Act 1955:[3] adult viewers are unnecessarily reduced to the level of what is suitable for children. The standard in both cases is overbroad, in the latter case in the sense that sale to children only should be covered, whilst here one needs some narrowing of the prohibition in terms of the film's indecency involving conduct 'with or towards' children.

The restriction on advertising would appear equally overbroad: it is

---

1   [1973] AC 854.

2   *Hansard*, H Lords Deb, 28 June 1978, vol.394, no.103, cols 330–1.

3   See chapter 5, protection of children.

surely sufficient to prohibit the advertising of material which *is* indecent. A factor here may be the protection of the gullible, who send off for material which is in fact quite innocuous, on the basis of advertisements themselves not indecent, but rather misleading as to the indecency of the principal materials. The Trades Descriptions Act 1968 makes it an offence to describe the quantity or composition of advertised goods in a false or misleading way. At the behest of the DPP therefore, coverage already exists in relation to such conduct.

Working on the basis that children do not 'enjoy a fully developed right to choose',[1] the Williams Committee came down heavily against the involvement of children in the production of pornography. Acknowledging that evidence presented to them suggested that 'young girls had the ability to exploit what they saw as a "good racket" and were quite capable of still growing up into well-adjusted women',[2] the committee nonetheless concluded that

> Few people would be prepared to take the risk (of long-term damage) where children are concerned and just as the law recognises that children should be protected against sexual behaviour which they are too young to properly consent to, it is almost universally agreed that this should apply to participation in pornography.[3]

The committee points out that most participation by children in the production of pornography would constitute an offence, and the area not so covered is 'even smaller in practice than on paper'. Nonetheless, it was desirable that such conduct be suppressed; it was also desirable that 'the pornographic product be suppressed as well as the original act, so as not to provide the incentive to pornographers to flout the sexual offence law, or to deal without inhibition in products which are imported from other legal jurisdictions'.[4] In these terms the committee recommended that it should be an offence to publish material which consists of:

> ... photographs and films whose production appears to the court to have involved the exploitation for sexual purposes of any person where either
> (a) that person appears from the evidence as a whole to have been at the relevant time under the age of

---

1 *Williams* para 6.69; see chapter 5, protection of children, for a full discussion.

2 *Williams* para 6.68.

3 Ibid.

4 Ibid.

225

sixteen ...'.[1]

What the committee appears to be saying is:

(a) that most sexual conduct involved in producing pornography involving minors is already an offence;
(b) that they consider that even though sexual intercourse with a girl under the age of sixteen (for example) is an offence, it should also be an offence to film the act where the girl is, or appears to be, under age; and
(c) that it should be an offence to distribute such a film.

The committee almost certainly faced a difficulty in arriving at this formulation: had they followed the approach suggested above, and linked prohibition on the taking of such pictures with existing controls of sexual conduct involving children, such filming would have been subject to control in terms of conduct involving those actually under age, and not a mere appearance thereof; the law's concern would have been conduct and not effect, thereby avoiding prior restraint considerations. But this would have been achieved by closing a loophole in existing law, and such law is couched in terms of indecency, a standard the committee wished to avoid.[2] The standard of 'exploitation' certainly appears to be an attractive one; it goes, after all, to the heart of society's concern in this area: the fact that because of their immaturity, children are peculiarly vulnerable to exploitation. Although there is general agreement that such films should be stopped, there are then a number of possible approaches: in terms of the present Act; in terms of the Williams recommendations; and in terms of coupling the prohibition to existing controls on conduct. Perhaps the most attractive of all would be the third, using the Williams standard of 'exploitation'. This, however, involves considerations beyond the Williams brief or the scope of this essay. It may well be, though, that the optimum answer lies in a restructuring of offences involving the sexual exploitation of children, to include a prohibition on filming, amongst other forms of conduct.

The age the committee has recommended as decisive is sixteen. They found that evidence on the age at which special protection for children is necessary, varied from sixteen to eighteen. In this instance, sixteen seems a reasonable choice, as it is after all the age of consent. Exploitation 'for sexual purposes' is perhaps not the best choice of phrase: the purpose may be financial gain. 'Sexual exploitation' might be a better term of reference in this regard. As far as the subsequent restraint on distribution is concerned, the committee would appear to

---

1 *Williams* para 13.4, subpara 19.

2 For further discussion, see displays, chapter 6, especially at p.182ff.

regard this as justified in terms of their general approach of rationally assessable harm: potential harm to children is such as to outweigh freedom of speech considerations, even though the prohibition is a general one, covering distribution, without exception in terms of audience, intention of the producer, or any other mechanism of variability.[1]

Although the question of prohibiting the production of certain forms of speech does not appear to have come before the American Supreme Court, a strong case could be made for such a measure's constitutionality. Were it accepted that the filming of children could be regarded as conduct together with other sexual offences against minors, one would be relieved of the entire prior restraint burden. Restriction would be concerned with, and aimed at, conduct and not speech, and the First Amendment could not then be invoked against it. The court has adopted this strategy with zoning restrictions,[2] where it has been argued that such restrictions are aimed at town planning, and impose the smallest possible restriction on speech. This approach could even more convincingly be argued here.

(ii)   *Adults.* As with the situation in respect of children prior to the 1978 Act, there is no prohibition, aside from various offences covering sexual conduct as such, on the filming of adult sexual activity. The question the committee had to resolve therefore was: should there be in this respect (in effect) a Protection of Adults Act?

One is concerned here with the effect of such participation on the models involved, and *not* with the effect of the material on a potential or actual audience. The committee's approach was in terms of conduct: if sexual conduct is lawful, is there any reason why the filming of it with a view to speech production should be unlawful? If the conduct when not filmed does not constitute exploitation, does the latter *ipso facto* import such considerations into the assessment? One is dealing with adults, who are presumably able to exercise mature consent, whether to exploitation or otherwise. Are there factors which *compel* participation in such conduct, thus vitiating consent and giving rise to exploitation? The committee's view was that generally such participation was, 'by ordinary criteria', voluntary.[3] In other words, although allegations were made — principally by Mr Raymond Blackburn — that participants in such work were subject to blackmail,[4] the committee

---

1   On the distribution prohibition, see p.174ff above.

2   See the section on zoning in relation to books and magazines, below; also *Young* v *American Mini Theaters* 427 US 50 (1976); chapter 14.

3   *Williams* para 6.70.

4   Ibid. para 6.69.

found no evidence to substantiate such assertions. Participation was indeed very probably voluntary even applying extraordinary criteria: although 'much employment is exploitation because people are obliged to do what they have no desire to do in order to earn their living',[1] the committee found no truth in the suggestion that 'no-one, knowing what was involved, and not under the direst pressure of economic or other necessity, would want to engage in such conduct'.[2]

If there is no exploitation, in the sense that participation is by adults who may exercise mature consent, often doing so in terms of a choice of ways of making a living and not in terms of dire economic pressure, justification in terms of exploitation was not considered possible. Should consent nonetheless be overridden, in terms of some harm to the participants, and irrespective of whether they are aware of this harm or not? The question here resolves itself into one of just what are such harms. Such assessment has presumably already been made in relation to the sexual conduct involved: it is difficult to see additional harms arising merely because of filming. The committee therefore concluded that no such general prohibition was required.

Where the conduct involved is already criminal, the position is rather different. The committee considered only one such case: so-called 'snuff' films, 'in which sadistic pornography is taken to the extreme of having an unsuspecting model actually injured, mutilated, and even murdered in front of the camera'.[3] Although the ambit of the defence of consent is not perfectly clear, most conduct of this sort is punishable in terms of present law. Society has predetermined and weighed the harms involved, and even if not covered in terms of complicity, there would accordingly seem to be a strong case for regarding the prohibition of the associated conduct of filming such activities as equally justified.[4] If the harms involved are considered sufficiently compelling, they are surely such as to justify the prohibition of such filming, which may in fact provide an incentive to the conduct in question. The committee did not apparently consider the question of the filming of illegal conduct any more broadly. The same reasoning would apply though: if the harms involved in a particular variety of sexual conduct are such as to justify its prohibition, the filming of such conduct might similarly be proscribed. The reason for this omission was probably the view, expressed elsewhere in the report,

---

1 *Williams* para 6.71.

2 Ibid. para 6.70.

3 Ibid. para 6.72.

4 Ibid. para 6.72.

that 'the present law on sexual offences itself contains anomalies ...'.[1] To tie recommendations for new prohibitions on conduct to what were felt to be possible anomalies, was thought undesirable, whilst a survey of existing law on sexual offences was clearly beyond the brief of the committee. The long term answer in terms of restricting such filming presumably lies in its being tied closely to such sexual offences as are deemed, after appropriate review, to be justifiable. Because of the vitiation of consent, one would be dealing with something akin to exploitation in such circumstances. Were it possible to formulate prohibitions generally in this respect, including that on filming, in terms of such exploitation, the filming restriction would have been assimilated as a conduct prohibition rather than a prior restraint. Restructuring sexual offences generally in terms of exploitation may be a remote possibility; acceptance of a prior restraint on speech production specifically may be inevitable.

Another approach to the prohibition of the production of pornography — essentially a prohibition on filming — is to tie it to a prohibition on the distribution of pornography. Because, in other words, the prohibition of such distribution is justified, so too might a prohibition as to its production. This is to approach the question from the speech rather than conduct viewpoint. The committee, in view of its rejection of further prohibitions on speech, was naturally biased against this approach. It would seem, in terms of censorship considerations, far preferable where possible to deal with prohibitions in terms of conduct. This area provides just such a possibility. Yet, in view of a final suggestion by the committee as to controls of this sort, the risk is run of breaking this conduct link: because of difficulties in prosecution, they felt the prosecution should not have the burden of proving that the material involved actual as opposed to simulated harm. Hence the final recommendation that prohibition should operate as to 'Material whose production appears to the court to have involved exploitation for sexual purposes of any person, where ... (b) the material gives reason to believe that actual physical harm was inflicted on that person'.[2] Once one prohibits the production of material on the basis of simulated harm, one breaks the link with conduct, and becomes concerned rather with the *effect* of material on its audience. The possible justifications for control are as a result rather different, and any control on production becomes assimilated into a control on distribution,[3] rather than the reverse being the case. In terms of the justifications raised above, this

---

1   *Williams* para 10.3.

2   Ibid. para 10.6.

3   In this regard, see p.174ff above.

229

control should be limited to material the production of which involves conduct in the form of physical harm, this possibly being widened to include other criminal offences. Whether wider prohibitions are justified will be considered in the final chapter.

2) *Post Office Regulation*

The Post Office Act 1953 specifically provides for the 'opening, detaining or delaying of a postal packet under the authority of this Act or in obedience to the express warrant in writing under the bond of a Secretary of State'.[1] Interceptions authorised in the latter manner would appear to be so authorised and made principally for evidentiary, rather than prior restraint purposes, and will be considered specifically in this respect.[2] What is of immediate concern here is just what is envisaged in terms of the phrase 'under the authority of this Act'.

In this regard, Section 11(1) of the 1953 Act makes it an offence[3] to send through the post 'indecent or obscene' articles. Section 8(3) of the Act provides for the restraint of anything illegally in the mail:

> If any postal packet is posted or sent by post in contravention of this Act or of any ... regulation made thereunder, the transmission thereof may be refused and the packet may, if necessary, be detained and opened in the post office and may be returned to the sender thereof or forwarded to its destination, subject in either case to any ... regulations as to additional postage or other charges or may be destroyed or otherwise disposed of as [the authority] may direct.

This would appear to some extent to mirror the position with regard to seizure of obscene materials in the United States mails.[4] The Comstock Act of 1873 provided — and continues to do so today — for the 'non-delivery' of such materials. Whatever Congressional intention may have been in this regard, by the 1880s the Post Office was exercising the power to censor the mails on an exclusionary basis. This the Supreme Court upheld: as Mr Justice Brandeis remarked in *Milwaukee Publishing Co v Burleson*:[5]

> Power to exclude from the mails has never been conferred in terms upon the Postmaster General. Beginning with the

---

1 Section 58(1).

2 See restraints not constituting prior restraints, below.

3 See distribution, chapter 5.

4 See chapter 10.

5 255 US 407 (1921) at 417.

Act of March 3, 1865 ... relating to obscene matter and the Act of July 27, 1868 ... concerning lotteries, Congress has from time to time forbidden the deposit in the mails of certain matter. In each instance, in addition to prescribing a fine and imprisonment as a punishment for sending or attempting to send the prohibited matter through the mail, it declared that such matter shall not be conveyed in the mail nor delivered from any Post Office nor by any letter carrier ... As a matter of administration the Postmaster General through his subordinates, [now] rejects matter offered for mailing or removes matter already in the mail, which in his judgement is non-mailable. The existence in the Postmaster General of the power to do this cannot be doubted. The only question which can arise is whether in the individual case the power has been illegally exercised.

The only limitation applied was that in inspecting and/or seizing first class mail, a search warrant is required.[1] The Court assumed not only the right of the Post Office to remove non-deliverable matter from the mails, but also apparently its right to examine mail to determine whether it was non-deliverable. The English position appears to be somewhat stronger as far as the Post Office is concerned, in that Sections 8 and 58 of the 1953 Act appear specifically to authorise the detention of matter unlawfully in the mail. It would appear that a Post Office official may, in terms of Section 8, seize a packet from the mail which has (for example) burst open, spilling allegedly indecent material over the sorting room floor. Section 58(1) of the 1953 Act provides an exemption from criminal liability for Post Office officials should they act in terms of the Section 8 authority. Section 64 of the Post Office Act 1969 appears however to cut across both this authorisation and exemption provided by the 1953 measure; the section is entitled 'Inviolability of the Mails', and provides that

> (1) Subject to the provisions of this section, a packet in the post, anything contained in a packet in the post and a mailbag containing a packet in the post shall (if it is not the property of the Crown) have the like immunity from examination under a power conferred by or under any enactment (whether passed before or after this Act), from seizure or detention under such a power, from seizure under distress or in execution and from retention by virtue of a lien, as it would have if it were the property of the Crown.

Section 64(3) contains certain exemptions from this provision in regard

---

1 To satisfy Fourth Amendment requirements: *ex parte Jackson* 96 US 727 (1877).

to seizure powers provided (under Sections 16, 17 and 26(6) of the 1953 Act) in relation to customs and excise. Assuming that Crown property enjoys inviolability from seizure or detention of any sort,[1] packets in the mail would appear to be similarly inviolate. The Post Office in evidence to Williams acknowledged that they had regularly up to 1978 utilised the specific provisions allowing mail coming from overseas to be opened for customs inspection.[2] However, as they informed the committee, '... they had misgivings about removing from the post in this way, on the basis of their own judgement — which they did not feel competent to make — of the material concerned, rather than the judgement of a court, and relying on a legal provision which was less than entirely clear in the way in which it sought to extend a domestic control to material posted beyond the jurisdiction of United Kingdom law'.[3] As far as seizures of domestic mail is concerned, the Post Office acknowledged that where packets burst open in transit or cannot be delivered, they are opened, although this occurs in only about fifty cases per year. The legal status of such seizures does not appear secure, whilst examination of the mail *on suspicion* that it contains prohibited material would very probably be unlawful. The Post Office themselves take the view that the Section 8 power does not extend to the opening of mail on this basis.[4]

Whatever the precise relationship of the various statutory provisions governing the inviolability of the mails, it is clear that prior restraints by the Post Office in terms of seizure from the mails is not a major threat to freedom of speech. It would appear to be operated solely in respect of those items the contents of which (through a packet bursting open, for example) are brought to the notice, whilst in transit, of Post Office officials. It is potentially operable, however, in respect of material imported via the mails, but not, even were the Post Office dramatically to change its views, to internal mail in the sense of such mail being subject to detention on suspicion.

---

1   The position in this regard is not clear. It may be that Crown property in the mails would be inviolate unless the statutory provisions concerned specifically extend to it. See e.g. S.A. de Smith *Constitutional and Administrative Law* (3rd edn, London 1977) at 119ff.

2   Paragraph 19 of the Overseas Letter Post Scheme 1971 applies the Section 8 (of the 1953 Act) seizure and disposition power of the Post Office to mail coming from overseas. Section 16 of the 1953 Act applies customs controls to material entering the country in postal packets, and enables the Treasury to make regulations governing the application of this control. Under the Postal Packets (Customs and Excise) Regulations 1975, Regulation 12 empowers customs to require the Post Office to open a packet for inspection. Once opened, of course, such a packet is clearly subject to the application of Section 8 powers.

3   *Williams* para 2.26.

4   Ibid. para 2.25.

Any such detentions and dispositions by the Post Office, on however narrow a basis, must nonetheless raise strong prior restraint objections. The 1953 Act, unlike the Customs provisions in this regard, does not require that the owner of the goods be notified of their detention, nor does it require that he be given a chance to challenge their unlawful character in the courts. Instead, 'The Post Office Act simply allows any postal packet opened to be returned to the sender or forwarded to its destination', or 'destroyed or otherwise disposed of'.[1] The possibility of judicial review does not appear ever to have been canvassed in relation to such detentions and/or dispositions; it would appear probable that the statutory power here would be regarded as an enforcement power, and therefore outside the scope of such review.[2] Without such judicial review one has in effect a quite arbitrary prior restraint.

The United States Supreme Court has taken its rulings on such prior restraints beyond judicial review as such, and has based them entirely on First Amendment prior restraint principles. Where material was seized from mails in the United States in terms of the Comstock Act it was forwarded to the solicitor for the US Post Office Department. If deemed obscene, the addressor would be notified to show cause within fifteen days why the material should not be disposed of. Usually no hearing was held; if the addressor proved difficult, a hearing was held in which the functions of prosecutor and judge merged in the person of the solicitor. The courts were less than happy with this: in 1945 the United States Court of Appeals in the District of Columbia used the Fifth Amendment (a fair trial) to brand as illegal seizure without a full hearing.[3] Congress followed this up with the Administrative Procedure Act, which required just such a hearing.[4] The restriction has been used less and less since then. However, it was not the Administrative Procedure Act or the federal statute relating to judicial review of administrative action[5] which put an end to use of the restriction, but rather constitutional, and more specifically First Amendment considerations.[6] Although these Post Office restraints have never specifically been ruled

---

1 *Williams* Appendix I, para 51.

2 S.A. de Smith *Judicial Review of Administrative Action* (4th edn, London 1980) at 216.

3 *Walker v Popenoe* 149F 2d 511 at 514 (DC Cir 1945).

4 5 USC Section 1001 *et seq*.

5 39 USC Section 3001 (f), referring to 5 USC chapters 5 and 7.

6 The courts appeared to be moving beyond the Administrative Procedure Act as early as 1960: in *Grove Press Inc.* v *Christenberry* 276 F2d 433 (2d Cir, 1960) the court appeared to regard review by the court *de novo* of administrative adjudication as possible; the Administrative Procedure Act does not apply where such review is possible.

unconstitutional by the Court, any use of them without adherence to *Freedman* requirements would clearly be found impermissible. The relevant statutes would seem virtually irredeemable in this respect and have not been amended; they are therefore no longer used.

An initial question as to the English position is whether prior restraint is necessary or justifiable in relation to the mails, either in terms of present controls or of those recommended above (pornography whose production involved those under sixteen years of age, or involved actual physical harm to participants; matter dealing with sexuality and/or violence in a manner unsuitable for children, when posted on an unsolicited basis, or to those who should reasonably have been apprehended to be under eighteen years of age).[1] Is it justifiable that the Post Office be permitted to open mail on suspicion, and destroy material unlawfully there? If one is to attach real weight to freedom of speech considerations, then as the Supreme Court has obliquely ruled, not only would a speedy subsequent judicial hearing on the merits be required, but an adversary hearing prior to detention might also be necessary, such detention serving only to preserve the *status quo*.[2] Were provision to be made for a search warrant for the police in such circumstances, with a forfeiture hearing in mind, undoubtedly a prior adversary hearing would be required.

Even were one to opt for the less controversial prior restraint of allowing the Post Office, after a forfeiture hearing, to destroy material spilt from packages broken in transit, the basic question is the same: does one wish to opt for a mechanism which punishes criminally for the conduct involved, or for one which provides potentially for the bulk destruction of material found in restricted circumstances, or itself subject to prohibition? The Williams Committee did not consider this question in relation to Post Office controls, but rather, broadly, in relation to forfeiture proceedings as such. Their conclusion was that in relation to restrictions on unsolicited mailing, and on mailing to those under eighteen years of age, control was aimed not at the material, but at the immediate circumstances of distribution;[3] with the prohibition on the distribution of pornography whose production involved minors, one is on the other hand concerned with the material, and not its circumstances of distribution.[4] In both cases the committee recommended against forfeiture proceedings: in the former case because one was

---

1   See p.174ff; pp.171–3.

2   To prevent the material disappearing, for example.

3   *Williams* para 9.46.

4   Ibid. para 10.19.

concerned with the particular circumstances of distribution, more than the material itself; with the latter, because the conduct was too serious to deal with civilly. Certainly prosecutions would seem more effective in the latter respect, in that they go to the source of the prohibited material, rather than merely removing it from circulation. One may add to these reasons the basic one that any prior restraint needs special justification.

Forfeiture proceedings are not the only form of prior restraint possible: the United States Supreme Court has upheld as constitutional a prior restraint system in relation to unsolicited mailings.[1] This allows the Post Office to order, on the individual recipient's request, the cessation of such mailings, an order which may be enforced by injunction. Without impugning the success of this scheme in the United States, its operation is no doubt expensive, and even if justifiable, would not seem to have such clear advantages over a criminal sanction as to make it an attractive alternative in English law.

Williams did however recommend the provision of search and seizure powers in relation to the two varieties of restriction/prohibition mentioned above;[2] these might be specifically extended to the mails. Were such provisions to be narrowly worded, seizures would be limited to materials specified in the search warrant. Statutory language would govern whether a magistrate was required to specify, on the face of the warrant, the title(s) he deems fit for seizure. One might conceivably have something close to a general warrant, dependent on such requirements; to require such specificity might, on the other hand, be to make the application of the law virtually impossible. What is of greater concern is whether the police, in executing the warrant, could seize multiple copies of the same work, or whether they would be obliged, where only one copy is available, for example, to make a copy of it and return the original; in other words, whether the seizure power was to be used for the gathering of evidence only, or whether it might provide an oblique form of prior restraint. The police may also have powers of seizure at common law to secure evidence; these may operate as an adjunct to an arrest or to a warrant issued under some other authority, for example; in other words, quite independently of the type of search warrant power discussed here. The American Supreme Court has acknowledged the necessity of seizures for evidentiary purposes, and although their use has been circumscribed, they may be used to effect

---

1   *Rowan* v *United States Post Office Department* 397 US 728 (1970); see distribution, chapter 5; also chapter 10.

2   Ibid. paras 9.45 and 10.17; see search and seizure later in this chapter, where it is argued that a search warrant provision is justified only in relation to the prohibition in question, and not the restrictions.

seizures of multiple copies, or of the sole available copy of a work, perhaps without making a copy or returning the original. What the search warrant powers should be in this regard, the extent of common law powers, and the constitutionally permissible extent of such powers in the United States, will be examined below in terms of search and seizure.

3)   *Customs controls*

The Customs and Excise Management Act 1979, besides providing for criminal penalties for the importation of prohibited goods, also provides (Section 49) that goods imported contrary to a prohibition are liable to forfeiture. Anything liable to forfeiture may in terms of Section 139, be seized[1] and detained by customs officers. Customs officers clearly have the power to inspect goods imported into the country; there is therefore no question of their right to open and inspect packages or containers. The Act goes beyond the Post Office provisions discussed above in another way: when any item is seized, the Commissioners are required in terms of Schedule 3 of the Act to give notice of this to the apparent owner (unless of course the item was seized in his presence). It entitles the owner, within one month, to contest the forfeiture. If no notice is given of an intention to contest, the goods may be forfeit without a court hearing; if notice is given, then the Commissioners are obliged to institute forfeiture proceedings. These are civil proceedings, and can be heard in the High Court or magistrates' court.

The prior restraint mechanism here operates in terms of the indecent or obscene standard, as well as that provided under the 1955 Children and Young Persons (Harmful Publications) Act. All legal restraint on the importation of material into this country is operated by customs and excise, as the Post Office, although empowered to detain goods illegally in mail from overseas, now no longer exercises this power.[2] The question here is, does one need both a criminal and a civil restraint, and if not, which of the two is preferable?

The United States relies in this regard solely on a civil measure.[3] The authorities detain goods, transmit them to the appropriate United States Attorney, who institutes judicial proceedings *in rem* for their forfeiture. The Customs Statute provides for a judicial hearing *de novo*; as a result the Administrative Procedure Act is inapplicable. Despite the

---

1   For a discussion of the powers of search and seizure in this regard, see 'Other Provisions' under Section 4(i), later in this chapter.

2   See Post Office regulation, above.

3   19 USC 1305.

prior restraint element, the Supreme Court has upheld the constitutionality of the Act, provided the hearings commence within fourteen days of seizure and are concluded within sixty days thereafter, unless the claimant is responsible for additional delays.[1] The *Freedman status quo* requirement would appear to be satisfied, and there would not appear to be any requirement for a preliminary adversary proceeding before detention. Such a requirement, imposed in the case of police search warrants, is in any case not the central aspect of prior restraint consideration, being perhaps more concerned with the Fourth Amendment requirements as to search and seizure.[2] It does not appear to have been canvassed here, probably because such a requirement would, practically speaking, make the application of any customs controls virtually impossible; such controls would not be operable without a general and immediate power to open, search and examine.

The English statute would very nearly satisfy these requirements, other than in respect of the Commissioners not being obliged to institute proceedings, and the time limitation. It might be argued that in view of the breadth of the standard employed here (the American statute operates in terms of standard obscenity)[3] the use of a civil control on its own is sufficient. The only criminal restriction recommended earlier in relation to customs controls was with regard to pornography the production of which involved minors, the occasioning of actual harm to participants, or perhaps, more broadly, the actual commission of crime. Williams' reasoning in relation to the latter was that the conduct was so serious that criminal penalties were apposite. They hence recommended generally against forfeiture hearings in this regard. Without explaining the distinction, they then go on to endorse the present customs forfeiture provisions as an addition to such criminal control.[4] The reasons for this are probably practical. If the conduct encompassed by the standard employed is so serious that one wishes to have criminal sanction, any seizure and detention of material would presumably be for evidentiary purposes only, unless one is to allow a prior restraint in via the backdoor. Customs seizures however often involve bulk seizures, or the detention of multiple copies, rather than the seizure of individual copies of books, films, etc. In the absence of a civil mechanism, what are Customs and Excise to do with that material not needed for prosecution purposes? They cannot send it back whence

---

1   See *United States* v *12 200ft Reels of Film* 413 US 123 (1973).

2   *Contra* however the fact that such a hearing is not required with seizures purely for evidentiary purposes: see search and seizure below.

3   *United States* v *12 200ft Reels of Film* 413 US 123 (1973) at 130, footnote 7.

4   *Williams* para 10.13. In respect of the recommended criminal penalty, see pp.173–4 above.

it came; to forward it to destination would be self-defeating. The same argument could be raised as to the mails, but there one is dealing with domestic transactions: the material, if not detainable as evidence of a crime, could at least be sent back to the addressor as non-deliverable. A civil control may be an inevitability here, presuming one wants control at all; if tightly drawn, perhaps along *Freedman* lines, the threat to freedom of speech is kept within strict bounds. The only real and probably unavoidable criticism, in these terms, is that the standard of proof is a civil and not a criminal one. Material might therefore be destroyed after a forfeiture proceeding, only to form the subject of an acquittal in later criminal proceedings. The only defence here is to operate in terms of standards as tightly drawn as possible.

4) *Books, magazines, photographs*

(i) *Search and seizure*. We are here concerned with prior restraint: in other words, with the ways in which, and extent to which, search and seizure can be used to effect such a restraint. The obvious way is as a prelude to a forfeiture hearing, a proceeding which depends on the earlier seizure. As was pointed out above in relation to Post Office controls, search and seizure, if it extends to the seizure of multiple copies of material, can, even if apparently an adjunct to the criminal process, still effect a prior restraint. It is not always easy rigidly to separate these two functions: in the discussion below an attempt will be made to do so; seizure for evidentiary purposes, which does not necessarily constitute a prior restraint, will be discussed at the end of this chapter.

Issue of a warrant: the major search and seizure provisions (other than customs provisions) in existence in this area at present are those provided by the Obscene Publications Act 1959 and by the Indecent Displays (Control) Act 1981. The 1959 Act specifies that:[1]

> If a justice of the peace is satisfied by information on oath that there is reasonable ground for suspecting that, in any premises in the petty sessions area for which he acts, or on any stall or vehicle within that area, being premises or a stall or vehicle specified in the information, obscene articles are, or are from time to time, kept for publication for gain, the justice may issue a warrant under his hand empowering any constable to enter (if need be by force) and search the premises, or to search the stall or vehicle, within fourteen days from the date of the warrant, and to seize and remove any articles found therein or thereon which the constable has reason to believe to be obscene articles and to be kept for publication for gain.

---

1   Section 3(1).

Only reasonable suspicion of a sale is required, whilst the articles must 'from time to time' be kept on the premises. The magistrate must, in issuing the warrant, be satisfied that reasonable cause has been shown,[1] both as to the material's obscenity and its prospective commercial distribution. Equally, he may be held to have acted judicially in this regard in accepting the assertions of one policeman, or in American parlance, 'the conclusory assertions of a single police officer'.[2] The 1981 Act makes, *mutatis mutandis*, the same provision. In terms of Section 2(3) only reasonable suspicion that an offence under the Act 'has been or is committed', is required. The magistrate should be satisfied in issuing the warrant that reasonable cause has been shown as to both the material's indecency, and its display in contravention of the Act. The measure is probably slightly broader than its Section 3(1) counterpart in that it is sufficient that there is reasonable cause to believe not only that an offence under the Act is being committed, but that such offence has been committed; in view of the 'from time to time' provision in Section 3(1), this distinction may be more illusory than real. As with the 1959 Act, a magistrate may, in issuing a warrant, accept the assertions of a single police officer.

The American Supreme Court has attempted, as far as the issue of a warrant is concerned, to separate the prior restraint and evidence gathering strands. In relation to the former, *Quantity of Books* made it clear that a prior adversary hearing is required. Fourth Amendment considerations are relevant to this, but prior restraint considerations may perhaps have been dominant, in that *Heller* v *New York* made it plain that such a hearing was not required with seizures for evidentiary purposes, provided that the warrant is issued after a determination of probable cause by a neutral magistrate, provided that copies of a film are made if only one is available, and provided that an adversary hearing is held promptly after the seizure, if the defendant so requests.[3] Although an adversary hearing is not required for the issue of a warrant in these circumstances, and although the judicial officer concerned is not required himself to have seen, for example, a film, something more than the assertions and conclusions of a single policeman are required. Each item to be seized must be specified, moreover, so as not to delegate the initial determination of obscenity to the police officer.[4]

---

1 See L.H. Leigh *Police Powers in England and Wales* (London 1975) at 175.

2 See e.g. *Marcus* v *Search Warrant* 367 US 717 (1961) at 731 and 732.

3 413 US 483 (1973) at 488–9 and 492–3.

4 *Marcus* v *Search Warrant* 367 US 717 (1961).

A preliminary adversary hearing is not the only limitation the Court has placed on search and seizure as a prelude to forfeiture: *Freedman* requires also that any temporary restraint prior to a final hearing (for example, a seizure prior to the forfeiture hearing) should be designed *only* to preserve the *status quo*. Quite what this means as far as warrants of this sort are concerned is not clear; presumably they should be issued only if, for example, there is reason to suspect that the materials might be removed. The requirement would appear to make forfeiture proceedings virtually inoperable, unless material was to be declared forfeit on the basis of sample copies. This would mean in effect that a warrant for seizure could only issue *after* a final determination at forfeiture hearings.

Seizures: (a) Under the 1959 Act: The warrant must be executed within fourteen days of issue. A question which arose as to the execution of Section 3 search warrants, was whether such a warrant empowered the police to make more than one search on the basis of a single warrant. The Court of Appeal,[1] although it noted that the phrase 'are kept' in the 1857 provision[2] had been broadened in Section 3(1) to 'are from time to time, kept', pointed out that the broadening phrase 'from time to time' had not been used in relation to the powers authorised by the warrant, as opposed to the power to issue it. These words had been specifically used in the former respect in, for example, the Misuse of Drugs Act 1971. The court concluded that other than by withdrawing the limitation as to daylight searches only, it was not Parliament's intention 'to impose a more onerous interference with the owner's right of privacy or right of property than had been enacted by the 1857 Act ...'.[3]

Once on premises, the police may search for and seize any articles which the constable reasonably believes to be obscene and to be kept for publication for gain. The wording of Section 3(1) is such that the magistrate is not under a duty to specify on the face of the warrant, the titles to be seized. One has in effect a general warrant. What has not been judicially tested is whether the seizure of multiple copies is sanctioned in terms of such a warrant. Seizures in terms of Section 3(1) are apparently for the purposes of forfeiture only, as Section 3(3) provides that any articles seized under 3(1) should be brought before a magistrate with a view to forfeiture proceedings, *or* returned to their owner. Despite the obvious prior restraint implications, the statutory language would not appear in any way to inhibit such multiple copy seizures:

---

1   *R v Adams* [1980] 1 All ER 473.

2   Obscene Publications Act 1857.

3   *R v Adams* [1980] 1 All ER 473 at 479.

'any articles' extends equally to multiple as opposed to single copies. There would not appear to be any obligation imposed to make a copy where only a single copy of the work is available; seizures of sole copies are a very effective prior restraint. There is no obligation to give a receipt, something which has given rise to considerable criticism. It would appear that the Metropolitan Police, at any rate, now operate in terms of scheduling all the articles seized from premises, a copy of which is supplied to the owner.[1] A general limitation recently urged upon the House of Lords in respect of Section 3(1) is that its provisions do not apply to obscene articles kept in this country for publication abroad. The House ruled that even though the obscenity of material awaiting export must needs be assessed for forfeiture purposes in terms of its potential audience abroad, potential publication to such audience was sufficient to satisfy Section 3 requirements.[2]

Nor are police seizure powers limited to the statutory provisions of Section 3. Lord Denning laid down in *Ghani* v *Jones*[3] two basic situations in which the police may seize property; these remarks were, it is true, *obiter dicta*, but they are very persuasive nonetheless. The first of the two situations which the Master of the Rolls identified is where no-one has been arrested or charged. This by implication extends to the situation where the police are on premises by virtue of a search warrant (not necessarily issued under Section 3), are there by consent, or perhaps — more controversially — are there unlawfully. In such a situation the police may in effect seize anything that is evidence of any (serious) crime committed by anyone.[4] Where an arrest has been made, the police may, in Lord Denning's view, seize anything which is evidence of any crime committed by the person arrested.[5] As there is no power of arrest under the Obscene Publications Acts,[6] any arrest in question here would be unrelated to obscenity. The question as far as prior restraint is concerned, is

---

1   Letter from the Assistant Commissioner, Metropolitan Police, 18 July 1979, in reply to a query as to present police practices in this respect.

2   *Gold Star Publications Ltd* v *DPP* [1981] 2 All ER 257.

3   [1969] 3 All ER 1700.

4   Ibid. at 1705.

5   Ibid. at 1702.

6   See arrest, below.

whether these common law powers allow the seizure of multiple copies, or of the only copy available. These powers would not appear to sanction the latter type of seizure, as the Master of the Rolls took the view that where possible a copy of material should be made and the original returned. Would this *caveat* prevent the seizure of multiple copies? The seizure of allegedly obscene articles has not been tested in these terms; it may be that the restriction as to making a copy applies only to the seizure of the sole copy available, and not to multiple seizures.

Such multiple copy seizures may however be impermissible at common law merely on the basis that all *Ghani*-sanctioned seizures are *a priori* for evidentiary purposes only. A court may take the view, however, that multiple copies of an article *are* of evidential value in terms of a charge of possession with a view to publication for gain. That the courts may not strictly apply the evidential value requirement is probably clear from *Malone* v *Commissioner of Police of the Metropolis*.[1] The police had here under warrant searched the plaintiff's house and had found a large number of allegedly stolen goods. These they had seized, together with English and foreign bank notes to the value of £10,000. The plaintiff was subsequently charged with handling stolen goods and conspiracy to do so dishonestly. His counsel was instructed that evidence as to the bank notes, their number, denominations, hiding place and discovery, was accepted by the plaintiff, and would not be contested at trial. The Court of Appeal nonetheless overruled the Divisional Court on the question of whether the bank notes were the best evidence on the offences charged. If this interpretation is correct, it would mean that the wide seizure powers provided under the common law may be utilised to effect seizures, which although arguably for evidentiary purposes, constitute nonetheless an at least incidental prior restraint. This would not appear to amount to any extension of seizure powers in respect of obscene materials where a Section 3 warrant is involved; it would have the effect of bestowing such seizure powers as incidental to the execution of other search warrants, arrests, or merely execution of duty, in the sense of presence on premises in the course of an investigation, for example. The only limitations to this, if correct, would be that the police should not seize goods if there is a reasonable refusal to hand them over. This has been interpreted as obliging the police to issue a receipt in such circumstances.[2] Possession of obscene articles with a view to publication for gain would have also

---

1   [1979] 1 All ER 256.

2   *Wershof* v *Metropolitan Police Commissioner* [1978] 3 All ER 540.

to be seen as 'a serious offence'. As the formulation allows the police potentially to seize anything that is evidence of any (serious) crime committed by anyone, the person from whom the material is taken need not necessarily be its possessor.

These potential powers may be coupled with a further statutory provision in the 1959 Act: Section 3(2) provides that

> A warrant under the foregoing subsection shall, if any obscene articles are seized under the warrant, also empower the seizure and removal of any documents found in the premises or, as the case may be, on the stall or vehicle which relate to a trade or business carried on at the premises or from the stall or vehicle.

This section is very widely worded, and allows the seizure of *any* document at all, irrespective of whether it relates to the suspect articles seized, or not. The police may seize from the premises all files, records, invoices, and 'even filing cabinets and pictures on the walls'.[1] An extreme example of the use of these powers, and one which gave rise to much criticism, was the seizure by the police in 1970 in the course of a raid on a cinema showing Andy Warhol's *Flesh*, of 'not only the film, but the projection equipment and even the theatre screen'.[2] These powers provide a clear basis for prior restraint quite unrelated to the offending material, in that the police can use them in effect to close down underground magazines, bookshops, etc. In that seizure is not limited to material which is necessarily of evidential value on any charge, nor to material potentially forfeit, these powers, as present constituted, seem unjustifiable and oppressive.

The Supreme Court in the United States has tried to separate prior restraint seizures from those aimed at securing evidence for a criminal prosecution. With regard to the former, they are permissible only to preserve the *status quo*: to prevent, for example, the disappearance of the material. The grounds on which material may be seized — or a prior restraint *per se* be imposed — prior to forfeiture, are thus narrow; perhaps so narrow as to make forfeiture proceedings almost inoperable. As far as evidentiary seizures are concerned, strict separation of prior restraint and the preservation of evidence for criminal trials is, as with the English common law powers under *Ghani*, difficult to achieve. The Supreme Court's position here is not clear, but it would seem that multiple seizures, if for use in evidence, would be permissible; such seizures

---

1   Robertson op.cit. at 90.

2   Ibid; *Hansard* H Lords Deb, 24 February 1970; HC Deb, 12 March 1970, vol.794, col. 1548; see also G. Zellick 'Two Comments on Search and Seizure under the Obscene Publications Act' [1971] *Crim L Rev* 504.

may have a prior restraint effect in terms of the seizure of a single copy of a work, should that be the only copy available. It is clear that a copy must be made of a film in these circumstances, as it may reach a wider audience; restriction would therefore constitute a more serious prior restraint.[1] It would seem that seizure other than that pursuant to a warrant issued in *Heller* terms, would be found unconstitutional. This was the view of the Court in *Roaden* v *Kentucky*,[2] where a seizure consequent to an arrest without warrant was found impermissible. The Court did remark that such seizure without previous showing of probable cause before a neutral magistrate may be permitted in a genuine 'now or never' situation;[3] the import of this has not been explained.

(b) Under the 1981 Act: As with the 1959 measure, a Section 2(3) warrant must be executed within fourteen days. In view of the Court of Appeal's ruling in *Adams* as to the impermissibility under the 1959 Act of multiple searches under a single warrant, it is probable that each warrant under Section 2(3) will be taken to authorise one search only.

The Act does not provide for any forfeiture procedure; seizure powers under a Section 2(3) warrant are therefore by implication for evidentiary purposes only. Seizure powers resemble those provided under Section 3 of the 1959 Act: once on premises, a constable may seize 'any article' which he reasonably believes 'to be indecent or to contain indecent matter and to have been used in the commission of an offence under this Act'. There is no duty on the magistrate issuing the warrant to specify the titles to be seized, there is not apparently any obligation on the police to make a copy where only a single copy of a work is available, nor to provide a receipt for articles seized. It is not clear where articles are seized under Section 3(1) of the 1959 Act, and then retained for evidentiary purposes, whether the seizure and subsequent detention, or the latter only, are common law based. Assuming that Section 3(1) empowers seizures for forfeiture purposes only, it may be that the entire transaction must needs be common law based. If so, the *Ghani* limitations that the offence involved should be a serious one, that a refusal to hand over the material should be unreasonable, and that sole copies of material should not be seized without providing a copy thereof, may apply. In this sense Section 2(3) of the 1981 Act may make somewhat broader provision. On the other hand, all articles seized must needs have been used in an unlawful display

---

1   The Court has taken a more serious view of seizures where they are of films, which are argued to reach a wider audience than printed material; the issue of the seizure of multiple copies of a film was before the Court in *Hicks* v *Miranda* 422 US 332 (1975); the Court did not reach the merits.

2   413 US 496 (1973).

3   Ibid. at 504; see *Walter* v *United States* 65L Ed 2d 410 (1980). Also chapter 12.

contrary to the Act, a requirement which will probably in practice inhibit the seizure of multiple copies.

In addition, those general common law powers of seizure for evidentiary purposes adhering in the police in respect, for example, of obscene materials, incidentally to the execution of other search warrants, arrests, or the mere execution of duty, have in effect been given statutory recognition in respect of indecent materials, Section 2(2) of the 1981 Act providing that

> A constable may seize any articles which he has reasonable grounds for believing to be or to contain indecent matter and to have been used in the commission of an offence under this Act.

The power of seizure provided by this section might operate incidentally to the execution of a search warrant other than one issued in terms of Section 2(3) of the Act, incidentally to an arrest, whether made under Section 2(1) of the Act[1] or not, or incidentally to the execution of duty, perhaps, controversially, even when such execution is unlawful. The subsection applies of course only to indecent material, but is in this respect wider than the *Ghani* provisions, in that the question of whether an offence under the 1981 Act is for these purposes a 'serious' one, has in effect been statutorily answered in the affirmative. There is moreover no exception in regard to a reasonable refusal to hand over the goods; the *Wershof* requirement of the issue of a receipt in this regard is thus of no force.

Subsequent disposition: The American Supreme Court has specifically provided in this regard, as the time scale and method of adjudication are all directly relevant to the extent of the prior restraint imposed. Where a seizure is made as a prelude to forfeiture, *Freedman* has laid down that a final judicial hearing must be instituted by the censor promptly. It is not clear just what would qualify as 'prompt'; in licensing terms, a procedure allowing 50–57 days for full decision-making was too long.[2] In terms of Customs controls, 74 days from seizure was permissible, but the Court made it clear that such limits vary with circumstances.[3] With seizures as a prelude to forfeiture, something less than 74 days would probably be required; how much less is not clear. Where seizure is for evidentiary purposes, an adversary hearing should be held promptly after seizure, if the defendant requests it. If a finding of obscenity is made at a forfeiture hearing, the materials would be

---

1 See Arrest, Section (ii) below.

2 *Teitel Films* v *Cusack* 390 US 139 (1968).

3 *United States* v *Thirty Seven Photographs* 402 US 363 (1971) at 373–4.

destroyed, whilst criminal statutes may similarly provide for destruction after a trial finding of obscenity.

The position in English law is somewhat less fortunate: material seized under Section 3 of the Obscene Publications Act may in practice be held for months, whilst the DPP decides whether to prosecute, or proceed instead to a forfeiture hearing. In *Cox* v *Stinton*,[1] a case which involved, under Section 1 of the Obscene Publications Act 1857, a delay of nine months between seizure and issue of summons, the Divisional Court refused to intervene to have the summons set aside. If a nine month delay is not unreasonable, one may be forgiven for pondering what is? A possible remedy in the case of such a delay would be an application for an order of *mandamus* to oblige the police to bring the property before a court in terms of Section 3(3), or to return it. Section 3(3) provides that

> Any articles seized under subsection (1) of this section shall be brought before a justice of the peace acting for the same Petty Sessions area as the justice who issued the warrant, and the justice before whom the articles are brought may thereupon issue a summons to the occupier of the premises or, as the case may be, the user of the stall or vehicle to appear on a day specified in the summons before a magistrates' court for that petty session area to show cause why the articles or any of them should not be forfeited ... Provided that this subsection does not apply in relation to any article which is returned to the occupier of the premises.

This subsection, and its predecessor, Section 1 of the Obscene Publications Act 1857, saw the growth of the so-called 'disclaimer' procedure, whereby the police would invite a shopkeeper to sign a document to the effect that he disclaimed ownership of the items seized from his shop. As only the occupier of the premises whence the material had been seized could intervene in a forfeiture proceeding, this ensured the absence of a troublesome contest, allowing the easy forfeiture and destruction of material seized. The practice would not appear to have had any clear statutory basis, as the then Metropolitan Police Commissioner admitted to the House of Commons Select Committee in 1957:

> it ... has no statutory authority behind it at all. It is really a means of avoiding the time and labour and expense of issuing summonses on booksellers inviting them to show cause why the books should not be destroyed, if a man says he is prepared to surrender his right to the articles and agrees

---

1   [1951] 2 KB 1021 at 1025.

that they ought to be destroyed.[1]

The committee recommended that no article should be destroyed without a court order. Although the 1959 Act made a submission to a court mandatory, in relation to the issue of a summons it substituted the word 'may' for 'shall'. The practice as a result, not surprisingly, continued. It amounted to little more than blackmail: if the bookseller did not sign, there was always the possibility of a full prosecution; with the open-ended nature of the law, few booksellers were likely to feel in a position to take such a risk. If, as seems to be the case, the police dealt with large quantitites of material in this way, the practice amounted to a bypassing of existing legal controls, and insofar as these controls might provide safeguards for material, their virtual subversion. The practice continued it would appear, until 1973, when the Court of Appeal in R v *Metropolitan Police ex parte Blackburn*[2] described it as undesirable, and probably illegal. The 1977 Criminal Law Act[3] amendment to Section 3(3), enabling the police to return articles, instead of bringing them before a court, did not seek, in the face of these judicial remarks, to confirm the procedure. The Metropolitan Police, as a result of these judicial remarks on its legality, no longer operate the disclaimer procedure, '... except in very rare circumstances. As an example, if a person should find obscene articles in the street and hand them in to a police station it is normal procedure to ask if he would be willing to disclaim the articles'.[4] Although the procedure may not be used at present, the remarks in *Blackburn* cannot be taken finally to have scotched it; its potential revival remains a possibility in the absence of statutory amendment. In the absence of this procedure, magisterial discretion would seem to extend only to the issue of a summons; if no summons is issued, presumably the court has discretion only to order the articles return.

After nothing more than a 'reasonable' delay then, material arrives before a court. The summons hearing before magistrates is not an adversary one, and neither the occupier of the premises whence the material was seized, nor any other interested party may defend the materials; even written representations are excluded.[5] There is no time limit as to how long may tolerably elapse between the issue of

---

1   Quoted in Paul O'Higgins *Censorship in Britain* (London 1972) at 50.

2   [1973] 2 WLR 43 at 53 per Lord Justice Phillimore.

3   Schedule 12.

4   Letter from the Assistant Commissioner, Metropolitan Police, 18 July 1979, in reply to a query as to the present police practices in this respect.

5   Robertson op.cit. at 95.

summons and the forfeiture hearing itself. There was some doubt as to whether the forfeiture hearing is itself an adversary proceeding. The 1959 Act has effected an improvement in the position of the defence in this regard, in that besides the occupier of the premises where the material was seized, the author, publisher and distributors may intervene: Section 3(4) provides that 'In addition to the person summoned, any other person being the owner, author or maker of any of the articles brought before the court, or any other person through whose hands they had passed before being seized, shall be entitled to appear before the court on the day specified in the summons to show cause why they should not be forfeited'.[1] A drawback here is that the Act does not provide for the notification to such interested parties of potential proceedings. Neither the police, the courts, nor the DPP will undertake such notification, even for example, when publishers' addresses are printed in the article itself.[2] This shortcoming has been raised in Parliament; in 1975 a Minister of State at the Home Office pointed out that 'In 1969 the Attorney-General of the day agreed that, in Section 3 proceedings against booksellers, it was not the Director's responsibility to contact the publishers of any material seized and to inform them of the seizure ... in the circumstances, I think that the initiative must rest with the bookseller to inform the publisher that proceedings have been set in train'.[3]

A variety of people are entitled then to intervene; if it is to be an adversary hearing, there must be an opposition. Lord Goddard in *Thomson* v *Chain Libraries Ltd* suggested that the police had no function at such a hearing: that it was in other words, a matter between the justices and respondent. Were this so, it might be left as a matter solely for the justices, for Section 3(3) provides that '... if the person summoned does not appear, the court shall not make an order *unless* service of summons is proved'.[4] If such service is proved, the hearing may proceed; in view of the absence of any mechanism for informing all interested parties, the absence of a defence representative may not be uncommon. Were the police to be excluded also, the matter would be entirely one for the justices. It must be remembered here that the magistrates issuing the summons and hearing forfeiture proceedings are members of the same Petty Sessions, and may in fact often be the same

---

1 See the Report of the 1957 Select Committee; quoted in Robertson op.cit. at 97–8.

2 Ibid. at 98.

3 Letter from the Solicitor-General to Sir Geoffrey Howe, 22 May 1975; quoted ibid.

4 [1954] 2 All ER 616 at 618; emphasis added.

officers. It has been argued that this possibly means a hearing before a biased tribunal. Lord Chief Justice Parker was adamant in his rejection of this:

> Justices must come to a *prima facie* view when the articles are brought before them, as these justices did. They are not determining the matter; they are merely deciding whether a summons should issue. It seems to me quite wrong to suggest that, because they have taken a *prima facie* view, they are in some way biased or incapable of approaching with an open mind the hearing of the summons. I feel that there is nothing whatsoever in that objection.[1]

The justices, should they double as adjudicators on both occasions, may not relish nonetheless reversing, in effect, their earlier view of *prima facie* obscenity in issuing a summons. Although the adjudication is in terms of the statutory definition of obscenity, with a work having to be assessed as a whole, and expert evidence on merit being available, each justice does not need to read every book.[2] The courts for some years moreover applied the obscenity test in such a way as, in effect, to disregard distribution altogether. Section 3(7) provides that in relation to forfeiture proceedings '... the question whether an article is obscene shall be determined on the assumption that copies of it would be published in any manner likely having regard to the circumstances in which it was found, but in no other manner'. The courts interpreted the latter phrase 'but in no other manner' as excluding evidence of the nature of the respondent's business, and his system of distribution.[3] Although the obscenity test (as interpreted) probably comes close to constant obscenity with pornography as far as distribution is concerned, this was to leave the relevant audience undefined. Presumably the assessment was in terms of the average person, as represented by the justices. This could serve only to heighten concern that might be felt at the disparities between such proceedings and criminal trials before a jury. This interpretation of Section 3(7) has been specifically disapproved by the Divisional Court in *Morgan v Bowker*, where Lord Parker held that regard should be had in circumstances to evidence given by a defendant 'as to the nature of his business and the methods employed by him'.[4]

The onus or burden of proof in forfeiture proceedings provides a

---

1   *Morgan v Bowker* [1964] 1 QB 507 at 515.

2   *Olympia Press v Hollis* [1974] 1 All ER 108; *contra Burke v Copper* [1962] 2 All ER 14 at 18.

3   Robertson op.cit. at 100.

4   [1964] 1 QB 507 at 516–7.

substantial disparity with criminal process, resting as it does on the accused.[1] *Dicta* in the *Thomson* case excluding prosecution evidence on the score of obscenity, have been taken to indicate a balance of probability standard in respect of such onus.[2] Indeed, if the burden of proof does fall on the respondent, it would scarcely be possible to require him to establish beyond a reasonable doubt the material's non-obscenity. All this nonetheless places a considerable burden on a respondent: he must persuade a tribunal with preconceived ideas on the subject that the material in question is not obscene. All the justices need think is that the material *may* be obscene: the onus after all is on the respondent to establish on balance that it is not. It is true that the *Thomson dicta* in this regard were made in terms of the 1857 Act. The provisions in both statutes as to seizure and the burden and standard of proof are however the same: respondents have 'to show cause' why the publications should not be destroyed. One aspect of the above that has been disapproved though, is the attitude to the presence and role of police prosecutors, whose functions in this respect were specifically approved in *Burke*.[3]

Thus, although some of the disparities as far as the application of the obscenity test as between forfeiture proceedings and criminal trials may have been ironed out, the former contrast strongly in a number of respects. Because of the absence of a system of notification, no-one may oppose forfeiture at all; where an interested party does appear, he may bear the burden of proof, and this possibly before a tribunal with preconceived ideas as to the question of 'fact' they are to decide. There may at worst be a decision by a partial adjudicator without any contest at all. Anxiety over the defects in the forfeiture system led to strong representations at the time of the passage of the Obscene Publications Act 1964, that interested parties to such proceedings should be given the opportunity to take their case, in the form of a true adversary hearing, before a jury. Nothing was done statutorily, but the following undertaking was given by the Solicitor-General, with the approval of the Attorney-General:

> ... if an article is seized under a warrant from a retailer or printer and if, before it is brought before the justices under section 3(3) of the 1959 Act, the publisher indicates his intention to continue publishing, whatever the result of any forfeiture proceedings may be, then, in the absence of any

---

1 *Thomson v Chain Libraries Ltd* [1954] 2 All ER 616 at 619.

2 Ibid. at 618.

3 [1962] 2 All ER 14.

> special circumstances, and subject to satisfactory evidence
> of an offence being available, it will ordinarily be the policy
> of the Director of Public Prosecutions to proceed against
> the publisher by way of prosecution rather than to pursue
> the forfeiture proceedings.[1]

Although the DPP told the Williams Committee that he regarded the undertaking as applying to literate works such as *Fanny Hill*, and to certain monthly magazines not produced in 1964, there had at the time of his evidence to them, been only one case in which an English publisher had sought to take advantage of the undertaking, and it was turned down because it did not satisfy the requirement of having been made before the magistrates' court proceedings had begun.[2] In view of the lack of a proper notification system under Section 3, the undertaking is virtually worthless.

The forfeiture proceeding differs from its American counterpart in that its use has increased greatly, and is not subject to any limitations in terms of the temporary restraint imposed prior to the hearing, other than those limited restraints on the issue of a warrant. There is no guarantee of a true adversary hearing before a final restraint is imposed, and there is no limit — beyond requirements of reasonableness — on the timescale involved. The latter point was one of the main criticisms — the other being the absence of access to a jury hearing — of the procedure advanced by Williams.[3] As was pointed out, even if the defendant won his case, he might have returned to him months after their original seizure, magazines now out of date and useless. Although much of this material probably does not go out of date in this way, the law is clearly unfair. The committee had the view put to them that this was the only practical way of dealing with pornography, and was therefore justified. This could be seen more as a criticism of obscenity law as such, rather than a convincing rationale of the type of procedure described above. Even an appeal of a forfeiture decision (under Section 3(5) of the Act) to the Crown Court cannot assuage misgivings. This is a considerable burden on an interested party, and although a check on cursory rulings by magistrates, cannot compensate for the uncertainties, and often oppressive effect of the prescribed forfeiture procedure.

We have so far been discussing the disposition of material in terms of a forfeiture hearing. Material may have been seized and/or retained with a view to a prosecution under the Obscene Publications Acts. On

---

1   House of Commons, Standing Committee F, 16 June 1964; Official Report 1963—4, vol.4, col.77; see *Williams* paras 2.16 and 2.17.

2   *Williams* para 2.17.

3   Ibid. para 2.18.

the assumption that Section 3(1) of the 1959 Act is concerned with the prosecution of forfeiture proceedings only, where material is seized under a Section 3(1) warrant and subsequently retained for use in a criminal prosecution, such retention — at least — will be common law based. Material may additionally have been seized under common law powers *per se*. In either case materials seized should be retained for no longer than is reasonably necessary, and then only if of evidential value; in view of *Malone* v *Commissioner of Police of the Metropolis*[1] the latter requirement would appear in reality to be a somewhat tenuous one. Assuming that the case proceeds to trial, the 1964 Act specifically provides that should there be a finding of possession with a view to publication for gain, the trial court should order the destruction of the obscene material;[2] the 1959 Act is silent on this score. The ultimate fate of the material, in the sense at least of its obscenity or non-obscenity, is determined in terms of a full adversary hearing. There is no guarantee of a speedy conclusion to this process however, whilst should the matter not proceed to trial, the material may well be returned to its owner many months after its initial detention. The burden of initiating proceedings for their return would in the interim fall on its owner. Such considerations would apply, *mutatis mutandis*, to seizures under Section 2(2) of the Indecent Displays (Control) Act 1981.

Other Provisions: The only other search, seizure and forfeiture provision in this area is provided by the Protection of Children Act 1978, Section 5. The section has been modelled closely on Section 3 of the 1959 Act; the discussion above (other than in relation to the standard employed) would be equally applicable to the former provision. There is in addition provision under the Customs and Excise Management Act 1979[3] that any customs officer may, having a writ of assistance, enter any building or place where 'there are reasonable grounds to suspect that anything liable to forfeiture under the customs and excise Acts is kept or concealed'. Thus any article found which is reasonably thought to have been unlawfully imported, and indecent or obscene in terms of the Act, may accordingly be seized. It is also provided that if reasonable cause in the above terms is shown to a Justice of the Peace, he may issue a search warrant whereby any officer 'or any other person named in the warrant' is authorised to enter, search and seize in the above terms.[4] Only reasonable suspicion as to the presence of the material in

---

1   [1979] 1 All ER 256 at 261−3.

2   Section 1(4).

3   Section 161(1).

4   Section 161(3).

question is required; clearly the conclusory assertions of a single officer are sufficient as to the issue of the warrant. A Section 161 warrant does not have to be executed within fourteen days, whilst it may be used to seize material with a view to forfeiture or subsequent prosecution. The titles in question need not be specified, whilst the authorisation under Section 161 extends to the seizure of single copies where only one copy is available, or to the seizure of multiple copies. Where the police are concerned, and provided that a contravention of customs regulation is seen as a serious offence, those common law powers enumerated in *Ghani* as to evidentiary seizures would be of equal application here.

The Customs and Excise Management Act provides two further search powers: officers may, on reasonable suspicion that they are carrying indecent or obscene articles imported in contravention of the Act, search vehicles or vessels,[1] or any person reasonably suspected of having such goods on him whilst entering or leaving the United Kingdom, or whilst in a transit area such as, for example, a dock or airport.[2] Where an individual who is to be searched in the above terms so requires, he must be taken before a Justice of the Peace or a superior officer or other person concerned; the latter shall then 'consider the grounds for suspicion and direct accordingly whether or not the search is to take place'.[3] A general power of seizure in relation to such goods is provided by Section 139 of the Act. Search and seizure powers in terms of vehicles or persons would then mirror in breadth those available in respect of premises. The question of the disposition of articles seized under the customs provisions is dealt with separately above.[4]

Law Reform: The Williams Committee did not recommend a forfeiture procedure either as to their recommended restriction on displays, nor as to the prohibition on the production or distribution of pornography the production of which involved minors or the occasioning of actual physical harm. In relation to the first they felt that it was the circumstances of publication, rather than the material, at which control was aimed; a criminal law control on such circumstances, rather than bulk destruction of the material, seemed appropriate. In relation to the proposed prohibition, this was thought enough as a deterrent only in terms of an exclusive operation: the conduct involved, in other words, is so serious as to merit only the attentions of the criminal law. When one takes into account the lengths to which the American

---

1   Section 163(1).

2   See Sections 164(1) and (4).

3   Section 164(2).

4   See chapter 7, Section 1(3): Customs Controls.

Supreme Court have gone to limit prior restraint, making in the process any forfeiture proceeding virtually inoperable, one is perhaps justified in demanding convincing argument that prior restraint is the better, or perhaps the only really effective method of dealing with the conduct in question. Freedom of speech, when seen in its constitutional dimension, must carry considerable weight, and is all the weightier in relation to prior, rather than subsequent restraints. It must be remembered that the First Amendment does not prevent seizures that are for evidentiary purposes, and that such seizures may be of multiple copies, nor does it, other than in the case of films, necessitate the return of the original, if only a sole copy is available.

Williams, although rejecting forfeiture,[1] did recommend that in relation to restriction on displays and sales in unrestricted premises the police be provided with a power of search and seizure because, although conduct such as selling openly from shelves would be obvious, there '... could well be other cases where restricted material is being sold more discreetly, from under the counter for example, and where evidence may be harder to obtain'.[2] They felt that such a power, 'to be exercised with the authority of a warrant issued by a magistrate', should also clearly exist in relation to the prohibition on the production and/or distribution of pornography the production of which involved minors or the occasioning of actual physical harm.[3] Their recommendations in respect of the former have been followed in the Indecent Displays (Control) Act 1981.

In view of the serious nature of the conduct falling within the prohibition, such powers seem more justified in this regard than in respect of the restriction on displays. If the prohibition and search power were appropriately worded, the seizure of multiple copies as evidence for a subsequent prosecution would be permissible, thus providing a sufficient power in relation to such material when held in bulk. This would clearly constitute a prior restraint. Such a provision would probably be constitutional in American terms provided the *Heller* conditions were observed. As far as English law is concerned, similar tightening of the prior restraint potential involved in such seizures would seem desirable. There is first the question of the issue of the warrant: although to require titles to be specified might make the use of this power a little difficult, one might, in prior restraint terms, wish for a stronger basis than 'the conclusory affidavit of a single police officer'. Second, one might well wish, again in prior restraint terms, to emphasise the require-

---

1   Other than in respect of customs controls: see above.

2   *Williams* para 9.45.

3   Ibid. para 10.17.

ment of such a neutral preliminary hearing in relation to common law powers of seizure external to a search warrant. Third, in view of the type of material involved, it might be appropriate to remove any obligation on the police to provide copies where only a sole copy is available. Fourth, some provision might be made as to retention of such materials prior to the trial, and the timespan involved. Either a preliminary adversary hearing might be held, or the statute might make clear that such materials were only to be held for a reasonable length of time and only if genuinely of evidential value. Some qualification of 'reasonable' and 'genuine' might be indicated to ensure a narrow interpretation by the courts. Fifth, Williams recommended that even if the giving of receipts on the spot for material seized was not always practicable, that the person '... from whom goods are seized should be given at the earliest opportunity a detailed record of what has been taken from him'.[1] Finally, such search and seizure provisions might be extended specifically to the mails.

(ii) *Arrest.* It may seem strange to regard a power of arrest as a potential prior restraint. Yet in the free speech area this is surely the (at least secondary) effect an arrest will have: once an arrest is effected and presuming subsequent detention, any possibility of publication before a subsequent criminal hearing is ended. The primary purpose and effect of an arrest power is presumably both to prevent the commission of a crime, and/or to ensure that the alleged criminal is brought to court. These two policy factors are reflected in the provisions governing continued detention after arrest and charge: Section 4(1) of the Bail Act 1976 provides that 'A person to whom this section applies shall be granted bail except as provided in Schedule 1 to this Act'. Accused people have a 'right' to bail, unless there are reasonable grounds for believing one of the exceptions applicable; the principal of these are listed in paragraph 2 of Schedule 1: that the defendant if released on bail would '... (a) fail to surrender to custody, or (b) commit an offence while on bail, or (c) interfere with witnesses or otherwise obstruct the course of justice, whether in relation to himself or any other person'.

The process of arrest and detention is manifestly an interference with individual liberty; the provision or non-provision of an arrest power in relation to a particular offence appears to be determined largely in terms of the seriousness of that offence. In other words, if the offence is sufficiently serious, it may be seen as pressing that someone reasonably suspected to be about to commit the offence be stopped, whilst it is equally important to ensure that alleged offenders be brought to justice. Before any decision is reached in relation to

---

1 *Williams* para 9.45.

offences in this area however, it is suggested that the prior restraint effect of arrest and the bail requirements be added to the question of interference with the freedom of the person. These may be weighed against the seriousness of the offence, and the view that the law should be enforceable. As long as a power of arrest or subsequent refusal of bail is based on the seriousness of the offence, but in particular on the need to ensure the alleged offender is brought to trial, any prior restriction on freedom of speech could be seen in the same light as can seizures of evidence for evidentiary purposes: in other words, a prior restriction, and not essentially a prior restraint. Once the question of the commission of an offence, or further offences, in the future becomes crucial however, then even though the offence may be serious, one has a prior restraint.

The Williams Committee remark in regard to their proposed restriction on offensive displays, that a power of arrest does not seem 'appropriate'.[1] In relation to the proposed prohibition on the production of pornography involving minors or actual physical harm to participants, they take the opposite view.[2] They appear to base their attitude in the latter respect principally on the difficulty of bringing offenders in this area to justice without an arrest power. The Metropolitan Police in evidence recorded that they had in 1973 searched 332 premises in terms of the Obscene Publications Acts, but that 93 of the men questioned in the process subsequently disappeared without trace. 'In other cases those responsible simply carried on trading normally until the case came to court, whereas if they had been arrested and bailed, the prospect of bail being revoked might have been a more effective deterrent against their continuing the offence.'[3] Certainly a safeguard in respect of any power of arrest provided in this area would be to enter a *caveat* in regard to the granting of bail: that is, unless the seriousness of the offence is felt to outweigh inhibitions against prior restraints, bail should be granted.

The Committee's recommendations as to a power of arrest in the former respect have not been followed. The Indecent Displays (Control) Act 1981, in instituting (it is noteworthy) the only arrest power in this area, provides that a constable may require of any person whom the constable reasonably suspects of *having* committed an offence under the Act, his name and address. If that person 'refuses or fails to do so or gives a name or address which the constable reasonably suspects to

---

1   *Williams* para 9.46.

2   Ibid. para 10.17.

3   Ibid.

be false, the constable may arrest him without warrant'.[1] This provision achieves a balance between considerations of individual liberty and prior restraint on the one hand, and on the other the need to bring offenders to justice, the seriousness of the offence, and the likelihood of the further offences. The question of the prior restraint aspect of arrest in this area does not appear to have been considered in the United States, where attention has focused rather on the question of the seizure of materials in such situations.

(iii)   *Declarations.* The first question here is to establish whether a declaration is a prior restraint at all. A declaration has no definite effect in the sense of imposing an obligation, and does not even have the effect of *autrefois acquit*. If however, one regards prior restraints a little more broadly, in the sense of including mechanisms capable of having a chilling effect on publication, it does not seem unreasonable to regard declarations as having a prior restraint effect. Certainly, a declaration which confirms that a proposed course of action is criminal very probably serves to inhibit such action.

It is doubtful whether declarations are of much significance here; in the first place, they are not generally given in relation to questions of fact; their relevance to obscenity or indecency determinations is correspondingly limited. Second, it is by no means clear that a declaration would be granted in order to determine criminal liability. In matters of public concern, the general rule would seem to be that an applicant should have a direct and substantial interest in the proceedings.[2] It would appear that the High Court has a residual authority to halt vexatious or oppressive proceedings.[3] It has been argued that once a declaration has been granted on a question of law, subsequent criminal proceedings on all fours would be vexatious.[4] This may well be correct; it does not answer the question of the rules governing the initiation of such proceedings for a declaration. It may be that a new class of circumstance will be recognised in which a delcaration may be obtained: where an applicant wishes to establish the criminality of his own actions, *locus standi* may be accorded on the basis of his clear, direct and substantial interest in the question of public concern involved. Were this to be the case, such standing would probably apply only where the allegedly criminal act had already been committed: it would

---

1   Section 2(1).

2   S.A. de Smith *Judicial Review of Administrative Action* (London 1980) at 509–10.

3   See double jeopardy, chapter 2.

4   D. Feldman 'Declarations and Control of Prosecutions', cited ibid.

seem that declarations are not available to establish criminality in terms of prospective conduct.[1] However, the authority for the grant of a declaration in these circumstances, even *ex post facto* the conduct in question, is slim.[2] Although the classes of situation in relation to which declarations may be issued is not a closed list, it may be that declarations are relevant here only if set on foot in terms of an already recognised situation.

Third, it might be possible for an individual to obtain a declaration as to the alleged criminality of the conduct of another. This would almost certainly be limited to past conduct; standing would moreover have to be established, and although the party seeking the declaration need not establish that a legal interest of his has been impaired, he must show a direct and substantial interest in the proceedings. Whether this could be done in terms of obscenity or indecency law is doubtful. Mr Raymond Blackburn established standing on the basis of having a wife and five children, and of being resident in the borough, in respect of *mandamus* proceedings against the Metropolitan Commissioner of Police and the GLC respectively.[3] It would seem that standing is less strictly viewed in such proceedings than in relation to declarations,[4] whilst it has been suggested that such matters adhere essentially to the Attorney-General.[5] There is of course always the possibility of action by the Attorney-General, or by relator. Declarations are a possibility in the United States in terms of obscenity determination, where it may be argued that such determinations are to a large extent a matter of constitutional law; there do not appear to be the same technical difficulties.[6] *Freedman* standards would presumably be applicable, at least as to prompt hearings, decision and burden of proof.

(iv) *Injunctions*. The initial problem here is to determine which varieties[7] (if any) of injunction constitute a prior restraint. In relation to interim or interlocutory injunctions, is disobedience to such an injunc-

---

1   *Imperial Tobacco Ltd* v *Attorney-General* [1980] 2 WLR 466 at 477–8; Feldman op.cit.

2   Feldman op.cit.

3   See *R* v *Metropolitan Commissioner of Police, ex parte Blackburn* [1973] 2 WLR 43; *R* v *GLC* [1976] 3 All ER 184.

4   De Smith op.cit. at 553, footnote 86.

5   Ibid. at 549; the matter was left open in *Gouriet* v *Union of Post Office Workers* [1978] AC 435 at 495.

6   See chapter 12.

7   See de Smith op.cit. at 434–5.

tion punishable as contempt of court, even though the second hearing finds that the publication in question (for example) did not transgress the standard in terms of which the initial restraint was issued? Mr Justice Frankfurter, in *Kingsley International Pictures Co. v Regents*[1] argued not. It was argued in *Vance v Universal Amusement Co.*[2] that an injunction of this type did not essentially involve a prior restraint at all, in the sense of imposing no greater burden than did a subsequent criminal sanction. The Court's *per curiam* judgement, however, struck down the Texas regulation which apparently allowed the temporary enjoining for an indefinite period of specific films after an *ex parte* showing, as not satisfying *Freedman* guarantees. In so doing they clearly regarded such an injunction as a prior restraint, taking the view that even were a film to be found non-obscene at a subsequent hearing, an exhibitor would still be liable for contempt of court were he to disobey the temporary injunction.[3] Another question in this respect is whether at subsequent proceedings for committal for disobedience to an injunction, the question merely of the breach itself is reviewed in terms of a criminal law standard of proof, or are the merits re-examined in these terms? The position in English law does not appear to be clear on this: although the breach of the injunction has to be established beyond a reasonable doubt,[4] Lord Wilberforce in *Gouriet* for example, objected to the use of injunctions to restrain breaches of the criminal law precisely because, in his view, different burdens of proof apply to the grant of the injunction and the question of breach.[5] Quite apart from this, one may yet have to do with a prior restraint, in the sense that any order of this sort surely throws a chilling effect over freedom of speech? Certainly the approach of the Supreme Court would appear to have been to regard such a provision as a prior restraint notwithstanding: the Rhode Island review scheme examined in *Bantam Books v Sullivan*[6] did not involve a mandatory prior restraint. The chilling effect of the review board's activities in reviewing publications not suitable for minors, and threatening prosecution in relation to those not amenable to their findings, was nonetheless clearly branded a prior restraint of speech.

---

1   360 US 684 (1959); see chapter 12.

2   63 L Ed 2d 413 (1980).

3   Ibid. at 420.

4   *Kent C.C. v Batchelor* (1977) P and CR 185.

5   *Gouriet v Union of Post Office Workers* [1978] AC 435 at 481.

6   372 US 58 (1963); chapter 12.

The operation of injunctions as prior restraints in this area would in any event seem limited. It has been made quite clear that an individual seeking an injunction to restrain the commission or continuance of an alleged criminal offence must show that the conduct in question violates a private legal right adhering to him, or perhaps, causes him special damage. The latter point was left open in *Gouriet* v *Union of Post Office Workers*;[1] if such a category is open, it appears to mean 'detriment attributable to an injury which is either distinct in character or significantly different in degree from any inconvenience suffered by other members of the public.[2] As was pointed out above in relation to declarations, Mr Raymond Blackburn has obtained orders of *mandamus* to enforce duties of a public nature in this area, on the basis of the composition of his family, and his area of residence; equally, it would seem that standing is much more strictly viewed in relation to injunctions: the House of Lords has made it clear that in *Attorney-General, ex rel, McWhirter* v *IBA*,[3] for example, Mr McWhirter should not have been accorded *locus standi* for the purposes of an interim injunction in relation to the broadcasting of an allegedly indecent programme.[4] The likelihood of an injunction lying to an individual is then remote.

It is of course open to the Attorney-General to institute proceedings for an injunction in such circumstances, or to allow a relator action: 'it seems that English courts will not refuse the Attorney-General an injunction to secure due compliance with the law except on very strong grounds'.[5] A number of arguments can be raised against the use of injunctions to secure compliance with the criminal law: 'disobedience to the injunction may result in imprisonment for an indefinite period without the benefit of trial by jury'.[6] Equally, the fairness of subsequent criminal proceedings may be affected by preceding civil hearings, and the publicity attached to them. This latter objection brings one back in fact to the question raised initially in this discussion: are injunctions prior restraints at all, in the sense that there is, before committal for breach, a review on the basis of a different standard of proof, proof beyond a reasonable doubt being required in respect of such latter decision? The position in English law does not appear clear on

---

1 [1978] AC 435; see de Smith op.cit. at 451, footnote 46.

2 De Smith op.cit. at 451.

3 [1973] AC 629.

4 *Gouriet* v *Union of Post Office Workers* [1978] AC 435 at 483, 495, 511 and 521–2.

5 De Smith op.cit. at 457.

6 Ibid.

this: if the stricter standard of proof applies only to the question of publication in breach of injunction, and not to the question of the nature of the publication, then unquestionably one has a prior restraint. The potential effectiveness of the latter is vastly enhanced, moreover, by the disparity (given the above assumption of different burdens of proof) between that applicable in criminal hearings, and that applicable in respect of injunctions: with interlocutory injunctions the standard is merely a balance of convenience.[1] Even were the reasonable doubt standard applicable *de novo*, one may still have a prior restraint, a consideration which may be added to the list of objections to the use of injunctions to restrain breaches of the criminal law in this area. Whether scattered *dicta* in, for example, *Gouriet* to the effect that the Attorney-General's discretion in this respect should not readily be enlarged,[2] will be followed, remains to be seen.

Injunctions have been utilised in American law, mainly in the form of statutory prior restraint schemes. Any such scheme must satisfy the requirements stipulated in *Freedman v Maryland*.[3] No such scheme exists in English law, and aside from the relevance of injunctions to the operation of public bodies such as local authorities (in terms of film censorship)[4] or broadcasting authorities,[5] the only apparent relevance for injunctions (or declarations) is in relation to the enforcement of the criminal law. Injunctions may however be granted in restraint of publication in this area, quite aside from questions of the enforcement of the criminal law, and in the absence of any statutory prior restraint scheme along American lines. A number of residents of Longmoore Street, Pimlico, recently brought an application before Chancery to restrain by injunction the continued operation of a sex shop which had opened on the corner of Longmoore Street and Wilton Road, Pimlico.[6] The basis of the claim was private nuisance, in the sense of the offence caused by such a business and its clientele to local residents constituting a material and unreasonable interference with the latters' comfort and

---

1 *American Cyanamid Co v Ethicon Ltd* [1975] AC 396; P. Wallington 'Injunctions and the Right to Demonstrate' 35 (1976) *Camb L J* 82.

2 [1978] AC 435 at 481, 490–1, 498–500 and 521; cf. also *dicta* by Lord Denning MR in *Imperial Tobacco Ltd v Attorney-General* [1979] 2 WLR 805 at 810 on the desirability of relator proceedings to determine whether conduct breaches the criminal law; the latter were expressly disapproved by Viscount Dilhorne in the House of Lords: [1980] 2 WLR 466 at 477–8.

3 *Supra*.

4 See below.

5 Ibid.

6 *Laws v Florinplace Ltd* [1981] 1 All ER 659.

enjoyment of their property; interlocutory relief was granted on a balance of convenience.

The decision neatly illustrates the difference a Bill of Rights can make to judicial process: freedom of speech formed no part of the court's reasoning in granting the injunction. As a result speech in this country is now subject to a clear prior restraint, a restraint which operates in terms of a standard that is virtually undefined. The restraint it is true, is a restriction rather than a prohibition: an injunction of this sort would operate (particularly if confirmed as permanent) as an indirect zoning mechanism. The court did not say that sex shops may not operate; it said rather — on an interlocutory basis — that such shops cannot operate in the type of residential area in question, their operation in such context constituting an offensive interference with the rights of local property owners. That the effect of such an order is indirectly to zone is clear when one considers that private nuisance remedies are open only to owners or occupiers.[1] Against this one must balance the fact that one is dealing with a prior restraint, which demands strong justification in freedom of speech terms. What are the justifications here? According to the court, the effect that the continued operation of the shop would have on the character of the neighbourhood, and the offence caused to residents by the knowledge that the business was being carried on on their doorstep.[2] The court was not necessarily, in other words, concerned with gratuitous offence; the rationale of the restriction involves a variety of offence which is borderline in rationally assessable harm terms. The standard employed is not clearly specified moreover, approximating it would appear to 'hard pornography'.[3] Whatever the position might be purely in terms of the law of private nuisance, had the court seen the application in terms of the above perspectives, it might well, even in the absence of a constitutionally sustainable right to free speech, have refused the application; unless that is, that it was satisfied as to the gratuitous offence caused by the shop's clientele to local residents.[4] Certainly at trial such application should not succeed on a balance of probabilities.

(v) *Administrative restraints.* The licensing of publications in Britain applied originally only to serious works, a distinction which prompted

---

1   Laws v *Florinplace Ltd* [1981] 1 All ER 659 at 664, quoting Lord Wright in *Sedleigh-Denfield* v *O'Callaghan* [1940] 3 All ER 349 at 364.

2   Ibid. at 667.

3   Ibid.

4   The shop in question did not carry offensive displays, whilst warning notices were posted for adults, those under eighteen years of age being denied entrance.

what was the country's first Obscene Publications Bill, a legislative attempt which also saw the word 'corruption' being used for the first time in this context. The Bill was drafted in 1580 by William Lambard, a magistrate and lawyer, and was probably motiviated more by a concern that the commercial burden of licensing be spread more evenly, than a concern with licentiousness. The Bill prophetically proposed the censorship of material which led to (*inter alia*) '... the intolerable corruption of common life and manners ...'.[1] The censorship in question was to be effected by a censorship board consisting of eight benchers of the Inns of Court. In the event it was never presented to Parliament, whilst the licensing of books finally expired in 1695. It was this historical background which Williams chose to emphasise when considering the opposing merits of subsequent and prior restraints with regard to proposed offence restrictions: despite precedents in Australia and New Zealand for the latter form of control over material unsuitable for children or offensive in public display, the committee felt that such controls would be 'quite unacceptable in this country'.[2] There are of course different ways in which such prior restraint might be structured; before discussing its endorsement or non-endorsement further, it may be instructive very briefly to examine two such systems operative elsewhere.

The Australian state of New South Wales[3] provides both an offence of publishing or displaying an indecent article, and a procedure for the classification of publications by appointed officials. The 1975 Act provides for the appointment of classification officers, who may classify material referred to them by the minister and/or the publisher. Classification is in terms of four categories: (a) unrestricted publications; (b) restricted publications; (c) direct sale publications; (d) child pornography. The publication, or possession for publication, of the latter is an offence. As far as category (c) is concerned, such publications cannot be displayed or exhibited publicly under any circumstances, and may only be sold a copy at a time, on the unsolicited request of someone over eighteen years of age. Category (b) may be displayed and/or sold within a shop which restricts entry to those over eighteen years of age. Both categories of publication must be 'completely wrapped in opaque wrapping', and cannot be advertised, although a warning notice outside the shop as to the possible offensiveness of its contents is permissible. The actual decision as to classification is made in terms of whether the publication relates to sex, drug

---

1   Quoted in Robertson op.cit. at 18.

2   *Williams* para 9.22.

3   See ibid., Appendix 3; Robertson op.cit. at 312—4.

addiction, horror, crime, cruelty or violence.[1] If the publisher or the minister disagrees with a classification, appeal may be had to the Publications Control Board, from whose decision a further appeal lies to the district court. If a declaratory judgement may be regarded as a prior restraint, this sort of system, which although to an extent voluntary in the sense that aside from the minister, requests to the Board come from the publisher, must, in view of the enforceability of the Board's decisions, constitute a similar restraint. Does this, or Williams' apparently traditional English deference to the past, automatically rule it out as far as English law is concerned? It has after all much to commend it: it is not, in the absence of ministerial action, mandatory; it may give publishers the opportunity to ascertain in advance potential liability in terms of the criminal law, both in respect of themselves, and their distributors and retailers; the public, at the same time, receives greater protection in the sense that an additional mechanism exists for filtering borderline material.

A number of modifications to the system are possible, whereby the prior restraint objections may perhaps to a considerable degree be allayed. The New South Wales system provides a criminal restraint in terms of indecency: the overbreadth of this standard is such as perhaps to pressure publishers to make use of the prior restraint. Were the tightly drawn standards recommended earlier as to the protection of minors, and the prevention of offence, to be utilised, this would not, to the same extent, be the case. If the Board were themselves to examine preferably all of such referrals, and do so with the aid of experts, reaching a decision in terms of the same standards applicable in the criminal law, and in terms of the same burden of proof, a publisher might have little to lose by using the system. Were one to add a *Freedman*-type requirement of a prompt judicial review *de novo*, with a jury, of the decision, he might well have much to gain. Although the tight time-scales envisaged in *Freedman* might be implemented, it is doubtful whether judicial review would be feasible in *every* case, as opposed to those appealed. A compromise, taking account of the partly voluntary nature of the system, would be to make mandatory judicial review in every case officially referred to the Board. Although the composition of such a Publications Control Board would inevitably be a matter of controversy, in view of the safeguards mentioned above, and in view of the fact that one is concerned with a restriction, and not a prohibition, such a system might prove a useful adjunct to the basic criminal prohibition. In view of the fact that the prohibition recommended above as to child pornography and pornography the production

---

1   South Australia, which operates a similar system, has issued regulations, quoted in Robertson op.cit. at 313—4, elaborating on the standard in list fashion.

of which occasions actual physical harm, covers the production of such material, this area is perhaps best left to the criminal law: any decision by the Board in such a case might well involve an assertion of criminality in relation to the publisher requesting the decision, were he to have been involved in the production of the material.

The licensing system operated in South Africa in relation to books, films and public entertainment,[1] forms a striking contrast to the Australian models. A Publications Control Board had been instituted in 1963 with respect to such forms of speech; its decisions were subject to judicial review on the usual grounds. This was not enough to satisfy the government, who in 1974 promoted a new Publications Act. Not only did the Act institute a very broad standard in terms of which decisions were to be made; it also removed the right to judicial review of such administrative decisions. A publication may be branded as undesirable by the Board of it

   (a) is indecent or obscene or is offensive or harmful to public morals;
   (b) is blasphemous or is offensive to the religious convictions or feelings of any section of the inhabitants of the Republic;
   (c) brings any section of the inhabitants of the Republic into ridicule or contempt;
   (d) is harmful to the relations between any sections of the inhabitants of the Republic;
   (e) if prejudicial to the safety of the State, the general welfare or the peace and good order.[2]

Appeal may be had from the Board to an Appeal Board, whose decisions are subject to the review of three judges. If the judges set aside a decision, it must be referred back to the Appeal Board, unless it is found to have been made *mala fide*, in which case the tribunal may substitute its own decisions for that of the Appeal Board. Like a court of law, the Appeal Board is obliged to give reasons, and in *Directorate of Publications* v *Brandwagpers*[3] outlined its approach, in a number of respects, to undesirability:

   (a) *Indecent or obscene*: a publication is indecent or obscene if it has the tendency to evoke lust or contains a disrespectful or morbid portrayal of sex or nudity or has the

---

[1] See J. Dugard *Human Rights and the South African Legal Order* (Princeton 1978) at 192–201.

[2] Section 47(2).

[3] A.P. 2/3/8/75 of 9 July 1975.

tendency to evoke sexual stimulation in regard to the portrayal or descriptions of violence, cruelty, or brutality.
(b) *Offensive to public morals*: this phrase covers material that is repugnant or that mortifies or pains and includes the use of swear words, blasphemy and foul language, or the portrayal of excessive violence.
(c) *Harmful to public morals*: this phrase concerns the portrayal of immorality as normal and natural, satisfying and right.[1]

The system imposes a prohibition rather than a restriction; this it does by means of a bald prior restraint, not itself subject to judicial review, other than of the most peculiar and ineffective sort. The basis of the system is moreover a standard so grossly overbroad as to render freedom of speech a privilege to be enjoyed only at the behest of the ruling Afrikaner elite. The censorious weight of the system illustrates in its extremity not only the dangers of prior restraint, but perhaps even more the basic political character of obscenity regulation.

(vi)   *Zoning.* There would not at present in England and Wales appear to be any planning law provisions which dilate specifically on the questions of public sexual morality.[2] Section 29(1) of the Town and Country Planning Act 1971 provides that an authority in considering planning applications, is required to have regard to the development plan, insofar as it is material, its policy in relation to the area and to any other material considerations. 'Material considerations' have been stipulated to be (in the Minister's Development Control Policy Note, No. 1 General Principles) 'genuine planning considerations related to the purpose of planning legislation, which is to regulate the development and use of land, and not to some extraneous purpose'.[3] The policy note adds a further caveat:

> Nor in general is it desirable that planning control should be used to secure objects for which provision is made in other legislation. It would be wrong, for example, to refuse permission for a betting office either because of a moral objection to betting or because it was thought that there were enough betting offices in the area already. The Betting,

---

[1] Dugard op.cit.; citations omitted.

[2] In this respect I am grateful to my colleague, Dr Harold Wilkinson, for a preview of his article 'Planning Law and Undesirable Activities', which has since appeared in the (1980) *New Law Journal* 1099.

[3] Wilkinson, op.cit.; such notes are strictly speaking not binding, being issued for guidance.

Gaming and Lotteries Act 1963 provides for the licensing of betting offices and makes the licensing authorities responsible for considering the demand for such facilities from place to place.

This is to presume, of course, that planning permission is required in relation to the proposed activity. Such permission is required generally in relation to development,[1] which is defined as 'the carrying out of building, engineering, mining or other operations in, on, over or under land, or the making of any material change in the use of any building or other land'.[2] Thus, provided the proposed premises are *already* used for the purpose of, for example, selling goods in retail trade, then this will fall within Class I of the Use Classes Order 1972 made by the Minister in terms of Section 22(2)(f) of the 1971 Act.[3] The order sets out some eighteen use classes, and provided change is within one of them, one does not have development as defined in the Act. The only potential complication here is that Class I (which deals with 'shops') specifies a variety of retail occupations which do not necessarily, but which may involve development, even though they on the face of it do not involve a change of use in the sense specified above. Such cases are then considered in terms of general principles, amongst which is the question of whether the change is material. This appears to involve very much the same sort of considerations stipulated above in relation to the granting of planning permission: what may be 'material', in other words, are questions specifically of increased traffic, noise and disturbance, or generally, interference with local amenity.[4]

Thus, were a proposed activity to fall within the restricted list in Use Class I, for example (which includes such exotica as tripe shops, cats' meat shops, and shops for the sale of hot food), considerations of materiality would apply in determining whether there was a change of use, and therefore development, in something of the same way they would in assessing planning permission. Such considerations should be related to planning, and not to extraneous questions, as the policy note discussed above, stipulated. It is clear from the generality of what may be considered material in terms of planning, however, that even though authorities would not appear to have the power to base decisions explicitly on such criteria as public morality, the latter may well be

---

1   There are a few exceptions, in relation to a resumption of previous use: see A.E. Telling *Planning Law and Procedure* (5th edn, London 1977) at 112–*et sequor.*

2   Town and Country Planning Act 1971, Section 22(1).

3   Telling op.cit. 92.

4   Ibid. at 103.

implicit in any one decision.[1] A recent decision in which the views of the Secretary of State clearly reflect this, is *Premises at Victoria Street, London*.[2] The case involved a property which had been used as a retail outlet of varied nature from about 1957 until 1974; it was then converted into a sex shop, for the sale of literature, appliances and films. Booths were provided upstairs for the viewing of the latter by prospective buyers. An enforcement notice alleged a change of use. The owners argued that the viewing involved did not differ from listening to records, or trying on clothes before purchasing them, even though a charge of ten pence was made for every one-and-a-half minutes' viewing. The minister ruled that the viewing was not incidental to the shop use; there was therefore a change of use, in relation to which planning permission was refused on the grounds (*inter alia*) that:

> While the nature of both the films shown and the goods sold at the premises is not in itself a matter that can be controlled under planning law, its effect on the character and amenities of the area is a matter that can properly be taken into account. In this case the change of emphasis from a sex shop to the showing of sex or pornographic films could well have a seriously adverse effect on adjacent businesses of a more generally attractive nature.

Although public morality may at least be an oblique consideration here, the question arises as to whether a more direct authority is necessary or justified. The question of such controls has arisen recently in relation to the question of prostitution.[3] The Wolfenden reforms in the law relating to prostitution have meant broadly that although soliciting (which includes prostitutes displaying themselves in the front of windows)[4] is illegal, as is brothel-keeping and the letting of premises by a landlord knowing they are to be used as a brothel, prostitution as such is not. The emphasis as far as the soliciting/prostitution distinction is concerned, is thus on the prevention of gratuitous offence, rather than the enforcement of any positive morality as to prostitution *per se*. This approach has not proven altogether satisfactory, however: the result has been in many parts of the country that groups of prostitutes operating from large premises have been broken up, and have spread into surrounding (usually residential) areas, with a serious resultant effect on such areas.

---

1 See Wilkinson op.cit.

2 [1980] *JPL* 58.

3 See A. Samuels 'Prostitution and Planning Law' [1980] *JPL* 578.

4 See Smith and Hogan op.cit. at 436.

The Derby Road area of Southampton is a notorious example, and has led the Southampton City Council to submit a report[1] embodying recommendations for the reform of the law in this area, to the Criminal Law Revision Committee. The report notes a number of adverse effects that have followed the dispersal of the operation of prostitutes into the Derby Road area as seen by residents in the area:

(i) Neighbours' lives are made intolerable by noise, arguments with clients, fights, potential clients looking for prostitutes and knocking on the wrong doors.
(ii) The possibility that the house next door may start up as a business may reduce the ability of the owner to sell his own house.
(iii) Clients kerb crawling, seeking prostitutes by night and day.
(iv) The ever-present anxieties about being molested or accosted, or the effect on children in the area.
(v) Peeping Toms and sightseers.
(vi) Race relations are adversely affected.
(vii) Part-time prostitutes are attracted into the area.
(viii) The openness and ease with which the prostitutes conduct their business makes the Police look ineffective.
(ix) The attraction of other unlawful activities into the area.

In addition to these problems, the area has been red-lined by building societies, which means that the improvement of housing, a key factor in attacking the social problems extant in the area, with ethnic minorities constituting up to 40 per cent of the population, is made, in present economic conditions, virtually impossible. The council has therefore recommended that such prostitution be removed from this type of area, but not that attempts be made to achieve this by suppressing it altogether; rather, prostitutes should be concentrated in adequate facilities outside residential areas. It would seem clear that the objections raised by Derby Road residents might be taken into account by planners in terms of local amenity, or more specific considerations such as offensive noise. Such reallocation is then probably not beyond the ambit of present planning law *per se*, which allows, it would seem, account to be taken, at least obliquely, of positive moral considerations in addition. The stumbling block is rather the criminal law prohibition on brothel-keeping, and hence the reference to the Criminal Law Revision Committee.

---

[1] Report of the Chief Executive to the Policy and Resources (Finance and General Purposes) Subcommittee of the Southampton City Council, as amended at City Council Meeting of 14 November 1979.

As far as sex shops, for example, are concerned, would present planning law, without grant of additional powers, enable such zoning to be implemented? There is no difficulty with the criminal law in the way there is in relation to prostitution; the answer therefore depends on the breadth of discretion allowed planners in terms of local amenity and/or other specific grounds of objection. Were such shops to constitute a rationally assessable source of offence, in the sense of noise or other interference with amenity, then discretion would presumably extend to the grant or refusal of planning permission in relation to it. Moral objections *per se* could be an implicit factor in such assessment; discretion appears to be sufficiently broad as virtually to allow a decision to be based implicitly on such considerations.[1] Obviously though, the more one could point to such a shop constituting a rational source of offence, the more likely it is that planning discretion would extend to its operation. However, provided the premises are already used for the retail trade, change from one trade to another does not require planning permission unless the new use falls within the exclusions to Use Class I. Running a sex shop does not at present fall within such exclusions, and unless development is involved, the opening of such an outlet would not then require planning permission.

A mechanism whereby zoning might indirectly be effected both in relation to prostitution and sex shops, is an injunction to restrain a private nuisance.[2] In *Thompson-Schwab* v *Costaki*[3] the plaintiffs were awarded an interlocutory injunction restraining the defendants from carrying on business as common prostitutes, on the basis that such activity 'constituted a sensible interference with the comfortable and convenient enjoyment of the plaintiffs' residences, having regard to the usages of civilised society and to the character of the neighbourhood'. Because private nuisance remedies adhere to owners or occupiers, the effect of an injunction of this sort is indirectly to zone open and notorious prostitution, at least as far as 'good class residential' areas are concerned. This is an avenue of attack open to those living in the Derby Road area of Southampton, for example. In practical terms the potential remedy is not likely to prove useful, as its utilisation would only deal with the problem on an individual, *ad hoc* basis, whilst potential plaintiffs are unlikely to bring many such suits before court. The remedy has recently been held[4] to be available against the operation of

---

1   *Contra*, Williams para 9.13.

2   See injunctions, Section 4(iv) above.

3   [1956] 1 All ER 652.

4   *Laws* v *Florinplace Ltd* [1981] 1 All ER 659.

a sex shop also, in respect of which its operation is likely to be far more effective: the defendant is more easily identifiable than is the case with prostitution, whilst an *ad hoc* remedy is appropriate in respect of individual retail outlets.

Law Reform: Although zoning is of limited application to the running of a sex shop or similar retail outlet at present, where planning permission is required, discretion may well, in terms of implicit cognisance of public morality, extend beyond what could be regarded as constituting, in offence terms, a rationally assessable harm. The same is apparently true in respect of private nuisance remedies: the court in *Costaki* emphasised that not all prostitution could be seen as constituting a nuisance, but rather that which is 'notorious and such as to force itself on the sense of sight at least of ... residents ...'.[1] This apparent concern with rationally assessable offence does not appear to have been sustained however: in *Laws* the court felt it was sufficient for the grant of relief that, quite aside from the potential offence occasioned by the clientele of the sex shop in question, the plaintiffs knew that a business in 'hard pornography' was being conducted on their doorstep,

Whether zoning or nuisance remedies are appropriate on this basis in respect of prostitution is a question which cannot be pursued here. As far as such restrictions on speech are concerned however, it is doubtful whether the prior restraints in question are justified. In terms of the restrictions recommended earlier[2] in relation to the protection of children or the prevention of offence, sex shops would not be permitted to display in their windows material harmful to minors. They would additionally, were they to sell restricted material, be obliged to display a warning notice to that effect, and to exclude minors completely from the premises. The Williams Committee felt that the offence potential of such premises was not adequately covered by such provisions. There were two clear alternatives: either to reduce the external obtrusiveness of such shops even further, or to subject them, via planning regulation, to some form of zoning regulation. The committee rejected the latter, and proposed, in implementing the former, that such shops be obliged to keep their windows completely blank.[3] It was argued earlier that such regulation would probably serve only to make those premises even more conspicuous than they would otherwise be. The committee is somewhat inconsistent in their choice of remedies, moreover, in that

---

1 [1956] 1 All ER 652 at 654 per Lord Evershed MR.

2 See protection of children, chapter 5; displays, chapter 6.

3 *Williams*, paras 9.13–9.15; such restrictions on appearance could also have been implemented by requiring planning permission for such premises, and attaching a condition as to external appearance to its grant.

they recommend that cinemas showing material restricted to adults, admission taking place only after adequate warning, should be subject to zoning regulation, at the complete discretion of the local authority.[1] The distinction here is elusive; it would seem preferable either to employ planning tools or to reject them. The type of offence occasioned by such premises is clearly on the borderline of what might be termed rationally assessable. One has to be careful not to include within the latter, offence which is more akin to objection to the private activities of others, as opposed to the type of harm occasioned by having material thrust upon one is public. Certainly the potential offence caused by sex shops, for example, is hardly comparable to the clearly intolerable strains placed upon the inhabitants of an area such as Derby Road.

It might therefore be best to leave planning provisons, with their possible relevance should planning permission be required, unchanged at present. Were the law in this respect to be shown in the future to be inadequate, as has perhaps been the law in relation to prostitution, changes might then be made to the Town and Country Planning Regulations. By contrast, the United States Supreme Court has, despite the First Amendment, allowed the constitutionality of zoning restrictions operated in terms of an 'adult' standard. Cinemas or book shops, for example, selling material suitable for adults, may constitutionally be zoned, such regulation being aimed at town planning considerations, and not at restriction of speech on a content basis.[2] The Court's approach here is open to criticism, because, skirting the First Amendment as it does, it allows restriction in terms of overbroad criteria. A preferable approach might be to meet the Amendment head-on, justifying such restrictions in terms of balancing, and stipulating both a narrowly drawn standard, and prompt judicial review in *Freedman* terms. Were zoning to be introduced in England and Wales, it is to be hoped that freedom of speech considerations would dictate similar caution in terms of planning law revision.

5) *Films*

(i) *Historical background*[3] — (A) *Prior restraint*. The first public exhibition in England of a film took place in 1896; such early film had

---

1 *Williams* para 12.38.

2 *Young* v *American Mini Theaters* 427 US 50 (1976); see further chapters 12 and 14.

3 See *Williams* Appendix 2.

a nitrate base, which on application of heat was highly inflammable.[1] The number of premises used for film shows grew rapidly, and the Home Office, responding to concern over public safety rushed through the Cinematograph Act 1909. Section 2(1) of the Act provides that

> A County Council may grant licences to such persons as they think fit to use the premises specified in the licence for the purposes aforesaid *on such terms and conditions and under such restrictions as, subject to the regulations of the Secretary of State, the Council may by the respective licences determine.*[2]

The legislation contemplated the imposition of conditions related to safety only;[3] the wider applicability of this licensing power seems to have been noted by only one parliamentary opponent of the Bill, who pointed out the possibility that it might be used to prevent seditious film exhibitions.[4] Such wider applicability was very quickly realised: in January 1910 the then London County Council decided to use the power to enforce Sunday observance in relation to cinemas. The Bermondsey Bioscope, open on a Sunday, was prosecuted, the Lord Chief Justice taking the view on appeal that Section 2 of the 1909 Act was 'intended to confer on the county council a discretion as to conditions which they will impose, so long as those conditions are not unreasonable'.[5] It would probably not have been unreasonable to have concluded at the time that cinema censorship had arrived.

By early 1911 the potential censorship power in relation to licence conditions had not been used in relation to the content of films; pressure for controls was, however, growing, the first example of a film being banned coming in July 1910, with the LCC informing licensees that it was undesirable that the film of the world heavyweight fight between Jack Johnson and James L. Jeffries should be shown. The unstated reason: it involved the first black world champion knocking out a white challenger.[6] Concern within the industry at the potential censorship hazard led in early 1912 to approaches to the Home Secretary, who declined to become involved in such a scheme. The industry

---

1 Robertson op.cit. at 258.

2 Emphasis added.

3 N.M. Hunnings *Film Censors and the Law* (London 1967) at 48.

4 *Hansard* HC Deb, 25 August 1909, vol.IX, col.2262.

5 *LCC v Bermondsey Bioscope Co Ltd* [1911] 1 KB 445; followed in e.g. *R v LCC ex parte London and Provincial Theatres Ltd* [1915] 2 KB 466.

6 Williams op.cit.

itself then set up the British Board of Film Censors, which began work on 1 January 1913. Licensing authorities were invited to give their support by, in effect, delegating their apparent censorship powers to the Board. By 1915 only thirty-five councils had imposed a BBFC certificate requirement for screening.

By 1915 pressure had grown for a centralised, statute-based system. In April 1916 the Home Secretary proposed just this to local authority representatives. Most accepted, but a minority of authorities wished to retain a local veto. This engendered opposition in the trade, and with a change of government in 1916, the scheme was abandoned. The BBFC's position was still far from secure: the most obvious weakness, besides the continued independence of many councils, was the question of the delegation of power to the Board. The Home Office had meanwhile issued model conditions to authorities, many of which then pursued their own censorship programme: 'No film shall be shown which is likely to be injurious to morality or to encourage or incite to crime, or to lead to disorder, or to be offensive to public feeling, or which contains any offensive representations of living persons'. The turning point for the Board came in 1921, with the High Court's decision in *Ellis* v *Dubowski*.[1] Middlesex County Council had shown the film *Auction of Souls*, which had not been given a BBFC certificate. It had added to the model conditions above the requirement 'or which has not been certified for public exhibition by the British Board of Film Censors'. The court found this condition unreasonable and *ultra vires*, as it involved the delegation of powers to the Board which might for any reason refuse a certificate and was unaccountable. Mr Justice Sankey (as he then was) intimated that provided the condition reserved the ultimate right of review to the authority, it might be *intra vires*. This led, on the advice of the Home Office, to the widespread adoption by councils of the so-called 'Sankey condition': 'No film – other than photographs of current events – which has not been passed for "universal" or "public" exhibition by the British Board of Film Censors shall be exhibited without the express consent of the Council'. The legal respectability of this condition was upheld in *Mills* v *LCC*[2] in 1924. The pattern of film censorship was thus set, and it is still operating today.

(B) *Subsequent restraints (a) Statutory and common law control of film exhibitions already subject to prior restraint.* The Obscene Publications Act 1959 defines obscenity in terms of a tendency to deprave

---

1 [1921] 2 KB 621.

2 [1924] 1 KB 213.

and corrupt 'persons who are likely ... to read, *see or hear* the matter contained or embodied'[1] in the article in question. An article is in turn defined[2] as anything 'containing or embodying matter to be read or *looked at* or both, any sound record, and *any film* or other record of a picture or pictures'. For the 1959 and 1964 Acts to apply to any potentially obscene article, however, publication (or at least the possibility thereof in the case of holding an article for publication for gain) is essential.[3] Section 1(3) of the 1959 Act defines publication: 'a person publishes an article who

> (a) distributes, circulates, sells, lets on hire, gives, or lends it, or who offers it for sale or for letting on hire; or
> (b) *in the case of an article containing or embodying matter to be looked at* or a record, *shows*, plays or *projects it*'.[4]

It has been emphasised by the Court of Appeal[5] that '... for the purpose of determining obscenity ... the persons referred to in Section 1(1) as 'likely to read, see or hear' are restricted to those who read, saw or heard as the result of such publication'. There was a proviso to paragraph (b) above, the importance of which was underlined by this ruling of the Court of Appeal; the proviso exempted from the operation of paragraph (b): (i) 'anything done in the course of a cinematograph exhibition ... other than one excluded from the Cinematograph Act 1909 by' Section 7(4) of that Act; and (ii) 'anything done in the course of television or sound broadcasting'.

The Obscene Publications Act 1959 set out then two basic categories or types of publication, the first involving sale, distribution, loan, etc., and the second covering the playing, showing or projecting, of the article in question, the second being subject[6] to a qualification with respect to cinematograph exhibitions, or sound or television broadcasts. The proviso to Section 1(3)(b) of the 1959 Act provided in effect that there was no publication in terms of the Act where the film-showing in question would amount to a cinematograph exhibition within the

---

1 Section 1(1); emphasis added.

2 Section 1(2); emphasis added.

3 This is so whether an offence under the Acts is in question, or whether it is merely a question of the seizure of the article(s) involved.

4 Emphasis added.

5 *Reference by the Attorney-General (No. 2 of 1975)* [1976] 2 All ER 753.

6 The Court of Appeal held that this proviso applies only to paragraph (b) and not to paragraph (a) as well: ibid. With respect to the proviso and its operation see The Law Commission Working Paper No. 57: Conspiracies relating to Morals and Decency (HMSO 1974) at 21–2.

meaning of the Cinematograph Act 1909.[1] This effectively excluded virtually all film shows or exhibitions from the purview of the Obscene Publications Act, as Section 1 of the Cinematograph Act 1909 provides that 'no cinematograph exhibition shall be given other than in premises licensed for the purpose'. Certain premises (under certain circumstances) are exempt from the licensing requirement: no film show on such premises (and/or in such circumstances, as the case may be) is a cinematograph exhibition within the meaning of the Act. These are:

(i) premises used occasionally and exceptionally only;[2]
(ii) buildings or structures of a moveable character (subject to a number of conditions);[3]
(iii) an exhibition given in a private dwelling house to which the public are not admitted on payment or otherwise;[4]

To these exemptions were added certain others by the Cinematograph Act 1952:

(i) Private exhibitions and free public exhibitions except when organised by or for a children's cinema club;[5]
(ii) Exhibitions given in premises by certain non-profit making societies (where so certified by the Commissioners of Customs and Excise).[6]

The Obscene Publications Act (via the proviso to Section 1(3)(b) applied *only* to the exception to the 1909 Act relating to exhibitions in private dwelling houses; this was the only film show or 'cinematograph exhibition' to which the Act applied. The Cinematograph Acts are silent as to the applicability of other measures. It was probably not open to argue that the Acts had implicitly excluded the potential operation of other statutes or the common law, for actions based on defamatory films (for example) had not been barred.[7] What common law or statutory controls might then have been applicable? It was probably open to the prosecution to bring charges such as obscene libel, keeping

---

1 *Reference by the Attorney-General (No. 2 of 1975)* [1976] 2 All ER 753.

2 Section 7(2).

3 Section 7(3).

4 Section 7(4).

5 Section 5(1)(a)(2).

6 Section 5(3)(4).

7 For example, *Youssoupoff* v *MGM* (1934) 50 TLR 581.

a disorderly house, keeping or showing an indecent exhibition,[1] corrupting public morals, or outraging public decency (if the latter two offences in fact exist). Available also would have been the charge of conspiracy (or possibly its inchoate relatives, incitement and attempt) to engage in such conduct.[2]

There was an obvious potential hazard in this system: provided the BBFC or local authority (as the case might be) operated prior restraint in terms of outrage or offence — in other words, in terms of the broadest legal test potentially applicable — there was no problem. If, however, they decided to apply a narrower standard, what was their position with regard to a possible transgression, occasioned by subsequent screening, of more broadly couched criminal restrictions? At the time of the passage of the 1959 Obscene Publications Act, the Lord Chancellor said in the House of Lords that it was unthinkable that entertainment already subject to censorship should be the subject of obscenity prosecutions. In 1975 the unthinkable came about, in that the DPP, after a complaint from Mr Raymond Blackburn, broke this long standing policy of non-intervention by (successfully) prosecuting the film *More About the Language of Love* in terms of common law offence of mounting an indecent exhibition.[3] The point of no return in terms of a full review of cinema censorship was probably reached in *R v GLC ex parte Blackburn*. Here the perennial Mr Blackburn, following the *Language of Love* success, brought proceedings against the GLC, and managed to elicit from the Court of Appeal, and particularly from Lord Denning, a glowing character reference for the standard of indecency. Not only had the 1959 Act 'misfired', but councils, were they to permit screenings which contravened the law, would be acting *ultra vires* their statutory powers. The Master of the Rolls went on to warn that if the GLC 'continue with their present wrong test, and in consequence give their consent to films which are grossly indecent, they may be said to be aiding and abetting a criminal offence'.[4]

The latter possibility was by no means as unlikely as might have been thought: in 1976 Mr Blackburn moved again. In the earlier prosecution in June 1975 of *More About the Language of Love* the film had been refused a BBFC certificate, but had been licensed by the GLC. Its counterpart, *The Language of Love*, had received both a BBFC certificate and a GLC licence. In instituting a common law prosecution

---

1 *R v Greater London Council, ex parte Blackburn* [1976] 1 WLR 550.

2 See chapter 3.

3 *Williams* para 4.32.

4 [1976] 1 WLR 550 at 560.

against the latter film, Mr Blackburn attempted to follow up Lord Denning's hint by having indicted both the President and Secretary of the BBFC. The Chief Metropolitan Magistrate refused to commit them for trial on the ground that certification was merely an expression of opinion and not a legal mandate.[1] The film's exhibitors were committed for trial at the Old Bailey charged with mounting an indecent exhibition. After jury acquittal, the prosecution was denounced from the bench in unusually strong terms, being described as 'shocking and appalling', and 'misguided'.[2]

All this very nearly saw the demise of cinema censorship. The GLC had for some time been unhappy about its role in such censorship. In June 1973, influenced by the new Chairman of the Council's Film Viewing Board, Mrs Enid Wistrich,[3] the council reviewed its functions in this respect, and recommended in late 1974 that as it was under no obligation to censor, it should cease to do so. This might well, in view of the influence of the GLC, have led to an abandonment of local authority film censorship for adults. In the event this recommendation was narrowly defeated in a council vote by a majority of 50 to 44 votes. The council therefore amended its rules to take account of the Court of Appeal's ruling on the non-applicability of obscenity as a standard, and has continued to exercise its censorship function.

The attempted Blackburn prosecution of BBFC officials led to an amendment of the criminal law with respect to films; it was not the only factor: cinema clubs were exempt from the Obscene Publications Acts and from cinema licensing, and had become in London in particular, a growth industry. Such clubs were subject only to the common law, which was both antiquated and often difficult to apply, as with the 'persistency' requirement in keeping a disorderly house for instance. In 1976 the Law Commission in its Report on Conspiracy and Criminal Law Reform[4] recommended, in conjunction with abolition of such common law offences, the extension of the 1959 Act to cover films. This was effected by Section 53 of the Criminal Law Act 1977.

(b) *Statutory and common law control of film exhibitions not subject to prior restraint.* As far as the exhibition of films was concerned, there were three categories involved: first the film show, which though subject to the Cinematograph Acts, escaped

---

1 See 'Film Censors facing the Crunch', *The Guardian*, 2 August 1975; quoted in Robertson op.cit. at 265.

2 *The Times*, 9 July 1976.

3 For a resumé of her experiences in this post, see her book *I Don't Mind the Sex, It's the Violence — Film Censorship Explored* (London 1978).

4 Report No. 76 (HMSO 1976); see chapter 3.

prior censorship through its exhibition (illegally) without a licence. Such film shows are subject to the fines prescribed under the Cinematograph Acts: besides this they would have been subject to the same common law and statutory controls that would have been applicable had they been licensed in the normal way. Second, one had the exception to the Cinematograph Acts that is covered by the Obscene Publications Acts: exhibitions in private dwelling houses to which the public are not admitted. Section 2(4) of the 1959 Act would have operated here, thus excluding any substantive, but not inchoate, common law offence. Third, one had those exceptions to the Cinematograph Acts not covered by the Obscenity Acts such as cinema clubs; here both the substantive and inchoate common law offences might have been of application.

(c) *Statutory and common law controls over the distribution, leasing, etc., of films.* In the light of the wording of Section 1(3) of the Obscene Publications Act 1959 it is not clear whether articles 'to be looked at' can be published only in those ways mentioned in paragraph (b) of the subsection, or whether such articles may be published in those ways listed in paragraph (a) of the subsection as well. The two paragraphs of the subsection are separated by a disjunctive 'or', which is immediately followed by the words '(b) in the case of an article containing or embodying matter to be looked at ...'. This would seem to suggest that the intention was '... for all articles containing "matter to be looked at" to be judged solely by the second paragraph, possibly because any dealing in the article as defined in paragraph (a) would not constitute a publication of visual matter properly so speaking'.[1] *Straker* v *DPP*[2] would appear indirectly to support this reasoning: the court held that since a photographic negative could not be 'shown, played or projected' it would not be published within the meaning of the Act. In so deciding, the court did not explicitly rule that paragraphs (a) and (b) were mutually exclusive: it rather ignored paragraph (a) completely.

In March 1974 Mr Edward Shackleton of the Nationwide Festival of Light initiated a prosecution of the film *Last Tango in Paris*, not in terms of its exhibition, but rather its distribution. The jury was at trial directed to acquit as the only publication involved was to the licensee of the cinemas and there was no evidence that it depraved and corrupted him. The question of whether a film could be 'published' in terms of the 1959 Act was referred by the Attorney-General to the Court of Appeal.[3] The court was quite clear that the screening of a film, in

---

1   Zellick [1971] *Crim L Rev* 126 at 133.

2   [1963] 1 All ER 697.

3   *Reference by the Attorney-General (No. 2 of 1975)* [1976] 2 All ER 753.

terms of the proviso to Section 1(3)(b) of the Act, could not constitute such publication. It was held also that the proviso applied only to paragraph (b) and not to paragraph (a) of subsection 1(3). This would seem to imply that paragraph (a) is of applicability to films, for were it not, any consideration of the proviso's applicability to it would, in view of the fact that the proviso deals only in terms of cinematograph exhibitions, have been entirely superfluous. The authority is slight, and despite the 1977 reform, the question apparently remains open.

Were the Obscene Publications Acts not to apply, it may be open to bring such charges as obscene libel, corrupting public morals, or outraging public decency (if the latter two offences exist), as well as conspiracy (and perhaps attempt and incitement) to engage in such conduct. Were the 1959 Act to apply, the inchoate offences only would be of applicability. Distribution through the post of indecent or obscene film is an offence under the Post Office Act 1953, whilst the Customs Consolidation Act 1876 prohibits the importation of indecent or obscene photographs or other articles; it was made clear in *Derrick v Commissioners of Customs and Excise* that the restriction applies to film transparencies and negatives.[1] In view of the proportion of films imported, and the probable absence of a public good defence under the customs provisions, this latter application is potentially a very significant one.

(ii) *Prior restraint currently applicable to films* (A) *Licensing*. The continued viability of the censorship arrangements established earlier this century in relation to the exhibition of films was threatened by the disappearance of inflammable film, the 1909 Act applying only to such film. Parliament, having in the interim presumably been converted to the desirability of this mode of censorship, stepped into the breach with the Cinematograph Act 1952. The new Act not only confirmed a wide power on the part of local authorities to impose conditions on the grant of a licence, but for the first time actually imposed a duty of censorship on licensing authorities in respect of 'works unsuitable for children'.[2] Although in practice local authorities continued to delegate the censorship powers to the BBFC, whose function was probably implicitly recognised in Section 3(1) of the 1952 Act, they are not obliged to accept the Board's decisions; indeed, the continued function of the Board still depends on the authorities retaining the last word, with

---

1   [1972] 1 All ER 993; films had for many years prior to this been seized under the Act: see Minutes of Evidence op.cit. Appendix A, at 49 (Memorandum submitted by Commissioners of Customs and Excise).

2   Section 3(1); see the Wheare Committee Report on Children and the Cinema, Cmnd 7945 (HMSO, May 1950).

Mills being approved in 1976 by Lord Denning in *R v GLC ex parte Blackburn*: 'I do not think the county councils can delegate the whole of their responsibility to the Board, but they can treat the Board as an advisory body whose views they can accept or reject; provided that the final decision — aye or nay — rests with the county council'.[1]

What has come closest to destroying the system as present constituted has probably been the question of the standard applicable by the authorities and/or the BBFC. The standard the Board applies is one aimed at excluding from public exhibition anything likely to impair the moral standards of the public, and anything likely to give offence to any reasonably minded members of the community;[2] this is in turn varied in terms of whether the film is a major one or not, for example. The standards applied by the Board are clearly influenced by the 'restraint that it operates only on the basis of the delegation of powers by local authorities. If it loses the confidence of those authorities its role vanishes. It must not reject films which most authorities, if appealed to, would allow, nor give certificates to those which most authorities would wish to ban.'[3] Such standards are then a curious amalgam: there is clearly reference to the law of the land; in addition, the Board has regard to its own often strong views on the social harms that might possibly flow from certain material, to the standards currently acceptable to the cinema-going public, but perhaps above all, to the 'political' element of ensuring the acceptability of its judgement to local authorities.[4] This latter aspect is presumably fortified by the various consultative committees that have from time to time been set up as between the Board, the industry and local authorities, to discuss (for example) the category system.[5]

The categories of certificates issued by the Board since 1970 are as follows:

X certificate : admission to view films is restricted to those over eighteen years of age.
AA certificate : admission is restricted to those over fourteen years of age.
A certificate : this denotes merely that parents/guardians should note that the film is not suitable

---

1 [1976] 1 WLR 550 at 554–5.

2 From a leaflet outlining the Board's work; quoted in P. O'Higgins *Censorship in Britain* (London 1972) at 82.

3 *Williams* para 3.26.

4 Ibid. paras 3.23–3.29.

5 Ibid. paras 3.30–3.32.

>   for children under fourteen years of age.
> U certificate : denotes that the film is considered suitable for anyone.[1]

The Board may in effect leave the final categorisation to the film maker, in the sense that the inclusion/exclusion of certain scenes determines whether it receives an A or an AA certificate.[2] In addition to examining completed films, the Board may often also find itself consulted in advance by film makers, who may be unwilling to place their money at risk by the cutting or even total banning of a film in its finished form.[3] The Board clearly does move with shifts in public standards: the figures for refusals of an X certificate show a decline from 6 per cent of those feature films submitted to the board in 1972, to 1 per cent in 1978.[4] It might be argued that the operation of the Board, with its clear dependence on local authority acceptance of its standards, and the relevance to both local authorities and the Board of current community standards, would mean a more or less homogeneous censorship pattern. Certainly most local authorities normally include a condition in their licensing provisions that films shall not be exhibited unless they have received BBFC certification.[5] Although Williams concluded that there had not been widespread dissatisfaction with the system,[6] such homogeneity cannot be claimed for it; indeed, disparities and occasionally even absurdities could be said to be a virtually institutionalised aspect of the system. One has first of all the fact of ultimate local authority discretion: although this may influence the Board towards homogeneity of result, it can pull in the opposite direction. Williams reported that some 72 authorities out of a potential total (for these purposes) of some 330, did in fact engage in their own censorship reviews, often reviewing all films granted an X certificate by the Board, or all those in relation to which an application has been submitted to the authority to review the Board's refusal of a certificate. In the process, some authorities may, as did the GLC for example, have operated in terms of an obscenity standard, which is rather narrower than the

---

1   *Williams*, para 3.19. The categories were changed to 18, 15, PG and U in 1983 but unfortunately too late for discussion in the main text of this book.

2   Ibid. para 3.20.

3   O'Higgins op.cit. at 84.

4   *Williams*, table, p.29.

5   For an example of such conditions, see extracts from the rules to be observed by holders of cinematograph licences made by the Justices of the Peace for the City of Cambridge 26 June 1970; quoted in O'Higgins op.cit. at 78.

6   *Williams* para 3.32.

criteria used by the Board.

Second, one may add to the potential disparity of standards employed the fact that decision, even if undertaken in terms of a single standard, is not undertaken by one body, nor necessarily even by bodies of a similar nature. Most of the censorship work that is done by local authorities is in fact not performed by specialist committees set up for this function. The task is rather added as an additional chore to the work of some other committee: in Brighton, for example, the Fire Brigade Committee – in which case the local fire chief may be invited to the viewing.[1] Not surprisingly, the system has produced some odd results in practice: in 1970 for example, the Board refused a certificate to the film *Language of Love*; the film was nonetheless granted a certificate by the GLC and by some 127 other authorities, and was approved by the Board itself three years later.[2] In 1968 Yoko Ono's film *Number Four*, 'which concentrated its attention on the human backside and was refused any certificate by the Board unless certain other portions of the human anatomy were deleted, received an X certificate from the Greater London Council and a U certificate from Birmingham'.[3]

Such disparities were basic to the Blackburn-instigated, and successful, prosecution of *More About the Language of Love* in 1975. Developments such as this could have done nothing to reassure councils such as the GLC, already doubtful about their exercise of a film censorship role. The subsequent *GLC* case although it may have clarified standards in the sense of excluding obscenity as one of them in this regard, could only have compounded dissatisfaction with the system, in the sense of obliging councils with doubts about whether to exercise censorship at all in relation to adults, to apply the potential catch-all test of common law indecency. Strains in the system were probably alleviated to some extent by the application, by virtue of the Criminal Law Act 1977, of statutory obscenity to the cinema. If the obscenity test was relevant before in the sense of obliquely ensuring, by virtue of its non-applicability to the exhibition of films, its own exclusion as a standard in this forum, this relevance will now presumably apply to exclude common law standards in this respect. If the 1959 Act has specifically been made applicable to films, this should be as relevant as its prior, and equally specific, non-applicability in this regard. If so, it is but a short step to concluding that obscenity as a standard is not only

---

1 O'Higgins op.cit. at 87, where numerous examples of such absurdities are set out.

2 *Williams* para 3.28.

3 O'Higgins op.cit.

applicable to film censorship, but is, in its own terms, exclusively applicable as such.

Appeal: It was remarked earlier that local authority discretion as to censorship is virtually absolute. It may nonetheless be subject to review by the courts. Although no statutory right of appeal was provided by the 1909 Act, councils had to observe the rules of natural justice and act reasonably. If the paucity of reported cases[1] in this regard bears any correlation to the number or success rate of appeals, applicants have not had a very happy time of it. A right of appeal to the High Court is now assured (in terms of Section 69 of the 1952 Act) to anyone aggrieved by a refusal or revocation of a licence. Applicants appealing to the High Court appear to have been more successful in terms of a condition some councils have recently attempted to impose: that prior notice be given to the council of the screening of any film accorded an X certificate by the BBFC. The courts have apparently taken the view that such a condition is in fact, in terms of the present circumstances of the film industry, unreasonable.[2] The courts have also made it plain[3] that the revocation of a film licence, a draconian power when taken in relation to the licensee's investment in the cinema, can only be made after a full investigation by members of the relevant council committee. Delegation of decision-making to the chairman of such a committee is invalid. In addition, the licensee must be given an opportunity to state his case, whilst the decision is to be taken only in relation to information that has been communicated to the licensee.

In regard to decisions as to the screening of particular films, although the court could not interfere in policy decision, it 'could and should intervene to ensure that the Council acted fairly and that it paid due regard to conflicting interests'.[4] A council has then presumably to see a film before refusing it a licence. Whether such considerations would require a council, on application, to reconsider a BBFC decision is not certain; presumably it should, as ultimate discretion remains *a priori* with the council. The likelihood of a court's overturning, in terms of reasonableness, a properly constituted decision, must seem remote: if the standard applicable is obscenity, then despite the legal test's emphasis on thought arousal, the inherent subjectivity of decision-making in terms of positive morality, must leave secure any but the

---

1   See e.g. *ex parte Stott* [1916] 1 KB 7.

2   *Williams* para 3.8.

3   *GLC* v *Langian Ltd*, Inner London Crown Court, 16 November 1977; quoted in Robertson op.cit. at 261—2.

4   *R* v *Liverpool Corporation ex parte Liverpool Taxi Fleet Operators Association* [1972] 2 QB 299.

most absurd council decisions. Although the probable application of a single standard would seem indicated since the 1977 amendment, such a standard, potentially applied by a wide variety of bodies, cannot, even with the possibility of judicial review, produce anything like uniform results.

(B) *Declarations*. These are not generally applicable in terms of determinations of fact, unless a decision of law involves an essential decision of fact perhaps.[1] There would not appear to be much room for direct application in the obscenity area in terms of prior restraint; declarations might, however, be obliquely relevant by virtue of their application to other, administrative, prior restraints, possibly be available to a distributor or cinema proprietor in relation to local authority refusals to licence films were the authority's decisions to be made in terms of indecency, a decision which would arguably be *ultra vires* statutory authority. This would depend in the first instance on the *locus standi* of the applicant;[2] although the Attorney-General would normally have such standing either in person or through a relator action, an individual might in this situation perhaps be deemed to have a direct and substantial interest in the administrative decision in question.

A further instance in which a declaration might be obtainable is in respect of a breach of a statutory duty by a local authority. If an authority ceased to exercise control over film exhibition altogether, this would be in contravention of Section 3 of the 1952 Act. Provided that this was a duty enforceable in the courts, and provided a private individual had *locus standi*, a declaration might be obtained. Although *locus standi* will not normally exist in relation to a legal duty of a public nature unless a private right has been invaded, or the applicant has suffered special damage,[3] and although *locus standi* in respect of declarations[4] and injunctions may be narrower than is the case with regard to prerogative orders, Mr Raymond Blackburn was held to have such standing with respect to a *mandamus* order against the Metropolitan Commissioner of Police in terms of enforcing the law against pornographic literature,[5] and against the GLC to prevent them licensing

---

1   S.A. de Smith *Judicial Review of Administrative Action* (4th edn, London 1980) at 508.

2   Ibid. at 486ff and 510.

3   *Gouriet v Union of Post Office Workers* [1978] AC 435.

4   Discretion in this respect in relation to declarations is probably wider than in relation to injunctions: de Smith op.cit. at 509.

5   *R v Metropolitan Commissioner of Police, ex parte Blackburn (No. 3)* [1973] 2 WLR 43.

the exhibition of indecent films.[1] In the former case, this standing appears to have rested on his having a wife and five children; in the latter, on the residence of Mr Blackburn and his family within the borough. In a recent ruling, Lord Denning MR managed to take a majority of the Court of Appeal with him in according *locus standi* to a body of tax payers who objected to the Inland Revenue granting an amnesty to certain casual workers in Fleet Street in respect of back taxes. He appeared to regard the question of standing as to a declaration to be on the same footing as in relation to the prerogative writs, and felt that the applicants had, as aggrieved tax payers, rather than mere busybodies, a sufficient interest for the purpose of judicial review.[2]

The situation in the United States in relation to declarations and films is no different from that existing in this regard in relation to books.

(C) *Injunctions*. *Locus standi* to obtain injunctions to prevent breaches of the criminal law are probably (in the case, for example, of cinema clubs) limited to the Attorney-General in person or through a relator action,[3] unless the criminal act violates a private right, or perhaps causes special damage[4] to the applicant. Much the same considerations would apply were an injunction sought as an alternative to a declaration where an authority acts *ultra vires*, perhaps in terms of the standard it applies to films, or were it to cease regulating films altogether, even in terms of children. The *locus standi* of an individual to seek an injunction in these latter circumstances is in fact not at all clear:[5] it may be narrower than is the case with declarations, and a court might hold that *locus standi* exists only where the individual concerned has 'a legal wrong redressible in an action for damages'.[6] The existence of alternative criminal law remedies would not appear to exclude equitable jurisdiction.

(D) *Zoning*. As far as film exhibitions not covered by the Cinematograph Act 1952 are concerned, the situation would be the same *mutatis mutandis*, as it is in relation to sex shops for instance. The 1909

---

1   R v *Greater London Council, ex parte Blackburn* [1976] 1 WLR 550; Lord Justice Bridge appeared to restrict standing here to ratepayers: at 567.

2   R v *Inland Revenue Commissioners, ex parte National Federation of Self-Employed and Small Businesses Ltd* [1980] 2 All ER 378.

3   See injunctions in relation to books, magazines, etc., above.

4   *Gouriet* v *Union of Post Office Workers* [1978] AC 435 left unclarified the law on this point: de Smith op.cit. at 451, footnote 46.

5   De Smith op.cit. at 509–10.

6   De Smith op.cit. at 460.

and 1952 Acts allow a council to grant a licence to such persons as they think fit to use the specified premises as a cinema subject to such terms and conditions, and under such restrictions as the council deems appropriate. If the latter part of this encompasses questions of safety and public morality, might it not be extended to zoning? This would be a question for the courts: would it be unreasonable and *ultra vires* the statute to refuse a licence in relation to certain premises because of possible offence to nearby residents, or in terms of a more pleasant environment? Although the section is widely drawn, the exercise of such discretion may perhaps be unlikely: it is perhaps a possibility though. The American zoning regime in relation to cinemas is no different to that applicable to book shops, for instance.

(E) *Search and seizure.* The 1959 and 1964 Acts both now apply to films as such. It may be that films may *only* be published in terms of Section 1(3)(b): there is a disjunctive 'or' between parts (a) and (b), and (b) follows this 'or' with 'in the case of an article embodying matter to be looked at ...'. If this is so, it does not rule out Section 3 operation, but merely means that it should be clear from the circumstances of seizure that publication for gain in terms of Section 1(3)(b) is intended by the possessor of the articles in question. American provisions on search and seizure are the same for films as books, except that in terms of *Heller* requirements, if it is desired to seize a single copy of a film for evidentiary purposes, a copy should be made, and the original returned.

(iii)   *Subsequent restraints currently applicable.* The morass of legal provision in this regard has since the 1977 amendment been largely avoided. Where films are shown in contravention of licencing provisions, Section 3 of the 1909 Act provides a criminal penalty. A variety of acts are contemplated here: showing films in unlicensed and non-exempt premises, showing banned films, breaches of safety requirements, etc. The maximum penalty on conviction is only £200, and only fifteen prosecutions took place in the four years between 1974 and 1978, for instance.[1] The distinction between commercial film exhibition and those exhibitions which are exempted dates back to the days of inflammable film: commercial users made use of 35mm film, which had an inflammable base; others tended to use 16mm film, which did not. When the 1952 measure was enacted, the Home Secretary made it clear in Parliament that he wished to maintain the exemption for 'non-commercial exhibitions organised by film societies and educational and

---

1   *Williams* para 3.9.

scientific bodies'.[1] What was not envisaged then was the growth of cinema clubs, which are mere stratagems adopted to avoid liability under licensing requirements. Williams reported that in terms of the statutory wording of the exemptions, it is difficult to prevent such circumventions; as a result, as the GLC reported, many such film shows are staged in unsafe premises. This loophole has been plugged in this latter regard in many areas outside London — Manchester, for example — where local legislation has been employed to require the registration of premises used for entertainment, and compliance with safety, but not censorship, requirements.[2] The 1973 Cinematograph and Indecent Displays Bill sought to alter the exemption, so that any film show 'promoted for private gain' would be subject to licensing. This attempt has not been resurrected.

Although cinematograph exhibitions as defined in the Cinematograph Act 1952, and given in a place required to be licensed under the Cinematograph Act 1909 are excluded from the ambit of the Indecent Displays (Control) Act 1981, cinema clubs do not appear to have been so fortunate. The latter measure[3] does not apply to those cinematograph exhibitions exempted from licensing requirements by the Cinematograph Act 1909; as far as the exemptions provided by the Cinematograph Act 1952 are concerned however, only that category of exempted exhibitions given by exempted organisations would appear to be excluded from the ambit of the 1981 Act. Shows exempt from licensing requirements in terms of non-admission of the public would nonetheless then be required to exclude in terms of indecency those under the age of eighteen and to provide warning notices.

In addition, film shows are subject to the Obscene Publications Acts 1959 and 1964. This change was effected by Section 53 of the Criminal Law Act 1977. Section 53(1) deletes the proviso to Section 1(3)(b) in terms of cinematograph exhibitions. Section 53(3) provides that no proceedings may be brought for an offence at common law (including conspiracy) in respect of a cinematograph exhibition alleged to be obscene, indecent, offensive, disgusting or injurious to morality. An indictment for statutory conspiracy in terms of Section 1 of the Criminal Law Act 1977 would lie, provided that the conspiracy relates to a substantive offence. Thus, provided corruption of public morals and outraging public decency are substantive offences, the common law

---

1 *Hansard* HC Deb, 21 October 1952, vol. 505, col. 870.

2 *Williams* paras 3.13 and 3.14.

3 Section 1(4)(e).

4 Section 1(4)(e)(ii).

has not, probably as the result of a drafting oversight, been completely excluded in this regard. The Law Commission recommended that film shows in private dwellings be excepted; this has not been implemented. The application of statutory obscenity to films is slightly narrower than the general application of the Act in one other respect: the public good defence provided by Section 53(6) of the Criminal Law Act omits the grounds of 'science' and 'other objects of general concern', in favour of those objects sanctioned by the public good defence in the Theatres Act, namely 'drama, opera, ballet or any other art, or of literature or learning'. The only other relevant statutory offence is the distribution or showing of indecent films of children, in terms of the Protection of Children Act 1978. The Act deals with films in precisely the same terms as it does photographs.[1]

(iv)   *Law reform.* Film censorship in the United States is largely a private operation, in the sense that it is undertaken by the Motion Picture Association of America, without any direct state involvement. The question of whether such private action falls within the First Amendment (which is concerned with state action) is considered below.[2] Were this system, which imposes censorship solely in favour of minors (those under seventeen years of age) to fall within the First Amendment, it would, together with those state schemes in operation, be subject to the full *Freedman* requirements described earlier.[3] This would ensure adherence to strict procedural requirements, and the application of an obscenity standard. As far as censorship in favour of children is concerned, this would appear permissible in terms at least of obscenity in relation to minors.[4] The system of film censorship at present operated in this country would, in these terms, clearly be unconstitutional. That it involves state action is hardly open to question, whilst no procedural safeguards are prescribed at all. The standard of obscenity is now perhaps obliquely imposed, if so avoiding to some extent the wide disparities of standard applied in the past by the various bodies potentially active in this regard.

In terms of law reform it is proposed to consider here principally the question of whether prior or subsequent restraints are more apposite in relation to films. There would not seem to be any reason why the standards recommended earlier in relation to the protection of

---

1   See production of pornography, above.

2   See non-legal prior restraints, below.

3   See search and seizure, in relation to books and magazines, earlier in this chapter.

4   See the protection of children, chapter 5.

children and the prevention of offence to adults should not apply here; the question whether restraints in wider terms than this are justified will be considered in relation to the question of general prohibitions, in the final chapter. Which then is preferable in relation to films: prior or subsequent restraint? As was remarked earlier, any prior restraint requires convincing justification. There are a number of possible justifications for such restraint here, which do not apply to the same extent to written or pictorial material. The first is one made strongly by Williams: that film is 'a uniquely powerful instrument' in the sense of producing 'an impact which no other medium can create'.[1] With film, patently offensive material may be thrust at the audience in a way, and in a context, which cannot but enhance the offensive impact that material may have; the same may be said of material unsuitable for children. A cinema audience is to a far greater extent a captive one than is generally the audience which might view offensive displays in public or in retail outlets. Once in a cinema, after having paid an ever-rising entrance charge, a viewer has to make a decision to get up and leave the darkened auditorium. There are not only both physical and economic pressures to sit it through, but parents accompanying children may find it both an embarrassing and difficult process in such circumstances to remove their children from what may, to the latter, be an unexpectedly intriguing experience.

It may be also that subsequent restraints would produce patchy enforcement in two directions: some film producers and distributors might attempt to disregard such provisions; others would take them seriously and tailor their offerings accordingly. Such tailoring would tend, because of the centralised nature of the industry, to have a considerable effect on film production and exhibition, and would in the process suffer from what is probably the central shortcoming of the present system: decision-making by widely differing groups and types of body or even individual. A factor which would tend to militate in favour of overkill on the part of producers and distributors is the amount of money involved in producing most films today. If a film were to be aimed at a particular type of audience, those footing the bill might well decide that the penalties involved in transgressing the standard of restriction which bounds its potential market would be so severe in terms of re-takes etc.,[2] that there might be a censorial overreaction, reducing much film fare to pap.

The sort of prior administrative control which obliges the submission of all films to be commercially exhibited to a board is not the

---

1 *Williams* para 12.10.

2 See *Williams* para 12.5.

only possibility however. A prior restraint system of the type endorsed herein[1] in relation to books and magazines, might be operable here. In terms of such a system, a subsequent restraint would operate, whilst submission to a control board would — unless referred by a nominated official — be voluntary. Such a system would provide cautious film producers and distributors with adequate reassurance, and would protect the public to a greater extent than would subsequent restraints operating on their own. It is probably no bad thing though that the public be provided, in view of the nature of the medium and the methods of marketing involved, with a uniform and hopefully consistent rating system. It is noteworthy that New South Wales, which employs a non-mandatory control system (other than in the case of official referral), has not extended this to films. The state's powers of censorship in this regard have been delegated to the Commonwealth Film Censorship Board, which appears to be something akin to a statutory version of the BBFC.[2]

If mandatory prior control of films is justified, the next question is just what sort of body should exercise this function? Williams reported that local control of films was 'overwhelmingly repudiated by our witnesses'.[3] A common argument in this regard, besides the question of commercial convenience, was that of the absurdity of people being prevented from seeing a film locally, only to drive a couple of miles into another authority to find it on show there. There is also the fact that at present any local authority wishing to vet films in its area faces practical difficulties in obtaining prior notice of the showing of a film.[4] Most authorities in evidence to Williams supported the ending of local controls. If this function is not to be exercised locally, but rather by a single body, the choice lies between the BBFC and a new statutory body. Williams concluded that although there was nothing to suggest that the former was 'unfit to continue the practice of film censorship', the only way in which the Board, a body without any direct legal authority, could fulfil this function would be to leave power with the local authorities, but provide that they might exercise it only by following Board rulings. This the committee, not surprisingly, felt was 'a highly artificial solution', and one which might give rise to legal objections in relation to the delegation of power. The committee did not feel that it would be proper to bestow legal powers of censorship di-

---

1 See administrative restraints in relation to books and magazines, herein.

2 See *Williams* Appendix 4.

3 Ibid. para 12.14.

4 Ibid. para 12.15.

rectly on the Board, a body which is not answerable to anyone for its conduct, and which has clear links, in the past at any rate, with the film industry.

Rather, a new statutory body called the Film Examining Board is proposed,[1] consisting of about twelve members, including representatives from the film industry, local authorities, educational experts, and so on. Examination of films would be by a small body of professional examiners, in terms of the policy laid down by the Board. The Board would hear appeals against their decisions.[2] Such appeals should be open to film distributors and individual members of the public; the Board should be required to view the film in the former case, but to have discretion whether to do so or not, in the latter. In order to extend normal safety controls to cinema clubs, which fall beyond the 1909 and 1952 Cinematograph Acts, it is proposed that films more explicit than those at present receiving an X rating, and suitable for adults only, should be publicly shown only in licensed cinemas. This would have the effect of bringing all commercial public showings under licensing control for safety purposes. The committee proposed that the exemption in the 1952 Act for film exhibitions of a non-commercial nature, should be retained.[3] Any cinema showing 'adult rated' movies would have to be specially designated for this purpose. The decision on allowing such cinemas, the committee felt, should be left entirely to the local authority's discretion.[4]

These proposals are open to criticism on a number of grounds: the first point is the standard to be employed. The committee proposes that Parliament should prescribe general criteria, but that the Board should lay down 'the policy to be adopted in censoring films'.[5] One of the major criticisms of the law operable in the obscenity area at present is its lack of certainty: this seems to perpetuate exactly this vice. It would seem both simpler and clearer to employ the standards recommended above in relation to the protection of children and the occasioning of offence to adults. The same problems arise in relation to the former standard as did with its proposed criminal law application: what age of child is to be taken as one's point of reference? Although this may perhaps in a trial be left, with expert help, to the jury, parents

---

1   *Williams* para 12.24.

2   Ibid. para 12.29.

3   Ibid. para 12.40.

4   Ibid. para 12.38.

5   Ibid. para 12.41.

require guidance as to the quality of films on offer. Williams suggests an 'accompanied by an adult' rating, to be set at the age of eleven. Thus a film rated U would be open to any child; a film rated 11A would be open to those under eleven years of age, only if accompanied by an adult; those rated 16 would not be open to anyone under sixteen years of age. No one under the age of eighteen would be admitted to a film rated 18, the equivalent of the present X rating.[1] It is noteworthy that with the present system of film rating, apart from the AA and X rating, restriction operates entirely at the discretion of parents. The proposed changes would roughly maintain this distinction. This is a question which has so far been avoided by the American Supreme Court: a line of cases[2] appears to establish that the power of the state in relation to children will supercede that of parents when one has to do with influences which are 'clearly' or 'inherently harmful' to 'the physical and mental health of the child'. *Ginsberg*,[3] which provided an exception to the average person test in terms of children (an exception whose viability in terms of the *Miller* hard-core pornography formulation, has since been cast in doubt), did not involve a clash between parental and state interests. The Court, however, quoted with approval the following remarks by Professor Henkin: 'While many of the constitutional arguments against morals legislation apply equally to legislation protecting the morals of children, one can well distinguish laws which do not impose a morality on children, but which support the right of parents to deal with the morals of their children as they see fit'.[4] The Supreme Court then would perhaps favour the rights of parents over those of the state; this would of course depend on the potential harm involved, and even in the event of a clash of interests, would presumably not invalidate at least the basic adult/minor restrictions.

Although the additional 'accompanied by an adult' category will clearly complicate the basic standard of harm to minors, this is perhaps inevitable; it is not binding in the sense that children, if accompanied, may see any film, unless it is rated 16 or 18. If a jury is to be trusted to reach, with the help of expert evidence, a sensible decision in this regard, the same should be true of the type of board in question. A principal concern must be, however, to attempt to achieve a sensible consistency of result with such ratings. Centralisation of decision will

---

1   *Williams*, paras 12.41 to 12.44.

2   *Meyer* v *Nebraska* 262 US 390 (1923); *Pierce* v *Society of Sisters* 268 US 510 (1925): *Prince* v *Massachusetts* 321 US 158 (1944); *Wisconsin* v *Yoder* 406 US 205 (1972).

3   390 US 629 (1968).

4   Ibid. at 639, footnote 7, citing L. Henkin 'Morals and the Constitution: The Sin of Obscenity', 63 (1963) *Colum L Rev* 391 at 413, footnote 68.

clearly aid this, as will the employment of tightly drawn standards, and expert aid in applying them. Crucial here must be the question of just how the Board's functions in this respect are properly to be performed, and what provision is to be made for appeals. It would seem improper for the Board to function, as Williams proposes, essentially — in terms of viewing films — as an appellate body. It would be preferable for such a body to review at least a proportion of all films submitted to it, as well as all films in relation to which an appeal has been made. In view of the fact that one is concerned with speech, it might be as well to go beyond the possibilities of judicial review in regard to the Board's decisions, and provide statutorily the possibility of a judicial review *de novo*, perhaps involving a jury, should this be desired. The approach of the American Supreme Court with prior restraints has been to view the issue as a constitutional one, pivoting on freedom of speech, rather than one to be seen in terms of judicial review of administrative action. Although the suggestion above would not satisfy *Freedman* requirements, it would ensure that the Board's activities were at least monitored by an independent agency. Such monitoring would correspond to the judicial role provided in the New South Wales system of administrative restraints described previously herein.[1] Both sides at such appeals could call expert evidence.

In terms of the Williams proposals the final rating category 18R would be a particularly vital one, as any cinema showing such films would need to be specially designated, and could be refused such designation entirely at the authority's discretion. Zoning may be justifiable on the basis of a number of potential harms such as offence and loss of local amenity. If zoning were to be considered justified, there would not seem any reason to exclude the cinema; what does seem unwarranted is the rejection by the committee of zoning in general, only then to endorse its importance in relation to the cinema. Zoning regulation should stand or fall in this area as a body, and not in terms of the medium of communication involved. Whether zoned or not, cinemas showing films rated 18R should, similarly to shops retailing matter patently offensive to reasonable people, display in a prominent place a warning notice about the nature of the film on offer, and should not admit anyone under the age of eighteen. It may well be, as with displays,[2] that the age of prohibition in respect of children could quite happily be set at sixteen, in which case the protection of the young and that of adults from gratuitous offence would be adequately achieved by

---

1   See administrative restraints on books and magazines, herein.

2   See chapter 5, Section I(3).

(in addition to the categories U and 11A) categories of 16 and 16R,[1] the category 18 dropping away altogether.

Such statutory prior restraint in terms of children, and restriction in terms of adults, would clearly not be constitutional in *Freedman* terms. Aside from problems of parental consent, restriction in favour of minors would, in *Ginsberg* terms, seem constitutional: that is, presuming that the Dallas ordinance involved in *Interstate Circuit Inc v Dallas*[2] was declared unconstitutional on the grounds of overbreadth, and not on the additional ground that it restricted, in terms of minors, distribution to adults, and presuming that the *Miller* hard-core pornography ruling has not scotched the *Ginsberg* exception altogether. The type of restriction proposed above would still fail constitutionally though, in terms of the *Freedman* requirement of a speedy judicial hearing in every case. It would simply not be possible to administer a system in terms of the standards recommended above, and subscribe to such a requirement. The constitutional alternatives are to leave film censorship in the United States in private hands, as at present;[3] or to justify the prior restraints advocated above in terms of the First Amendment. The first of these options involves dangers of the application of overbroad standards, and the absence of procedural safeguards; in view of the Court's attitude towards prior restraints this is perhaps at present the only viable option.

The final question for consideration here is whether subsequent restraint should also be applicable to films. With the inclusion in terms of public exhibitions of cinema clubs, virtually all cinema showings would be subject to licence. Williams proposes that it should be an offence to exhibit publicly a non-certificated film, or to exhibit a certificated film in terms other than those attaching to the certification.[4] It should also be an offence not to display notice of certification in the designated manner. The committee rejected the proposal that in addition to the cinema licensee being liable to prosecution if those under age are admitted, that the young people involved should themselves bear some of the criminal onus. As with restrictions on retailers, and despite the difficulties of administering restriction in practice, the committee determined that in their view criminalisation was not appropriate in this respect. Is it necessary, in addition to such offences, that the criminal

---

1   16R approximating to the 18R category proposed by Williams, which combines the minimum age with an indication — in respect of adults — of restriction.

2   390 US 676 (1968); see the protection of children, chapters 5 and 14.

3   See non-legal prior restraints, below.

4   *Williams* para 12.49.

measures proposed earlier in relation to protecting minors and preventing offence, be applicable? The committee recommended not,[1] and in view of the possibility, in present law, of charges of criminal complicity against councils and the BBFC, this seems a sensible approach.

6)   *Live shows*

In terms of the Theatres Act 1968, Section 1(2), a local authority may refuse a theatre a licence on the grounds of safety etc., but not in terms of the content of a play. All administrative prior restraint is therefore excluded in relation to the theatre;[2] the only other prior restraint that appears potentially of serious relevance is injunction. The discussion in this regard previously in this chapter in relation to books and magazines would be of equal application here. The rejection of prior restraints in this respect seems sensible: not only may productions be more easily tailored than are films, once distributed, but the practicalities of prior restraint would be altogether more difficult to manage in the case of the theatre.

Theatre, as we have seen, does not cover the gamut of what may be termed 'live shows'. In terms of the distinction drawn earlier between conduct and speech,[3] the former falls beyond the scope of this enquiry. The distinction is one of fact, and not always easy to draw: hence the consideration of subsequent restraints in relation to live shows earlier,[4] and their inclusion here. As was argued earlier, the control of shows constituting conduct rather than speech, does not raise, primarily, freedom of speech considerations. As a result, prior and subsequent restraints may perhaps be more easily justified, particularly in terms of the public order considerations such entertainment may potentially raise. Thus prior restraint of such shows would be permissible in American terms as falling outside the First Amendment; prior or subsequent restraint may be couched in terms other than obscenity. In this country there do not appear to be any such restraints operative. There are licensing provisions in relation to establishments providing dancing and music, for example; generally they are aimed at ensuring observance of safety and health regulations. The Greater London Council in licensing such establishments imposes a condition that

---

1   *Williams,* para 12.47.

2   See the Report of the Joint Committee on Censorship of the Theatre (HMSO 1967).

3   See substantive common law offences, chapter 3; live shows, chapter 6.

4   Chapter 6.

those under eighteen years of age be excluded.[1] To extend such licensing requirements to cover the content or nature of such shows might in fact be a most effective sanction, which might operate in conjunction with the subsequent restraints proposed previously herein. Rather than such shows being reviewed by a controlling body beforehand, a process which would hardly be practical in terms of the nature of the entertainment and the establishments staging them, the grant of a licence might be made conditional on the establishment not staging shows which either were contrary, in the authority's view, to prescribed standards, or which had formed the subject of a successful criminal prosecution. The standards employed in the former instance could be the same as those recommended for subsequent restraint, and such findings might be open to judicial review. Zoning might equally, particularly in terms of the public order dimension raised by such shows, be a valuable tool in their regulation. It may be that licensing provisions would provide local authorities with discretion in this regard.

7) *Television and sound broadcasting*

(i) *Subsequent restraints.* The Criminal Law Act 1977, in revoking the proviso to Section 1(3)(b) in terms of cinematograph exhibitions, left intact the second proviso thereto as to television[2] and sound broadcasts. The 1959 Act is not therefore applicable to such broadcasts. It may, however, apply to the distribution of films to television studios or personnel. This point was never clearly settled in relation to cinematograph exhibitions: although the Act did not apply to public film showings, it may well have applied to the distribution process antecedent to such showings. A consideration which would exclude such application is the disjunctive 'or' between subparagraphs (a) and (b) of subsection 1(3): it may be that articles embodying matter to be looked at can only be published, under the Act, in terms of Section 1(3)(b).[3]

As regards broadcasting itself Section 2(4) of the 1959 Act has no application; thus any common law offence apposite might be charged. Possibilities here are publishing an obscene libel, outraging public decency, mounting an indecent exhibition, keeping a disorderly house, or (if it is a substantive offence) corrupting public morals. Outraging public decency and its more specific manifestations require a public aspect;[4] this extends to the inside of premises, and the fact that tele-

---

1 *Williams* para 11.7.

2 See generally C.R. Munro *Television, Censorship and the Law* (Farnborough 1979).

3 See search and seizure in relation to films, above.

4 See outraging public decency, chapter 3.

vision is shown in 'public' places, such as public houses, for example, may well be sufficient here.[1] Application of Section 1 of the Indecent Displays (Control) Act 1981 to television and sound broadcasts has been specifically excluded however.[2]

(ii) *Prior restraints* (a) *Administrative regulation*.[3] Although the BBC is not statutorily required not to offend decency or good taste in terms of its programmes, the government of the day in fact has extensive powers over the Corporation. The Corporation is subject to the Wireless Telegraphy Act 1949 and its Charter of Incorporation, as well as its licence and agreement with the Postmaster-General. In these terms, government powers include both the financial and technical aspects of the Corporation's running. In addition, the Postmaster-General may (under clause 12(4) of the licence) 'from time to time by notice in writing require the Corporation to refrain from sending any matter or matter of any class specified in such notice'. In 1964, for example, the BBC was directed via such a notice to 'maintain standards of good taste and decency'. The Corporation is thus not only authorised to do so, but is actually required to exercise its own internal censorship. Its discretion, in the sense of the guidelines under which it operates, is very broad: ultimate censorship power rests with the Postmaster-General however; his discretion is absolute.

Within the Corporation, producers who foresee offence being caused by a programme, will consult their seniors, such matters perhaps going as high as the Director-General. Internal directions on such questions are supposedly aimed at the Corporation occupying the middle ground as far as controversial questions of taste or propriety are concerned. Examples of such internal self-censorship, and there are many of them,[4] include drama, entertainment and factual programmes being cut or banned altogether. The television critic of the *Financial Times* has remarked in this regard that 'It is depressing that the subjects of programmes which are being suppressed in the 1970's are so often the very same subjects which have been upsetting the bigots for centuries: God, sex and Ireland'.[5] These in turn perhaps point to a deeper thread: a form of political censorship in the sense of a distaste for anything which

---

1   See Munro op.cit. at 97.

2   Indecent Displays (Control) Act 1981, Section 1(4)(a).

3   See Munro op.cit. especially chapters 2, 3, 6 and 7.

4   For an extensive examination of internal censorship pressures and decisions, see Munro op.cit., chapter 7.

5   Christopher Dunkley, *Financial Times*, 15 June 1977; quoted in Munro ibid. at 159.

challenges the establishment and its proclaimed views.[1] If this is correct, internal Corporation control would seem to go far beyond such considerations as protecting children or preventing offence in terms of graphic representations, and is aimed basically rather at the preservation of basic positive morality, both religious, sexual and political, if these are separable. This bias is scarcely surprising: although the blunt instruments of government censorship have been used very seldom indeed in relation to broadcasting,[2] their existence is obviously an incentive to restraint. In fairness, though, the Corporation has been conscious of the need for, and is statutorily[3] obliged to be impartial; the bias is probably not so much party political, as one in favour of the broad mainstream of consensus, political and otherwise, in the society. This is strongly reinforced by the external and informal pressures[4] brought to bear on the Corporation by government, politicians and vociferous lobbies, such as the National Viewers' and Listeners' Association, and its General Secretary, Mrs Mary Whitehouse.

A number of things are clear from all this: in the first place it is quite obvious that television is subject to extensive administrative censorship in fact; second, this censorship is not so much a formal restriction imposed by government, as something which is principally the result of internal, and largely informal, external pressures. Third, it is clear that the level of such self-censorship depends in reality to a large extent on the nature of the people leading the Corporation and on the *laissez faire* attitude of the government. Mrs Whitehouse put her finger on the relevance of the former when she described Sir Hugh Greene, Director-General during the 1960s, as the individual 'who above all, was responsible for the moral collapse which characterised the sixties and seventies'.[5] Although the substance of her remark is best seen in context with other of her observations, such as the condemnation of a television series which treated Darwin's Theory 'as though it were a fact',[6] and suggestions that pornography is communist-inspired in order to undermine the West,[7] her identification of personality in the Corporation, government and the lobbies as a strong determinant is

---

1 Munro op.cit. at 159.

2 Ibid. at 14—15, 33—4.

3 At least as far as proceedings in Parliament are concerned.

4 Munro op.cit., chapter 6.

5 Mary Whitehouse *Whatever Happened to Sex?* (Hove 1977) at 17; quoted ibid. at 133.

6 *The Sunday Times* 12 February 1978; quoted ibid.

7 Mary Whitehouse *Who Does She Think She Is?* (London 1971) at 65 and 127; quoted ibid.

surely correct.

Although this is certainly true of the IBA, their situation is a little more closely defined statutorily: amongst other legal duties, the Independent Broadcasting Authority Act 1973 provides that

> It shall be the duty of the Authority to satisfy themselves that, so far as possible, the programmes broadcast by the Authority comply with the following requirements, that is to say: (a) that nothing is included in the programmes which offends against good taste or decency or is likely to encourage or incite to crime or to lead to disorder or to be offensive to public feeling.[1]

The authority is by Section 5(1) required to draw up and observe a code giving guidance as to the showing of violence. Final legal control of what is broadcast is placed by the Act in the hands of the government; once again discretion is absolute: the 'Postmaster-General may at any time by notice in writing require the Authority to refrain from broadcasting any matter or classes of matter specified in the notice ...'.[2] There was some doubt as to whether the wording of the Independent Broadcasting Act 1973, Section 4(1), was such as to render the duties imposed susceptible to judicial enforcement. The form of words employed have been taken as having made the authority the sole judge in such matters.[3] The Courts' attitude towards subsection 4(1) was put to the test in 1973 when Mr Ross McWhirter attempted to obtain an injunction against the IBA to prevent the showing of an ATV programme about artist Andy Warhol, on the grounds that it offended good taste and decency, contrary to Section 4(1)(a) of the 1973 Act. Aside from the question of *locus standi*, and from the question of the grant of the injunction, it was clear that Section 4(1) was not regarded by the courts as precluding judicial enforcement.[4]

The IBA has not been reticent in exercising these powers; the result has been that independent television is subject to even more pervasive internal pressures than is the BBC, as these pressures are applied at two levels: within the television company concerned, and then by the IBA. The Annan Report[5] in 1977 criticised the extent to which the IBA

---

1 Section 4(1)(a).

2 Section 18(3).

3 Munro op.cit. at 50–1.

4 See *Re McWhirter* reported in *Attorney-General, ex rel, McWhirter* v *IBA* [1973] 1 QB 629.

5 Report of the Committee on the Future of Broadcasting chaired by Lord Annan (HMSO 1977) Cmnd 6753, chapter 12.

involved itself in this way. This criticism has subsequently been rejected governmentally: the 1978 White Paper on Broadcasting[1] did not mirror the committee's views, and no proposals to amend the legislation were made. Such amendment would clearly be necessary were such a change to be effected, as at present the IBA is under a clear statutory duty to censor offensiveness.

(b) *Declarations* will generally not be given in relation to questions of fact, and their relevance to obscenity or indecency determinations is therefore limited. A declaration might be obtained, however, in a sense to reinforce administrative prior restraint: in other words, were the BBC or the IBA to breach their statutory duty in terms of programme control, judicial intervention is possible.[2] The statutory duty in question must needs be enforceable in court: the more precisely framed obligations on the Independent Broadcasting Authority in relation to programme control would seem amenable to such enforcement; such control in the case of the BBC is self-imposed. A second requirement here is *locus standi*: unless the applicant can show that a private right is involved, or that he suffers special damage beyond that suffered generally,[3] an individual is unlikely to be found to have standing here. Standing has been conceded in terms of *mandamus* by virtue of residence in the relevant area, or the extent of family obligations (in relation to Mr Blackburn and his family in each case);[4] *locus standi* requirements here are probably narrower. Having said this, in a recent Court of Appeal decision[5] Lord Denning MR managed to take a majority of the court with him in according standing for judicial review to a body of taxpayers aggrieved at a tax amnesty granted by the Inland Revenue to certain Fleet Street casual workers. Quite where the line is drawn in any one instance is difficult to predict.

In terms of the standards enforced in relation to programmes, although the BBC is not under a statutory obligation to enforce a particular standard, were the Corporation to opt for obscenity in decision-making, then the reasoning in *R v GLC ex parte Blackburn*[6] would seem apposite, in that the statutory exception of television broadcasting from the purview of the 1959 Act may well found a decision that

---

1 Broadcasting Cmnd 7294 (HMSO July 1978).

2 See Munro op.cit. at 22 and 50.

3 De Smith op.cit. at 509.

4 See declarations in terms of films, above.

5 *R v Inland Revenue Commissioners, ex parte National Federation of Self-Employed and Small Businesses Ltd* [1980] 2 All ER 378.

6 [1976] 1 WLR 550.

indecency is the applicable standard in relation to such broadcasting. Were standing to be accorded to an individual, such assertion might lie through an order of *mandamus* or possibly a declaration; even though individuals may not have standing in relation to declarations in terms of public rights, the Attorney-General may act in the public interest,[1] or consent to a relator action.

(c) *Injunctions*. As was remarked in relation to films earlier, an individual does not normally, in the absence of breach of private right or, perhaps, some special damage to him, have *locus standi* in terms of preventing by injunction a breach of the criminal law. Similar considerations would appear to apply to a wrongful act or omission by a public body; although the Court of Appeal granted an interim injunction in the *McWhirter*[2] case, the House of Lords, as well as more cautious *dicta* in the second decision in the Court of Appeal, have made it clear that this was an error.[3] This of course would probably not preclude the Attorney-General suing, or permitting a relator action.[4]

(iii) *Law reform*. Accountability in terms of the courts is clearly limited; it exists rather in an ultimate sense in terms of public opinion, and more immediately in terms of informal external pressures. A number of questions may be posed as to the future of broadcasting censorship: in the first place, should there be censorship of broadcasting at all? Second, presuming an answer in the affirmative, should there be both subsequent and prior restraints? Although some censorship would seem appropriate at least in terms of protecting children, it is not proposed to embark on a discussion of the basic question here. This would seem legitimate in view of the fact that broadcasting restraints are generally seen as raising their own particular policy considerations that do not apply elsewhere in the area under consideration; principal among these is the fact that air waves are limited in number. In the United States, the Supreme Court has developed a distinct area of constitutional jurisprudence with regard to broadcasting restrictions: in terms of the so-called fairness doctrine, broadcasting companies are able to exercise prior restraint in a way which would not be acceptable in First Amend-

---

1   De Smith op.cit. at 453 and 489.

2   *Attorney-General, ex rel, McWhirter* v *IBA* [1973] 1 QB 629.

3   *Gouriet* v *Union of Post Office Workers* [1978] AC 435 at 483, 495, 511 and 521–2. Were the broadcast in question to have constituted a criminal offence, then the ruling is in line with *Thorne* v *BBC* [1967] 1 WLR 1104, where an injunction to prevent the BBC disseminating allegedly racist propaganda was denied an individual; enforcement under the Race Relations Act 1965 was, however, at the Attorney-General's discretion.

4   De Smith op.cit. at 453.

ment terms in relation to speech in other media form.[1]

Assuming that some prior restraint is permissible, three observations may be made: in the first place, it seems anomalous that the statutory duties imposed on the broadcasting authorities in this country differ. Second, that those standards at present statutorily prescribed might be more tightly drawn, and third, that in view of experience in relation to film censorship, the exclusion of subsequent restraints may seem indicated. The Annan Committee in fact recommended in relation to the new fourth channel in this country that the Open Broadcasting Authority be relieved of restrictions in terms of good taste, and that its broadcasts be subject only to the law of obscenity.[2] This is to assume that obscenity law remains on the statute book; it is also to conclude that considerations of the protection of the young, and the prevention of gratuitous offence may be satisfied without prior restraint. The latter would in any event be a reality, as decisions would have nonetheless to be made. The committee recommended a very much stronger element of public accountability in this respect, in terms of regular public hearings.[3] Although the government has since announced that the familiar restrictions in terms of offensiveness will apply to the OBA,[4] the idea of greater public accountability is perhaps one feasible way in which the inherent secrecy of the present system might to some extent be ameliorated.

8) *Non-legal prior restraints*

Such restraints have a long history, and have often proven just as effective — if not more so — as their legal counterparts in suppressing the publication of speech. Obvious examples include library censorship, and sales policies on the part of monopolistic or oligopolistic retailers. Two early, and most effective examples of such controls in Britain were Charles Mudies' monopoly of libraries and W.H. Smith's monopoly of railway bookstalls.

Two problems arise in identifying and commenting on restrictions potentially falling within this area. The first is whether the restriction is a legal or non-legal one; the second is whether the restriction involved actually constitutes a prior restraint or not. In the United States, the first of these questions assumes a constitutional significance: the First Amendment prohibits any legal restriction ('Congress

---

1 See S.J. Stephens *The Fairness Doctrine and the Media* (Berkeley 1978).

2 Annan Report, chapter 4, para 30.

3 Ibid., chapter 6, para 30; chapter 16, para 50.

4 Broadcasting (HMSO 1978) Cmnd 7294, para 100.

shall make no law ...') on the press or freedom of speech. Most legislatively-based restrictions are clearly potentially subject in these terms to First Amendment review. Conversely, any non-legal restraint would by implication appear not to raise First Amendment considerations, and in these terms at any rate, to be *prima facie* permissible. It has been argued recently that constitutional protection is not so clear-cut; that the First Amendment in fact guarantees for example, a right of access to the media. It was argued that newspapers enjoying a monopolistic position because of their operation in an area of vital public concern, for instance, were engaged in state action;[1] private restrictions on the media were in these terms translated into governmental action, subject to First Amendment guarantees. There are three principal ways in which private action has been argued to become state action for First Amendment purposes. The Court has apparently set its face against all three.[2]

The first avenue of attack here was state enforcement: if the state enforced private action restricting on freedom of speech, this was argued[3] to constitute state action. Thus, if one leased property to a bookseller on condition that he did not stock certain material, would the enforcement of such a covenant in the courts constitute state action? Allowing this argument might seriously interfere with a free market place of ideas; the Court has made it clear that the First Amendment is not there to enforce neutrality on private persons.[4] The second avenue of attack is that where governmental functions are delegated to private parties, consequential private action may be seen as state action. The Court in *Hudgens* v *NLRB*[5] did not overrule *March* v *Alabama*,[6] a case in which the private actions of an oil company, by virtue of its running an entire town, were seen as state action, and therefore subject to First Amendment limitation. Equally, private action in excluding picketers from a shopping mall would not fall into the same category. The distinction between these two situations has not been

---

1   The First Amendment is applicable to state, as opposed to federal action via the Fourteenth Amendment: 'No State shall make or enforce any law ...'.

2   For a full discussion of the case law and the literature available in this area generally, see F. Schauer 'Hudgens v NLRB and the Problem of State Action in First Amendment Adjudication', 61 (1977) *Minn L Rev* 433.

3   See especially *Shelley* v *Kraemer* 334 US 1 (1948).

4   See *Lloyd Corp* v *Tanner* 407 US 551 (1972); *CBS* v *Democratic National Committee* 412 US 241 (1974). The issue of state enforcement did not arise in *Hudgens* v *NLRB* 424 US 507 (1976) as none of the picketers in the shopping mall was arrested or charged.

5   424 US 507 (1976).

6   326 US 501 (1946).

clearly enunciated by a majority on the Court: a suggestion in this regard is that where the delegation is so extensive as to allow private interests to control the flow of information into a community, then that private conduct will be seen as state action.[1] For our purposes private action is in this sense unlikely to be subject to First Amendment limitations.

A final avenue of approach is that mentioned in introducing this discussion: where private action is monopolistic, and if it concerns a vital public concern such as the purveying of news, it acquires a public aspect; as a result it is, as state action, subject to the First Amendment and whatever constitutional limitations on speech restriction it imposes. This is a quite distinct line of reasoning from that which argues a right of access to the media on the basis of First Amendment language, in the sense of the separate specification of freedom of the press.[2] The Court has on several occasions refused to apply such an affirmative view of the First Amendment: in *Miami Herald* v *Tornillo*, for example, a Florida right-to-reply statute was declared unconstitutional. Although the Court affirmed that the constitution does not require the subordination of personal or economic interests in this way,[3] the decision probably rests on the First Amendment freedom of the press specification; the right-of-reply statute was seen as a means by which the state might dictate what a newspaper should print. After *Hudgens*, however, the probability of private censorship being classified as state action, and therefore subject to the First Amendment, seems slim; the state action doctrine has been narrowed so far that such application would seem remote.[4]

It has been suggested[5] that such limitation of the application of the First Amendment is in fact dictated by First Amendment considerations: if access to the media were provided, then as in *Tornillo*, this would require legislative prescription, thus infringing the operators' First Amendment rights. Such prescription might of course be essayed by the Court. Second, it is argued that to regard private action as state

---

1   Schauer op.cit. at 455.

2   See Nimmer 'Introduction — Is Freedom of the Press a Redundancy: What Does it Add to Freedom of Speech?' 26 (1975) *Hast. L.J.* 639; Stewart 'Or of the Press' ibid. at 631; Lange 'The Speech and Press Clauses' 23 (1975) *UCLA L Rev* 77.

3   418 US 241 (1974) at 256; see also *CBS* v *Democratic National Committee* 412 US 94 (1972).

4   See Schauer op.cit., especially at 459—60.

5   Ibid.

action in this context, is to interfere in the market place of ideas, thus assaulting a fundamental First Amendment rationale. This perhaps ignores the economic realities of that market place. Even if the present administrations in Britain and the United States succeed in 'rolling back the frontiers of the State', it is difficult to see that they will be able to do much about economic realities such as economies of scale. Rather than being justified in First Amendment terms, the Court's action on this issue is perhaps best seen simply as a policy of judicial restraint, convenience, or conservatism, or a combination of these.

Assuming that private action is largely immune from First Amendment limitation, perhaps the principal example of such censorship in the United States, the motion picture rating system, would seem constitutionally permissible. The scheme, which covers some 92 per cent of all films shown commercially in the United States,[1] imposes censorship in terms of what is suitable for minors: specifically those under seventeen years of age.[2] It has been argued strongly that the system should be classified as state action on one or all three of the grounds discussed above.[3] Despite the limitation of the state action doctrine by the Court, the film censorship scheme is such that it might, even on the basis of narrowly interpreted criteria, qualify on at least one of these bases as state action; possibly the most likely basis in this respect is the monopolistic position, in a regulatory sense, of the Motion Picture Association of America. It can always be argued that if material is not published in one newspaper or magazine, it may be acceptable to another publication. The film regulation system ensures that very few films indeed escape its ministrations. If any aspect of private censorship were to be made subject to the First Amendment in this way, the MPAA film censorship scheme is perhaps the most likely candidate. The principal advantage of the application of First Amendment standards here would not be an abolition of such controls, but rather the imposition of procedural safeguards, and perhaps even more important, narrowly drawn standards. The MPAA, in order to achieve flexibility, does not at present even publish the criteria it applies. As the system does have considerable drag in terms of adults: although they are not barred from X rated films, the exclusion of children imposes an economic burden on producers, whilst new areas of film exhibition, such as cable television

---

1   See J. Freedman 'The Motion Picture Rating System of 1968: A Constitutional Analysis of Self-Regulation by the Film Industry', 73 (1973) *Col L Rev* 185. This figure has been put lower at 80–85 per cent: *Williams* para 12.3.

2   Films unsuitable for minors receive an X certificate.

3   Freedman op.cit.

and airline in-board film shows, often exclude X rated films.[1] Such film censorship contrasts with the position in England where although there is no statutory basis for the British Board of Film Censors, local authority licensing is statute-based and lawful, and in the case of children, mandatory. The English system as it stands at present would not fall outside First Amendment protection were it to be duplicated in the United States.[2]

Perhaps the other outstanding example of such censorship in the United States to attract legal comment is that imposed by libraries or allied institutions. Considerable concern has been expressed recently by the American Library Association for example, at censorship aimed at public school library and textbook selections, and said to constitute the 'most massive, vicious and sophisticated censorship since McCarthyism of the 1950's'.[3] On the East Coast, Long Island's free school district board axed Desmond Morris's *The Naked Ape* and Jonathan Swift's essay *A Modest Proposal*, on the grounds that they are 'anti-American, anti-Christ, anti-Christian, anti-Semitic, and just plain filthy'. The Cedar Lake, Indiana, school board banned the *American Heritage Dictionary*, as other school boards have done, because it included amongst its 155,000 entries 'bed, verb transitive' as vernacular for having sexual intercourse. Where such censorship is imposed by public bodies, the First Amendment may well be applicable. The question of such library censorship brings into play, however, a different constitutional consideration: that of academic freedom. At the risk of drawing arbitrary boundaries, it is not proposed to pursue this any further;[4] suffice it here to point out that most private censorship, beyond the two principal examples cited above, would apparently escape First Amendment limitation.

The position in English law as regards private censorship is clear: although such censorship may be argued to raise philosophical and constitutional questions with regard to freedom of speech, in the absence of a constitutional guarantee of such freedom, there can be no question (in these terms at any rate) of the illegality of such censorship. Although private censorship may not be unconstitutional in American First Amendment terms, it has to be private: in other words, 'non-legal', in the sense of not having directly or indirectly a legislative basis; any such basis would clearly resurrect arguments of state action. This is

---

1   See Friedman op.cit. at 202–6.

2   See law reform, films, above.

3   *The Sunday Times*, 20 April 1979.

4   See in this regard, e.g. 10 *Connecticut L Rev* 747.

not the case in Britain; as a result, there is no specific inhibition on public, statute-based bodies engaging in what may be termed quasi-private prior restraint, in the sense that such regulation is indirectly statute-based, but is not itself based on specific legal provision.

It is not possible here to explore in any detail private censorship in England.[1] All that can be done is to give some examples of the types of private, and often very effective, prior restraints operative. A recent example of a purely private operation is the British Adult Publications Association. This was formed in May 1977, and includes nine out of the thirteen main sex magazine publishers in Britain, nearly all the distributors, and some retailers.[2] The Association has set up a Publications Control Board, and has laid down guidelines, based on trial court findings of obscenity, as to what is or is not permissible. The Board is to apply these guidelines in different cases, and has as its part time President, the former Secretary of the British Board of Film Censors, Mr John Trevelyan. The sanction exercised by the Board is in terms of distribution: anything given the thumbs-down by the Board will not be distributed to retailers; such sanction could be extended to the title should the magazine continue to flout guidelines. Such sanctions had by September 1978 been implemented in four cases, and certain magazines had ceased publication. It is a little early to say how effective the Association is as a censorship mechanism: the DPP thought there was little difference between publications before and after its initiation.[3] Certainly its guidelines and compliance with them are irrelevant as far as prosecutional authorities are concerned.

An example of potential speech restriction by a public, rather than purely private body, may be seen in the recent controversy over the London staging by the National Theatre of Mr Howard Brenton's *The Romans in Britain*.[4] The play with its theme of the Roman occupation of Britain, and parallels with the present 'occupation' of Northern Ireland, includes scenes of homosexual rape and violence, and has been advertised as unsuitable for children. Sir Horace Cutler, leader of the Greater London Council, walked out of a preview at the Olivier Theatre, and later telegrammed the National Theatre threatening to terminate the theatre's £630,000 annual grant from the Council. This type of potential restriction takes us back to a basic point initially raised as to private censorship: besides its non-legal aspect, does the conduct in

---

1   In this respect see particularly Paul O'Higgins *Censorship in Britain* (London 1972).

2   See *Williams* paras 4.21 and 4.22.

3   Ibid.

4   See *The Times*, 18 and 20 October 1980; *The Sunday Times*, 19 October 1980.

question in fact constitute a prior restraint? It might be argued that the theatre in this example, even were the money withdrawn, would not be restrained from staging plays. The putative restriction is prior to publication; does it constitute a restraint on publication? This is clearly a question of degree; in *Bantam Books v Sullivan*[1] the Supreme Court was faced with a very similar decision: was the operation of a Rhode Island legislature-created board, set up to investigate publications unfit for youth, a prior restraint? The board did not license, rather notifying publishers of material's unsuitability for the young, and compiling black-lists and issuing threats of prosecution in the event of non-compliance. The Court took the view that the chilling effect of such activities was such as to constitute a prior restraint. In an equivalent of the GLC case mentioned above, the same view might well be taken. The effectiveness of the GLC's threat may possibly be gauged in terms of the theatre's reaction: four days after its delivery, Sir Peter Hall, the National Theatre's Director, indicated that the play might be taken off; he did not disclose precisely what had prompted this change of attitude, which has to be measured against buoyant box office sales.

A final example of quasi-private prior restriction, arguably a restraint, is that potentially effected by the British Film Fund Agency. Under the so-called Eady Levy, a levy on cinema admissions is collected (in terms of the empowering legislation, the Cinematograph Films Act 1957 and the Films Act 1970) by Customs and Excise at four-weekly intervals from cinemas. The present rate of levy is one-ninth of the excess over 17½ pence of payments for admission (the amount paid for admission, less VAT). Cinemas taking less than £1,100 per week are exempt from the levy. The funds collected are paid over to the British Film Fund Agency. It may, subject to the approval of the Secretary of State for Trade, and after consultation with the Cinematograph Film Council, make grants from the fund to the Children's Film Foundation, the British Film Institute, the National Film School, and the National Film Finance Corporation. The remainder may similarly be distributed to the makers of eligible British quota films, in proportion to their films' earnings in Britain. Films will normally be 'eligible' provided these are of a width exceeding 16mm, are not television films, are not made for or by a government department, and are not films consisting wholly or mainly of photographs, which when taken were essentially means of communicating news. The requirements for registration as a British quota film concern principally the location of the studio used, the nationality of the maker, and costs of production.

---

1   372 US 58 (1963).

In addition, films made principally as advertisements are exempt, as are certain news films, and any films made before 1 April 1938. On the face of it grants should be made to film makers without regard to the content of the film. To make money available to films the making or publication of which involves a criminal offence, might well be a breach of statutory duty. Beyond this no distinctions would appear to be statutorily envisaged, and the fund would appear to have made money available in relation to soft-core pornographic, or as the Department of Trade prefers to refer to them,[1] 'sexploitation' films. During the six-month period March to August 1979 about £300,000 was allocated to such films.[2] Pressure has arisen from a number of MPs, sectors of the film industry and others, in this regard; the government has as a result attempted to exclude grants to films exploiting sex and/or violence. The extent to which this has been done, and the criteria on which such distinctions are based, have not been made public, the Department of Trade merely acknowledging that grants to such films had been made in the past.[3]

Private censorship then, although one cannot explore its extent or effects further here, is probably both widespread and effective; it is also often very much more difficult to identify and quantify. The absence of constitutional guarantees in Britain means that examples of it, probably subject to First Amendment limitation in the United States, escape judicial constitutional review. Equally, the application of First Amendment guarantees to such censorship very often raises serious problems; it may be that despite its potential constitutional significance, it is something which cannot in a free society, constitutional guarantees or not, be eradicated or even seriously curbed.

II Prior restriction not constituting a prior restraint

Seizures for evidentiary purposes

It is very difficult to draw a rigid distinction between such seizures and those effecting a prior restraint. Indeed, if viewed from the stance that any seizure prior to publication for whatever purpose constitutes a

---

1 The Department takes the view that no pornographic films 'as we understand the word' are shown to the public in this country. In the Department's view, cheaply made 'sexploitation' films are apparently a category distinct from soft-core pornography; letter from Mrs E.M. Crawford-Price, Films Branch, Department of Trade, 14 December 1979, in answer to a query as to the allocation of funds to such films.

2 *The Daily Telegraph*, 10 November 1979; details of individual films receiving payment are published in the department's journal *Trade and Industry*.

3 Letter from E.M. Crawford-Price op.cit.

prior restraint, no such distinction exists. It would seem legitimate though to regard seizures aimed at the securing of evidence, and with only the minimal prior restraint impact, as where one only of a number of copies of a work is taken, as not constituting a prior restraint. The reasoning, although not explicit, on the American Supreme Court's part in this respect, is probably that such powers and their exercise are aimed at the promotion of proper criminal process, and not the inhibition of speech; their impact on speech is minimal, and they are therefore constitutional. This line of reasoning is parallel to that employed by the Court in *Young* in relation to zoning. It becomes a little strained where multiple seizures, or the seizure of the only copy of a work, are involved. As a result the Court has laid down in *Heller* additional safeguards to minimise prior restraint effects. No such distinctions have been drawn in English law. Dependent on the couching of the offences in question, such seizures may be difficult to avoid; if forfeiture proceedings were to be abandoned as a mechanism of restraint, such seizures might, in judiciously chosen cases, provide a useful weapon in the law's armoury. If so, careful monitoring and limitation of prior restraint effects would seem essential.[1]

A form of seizure aimed at the securing of evidence for criminal prosecution, but in relation to which monitoring is to say the least, unlikely, is that effected under warrant authorised by a Secretary of State. Such interceptions are generally authorised at the request of the police, customs and excise, and the security service.[2] In the case of the police and customs and excise, a 'really serious crime' should be involved, other methods should have proven inadequate, and an arrest and conviction should be facilitated by the interception. Although such interceptions might be authorised in relation to offences in this area, its employment as a prior restraint is not very probable.

---

1 See search and seizure, law reform, above.

2 See the Report of the Committee of Privy Councillors on the Interception of Communications (HMSO 1957) Cmnd 283; The Interceptions of Communications in Great Britain (HMSO April 1980) Cmnd 7873.

8 Enforcement of the law

Discretion to prosecute[1] adheres in England and Wales principally to three varieties of potential prosecutor: a private individual, the police, or the law officers. Judicial control in this area in the sense of halting prosecutions has been very briefly alluded to earlier;[2] one's immediate concern here is which of the potential prosecutors mentioned above are relevant in relation to the offences discussed so far, and the extent to which their discretion not to prosecute is absolute.

I) The law officers

Authority vests here in the Attorney-General, who is in turn responsible to Parliament. The Director of Public Prosecutions acts under the direction of the Attorney-General. The former has a small staff which collects information about offences; the Director provides advice to chief officers of police, and is himself under a duty to prosecute in certain cases, whilst having a discretion so to do in others: the latter extends to intervention in summary or indictable proceedings should

---

1 See generally D.G.T. Williams 'Prosecution, Discretion and the Accountability of the Police' in R. Hood (ed.) *Crime, Criminology and Public Policy* (London 1974) at 161–95, and authorities cited there.

2 See Double Jeopardy, chapter 2.

313

he think fit so to do.[1] Challenge to the non-exercise of these powers through judicial review would seem unlikely.[2] The only other apparent avenue of attack would be for an individual to request a court to interpose to prevent a breach of the criminal law by issuing an injunction for example. It would seem clear that the possibility of obtaining an injunction or declaration in these circumstances is very limited: although the position may not be quite as curtailed in relation to declarations, an applicant would probably have to demonstrate either the infringement of a legal right adhering to himself, or perhaps, special damage sustained by himself. Whether an individual would be in a position to establish *locus standi* must seem rather doubtful.[3] The same may be said of the probability of obtaining an order of *mandamus* compelling the Attorney-General to exercise his discretion properly.[4]

Proceedings may be instituted at present only by or with the consent of the Attorney-General in relation to the following offences:

(i) The Theatres Act 1968;
(ii) The Children and Young Persons (Harmful Publications) Act 1955;
(iii) The Judicial Proceedings (Regulation of Reports) Act 1926;
(iv) Section 4(3) of the Criminal Law Act 1977 applies to prosecution for conspiracy (in terms of the Act) to commit other offences, any consent requirement applying to the offences themselves.[5]

Proceedings may at present be instituted only by or with the consent of the Director of Public Prosecutions in relation to the following offences:

(i) The Obscene Publications Act 1959 and 1964, where the prosecution relates to a film of 16mm or more;
(ii) The Unsolicited Goods and Services Act 1971, where the prosecution is for the sending of unsolicited circulars;
(iii) The Protection of Children Act 1978;
(iv) Sections 4(1) and 4(2) of the Criminal Law Act 1977 require the consent of the DPP (or in some cases the

---

1   Prosecution of Offences Act 1908, Section 2(3).

2   Report of the Committee on Obscenity and Film Censorship (HMSO 1979) at 171; hereafter cited as *Williams*.

3   See declarations and injunctions as prior restraints in relation to books and magazines, chapter 7.

4   Williams op.cit. at 178–9.

5   See E. Griew *The Criminal Law Act 1977* (London 1978) at 45/4.

Attorney-General) to prosecute for conspiracy (in terms of the Act) to commit summary offences. (Section 4(3), as noted on previous page, applies to such conspiracy charges the consent requirements adhering to the offences themselves.)[1]

In addition,
(i) Proceedings may be instituted only by order of the Commissioners in relation to offences under the Customs Acts;
(ii) Search warrants under the Obscene Publications Acts and the Protection of Children Act may be issued only on application by a constable or by or on behalf of the DPP; a forfeiture order (other than one following a conviction) under the former Acts may be made in relation to a 16mm or wider film only where the application for the warrant was by or on behalf of the DPP.

II) The police

Theoretically every police prosecution is a private one; this is not any longer a realistic representation of police proceedings however.[2] Apart from cases involving the law officers, ultimate responsibility for law enforcement adheres to chief officers of police. Forces generally observe their own internal procedures: with the Metropolitan Police for example, it was usual for search warrants under the 1959 Act to receive the prior approval of a Detective Inspector of the obscene publications squad.[3] The squad generally followed its own rules of thumb in seeking out what might be seen as 'filth for filth's sake'. In 1978 'erections, labial, anal oral, child, animal, and group sexual depictions were the main taboo subjects'.[4] However in any case likely to involve publicity, consultation was to be had at senior level before action was taken; police officers were directed to proceed carefully in such cases.[5] Although procedure and criteria for prosecution varied from force to force, Section 6(2) of the Prosecution of Offenders Regulations 1946

---

1 Griew op.cit. at 45/4.

2 Williams op.cit. at 169.

3 G. Robertson *Obscenity* (London 1979) at 82.

4 Ibid. at 82.

5 Ibid.

required that

> The chief officer of police shall also report, as respects offences alleged to have been committed within his police district, to the Director of Public Prosecutions ...
> (d) cases of obscene or indecent libels, exhibitions or publications, in which it appears to the chief officer of police there is a *prima facie* case for prosecution.

This did not actually require all prosecutions to be stayed pending such report; this was often in fact done for reasons of prudence, the police perhaps fearing the subsequent intervention of the DPP. In the Metropolitan area there was an arrangement that all Section 2 and 3 proceedings under the Obscene Publications Act 1959 would in fact be conducted by the Director under his power (in terms of Regulation 1(c)) of prosecution 'in any case which appears to him to be of importance or difficulty or which for any other reason requires his intervention'. The 1946 Regulations have since been replaced by the Prosecution of Offences Regulations 1978, which came into force in January 1979. Section 6(2) requires the chief officer of police to furnish the Director with information 'as to such other cases as the director ... may from time to time specify ...'.

In December 1978, the Commissioner of Metropolitan Police wrote to the Director adding to the list of such cases 'offences involving obscene exhibitions or publications'. This latter addition was made because of the revocation, before the new regulations entered into force, of regulation 6(1)(g), which contained provisions corresponding to the former 6(2)(d). At the same time new arrangements were agreed between the Director and the Commissioner: as obscenity prosecutions were no longer to be referred as a matter of course to the former, district police officers were now to be required to report to the obscene publications branch on test purchases, before applying for a Section 3(1) warrant. The branch advised them as to whether prosecution or forfeiture proceedings should be brought; this was advice only, and not binding. The original centralisation of prosecutions — in the Metropolitan area at least — under the DPP has thus been changed, although the police still consult the Director, and proceedings may still be brought by him.

Is this system, or the use of discretion in terms of it, open to challenge in the courts? Discretion in this area may be exercised in terms of many criteria, and in relation to several aspects of prosecution: 'Apart from the initial decision whether to prosecute or not, it has to be considered whether one or more offenders should be charged, whether one or more offences should be alleged, and whether summary or indictable trial should be sought. At each stage of the decision there are numerous factors which may be relevant, including the trivial or technical nature of the offence, the obscurity or antiquity of the law, and the current state of public feeling'.[1] Courts may well exercise control over the exercise of this discretion in terms of the sentences they impose, advice they offer as to future prosecutions and their views of the present one.[2] Can the courts interfere in a more direct way? Mr Raymond Blackburn has been active over the last twelve years in attempting no fewer than three times to persuade the courts to reverse policy decisions taken by the Commissioner of Metropolitan Police. In his first application for an order of *mandamus* he sought the revocation of a decision not to prosecute clubs 'for breach of the gaming laws unless there were complaints of cheating or they had become haunts of criminals'.[3] The application would probably, despite the view that standing to make such applications adheres to the Attorney-General,[4] have succeeded; in the event, counsel for the respondent undertook to revoke the policy. The second *Blackburn* case[5] concerned the proper enforcement of the Obscene Publications Act 1959. The Court of Appeal declined to intervene, and indicated that it would do so only in extreme cases.[6] It would in fact be difficult for the courts to intervene in this area, as it would 'be difficult to isolate the point at which prosecution discretion must be exercised: for there is the earlier stage of whether, when and how to investigate or pursue inquiries and the discretion decisions there depend upon an overall appreciation of priorities'.[7] As Lord Justice Roskill remarked in the second *Blackburn* case: 'It is no part of the duty of this court to presume to tell the respondent how to conduct the affairs of the Metropolitan Police, nor how to deploy his all too limited resources at a time of ever-increasing crime, especially crimes of violence in London'.[8]

An allied aspect of the court's attitude in the second *Blackburn* case

---

1   Williams op.cit. at 175; citations omitted.

2   Ibid. at 175–6.

3   *R v Metropolitan Police, ex parte Blackburn* [1968] 2 QB 118 at 134, per Lord Denning MR.

4   S.A. de Smith *Judicial Review of Administrative Action* (4th edn London 1980) at 549.

5   *R v Metropolitan Police Commissioner, ex parte Blackburn (No. 3)* [1973] 1 All ER 324. In fact the second *Blackburn* case occurred in 1968, and involved contempt of court: [1968] 2 QB 150; for present purposes (*No. 3*) will be referred to as the second *Blackburn* case.

6   Ibid. at 331 per Lord Denning MR.

7   Williams op.cit. at 181.

8   [1973] 1 All ER 324 at 338.

was its unwillingness to overturn the police practice of basing prosecutions on the advice of the DPP. The disclaimer procedure operated by the police in relation to forfeiture procedure was however specifically disapproved.[1] Mr Blackburn described both the Prosecution of Offences Regulation requiring reference of cases in this area to the DPP, and the practice of relying on his advice, as 'the incredibly stupid bureaucratic rules which prevent ordinary police officers from doing their duty and involve them in waste of time'.[2] His feelings in this regard were so strong that five years after his first attempt, Mr Blackburn was back in the Court of Appeal arguing the disastrous record of the Metropolitan Police in enforcing the 1959 Act.[3] He would appear this time to have concentrated on the procedures employed; unfortunately for Mr Blackburn the regulations were changed in 1978; before their coming into force, regulation 6(1)(g) requiring reference of such cases to the DPP had, according to police counsel in the case, been dropped because the Director was not able to cope with the amount of seizures. The Court of Appeal felt that not only had little changed since his initial application to them in this regard, but also the change in the regulations could serve only to weaken his case. The arrangements at present in force between the police and Director, together with the role of the obscene publications branch, were within the Commissioner's discretion, and would not be questioned by the court.[4]

Thus although it would appear that an individual has standing in this respect (this issue was left open in the first *Blackburn* case, but was accorded on the basis of Mr Blackburn's having a wife and five children in the second case, and on his status as a ratepayer in the *GLC* case), the courts are most unlikely to second-guess the police, other perhaps than in cases of clearly formulated and controversial policy.

III) Individuals

There clearly adheres to private individuals a right of prosecution; some

---

1   See search and seizure in relation to books and magazines, chapter 7.

2   *R v Metropolitan Police Commissioner, ex parte Blackburn (No. 5), The Times* (Law Report) 30 November 1979; *Blackburn (No. 4)* was a *mandamus* application brought to secure the proper standard by the Greater London Council in the course of film censorship: *R v Greater London Council, ex parte Blackburn* [1976] 1 WLR 550; see film censorship, chapter 7.

3   Ibid.

4   Ibid.

appear to regard this as a fundamental constitutional principle;[1] insofar as it ties in with the constitutional position of the police, it probably is. Despite its possible disfavour with the courts,[2] it was described by the Minister of State at the Home Office during committee proceedings on the Cinematograph and Indecent Displays Bill 1973 as 'a cherished right'.[3] It is worth recalling that in this area, the exercise of such cherished right extends potentially to the following offences:

(i) The Obscene Publications Acts, where the offence does not involve film of 16mm in width or more;
(ii) The Post Office Act 1953;
(iii) The Unsolicited Goods and Services Act 1971, where the prosecution does not concern unsolicited circulars;
(iv) The Indecent Displays (Control) Act 1981;
(v) Any offence at common law.

Private prosecutions in relation to these offences have increased in recent years: a number of examples have already been discussed, such as the Shackleton prosecution of the distributors of *Last Tango in Paris*, the Blackburn prosecution of *More About the Language of Love*, and the latter's attempted prosecution of BBFC officials in relation to the sister film, *The Language of Love*. Beyond limited judicial control in individual cases, such prosecutions are not subject to any restraint, other than the intervention of the DPP or (unusually) the entry of a *nolle prosequi* by the Attorney-General. As has been pointed out, even were the Parliamentary assurances given by the law officers in relation to prosecutions for conspiracy to corrupt public morals to be regarded as carrying any real weight, the right of private prosecution in relation to such conspiracy detracts, to say the least, from any substance they may have.[4]

IV) Practice, policy and censorship

It is quite clear that there are considerable disparities around the country in the enforcement of the Obscene Publications Acts. An obvious reason for this is the uncertainty as to just what is or is not

---

1 Williams op.cit. at 166.

2 See e.g. Lord Justice Edmund Davies in *R v Metropolitan Police Commissioner, ex parte Blackburn* [1968] 2 QB 118 at 149.

3 HC Standing Committee B, 10th sitting, 17 January 1974, col.472; quoted in Williams op.cit. at 166.

4 *Knuller* v *DPP* [1972] 3 WLR 143 at 170 per Lord Diplock; see Williams op.cit. at 177.

obscene. The *Inside Linda Lovelace* case for example, led the Metropolitan Police to express the view to Williams that 'the law was unlikely to be invoked again against the written word'.[1] Although the acquittal there may have been based on the psychotherapeutic defence, since declared inadmissible, there is little doubt that predictions as to the obscenity of material are difficult to make. Prosecutors are often understandably reluctant to embark on obscenity prosecutions. They have an extensive alternative armoury, it might be argued; this is certainly true with respect to the extremely wide common law offences applicable both to obscene publications and indecent displays, and the statutory provision with regard to the latter. Again though, prosecutions may be subject to inhibition: there are, for what they are worth, the law officers' assurances and practice direction in relation to conspiracy; many of the offences concerned are of some antiquity, whilst there seems, perhaps as a result of its breadth and its application in contexts not involving gratuitous offence, to be something less than a consensus in society on just what is indecent.

The result of all this is patchy enforcement: many people in society probably no longer have any real idea of what they or the law comprehend as obscene or indecent. If many of the attractions found in Soho for example, do not constitute indecent exhibitions, it is difficult to imagine what would; much of what is sold in sex shops is obscene at least in the colloquial sense. It may be that society is moving towards, or has reached, a new pluralism in regard to such matters;[2] the law in its present form, aimed at enforcing positive morality, not surprisingly has varied and unpredictable results. This does nothing to improve the public's view of the law, a policy factor of paramount importance in any society; it also places a quite unfair burden on prosecutional authorities, who, whatever they do, attract scorn and ridicule from one or other group or individual concerned with such matters. This odium would often be better directed at those ultimately responsible for policy in this area. This burden was clearly recognised, insofar as the police are concerned, in the second *Blackburn* case.[3] Some of those who have criticised the police in respect of non-prosecution, have themselves had scorn heaped upon them for their attempts to bring private prosecutions in this area.[4] Whatever one may think of their censorious

---

1   *Williams*.

2   See chapter 15.

3   R v *Metropolitan Police Commissioner, ex parte Blackburn (No. 3)* [1973] 2 WLR 43.

4   Robertson op.cit. at 85–7.

aims, such scorn would again seem misdirected: it is the law, and/or the prosecutional system which is at fault. Such individual efforts may in fact have proven valuable: although this was scarcely what he had in view, Sir Cyril Black MP's successful institution of forfeiture proceedings against a London bookseller in 1967 with regard to *Last Exit To Brooklyn* (despite the DPP's having initially declined to prosecute) resulted in not only the subsequent prosecution of Calder and Boyars, but also the amendment — by Section 25 of the 1967 Criminal Law Act — of the provision as to standing in respect of forfeiture proceedings, private applications being abolished. Equally Mr Blackburn's attempted prosecution of BBFC officials in relation to the film *The Language of Love* was instrumental in bringing about the Criminal Law Act 1977 amendment applying the Obscenity Acts to films, thereby probably having the incidental result of reversing Mr Blackburn's earlier success in the *GLC* case as to indecency constituting the proper standard for local authority film censorship.[1]

There would seem little point in dwelling on possible reform of prosecutional discretion in terms of the present system. Even were one to centralise prosecutions in order to achieve more uniform results, the law scarcely permits of the latter. When Calder and Boyars submitted *Last Exit To Brooklyn* to the DPP in 1966 for advice, they received no help whatever, the reply ending thus: 'If you find — as I am afraid you will — that this is a most unhelpful letter, it is not because I wish to be unhelpful but because I get no help from the Acts'.[2] A decade later a new Director was no more helpful, publishers being routinely informed that he could not guide them 'because of the generally recognised uncertainty in the operation of the law in this field'.[3]

What is perhaps more useful is to consider the offences recommended above, and the optimum prosecutional machinery in relation to them.[4] This is not the place to attempt an analysis of the constitutional status of the police or a reform of the prosecutional system in England and Wales: prosecution will be considered only from the narrow angle of the offences involved. As far, in the first place, as private prosecutions are concerned, Williams recommended that neither offence restrictions nor prohibitions on the production of pornography

---

1   *R v GLC, ex parte Blackburn* [1976] 1 WLR 550.

2   *R v Calder and Boyars* [1968] 1 QB 151 at 165.

3   Quoted in A.F. Wilcox *The Decision to Prosecute* (London 1972) at 6; see Robertson op.cit. at 85.

4   Should any general prohibitions be felt justified, this aspect of their enforcement will be considered then: see chapter 15.

accord the right of private prosecution. In regard to the latter, although offence may properly be determined by use of a reasonable person standard, there are those in the community, the committee felt, who are more tender than others; it is not right they should have access to the levers of prosecutional process. Insofar as the latter is concerned, the offence was felt to be too serious, whilst there is the added factor that one is concerned here with a prohibition and not a restriction.[1] An additional factor militating against private prosecution is the desirability of achieving more uniform results. In 1958 the Select Committee on Obscene Publications considered whether to except, in order to provide uniformity of enforcement, obscenity law from the ambit of private prosecution; such exception was not made, the Attorney-General at the time taking the robust view that 'Uniformity in the administration of the law is a matter for the courts themselves and should not, in my view, be achieved by interposing the decisions of the law officers of the executive between them and the law they administer'.[2] Uniformity is a matter for the jury which may be said to operate quasi-legislatively in this area, thus not constituting anything like an infallible barometer of criminality; although someone has to take the decision to prosecute, and although the recommended offences are far more narrowly drawn than present law, there is much to be said for not testing jury fallibility in respect of uniformity by allowing private prosecutions. The latter may thus preferably be excluded in relation to all the offences recommended above in respect of the prevention of offence, the protection of children, the control of the production of pornography, live shows, and cinema licensing offences. As Williams pointed out, individuals can always agitate for prosecution, or, if the latter is entrusted to the police, institute proceedings for judicial review of police action or inaction.[3]

One is left with a choice between a centralised control on prosecutions and leaving them in the hands of the police. There are a number of possible objections to the latter: one is the possibility in this respect of police corruption. This question has been the subject of both police and public concern, and has resulted in a number of prosecutions of officers in recent years, particularly in the Metropolitan Police. Although corruption may extend its tentacles into virtually any aspect of police work, the obscene publications branch is perhaps particularly

---

1   *Williams* para 9.49 and 10.20; recommendations in this respect in relation to restriction and prohibition on live shows, and restriction in relation to films follow these recommendations on a restriction/prohibition distinction basis.

2   Memorandum to Select Committee on Obscene Publications, HC Paper 123—1, at 23—4; quoted in Robertson op.cit. at 86.

3   *Williams* para 9.50.

susceptible: those engaged in vending the material concerned often make enormous profits; bribery is all the more a potential hazard as a result of the limited centralisation of obscenity procedures under the obscene publications branch. In November 1976, March 1977 and June 1977, a number of members of the squad, both senior and junior, were charged with accepting bribes in relation to the purveying of pornography in London's West End.[1] It must be admitted though that considerable efforts have been made to eradicate such corruption within the Metropolitan Force; although Mr Blackburn made allegations to Williams of 'continuing and massive corruption' in the West End of London, he did not bring forward any evidence to substantiate such allegations.[2] One has also the fact that the restrictions and prohibitions in question here are not aimed at the suppression of pornography (other than where minors or the occasioning of actual physical harm is involved in its production); the applicable law, more tightly drawn and narrowly based than is present law in this area, would perhaps be far less likely to give rise to attempts to corrupt the police.

A more substantial point is the desire, with restrictions and prohibitions on speech, for uniformity of enforcement; this brings one to the question of the status and accountability of the police.[3] Although responsibility for prosecution lies today in England and Wales chiefly in the hands of the police, there is no national police force, nor is there a system of public prosecutors as in Scotland. A measure of control is effected over police prosecution policies by the courts and the possibility of judicial review, although this could hardly be claimed to be of the sort likely to encourage prosecutional uniformity. There are possibilities of supervision of police policy as formulated by chief officers, by police authorities, whilst considerable power is in fact exercised by the Home Secretary in relation to such officers.[4] Perhaps the principal influence however was that exercised by the DPP; although chief officers may seek his advice on prosecutions in this area, reference of cases to him is no longer mandatory. This can serve only to weaken the unifying influence he exerted in terms of the administration of the law. Williams recommended that because of the seriousness of the offence, and because it involved a prohibition and not a restriction, controls on the production of pornography and live shows should be left to the DPP. Because offence restrictions are not

---

1   *Williams* para 4.15.

2   Ibid. para 4.16.

3   Ibid. at 184—8.

4   Ibid. at 191—2.

particularly serious, being recommended as triable only by magistrates, and because centralisation raises criticisms of a censorship function by the authority concerned, police prosecution of the latter variety of offence was urged.[1]

Allegations of censorship are probably the chief objection to centralised prosecution being imposed uniformly in relation to recommended offences. The DPP at present operates a grading system in terms of obscene publications for example, Grade 3 being the most extreme, principally imported hard-core pornography. Grade 2 includes many explicit magazines, and Grade 1, naturist magazines and publications of a milder sort.[2] Despite this classification system, and despite having responsibility until recently, at least in the Metropolitan area, for prosecutions in this area, the Director was often apparently not in a position to venture an opinion as to the permissibility of a particular book. In terms of standards of this sort, the censorship criticism carries real weight. If on the other hand, the offences already proposed are sufficiently narrowly drawn to be entrusted, despite censorship misgivings, to the police, there would seem little reason why they should not adhere, in prosecution terms, solely to a nominated law officer. Such centralisation has already taken place with a number of offences in this area, and has been recommended by the Royal Commission on the Press[3] in relation to obscenity, blasphemy, sedition and criminal libel, where action is contemplated against a newspaper. This progression may perhaps profitably be continued in relation to law reform in this area.

---

1   *Williams* paras 9.47 to 9.49.

2   Ibid. para 4.6.

3   Report of the Royal Commission on the Press (HMSO 1977) Cmnd 6810, paras 48 and 50.

9 The constitutional dimension

The constitutional importance of freedom of speech has been briefly rehearsed in discussing prior restraints. A further factor which may be seen to have a similar dimension is privacy. Although there is no formal guarantee in the form of a Bill of Rights in respect of either of these concerns, a case such as *Entinck* v *Carrington*,[1] although concerned with the exercise of arbitrary executive authority, did strongly assert the fundamental importance of the inviolability of property:

> The great end, for which men entered into society, was to secure their property. That right is preserved sacred and incommunicable in all instances, where it has not been taken away or abridged by some public law for the good of the whole. ... If no such excuse can be found or produced, the silence of the books is an authority against the defendant, and the plaintiff must have judgement.

It must be conceded that such property interest was already recognised in the form of the law of trespass; in the absence of this, no right of privacy exists which can be cited as rendering invasions such as telephone tapping unlawful;[2] the court may also have been emphasising the importance of physical property rather than the privacy which may

---

1   (1765) 19 St Tr 1030.

2   *Malone* v *Commissioner of Police for Metropolis (No. 2)* [1979] 2 All ER 620.

325

be enjoyed in relation to it. As an assertion of the fundamental importance of an Englishman's home being his castle, the case is at least oblique authority for the constitutional importance, in a residual sense, of privacy.

The two principal aspects of individual freedom relevant in this area may then, even in the absence of written constitutional guarantees, be argued to have a constitutional significance which can serve only to render them all the weightier when set against one or other policy consideration underlying a censorship restriction. The same may be said of a number of the criticisms raised earlier in relation to offences in this area: the principle of legality, in this context better known as the rule of law, is a fundamental constitutional doctrine; insofar as constitutional theory in this country is still essentially Diceyan, it in fact constitutes, together with the doctrine of Parliamentary sovereignty, one of the two fundamentals of the British Constitution. Strictures against overbreadth are not merely representative of the plaintive desires of libertarian philosophers for a better world. The same can to an extent be said of the question of the legal enforcement of morality: in view of the sovereignty of Parliament, this cannot in any sense be argued to be unconstitutional; misgivings may be aired however in relation to the assertion by the House of Lords in *Shaw* v *DPP*[1] that the courts are *custos morum* of the nation. It must be conceded that this claim was subsequently abandoned in *Knuller* v *DPP*;[2] two of the three offences affirmed in the process however, remain.

The ruling in *Shaw* offers perhaps an interesting comparison with the approach of the American Supreme Court in this area. One's comments here must depend to some extent on what one takes to be judicial restraint: in the American system it might be seen as a constitutional court's interpreting a Bill of Rights restrictively so as to impinge as little as possible on legislative activity. A bill might also be used positively by the court to, in effect, create law. There are numerous examples of the Supreme Court in the United States acting in this capacity; a refusal to engage in such judicial creativity might equally be seen as judicial restraint. The Court has in the obscenity area been remarkably restrained: although it has in effect asserted obscenity as the only permissible standard, and therefore struck down legislation employing other criteria, obscenity regulations have not generally, aside from periodic modification, been subject to the full rigours of First Amendment justification.[3] As far as positive prescription is concerned,

---

1 [1960] AC 220.

2 [1972] 3 WLR 143.

3 See below and chapter 14, in particular.

the Court has been relatively inactive, other than in respect of the elaborate prior restraint prescriptions advanced in recent years.

This contrasts remarkably — in view of the constitutional disparity — with the English situation, and particularly *Shaw*. The English courts have made it plain that under the present dispensation it is no part of their function to question Acts of Parliament;[1] one might have expected that any comparison in terms of judicial law-making would, today, be equally difficult to make; as Sir Robert Megarry VC remarked in *Malone*:

> ... it is no function of the courts to legislate in a new field. The extension of the existing laws and principles is one thing, the creation of an altogether new right is another. At times judges must, and do, legislate; but as Holmes J. once said, they do so only interstitially, and with molecular rather than molar motions: see *Southern Pacific Co. v Jensen* (1917) 244 US 205, 221, in a dissenting judgement. Anything beyond that must be left for legislation. No new right in the law, fully-fledged with all the appropriate safeguards, can spring from the head of a judge deciding a particular case: only Parliament can create such a right ...[2]

Mr Justice Holmes was probably understating the Supreme Court's position; he was certainly very much more cautious than Viscount Simonds in *Shaw*, who asserted a clear law-making authority vesting in the courts as *custos morum*.[3] Although the offence of conspiracy to corrupt public morals might be argued to be based on precedent, it very possibly is an example of just such judicial creativity.

Although there are no assertable constitutional rights, the constitutional dimensions argued above may at least weigh the scales against censorship regulation. They may receive additional weight, or perhaps even, obliquely, the unexpected status of judicial assertability either as a result of a number of international commitments entered into by the United Kingdom in recent years, or as a result of the introduction into this jurisdiction of a Bill of Rights.

---

1   *Pickin v British Railways Board* [1974] AC 765.

2   [1979] 2 All ER 620 at 642–3.

3   [1962] AC 220.

I) Commitments in international law only

(i) *The European Convention on Human Rights*

The Convention for the Protection of Human Rights and Fundamental Freedoms[1] (generally known as the European Convention on Human Rights) came into force in 1953. The convention, although binding in international law on the United Kingdom from this time on, made little impact within the country for two principal reasons: it was not (and is still not)[2] part of the law of the land, and cannot be pleaded in an English court, although it may of course be persuasive authority; the United Kingdom moreover had not accepted the right of individual petition under the Convention. The latter shortcoming was rectified in 1966, with the acceptance on the United Kingdom's part of individual petition (a right which is not available under any other international instrument), as well as the compulsory jurisdiction of the European Court of Human Rights.[3] Article 10 of the convention deals with freedom of expression, providing that:

(1) Everyone has the right to freedom of expression. This right shall include freedom to hold opinions and to receive and impart information and ideas without interference by public authority and regardless of frontiers. This Article shall not prevent States from requiring the licensing of broadcasting, television or cinema enterprises.

(2) The exercise of these freedoms, since it carries with it duties and responsibilities, may be subject to such formalities, conditions, restrictions or penalties as are prescribed by law and are necessary in a democratic society, in the interests of national security, territorial integrity, or public safety, for the prevention of disorder or crime, for the protection of health or morals, for the protection of reputation or rights of others, for preventing the disclosure of information received in confidence, or for maintaining the authority and impartiality of the judiciary.

The first appeal in the obscenity area to the European Court of

---

1 On this see generally J.E.S. Fawcett *The Application of the European Convention on Human Rights* (London 1974); F.G. Jacobs *The European Convention on Human Rights* (London 1975). Also *Williams*, Appendix I, at 185—7.

2 See e.g. *R v Home Secretary, ex parte Bhajan Singh* [1976] 1 QB 198.

3 Cmnd 8969, European Treaty Series No. 5.

Human Rights followed close on the heels of the acceptance in 1966 by the United Kingdom of the right of individual petition. It followed a conviction under Section 11 of the Post Office Act 1953.[1] The application, perhaps not surprisingly, was dismissed: the exception embodied in Article 10(2) in favour of 'health or morals' is so broad as virtually to rule out the Convention as an avenue for the control of local obscenity regulation. Confirmation of this came in 1976 with *The Little Red Schoolbook*[2] case. The application stemmed from the seizure and destruction of a manual giving advice, primarily to schoolchildren, on a number of topics including sex, and the subsequent prosecution and conviction (under the Obscene Publications Acts 1959 and 1964) of its publisher. The application was accepted by the Commission, but was rejected in its principal contentions by the Court. A national government is entitled to take such measures as are necessary to protect public morals; in the Court's view the aim of the legislation was therefore permissible, whilst the measures in question could not be said to be unnecessary; the same reasoning applied to the decisions applying the legislation. In particular, said the Court:

> It is not possible to find in the domestic law of the various Contracting States a uniform European conception of morals. The view taken by their respective laws of the requirements of morals varies from time to time and from place to place, especially in our era which is characterised by a rapid and far-reaching evolution of opinions on the subject. By way of their direct and continuous contact with the vital forces of their countries, State authorities are in principle in a better position on the exact contents of these requirements as well as on the 'necessity' of a restriction or penalty intended to meet them.[3]

A subsequent attempt was made to obtain a favourable ruling from the Court with regard to *The Little Red Schoolbook's* suppression, this time not in terms of freedom to impart information and ideas, but rather in terms of freedom to be in receipt thereof. The application was on this occasion rejected in view of the fact that a revised edition — having had in the process of revision only eighteen lines deleted — of the manual had been available in Britain since the initial prosecution. There do not appear to have been any applications in the obscenity

---

[1] *Straker* v *United Kingdom* application no. 3003/66 D 19269.

[2] *Handyside* v *United Kingdom* application no. 5493/72, *Publications of the European Court of Human Rights* Series A: Judgments and Decisions vol. 24, no. 20.

[3] Ibid.

area since.

(ii)   *International Covenant on Civil and Political Rights*

This was adopted by the United Nations in 1966, and was both ratified by the United Kingdom, and came into force, in 1976. In the field of freedom of expression the rights are very similar to those embodied in the European Convention. An optional protocol permitting individual complaints to the Human Rights Committee established in terms of the covenant has not been ratified by the United Kingdom; complaints against this country may be brought by other state parties accepting a similar obligation. The relevance of this obligation to domestic obscenity law would seem to mirror that of the European Convention.

(iii) *The Universal Declaration of Human Rights*

This was adopted by the United Nations in 1948, and provides by Article 29 for freedom of expression. This is qualified by an exception in favour of 'meeting the just requirements of morality, public order and the general welfare in a democratic society'; the convention is not enforceable.

There are also a number of international commitments entered into by the United Kingdom which tend in the opposite direction; in the direction in other words, of obliging obscenity controls:

(iv)   *The International Agreement for the Suppression of Obscene Publications*

This was signed in 1910 and ratified by the United Kingdom in 1911; it has subsequently become an instrument of the United Nations. It provides basically for the national co-ordination of information relevant to the suppression of trade in obscene materials, and the international sharing of such data. Williams record that the convention is of little practical relevance.[1]

(v)   *The International Convention for the Suppression of the Circulation of and Traffic in Obscene Publications*

The convention was signed in 1923 and ratified in 1925 by Britain; it also has since become an instrument of the United Nations. Under Article 1, contracting parties agree to suppress trade in obscene articles; the Obscene Publications Acts and customs regulations would appear to satisfy this obligation. The convention provides additionally for the international exchange of information, using the authorities

---

1   *Williams* Appendix I, p.187.

specified in the 1910 Agreement. This latter aspect does not appear to have been used in recent years.[1] It is perhaps noteworthy that the United States is not a signatory, whilst Denmark repudiated the treaty in 1968, as did the Federal Republic of Germany in 1975.

(vi) *The Universal Postal Convention*

This was signed in 1974. Article 33 prohibits the use of the letter post for the carriage of obscene or immoral items, or the carriage in international mails of items prohibited in their country of destination. Although the Post Office stressed to Williams the practical difficulties of enforcement, the latter noted that Denmark (for example) had retained a domestic prohibition of the latter sort, despite removing general obscenity controls; law reform was recommended to follow the same course in England and Wales.[2]

II) The Treaty of Rome and the European Community Act 1972

Unlike the European Convention above, the Treaty of Rome has been made a part of English law via the European Communities Act 1972. The defence has recently been advanced at trial and on appeal from conviction under customs regulations, that Article 9 of the Treaty of Rome, which provides for the free movement of goods between member states, accordingly takes precedence over the prohibition under Section 42 of the Customs Consolidation Act 1876 (as enforced by the Customs and Excise Act 1979) against the importation of obscene or indecent material. Because interpretation of the Treaty of Rome was involved, the House of Lords, on hearing argument, referred,[3] *inter alia*, the following questions to the European Court of Justice: besides the provisions of Article 9:

(i) Was a prohibition on pornographic imports equivalent to a quantitative restriction on imports, outlawed in terms of Article 30(2);
(ii) If so, was a prohibition on obscene or indecent imports from another member state permissible in terms of Article 36, despite variations between the laws of constituent parts

---

1 *Williams* Appendix I, p.187.

2 Ibid.; see the Post Office Act 1953, chapter 5.

3 Without giving a reportable judgement to that effect; but see [1979] 2 CMLR 49.

of that state;[1]
(iii) Even if justified on public morality grounds, was the prohibition not a discriminatory restriction on trade; and
(iv) whether in view of Article 234g of the Treaty such prohibitions could be justified on the grounds of obligations under the 1923 Convention on the suppression of trade in obscene articles and the Universal Postal Convention 1974?

The European Court reversed the Court of Appeal on ground (i); such prohibition, although quantitative, was covered by Article 36, and regional variations within the United Kingdom did not affect this. As to the third question, the Court concluded that the internal laws of the United Kingdom in this area

> ... had as their purpose the prohibition, or at least the restraining, of the manufacture and marketing of publications or articles of an indecent or obscene character. In these circumstances it is permissible to conclude, on a comprehensive view, that there is no lawful trade in such goods in the United Kingdom. A prohibition on imports which might in certain respects be more strict than some of the laws applied within the United Kingdom could not therefore be regarded as amounting to a measure designed to give indirect protection to some national product or aimed at creating arbitrary discrimination between goods of that type depending on whether they were produced within the national territory of another member state.[2]

The United Kingdom was therefore not precluded from fulfilling other treaty obligations. The Court in the process rejected two potentially telling arguments by the defendants: the first was that before a restriction can be based on rules of public morality, there must exist clearly defined rules or public policy with regard to the latter. This they contended was something the European Court had required in *Van Duyn v Home Office (No. 2)*[3] in relation to Article 48: although for the activities of an organisation to be considered socially harmful it need not be declared unlawful, some clearly defined policy must have been

---

1 Article 36 provides that the restrictions of Article 30 and other articles 'shall not preclude prohibitions or restrictions on imports ... justified on grounds of public morality, public policy, or public security ... .

2 *R v Henn, R v Derby* [1980] 2 All ER 166 at 193.

3 [1975] 3 All ER 190.

exhibited by the relevant authorities towards the organisation. In view of the repudiation by the last Labour Government of the standard of indecency, together with the appointment of Williams, their claim that no such consistency has been exhibited domestically was probably correct.

A further submission that appears equally apt is that United Kingdom law does not prohibit the manufacture or dissemination as such of indecent articles; with respect, the European Court's view of domestic law in this respect is wrong. The Court presumably wished to avoid the difficulties that a ruling in the affirmative here would have raised. The House of Lords, applying these answers, dismissed the appeal; the customs restriction thus remains intact.[1] Had the answer of the European Court been in the affirmative, this would have meant, by virtue of implied repeal effected by Section 2(4) of the European Communities Act 1972, that the customs provisions would necessarily have given way to European law; allowing the former supposition, had the case arisen in terms of the 1979 Customs and Excise Management Act, a nice question of statutory interpretation and constitutional law would have arisen. The prohibition would presumably be seen as being imposed by the 1979 Act; allowing this though, national courts would have been faced with a conflict between the Treaty of Rome and a post-1972 statute: the outcome would be a little difficult to predict.

III) A Bill of Rights

Aside from considerations of international obligations in terms of the European Convention on Human Rights and Fundamental Freedoms, and the situation in Northern Ireland, perhaps the principal concern evidenced in the growing volume of literature[2] on the question of a Bill for this country is whether the present constitutional dispensation is still adequate today. It may be that the legislation-based growth of government has been and will be such that many fundamental freedoms cannot be entrusted, even if one takes the view that Parliament will be peopled by those committed to a relatively benign democracy, to the reality of residual liberties. Disquiet over the adequacy of constitutional provision in this regard is hardly to be assuaged by reference to the Rule of Law, which, besides being toothless with respect to judicial utilisation in relation to legislation, very probably does not lend itself

---

1 See customs regulation, chapters 5 and 7.

2 See e.g. M. Zander *A Bill of Rights?* (Chichester 1975); P. Wallington and J. McBride *Civil Liberties and a Bill of Rights* (Belfast 1976); F.A. Mann 'Britain's Bill of Rights' 96 (1978) *LQR* 512; J. Jaconelli *Enacting a Bill of Rights* (Oxford 1980).

to the guarantee of specific liberties; although the link is not generally spelt out, such disquiet may well be echoed in proposed jurisprudential formulations in terms of fundamental rights, rather than utilitarian maximisation of the majority good.

The introduction of a Bill of Rights into the law of this country would raise all manner of problems:[1] does one wish the judiciary to wield the power such a Bill might vest in them? This in turn depends on the type of Bill one favours: a substantive Bill as in the United States would probably vest real power in the constitutional court; a procedural Bill, as one has in Canada at present, would probably require only that the legislature concentrate its mind on the implications, in Bill of Rights terms, of contemplated legislation, and provide procedurally for the Bill to be overridden. Again, does one wish to provide a form of higher law, or does one wish merely to employ for such a Bill the usual legislative form; allied to this is the question of entrenchment in the sense not of putting the Bill into writing, but rather in the sense of the procedural requirements for its repeal. One cannot here embark on such discussion; equally, one is comparing censorship provisions in terms of public sexual morality in a substantive Bill of Rights jurisdiction, with the same question within a residual liberties constitutional framework. An obvious question is what difference has the Bill of Rights made to regulation in the United States, as opposed to regulation in Britain, and more specifically England and Wales? The answer may not necessarily take the Bill of Rights debate very much further, as one is talking here only of one area of law; it is at least illustrative of what a court may do with a Bill of Rights provision such as the First Amendment. What has become clear in preceding chapters, and what will emerge in those to follow, is the need, in both jurisdictions, despite the constitutional disparity, for law reform in this area; whether this reform is best pursued, and/or effected through a constitutional court or a legislature is a question which must itself be pursued elsewhere.

The differences that the First Amendment as interpreted by the Supreme Court has effected in this area of law in the United States, as compared to the situation in England and Wales,[2] may perhaps be seen on two levels. The first of these is the question of the legal definition of obscenity: in terms of this, the sharp end of the law, is obscenity law more lenient or more restrictive in one jurisdiction than the other? The second is the effect of the First Amendment on, and its accommodation of, the basic policy issues raised earlier in relation to obscenity regulation.

---

1   See especially Jaconelli op.cit.

2   See R.D. Davidow and M. O'Boyle 'Obscenity Laws in England and the United States: A Comparative Analysis' 56 (1977) *Neb L Rev* 249.

As a result of the basic exception approach to the First Amendment, the definition of obscenity is of direct constitutional concern in the United States. Aside from such definition and its status, two singular distinctions have emerged between the two jurisdictions in terms of this exception approach. The first is the elimination of all standards other than obscenity. The Court has not specifically ruled that obscenity is the only constitutionally permissible standard;[1] on the other hand it would seem that this is in practice the case. By contrast, English law has allowed a proliferation of standards, principally obscenity, indecency, and obscenity where used in a context other than the Obscene Publications Acts. As far as standards other than obscenity are concerned, the only variety clearly constitutionally permissible is that of 'adult', used in relation to zoning requirements. Such constitutionality was only arrived at by the Court's regarding such restrictions as being aimed at town planning and not censorship, thus not constituting a prior restraint in First Amendment terms at all.[2] The second major distinction is in respect of prior restraint. Administrative regulation of obscenity is itself, in terms of constitutional strictures on prior restraint, closely regulated, and may only operate under the most stringent procedural safeguards for speech and its propagators. Administrative restraints under the Obscene Publications Acts provide a dismal comparison: there are no external (to the statutes) procedural limitations at all, whilst the statutorily provided safeguards are extremely limited.

We turn now to a more specific comparison of the obscenity definition; this may seem a little premature, as American law has not been considered in detail; reference may be had to succeeding chapters in this regard, as this does seem an apt point at which to conclude just which of the two tests is the more stringent.

(i) *Applicability*

(a) Intention requirements as far as the publisher is concerned are almost exactly parallel: intention as to literal publication is presumed, as is knowledge of the legal test for obscenity. Two areas of common uncertainty had existed in relation to whether or not *mens rea* was required as to material's obscenity, or as to the nature or content of the material. It is now clear that neither jurisdiction require the former; in regard to the latter English law has adopted a negligence (rather than strict liability as such) standard. American jurisprudence is somewhat less strict, requiring *mens rea* (or *scienter*) in the normal way in this respect. The major difference in this regard is that the

---

[1] See *Interstate Circuit, Inc* v *Dallas* 390 US 676 (1968).

[2] See chapter 14.

American test allows the publisher's intention to be taken into account in assessing the obscenity of the material in question. This goes beyond the question merely of a commercial motive: if the publisher markets the material in such a way as solely to emphasise its erotic appeal, he may be said to be pandering. Although commercial exploitation is a factor which may be taken into account in assessing the viability of an obscenity prohibition, such relevance assumes *a priori* that some harm is involved in the publication of pornography.[1] The Court has carefully, via the exception approach, avoided discussion of such issues; as a result, the rationales of the relevance of pandering are somewhat contrived: commercial exploitation is argued to promote the prurient interest; or, more convincingly, it has been ruled to be relevant in terms of estoppel — once a publisher has proclaimed prurient appeal, he is estopped from later denying its existence. Pandering is however only relevant in 'close' cases, and with the cutting-edge of the First Amendment set in terms of patent offensiveness, it is difficult to conceive of a close case in which the question of prurient appeal is decisive. In reality the Court has allowed the jury some room for variability in obscenity assessments in terms of their dis/approval of the marketing methods employed in relation to the material in question.

(b) Possession in the home is not covered in terms of the American test; the English statutes are slightly narrower, excluding possession *per se*, unless there is possession with a view to publication for gain.

(ii)   *The standard applied*

(A) *Effect*. (a) The effect in question in English law falls into two parts: the immediate effect on the audience involved, and second, that effect's im/morality. The emphasis in the law, with the aversion defence and the strictures on recorruption, is on thought arousal as being sufficient in these terms; this makes the jury's task difficult in the sense of moving with more liberal community standards: consequential action is not required, and should they feel that thought arousal is not corrupting, the only apparent alternative, other than a finding of non-obscenity, is to decide in terms of offensiveness. The latter is however more concerned with affront to community standards than effect on a particular audience, and should not strictly form the basis of an obscenity decision. An American jury is concerned only with prurient appeal in the effect sense; patent offensiveness is something which stems from material's incompatibility with positive morality, and is not judged in terms of effect on an audience.

(b) As attention has concentrated on pornography, and with the

---

1   See chapter 15.

emphasis on thought arousal in English law, distribution has become increasingly irrelevant. The aversion defence emphasises the need for thought arousal, and clearly excludes any decision entirely in terms of offensiveness. The defence employs an average person standard, and, as was argued earlier,[1] were this — with exceptions for deviants and minors — to be extended to Section 2 enquiries as a whole, the difference occasioned would probably in practice be only marginal. Such average person standard is undefined. With pornography, which cannot boast literary or artistic merit, effect, and therefore obscenity, is thus very close to a constant. Even where the test purports to rest on effect then, one's inquiry is rather more akin to one in terms of the nature of the work — is the material pornographic or not?

The American test prescribes virtual constancy for effect: not only is the effect a predetermined one, thus making questions of recorruption irrelevant, but assessment is in terms of the average person. The only avenues for variability here are the exceptions to the average person standard conceded by the Court in relation to deviants and minors; the *Miller* hard-core pornography ruling has cast some doubt over the viability of the latter. Another avenue of variability for effect — in theory at any rate — is the presence of pandering; this scarcely has any bearing on effect in practice however. The Court has attempted to break free to some extent from this constant effect test by prescribing a fairly wide definition of the average person, and stipulating that the average person is to be assessed in terms of local and not national standards. In regard to the breadth of the standard, it is to comprise a composite of the community, but is to exclude minors; 'local' has not been defined, and may in fact be state-wide. In terms of prurient effect, the latter change is unlikely to make very much difference to constancy. Thus in American law also, the effect inquiry is akin to one as to the nature of the material: is it pornographic or not?

(c) With English law a mere tendency to the effect in question is sufficient: this phrase has not appeared in American tests since *Roth*. It may be tautologous, but could well be argued to couch the effect requirement in a form more easily satisfied.

(B) *The nature of the work.* (a) Early law had generally in both America and England been based solely on an assessment of effect. Such assessment could be and often was, based on isolated excerpts from the material in question. Changes in society's 'critical point of compromise' forced both systems at roughly the same stage, the 1930s to 1950s, to narrow the test by considering material as a whole, a change which in turn made some consideration of literary or other

---

[1] Chapter 2.

merit virtually inevitable. Under most pre-*Roth* American tests, consideration of the work as a whole went hand-in-hand with a relevance for the work's merit, and this is the essence of the change introduced into English law by the Obscene Publications Act 1959: although a work is hereby considered as a whole specifically in relation to its obscenity, literary or other merit then being weighed against this, the result is very similar. With the *Roth* test, prurient appeal is to be assessed in terms of the work as a whole, whilst a work's merit, although only implicitly recognised, has since acquired clear status via the First Amendment value factor. The additional requirement that a work's dominant theme only is to be relevant, thereby giving the assessment of material as a whole a slightly more generous slant, has never been part of English law, and is now, since *Miller*, no longer part of the Supreme Court's formulation.

(b) Literary or other merit, in its initial canvass in English law — in the *Secker* case — was apparently a factor to be weighed up by the jury in assessing obscenity; this was the approach that had already been adopted in several American jurisdictions in this regard. Under the Obscene Publications Act this balancing continued, literary or other merit now being balanced against obscenity, rather than in assessment of it. *Roth* (as subsequently interpreted) introduced changes as to the American formulations however: in terms of the basic First Amendment 'exception' approach, social value became an absolute factor: any social value at all precluded proscription, whilst balancing in terms of this First Amendment value factor was clearly impermissible. Aside from the question of balancing such values, the public good defence under the 1959 Act is in contrast limited *sui generis* to literary, artistic, scientific or educational value, and does not therefore encompass the psychotherapeutic value of the material. The American approach was substantially altered in *Miller* however: those values relevant in this context would appear to have been limited — as with the English Section 4 defence — to literary, artistic, scientific or political merit; such merit has to be serious. Thus although the First Amendment value factor apparently remains an absolute, balancing is to some extent permitted.

(c) The author's intention in writing the material is relevant in both jurisdictions in terms of assessing literary or other merit. It may also be of relevance in a determination of just what, in an assessment of material as a whole, should be regarded as the whole in question.

(d) The American test has taken its emphasis on the nature of the material even further than the near-absolute determinative nature of the value factor: there is an additional requirement of patent offensiveness — or the stricture that only hard-core pornography is to be proscribed. This, plus the value factor, places the emphasis of the test unmistakably on the nature of the material rather than its effect.

Although both systems have shifted emphasis from effect to the nature of the material, this shift has been less marked with the English test: effect is not as close to a constant, with marginally greater relevance for distribution. There is no patent offensiveness requirement, and assessment in terms of offensiveness is probably not strictly permissible. Not only this, but there is greater scope for the effect factor in the sense that the jury has far greater discretion in terms of balancing effect against value. Even with the American test though, effect is far from irrelevant: although an inquiry in terms of constant effect is virtually one in terms of the nature of the material, prurient appeal must be present; the test does not operate solely in terms of patent offensiveness, and something akin to the English aversion defence applies, in the sense that should the patently offensive nature of material be such as to obviate the possibility of any prurient appeal, such material cannot be found obscene. Effect then determines at least the outside perimeters of the law's permissible area of application. The role of effect in defining such perimeters is quite clear in American law in that the law encompasses only sexual impurity; in terms of prurient appeal, extension to anything beyond would seem unlikely. In English law this emphasis is not as specific as a requirement of a prurient appeal; the English test has thus proven sufficiently malleable to extend to drug-taking and violence for example.

(iii) *Jury decision*

(a) Although expert evidence is admissible in both systems, there are considerable variations in the scope of such admissibility. The English courts have accepted admissibility only in relation to the defence of public good; such evidence has been rigorously excluded on the question of obscenity, other than in one isolated instance involving the effect of material on children. The American courts have been a good deal more permissive, in that evidence has been allowed not only as to the value factor, but also on the questions of prurient appeal and patent offensiveness. The broadened use of expert testimony, a factor militating towards constant obscenity, was supposedly based on the employment of a national community standard, something clearly beyond the experience of the average juror. With the introduction of local standards, the Court has predictably taken the view that the use of such testimony should be limited, in that such standards are within the knowledge of jurors; such limitation however must depend in each instance on what is meant by 'local': if this is taken as state-wide, standards may well still be beyond the average juror's experience.

(b) In terms of its constituting a finding of fact, a jury determination is not in English law generally subject to appellate review.[1] As a result of the constitutional status of the definition of obscenity in American law, determinations of obscenity are reviewable by the Supreme Court. Jury discretion in the United States is further limited in that the First Amendment value factor is close to being an absolute, whilst it is not open to a jury to find obscene (other, perhaps, than in terms of pandering) material which appeals to the prurient interest, but is not patently offensive. Discretion is fairly broad in the other direction however, as the phrases 'patently offensive' — particularly in view of the fact that one is talking not of a restriction on public display, but a general prohibition — and 'hard-core pornography' cannot be described as tightly drawn. The Court, conscious of this, attempted to limit the overbreadth of patent offensiveness by requiring that obscenity statutes list the sexual conduct in question. The *Miller* list merely gives examples, it has been held subsequently, and patent offensiveness in the sense of affront to community standards remains itself a broad standard.

The jury retains far greater discretion with the English test in relation to material with some merit: the public good defence is in no way an absolute. With material without merit, there is no requirement of patent offensiveness. With the effect requirement a virtual constant in relation to much so-called soft-core pornography, the ambit of proscription is very wide. Although the commercial motives of the publisher, which can provide an additional basis for variability in American law, are irrelevant, expert evidence, which undoubtedly tends towards a constant result, and in practice towards a reduction in unfettered jury discretion, is probably more tightly controlled in English law. Standards in English law are judged locally, a term which in the United States may imply for example, state-wide standards, again a factor tending towards constancy. Juries thus have considerable discretion should they wish to proscribe. The test has however, with its emphasis on thought arousal, become to an extent identified with a particular variety or level of positive morality; although a jury retains discretion in terms of a finding of im/morality, action is not necessary, whilst offensiveness is strictly speaking not relevant. In a period of changing and diversifying positive morality, the law has become to an extent ossified, making the jury's task a very difficult one, and results unpredictable.

The English obscenity test is clearly then the more potentially

---

1   Unless (in the case of the Court of Appeal) the court thinks 'that the verdict of the jury should be set aside on the ground that under all the circumstances of the case it is unsafe or unsatisfactory': Section 2(1)(a) of the Criminal Appeal Act 1968. See *R v Cooper* [1969] 1 QB 267. In civil cases, it would appear that the appeal court must be convinced that the decision by the lower court is 'wrong'. See *SS Houtestroom (Owners) v SS Sagaporack (Owners)* [1929] AC 37. See also, for example, Parker C.J. in *Burke v Copper* [1962] 2 All ER 14 at 18.

censorious. The American test on the other hand clearly allows a jury more accurately to reflect contemporary community standards, in the sense that decision is in terms primarily of the only other apparent — besides action or thought arousal — basis therefore in this area: offensiveness.

One may look at the question of what difference a Bill of Rights has effected in this area in the United States as opposed to England and Wales, on quite a different level: rather than comparing the tests in a practical sense, one may compare them in policy terms. To what extent have the major questions of policy raised earlier in relation to English obscenity law, been relevant to the American formulations, and to what extent has the law accommodated such relevance? Let us begin here with the basic policy question of whether the law should enforce positive morality, and if not, whether any other rationale can be found for obscenity prohibitions. Both obscenity and conspiracy to corrupt public morals are clearly concerned with the enforcement of such morality; can the same be said of the *Roth* test? Both appeal to the prurient interest and patent offensiveness, when assessed in terms of a general prohibition, can hardly be seen as concerned with anything other than positive morality. Not only does the law enforce positive morality, but the jury reaches a decision in terms of positive morality. This approach was initially abandoned with the *Roth* test; it was felt necessary to add the requirement of patent offensiveness however, a requirement that is assessed not in terms of a rationally assessable harm caused by the offensiveness of displays or material thrust upon an unwilling audience, but rather in terms at best of affront to positive morality, and at worst, mere taste.

The Supreme Court has however carefully managed to avoid the policy question implicit in this: by means of the exception approach it has contrived to regard obscenity as something outside First Amendment protection. The question of justifying restriction in terms of rationally assessable harms or positive morality has been carefully avoided. The former would require not only a rationally assessable harm, but a rational connection between the restriction and the harm or governmental objective in question. Even if one skirts the First Amendment in this way, a rational connection in the latter sense is required in terms of Fourteenth Amendment due process. Yet the Court has largely avoided discussion even of this requirement. The introduction of patent offensiveness has however threatened this entire structure: if material which has no merit, but is not patently offensive, is within First Amendment protection where does this leave the exception approach? One has also the question of the protection of children for example: the Court in admitting this exception, excluded from First Amendment protection material normally covered; the only logical answer is that the Court was here balancing harm to minors against the latter's First Amendment rights. The obscenity definition itself moreover, as interpreted in *Miller*, allows balancing in the sense that the First Amendment value factor is no longer an absolute. Nor is the First Amendment the only constitutional provision relevant here: privacy is clearly relevant, not only in terms of the home, but of one's mail, and possessions in customs; it may also be a factor which can be weighed against obscenity prohibition in general in the sense of the latter's interference with personal development. The Supreme Court has not managed to avoid the privacy issue altogether, but has, without convincing rationale, excluded its relevance to customs controls for example. The same may be said of pandering — the rationale in terms of prurient interest is unconvincing: it may be that commercial exploitation is a factor legitimately to be taken into account in relation to regulation in this area; this cannot convincingly be done, unless the entire question of the enforcement of morality and the rationale of obscenity prohibition is entered into in terms of due process, the First Amendment, and privacy.

Decision in terms of morality raises the question of overbreadth. The Court has been particularly sensitive to this issue, ruling out standards other than obscenity. Additionally the Court attempted with the *Roth* test as initially formulated to exclude decision in terms of morality altogether, by defining the effect in question — the arousal of prurient interest. Although this was modified by the introduction of the requirement of patent offensiveness, the Court attempted to ensure something close to constant obscenity: expert evidence was admitted, an average person standard was applied, and that in relation to national, and not local standards. The value factor also, in terms of the exception logic, could be only an absolute, whilst commercial motives in marketing were irrelevant. By the 1970s constant obscenity, perhaps determined in terms of the more influential, sophisticated, and probably liberal parts of the country, was tending towards minimal obscenity. Hence the emphasis by the Burger Court on local standards, the reaffirmation of pandering, and the tightening-up on the admissibility of expert evidence. All of which led to sensitivity in terms of possible overbreadth; hence the rather ineffectual attempt in *Miller* to limit patent offensiveness in terms of listing the sexual conduct the depiction of which is to be proscribed. The final policy question raised earlier in relation to English law was that of strict liability: the position in American law mirrors (virtually) the English position, whilst once again the policy issues remain unsifted.

One has then not only, in view of respective development taking place thousands of miles apart and in two different legal jurisdictions, a perhaps surprising — despite a common historical background in this area — congruence in terms of the practical application of the law, but also of the basic policy questions involved, and the extent to which these have been explored and discussed. One quite obvious difference though, stemming simply from there being a Bill of Rights of the substantive sort in the United States, is that issues such as freedom of speech and privacy are not only constitutionally guaranteed, but may be asserted by the constitutional court; in this country such questions are essentially for the legislature. Not only this, but the policy issues involved may be seen in English law as criminal law concerns, as constitutional questions, or as jurisprudential problems; administrative law is not to be forgotten in terms of prior restraints and their administration in particular. In the United States the basic freedoms concerned, together with the policy questions just raised, may all be seen in terms of constitutional law. In other words, if the exception approach to obscenity is to be abandoned, some other First Amendment rationale, probably involving questions of justification, must needs be found if the offences are to remain. The question of overbreadth may equally be seen as a question either of due process, or impingement on First Amendment guarantees, whilst prior restraints are governed specifically by First Amendment based requirements. In the following chapters we will be concerned with constitutional law, and particularly the First Amendment: within this framework, an attempt will be made to trace the actual definition of obscenity, which with the exception approach, has assumed First Amendment status, as well as to follow through those central policy questions discussed above. Before embarking directly on the constitutional setting of obscenity law in the United States, it must be remembered that no Supreme Court ruling was given in this area until *Roth* in 1957. It is necessary therefore to trace very briefly the preliminary background development in both state and federal courts, and to ask to what extent, despite the absence of a clear ruling on the constitutional position, the courts considered, discussed, or accommodated basic problems of policy in this area.

10 State and federal obscenity controls

I   State controls

Most of the American colonies had prior to the War of Independence legislated against certain forms of expression: of the fourteen states that ratified the Constitution in 1792, thirteen had, for example, statutorily provided for the prosecution of libel, blasphemy and profanity. The New England colonies in particular exhibited something of a preoccupation with the preservation of Puritan orthodoxy in matters of religious observance and sexual morality.[1] In the latter regard, Massachusetts was to pre-empt developments in English law: in 1712 a statute was enacted making it criminal to publish 'any filthy, obscene or profane song, pamphlet, libel, or mock sermon in imitation or mimicking religious service'.[2] Massachusetts formed a model in this respect for the statutory enactments of a number of other colonies.[3]

Applicable also at this stage (although it is by no means certain to what extent there was actually reception into the colonies or states as they later became) was English statute and common law, where not

---

1   See in this regard e.g. Joseph H. Smith and Thomas G. Barnes *The English Legal System: Carryover to the Colonies* (1975).

2   Acts and Laws of the Province of Massachusetts Bay cCV Sect 8 (1792); Prov St 1711–12 C6 Sect 12, 1 Prov Laws 682.

3   See e.g. Smith and Barnes op.cit.

clearly excluded by differences in surroundings and circumstances.[1] It was in fact under the English common law as received into Pennsylvania that the first recorded obscenity prosecution in America took place: in 1815 in Philadelphia a group of businessmen who exhibited a painting 'representing a man in an obscene, impudent and indecent posture with a woman' were convicted on the authority of *R v Curl*[2] of publishing an obscene libel.[3] It must be remembered, however, that under the Constitution of the United States as interpreted by the Supreme Court[4] no misdeed is punishable by the federal courts on the basis that it is recognised as a common law crime; any reception of the common law was to take place only through statutory re-enactment. Many of the states came to apply the same rule;[5] certain states continued to allow punishment under the common law even without statutory mention, but today the difference is slight, as by the end of the nineteenth century most common law offences were included in the statutes of the several states.[6] The prosecution in *Sharpless* was almost certainly under the common law only because the relevant statute did not cover paintings.[7] The first state obscenity law, proscribing the publication of 'lewd or obscene' material, was in fact enacted in Vermont in 1821;[8] in Massachusetts, an unofficial organisation, The New England Watch and Ward Society, kept a constant lookout for possible threats to the community's welfare. Although one cannot push the generalisation too far, prior to the Civil War the New England preoccupation with the enforcement of orthodox sexual morality does however not seem to have spread widely to other states or areas of the

---

1   See Rollins and Perkins *Criminal Law* (3rd edn) at 23.

2   (1727) 2 Strange 788.

3   *Commonwealth v Sharpless* 2 S and R 91 (Pa Sup Ct 1815).

4   *US v Hudson and Goodwin* 7 Cranch 32 (1812); upheld (without argument) in *US v Coolidge* 1 Wheat 415 (1816).

5   See e.g. *Mitchell v State* 42 Ohio St 383 (1884); *State v Campbell* 217 Iowa 848 (1934).

6   Rollins and Perkins op.cit. at 25.

7   The same can be said of the second reported obscenity conviction in the United States, *Commonwealth v Holmes* 17 Mass 336 (1821), on this occasion in Massachusetts in 1821, for the sale of a book that was to become the 'prima ballerina of obscenity law': John Cleland's *Memoirs of a Woman of Pleasure*, perhaps best known as 'Fanny Hill' (the edition in this case contained illustrations as well as text). This was the last recorded obscenity prosecution under the common law in the United States.

8   Laws of Vermont, 1824, C XXXII, No. 1 Sect 23.

country.[1] Certainly the main impetus for the enactment of obscenity regulations, and/or their enforcement, appears to have arisen after the war: the number of prosecutions before the Civil War appears relatively limited.[2]

The Civil War was to prove a turning point, the tide thereafter running strongly in favour of state regulation to preserve orthodox sexual morality, the breaching of which was often seen as a threat to the established order, both religious and political: 'The financial scandals, the vulgar and lax social behaviour, and the flagrant immorality of the years immediately after the war led to a powerful reaction. "The voice of the reformer was heard in the land. The stage was set for a stern and rigorous revival of the spirit of the Puritan forefathers".'[3] The Massachusetts Watch and Ward Society could thus begin to court powerful allies elsewhere in the United States.[4] Of these, perhaps the best known was Anthony Comstock, 'Roundsman of the Lord',[5] who during the course of his forty-year campaign to purify American literature under the banner 'MORALS, Not Art or Literature',[6] succeeded in having destroyed 'something over fifty tons of vile books; 28,425 pounds of stereotype plates for printing such books; 3,984,063 obscene pictures; 16,900 negatives for printing such pictures'.[7] The year 1873 was particularly successful for Comstock: he founded the New York Society for the Suppression of Vice, and also, after a long campaign, succeeded in pushing through Congress the first piece of federal obscenity regulation, the so-called Comstock Act.[8] The Act, declaring certain books and other matter non-mailable, was finally urged through a busy Congress on the final day of session, after a campaign in which opponents were tarred with the brush of lechery and held up as

---

1 See however e.g. *People* v *Gerardin* 1 Mich 90 (1848); *Bell* v *State* 31 Tenn 42 (1851). For other examples see F. Schauer *The Law of Obscenity* (1975) p.11.

2 See *Paris Adult Theater I* v *Slaton* 413 US 49 (1973) at 104, per Brennan, J.

3 William B. Lockhart and Robert C. McClure 'Literature, The Law of Obscenity, and the Constitution' 38 (1954) *Minnesota L Rev* 295 at 325; quoting Heywood-Broun and Margaret Leech *Anthony Comstock: Roundsman of the Lord* at 76 (1927).

4 On the growth of the vice society movement in the United States generally, see P.S. Boyer *Purity in Print, the Vice Society Movement and Book Censorship in America* (New York 1968).

5 Broun and Leech op.cit.

6 Ibid.

7 Charles G. Trumbull *Anthony Comstock, Fighter* (1913) at 239; Comstock personally approved this biography. Quoted in Leo M. Alpert 'Judicial Censorship of Obscene Literature' 52 (1938) *Harv L Rev* 40 at 57.

8 Rev St Sect 3893 (1873).

abetting the defilement of American youth and womanhood. On the day of the Act's passage, its author made a diary entry: 'Oh how can I express the joy of my soul or speak the mercy of God'.[1] The Act is significant for state regulation of obscenity in that its definitive terminology (obscene, lewd, lascivious and indecent)[2] formed the basis or the model for a number of subsequent state enactments; Comstock succeeded for example in pushing through the New York state legislature a similarly comprehensive measure.[3]

The approach of the New York courts[4] to the interpretation of this statute, and indeed the approach adopted on the whole by other state[5] and federal courts[6] when faced with similar statutory language, was to take all the words describing what is proscribed as synonymous, and as meaning collectively 'obscene' or 'tending to obscenity'. The need for judicial embellishment was clear: the New York courts within three years of the passage of the obscenity statute introduced into New York common law[7] the *Hicklin* test in defining the word 'obscene'.[8] This was the test's first appearance in American state jurisprudence, and its second in American obscenity regulation as a whole.[9] This definition was never to establish an undisputed ascendancy in New York however: a further test was enunciated: 'Whether the matter tends to excite lustful and lecherous desires'. The confusion was compounded in *People* v *Seltzer*,[10] a case involving a copy of *Cassanova's Homecoming*: the court here not only compromised in asserting the applicability of both the *Hicklin* and lustful desires tests, but added a third to their number:

---

1 Quoted in Charles Rembar *The End of Obscenity* (1969) at 31.

2 By a later amendment the word 'filthy' was added to these four.

3 New York Penal Law Sect 1141 subsect 1 (1884).

4 For example, in *People* v *Muller* 96 NY 408, 48 Am Rep 635 (1884); *People* v *Eastman* 188 NY 478, 81 NE 459; *People* v *Seltzer* 122 Misc 329, 203 NYS 809 (1924).

5 For example, *Commonwealth* v *Herald Publishing Co.* 108 SW 892 (Kentucky); *Anderson* v *Hattiesburg* 94 S163 (Missouri); *Wood* v *State ex rel Boykin* 45 Ga App 783, 165 SE 908 at 911 (Georgia).

6 For example, *US* v *Bennett* 24 Fed Cas 1093 No. 14, 571 (SDNY 1879).

7 The term common law is still applicable in United States jurisprudence in this area, and covers principally the body of the law handed down by the courts in the course of statutory interpretation.

8 In *People* v *Muller* 96 NY 408, 48 Am Rep 635 (1884).

9 The first was in 1879 in *US* v *Bennett* 24 Fed Cas 1093, No. 14, 571 (SDNY 1879).

10 122 Misc 329, 203 NYS 809 (1924).

'To summarise the general, though not exclusive rules as aids to interpretation: the penal provision prohibits the publication of lewd, lascivious, salacious, or obscene writings, the tendency of which is to excite lustful and lecherous desires; likewise it prohibits the publication of those writings whose tendency is to deprave and corrupt minds open to immoral influences and who might come into contact with it. It is also offensive to the section if the matters charged as obscene are so filthy and disgusting as to be revolting to those who may have occasion to read them'.[1] A fourth possibility was later added: was the effect of the material to tend to lower the standards of youth as to sexual relations?[2] Although confused, the position in New York was representative of the condition of most state jurisdictions at this time;[3] of the multiplicity of definitions in use, that perhaps most common was the lustful and lecherous desires test;[4] this failed also to gain anything like general acceptance. Many of the tests were in fact cited individually, as alternatives, or even in hybrid form. Despite the apparent disparities, one finds that certain of the fundamentals of the *Hicklin* test were followed in most jurisdictions, even though on the face of it they may have been applying quite another test:

(1) All the tests in use had in common the fact that they were basically attempts to define what effect material should have on its readers (or viewers) in order that it might be defined as obscene. The effect necessary apparently varied from state to state and from test to test. As a result, with rare exceptions,[5] it was early on established by state courts that vulgar or coarse language was not enough to constitute obscenity;[6]

---

1   203 NYS 809 (1924) at 814.

2   *People* v *Wendling* 258 NY 451, 180 NE 169 (1932).

3   See e.g. *State* v *Pfenninger* 76 Mo App 373 (1883); *Commonwealth* v *Landis* 8 Phila 453 (1870).

4   Cf. e.g. *State* v *Pfenninger* 76 Mo App 373 (1883): *State* v *MacSales Co* Mo App 263, SE 2d 860 (1954): *People* v *Eastman* 188 NY 478, 81 NE 459 (1907): *People* v *Brainard* 192 App Div 816 183 NYS 452 (1920).

5   For example, *People* v *Seltzer* 122 Misc 329, 203 NYS 809 (1924); Courts on occasion held that the words filthy, indecent or disgusting (usually taken as being synonymous with 'obscene') included vulgar and offensive language: e.g. *Commonwealth* v *Donaducy* 33 Erie 330 (Pa 1949).

6   See e.g. *People* v *Muller* 96 NY 408, 48 Am Rep 635 (1884); *People* v *Eastman* 188 NY 478, 81 NE 459 (1902); *People* v *Wendling* 258 NY 451, 180 NE 169 (1932); *Commonwealth* v *Dowling* 14 Pa CC 607 (1894); *Commonwealth* v *Gordon* 66 Pa D + C 101 (1949) Affd *sub nom Commonwealth* v *Feigenbaum* 166 Pa Super 120, 70 A 2d 389 (1950); *Bantam Books* v *Melko* 25 NJ Super 292, 96 A 2d 47 (1953); *Adams Theatre Co* v *Keenan* 12 NJ Super 267, 96 A 2d 519 (1953); *Commonwealth* v *Isenstadt* 318 Mass 543, 63 NE 2d 840 (1945): *Attorney-General* v *Book Named 'Forever Amber'* 323 Mass 302, 81 NE 2d 663 (1948).

obscenity was in fact concerned with sexual impurity only: consideration of violence or drug-taking for example was thus effectively precluded. Sexual impurity, as the effect in question, could apparently sufficiently exist in the mind of the reader or viewer: although the courts did not often specify that it was sexual thoughts with which they were concerned,[1] there was equally nothing in most of the tests to limit their operation to subsequent conduct.[2] Discussion of the justification for obscenity regulation was both sparse and crude, little more being said than to approve it in terms of state power to protect morality and health. The attendant problem of causation was not considered, its presence apparently merely being assumed. There was a general agreement also that for a book to violate one or other statute, it need have only a tendency[3] to create an effect in the mind of the reader.

(2) The designation of the most susceptible as the standard group in general distribution was clear in certain state statutes (for example, that of Massachusetts with the phrase 'or manifestly tending to the corruption of youth');[4] in yet other jurisdictions such application clearly followed the adoption of the *Hicklin* test,[5] or where an alter-

---

1   *People* v *Brainard* 192 App Div 816, at 820, 183 NYS 452 at 456 (1920); *People* v *Viking Press* 147 Misc 813 at 816, 264 NYS 534 at 536 (Mag Ct 1933).

2   The *Hicklin* test embodies no such limitation; although the test was probably intended to denote moral corruption, the court may well have regarded thoughts as sufficient: Cockburn CJ spoke of the tendency to 'deprave and corrupt those whose minds are open to such immoral influences', and added that something of such nature 'would suggest to the minds of the young of either sex, or even to persons of more advanced years, thoughts of a most impure and libidinous character'. *R* v *Hicklin* LR 3 QB 360 at 371 (1868). Other tests were no different: e.g. tendency 'to excite impure imagination' (*People* v *Muller* 96 NY 408, 48 Am Rep 635 (1884); *People* v *Viking Press* 147 Misc 813, 264 NYS 534 (Mag Ct 1933); 'to excite lustful and lecherous desires' (*People* v *Brainard* 192 App Div 816, 193 NYS 452 (1920)): 'to stir sex impulses or lead to sexually impure thoughts' (*People* v *Vanguard Press* 192 Misc 127, 84 NYS 2d 427 Mag Ct 1947)); 'inciting lascivious thoughts or arousing lustful desire' (*Commonwealth* v *Isenstadt* 318 Mass 543, 62 NE 2d 840 (1945)). Contrast 'obscenity is such indecency as is calculated to provoke the violation of the law and the general corruption of morals' (*State* v *Pfenninger* 76 Mo App 373 at 377 (1883)).

3   The tendency requirement was on occasion statutorily enacted, as with the Massachusetts regulations (e.g. RL Ch 212, sect 20). Otherwise it was asserted (either as part of the *Hicklin* test or some other obscenity definition) by the courts in the course of defining obscenity: see e.g. *People* v *Muller* 96 NY 408 at 411, 48 Am Reps 635 at 637 (1884); *Commonwealth* v *Landis* 8 Phila 453 (1870); *People* v *Brainard* 192 App Div 816, 193 NYS 452 (1920); *People* v *Wendling* 258 NY 451, 180 NE 169 (1932).

4   See e.g. *Commonwealth* v *Buckley* 200 Mass 346, 86, NE 910 (1909).

5   See e.g. *Commonwealth* v *Calloway* 171 Ky 521, 188 SW 628; *People* v *Pesky* 230 App Div 200, 243 NYS 193 (1930).

native test was employed, was usually emphasised by the court.[1] The second aspect of distribution, that is distribution to particular groups, and its relevance in varying material's obscenity, was not apparently considered by courts or legislatures.

(3) It was sufficient under *Hicklin* for an entire work to be held obscene, that some passages from it were of a 'libidinous' character. It was not only courts applying the English test[2] that took this position; in Massachusetts for example it was rigorously applied: in *Commonwealth* v *Friede*[3] involving Theodore Dreiser's *An American Tragedy*, the prosecutor was permitted to read selected passages to the jury, refusing a reading of the entire story, and excluding evidence of the theme because of the length and because children might only read selected passages and not the whole book.

(4) Lord Cockburn's rule provided no exception on the grounds of literary, artistic or scientific merit; state obscenity statutes were generally equally uncompromising, and the courts displayed little eagerness to innovate in this regard.[4]

(5) The *Hicklin* test established the irrelevance of the author's motive. This was apparently generally accepted. In view of the fact that literary merit was irrelevant, there would equally be little room for the relevance of the author's intention, in the sense of intention to produce serious literature for example.[5]

(6) The position of the publisher with regard to intention was somewhat uncertain. He would presumably have to intend to publish (literally), and his knowledge of the law would be presumed. Whether he needed also to be aware of the nature of the publication, and/or its obscenity is not clear, although indications were that strict liability would apply in both instances.[6]

---

1 See e.g. *Ultem Publications* v *Arrow Publications* 166 Misc 645, 2 NYS 2d 933 (1933); *People* v *Wendling* 258 NY 451, 180 NE 169 (1932); *Commonwealth* v *Havens* 6 Pa CC 545 (1889); *Commonwealth* v *Magid and Dickstein* 91 Pa Super 573 (1927).

2 For example, *People* v *Muller* 96 NY 408 (1884). This involved an indictment for selling photographs, but the court held that the traditional test applied to photography as well as books.

3 271 Mass 318, 171 NE 472 (1930); also see for example *Commonwealth* v *Buckley* 200 Mass 346, 86 NE 960 (1909).

4 For example, *Commonwealth* v *Buckley* 200 Mass 346, 86 NE 910 (1909); *Commonwealth* v *Friede* 271 Mass 318, 171 NE 472 (1930).

5 *Contra* however *People* v *Muller* 96 NY 408, 48 Am Rep 635 (1884).

6 'A mistaken view of the defendant as to the character and tendency of the book, if it was in itself obscene and unfit for publication, would not excuse his violation of the law'. *Comm* v *Landis* 8 Phila 455 (1870).

(7) Expert evidence was not admissible under the *Hicklin* rule, and most state courts adopted this approach.[1]

(8) Obscenity was a matter for the jury.[2] A distinction in terms of jury discretion that was not apparently recognised was that between a test which prescribed the immediate effect a jury was to look for, jury discretion ending with such a determination, and a test which allowed the jury to determine corruption, in the sense of isolating an immediate effect, and then determining its im/morality. The latter quite clearly provides a jury with a much wider discretion.

(9) Lastly, possession was often sufficient for liability under state statutes.[3]

The constitutionality of regulation

As far as state control of obscenity was concerned, a potentially profound change was introduced by the Supreme Court in 1925 in *Gitlow* v *New York*,[4] when the Court finally gave a firm ruling that the First Amendment is (by virtue of the Fourteenth Amendment) applicable to state power: this has been confirmed in a line of subsequent decisions.[5] The restriction thus imposed was parallel to that placed on federal authority,[6] with the apparent result that no state legislature could pass a measure restricting freedom of speech. Was all control of obscenity as a result unconstitutional? The Supreme Court ruled not: in the very

---

1   For example, *People* v *Muller* 96 NY 408 (1884); *People* v *Seltzer* 122 Misc 329, 203 NY 809 (1924); *McAnany* v *Henrice* 238 No. 103, 141 SW 633.

2   *People* v *Muller* 96 NY 408, 48 Am Rep 635 (1884); *Dreiser* v *John Lane & Co* 183 App Div 773, 171 NYS 605 (1918); *People* v *Seltzer* 122 Misc 329, 203 NYS 809 (1924); *People* v *Pesky* 254 NY 373, 173 NE 223 (1930); *Commonwealth* v *Isenstadt* 318 Mass 543, 62 NE 2d 840 (1945); *Commonwealth* v *Landis* 8 Phila 453 (1870); *Davidson* v *State* 19 Ala App 77, 95 So 54 (1923); *State* v *Weitershausen* 11 NJ Super 487, 78 A 2d 595 (1951); *People* v *Wepplo* 78 Cal App 2d Series S 959, 178 P 2d 853 (1947); *King* v *Commonwealth* 313 Ky 741, 233 SW 2d 522 (1950); *State of Florida* v *Clein* 93 So 2d 876 (1957). An exception to this general rule was where the accused (as in Massachusetts) was permitted to go for trial by a single judge rather than judge plus jury: see *Commonwealth* v *Isenstadt* 318 Mass 543, 62 NE 2d 840 at 849 (1945).

3   See note: 'More Ado about Dirty Books' 75 (1966) *Yale LJ* 1364 App I.

4   268 US 652 (1928).

5   *Near* v *Minnesota* 283 US 697 (1931); *Stromberg* v *California* 283 US 359 (1931); *Grosjean* v *American Press Co.* 287 US 233 (1936); *De Jonge* v *Oregon* 299 US 353 (1937); *Lovell* v *Griffin* 303 US 444 (1938); *Schneider* v *State* 308 US 147 (1939); *Joseph Burstyn* v *Wilson* 343 US 495 (1952).

6   *Thornhill* v *Alabama* 310 US 88 (1940); *Chaplinsky* v *New Hampshire* 315 US 578 (1942); *Pennekamp* v *Florida* 328 US 331 (1946); *Winters* v *New York* 333 US 507 (1948).

case[1] in which the Court had finally recognised the applicability of the First Amendment to state power, obscenity was held to be an exception to the general protection so afforded.[2] The Supreme Court in this and subsequent opinions[3] evaded the discussion of the fundamental question of the constitutionality of obscenity censorship by merely assuming that such expression is not protected; the question only came squarely before the Court in 1957; such discussion had to wait until then.[4] Even assuming that obscenity is an exception to the First Amendment, state obscenity statutes were still open to attack on several further constitutional grounds:

(a) As obscenity was an exception to the First Amendment, the question of the admissibility, in First Amendment terms, of the state objectives underlying obscenity regulation was strictly speaking irrelevant. It might alternatively have been asked, quite apart from the First Amendment, whether such regulation fell within state powers at all. Although the courts had not been particularly explicit about state objectives in this area, it was clear that obscenity regulation was aimed at the enforcement of public morality. The courts, in these terms, tended to dispose of this initial question with dispatch: as the so-called police powers of the states extend to and include 'everything essential to public safety, health and morals';[5] obscenity statutes in their turn were 'manifestly ... designed to promote the public morals, and in a broad

---

1   *Gitlow* v *New York* 268 US 652 (1925).

2   There had, in fact, been a few earlier and rather cryptic statements to this effect: see *ex parte Jackson* 96 US 727 (1877), a case involving the application of the First Amendment to Congressional action; in *Public Clearing House* v *Coyne* 194 US 497 at 508 (1904) the Court remarked in connection with the Federal Obscenity Statute that 'its constitutionality has never been attacked'; see also e.g. *Fox* v *State of Washington* 236 US 273 (1914).

3   For example, *Winters* v *New York* 333 US 507 at 570 (1928); *Chaplinsky* v *New Hampshire* 315 US 568 at 581 (1942); *Beauharnais* v *Illinois* 343 US 250 at 266 (1952).

4   The question of First Amendment theory will be discussed in more detail later. It is interesting to note, though, that the question of the constitutionality of state obscenity controls could in many states have been raised even before *Gitlow*. This by virtue of the guarantees of freedom of expression (similar to those embodied in the First Amendment) which many state constitutions contained: Article I Section II of the Ohio Constitution (for example) provides that: 'Every citizen may freely speak, write and publish his sentiments on all subjects, being responsible for the absue of the right; and no law shall be passed to restrain or abridge the liberty of speech, or of the press' (cf. also e.g. Art I Section 7 of Pennsylvania Constitution). Such guarantees and the consequent question of the constitutionality of obscenity controls do not appear to have been raised before state courts however. For further examples of such guarantees see T. Schroeder *Obscene Literature and Constitutional Law* (New York 1911) chapter 10.

5   *Lawton* v *Steele* 152 US 133 at 136 (1894).

sense the public health and safety'.[1] There was less than universal agreement, however: a Pennsylvania court in what was later to become an oft-quoted (if not followed) judgement, came to the conclusion, after an extensive review of previous decisions, that the state police power may be applied to regulate publications on the ground of obscenity

> ... only where there is a reasonable and demonstrable cause to believe that a crime or misdemeanour has been committed or is about to be committed as the perceptible result of the publication and distribution of the writing in question: the opinion of anyone that a tendency thereto exists or that such a result is self-evident is insufficient and irrelevant. The causal connection between the book and the criminal behaviour must appear beyond a reasonable doubt. The criminal law is not, in my opinion, the 'custos morum' of the King's subjects: it is only the custodian of peace and good order that free men and women need for the shaping of their common destiny.[2]

This ruling was confirmed *per curiam* by the Pennsylvania Supreme Court,[3] but was not followed (or even mentioned in this regard) in other jurisdictions.

(b) Assuming the acceptability of state objectives in this area, a second potential avenue of attack lay in the connection between the regulation and the state objective in question. Again, because obscenity regulation constituted an exception to the First Amendment, a connection in terms of a clear and present danger — a requirement in respect of restriction on (for example) expression affecting national security — was not strictly required.[4] Mr Justice Bok would appear to

---

1 *Commonwealth* v *Allison* 277 Mass 57 at 63, 116 NE 265 (1917); confirmed in *Commonwealth* v *Isenstadt* 318 Mass 543 at 551, 62 NE 2d 840 at 848 (1945); see also *State* v *McKie* 73 Conn 18, 45 A 409; *Burke* v *Kingsley Books* 208 Misc 150, 142 NYS 2d 735 (1955).

2 *Commonwealth* v *Gordon* 66 Pa D + C 101 (1949), per Mr Justice Bok.

3 *Sub nom Commonwealth* v *Feigenbaum* 166 Pa Super 120, 70 A 2d 389 (1950).

4 On the clear and present danger test, see chapter 14.

have been asserting something close to clear and present danger,[1] however, with his requirement of a connection sustainable beyond a reasonable doubt. Quite apart from the First Amendment, however, it might have been asked whether there was, in Fourteenth Amendment due process terms, a reasonable or rational connection in any given case between the state's objectives and the restriction imposed. This question was particularly relevant in relation to the employment in much state obscenity regulation of the most susceptible person test: could there be said to be a rational connection between a regulation in favour of minors, but which imposed a prohibition on the material concerned in relation to adults also? Despite the fact that it was well settled that the state police power may be exercised only when the public required such interference, and not in the interests of a particular class,[2] doubts as to the constitutionality of obscenity regulation at least in terms of the most susceptible person approach were in these terms raised in only one case, *State* v *Lerner*,[3] an Ohio decision handed down in 1948. Here the court merely applied the general rule to obscenity regulation: 'The police power may not be exercised for the benefit of the few in disregard of the many'.[4] The statute in question prohibited sales to adults even though the undesirable effect in question was on the immature; the rational connection was therefore absent. This approach was not emulated by other state courts, however; it was only in 1957 in *Butler* v *Michigan*[5] that the Supreme Court moved to adopt

---

1   The test would appear to have been considered in only one obscenity case in the Supreme Court, *People* v *Doubleday* quoted in 17 *US Law Week* (Supreme Court Section 3118), a *per curiam* decision, in which Mr Justice Rutledge remarked orally:

> Before we get to the question of clear and present danger, we've got to have something which the State can forbid as dangerous. We are talking in a vacuum until we can establish that there is some occasion for the exercise of the State's power ... Yes, you must first ascertain the substantive evil at which the statute is aimed, and then determine whether the publication of this book constitutes a clear and present danger ... It is up to the state to demonstrate that there was a danger, and until they demonstrate that, plus the clarity and imminence of the danger, the constitution prohibition would seem to apply.

Not only was the decision *per curiam*, but these remarks do not appear to have been made within the context of the Court's exception approach to obscenity, an approach which was merely emphasised in a routine way four years later in *Beauharnais* v *Illinois* 343 US 250 (1952). It is perhaps significant that the Court in *Doubleday* nonetheless affirmed a trial court conviction based on a mere tendency test, something hardly in accordance with a clear and present danger approach.

2   See *Lawton* v *Steele* 152 US 13 (1894) at 17.

3   81 NE 2d 282 (Ohio 1948).

4   Ibid. at 289.

5   352 US 380 (1957); *Ginsberg* v *New York* 390 US 629 (1968); see *infra* chapter 12.

the *Lerner* approach. Due process requirements were equally applicable to adult obscenity regulations; this issue has been dealt with only twice by the Supreme Court, and only to affirm the existence of the required rational connection.[1]

(c) Fourteenth Amendment procedural due process demands that any statute rendering conduct criminal must not be vague, indefinite, or overbroad.[2] The law must be sufficiently certain; statutes, where not narrowly drawn, are likely to be declared void for uncertainty as violating the procedural due process requirement of the Fourteenth Amendment.[3] Where the statutes in question impose restrictions on expression, however, a First Amendment dimension is added. In view of the preferred position of free speech — which allows a court to neutralise the presumption normally indulged in favour of a statute's constitutionality, should it in some way impinge on freedom of expression[4] — and the Court's consciousness of the 'chilling effect'[5] even of obscenity statutes drawn sufficiently narrowly, any statutory provision in this area is likely to be subjected to a close judicial scrutiny in order to ensure that it does not prohibit both protected and unprotected speech by being overbroad,[6] or by not giving adequate notice of what it prohibits.[7] In *Winters* v *New York*[8] the Court was faced with a criminal statute prohibiting the dissemination of 'accounts of "bloodshed, crime and lust" '.[9] The New York Court of Appeals limited the application of the statute to stories which would 'become vehicles for inciting

---

1 See Mr Justice Harlan in *Roth* v *United States* 354 US 476 (1957); Chief Justice Burger in *Miller* v *California* 413 US 15 (1973); *Paris Adult Theater I* v *Slaton* 413 US 49 (1973) at 57–62.

2 Overbreadth and vagueness may be dealt with as separate concepts (see e.g. Schauer op.cit., chapter 8); as related concepts, however, they are often indistinguishable, and for this reason will be dealt with together here.

3 See e.g. *Lanzetta* v *New Jersey* 306 US 457 at 485; this is as opposed to substantive due process, a phrase that came to connote more 'fairness' than procedural acceptability.

4 Cf. *Herndon* v *Lowry* 301 US 242 (1937); *United States* v *Carolene Products Co.* 304 US (1938) 144 at 152, footnote 4; *Thornhill* v *Alabama* 310 US 88 (1940); *Thomas* v *Collins* 323 US 576 (1945) at 530.

5 See generally note 'The chilling effect in Constitutional Law' 69 (1969) *Colum L Rev* 808; also *Smith* v *California* 361 US 147 (1959) at 150–4; *Paris Adult Theater I* v *Slaton* 413 US 49 (1973) at 92–3, per Brennan, J. dissenting.

6 See note 'The First Amendment Overbreadth Doctrine' 83 (1970) *Harvard L Rev* 844.

7 See note 'The Void-for-Vagueness Doctrine in the Supreme Court' 109 (1960) *U Pa L Rev* 67.

8 333 US 507 at 512 (1948).

9 Then New York Penal Law Sect 1141, subsect 2.

violent and depraved crimes against the person ...'.[1] The Supreme Court nonetheless held the statute indefinite and overbroad, and struck it down as violating procedural due process; the Court went out of its way, however, to emphasise that Section 1141—1 of the New York Penal Law, the obscenity statute, was itself sufficiently certain:

> The impossibility of defining the precise line between permissible uncertainty in statutes caused by describing crimes by words well understood through long use in criminal law — obscene, lewd, lascivious, filthy, indecent or disgusting — and the unconstitutional vagueness that leaves a person uncertain as to the kind of prohibited conduct — massing stories to incite crimes — has resulted in three arguments of this case in this Court.[2]

This ruling, in view of the fact that the Court had placed obscenity outside the protection of the First Amendment, without offering any definition of 'obscene', is hardly surprising. It effectively closed the question of the constitutionality, in terms certainly of vagueness, and almost certainly of overbreadth, of the word 'obscene', at least as far as state courts were concerned.[3]

In only one subsequent case[4] did the Supreme Court reverse an obscenity judgement in circumstances such that it might be supposed that the Court did not regard the standard of obscenity as satisfying the minimum requirement of certainty and definiteness: one can say no more than this with regard to the *per curiam* ruling in *Holmby*: it might equally well have been based on a determination by the Court that the film involved was not in fact obscene. The word 'obscene' then was sufficiently definite; in contrast the word 'sacrilegious', used in a statute[5] imposing prior restraint on '... obscene, indecent, immoral, inhuman and sacrilegious' films was held too vague,[6] whilst the word 'immoral' and the phrase 'tend to corrupt morals' were found over-

---

1   *People* v *Winters* 294 US 545 at 550, 63 NE 2d 98 at 100 (1945).

2   *Winters* v *New York* 333 US 507 (1948) at 518; see also *Chaplinsky* v *New Hampshire* 315 US 568 (1942) at 571—2.

3   See e.g. *Burke* v *Kingsley Books* 208 Misc 150, 152 NYS 2d 461 (1956); *Brown* v *Kingsley Books* 1 NY 2d 177, 134 NE 2d 461 (1956); *American Civil Liberties Union* v *City of Chicago* 2 Ill 2d 334, 121 NE 2d 585 (1954).

4   *Holmby Productions* v *Vaughn* 350 US 870 (1956).

5   New York Educational Law, Sect 122.

6   *Joseph Burstyn* v *Wilson* 343 US 495 (1952).

broad.[1] Following this case, the relevant portion of the New York Education Law was amended, the terms 'immoral' and 'tend to corrupt' now being defined as denoting in this context 'a motion picture or part thereof, the dominant purpose or effect of which is erotic or pornographic; or which portrays acts of sexual immorality, perversion, or lewdness, or which expressly or impliedly presents such acts as desirable, acceptable or proper patterns of behaviour'.[2] In a subsequent prosecution[3] of a film version of D.H. Lawrence's *Lady Chatterley's Lover* on the grounds of its immorality in advocating adultery as proper behaviour, the Court, despite the statutory elaboration, once again rejected the standard, implicitly on the grounds of overbreadth: the statute as applied had 'reached beyond obscenity and pornography to the advocacy of ideas'.[4]

The Court thus by implication would appear to have clarified earlier uncertainty in terms of permissible definitions of obscenity: although the term obscene was not overbroad, and although the Court had not itself offered a definition of obscenity, any definition in terms of corruption of public morals would implicitly have been overbroad. It would appear then that although the standard of obscenity was constitutionally permissible, any elaboration on it allowing jury decision in terms of positive morality as such, probably would not. The *Hicklin* test was thus by implication ruled out of court: the implication was sufficiently oblique, however, for many states employing definitions in terms of morality to continue so to do.

By 1954 there were in fact at least fourteen judicial definitions of obscenity in use.[5] Although state courts did not generally employ the potential constitutional controls available to reduce this confusion, and perhaps to reconcile such restrictions with the demands of constitutional guarantees against overbreadth or irrational prohibition, there seems nonetheless to have been by the 1940s and 1950s a strong feeling that

---

1 *Commercial Pictures Corp* v *Regents* 346 US 587 (1954); see also *Superior Films* v *Department of Education*, ibid. Both decisions were *per curiam* and may well have been based on a finding that the films were not 'immoral', nor did they 'tend to corrupt morals', as the case might be. See also *Gelling* v *Texas* 343 US 960 (1952) where the standard was that a motion picture was 'of such a character as to be prejudicial to the best interests of the city'.

2 New York Education Law, Section 122(a).

3 *Kingsley Int. Pictures Corp* v *Regents* 360 US 684 (1959).

4 Schauer op.cit. at 157–8; see chapter 12.

5 See W. Gellhorn *Individual Freedom and Governmental Restraint* (Baton Rouge 1956) at 59.

'modernisation' was necessary in relation to obscenity law.[1] The principal of these changes was the introduction of a defence of literary or artistic merit, a change which was in many jurisdictions effected, as in England, quite independently of any constitutional guarantees. Perhaps the first of the *Hicklin* characteristics to be unequivocally axed judicially was the most susceptible person aspect of obscenity tests:

(1) By the mid-1950s both the New York and Massachusetts courts had adopted a similar approach in this regard: the abnormal were to be excluded, whilst in general distribution, the effect was to be judged on all those reached, and not merely a particular section; particular distribution was not considered.[2] In Pennsylvania the most susceptible person rule had been specifically affirmed by the courts,[3] but was overturned in *Commonwealth* v *Gordon*:[4] the court laid down the standard as that of the average modern reader. Judge Bok's lead was followed in a number of jurisdictions;[5] some however retained the old approach.[6]

(2) With the assertion of an average person, or a composite average person standard, certain state courts had begun the trend, later to become so marked in Supreme Court obscenity jurisprudence, towards constant rather than variable obscenity. A further factor in this regard, in relation to which there was probably greater agreement, was the question of a work-as-a-whole rule; although the latter had been

---

1   For a comprehensive account of this shift in public opinion, and in particular the decline of the vice societies in the late 1920s and 1930s, see Boyer op.cit. chapters 6–9.

2   See e.g. *Brown* v *Kingsley Books* 208 Misc 150, 142 NYS 2d 735, (1955); *Attorney-General* v *Book Named 'Serenade'* 326 Mass 324, 91 NE 2d 259 (1950).

3   As late as 1940 in *Commonwealth* v *New* 142 Super 358, 16 A 2d 259 (1940).

4   66 Pa D + C 101 at 116 (1949); affd *sub nom Commonwealth* v *Feigenbaum* 166 Pa Super 120, 70 A 2d 389 (1950).

5   For example, the Superior Court of New Jersey in *Bantam Books* v *Melko* 125 NJ Super 282, 96 A 2d 47 (1953); the Supreme Court of Illinois in *American Civil Liberties Union* v *City of Chicago* 3 I11 2d 334, 121 NE 2d 585 (1954).

6   The Supreme Court of Missouri in 1954 in *State* v *Becker* 364 Mo 1079, 272 SW 2d 283 (1954), for example, after speaking of the effect of the publications 'in their entirety upon persons of average human instincts', quoted with approval the *Hicklin* test, and then went on to remark that it could not '... disregard an unambiguous enactment which has as its obvious purpose the protection of the morals of the susceptible into whose hands these publications may come'.

adopted by a number of states by the 1940s,[1] many retained in their statutes the partly obscene rule.[2]

(3) Judging the work as a whole constituted a more fundamental shift in emphasis than the courts were willing, initially at any rate, to acknowledge: literary merit, they asserted again and again, was not a defence to an obscenity charge; obscene material was not to be sanctioned.[3] Yet the process of assessing a book as a whole would needs involve an assessment and a weighing-up of its merits against its demerits; it in other words opened the way not only for the admission of literary worth as a relevant factor, but also involved a tacit admission by the courts that some prurient appeal was permissible. The book-as-a-whole rule was an advance, but the position still remained rather ill-defined; the relationship of literary merit to a work's obscenity or partial obscenity was less than clear; as a result, different jurisdictions attached very different weight to this factor.

(4) Consideration of a work as a whole opened the way also for an assessment of the author's sincerity of purpose being taken into account; this follows on any consideration of literary worth. The position with regard to sincerity was much the same as with artistic merit: the courts would weigh this (together with literary worth or any other factors to be taken into account) against 'the objectionable passages' the book might contain.[4] Obversely, an absence of sincerity was likely

---

1 For example, New York in *Halsey* v *New York Society for Suppression of Vice* 234 NYI, at 4, 136 NE 219 at 220 (1922); Massachusetts in *Commonwealth* v *Isenstadt* 318 Mass 543, 62 NE 2d 840 at 844 (1945); Pennsylvania in *Commonwealth* v *New* 142 Pa Super 358, 16 A 2d 437 (1940), confirmed in *Commonwealth* v *Gordon* 66 Pa D + C 101 (1949) affd. *sub nom Commonwealth* v *Feigenbaum* 142 Pa Super 358, 16 A 2d 437 (1950); Ohio in *State* v *Lerner* 81 NE 2d 282 (1948); New Jersey in *Bantam Books* v *Melko* 25 NJ Super 282, 96 A 2d 47 (1952); and Illinois in *American Civil Liberties Union* v *City of Chicago* 3 I11 2d 334, 121 NE 2d 585 (1954).

2 Conn Rev Gen Stat Sect 8567 (1949); Del Rev Code c 70 Sect 2555 (1935); Fla Stat Sect 847.01 (1951); Iowa Code Sect 725.4 (1950); Me Rev Stat C121 Sect 24 (1944); Mich Stat Ann Sect 28.575 (1938); Ohio Gen Code Sect 13035 (1935); RI Gen Laws c610 Sect 13 (1938); Sc Code Sect 16–415 (1947); Va Code Sect 18–113 (1950); W.Va Code Ann Sect 60 66 (1949); Wis Stat Sect 351.38 (1951); c.f. Ark Stat Ann Sect 41–2704 (1947); Colo Stat Ann C48 Sect 217 (1935) as amended Colo Laws 1937 p.504 Sect 2; Md Code Ann Art 27 Sect 574 (1951).

3 *Commonwealth* v *Isenstadt* 318 Mass 543, 62 NE 2d 840 at 846 (1945); cf. also *People* v *Viking Press* 147 Misc 813, 244 NYS 534 (Mag Ct 1933); *People* v *Berg* 241 App Div 543, 272 NYS 586 (1934); *People* v *Muller* 155 Misc 446, 279 NYS 583 (Mag Ct 1935); *People* v *Gotham Book Market* 158 Misc 240, 285 NYS 563 (Mag Ct 1936); *Ultem Publications* v *Arrow Publications* 166 Misc 645, 2 NYS 2d 933 (1936); *People* v *Finkelstein* 114 NYS 2d 810 (Mag Ct 1953).

4 *Commonwealth* v *Isenstadt* 318 Mass 543, 62 NE 2d 840 (1945); *People* v *Pesky* 230 App Div 200, 243 NYS 193 (1930); *People* v *Berg* 241 App Div 543, 272 NYS 586 (1934); *Sunshine Book Company* v *McCaffrey* 112 NYS 2d 476 (1952); *Kingsley Books* v *Brown* 1 NY 2d 177, 134 NE 2d 461 (1956); *Adams Theatre Company* v *Keenan* 12 NJ 267, 96 A 2d 579 (1953); *American Civil Liberties Union* v *City of Chicago* 3 I11 2d 334, 121 NE 2d 585 (1954).

to tip the balance against a particular work.[1] Certain jurisdictions, Massachusetts for example, were here (as with literary merit) less generous than others in the weight they attached to this factor; some courts, however, went so far as to suggest that a book 'cannot be obscene unless it is written with a pornographic purpose'.[2] This, however, would have established a defence of mistake, and most courts, although taking intention into account, stopped short of this. It had, in addition, been suggested[3] that where an author's purpose in writing was one of mere gain, that this should be a strong factor in favour of condemning the work, and was not to be equated with 'a legitimate and useful purpose'. This was not followed, however, whilst the Supreme Court had ruled that the fact that works are published for gain does not exclude them from First Amendment protection.[4]

(5) How should a court ascertain an author's purpose or the literary worth of his production? The author can testify as to his objects,[5] but clearly the court's resort is to the book itself, and to the testimony of expert witnesses.[6]

Despite such development, state regulation of obscenity remained fragmented: not all states had followed the trends outlined above: in the absence of Supreme Court ruling on these issues, there was nothing, other than public opinion, to oblige them so to do. The logic of the Court's own position moreover demanded further elucidation in the sense of a constitutionally approved definition of obscenity: if obscenity was an exception to the First Amendment, and therefore outside the Amendment's protection, the definition of obscenity employed was crucial, and itself assumed a constitutional status. As one entered the 1950s it was thus unlikely that the Supreme Court would for very

---

1   For example, *People* v *Pesky* 230 App Div 200 at 204, 243 NYS 193 at 197 (1930).

2   *Commonwealth* v *Gordon* 66 Pa D + C 101 (1949); affd *sub nom Commonwealth* v *Feigenbaum* 166 Pa Super 120, 70 A 2d 389 (1950); *People* v *Gotham Book Market* 158 Misc 240, 285 NYS 563 (Mag Ct 1936).

3   In *Commonwealth* v *Landis* 8 Phila 453 (1870), for example.

4   *Grosjean* v *American Press Co* 297 US 233 (1936); *Thomas* v *Collins* 323 US 576 (1945); see chapter 11.

5   Employed in *People* v *Vanguard Press* 192 Misc 127, 84 NYS 2d 427 (Mag Ct 1947); *People* v *Creative Age Press* 192 Misc 188, 79 NYS 2d 198 (Mag Ct 1948).

6   For example, *in re petition of Trustees of Worthington Co* 30 NYS 36 (1894); *Halsey* v *New York Society for Suppression of Vice* 234 NY 136, 136 NE 219 (1922); *People* v *Berg* 241 App Div 543, 272 NYS 586 (1934); *People* v *Larsen* 5 NYS 2d 55 (1938); *Attorney-General* v *Book Named 'God's Little Acre'* 326 Mass 281, 93 NE 2d 819 (1950); *State of Delaware* v *Scope* 86 A 2d 164 (1952). But see *State* v *Becker* 364 Mo 1079, 272 SW 2d 283 (1954) in which expert evidence was held inadmissible.

much longer be able to avoid entering the obscenity area. Before moving on to the Court's attempt in *Roth* to resolve the problems such entry raised, balance at least demands an examination of the development of federal obscenity jurisprudence prior to 1957.

II Federal obscenity controls

Public health and moral welfare was, and is, primarily the concern of state governments. The jurisdictional basis of federal controls in the area of obscenity have as a result been primarily the control of the mails or of interstate commerce.[1] Federal concern with obscenity first developed as a result of the growing circulation of French postcards in the mid-nineteenth century. This parallels a similar English concern;[2] the federal customs law of 1842[3] predates the equivalent English Act of 1853 by eleven years however. The statute barred the importation of 'indecent and obscene prints, paintings, lithographs, engravings and transparencies'. Enforcement, perhaps mirroring the general lack of concern with obscenity in the pre-Civil War period, was sparse.[4] The aftermath of the war was to bring changes in this area, the first of them materialising as early as 1865 — in the middle of reconstruction — in the form of the first legislation relating to obscenity in the mails. This was the first federal criminal statute to deal with obscenity, and provided that

> No obscene book, pamphlet, picture, print, or other publication of a vulgar and indecent character, shall be admitted into the mails of the United States; any person or persons who shall deposit or cause to be deposited, in any post office of the United States, for mailing or for delivery, an

---

1 For a more extensive treatment of the history of federal regulation in this area see J. Paul and M. Schwartz *Federal Censorship: Obscenity in the Mail* (1961); Paul 'The Post Office and Non-Mailability of Obscenity, An Historical Note' 8 (1961) *UCLA L Rev* 44; Paul and Schwartz 'Obscenity in the Mails: A Comment on some problems of Federal Censorship' 106 (1957) *U Pa L Rev* 214; de Grazia 'Obscenity and the Mail: A Study of Administrative Restraint' 20 (1955) *Law and Contemp Prob* 698; note 'Obscenity and the Post Office: Removal from the Mail under section 1461' 27 (1960) *U Chi L Rev* 354; Zuckman 'Obscenity in the Mails' 33 (1960) *So Cal L Rev* 171; Frederick F. Schauer *The Law of Obscenity* (1976) chapters 1 and 9.

2 A. Craig *Suppressed Books, A History of the Conception of Literary Obscenity* (1963) at 36—7; D. Tribe *Questions of Censorship* (1973) at 60—5; *The Reports of the Commission on Obscenity and Pornography* (New York Times edn (1970)) at 351.

3 5 Stat 566 Sect 28 (1842): amended by 11 Stat 168 (1857).

4 For an early application of the statute see *United States v Three Cases of Toys* 28 Fed Cas 112 (No 16499) (SD NY 1843).

obscene book, pamphlet, picture, print, or other publication, knowing the same to be of a vulgar and indecent character, shall be deemed guilty of a misdemeanour, and by being convicted thereof, shall for every such offence be fined not more than five hundred dollars, or imprisoned for not more than one year, or both, according to the circumstances and aggravations of the offence.[1]

Once again, enforcement was sparse, and it was left to Anthony Comstock to bring about both a revision of the legislation[2] and the first concerted effort to enforce it.[3] His efforts resulted in the enactment in 1873 of a measure entitled 'An Act for the Suppression of Trade in, and circulation of, Obscene Literature and Articles of Immoral Use', perhaps better known as the Comstock Act.[4] The customs statute was correspondingly broadened to include books and pamphlets as well as pictorial matter, while three years later, in 1876, Post Office censorship was apparently specifically authorised in the alteration of the statute to declare all obscene matter 'non-mailable' and prohibiting its delivery.[5] Comstock was not only instrumental in furnishing the tools of censorship: as a special agent of the Post Office Department his aggressive and energetic investigations ensured the

---

1   13 Stat 507 Sect 16 (1865).

2   There had been a minor change to the 1865 statute which prohibited the carrying in the mail of any 'letter upon the envelope of which, or postcard upon which scurrilous epithets have been written': 17 Stat 302 Sect 148 (1872). This was discarded by the Act of 1876, 19 Stat 90 (1876) but was re-introduced into the postal laws in 1888, 25 Stat 188 (1888), in a measure that made it clear that obscene or scurrilous matter on the outside as well as the inside of mail was prohibited. Later the same year this prohibition was enacted as a separate postal crime, 25 Stat 496 (1888). The measure, codified, as amended, exists today as 18 USC Sect 1463 (1975 supp). The courts have held that this section incorporates only obscenity as legally defined: *United States* v *Davis* 353 F 2d 614 at 615 (2d Cir 1965) cert denied 384 US 953 (1964). The statute is little used and *Davis* is the last reported case.

3   For a fuller account of Comstock's activities see H. Brown and M. Leech *Anthony Comstock: Roundsman of the Lord* (1927), C. Trumbull *Anthony Comstock, Fighter* (1913), quoted in Kilpatrick *The Smut Peddler* (1960), at 35–44; P. Boyce *Purity in Print: The Vice Society Movement and Book Censorship in America* (1968).

4   17 Stat 596 (1873).

5   19 Stat 90 Sect 1 (1876): 'Every obscene publication etc. is declared to be non-mailable matter and shall not be conveyed in the mails or delivered from any post office or by any letter carrier'. It is by no means certain whether the amendment was intended to authorise independent administrative censorship, and it may (although this does not explain the prohibition against delivery) be that it was merely intended to correct a drafting error in the 1873 Act whereby the mailing of books (as opposed to articles or things) appeared to fall outside the sanction imposed by the Act: see James C.N. Paul 'The Post Office and Non-Mailability of Obscenity: An Historical Note' 8 (1961) *UCLA L Rev* 44 at 57–8. In connection with this and the development of civil sanctions by federal agencies, see chapter 12.

frequent seizure and destruction of material,[1] whilst prosecutions were commonplace. Comstock's campaign was over time aided by the growth in federal powers under the commerce clause; federal powers to control obscenity tended to expand in tandem with the latter: in 1897 a criminal statute prohibited the importation into the United States, or the transportation across state lines of obscene material by means of a common carrier or express company.[2]

The statutes,[3] and more particularly the Comstock Act (which

---

1   For such civil sanctions, see chapter 12.

2   29 Stat 572 (1897). Interstate transportation of obscene materials by means other than the post has become increasingly common, and the 1897 Act, modified several times over the years, (33 Stat 705 (1905); 35 Stat 1138 (1909); 41 Stat 1060 (1920); 62 Stat 768 (1948); 64 Stat 194 (1950); 72 Stat 962 Sect 2 (1958); 84 Stat 1973 (1971); existing now as 18 USC Sect 1462) has been increasingly used. The statute covers the knowing use of such carriers or the knowing taking of materials from them; knowledge of the character of the material is required. The insertion of the verb 'uses' for 'deposit' by the 1958 Amendment ensures that this offence is a continuing one and may be prosecuted where the material originates, is received or through which it passes: see e.g. *Gold* v *United States* 378 F 2d 588 (9th Cir 1967). For the elements of the offence (besides the obscenity of the material), such procedural aspects, and the difficulties of proof, see Schauer op.cit. at 181–2. The statute was joined in 1955 by a further measure which outlaws the interstate transportation of obscene material for the purposes of sale or distribution: 69 Stat 183 Sect 3 (1955), 18 USC Sect 1465. The statute also authorises the seizure and destruction of the materials in question, but this has been held to apply only after a conviction: *United States* v *50 Magazines* 323 F Supp 395 (DRI 1971). Sale or distribution has been taken to mean any commercial purpose, and the statute thus encompasses the forwarding of films from distributor to exhibitor. Knowledge of the character of the materials is again required. For the elements of the offence (other than obscenity of the materials), procedural aspects and difficulties of proof, see Schauer op.cit. at 183–4. Both statutes have been held constitutional 18 USC 1462: *United States* v *Orito* 413 US 139 (1973); 18 USC 1465: e.g. *United States* v *New Orleans Book Mart, Inc* 490 F 2d 73 (5th Cir 1974) cert denied 419 US 801. Obscene here has the same meaning as it does under the Comstock Act.

3   For the history of the Customs Statute (a purely civil sanction) see below. Certain other measures have been added more recently: 26 USC Sect 5723d (The Inland Revenue Code) prohibits indecent or immoral pictures, prints, or representations in or on cigarette or tobacco packages; the statute does not appear to have been enforced. The only other federal criminal statute in this area was added in 1968 (47 USC Sect 223) and prohibits the making of 'obscene, lewd, lascivious, filthy or indecent' telephone calls in interstate or foreign commerce. This statute probably relates, however, to the control of offensiveness, rather than obscenity; its constitutionality may be open to doubt in terms of *Cohen* v *California* 403 US 15 (1971); see chapter 14.

despite modifications remains substantially similar today)[1] did not define obscenity, but merely listed apparent synonyms therefor. Judicial interpretation is thus significant; those cases initially arising under the Comstock Act were concerned with both the constitutionality of the Act and various procedural issues arising under it. In *United States v Bott*[2] for example[3] the defendant argued that despite his having mailed a contraceptive powder, he had no intention of promoting birth control. The court ruled such intention unnecessary, and confirmed the constitutionality of the statute, Congress having the power to regulate the mails; despite the applicability of the First Amendment to the federal government, free speech issues were not raised. The constitutionality in First Amendment terms of federal legislation had by the

---

1   In 1908 'indecent' was defined to include 'matter of a character tending to incite arson, murder or assassination' 35 Stat 416 (1908); see also 36 Stat 1339 Sect 2 (1911); 62 Stat 768 (1948); 64 Stat 194 Sect 2 (1950); 19 Stat 183 (1955); 72 Stat 962 Sect 1 (1958); 84 Stat 1973–1974 (1971). The last amendment removed the bar to the mailing of materials and articles relevant to birth control, probably as a result of *Griswold* v *Connecticut* 381 US 479 (1965). In the light of *Roe* v *Wade* 440 US 113 (1973) and *Bigelow* v *Virginia* 95 S. Ct 2222 (1975), the sections concerned with articles etc. relevant to abortion would surely be unconstitutional? No prosecution has been brought in this area for over thirty years. The statute exists today as 18 USC Sect 1461. The 1955 amendment substituted the word 'uses' for 'deposit' as far as the mails were concerned. As a result the offence is a continuing one and may be prosecuted anywhere it commenced, continued or was completed. See note 'Multi-Venue and Obscenity Statutes' 115 (1967) *U Pa L Rev* 399. For other elements of the offence (besides obscenity of materials), procedural aspects and difficulties of proof, see Schauer op.cit. at 175–6.

2   24 F Cas 1204 (No.14,626)(CCSDNY 1873). The defendant's intention as to legal obscenity of the material was irrelevant; this is much in line with rulings that an author's intention as to obscenity is similarly irrelevant. With distribution perhaps even more than authorship becoming the law's concern, there may in fact with such postal laws be two questions as to intention: that of the author, and that of the distributor. The distributor was here required to know the character of the material, and this (scienter) requirement has been established as a constitutional standard in such proceedings; see chapter 11.

3   Another important procedural issue was the question of letters: the 1873 version of the Act did not include letters, but spoke of 'writings'. In 1895 the Supreme Court in *United States* v *Chase* 135 US 255 (1895) held that letters were not included. As a result the statute was amended to include them: in 1896 *Andrews* v *United States* 162 US 420 (1896) held them clearly covered by the amendment. In *Grimm* v *United States* the Act was held to cover letters advertising objectionable matter, even if the letters themselves were not obscene. It has become the policy of the department to enforce as to private letters only in particular cases (as with relationships involving minors, for example). A defendant may apparently not enforce this policy however: *Spellmain* v *United States* 413 F 2d 527 (9th Cir 1969) cert denied 396 US 930 (1969), unless the government's motives in selectional prosecution are suspect: *United States* v *Oaks* 508 F 2d 1403 at 1404 (9th Cir 1974). In a Supreme Court *per curiam* decision in *Redmond* v *United States* 384 US 204 (1966) Mr Justice Stewart (joined by Mr Justice Black, Mr Justice Douglas concurring) was of the opinion that convictions involving private letters were unconstitutional (at 265). See also *Cox* v *United States* 370 F 2d 563 (9th Cir 1967). See generally Ludwig 'Private Correspondence Under the Mail Obscenity Law' 41 (1964) *Denver LCJ* 152: note 'Private Correspondence and Federal Obscenity Prosecution' 4 (1967) *San Diego L Rev* 76.

end of the nineteenth century been clearly challenged in only one case: *United States* v *Harmon*,[1] in 1891. The Supreme Court continued to assume that obscenity was outside the scope of First Amendment protection, and that therefore no constitutional question was raised.[2] The first court pronouncement specifically on the obscenity issues involved was handed down in 1879; in *United States* v *Bennett*, a Federal Court of Appeals had to consider the mailing of a copy of a book entitled *Cupid's Yokes, or the Binding Forces of Conjugal Life*; in so doing the court imported into American jurisprudence the *Hicklin* test, a formulation that was followed in a line of subsequent decisions.[3] The central aspects of the *Hicklin* test thus became established in federal jurisprudence: the effect of the material was central; the arousal of thoughts was sufficient to constitute corruption, subsequent conduct not being necessary.[4] Such effect was to be measured in terms of the most susceptible; in the process the material in question had not necessarily to be assessed as a whole. Literary merit was no defence, and expert evidence was inadmissible; the author's intention was similarly irrelevant.[5] Obscenity was a matter for the jury,[6] and a mere tendency to the effect in question was sufficient. There was general agreement also that words such as 'indecent', 'filthy', 'lascivious' and

---

1   45 F 414 at 416 (D Kan 1891) revd on other grounds 50 F 921 (1892).

2   See *ex parte Jackson* 96 US 727 (1877); *in re Rapier* 143 US 110 (1892); *Hoke* v *United States* 227 US 308 at 321 (1913); *Caminetti* v *United States* 242 US 470 (1917); *Brooks* v *United States* 267 US 432 at 437 (1925). In so doing, the Court showed little inclination to define such exception: in *Rosen* v *United States* for example Justice Harlan upheld the trial court test that material was obscene were it 'to suggest or convey lewd and lascivious thoughts to the young and inexperienced': 161 US 29 (1896) at 43. In the same year the Court, in the course of declaring that vulgarity was not synonymous with obscenity, quoted the traditional *Hicklin* test: material had an obscene tendency when 'calculated to corrupt and debauch the mind and morals of those into whose hands it might fall'. 161 US 446 (1896) at 451 *Swearingen* v *United States*.

3   For example, *United States* v *Chesman* 19 F 497 (CCES Mo 1881); *United States* v *Bebout* 28 F 522 (ND Ohio 1886); *United States* v *Wightman* 29 F 636 (D Pa 1887); *United States* v *Clarke* 38 F 500 (Ed Mo 1889); *United States* v *Harmon* 45 F 414 (D Kan 1891) (reversed on other grounds 50 F 921); *United States* v *Smith* 11 F 663 (CCkg 1882); *United States* v *Males* 51 F 41 (D Ind 1892); *Swearingen* v *United States* 161 US 446 at 451 (1896).

4   See e.g. *United States* v *One Book Entitled 'Contraception'* 51 F 2d 525 at 528 (SDNY 1931).

5   With such legislation it was not only the author's intention that was relevant; the Supreme Court in *Rosen* v *United States* 161 US 29 (1896) settled the issue: a mailer must know the character of the materials, even if he did not know that they were legally obscene, see *supra* note 2, p.365.

6   Cf. e.g. *United States* v *Clarke* 38 F 500 at 501 (Ed Mo 1892); *Rosen* v *United States* 161 US 29 at 42 (1896); *Dunlop* v *United States* 165 US 486 (1897).

'lewd' should be taken as synonymous for 'obscene',[1] whilst 'obscene' itself signified sexual impurity only.[2] Subjects such as violence or drug-taking were thus excluded, as was mere abuse,[3] blasphemy,[4] or vulgarity.[5]

As early as 1913 Judge Learned Hand in *United States* v *Kennerley*, although following the traditional test evidenced clear dissatisfaction with the traditional approach:

> ... I hope it is not improper for me to say that the rule as laid down, however consonant it may be with mid-Victorian morals, does not seem to me to answer to the understanding and morality of the present time. ... I question whether in the end men will regard that as obscene which is honestly relevant to the adequate expression of innocent ideas and whether they will not believe that truth and beauty are too precious to society at large to be mutilated in the interests of those most likely to pervert them to base uses. Indeed, it seems hardly likely that we are even today so lukewarm in our interest in letters or serious discussion as to be content to reduce our treatment of sex to the standard of a child's library in the supposed interest of a salacious few, or that shame will for long prevent us from the adequate portrayal of some of the most serious and beautiful sides of human

---

1 One statutory exception here was the amendment to the Comstock Act of 1908 to include 'matter of character tending to incite arson, murder or assassination' 35 Stat 416 (1908). Only a few courts have given the words 'filthy', 'indecent' or 'disgusting' a separate meaning: see e.g. *United States* v *Limehouse* 285 US 424 (1932).

2 See e.g. *Swearingen* v *United States* 161 US 446 (1896).

3 See *United States* v *Smith* 11 F 663 (CCKy 1882); rulings were not always consistent however: see e.g. *United States* v *Davis* 38 F 326 (W D Tenn 1889) (reference to someone as a 'radical' held obscene); *United States* v *Olney* 38 F 328 (W D Tenn 1889) (invitation 'to go to hell' held obscene).

4 See *United States* v *Moore* 104 F 78 (D Ky 1900).

5 See *Swearingen* v *United States* 161 US 446 (1896). It is clear, however, that the use of such language has had an important bearing on certain decisions: in *United States* v *Dennett* 39 F 2d 564 (2d Cir 1930) for example the 'decent' language of the sex instruction booklet involved was emphasised by the court, whilst conversely the language used in Henry Miller's *Tropic of Cancer* and *Tropic of Capricorn* undoubtedly played a part in the court's decision in *Besig* v *United States* 208 F 2d 142 (9th Cir 1953) that the works concerned were in fact obscene. Although not explicitly stated then, federal courts would appear to have adopted the approach of taking vulgarity into account in assessing obscenity, even though vulgarity was not *per se* obscene. This approach was clearly adopted in *United States* v *Rebhuhn* 109 F 2d 512 (2d Cir 1940) in relation to works consisting primarily or entirely of vulgarity; the same court nine years later seemed unable to solve the dilemma that 'the duller the book, the more its lewdness is to be excused or at least accepted': *Roth* v *Goldman* 172 F 2d 789 (2d Cir 1949).

nature ... Should not the word 'obscene' be allowed to indicate the critical point in the compromise between candor and shame at which the community may have arrived here and now? ... To put thought in leash to the average conscience of the time is perhaps tolerable, but to fetter it by the necessities of the lowest and least capable seems a fatal policy.[1]

Federal courts were not, however, to put such objections into operation until the 1930s,[2] the major break coming however with the *Ulysses* cases of 1933 and 1934: here the trial court clearly rejected the most susceptible person rule.[3] This was affirmed[4] by the Circuit Court of Appeals: assessment was to be effected in terms of the dominant effect[5] of a work on the average person,[6] taking account of the relevancy to theme of any 'objectionable' passages, the literary worth of the material (as attested by expert evidence) and the author's sincerity of purpose.[7] Federal courts had then arrived at very much the same position as had state courts in regard to obscenity; they appeared content moreover to accept the Supreme Court's exception approach at

---

1   209 F 119 (SD NY 1913) at 120–1.

2   The so-called 'community standards' test propounded by Judge Hand in *Kennerley* was not itself to be applied until 1940: see *Parmelee* v *United States* 109 F 2d 729 (DC Cir 1940).

3   *United States* v *One Book Called 'Ulysses'* 5 F Supp 182 (SD NY 1933) at 184; see also *Walker* v *Popenoe* 149 F 2d 511 at 512 (DC Cir 1945).

4   *United States* v *One Book Entitled 'Ulysses'* 72 F 2d 705 (2nd Cir 1934) at 708.

5   The dominant effect test is more generous than the book-as-a-whole approach, at least as followed in *Commonwealth* v *Isenstadt* 318 Mass 543, 62 NE 2d 840 (1945) for example: a book might well pass the dominant effect test and fail (in the light of objectionable passages) from the book-as-a-whole point of view (at least as applied by the Massachusetts courts). The federal courts would seem here to have allowed themselves something of a similar loophole, in that although only one of the factors to be taken into account in assessing the dominant effect, such disproportionate weight could be attached to a few isolated 'objectionable' passages in a work, as effectively to distort the dominant effect assessment. Take the remarks of the United States Court of Appeals for the Ninth Circuit in *Besig* v *United States* 208 F 2d 142 at 146 (9th Cir 1953): 'We agree that the book as a whole must be obscene to justify its libel and destruction, but neither the number of "objectionable" passages nor the proportion they bear to the whole book are controlling. If an incident, integrated with the theme or story of a book, is word-painted in such lurid and smutty or pornographic language that dirt appears as the primary purpose rather than the relation of a fact or adequate description of the incident, the book itself is obscene'.

6   The *Hicklin* test (if perhaps disguised) continued to appear: see e.g. *Burstein* v *United States* 178 F 2d 665 (9th Cir 1949); *United States* v *Two Obscene Books* 99 F Supp 760 (ND Calif 1951) affd *sub nom Besig* v *United States* 208 F 2d 142 (9th Cir 1953).

7   See e.g. *United States* v *Levine* 83 F 2d 156 (2nd Cir 1936); *Parmelee* v *United States* 113 F 2d 729 (DC Cir 1940); *Walker* v *Popenoe* 148 F 2d 511 (DC Cir 1945).

face value: as a result the question of the permissibility of the enforcement of morality, of the application of strict liability, and of overbreadth were, in First Amendment terms, seen as virtually irrelevant.

Despite the failure of federal courts to explore the potential constitutional angles in relation to obscenity, one of their number did display, in the midst of the piecemeal reforms outlined herein, a remarkable prescience with regard to the latter's future. Although such reforms may have accommodated shifts in community standards, the Supreme Court's strictures on the overbreadth of 'immorality' as a standard made unlikely any constitutionally approved definition of obscenity in terms of corruption. Any such definition handed down by the Supreme Court would probably then be in terms of a defined effect engendered by material dealing with human sexuality. The inducement of consequential action was most unlikely to be selected as the relevant effect; the choice very clearly would probably be in terms of thought arousal. Even if such a definition allowed a role for literary or artistic merit, what would the position be were community standards to shift once again, in the sense of not viewing so-called soft-core pornography — material without merit, and satisfying thought-arousal requirements — as obscene? Any definition of obscenity in the above terms would in effect have become ossified, no longer capable of accurately reflecting community standards; with the emphasis in English law on thought arousal, this is very much, despite apparent jury discretion, the position under the 1959 Obscene Publications Act. Probably with this type of development in mind, Judge Hand returned in *Parmelee* v *United States* to his so-called 'community standards' test first propounded in *United States* v *Kennerley*[1] in 1913; particularly in respect of pictorial matter, the court asked, 'Should not the word obscene be allowed to indicate the present critical point in the compromise between candor and shame at which the community may have arrived here and now?'[2]

The court was here perhaps anticipating the type of development and shifts in community standards which led the Supreme Court, after enunciating an obscenity definition in *Roth*,[3] to modify this only five years later in *Manual*[4] by adopting the patent offensiveness requirement, in effect thereby, in part at any rate, approving Judge Hand's 'critical point of compromise' formulation. This is to anticipate the

---

1   209 F 119 (SD NY 1913).

2   109 F 2d 512 at 514–5 (2d Cir 1940).

3   *Roth* v *United States* 354 US 476 (1954).

4   *Manual Enterprises* v *Day* 370 US 478 (1962).

Roth formulation, however: it is to this that we turn next.

11 The *Roth* test

An opportunity for the Supreme Court to pronounce in the obscenity area, other than merely to assert the exception approach, had gone by the board in *Doubleday and Co v New York*,[1] when the Court had divided evenly and (following tradition) had consequently not handed down an opinion. It was only in 1957 that the Court was to hand down its first important decision in the obscenity area in *Butler v Michigan*.[2] *Butler* was in fact originally brought as a test case involving the sale in Detroit of John J. Griffin's *The Devil Rides Outside*. The test the assistant prosecutor (as was his practice) applied in arriving at an assessment of the book was simple: if he did not want his young daughter to read the book, it was illegal.[3] At first instance, the constitutional arguments advanced were summarily dismissed, the constitutionality of the statute being upheld on the ground of the restriction being no more than a justifiable exercise of state police power to protect the health and welfare of citizens. The statute in question prohibited the publication of any book *containing* such material as might tend 'to incite minors to violent or depraved or immoral acts, manifestly tending to the corrup-

---

1 335 US 848 (1948).

2 352 US 380 (1957).

3 The prosecutor's daughter was eleven or twelve at the relevant time; see Lockhart and McClure 'Censorship of Obscenity: The Developing Constitutional Standards' 45 (1960) *Minnesota L Rev* 5 at 14–15.

tion of youth'.[1] Butler based his appeal to the Supreme Court on several constitutional grounds: that the statute violated the First and Fourteenth Amendments to the constitution of the United States for three reasons:

(a) it prohibited the sale to any adult of a book unsuitable for minors;
(b) its prohibitions were too vague and indefinite; and
(c) it precluded consideration of the work as a whole.

In an unanimous decision the Court, relying solely on his first point of appeal, reversed Butler's conviction. Mr Justice Frankfurter, delivering the opinion of the Court, after pointing out that the conviction was not based on a narrower Michigan statute specifically aimed at the sale of obscene material to children,[2] remarked:

> We have before us legislation not reasonably restricted to the evil with which it is said to deal. The incidence of this enactment is to reduce the adult population of Michigan to reading only what is fit for children. It thereby arbitrarily curtails one of those liberties of the individual, now enshrined in the Due Process Clause of the Fourteenth Amendment, that history has attested as the indispensable condition for the maintenance and progress of a free society.[3]

The decision was couched primarily in terms of substantive due process: Fourteenth Amendment due process (particularly in view of the preferred position of free speech) demands a rational connection between a statutory restriction and the governmental objective in question. In accepting that the restriction of the sale of material to adults merely because of its unsuitability for the immature did not demonstrate such a connection,[4] the Court was in fact adopting an approach initially canvassed in *State* v *Lerner*.[5] As far as First Amendment theory was concerned, the contribution of the decision was negligible, obscenity being implicitly taken as an exception to the general constitutional guarantee.

---

1 Michigan Penal Code S343; the statute (other than for the book as a whole point) was patterned on the pre-1945 Massachusetts statute, and was thus typical of many state obscenity statutes of this time.

2 *Mich Stat Cum* S750–142 and 750–143.

3 *Butler* v *Michigan* 352 US 380 (1957) at 383–4.

4 It was to be some time before all states fell into line with this constitutional ruling; see Lockhart and McClure op.cit. at 17–18.

5 81 NE 2d 282 (Ohio 1948): see chapter 10.

It was only in 1956 in two cases that were heard and decided together[1] that the Court finally reached the basic constitutional issues involved. Samuel Roth, a mail order dealer in erotica, sold through the New York City mails a monthly magazine called *Good Times, a Review of the World of Pleasure*, and a quarterly magazine called *American Aphrodite*. He was eventually indicted (in a twenty-six count indictment) for violating the federal statute[2] by mailing obscene matter (and advertisements for such matter). At the trial, the judge defined obscenity for the jury as

> that form of immorality which has relation to sexual impurity and has a tendency to excite lustful thoughts ... The matter must be calculated to corrupt and debauch the minds and morals of those into whose hands it may fall. It must tend to stir sexual impulses and lead to sexually impure thoughts.[3]

The material was to be judged as a whole, and the most susceptible person test was not to apply in determining its effect; literary value was ignored. On this basis, Roth was convicted, and the conviction was upheld by the Court of Appeals.[4] On appeal, four main issues were raised: whether the federal statute contravened First Amendment guarantees; whether it was too vague to satisfy due process requirements; whether it contravened the First, Ninth and Tenth Amendments by usurping powers reserved to the states and the people; and finally, whether the publications in question were in fact obscene or not. The Court limited the writ to the first of these three.

David Alberts and his wife Violet operated (out of Los Angeles) a business very similar to Roth's, the only distinction being that their material had no pretensions — as did Roth's — to any literary merit whatever.[5] They were charged with advertising and selling obscene materials in violation of the California obscenity statute, which did not attempt a definition of obscenity, but merely provided that:

> Every person who wilfully and lewdly, either ...
> 3. ... keeps for sale or exhibits any obscene or indecent writing, paper or book ... or

---

1   *People* v *Alberts, United States* v *Roth* 354 US 476 (1957); for an in-depth analysis of these cases see Lockhart and McClure op.cit. at 19ff.

2   18 USC 1461 (1958).

3   Record at 25–6; quoted in Lockhart and McClure op.cit. at 20.

4   *United States* v *Roth* 237 F 2d 796 (2d Cir 1956).

5   For a description of the relevant materials see Lockhart and McClure op.cit. at 23–4.

4. ... publishes any notice or advertisement of any such writing, paper, book, picture, print or figure;

6. ... is guilty of a misdemeanour.[1]

Alberts[2] was convicted, and the conviction was affirmed by the appellate department of the superior court.[3] The obscenity standard employed by the trial court is by no means clear: reference was made to dictionary definitions of obscenity, the *Hicklin* test, and the formula given in *Ulysses*. The court also referred to a decision of the appellate court, *People* v *Wepplo*, in which obscenity had been defined as that which 'has a substantial tendency to deprave or corrupt its reader by inciting lascivious thoughts or arousing lustful desires'.[4] Which of these was actually applied, the court did not specify. In the Supreme Court Alberts raised the same basic issues as had Roth; once again the obscenity of the particular publications was not reached,[5] and the Court was faced with two basic issues:[6] whether the federal and Californian obscenity statutes '*on their faces and in a vacuum* violated the freedom of expression and the definiteness guarantees of the United States Constitution'.[7] The stage was thus set at last for a definitive pronouncement by the Court on obscenity and First Amendment theory. Definitive the opinion of the Court was, but to most First Amendment theoreticians, probably disappointing. In outlining the issue before the Court, Mr Justice Brennan (delivering the majority opinion) presaged the choice by the Court of perhaps the crudest of all free speech theories so far advanced: 'The dispositive question is whether obscenity is utterance within the area of protected speech and

---

1   *Calif. Penal Code Ann* S311 (1955).

2   Mrs Alberts was acquitted on the ground that she had acted under her husband's direction.

3   *People* v *Alberts* 138 Cal App 2d 909, 292 P 2d 90 (1955).

4   78 Cal App 2d 959T 178 P 2d 853 (1947).

5   The Court was not entirely without a point of practical reference though: the Solicitor-General pleaded that there were three categories of material caught by the federal statute: (a) 'novels of apparently serious literary intent' caught because of explicit sexual description: these constituted less than 2 per cent of items founding convictions under the statute; (b) borderline material: primarily photographic – this accounted for less than 10 per cent; and (c) hard-core pornography, constituting perhaps 90 per cent of material in question. 'Then to make sure the Court understood what he meant by "hard-core pornography", the Solicitor-General sent to the Court a carton containing numerous samples of actual hard-core pornography'; Lockhart and McClure op.cit. at 26.

6   Alberts raised the question whether the statute as applied to the mails, infringed a federal preserve; this and the federalism issue raised by Roth, are not relevant here.

7   Lockhart and McClure at 25 (emphasis in original).

press'.[1] This question the Court decided in much the same way as it had in the past: obscenity was assumed to be beyond constitutional control. Although 'All ideas even having the slightest redeeming social importance — unorthodox ideas, controversial ideas, even ideas hateful to the prevailing climate of opinion'[2] — are protected, utterances that 'form no essential part of any exposition of ideas'[3] are not. Obscenity, which is 'utterly without redeeming social importance',[4] falls into the latter category, and is therefore not constitutionally protected.

The Court's reasoning here is open to criticism on a number of grounds:[5] it appears to make an assumption of infallibility with regard to obscenity and its social worth; such material might be argued to embody views that are inimical to established norms of sexual conduct, and may not be completely without worth in the sense of dealing in ideas. Second, the ruling appears to regard the First Amendment as based solely on the market place of ideas concept; equally basic may be the ideal of freedom of individual development. Pornography may be argued to aid certain individuals in this regard. Third, the social value reasoning presumably meant that material with *any* such value would fall within First Amendment protection: it might possibly be open in these terms to argue the psychotherapeutic value of certain materials. Fourth, the approach inevitably concentrates attention on the permissible definition of obscenity: as decisions in terms of this definition have a constitutional status, they presumably would, as Mr Justice Harlan pointed out in *Roth*, be open to Supreme Court review. Not only would this place an unreasonable burden on the Court, but it would tend towards a constancy of the decision from which the Court might in later years wish to escape. In these terms, any consideration of governmental aims behind obscenity controls, and their permissibility in First Amendment terms was clearly superfluous.

The dissenting opinions in *Roth* are perhaps some 'index of the unpersuasive quality of the majority opinion and the full complexity of the issue presented to the Court'.[6] Perhaps the most interesting dissent came from Justice Harlan, whose misgivings about the majority app-

---

1   *Roth* v *United States* 354 US 476 (1957) at 481.

2   Ibid. at 484.

3   *Chaplinsky* v *New Hampshire* 315 US 568 (1942); quoted by the court in *Roth* ibid. at 485.

4   *Roth* op.cit. at 484.

5   See chapter 14 for a fuller discussion of the exception approach and First Amendment theory generally.

6   H. Kalven 'The Metaphysics of the Law of Obscenity' 1960 *Supr Crt Rev* 1 at 17.

roach were made clear in his opening sentence: 'I find lurking beneath its disarming generalisations a number of problems which ... leave me with serious misgivings as to the future effect of today's discussion'.[1] His basic objection to the majority view was that it avoided, and would allow avoidance in the future, of the basic constitutional issue:

> This sweeping formula appears to me to beg the very question before us. The Court seems to assume that 'obscenity' is a peculiar genus of 'speech and press', which is as distinct, and classifiable as poison ivy is among other plants. On this basis the *constitutional* question before us simply becomes, as the Court says, whether 'obscenity', as an abstraction, is protected by the First and Fourteenth Amendments, and the question whether a *particular* book may be suppressed becomes a mere matter of classification, of 'fact', to be entrusted to a fact finder and insulated from independent constitutional judgement.[2]

Justice Harlan had never favoured the incorporation of the First Amendment with regard to the states; his answer to the constitutional problem probably reflects this: a distinction should be drawn, he argued, between the application of the First Amendment to the states, and its application to federal authority. The former, he argued, should be less stringent than the latter. He therefore concurred in *Alberts*, remarking:

> Nothing in the Constitution requires California to accept as truth the most advanced and sophisticated psychiatric opinion. It seems to me clear that it is not irrational in our present state of knowledge, to consider that pornography can induce a type of sexual conduct which a state may deem obnoxious to the moral fabric of society.[3]

Justice Harlan would therefore allow state regulation of obscenity provided that such regulation was not irrationally based; that is, mere substantive due process would apply. There does appear to be an additional (implied) restraint in that the exercise of police power would appear to be limited (in this area) to control of conduct, and not of thoughts; this restriction is (in Judge Harlan's formulation) more theoretical than real, as an assumption of a casual connection between obscene material and conduct is not felt to be irrational (and therefore

---

1 *Roth* v *United States* 354 US 476 (1957) at 496.

2 Ibid. at 497 (emphasis in original).

3 Ibid. at 501–2.

unconstitutional). He also goes on to state that even if subsequent conduct cannot be shown, a state may validly restrict the distribution of obscene materials on the ground that they erode the moral fabric of society. He appears to be the only member of the Court to deal, aside from its specific *Butler* application, with the due process demands of a rational connection between permissible governmental aim and the regulation in question. In view of his opposition to incorporation, his view of the constitutionality of state regulation of obscenity is perhaps best seen in due process terms. If seen in terms of the First Amendment, his formula amounts to no more than the old bad tendency test, first formulated in *Gitlow* v *New York*, and long since discarded, in terms of which a state '... in the exercise of its police power may punish those who abuse this freedom of speech by utterances inimical to the public welfare, tending to corrupt public morals, incite to crime, or disturb the public peace, ...'.[1]

This can hardly be seen as adequate in First Amendment terms: insofar as it merely restates due process demands, it renders the Amendment virtually superfluous. Justice Harlan would appear, viewing his state formulation in First Amendment terms, to be rejecting the two-tier or exception approach. His attitude to federal regulation was in this respect less than clear: here the approach is in terms of vagueness rather than social values: the federal statute in *Roth* was unconstitutional (argued Judge Harlan) because it was so widely couched as to cover what might well be protected speech. What may be proscribed is cryptically described as 'hard-core pornography'. Implicit in this is an acceptance (in this area, at any rate) of the Court's classification of obscenity as an exception to First Amendment protection.[2] Besides the inadequacy of the bad tendency approach, and his rather glib assumption of a due process rational connection, this approach is open to a number of criticisms: first, it would probably prove an unnecessary complication to have to decide not only which articles of the Bill of Rights are incorporated into the Fourteenth Amendment (a task the Court has found difficult enough as it is), but also to decide how much of each one is so incorporated.[3] Second, no First Amendment reconciliation is offered with federal restrictions at all, whilst in addition the term 'hard-core pornography' is not defined.

In terms of the majority approach, considerations of policy aims permissible in First Amendment or due process terms was largely

---

1   268 US 652 (1927) at 667; see chapter 14.

2   This despite his apparent rejection of this approach; ibid. at 507.

3   Mr Justice Harlan had himself always opposed the concept of incorporation.

avoided: the Court declined to elucidate on the meaning of 'without social value', for example. In the same way the admission by the court of thought arousal as being sufficient might point towards governmental objectives such as safeguarding moral welfare; this is by no means explicit, and cannot relieve the Court of the burden of closer identification. In fact, not a single member of the majority in *Roth* would appear to have identified the values or objectives in question,[1] other than a rather vague assertion that any benefit that may be derived from obscene utterances '... *is clearly outweighed by the social interest in order and morality*'.[2] In this regard the exception approach would appear to differ radically from most other First Amendment theory developed by the Court, all of which appears to involve (to one extent or another) a roughly utilitarian approach in that elucidation (in varying degrees) of governmental aims and the harm to be avoided is required, if only in the sense that a connection between the policy aim in question and the restriction need be shown.[3] As a result, aside from the *Butler* ruling, no consideration was given to the question of the necessary relationship between such aims as might be advanced and the regulations in question; elucidation of such relationships in the absence of an exploration of the relevant aims was hardly possible. As far as Justices Black and Douglas were concerned, such considerations were, in view of the absolute nature of the First Amendment ('Congress shall make no law ...'), irrelevant. Any weighing of policy aims, or the creation of exceptions to the Amendment were in their view no answer to a clear statement that speech should be free.[4]

The exception approach adopted by the majority does not however permit the complete avoidance of policy issues and their accommodation to First Amendment concerns. As obscenity is an exception to the constitutional guarantee, attention immediately and inevitably fastens on its definition. The traditional view was that the application of any such definition was a determination of fact, and therefore a matter for a jury. As Justice Harlan's dissent points out, once a definition of obscenity has received constitutional status, unless the constitutional issue is to be relegated to a back seat, such determination can no longer be left with a jury. In other words, the Court, by adopting the exception approach, has not avoided the problems of balancing conflicting

---

1   See note 'More Ado About Dirty Books' 75 (1966) *Yale LJ* 1364; Elias 'Sex Publications and Moral Corruption: The Supreme Court Dilemma' 9 (1967) *Wm and M L Rev* 392.

2   *Roth* v *United States* 354 US 476 (1957) at 484–5 (emphasis in the original).

3   See chapter 14.

4   *Roth* v *United States* 354 US 476 (1957) at 514; see further chapter 14.

interests. Instead of the Court engaging in a process of constitutional balancing with regard to obscenity *statutes*, the application of which and balancing inherent therein being left to a jury, it must now in *each case* determine obscenity as a constitutional issue. Instead of the Court first balancing freedom of speech against governmental objectives with regard to the statute, the jury then balancing the obscenity of the publication against its literary merit (and other such factors) in applying the statute, the processes have been elided into one. The exception approach by no means eliminates balancing;[1] what it does do is to allow the avoidance, by focusing attention on a definition, of any explicit statement of governmental aims.

And what of the question of overbreadth? The exception approach focuses attention on the definition of obscenity; any overbreadth inherent in the latter should be subject, in terms of Fourteenth Amendment due process and the First Amendment, to the closest scrutiny. Previously the Court had simply affirmed obscenity as an exception to the First Amendment, without offering a constitutionally approved definition of the former; this time overbreadth considerations proved too demanding, and the Court finally entered the obscenity arena, handing down a definition of obscenity substantially similar to that advanced by the American Law Institute: 'Whether to the average person, applying contemporary community standards, the dominant theme of the material taken as a whole, appeals to the prurient interest'.[2] As far as overbreadth was concerned, 'All that is required is that the language of the statute conveys sufficiently definite warning as to the proscribed conduct when measured by common understanding and practices'.[3] The definition of obscenity formulated, the Court felt, fulfilled these requirements. It remained to be seen whether the definition, as interpreted and applied, would satisfy overbreadth criticisms any more than had its state and federal jurisdiction predecessors. Interpretation of the test might well affect also the basic exception approach, particularly in terms of the potential difficulties in relation to the latter mentioned earlier. Any instability in relation to the basic exception approach might in turn of course jeopardise the Court's position of avoiding the basic policy questions at issue here, either in terms of governmental aims, or their necessary relationship to obscenity

---

1   In fact it may oblige the Court to engage in balancing, whereas under the balancing test the Court might in fact avoid this duty altogether: this would be the case where the Court defers to the relevant legislative determination.

2   *Roth* v *United States* 354 US 476 (1957) at 489; cf. at 487 and footnote 20, citing the ALI Model Penal Code S207.10(1) (Tent. draft no. 6 (1957).

3   Ibid. at 491; quoting *United States* v *Petrillo* 323 US 1 (1947).

regulations. We turn now to examine the *Roth* definition, as interpreted; this may perhaps conveniently be done under the following heads:

I)   Applicability

1   *Forms of speech*

Obscenity regulation may apply to any form of speech, whether written, pictorial, in film form, or any other; material consisting of the written word is not constitutionally excepted.

2   *Intention*

As far as the publisher's intention was concerned, the position remained somewhat murky: federal courts would appear to have required a literal intention to publish, and to have presumed a knowledge of the law; although intention as to obscenity was not required, knowledge of the nature of the material was. State courts appear to have adopted the same approach, but to have been divided on the latter point. *Roth* left the constitutional position open. Chief Justice Warren (dissenting) in *Roth*, laid particular emphasis on the defendant's intentions, rather than on the nature of the material, more specifically noting that both defendants were '... plainly engaged in the commercial exploitation of the morbid and shameful craving for materials with a prurient effect'.[1] What the Chief Justice appears to have been proposing here is that for liability, a publisher should not only have intention as to obscenity, but also in fact have as his object commercial gain. In raising the relevance of a commercial motive, the Chief Justice was attempting to reopen a question apparently already settled: that the profit motive should be irrelevant.[2] Although his views were not accepted in *Roth*, they were partially followed in *Ginzburg* v *United States*[3] some nine years later. Here the Supreme Court affirmed the relevance of pandering:[4] in other words, where pornography is sold in a commercially exploitative manner, this may be taken into account in assessing the prurient appeal of the material. The Court did not adopt the Chief Justice's view in *Roth* that such a motive should be, in effect, a require-

---

1   *Roth* v *United States* 354 US 476 (1957) at 496.

2   See p.359.

3   383 US 863 (1966).

4   On pandering, see the section on effect, below.

ment for a finding of obscenity.

Although the author's intention had been accepted as relevant, together with literary merit, in assessing a work's obscenity or non-obscenity, both state and federal courts continued to assume that intention as to obscenity was not necessary for publication.[1] This issue, in view of the fact that virtually all obscenity statutes operated primarily in terms of publication,[2] was clearly a central one. It also involves the question of the desirability, in terms of criminal jurisprudence, of the imposition of partial strict liability, particularly in a potential First Amendment area. The issue of intention first came before the Court in 1959 in *Smith* v *California*.[3] Eleazar Smith had been convicted under a Los Angeles ordinance making it a crime for anyone to have in his possession, for sale, any obscene or indecent writing or book. On appeal, he raised a number of issues, amongst them the assertion that the ordinance was bad because it did not require intention on the publisher's part. The majority opinion (by Mr Justice Brennan), in view of the fact that the Court had already upheld strict liability in relation to drug legislation,[4] could not declare the statute's operation unfair to the bookseller. The opinion was couched rather in First Amendment terms: if the statute were upheld the publisher would '... tend to restrict the books he sells to those he has inspected: and thus the state will have imposed a restriction upon the distribution of constitutionally protected as well as obscene literature'.[5] Although the Court was clearly conscious of the chilling effect on speech of not requiring *mens rea*, it was not prepared to go so far as to define just what in the form of intention was required; in striking the Los Angeles ordinance down, it opted for a requirement of knowledge as to the nature of the material.[6] The apparent doubt left in this respect in Smith has since been resolved: in *Hamling* v *United States*[7] the Court specifically affirmed that

---

1 See note 'The Scienter Requirement in Criminal Obscenity Prosecutions' 41 (1966) *NYUL Rev* 791.

2 Possession was, however, very often sufficient: see note 'More Ado About Dirty Books' 75 (1966) *Yale LJ* 1364 at 1410 (Appendix II); also the section on possession, below.

3 361 US 147 (1959).

4 *United States* v *Balint* 258 US 250 (1922).

5 *Smith* v *California* 361 US 147 (1959) at 153; see F. Schauer 'Fear, Risk and the First Amendment: Unravelling the Chilling Effect' 58 (1978) *Boston UL Rev* 685 at 719.

6 See also *Rosen* v *United States* 161 US 29 (1896).

7 418 US 87 (1974).

It is constitutionally sufficient that the prosecution show that a defendant had knowledge of the contents of the materials he distributed, and that he knew of the character and nature of the materials. To require proof of a defendant's knowledge of the legal status of the materials would permit the defendant to avoid prosecution by simply claiming that he had not brushed up on the law. Such a formulation of the scienter requirement is required by neither the language of 18 USC 1461 nor the Constitution.[1]

A number of state laws were altered following *Smith*: in most cases the courts merely construed the regulation in question as incorporating a requirement of intention or scienter as to the nature of the material.[2] What the court has not discussed is the chilling effect of applying strict liability as to the question of obscenity; to refuse the requirement of full *mens rea* is surely to admit, implicitly, the overbreadth of the obscenity standard.

3   Publication/possession

With most state statutes,[3] and federal restrictions, possession was generally sufficient for liability; this the *Roth* holding left undisturbed. The penalisation of possession raised potentially the question of the individual right to privacy;[4] it was nonetheless not until 1967 that the Court first alluded to such relevance: in a *per curiam* decision in *Redrup* v *New York*[5] the Court, in indicating a preference for minimal restriction, emphasised (*inter alia*) the central nature of privacy to restriction, in the sense that individuals are entitled to protection from unwilling exposure to material. It was not long before the *Redrup* hint at the significance attached by the Court to privacy in the obscenity area bore some more tangible fruit. In 1969 in *Stanley* v *Georgia*,[6] the court reversed Stanley's conviction under a Georgia statute for the possession of obscene matter, the matter in question being three reels of 8mm film found in his home during the course of a police search into his alleged

---

1   418 US 87 at 123–4.

2   See e.g. *Hamling* v *United States* 418 US 87 (1974) construing 18 USC 1461. As to the difficulties of proof in regard to intention, see Schauer op.cit. at 224–6; also note *NYU L Rev*, op.cit.

3   See note 'Much Ado About Dirty Books' 75 (1966) *Yale LJ* 1364, Appendix II.

4   For a fuller discussion, see privacy, chapter 5, also chapter 14.

5   385 US 767 (1967).

6   394 US 557 (1969).

bookmaking activities. The Court, in an opinion written by Mr Justice Marshall, declared that 'mere private possession of obscene matter cannot constitutionally be made a crime'.[1] The judgement, based principally on the First Amendment, disclaimed any wholesale repudiation of *Roth*; rather, the obscenity exception laid down in *Roth* was held to apply to commercial distribution of obscenity, and not to its private possession. This raised two difficulties: (a) The Court did not make its attitude towards the 'exception' approach clear: was it creating an exception to an exception? In other words, was obscenity an exception to First Amendment protection, and therefore subject to restriction, with the exception of obscenity merely in private possession? Or was it narrowing the *Roth* exception down radically, in the sense that obscenity *was* now protected, other than when commercially distributed?[2] (b) Whatever the answer, even more significant was the Court's attitude to any exception which might exist. The Court had so far carefully avoided any pronouncement on the justifications for obscenity laws: the *Roth* exception approach made all this technically unnecessary. This attitude Mr Justice Marshall now abandoned: whilst purporting to accept (in one form or another) the exception approach, he proceeded to explain why the restriction of private possession of obscenity fell foul of the First Amendment. Such expression was protected because

> (i) a causal connection between it and action ('deviant sexual behaviour or crimes of sexual violence') cannot be shown:
>
> 'given the present state of knowledge, the state may no more prohibit mere possession of obscenity on the grounds that it may lead to antisocial conduct than it may prohibit possession of chemistry books on the ground that they may lead to the manufacture of home-made spirits.'[3]
>
> (ii) in the absence of evidence of such casual connection (thereby justifying restriction in terms of subsequent action), restriction may not be based on moral censure of a person's thoughts:
>
> 'Whatever the power of the state to control public dissemination of ideas inimical to the public morality, it cannot

---

1   394 US 557 (1969) at 559.

2   See Katz 'Privacy and Pornography: Stanley v Georgia' (1969) *Supr Crt Rev* 203 at 210—11. It may well be that the latter was intended: 'This right to receive information and ideas, regardless of their social worth ... is fundamental to our free society': per Marshall J, ibid. at 564.

3   *Stanley v Georgia* 394 US 557 (1969) at 559.

constitutionally premise legislation on the desirability of controlling a person's private thoughts.'[1]

Because no justification existed for the control of private possession of obscenity, only the commercial distribution of such material should be restricted. A number of justifications were cited:

(i) the protection of juveniles;
(ii) the obtrusion into the privacy of the general public, presumably in the sense that although unwilling, a person might be forced to look at or hear objectionable material.

The opinion followed closely the pointer in *Redrup*; the emphasis had shifted away from the effect of the material or its nature, and emphasised rather the protection of privacy, the commercial exploitation aspect, whether adults are consenting or not, and the protection of children. This in turn opened the way for the virtual removal of obscenity controls: if sales of material did not affect minors, and the adults concerned were consenting, could restriction be justified merely in terms of commercial exploitation? A Massachusetts federal court (for example) took the view that it could not:

> It is difficult to think that if Stanley has a constitutional right to view obscene films, the Court would intend its exercise to be only at the expense of a criminal act on behalf of the only logical source, the professional supplier? ... If a rich Stanley can view a film or read a book, in his home, a poorer Stanley should be free to visit a protected theater or library. We see no reason for saying that he must go alone.[2]

In these terms there can be little relevance for an aspect such as pandering, with its emphasis on effect. Indeed, the entire *Roth* formulation (as elaborated by later cases) must fall away; in proscription terms, effect and nature of material are irrelevant: the rejection by the Court of the action and morality justifications ensure this. Justifications are now in terms of individual consent, or the protection of juveniles, neither of which require the elaborate *Roth* structure.[3] Although the boundary between private possession and commercial distribution was not clearly defined, the inference undoubtedly was that commercial distribution where it affected

---

1   394 US 557 (1969) at 559.

2   *Karalexis* v *Bryne* 306 F Supp 1363 (D Mass 1969).

3   Restriction in terms of minors could be essayed in terms of a definition of minors' rights under the First Amendment, for example.

privacy[1] or juveniles, was proscribable, but that otherwise restrictions would probably be unlawful — as for example where material is seized under customs regulations, even though it is destined only for private perusal by an adult.

II) The standard applied

1) *Effect*

(i) *Its nature*. Thoughts rather than conduct were apparently regarded as a sufficient effect: the court in *Roth* defined — in a footnote — material appealing to the prurient interest as 'material having a tendency to excite lustful thoughts', and went on to cite a dictionary definition of 'prurient': '... itching; longing; uneasy; with desire or longing; of persons, having itching, morbid, or lascivious longings; of desire, curiosity, or propensity, lewd ...'.[2] Mr Justice Harlan pointed out that the American Law Institute expressly rejected 'the prevailing test of obscenity of tendency to arouse lustful thoughts or desires'[3] as being too broad. Presumably then, the majority, in adopting the ALI test, regarded the old test as unconstitutional? This is not expressly stated, it is rather merely remarked that 'the prurient test' supplies adequate safeguards.[4] Insofar as the court upheld convictions under the old lustful thoughts variety of test, whilst at the same time apparently regarding the new test as the constitutional standard, there is apparently something of a contradiction here in *Roth* and *Alberts*; unless of course the court simply disregarded the distinction drawn in this respect by the Law Institute. Certainly Justice Brennan would appear to have equated the new test with the lustful thoughts variety of test established in case law.[5]

One clear constitutional result of the majority opinion was that in view of the prurient interest ruling, obscenity relates to human sexuality only; the constitutionality of statutes prohibiting mere vulgarity or depictions of violence could not be based on the obscenity exception, an argument that had previously been potentially an open one. This was confirmed by the court in *Cohen* v

---

1 See especially privacy, chapter 5; also chapter 14.

2 *Roth* v *United States* 354 US 476 (1957) at 487, footnote 20.

3 Ibid. at 499.

4 Ibid. at 489.

5 See Lockhart and McClure op.cit. at 56—7.

California[1] in 1971; in relation to a conviction for the wearing in a court house lobby of tee-shirts bearing the inscription 'Fuck the draft', the Court remarked:

> This is not ... an obscenity case. Whatever else may be necessary to give rise to the State's broader power to prohibit obscene expression, such expression must be, in some significant way, erotic ... It cannot plausibly be maintained that this vulgar allusion to the selection system would conjure up such psychic stimulation in anyone likely to be confronted with Cohen's crudely defaced jacket.

The Court could have approached the case from a narrower standpoint: that such offensiveness may constitutionally be restricted, unless perhaps it is used in connection with some ideas, political or otherwise; this would have meant the admission of controls on offensiveness, rather than obscenity, something the Court was not prepared to do.[2]

The Court had predictably avoided a definition of obscenity which explicitly allowed decision in terms of immorality. The standard, as a result, did not exhibit the same overbreadth as does its English counterpart, for although emphasis in the law with the latter is on thought arousal, the jury still apparently retains discretion in terms of 'corruption'. As the emphasis shifts more and more to pornography, written and bought for titillation, so the effect in terms of thought arousal, comes closer in distribution terms to being a constant. As was argued in the previous chapter, Judge Hand may well have foreseen the possible ossification of the law in these terms, thus recommending a critical point of community compromise test. This trend towards constancy for the effect factor was accentuated by the adoption in 1966 in *Ginzburg* v *United States*[3] of the concept of pandering. Ralph Ginzburg, a New York publisher, announced in 1961 (with the mailing of five million advertisements) the publication of *Eros*, 'The magazine of sexual candour, which has been made possible as a "result of recent court decisions that have realistically interpreted America's obscenity laws and that have given to this country a new breadth of freedom of expression" '.[4] In 1963 Ginzburg was indicted under 18 USC Section 1461 for the publication, not only of *Eros*, but also *Liaison*, a

---

1   403 US 15 (1971).

2   See zoning, chapter 12, and offensiveness, chapter 14.

3   383 US 463 (1966).

4   P. Magrath 'The Obscenity Cases: Grapes of Roth' *1966 Supr Crt Rev* 7 at 25, quoting *Eros* advertising brochure.

bi-monthly newsletter dealing with sex, and a book entitled *The Housewife's Handbook on Selective Promiscuity*, which purported to be 'A woman's candid sexual autobiography from age three to thirty-six'.[1] The subsequent Supreme Court ruling was the first in which a finding of obscenity was upheld by the Court, and also the first majority opinion in an obscenity case since *Roth*. Mr Justice Brennan (joined by Chief Justice Warren, and Justices Clark, Fortas and White) gave the opinion of the Court. The materials clearly were not without some social value, nor was there any showing of patent offensiveness; despite their appeal to the prurient interest, they should have been found not obscene. Instead, the Court adopted the view that the conduct of the defendant is central to the resolution of any obscenity hearing. According to Justice Brennan, Ginzburg was 'engaged in the sordid business of pandering'; this he defined by quoting Chief Justice Warren's opinion in *Roth*: '... the business of purveying textual or graphic matter openly advertised to appeal to the erotic interest of their customers'.[2]

Chief Justice Warren's suggestion in *Roth* that 'the conduct of the defendant is the central issue, not the obscenity of a book or picture',[3] was not accepted; commercial exploitation, re-emphasised in *Stanley*, was not essential for a finding of obscenity, but was at least relevant to it. Pandering was to be relevant to a determination of obscenity in that the advertisement or portrayal of the material as erotic '... stimulated the reader to accept them [the materials in question] as prurient; he looks for titillation, not for saving intellectual content'.[4] The Court was not prepared to break with *Roth*; pandering if it was to be relevant had to be dovetailed into the *Roth* formulation. This was attempted by arguing its relevance to the arousal of prurient interest, the manner of publication[5] putting the audience in the mood to have their prurient interest stimulated. Pandering was in effect an attempt on the Court's part to provide an alternative to the increased emphasis placed (via the value factor and patent offensiveness requirement) on the nature of the material. Professors Lockhart and McClure were some of the first to canvass the concept of pandering, but only in a peripheral

---

1   Magrath, op.cit. at 27. Despite the titles, there was considerable expert evidence led at to the trial as to the value and serious purpose of the works in question.

2   *Ginzburg v United States* 383 US 463 (1966) at 467; 354 US 476 at 485–96.

3   Ibid. at 475.

4   Ibid. at 470.

5   For examples of the varieties of marketing technique (or manner of distribution) relevant here, see Schauer *The Law of Obscenity* 84–5.

way;[1] they pointed out that the average person standard involved difficulties: with it, material appealing to the prurient interest of particular groups, such as minors or deviants, could not be found obscene. This they proposed to remedy by rendering material's obscenity variable, in the sense of taking into account, with particular distribution, the appeal it might have to the group in question. They also proposed that restriction be limited to hard-core pornography: this raised problems, as material not classifiable as hard-core might nonetheless well appeal to the prurient interest of the young. This point they attempted to cover by describing material in question as being 'treated' — by its publisher — as hard-core pornography. They did not develop the pandering aspect further than this. An alternative argument for the relevance of pandering, also taking as its point of departure the manner of marketing or distribution, infers from this not a susceptibility to prurient interest stimulation, but rather an intention on the part of the publisher to purvey pornography or obscenity; he is then estopped from denying these conclusions: '... where the purveyor's sole emphasis is on the sexually provocative aspects of his publications, a court could accept his evaluation at face value'.[2] The authority cited by Mr Justice Brennan in support of the relevance of pandering was scanty; he felt that a 1940s Court of Appeals decision, *United States* v *Rebhuhn*[3] was 'a persuasive authority for our conclusions';[4] *Rebhuhn* had involved a prosecution for sending obscene materials through the mails. The advertising for the materials in question the Court of Appeals found, were appeals 'merely to catch the prurient ... The books were not obscene *per se*; they had a proper use, but the defendants woefully misused them, and it was that misuse which constituted the *gravamen* of the crime.[5]

Rebhuhn was not mentioned in *Roth*, where thirteen cases were cited as examples of the approved obscenity formula;[6] to regard *Rebhuhn* as settling the question of pandering seems questionable. Pandering was, moreover, to be of relevance only in 'close cases'; quite what this meant is obscure: did it mean (as the *Ginzburg* opinion appears to imply) that a work that had prurient appeal and was

---

1   See Lockhart and McClure 'Censorship of Obscenity: The Developing Constitutional Standards' 45 (1960) *Minnesota L Rev* 5 at 68—88.

2   *Memoirs* v *Massachusetts* 383 US 413 (1966) at 420.

3   109 F 2d 512 (2d Cir 1940).

4   *Ginzburg* v *United States* 383 US 463 (1966) at 472.

5   *United States* v *Rebhuhn* 109 F 2d 512 (2d Cir 1940) at 514—5.

6   354 US 476 (1957) at 489, note 26.

patently offensive, but perhaps had some social value, could be proscribed under the pandering concept? This was to do violence to the basic *Roth* 'utterly without social value' formulation as elaborated in *Manual* and *Jacobellis*.[1] What may have been meant was that a work which has no value, and has prurient appeal, may be proscribed despite an absence of patent offensiveness.[2] Both Justice Stewart and Justice Harlan strenuously dissented from the majority view on pandering, principally on the ground that the materials in question were not hard-core pornography, not being patently offensive, and having some social value. Mr Justice Douglas' dissent, whilst reiterating his stand that the First Amendment protects all speech, dismissed with a trenchant comment the pandering concept:

> This new exception to the First Amendment condemns an advertising technique as old as history. The advertisements of our best magazines are chock-full of thighs, calves, bosoms, eyes, and hair, to draw the potential buyer's attention to lotions, tyres, food, liquor, clothing, autos, and even insurance policies. The sexy advertisement neither adds to nor detracts from the quality of the merchandise being offered for sale. And I do not see how it adds to or detracts one whit from the legality of the book being distributed. A book should stand on its own, irrespective of the reasons why it was written or the wiles used in selling it. I cannot imagine any promotional effort that would make chapters 7 and 8 of the Song of Solomon any the less or any more worthy of First Amendment protection than does its unostentatious inclusion in the average edition of the Bible.[3]

Justice Douglas' comment does not appear unreasonable: the justifications advanced for the relevance of pandering appear to be little more than excuses for the Court to find relevant in an obscenity assessment the commercial exploitation factor. The argument that pandering is relevant in terms of its relationship to prurient appeal is without any real foundation: it is difficult to imagine that in any close case, prurient appeal would not already be present. It was to narrow down the test beyond the presence of such appeal that the patent offensiveness requirement was introduced. The estoppel justification amounts to no more than an indirect disapproval of commercial exploitation

---

1   See Section (II)(2) below.

2   For the procedural problems raised by pandering, see Schauer *The Law of Obscenity* at 86–7.

3   *Ginzburg* v *United States* 383 US 463 (1966) at 482–3.

in this area.[1] Although pandering is in practice a mechanism of variability in relation to obscenity determination, in terms of the court's prurient appeal reasoning, it is rather an agency tending to promote a constant result with regard to the latter.[2]

(ii)   *Distribution.* Many jurisdictions (New York, for example) were via either statute or court ruling, still applying the most susceptible person approach. *Butler* ruled this unconstitutional on due process grounds; this was clearly sustained in First Amendment terms in the *Roth* definition: the standard is the average person, not the abnormal or immature. The Court did not make itself clear here: is the average person obscenity law's equivalent of the law of tort's reasonable man (as canvassed by Judge Woolsey in *Ulysses*)[3] or is one here concerned with a composite of all those in the community?[4] In other words, is the law concerned with the effect of material on the 'average' man, or rather the average effect of the material on all those whom it is likely to reach? The composite approach is the more rigorous of the two, and may not be very far removed from the rejected most-susceptible-person standard. The extent of the change in terms of general distribution was not altogether clear. Although both standards would probably yield, in terms of thought arousal, a near constant result with pornography, a ground of possible variability is the nature of the relevant community in terms of which such average person assessment is to be made: is it, in other words, a locally or nationally assessed standard? This also the Court did not specify. State and federal courts had generally not taken into account the question of particular distribution, in the sense of material going to an audience of minors or deviants, and the appropriateness of an average person assessment in such circumstances; here also, the Court did not apparently apply itself to the potential problem.

It was the latter question which forced one of the earliest departures from the original *Roth* test: the Institute for Sex Research at Indiana University had placed an order, in connection with work begun by Dr Alfred Kinsey, for a package of clearly hard-core pornographic materials. The materials were seized as being obscene under the Tariff Act 1930. The lower federal court was placed in a difficult position, finally distinguishing *Roth* on the grounds that the average person

---

1   Whether such disapproval is itself justified will be discussed later: see chapter 15.

2   *Contra* F. Schauer 'The Return of Variable Obscenity' 28 (1977) *Hastings LJ* 1275.

3   *United States* v *One Book Called 'Ulysses'* 5 F Supp 182 (SD NY 1933) at 184, affd 72 F 2d 705 (2d Cir 1934).

4   See for example *Commonwealth* v *Isenstadt* 318 Mass 543, 62 NE 2d 840 (1945).

standard is applicable only to materials available to the public at large; in the context of their distribution for scientific research, no prurient appeal was aroused, and they were therefore not obscene.[1] This was broadly the approach advocated in this regard by Professors Lockhart and McClure,[2] and was finally adopted by the Court in 1966 in *Mishkin* v *New York*.[3] Edward Mishkin, a New York publisher, was indicted under the New York obscenity law for publishing, and possessing with intent to sell, predominantly sadistic materials. Typical of the fifty titles in question were *Dance with the Dominant Whip*, *Bound in Rubber*, and *Sorority Girls' Stringent Initiation*. Mishkin argued that as the appeal of such material was primarily to the prurient interest of deviants, and not to that of the average person — whom the material would tend to disgust — the materials were not obscene. The Court here had little choice other than to depart from the *Roth* test: the materials were without merit, were patently offensive, but did not appeal to the average prurient interest. Mr Justice Brennan (speaking for the court) affirmed the proscription of the materials, saying that the Court was 'adjusting' the *Roth* test 'to social realities by permitting the appeal of this type of material to be assessed in terms of the sexual interests of its intended and probable recipient group'.[4]

The exception created as to the average person standard only applies to distribution to 'a clearly defined deviant group, rather than the public at large'; Mr Justice Brennan made it clear by his reference to a standard psychiatric textbook,[5] that the Court intended medical categories of deviance only to be used. Courts have subsequently accepted homosexuality, sado-masochism, bondage, and bestiality as activities constituting such defined areas of deviance.[6] Proof that the materials go primarily to such groups is not necessary: it is enough that the group in question should appear the probable recipient.[7] Variability

---

1 *United States* v *31 Photographs* 156 F Supp 350 CSDNY (1957).

2 Lockhart and McClure op.cit. at 72ff; they did not feel that the average person standard was particularly relevant: they based this on an apparent assumption that hard-core pornography did not appeal to the average person. Their analysis therefore was confined to particular distribution, general distribution not being regarded as a practical problem.

3 383 US 582 (1966).

4 Ibid. at 589.

5 Ibid.; note 8.1 S. Arieti (ed.) *American Handbook of Psychiatry* 593–604 (1959).

6 See Schauer *The Law of Obscenity* at 79.

7 *United States* v *Manarite* 448 F 2d 583 at 592, cert. denied 404 US 947 (1971); this at least would be required for this development not to amount to a limited reinstatement of the most susceptible person test with general distribution.

of obscenity in terms of the audience to whom distribution takes place was to receive added relevance two years later in *Ginsberg* v *New York*.[1] What was the position of material which was not proscribable under the average person standard, but which might be said to appeal to the prurient interest of the immature? This question had been referred to in an aside in *Butler* v *Michigan*,[2] where the Court had noted in a pointed way that Michigan in fact had a statute designed to deal with the distribution to minors of harmful material.[3] An even more specific pointer as to the Courts' attitude in this regard emerged in *Jacobellis* v *Ohio* when Mr Justice Brennan remarked:

> We recognise the legitimate and indeed exigent interest of states and localities throughout the Nation in preventing the dissemination of material deemed harmful to children. But that interest does not justify a total suppression of such material, the effect of which would be to reduce the adult population ... to reading only what is fit for children ... State and local authorities might well consider whether their objectives in this area would be better served by laws aimed specifically at preventing distribution of objectionable material to children, rather than at totally prohibiting its dissemination.[4]

Professors Lockhart and McClure had urged that a variable approach be adopted in this regard: if this meant proscribing material that was not hard-core pornography, then pandering might be relevant, in that the material might be seen as having been 'treated' as hard-core pornography.[5] The Court faced the issue with their review of Sam Ginsberg's conviction under a New York statute for the distribution of material 'harmful to minors', minority being fixed in this instance as being under the age of seventeen; the materials in question had already been found non-obscene in terms of the average person standard.[6] Not unexpectedly, in view of *Mishkin*, the court accepted yet another exception to the average person approach: a state may with distribution

---

1 390 US 629 (1969).

2 352 US 380 (1957).

3 Ibid. at 383.

4 378 US 184 (1964) at 195.

5 Lockhart and McClure op.cit. at 79–80.

6 *Ginsberg* v *New York* 390 US 629 (1968) at 634. One of the magazines, *Sir*, had been found non-obscene in *Gent* v *Arkansas* 386 US 767 (1967), a companion case to *Redrup* v *New York* 385 US 767 (1967).

to minors '... adjust the definition of obscenity to social realities by permitting the appeal of this type of material to be assessed in terms of the sexual interests ... of such minors'.[1] The court had an alternative to this adjustment of the obscenity test: the material could have been acknowledged as being within First Amendment protection, but the state interest involved in preventing such dissemination to children could have been invoked to justify restriction.[2] Such an exploration of minors' First Amendment rights would have meant a novel digression (in this area at any rate),[3] one that would probably have involved an intimate exploration of state objectives, and the justifications for restrictions in this area, a debate the Court (with the exception of Justices Douglas and Harlan) had so far assiduously avoided. The *Ginsberg* opinion also necessarily raised the question of Fourteenth Amendment due process: although obscene, was there a rational connection between the restriction imposed and the state objective in question? *Butler* v *Michigan*[4] had held that no such connection existed in relation to a statute restricting general circulation in terms of minors' susceptibilities; here the necessary relationship was held to subsist between the type of materials involved and harm to minors.

Material must under the *Ginsberg* approach be obscene:[5] besides appealing to the prurient interest of minors, it must therefore also be patently offensive, and should also be utterly without any social value. The New York statute upheld by the court was concerned with material dealing with sexuality, which was harmful to minors in that it

(i) predominantly appealed to the prurient, shameful, or morbid interests of minors, and
(ii) was patently offensive to the prevailing standards in the adult community ... with respect to what was suitable material for minors, and
(iii) was utterly without redeeming social importance for minors.[6]

It is then constitutional to assess patent offensiveness in terms of what

---

1   390 US 629 (1968) at 638.

2   See Krislov 'From Ginzburg to Ginsberg: The Unhurried Children's Hour in Obscenity Litigation' 1968 *Supr Crt Rev* 153 at 180; see pp.481ff.

3   See *Wisconsin* v *Yoder* 406 US 205 (1972); see restrictions not constituting prior restraints, chapter 7.

4   352 US 380 (1957).

5   390 US 629 (1968) at 642–3.

6   New York Penal Law S484 h(1)(f).

reasonable adults would find offensive that a child should see, whilst First Amendment value is to be determined in terms of minors themselves. Although the Court did not say that other definitions of 'obscene for minors' are definitely excluded, an indication of what was not considered suitable in this respect was given in the companion case of *Interstate Circuit, Inv.* v *Dallas*.[1] Involved here was a Dallas city motion picture licensing scheme employing a standard in terms of which licences might be refused by a licensing board according to whether the films were (in its view) 'not suitable for young persons'. The ordinance gave an elaborate definition of what might be considered unsuitable in this sense.[2] The Court clearly distinguished the Dallas standard from that in *Ginsberg*, in that the latter defined the phrase 'harmful to minors' in terms of the *Roth* test (as interpreted) for obscenity, merely substituting the standard of minors for that of the average adult in the process. Although the Court did not reach the question whether obscenity is the only constitutionally permissible standard in this area, in view of the fact that alternatives had here and in other rulings, regularly been held unconstitutional, the result appears to be much the same. Even though it is not clear which portions of the Dallas standard were rejected, the case is probably best seen in terms of vagueness or overbreadth.

A number of uncertainties exist in relation to the *Ginsberg* formulation: first there is the question of just what age group it is that forms the standard against which prurient appeal to minors is to be judged. There does not appear to be any constitutional guideline here; it would probably be the average minor. Certainly some median would seem indicated or the statute might fall foul of Fourteenth Amendment due process. Quite what age the median should be remains uncertain. Second, one has the question of the Court's basic First Amendment approach: material surely either has social value in terms of the exception approach, or it does not; there seems little logic in arguing that material normally within the protection afforded by the First Amendment suddenly loses this value because of distribution to minors. Third, one has difficulty in terms of the approach suggested by Mr Justice Stewart in *Jacobellis* v *Ohio* and by Professors Lockhart and McClure: that obscenity regulation should be concerned principally with hard-core pornography. It would seem probable that the requirement of patent offensiveness corresponded more and more closely in practice with this hard-core formulation. The phrase hard-core porno-

---

1   390 US 676 (1968); see also *Rabeck* v *New York* 391 US 462 (1968) where the standard invalidated was in terms of an appeal 'to the lust of persons under the age of eighteen years or to their curiosity as to sex or the anatomical differences between the sexes'.

2   Ibid. at 681–2.

graphy may well be a mechanism to avoid criticisms of overbreadth in relation to patent offensiveness; any relaxation of such standards in favour of minors therefore creates constitutional difficulties.

What the Court appeared to wish to do in *Ginsberg* was to have their cake and eat it: if the exception approach was to be maintained, the concession in relation to children should have been avoided; once made, the exception approach is compromised to the extent that the Court was in reality balancing the interests of minors against the First Amendment rights of the latter. This is exactly what Mr Justice Stewart did: although material may have been protected, '... a State may permissibly determine that, at least in some precisely delineated areas, a child ... is not possessed of that full capacity for individual choice which is the presupposition of First Amendment guarantees'.[1] It would have been preferable had the rest of the Court followed this approach. That suggested by Professors Lockhart and McClure — that where material is treated as hard-core pornography by its distributors the courts (presumably via estoppel) may hold them to such pandering — was not accepted; the exception approach to the protection of minors was to result in the probable unconstitutionality of such protection.[2]

With regard to the uncertainty in *Roth* as to whether the average person is a composite of the community or not, Mr Justice Brennan in *Ginzburg* specifically rejected the trial judge's definition of the relevant community as including (and emphasising) children and psychotics.[3] It would appear, although a reasonable man standard has not been ruled out, that the average person standard is to be assessed in terms of an averaging of the effect of material on all sections of the community, none having a predominant influence.

In *Roth* terms, prurient appeal was to be assessed in terms of contemporary community standards; was this a possible avenue of variability? Such effect was not something to be judged in terms of the jury's own standards; prurient appeal had rather to be assessed in terms of the hypothetical average person, applying contemporary community standards. The phrase 'contemporary community standards' was, however, dropped by the court in *Memoirs* in relation to prurient appeal. It has been argued[4] 'that this omission constituted an admission by the

---

1   390 US 629 (1968) at 642–3.

2   See chapter 13.

3   *Ginzburg v United States* 383 US 463 (1966) at 466, footnote 5.

4   See Schauer 'Reflections on "Contemporary Community Standards": The Perpetuation of an Irrelevant Concept in the Law of Obscenity' 56 (1978) *N Car L Rev* 1 at 16.

Court of its irrelevance in this context'; in other words, most hard-core pornography, written and bought for its titillation effect, has a more or less constant prurient appeal, even given shifts over time and space in regard to its communal point of reference.[1] This is probably correct, and would certainly accord with the initial use of the community standards concept by Judge Learned Hand in *United States* v *Kennerley*.[2] Learned Hand here argued that community standards had changed to an extent sufficient to justify the consideration of literary or other merit. Such changes in community standards had clearly not been reflected in the prurient appeal factor; to narrow the test to coincide with shifts in standards, consideration of literary merit was necessary. Community standards have probably for decades been virtually irrelevant to an assessment of prurient appeal, this being so whether such standards be national or local. Once the point was reached that pornography had become the standard for proscription, prurient effect may surely be presumed in terms of the average person standard to be a constant? In the absence of a clear requirement as to community standards, federal courts and most state courts in practice applied a national standard with regard to prurient appeal.

(iii) *Mere tendency*. With many state and federal rulings, a mere tendency to the effect in question was sufficient. Were one to consider the policy questions involved in the obscenity area, together with the question of a necessary connection between aim and regulation, any test in terms of a mere tendency would be more difficult to sustain. *Roth* omitted any reference to such tendency only requirements.[3]

2) *The Nature of the material*

(i) *Work as a whole*. The *Roth* definition confirmed another general state and federal practice in this area: the insistence that a work be judged as a whole was clearly upheld. To satisfy the prurient appeal requirement, such appeal had to be the work's dominant theme. What was not clear was the position with regard to a magazine or newpaper containing a number of articles: is the publication to be taken as a whole, or may each article be scrutinised separately? This question

---

1 Clearly this argument cannot be pressed to extremes: given changes over considerable periods of time, or shifts geographically as broad as from one society to another, prurient appeal may vary. Within reason, however, much erotica is likely in this regard to maintain a constant status.

2 209 F 119 (SD NY 1913) at 120–1.

3 Although material appealing to the prurient interest was defined in a footnote as 'material having a tendency to excite lustful thoughts'. *Roth* v *United States* 354 US 476 (1957) at 487, footnote 20.

arose in *Ginzburg* v *United States*[1] in that one of the publications involved, *Eros*, consisted of fifteen articles. Of these, the lower court had found four obscene and eleven inoffensive. It was argued that the issue should be dealt with as a whole. The Court did not deal with the question specifically, but by affirming the conviction, indirectly upheld the lower court's approach of taking the articles singly. It has been suggested that this should be the approach where the various articles are not interrelated;[2] a relevant factor here must be the intention of the publisher: it may be quite clear from a publication that the intention was to put in serious work merely to save the rest. In these circumstances, the articles would not be interrelated, and could be assessed separately.

The same may be said of what is probably an even more difficult problem in this respect: the question whether articles — particularly in underground newspapers, for example — are themselves severable. In other words, where an article consists of text and graphics, the text having clearly been inserted merely in an attempt to legitimate the rest, can the text be severed, and an exception made to the work as a whole rule? The Court faced this issue in *Kois* v *Wisconsin*.[3] The approach adopted was one of rational relation: where the portions of the article are in no way related, severability is possible;[4] the publisher's intention was not apparently considered to be decisive in this regard. The question of dominant theme may be indirectly relevant here, in that the question of what is taken as the whole may be crucial in relation to the question of theme, or vice versa.

(ii) *Literary or other merit.* Consideration of the work as a whole almost inevitably results in consideration of literary or artistic merit or the author's intention or sincerity of purpose. The *Roth* test implicitly recognised this: a work may be proscribed if its 'dominant theme' appeals to the prurient interest. As Justice Brennan has more recently put it: '... the thrust of the constitutional protection is to forbid government to suppress material that, although having sex as its subject, advocates ideas, or possesses literary or scientific or artistic values or any other form of social importance'.[5] This reaffirmed the approach

---

1   383 US 463 (1966).

2   Schauer *The Law of Obscenity* at 108.

3   408 US 229 (1972).

4   Ibid. at 231.

5   W. Brennan 'The Supreme Court and the Meiklejohn Interpretation of the First Amendment' 79 (1965) *Harv L Rev* 1 at 7.

adopted in a number of jurisdictions, although in certain cases it did involve a subtle shift in approach.[1] Although this is by no means clear from *Roth*, in order to ascertain the dominant theme of material, a court was presumably required to balance the merits of the material against its demerits. If this is the case, it raises serious problems in terms of the Supreme Court's basic First Amendment approach to obscenity: obscenity is an exception to First Amendment protection because it is 'utterly without redeeming social importance'; that is, it plays no part in bringing about that 'political and social change desired by the people'.[2] In these terms material would have to be utterly without value in terms of the purveying of ideas in order to be suppressed: that is, *any* literary or other merit would be sufficient for its rescue.

The difficulty inherent in allowing, in terms of the exception approach, the proscription of material with some literary or artistic merit was acknowledged by the author of the *Roth* majority opinion in *Jacobellis* v *Ohio*:[3] obscenity was unprotected only because it was 'utterly without redeeming social importance'; material with literary, artistic, scientific or other value was as a result constitutionally protected despite its possibly dominant prurient appeal. As a result, there was to be no weighing-up of social importance against prurient appeal; the existence of any social value in the material was conclusive, irrespective of the prurient appeal. This emphasis was clearly restated in *Memoirs* v *Massachusetts*,[4] perhaps the best known of the 1966 trilogy of cases, in which the Court was faced with that perennial of obscenity adjudication, John Cleland's *Memoirs of a Woman of Pleasure* — perhaps best known as *Fanny Hill*. Once again, Justice Brennan (joined here only[5] by Chief Justice Warren and Mr Justice Fortas) gave the

---

1 Massachusetts courts, for example, did not disregard literary merit, but attached relatively little weight to it: even though it outweighed any prurient appeal (that is, the dominant theme was other than a prurient one), the work could still be proscribed, provided the objectionable passages could be said to be 'characteristic' of the whole. A shift in emphasis was required of such courts. The same can be said of courts operating an exception in favour of 'the classics'; New York is an example here: despite an equivocal attitude to the defence of literary merit, this 'exception' was sustained. This sort of equivocation was now unnecessary, as the dominant theme of such works is presumably not their prurient appeal. Federal courts had also operated this approach: for this and a succinct statement of its illogicality, see the opinion of Judge Frank (in the court below) in *Roth* F 2d 796 at 819—20 (2d Cir 1956).

2 *Roth* v *United States* 354 US 476 (1957) at 477.

3 378 US 184 (1964).

4 383 US 413 (1966).

5 The Court has subsequently held that this acted as a holding of the Court: see *Marks* v *United States* 430 US 188 (1977).

prevailing opinion; the *Roth* test (as subsequently elaborated) requires that three elements must coalesce:

> (a) the dominant theme of the material taken as a whole appeal to the prurient interest in sex;
> (b) the material is patently offensive because it affronts contemporary community standards relating to the description or representation of sexual matters; and
> (c) the material is utterly without redeeming social value.[1]

Justices Clark and White strongly dissented[2] as to the 'utterly without social value' test: to Justice Clark, this was a manufacture of Justices Brennan and Goldberg in *Jacobellis*; it formed no part of the *Roth* formulation, which gave relevance to social value in terms of its being balanced against the material's prurient appeal. In *Jacobellis* v *Ohio*,[3] moreover, Mr Justice Brennan had defined social value very broadly indeed: it comprised the advocacy of ideas, literary, artistic, scientific value; or 'any other form of social importance'. This presumably opened the way for the consideration of psychotherapeutic defences, the result of which might be to render virtually all pornographic material permissible. This specific argument appears to have been discussed only by Mr Justice Black in *Memoirs*.

As social value represents the First Amendment value factor, it is not something to be assessed in terms of a particular audience, hypothetical or otherwise. Nor presumably, although the Court did not make this clear, was the value factor to be assessed specifically in terms of contemporary community standards; it has certainly never been ruled that local standards should apply. Indeed so to rule would make First Amendment values dependent on local variations, something that would presumably be constitutionally unacceptable.[4] All federal and most state courts adopted a national standard in this respect following *Jacobellis*.

(iii) *Patent offensiveness.* It was *Manual Enterprises* v *Day*,[5] decided only five years after *Roth*, that saw perhaps the most significant departure from the original *Roth* formulation: a splintered Court reversed a Post Office ban (as non-mailable) on three homosexual magazines,

---

1   383 US 413 (1966) at 418.

2   Ibid. at 445 and 461–2.

3   378 US 184 (1964) at 191.

4   See Schauer *The Law of Obscenity* at 125–6.

5   370 US 478 (1962).

MANual, *Trim* and *Grecian Guild Pictorial*. Mr Justice Harlan, who produced the prevailing opinion, was faced principally with the problems raised by the average person formulation: the magazines were distributed to homosexuals, and the average person would probably not find them alluring; on a straight application of the test they would therefore be held not obscene. This would mean that material with an average person appeal and with some literary merit — the articles in *Manual* apparently had none — but not such as to outweigh their prurient appeal, might be proscribed, whilst material without merit, but with deviant appeal, would pass muster. This the Court could not countenance; Mr Justice Harlan's answer was to graft onto the *Roth* test the requirement of patent offensiveness: material to be proscribed had to have prurient appeal *and* be patently offensive. *Manual* had concerned a federal statute (18 USC 1461) and thus Mr Justice Harlan's remarks applied only to the statute in question; one has also the consideration that Harlan believed in a distinction between state and federal power in this regard: the requirement of patent offensiveness would appear to correspond fairly closely to hard-core pornography, the standard recommended by Harlan as to federal, but not state, restriction. This uncertainty was resolved by the endorsement in the plurality opinion in *Jacobellis* v *Ohio* of the patent offensiveness requirement with respect to both state and federal prosecutions; material without social value had additionally to be patently offensive, a requirement that was inherent in the *Roth* formulation:

> It should be recognised that the *Roth* standard requires *in the first instance* a finding that the material 'goes substantially beyond customary limits of candor' in description or representation of such matters.[1]

The requirement of patent offensiveness has never been satisfactorily defined by the Court. When first suggested by Mr Justice Harlan in *Manual*, it was equated with the phrase 'substantially beyond customary limits of candor', as found in the Model Penal Code of the American Law Institute,[2] and as adopted in *Roth*. This was followed by Mr Justice Brennan in *Jacobellis*, who elaborated it as 'a deviation from society's standards of decency'.[3] A further restatement was forthcoming in *Memoirs*: 'material is patently offensive because it affronts contemporary community standards relating to the description or representation of sexual

---

1   378 US 184 (1964); confirmed in *Memoirs* v *Massachusetts* 388 US 413 (1966).

2   ALI *Model Penal Code* Sect 251.4 (1962).

3   *Jacobellis* v *Ohio* 378 US 184 (1964) at 191–2.

matters'.[1] None of these definitions is particularly informative; on the other hand, the requirement had clearly been added to restrict the scope of the obscenity definition: insofar as it pointed towards material without merit, with prurient appeal, and which was patently offensive, it pointed towards hard-core pornography.[2] Two members of the Court had in fact opted for a straight hard-core pornography obscenity test: the term was first used in this respect by Mr Justice Harlan with regard to federal prosecutions only. He did not attempt to define the phrase, but acknowledged having taken it from a government brief, which described it as

> commercially-produced material in obvious violation of present law ... This material is manufactured clandestinely in this country or abroad and smuggled in. There is no desire to portray the material in pseudoscientific or 'arty' terms. The production is plainly 'hard-core' pornography, of the most explicit variety, devoid of any disguise. Some of this pornography consists of erotic objects. There are also large numbers of black and white photographs, individually, in sets, and in booklet form, of men and women engaged in every conveivable form of normal and abnormal sexual relations and acts. There are small printed pamphlets and books, illustrated with such photographs, which consist of stories in simple, explicit words of sexual excesses of every kind, over and over again. No one would suggest that they had the slightest literary merit or were intended to have any. There are also large numbers of 'comic books', specifically drawn for the pornographic trade, which are likewise devoted to explicitly illustrated incidents of sexual activity, normal or perverted ... It may safely be said that most, if not all, of this type of booklets contain drawings not only of normal fornication but also of perversions of various kinds.
> The worst of the 'hard-core' pornographic materials now being circulated are the motion picture films. These films, sometimes of high technical quality, sometimes in color, show people of both sexes engaged in orgies which again include every form of sexual activity known, all of which are presented in a favourable light. The impact of these pictures on the viewer cannot easily be imagined. No form of incitement to action or to excitation could be more

---

1   *Memoirs* v *Massachusetts* 383 US 413 (1966) at 418.

2   P. Magrath 'The Obscenity Cases: Grapes of Roth' 1966 *Supr Crt Rev* 7 at 19 and 72.

explicit or more effective.[1]

Such descriptions are hardly more informative than Mr Justice Stewart's famous *Jacobellis* dictum in this regard: 'I know it when I see it'.[2] Two years later in *Ginzburg*, Mr Justice Stewart, once again unable to advance a definition, adopted the description afforded the Court by the Solicitor-General:

> Such hard-core pornographic materials include photographs, both still and motion picture, with no pretence of artistic value, graphically depicting acts of sexual intercourse, including various acts of sodomy and sadism, and sometimes involving several participants in scenes of orgy-like character. They also include strips of drawings in comic-book format grossly depicting similar activities in an exaggerated fashion. There are, in addition, pamphlets and booklets, sometimes with photographic illustrations, verbally describing such activities in a bizarre manner with no attempt whatsoever to afford portrayals of character or situation and with no pretence to literary value. All of this material ... cannot conceivably be characterised as embodying communication of ideas or artistic values inviolate under the First Amendment ...[3]

All that emerges from such descriptions is that the material in question lacks any literary or artistic value, and depicts sexuality in a graphic, or presumably, patently offensive, manner. One is concerned, with patent offensiveness, not with effect, but rather with the nature of the material. On what basis would such material be found offensive? Significantly, one is concerned here not with a restriction in terms of material being thrust upon an unwilling audience, but rather a prohibition. The question is, does the material at issue, irrespective of the context of publication, affront recognised community standards? Because of the irrelevance of context, such offensiveness cannot be regarded as a rationally assessable harm, and one is therefore concerned, at best, with the enforcement of positive morality, and at worst with decision in terms of mere taste.[4] Patent offensiveness was almost certainly added to the test to enable juries more accurately to reflect community standards than did a straight prurient appeal test. In making

---

1   Brief for the United States 37–38, *Roth* v *United States* 354 US 476 (1957); cited in Schauer *The Law of Obscenity* at 109–10.

2   *Jacobellis* v *Ohio* 378 US 184 (1964) at 197.

3   Brief for the United States 37–38, *loc.cit.*

4   On the question of offence as a rationally assessable harm, see pp.117ff and 182ff.

this accommodation, the Court opened the test once more to criticism in terms of overbreadth. In an area as subjective as that of positive sexual morality, and in terms of a blanket prohibition rather than a restriction on gratuitous offence, a standard such as patent offensiveness or hard-core pornography is possibly even more open to overbreadth criticism than are standards clearly couched in terms of corruption of public morality:[1] the latter at least rest on public morality; offensiveness in this form may be a matter merely of individual or local taste.[2]

A number of mechanisms might be employed to narrow down this overbreadth: first, one might apply an average person standard in assessing patent offensiveness. The Court has never specifically required this; equally, one is not concerned with offensiveness with an effect on a particular audience. In practice the jury assesses such offensiveness in community terms, which would presumably approximate to an average person's view of community standards. Second, the relevant community might be specified as a notional one, thus tending to obviate regional disparities. Mr Justice Harlan first espoused national standards as to prurient appeal and patent offensiveness in *Manual*; he did so only in the context of federal laws. His views were endorsed as to such national assessment in *Jacobellis*, both as to state and federal regulation. Mr Justice Brennan followed Chief Justice Marshall's famous *dictum* in *McCulloch* v *Maryland*:[3] it '... is, after all, a national constitution we are expounding'.[4] To hold otherwise, he argued, would be to restrict national distribution of materials, as no distributor would wish to risk isolated prosecutions, under local standards, in those communities with a stricter than average standard. The opinion's strictures in this regard did not command a majority on the court;[5] despite the absence of firm authority on this issue, however, following *Jacobellis*, all federal courts and most state courts adopted a national

---

1   See pp.89ff.

2   As positive morality may be based on disgust for example, the line between taste and such morality is not always easy to draw.

3   17 US (4 Wheat) 316 (1819).

4   378 US 184 (1964) at 195.

5   Justice White concurred without opinion, whilst Justices Black, Douglas and Stewart did not in their concurrences discuss the community standards issue, the former two Justices merely reaffirming their position that the First Amendment prohibits all obscenity censorship. Chief Justice Warren in a dissenting opinion joined by Justice Clark, disagreed with the national standard test, principally because he felt that as a reference point it was unascertainable. Even Justice Harlan in his dissent disagreed with the ruling, reiterating his view that different standards should apply to federal and state agencies in the obscenity area.

standard in regard to patent offensiveness. A third possibility in terms of avoiding overbreadth was to provide a definition of patent offensiveness, or to adopt a list type approach, giving examples of what may or may not be considered offensive in this manner. Both of these alternatives the court avoided, preferring to leave the requirement to speak for itself.

Although the requirement of patent offensiveness probably allowed juries to reflect more accurately community standards, its introduction heralded further First Amendment problems. Not only was it open to overbreadth criticisms, but it also compromised the logic underlying the First Amendment exception approach: this proclaimed that material which appealed to the prurient interest and was without social value, fell outside the First Amendment; yet one now finds that material of this type, but which is not patently offensive, falls within the Amendment's protection. Material, in other words, which in terms of the exception logic should not be protected, falls within the Amendment's ambit. The logic is difficult to discern.

(iv)   *Author's intention.* The author's intention in writing the material remained relevant to the assessment of the material's value. Some relevance is also possible in deciding what constitutes the 'whole', in an assessment of the work as a whole.

III)   **Jury decision**

1)   *Expert evidence*

The ruling accepted in most jurisdictions that expert evidence was admissible in determining literary merit (for example) apparently remained unchanged. Mr Justice Frankfurter took the view in *Smith* that 'the defence should be free to introduce appropriate expert testimony',[1] such evidence being appropriate where the standards or concepts employed were beyond the jury's scope of personal reference. As a result such testimony not only remained relevant (and after *Memoirs* was often vital) in regard to social value, but in addition, with the proliferation of concepts in the test for obscenity (prurient appeal, patent offensiveness, and lack of social value) became broader-based, very largely because these standards were generally judged by a national or, to the jury, external, standard. Such evidence was held admissible in particular in regard to the assessment of prurient interest in the case of minors and deviants, where it was argued that psychiatric

---

1   *Smith* v *California* 361 US 147 (1959) at 167.

evidence was necessary to aid the jury with an assessment perhaps outside their immediate experience.[1] Expert evidence may also be admissible in relation to the work as a whole requirement: the author's or publisher's intention may be relevant here in assessing what should be taken as the 'whole', and evidence of this may be adduced.[2] Evidence on whether a prurient appeal is harmful, or on the question of material's obscenity has generally been excluded;[3] the very much widened use of expert testimony may come down to very much the same thing, particularly if the test, applied in terms of such evidence, results in a virtually constant result.

2)   *Jury discretion*

Obscenity remained a matter for the jury: this was reflected in the fact that expert evidence was not admissible on this issue. Yet how much remained in fact for jury determination or discretion? The prurient effect factor, assessed in terms of the average person, and in practice in terms of a national standard, was, with pornography, very close to a constant, other than in respect of the exceptions to the average person test. Pandering, although a mechanism for variability in practice, would in terms of the Court's reasoning, merely reinforce the trend towards a constant prurient appeal. The social value factor was an absolute, any balancing being excluded, and was assessed probably in national terms. Patent offensiveness gave the greatest scope for subjectivity, but even here, as with the other two elements of obscenity, expert evidence was probably admissible, whilst such offensiveness was generally assessed in terms of a national standard. Obscenity, then, probably came close to being a constant — a constant synonymous with hard-core pornography. This trend towards constancy received a further boost in terms of the Court's implicit assumption since *Roth* of the right to review trial court decisions in this area. The issue had been raised by Mr Justice Harlan in *Roth*,[4] when he pointed out the role the Court was creating for itself in this regard. He returned to this in *Memoirs* v *Massachusetts*, remarking

> A final aspect of the obscenity problem is the role this Court is to play in administering its standards. ... Short of

---

1   See Schauer *The Law of Obscenity* at 284—5.

2   As to the basic political theme of an underground newspaper, for example: see *Kois* v *Wisconsin* 408 US 229 (1972).

3   Schauer *The Law of Obscenity* at 279—81.

4   See also Mr Justice Black (concurring) in *Kingsley International Pictures Corp* v *Regents* 360 US 684 (1949).

saying that no material relating to sex may be banned, or that all of it may be, I do not see how this Court can escape the task of reviewing obscenity decisions on a case-by-case basis.[1]

Future development

Supreme Court decisions in the obscenity area had since *Roth* clearly involved agonising and difficult decisions for the Justices. From *Smith* onwards, with a few exceptions, the Court was very often fragmented. Professors Lockhart, McClure[2] and Kalven[3] had all predicted, despite the uncertainties inherent in *Roth*, that obscenity adjudication would move towards the proscription of hard-core pornography. Just how close did all this leave the Court to this predicted position? With the cutting edge of the test set in terms of patent offensiveness, and with the emphasis on the nature of material rather than its effect, the answer was, very close indeed. In no case between 1957 and 1966 did the Supreme Court uphold a finding of obscenity, whilst between 1967 and 1973 the Court issued thirty-one so-called *Redrup* reversals, the term stemming from a *per curiam* opinion of the court in *Redrup* v *New York*.[4] The Court in *Redrup* reviewed three state cases involving magazines with titles such as *Lust Pool, Shame Agent, Gent, Modern Man, High Heels,* and *Spree;* the Court reversed the judgement in each case, but only after acknowledging that this conclusion had been reached by the Justices by divergent constitutional routes: 'Whichever of these constitutional views is brought to bear upon the cases before us, it is clear the judgements cannot stand'.[5] What were the various constitutional avenues open to the Justices? Accepting the basic 'exception' approach propounded by *Roth* (and thus excluding the position of Justices Black and Douglas that only a clear and present danger of action justifies restriction in this area) five possibilities appeared to be open:

1   Professors Lockhart and McClure advocated the proscription of hard-core pornography in terms essentially of distribution to particular groups: general distribution was not seen as particularly relevant, as their basic assumption was that porno-

---

1   383 US 413 (1966). See also Mr Justice Brennan in *Jacobellis* v *Ohio* 378 US 384 (1964), quoting Lockhart and McClure op.cit. at 119.

2   Lockhart and McClure op.cit.

3   H. Kalven 'The Metaphysics of the Law of Obscenity' 1960 *Supr Crt Rev* 1.

4   386 US 767 (1967).

5   Ibid. at 771.

graphy does not appeal to 'sexually mature' adults. With their formulation, variable obscenity in relation to particular distribution only would be relevant; constant obscenity would play no part. The Court assumed, however, that appeal to the sexually mature is possible, and thus combined constant and variable obscenity; with general distribution the average person standard applied, obscenity thus being constant; with particular distribution to deviants and minors, variable obscenity applied.

2   Material may only be suppressed when the three factors of lack of social value, patent offensiveness, and prurient appeal coincide. In a 'close case' — presumably where prurient appeal or patent offensiveness is absent — pandering may be relevant.[1]

3   Material may be suppressed if appealing to the prurient interest; pandering may be relevant.[2]

4   Material may be suppressed at the federal level if hard-core pornography; at the state level, suppression should be on the due process rational basis standard.[3]

5   Only hard-core pornography may be suppressed.[4]

All this was hardly calculated to inspire confidence either in the Court or its obscenity rulings. Perhaps as Mr Justice Stewart announced, the *Roth* opinion could be read 'in a variety of ways', because the Court was 'trying to define what was indefinable'.[5] Not only was the credibility of the obscenity test at an all-time low, but the basic First Amendment exception approach was itself looking increasingly battered. As has already been argued, the introduction of a patent offensiveness requirement sat very ill with the reasoning underlying this approach. Such reasoning resulted moreover in a virtually open-ended and absolute social value factor: to determine that material is utterly without any social importance is probably in many instances to make an assumption of infallibility. One has also the difficulties created by the exception for minors in *Ginsberg*: the Court's logic in holding that material normally within First Amendment protection may fall outside it when distributed to minors is difficult to sustain. It would have been far better had the Court more openly acknowledged the balancing of interests in which it was engaging in this instance. To

---

1   Chief Justice Warren, Justices Brennan and Fortas.

2   Justices Clark and White.

3   Mr Justice Harlan.

4   Mr Justice Stewart.

5   378 US 184 (1964) at 197.

complete the catalogue of fallibility, one has finally *Stanley*: if privacy ensured an unfettered right to possession of pornography in the home, this had clear implications for customs restrictions, and possibly the privacy of private possessions outside the home. In First Amendment terms it was by no means clear whether *Stanley* was upholding the *Roth* exception approach or not. If it was not, this brings the Court into the arena of justification and policy consideration; if it was, the distinction between possession in the home and commercial exploitation of pornography is a little obscure.

In reality of course, the exception approach did not allow the Court to avoid balancing: it was clearly engaged in the latter in *Ginsberg*, whilst the exception approach, resulting in the Court's becoming the ultimate arbiter in terms of obscenity definition, meant that the Justices were in fact engaged in balancing in each and every obscenity decision they handed down. Most of the Court had studiously avoided any explicit discussion of the policy questions behind obscenity regulation; such discussion as there was tended to the view that such regulation was not in principle sustainable. Justice Douglas in his *Roth* dissent had taken the position that obscenity restriction was justifiable only if it led to criminal action. As there was, he concluded, no evidence of such a causal link, the First Amendment precluded proscription of the relevant materials. This opinion he reiterated in *Memoirs*,[1] only to arouse strong dissent on the part of Justice Clark. The latter adduced evidence from a number of experts, police officials, and the clergy[2] that material appealing to the prurient interest leads to antisocial behaviour. If 'social value' is to be a part of a test of obscenity he argued, such evidence of the antisocial tendencies of material is equally admissible in evidence. Mr Justice Douglas, in reiterating his belief that no causal link had been empirically established, answered that pornographic material very often served as a safety valve, and 'would in many cases provide a substitute — not a stimulus — for antisocial conduct'. Justice Douglas' views were clearly endorsed by Mr Justice Marshall in *Stanley*, at least with respect to non-commercial distribution. Whether the distinction between commercial and non-commercial distribution could in principle sustain obscenity regulation should the court finally abandon the exception approach and opt for an assessment in policy terms, remained to be seen. The Court had in fact given a fairly clear hint of the policy factors it regarded as pre-eminent in this area: although only *per curiam*, the Court in *Redrup* listed three

---

1   483 US 413 (1966) at 431.

2   For a summary of the evidence see Magrath op.cit. at 49—51; on the question of causation generally, see chapter 16.

factors as central to regulation:
- (a) state concern for juveniles;
- (b) the right to individual privacy in the sense of entitlement to avoidance of unwilling exposure to material; and
- (c) pandering.[1]

Even assuming that all of these policy factors are sustainable, they do not individually, or collectively, justify the type of blanket prohibition at present constitutionally sanctioned. The Court may have been moving in principle towards an abandonment of the exception approach and the formulation of more narrowly based restrictions; certainly the Court's rulings on obscenity appear (perhaps reflecting a shift in positive morality) to have moved in this period beyond a hard-core pornography standard towards minimal restriction, in that most of the thirty-one *Redrup* reversals involved material apparently of a hard-core variety. Whether the court's proceeding in this way was satisfactory is open to doubt; the pointers above were not more than pointers. Meanwhile, although the court might in fact deal with hard-core pornography only, or be perhaps even more permissive than this, basic constitutional approaches were numerous and fragmented; so much so that a leading commentator described the Court's efforts as having turned obscenity law into 'a constitutional disaster area'.[2] Clearly, some synthesisation of approaches was required; the perennial obscenity regulation problems in the meanwhile remained: the articulation of policy objectives had been avoided; a rational connection between valid objectives and the regulations in question had merely been assumed (other than by Justice Harlan in *Roth*); despite the strong trend towards constant obscenity, overbreadth remained a problem, particularly in respect of patent offensiveness; and finally the appropriateness of strict liability — an issue not unrelated to overbreadth — to speech restrictions was merely assumed. Before examining, in the light of such factors, post-*Stanley* obscenity jurisprudence, it is proposed briefly to turn to the prior restraints operative and/or permissible in this area.

---

1 *Redrup* v *New York* 385 US 787 (1967).

2 Magrath op.cit. at 59.

12 Prior restraint in the USA

The technique of prior restraint[1] – that is, official restriction on speech imposed in advance of publication, as opposed to subsequent restraint, which involves the imposition of post-publication penalties – has long been utilised by authority. In England, the immediate source of the American doctrine of prior restraint, for almost two centuries prior to 1695 printing, initially developed under royal sponsorship and later granted as a crown monopoly, was rigorously controlled. By the end of the seventeenth century however the licensing system had broken down;[2] by the mid-eighteenth century freedom from licensing began to assume the status of a central constitutional principle.[3] Developments in America were very much parallel, if a little later: by the early eighteenth century the licensing laws had broken down,[4] whilst there

---

1   I have drawn heavily on T. Emerson 'The Doctrine of Prior Restraint' 20 (1955) *Law and Contemp. Probs* 648; F. Schauer *The Law of Obscenity* (1967) chapters 11 and 12, and 'Fear, Risk and the First Amendment: Unravelling the "Chilling Effect" ' 58 (1978) *Bost U L Rev* 685 at 725–30. See also *Annotation: Comment Note* 'Validity of Procedures Designed to Protect the Public against Obscenity' 5 ALR 3d 1214.

2   For the background, see Thomas Macaulay *The History of England*, vol.4 at 125 (1879, Heron edn, London 1975).

3   W. Blackstone *Commentaries* vol.4 at 151–2; see also J. Milton *Areopagitica* 48 at 136 (J.C. Suffold ed., 1968).

4   Clyde Duriway *The Development of Freedom of the Press in Massachusetts* (1906) chapters 1–5; cited in Emerson op.cit. at 651, footnote 12.

can be no doubt that the First Amendment was intended to outlaw prior restraint. It was in fact argued that the First Amendment precluded (in Blackstonian terms) *only* prior restraint.[1] This and other basic First Amendment issues had to wait nearly one hundred and thirty years for resolution: it was with World War I and the Espionage Act that the Supreme Court began exploring the free speech area. In 1919 the First Amendment was held[2] to cover subsequent as well as prior restraint. It was another twelve years before the Court reached any discussion of the latter doctrine. In *Near* v *Minnesota*[3] the Court faced an apparently clear case of prior restraint: the legislation in question provided that any person publishing an 'obscene, lewd and lascivious', or a 'malicious, scandalous and defamatory' newspaper or periodical 'is guilty of a nuisance'. At the instance of the state, the courts could issue an injunction prohibiting such a nuisance: disobedience was punishable as contempt of court. The newspaper involved, *The Saturday Press*, was enjoined from publishing further 'malicious, scandalous and defamatory' articles. On appeal the Supreme Court held that the statute constituted a prior restraint; it therefore violated First Amendment protection and was unconstitutional. This apparently definite ruling was qualified, however: the prohibition against prior restraint did not apply in certain exceptional cases, and the Court in giving examples of these listed obstruction of the conduct of war, obscenity and incitement to violence.[4]

The ruling left much unresolved: it is by no means clear what the Court meant in baldly, and without authority, asserting obscenity as an exception to the general guarantee against prior restraints. Literally speaking, such assertion does constitute an exception to the broad principle that only subsequent restraint is permissible. The prior restraint doctrine only has validity, however, in terms of the First Amendment; if obscenity is outside First Amendment protection, any prior restraint of such obscenity does not raise (in First Amendment terms) a prior restraint issue. In these terms the *Near* obscenity exception is no exception at all. This is to make one crucial assumption: that the determination of obscenity is in all cases a constant. Such determination involves both substantive and procedural elements: what is obscenity, and how and by whom is it determined? Presuming that a uniform definition of obscenity is employed, the prior restraint ques-

---

1   See Zachariah Chafee *Free Speech in the United States* (1941) at 9–12.

2   In *Schenck* v *United States* 249 US 47 (1919).

3   283 US 697 (1931).

4   Ibid. at 716.

tion resolves itself into one of procedure. The relevant question is not so much whether civil regulation — as opposed to criminal process — is permissible or not: it is rather what *form* of procedure is involved. Uniformity of determination would involve employment of procedure of a criminal process variety, which with all its constitutional safeguards is clearly constitutionally acceptable. The use of any more summary procedure would convert any apparent prior restraint into a real one: material might well be suppressed, which, via a full determinative process, would be held protected. The question is, what form(s)[1] of prior restraint is/are permissible?

This is precisely the area that *Near*, with one exception, left unexplored. The exception relates to the type of prior restraint which operates by enjoining on the basis of past conduct the future showing of (say) obscene films by a cinema. This type of injunction was apparently at issue in a recent case before the Supreme Court. One must say apparently, because it is not clear whether the Texas regulatory system at issue in *Carol Vance* v *Universal Amusement Co., Inc.*[2] imposed a blanket restraint of this sort on future showings, or whether it operated in relation to particular films. The system was found to constitute an impermissible prior restraint, apparently on the latter basis;[3] the Court appeared to accept, however, that the former type of regulation, which is based on past rather than present conduct, and which therefore imposes a potential penalty without reference to the obscenity of particular material, falls outside the obscenity exception as to prior restraints permitted by *Near*. This clearly follows from the reasoning in *Near*: if obscenity is an exception to the First Amendment, any film determined to be obscene may legitimately be subject to prior restraint; the outstanding question is how such a determination of obscenity is to be made. With the blanket type injunction based on past conduct, should a film be shown which is subsequently found obscene, the exhibitor will be liable for contempt of court for breaking the injunction, a restraint imposed not in relation to the film in question, but in relation to past showings of other films altogether. The initial restraint was not imposed on the basis of the material in question in other words; the prior restraint operates to an extent on a basis other than a determination that the particular material is obscene, and therefore non-speech. The argument that such a measure is not a prior restraint at all as it imposes no more onerous a burden than subsequent criminal restraint, was not specifically dealt with by the Supreme

---

1   In this regard see Emerson op.cit. at 655—60.

2   63L Ed 2d 413 (1980).

3   See injunctions, below.

Court, the *per curiam* opinion accepting the United States Court of Appeals for the Fifth Circuit's view that a temporary restraining order could be issued under the system in relation to named material. Justice White (joined by Justice Rehnquist), taking the Texas measure as not being aimed at named films, espoused this view in arguing (in his dissent) the regulation's constitutionality. This argument would clearly fail were the burden of proof in subsequent contempt proceedings to differ from that imposed in criminal proceedings generally, or were it to be shifted to the defendant, for example. The United States Court of Appeals for the Fifth Circuit majority was in some doubt on the latter issue. In general, were such a hearing to provide full criminal trial safeguards, the only bar to the constitutionality of such blanket injunctions would be their basis in past conduct.

A number of prior restraints (both state and federal) were in operation at the time of *Near* in the obscenity area. They were principally book and magazine regulation, motion picture censorship, post office regulation and customs restrictions; some related to the prior restraint of particular or named materials, and attention inevitably focused on the procedures constitutionally required for a valid prior restraint of this sort. The emergence of a clear picture in this respect was to be spread over the next thirty years. After *Near*, several jurisdictions[1] outlawed attempts at informal censorship by means of police threats of criminal prosecution. It was not until 1957 that the Supreme Court was once again to deal with a prior restraint issue. In *Kingsley Books, Inc.* v *Brown*[2] the Court was faced with a New York statute which provided for injunctions against the sale of certain publications found to be obscene (as well as the seizure and destruction of such materials). Disobedience was punishable as contempt of court. Kingsley and the other book dealers concerned did not challenge the trial court's finding of obscenity with regard to the materials in question (a series of books called *Nights of Horror*);[3] the sole issue was whether the statute

---

1   See *Bantam Books* v *Melko* 25 NJ Super 292, 96 A 2d 47 (1953); *New American Library* v *Allen* 114 F Supp 823 (ND Ohio 1953); *contra Sunshine Book Co* v *McCaffrey* 112 NY Supp 2d 476 (Sup Crt 1952).

2   354 US 436 (1957).

3   The trial judge described the material thus: '*Nights of Horror* makes one contribution to literature. It serves as a glossary of terms describing the private parts of the human body ... the emotions sensed in illicit climax and various forms of sadistic, masochistic and sexual perversion. ... Perverted sexual acts and macabre tortures of the human body are repeatedly depicted ... These gruesome acts include such horrors as cauterising a woman's breast with a hot iron ... completely singeing away body hairs ... *ringing* the nipple of the breast with needles ... sucking a victim's blood was pictured ... and putting honey on a girl's breast, vagina and buttocks — and then putting hundreds of great red ants on the honey'. *Burke* v *Kingsley Books, Inc* 208 Misc 150 at 158–9, 142 NY Supp 2d 735 at 742–3 (1955).

imposed an unconstitutional prior restraint on publication. *Kingsley* in fact took the matter no further than did *Near*; rather than firmly insisting either on a uniform procedure with full constitutional safeguards (thus taking the narrower view that the exception in *Near* was more apparent than real) or ruling that some variation (at the same time specifying just what this was) was permissible, the Court sought to uphold the statute, principally by distinguishing *Near*. This they did partly on the basis that the *Kingsley* statute provided for a preliminary (to the issue of even a temporary injunction) adversary hearing to determine obscenity in relation to particular materials; the *Near* statute on the other hand provided for the enjoining, on the basis of past conduct, of future publications not yet determined to be outside First Amendment protection. Although such determination was an important point of distinction, the *form* of determination and subsequent procedure required was not alluded to; Justice Brennan dissented, however, specifically on the ground that a jury trial should constitutionally be required in all obscenity determinations, civil or criminal.[1] Mr Justice Frankfurter, delivering the majority opinion in *Kingsley Books*, concluded that the procedure involved was not in fact a prior restraint at all; one of his grounds for this was the argument that an injunction and later contempt proceedings leave the disseminator free to continue sale subject only to subsequent contempt consequences if the materials are *at that stage* found obscene, and thus differ little from subsequent criminal restraint. This is based on the assumption that contempt consequences follow only if the materials are subsequently found to be obscene.[2]

In the decade following *Roth*,[3] motion picture censorship was a prior restraint issue that was regularly to come before the court. Censorship of films was something that had (since 1915) been beyond First Amendment challenge: in *Mutual Film Corp* v *Industrial Commission*[4] the Supreme Court had held motion pictures to be merely commercial entertainment, and not a form of expression subject to constitutional protection: '... the exhibition of moving pictures is a business pure and simple, originated and conducted for profit, like other spectacles, not to be regarded, or intended to be regarded ... as

---

1 This has since been specifically rejected: the Court in *Alexander* v *Virginia* 413 US 836 (1973) held that a jury trial is not necessary in civil proceedings. The type of litigation (obscenity proceedings) did not affect this.

2 On this aspect of *Kingsley*, see motion pictures, below.

3 354 US 436 (1957).

4 236 US 230 (1915).

part of the press of the country or as organs of public opinion'.[1] This was overruled only in 1952 in *Burstyn* v *Wilson*,[2] which placed motion pictures squarely within First Amendment protection. In the meanwhile, in the absence of constitutional controls, prior restraint by officialdom (principally via the requirement of advance approval) had established itself; some constitutional reconciliation was needed. *Burstyn* made clear that films were protected, and that the doctrine of prior restraint was as a result applicable to them; the final ground of decision in the case was somewhat narrower, however: the statutory standard employed — 'sacrilegious' — was held not to constitute an exception (in *Near* terms) to the general rule against prior restraints. The question 'Whether a state may censor motion pictures under a clearly drawn statute designed and applied to prevent the showing of obscene films'[3] was expressly left open. In three *per curiam* decisions[4] the Court subsequently held invalid prior restraints based on the following standards: 'prejudicial to the best interests of the people'; 'immoral'; 'sexually immoral'; and 'harmful'. These added nothing to the position of obscenity in this context, probably being based on the constitutional validity of such standards as subsequent restraints.[5]

Kingsley Int's Pictures Corp v *Regents*[6] decided in 1958, yet again did little to clarify the prior restraint position. The New York Board of Regents (under a statutory licensing scheme) refused Kingsley Pictures a licence to exhibit a motion picture version of D.H. Lawrence's *Lady Chatterley's Lover*. One of the statutory standards of prohibition was whether the film was 'immoral'. A recent amendment had defined 'immoral' as including 'acts of sexual immorality ... expressly or impliedly ... presented as desirable, acceptable or proper patterns of behaviour'.[7] On appeal to the Supreme Court *Kingsley Pictures* raised two major

---

1   236 US 230 (1915) at 244.

2   343 US 495 (1952).

3   343 US 495 (1952) at 506.

4   *Gelling* v *Texas* 343 US 960 (1952); *Superior Films* v *Dept of Education* and *Commercial Pictures* v *Regents* 346 US 587 (1954).

5   Certainly Mr Justice Marshall, delivering the opinion of the Court in *Interstate Circuit, Inc.* v *Dallas* 390 US 676 (1968) regarded these cases (together with *Holmby Productions, Inc.* v *Vaughan* 350 US 870 (1955)) as being based on the unconstitutional vagueness of the standards employed; see overbreadth, chapter 10.

6   360 US 684 (1959).

7   Ibid. at 685; the amendment was added following the Court's *per curiam* decision in *Commercial Pictures Corp* v *Regents* 346 US 587 (1954) involving the same standard ('immoral'). See pp.357ff.

issues: prior restraint and vagueness. The majority held the relevant portion of the statute unconstitutional on a different ground, however: taking the refusal of the licence to be based on the ground that the picture portrayed 'adultery as proper behaviour ... under certain circumstances',[1] Mr Justice Stewart (delivering the opinion of the Court) remarked

> It is contended that the State's action was justified because the motion picture attractively portrays a relationship which is contrary to moral standards, the religious precepts, and the legal code of its citizenry. This argument misconceives what it is that the Constitution protects. Its guarantee is not confined to the expression of ideas that are conventional or shared by a majority. It protects advocacy of the opinion that adultery may sometimes be proper, no less than advocacy of socialism or the single tax. And in the realm of ideas it protects expression which is eloquent no less than that which is unconvincing.[2]

The majority were clearly excluding 'immoral' as a standard for exception from First Amendment guarantees;[3] as a synonym for 'obscene' it was also clearly overbroad. Beyond this the ground of decision amounted to nothing more specific than a broad affirmation of freedom of speech. Essentially the same prior restraint issue came before the Court once again two years later in *Times Film Corp* v *Chicago*.[4] Here a city ordinance required all films to be submitted for approval prior to screening. On this occasion the Court reached the prior restraint issue, taking the matter further than had *Kingsley Books* with the admission that the scheme (although finally upheld) did constitute a prior restraint.[5] The advance was a limited one, however; the scheme (remarked the Court) was not unconstitutional, provided adequate safeguards and appropriate standards were applied; once again, no statement was forthcoming as to what was (or was not) adequate.

---

1   360 US 684 (1959) at 687.

2   Ibid. at 688–9.

3   See Kalven 'Metaphysics of the Law of Obscenity' 1960 *Supr Crt Rev* 1 at 34, footnote 104.

4   365 US 43 (1961).

5   For the distinction subsequently drawn in this respect between books and films, see books, below.

I)   Procedural standards defined

The demands on the Supreme Court for clarification continued: Missouri had at this time a special statutory scheme for the seizure and destruction of obscene materials. On receipt of a sworn complaint, a judge or magistrate could, after an *ex parte* hearing, and without giving the owner of the property notice, issue a search and seizure warrant. Final destruction could take place only after a hearing, but no time limit was imposed in relation to the holding of the latter. In *Marcus* v *Search Warrant*[1] the Court was asked to review the seizure (under this procedure) of 11,000 copies of 280 different publications. Mr Justice Brennan, delivering the opinion of the Court, held the procedure unconstitutional on the basis that there was no requirement of an adversary hearing prior to seizure, the warrant in fact being issued 'on the conclusory assertions of a single police officer'.[2] This was upheld in *A Quantity of Copies of Books* v *Kansas*:[3] here certain of the materials had been examined by a judge in a preliminary *ex parte* hearing. This was constitutionally insufficient: before the seizure of material there must be a stage in the procedure 'designed to focus searchingly on the question of obscenity';[4] that is, where all (or virtually all) the copies of a publication are seized, an adversary hearing. It was unsuccessfully argued in *Quantity* that the limited time allowed between seizure and subsequent hearing[5] removed any possible objection to the procedure. This assumes a rapid conclusion of the subsequent hearing, and makes no allowance for any appeal, throughout which (often protracted) period the materials in question may remain in the hands of the authorities.

The issues raised by this argument — the circumstances of imposition of a *final* (rather than *preliminary*) prior restraint — were firmly before the Court a year later in *Freedman* v *Maryland*.[6] A ruling was here required on the validity of procedures followed by the Maryland State Board of Censors in their censorship of motion pictures shown in the state. The procedures in question provided that any motion picture

---

1   367 US 717 (1961).

2   Ibid. at 731 and 732; the word 'conclusory' is used in the sense of conclusions being drawn from the facts.

3   378 US 205 (1964).

4   Ibid. at 210–11: the quotation is from *Marcus* v *Search Warrant* 367 US 717 (1961) at 732.

5   Not more than twenty days; 378 US 205 (1964) at 221.

6   380 US 57 (1965).

had, prior to screening, to be submitted to the Board; no time limit was imposed for Board decision. Although an appeal from their decision to the courts was *permitted*, there was no statutory requirement for judicial participation in the censorship process; in the case of an appeal to the courts, no time limit was set for decision. A *final* restraint could then (depending on the disseminator) be imposed without any judicial participation at all. This the Supreme Court ruled unconstitutional. The focus was now firmly put on the final restraint hearing:

> Any restraint imposed in advance of a final judicial determination on the merits must similarly be limited to the preservation of the status quo for the shortest period of time compatible with sound judicial determination. Moreover, we are well aware that, even after expiration of a temporary restraint, an administrative refusal to license, signifying the censor's view that the film is unprotected, may have a discouraging effect on the exhibitor ... therefore, the procedure must also assure a prompt final judicial decision, to minimise the deterrent effect of an interim and possibly erroneous denial of license.[1]

Thus any prior restraint can finally be imposed only by judicial process; progress towards such determination must be speedy, and the burden of initiating judicial review and of proving that the film is unprotected speech lies on the censor, not the owner of the materials. Any temporary restraint prior to a final decision must be designed only to preserve the *status quo*. This apparently in no way affected the requirement of a preliminary adversary hearing, even though such requirement was not specifically included.[2]

Here were fairly clear guidelines: how did they affect the various areas and types of prior restraint in operation? One such area — detention of mail by the Post Office — was as a result soon to drop away altogether.

1) Post Office restraints

The Post Office Department operated some of the earliest prior

---

1   380 US 57 (1965) at 59.

2   The Court did suggest the New York procedure in *Kingsley Books* as a guide; this provided for a judicial determination following an adversary hearing before any restraint was imposed. Compliance with such a requirement would be difficult in respect of licensing procedures however: here an adversary hearing before a licensing board would seem sufficient.

restraints in this area. The 1865 Postal Statute[1] had spoken in terms of all obscene publications deposited or discovered in the mails being 'seized and destroyed or otherwise disposed of, as the Postmaster General shall direct'. The Comstock Act similarly provided in 1873 (and continues to do so today) for the 'non-delivery' of such materials. Whatever congressional intention with respect to such phrases may have been,[2] by the 1880s the Post Office was exercising the power to censor the mail on an exclusionary basis; such censorship was upheld in *Milwaukee Publishing Co v Burleson*[3] in 1921. The only circumscription of this power was that for the inspection and seizure of first class mail a search warrant was to be required;[4] this still applies today. Where mail was intercepted, it was transmitted to the solicitor for the United States Post Office Department at Washington DC for review of the decision that it was obscene. The solicitor would make the final decision, which would be imputed in law to the Postmaster General. If the mail was deemed obscene, then the addressor would be notified, and unless he could 'show cause' within fifteen days as to why the matter should not be disposed of as non-mailable, it would be destroyed. Usually no hearing was held; if an addressor proved difficult, the solicitor might schedule a hearing in which the functions of prosecutor and judge would be merged in his person. It was open to interested parties to resort to the courts,[5] but expense almost always precluded this.

Such censorship, even if justified in terms of the legislation, raised questions of a constitutional nature: prior restraint, a fair and impartial trial, and subjection of expression to the arbitrary judgement of one person. In 1945 the due process requirement of the Fifth Amendment (a fair trial) was used by the United States Court of Appeals in the District of Columbia to brand the seizure of materials without a hearing illegal.[6] The Post Office ignored this ruling. A year later Congress passed the Administrative

---

1   See chapter 10; also post office regulation, chapter 7.

2   It would seem unlikely that Congress applied its collective mind to the censorship potential here at all: see J. Paul 'The Post Office and Non-Mailability of Obscenity, An Historical Note' 8 (1961) *UCLA L Rev* 44.

3   255 US 407 at 417 (1921).

4   To satisfy Fourth Amendment requirements: *ex parte Jackson* 96 US 727 (1877).

5   As e.g. in *Levinson v Summerfield* Civil Action No. 976–55 (DDC 1955) where a suit was filed for an injunction compelling the return of a rare volume of Aristophanes' *Lysistrata* which had been seized as obscene. When the plaintiff refused the Postmaster General's offer of a hearing, the volume was returned.

6   *Walker v Popenoe* 149 F 2d 511 at 514 (DC Cir 1945).

Procedure Act,[1] which required just such a hearing. The courts overruled department arguments that the Act did not apply to postal proceedings, and went on to assert that the hearings in question should take place before any censorship action.[2] This severely hampered the effectiveness of this sanction, as a distributor could continue mailing whilst the hearing continued. The Post Office thus continued to resort to interim mail impounding: the sanction was however used less and less. It is today embodied in that section of the US Code dealing with Postal Services, which reaffirm that 'matter the deposit of which in the mails is punishable under section ... 1461 [the Comstock Act] ... of title 18 is non-mailable',[3] and that proceedings concerning the mailability of matter shall be conducted in accordance with the Administrative Procedure Act and the federal statute relating to judicial review of administrative action.[4] Any use of this sanction is now unlikely, as the Supreme Court would probably declare any such use (or the sections authorising it) unconstitutional as not providing sufficient safeguards against the dangers of prior restraint.[5]

Yet another weapon the department possessed was that of the mail block. This was statutorily authorised in relation to obscenity in 1950; under the legislation in question, the department could sever *in toto* and indefinitely *all* mail addressed to anyone believed to be dealing in obscenity.[6] Within two years the courts had held the Administrative Procedure Act applicable;[7] the department continued interim blocks, despite lacking any statutory authority so to do. Mr Justice Douglas in *Stanard* v *Oleson*[8] expressed disquiet at the operation of such interim blocks. The result was legislation authorising the practice, but only for a twenty day period.[9] This was watered down in 1960, in that such an interim measure became possible only after court authorisation.[10] The mail block provision exists today as 39 USC Section 3006, whilst

---

1   5 USC Sec 1001 *et sequor*.

2   See J. Paul and M. Schwartz, *Federal Censorship: Obscenity in the Mail* (1961) at 96–7.

3   39 USC Sect 3001 (a) Supp 1975.

4   39 USC Sect 3001 (f) referring to 5 USC chapters 5 and 7.

5   See the Court's holding as to mail blocks in *Blount* v *Rizzi* 400 US 410 (1971).

6   39 USC Sect 459a (Supp 1952).

7   *Door* v *Donaldson* 195 F 2d 764 (DC Cir 1952).

8   74 Sup Ct 768, 98L Ed 1157 (1954).

9   39 USC Sect 259(a), 259(b), and 259(c).

10 PL 673, 86th Congress, 2nd Session 1960, amending 39 USC 259(b) and 259(c).

the authorisation of interim blocks exists in 39 USC Section 3007. The use of blocks received a serious setback when in 1955 the Court of Appeals for the District of Columbia ruled that only mail directly connected with specific materials found (after hearing) to be obscene could lawfully be the subject of any such block.[1] It was on the constitutional rack of prior restraint that the sanction was finally to be broken, however: in 1971 in *Blount* v *Rizzi* the Supreme Court ruled that neither section of the code provided a sufficient protection against the dangers of prior restraint,[2] and were therefore unconstitutional. Neither statute has been amended and thus can no longer be used.

The department was also to be denied the sanction of a refusal of second class mailing privileges to those felt to be disseminating obscenity. This sanction developed around the turn of the century without any statutory authorisation at all: those putting out non-mailable matter had their cheap rate privileges revoked and as a result faced collapse. The exercise of the power received early confirmation in *Milwaukee Publishing Co. Inc.* v *Burleson*.[3] By 1945 the Court had substantially changed its views: without overruling the earlier case, it warned[4] that 'grave constitutional questions' were immediately raised 'should the government continue to exercise this power'; the practice was subsequently abandoned. The only civil sanction remaining to the Post Office today was added in 1967; the measure permits the department to allow an addressee to refuse mail which he 'in his sole discretion believes to be erotically arousing or sexually provocative'.[5] Upon receipt of the proper notice[6] the postal services will order the sender to cease sending any further such materials to the person in question, and this order may be enforced by federal court injunction. The statute reaches not only the legally obscene, but also anything objectionable to the addressee personally; its constitutionality was soon challenged, but the right of the individual to privacy was such as to limit the senders' First Amendment freedom to communicate (ruled

---

1   221 F 2d 42 (DC Cir 1953) affirming 128F Supp 564 (DDC), cert denied 74 Sup Ct 661 (1955). This was confirmed in *Tourlanes Publishing Co* v *Summerfield* 231F 2d 773 (DC Cir 1956), cert denied 352 US 912 (1956).

2   400 US 410 (1971) affirming 305 F Supp 634 (CD Cal 1969) and 206 F Supp 1023 (ND Ga 1969).

3   255 US 407 (1921).

4   *Hannegan* v *Esquire* 327 US 146 (1946).

5   Now 39 USC Sect 3008 (Supp 1975).

6   Procedures are set out in 39 CFR Section 916.1 *et sequor* (1975).

the Supreme Court).[1] Two further related statutes[2] provide that a sexually oriented advertisement sent by mail should be marked as such;[3] anyone not wishing to receive such material may place his name on a list (available to senders) and nothing may be sent to him once his name has been on the list for more than thirty days.[4] The Supreme Court has not determined the constitutionality of these measures, but they have been upheld in this regard by lower federal courts.[5]

II) Customs controls

Customs regulation[6] in the United States is an entirely civil concern: detention under the customs statute is by customs authorities who transmit information about the material to the appropriate United States Attorney, who institutes proceedings (*in rem*) for a judicial determination of obscenity, upon which the materials can be destroyed. There is apparently no need for an assertion of procedural due process via the Administrative Procedure Act.[7] In practice 'assent to

---

1 *Rowan* v *United States Post Office Department* 397 US 728 (1970); 'The Supreme Court, 1969 Term' 84 (1970) *Harv L Rev* 1 at 177. On the statute generally see note: 'Federal Pandering Advertisements Statute: The Right of Privacy versus the First Amendment' 32 (1971) *Ohio St LJ* 149; Zellick 'Offensive Advertisements in the Mail' [1972] *Crim L Rev* 724.

2 39 USC Sects 3010 and 3011; Sect 3011 provides for the judicial enforcement of 3010.

3 Postal regulations provide that the notice as to the character of the material must appear on the outside of the envelope or on the outside of an inside envelope: 39 CFR Sect 124.9 (1974).

4 If the mail is sent on an unsolicited basis, the sender must subscribe to the list, for which he pays on an allocation basis, payment not to exceed $100,000 per annum.

5 *Pent-R-Books, Inc.* v *United States Postal Services* 328F Supp 297 (SD NY 1971); *Universal Specialities, Inc.* v *Blount* 334F Supp 52 (CD Cal 1971).

6 The current statute is 19 USC 1305, which derives from 38 Stat 194 (1913), superceded by 42 Stat 937 (1922); and the Tariff Act 1930 Sect 305, 46 Stat 688 (1930) as amended by 62 Stat 862 (1948); 84 Stat 287 (1970) and 84 Stat 1973 (1971). The 1930 amendment provided an exception in that 'The Secretary of the Treasury may, in his discretion, admit the so-called classics or books of recognised and established literary or scientific merit, but may, in his discretion, admit such classics or books only when imported for non-commercial purposes'. This amendment is today irrelevant, as in the light of *Roth* v *United States* 354 US 476 (1957) such books cannot constitutionally be deemed obscene.

7 The Tariff Act provides an importer with the right to a trial *de novo* and the Administrative Procedure Act (5 USC 1005) does not apply to administrative adjudications that the court can review *de novo*. As far as Post Office proceedings were concerned, there was some confusion as to whether such *de novo* review of administrative findings was possible or not. Following *Grove Press, Inc.* v *Christenberry* 276 F 2d 433 (2d Cir 1960) such review would seem possible, even though it would contradict the need (perhaps) for the applicability of the Administrative Procedure Act.

forfeiture' forms were issued to importers, who more often than not would sign them: the goods were then dealt with in bulk in a subsequent judicial proceeding, with the result that the prosecutor and judge seldom examined the materials in question.[1] Those importers who wished to risk the expense involved could of course refuse and take their case to court.

The Supreme Court has twice upheld the constitutionality of the Act, and in so doing found a way around the prior restraint element clearly present in the procedures involved: the statute was interpreted as requiring that forfeiture proceedings commence within fourteen days of seizure and be concluded within sixty days thereafter, unless the claimant was responsible for any additional delays.[2] Although such procedures may satisfy the *status quo* requirement of *Freedman*, they do not satisfy *Marcus* and *Quantity*, in that there is no provision for a preliminary adversary hearing. It can only be assumed that customs regulation constitutes a not illogical exception to the rulings in these two cases.[3] Although the constitutionality of these regulations has been clearly upheld, this was done at the expense of the logic in *Stanley* v *Georgia*: there would not seem to be any reason in principle why the exclusion of obscenity regulation on a privacy basis from the home should not extend to one's private possessions when in the mails, in interstate shipment, or as here, in the customs system. Although the Court's concern in *Walter* v *United States*[4] was with the searching, and subsequent viewing by agents without warrant, of an interstate shipment of films, the majority opinion regarded such official examination as an invasion of the legitimate expectations of privacy of the consignor as to the packages. This, despite the fact that the situation extended far beyond privacy in the home; such remarks must raise, obliquely at least, some doubt as to the constitutionality of present customs restraints?

---

1   See Paul and Schwartz op.cit. at 88 and 274.

2   See *United States* v *Thirty-Seven Photographs* 402 US 363 (1971) at 367–75: *United States* v *12 200ft Reels of Film* 413 US 123 (1973). The definition of obscenity in such hearings is the same as that under the Comstock Act (*12 Reels* at 130 note 7); there is obviously no scienter requirement. Because of the non-criminal nature of the proceedings, obscenity need only be proven by a preponderance of evidence rather than beyond a reasonable doubt: *United States* v *One Reel of 35mm Color Motion Picture Film Entitled 'Sinderella'* 369 F Supp 1082 (1972) affd 491 F 2d 956. The burden of proof remains on the government: *United States* v *One Book Entitled 'The Adventures of Father Silas'* 249 F Supp 91 (SD NY 1966).

3   Contra e.g. *United States* v *18 Packages of Magazines* 238 F Supp 846 (1964) on 19 USC S 1304.

4   65 L Ed 2d 410 (1980); see privacy pp.159–66.

III)   Motion picture censorship

The principal means of restraint here are licensing procedures, injunctions and seizures. The most common of these is probably licensing. Such schemes, providing for prior submission of films to an administrative agency (either with a view to outright prohibition, or to official classification) are constitutional provided they subscribe to *Freedman* standards. A preliminary judicial adversary hearing is not required: clearly any insistence on such a procedure would render the system unworkable. Administrative censorship remains constitutional, but in view of the requirement of a prompt judicial hearing, it exists more in form than in substance: such systems are in fact no longer used. As far as time limitations are concerned, the Court in *Teitel Films* v *Cusack*[1] held unconstitutional a procedure which allowed from fifty to fifty-seven days for the full decision-making process; a judicial decision was required earlier than that. There is no obligation to provide an equally prompt procedure on appeal, however.[2]

Licensing systems may also[3] be aimed not at regulation on a film-by-film basis, but on an establishment-by-establishment basis. There is no reason why cinemas should not be required to be licensed, and the incidence of such regulation may be to curtail in some way the dissemination of speech. The most obvious would be to make the licence conditional on the non-showing of material determined to be legally obscene to adults, or alternatively to minors. Such determination would have to be via the criminal process, or at least (presumably) via a scheme providing the full procedural safeguards of *Freedman*. A licence may not be made conditional on the type of non-legally obscene material shown: this was made clear in *Erznoznik* v *City of Jacksonville*[4] involving a Jacksonville municipal regulation declaring it a public nuisance to exhibit '... any motion picture, slide, or other exhibit in which the human male or female bare buttocks, human female breasts, or human bare pubic areas are shown, if such a motion picture, slide, or other exhibit is visible from any public street, or public place'.

The ordinance clearly extended to protected speech; any control of

---

1   390 US 139 (1968).

2   Cf. e.g. *Interstate Circuit, Inc.* v *Dallas* 390 US 676 (1968).

3   Another form of licensing, copyright, may be used indirectly to discriminate against obscenity. A discussion of this area is beyond the scope of the present review; on this however, see the authorities cited in Schauer op.cit. at 243, footnote 86; also J. Phillips 'Copyright in Obscene Works: Some British and American Problems' 6 (1977) *Anglo-American L Rev* 138.

4   422 US 205 (1975); see also *Southeastern Productions* v *Conrad* 420 US 546 (1976); *Interstate Circuit, Inc.* v *Dallas* 390 US 676 (1968).

such speech on a content basis[1] contravenes First Amendment protection, and is therefore unconstitutional. Although the restriction in question was a municipal regulation rather than a licence, the reasoning would be equally applicable in both areas. There were three further options open to the Court in this case: one was simply to declare the standard overbroad, thus in essence asserting the exclusivity of obscenity in this regard. Another would have been to find this, or a more narrowly drawn standard, constitutional in terms of the protection of minors, and/or the prevention of gratuitous offence to adults. A third would have been to view the regulation as aimed at some legitimate governmental purpose, such as preventing the distraction of motorists, and not at censorship at all. If one could additionally take the view that the measure had minimal impact on speech, its constitutionality would be, if a little artificially, assured. These are all arguments as to the constitutionality of particular standards, and would be of equal force were the standards to be used in subsequent as in prior restraints: the question of constitutionality in relation to such policy factors will be considered later.[2]

Assuming a constant obscenity standard, would a licensing provision of this sort constitute nonetheless an impermissible prior restraint? Such a regulation is similar to the blanket type of injunction discussed earlier in this chapter, which prohibits future activity on the basis of past conduct. This is essentially a nuisance[3] approach: assuming that the burden of proof at the relevant hearing is the same as that required in criminal trials, it is nonetheless perhaps surprising, in the light of *Near* v *Minnesota*, to find such a procedure extant. It has been held unconstitutional by a number of lower courts, and came before the Supreme Court in *Hoffman* v *Pursue*,[4] where the decision was not on the merits. Its most recent appearance before the Court in *Vance* v *Universal Amusement Co.*[5] may have been equally inconclusive, as the *per curiam* opinion of the Court appears to be based on the assumption that the Texas regulation is aimed at the enjoining of particular films; this makes a difference, in that such a system is

---

1   See Karst 'Equality as a Central Principle in The First Amendment' 43 (1976) *U Chi L Rev* 20.

2   See chapter 14 in particular; also chapters 5 and 6.

3   See generally D. Rendleman 44 (1977) *U Chi L Rev* 509.

4   420 US 592 (1975); the decision was in terms of federalism principles: the case was remanded to the district court to consider whether state process should not first have been completed before relief was sought in the federal courts.

5   63L Ed 2d 413 (1980).

clearly distinguishable from a subsequent criminal restraint on the basis that any showing of an enjoined film is punishable as a contempt of court, whether the film is subsequently found obscene or not. This is clearly not the case with a blanket injunction or licensing regulation along nuisance lines. If it is to be found an unconstitutional, or in other words a prior, restraint this must presumably be on the basis of a difference in the burden of proof at a subsequent hearing and that imposed in criminal process, or more substantially, the reasoning in *Near*. As of present, the issue apparently remains open.

Film seizures would be subject to the rules laid down in *Marcus*, *Quantity*[1] and *Freedman*. These standards, if collectively adhered to, reduce the scope for the use of seizure drastically. If a preliminary adversary hearing is held prior to seizure and a full hearing on the merits before destruction, constitutional standards are satisfied. There would seem to be little advantage in employing such a procedure in preference to normal criminal process.[2] Any seizure prior to hearing on the merits would, via *Freedman*, be required merely to preserve the *status quo*; the seizure would thus presumably be limited to the prevention of removal, alteration or destruction of the materials in question.

As far as injunctions are concerned, the initial question is whether they constitute a prior restraint at all. This question has been explored in relation to the blanket nuisance-type injunction. What of injunctions aimed at named materials? Mr Justice Frankfurter in *Kingsley Books, Inc.* v *Brown*[3] took the view that injunctions of this sort do not constitute prior restraints at all, as a subsequent finding of non-obscenity as to the material would obviate any contempt penalties. The sanction in other words, does not differ from that imposed by constitutionally acceptable subsequent criminal sanctions. Doubts have been expressed as to the correctness of this view, doubts which were upheld by the majority opinion of the Court in *Vance*.[4] The Court here clearly distinguished such a system from subsequent criminal restraint on the basis that contempt liability *will* apply, despite a subsequent

---

1   Although *Marcus* and *Quantity* applied specifically to books, their reasoning would appear equally applicable to films: see *Heller* v *New York* 413 US 483 (1973).

2   *Contra Kingsley Books, Inc.* v *Brown* 354 US 436 (1957) at 442; *Paris Adult Theater* v *Slaton* 413 US 49 (1973) at 55. Provided the relevant criminal statute provides for destruction, the material may be treated as contraband, and destroyed: see e.g. *Hicks* v *Miranda* 422 US 332 (1975).

3   354 US 436 (1957); see also in relation to the *Kingsley* system Cheif Justice Warren (dissenting) in *Times Film Corp* v *City of Chicago* 365 US 43 (1961).

4   See comment 'Free Speech and Obscenity: A search for Constitutional Procedures and Standards' 12 (1965) *UCLA L Rev* 532 at 535 footnote 27. *Carol Vance* v *Universal Amusement Co. Inc.* 63 L Ed 2d 413 (1980); see pp.412ff.

finding of non-obscenity. An alternative issue not dealt with would be the standard and burden of proof at a subsequent hearing. Accepting such injunctions as prior restraints, the normal *Freedman* rules would apply; any shortfall in the system would, as in *Vance*, render it unconstitutional. Thus no final injunction may issue without a full hearing on the merits, any temporary injunction must essay only to preserve the *status quo*, and must itself be preceded by a preliminary adversary hearing. All this is not without its difficulties (which might apply also to seizures): in certain circumstances the requirement of a preliminary adversary hearing may make even the preservation of the *status quo* impossible, as (for example) when the defendant is likely, on notice of the proceedings, to remove, alter or destroy the materials. These guidelines have as a result not always been followed: certain courts have permitted preliminary *ex parte* hearings, and preliminary restraints that proceeded beyond the preservation of the *status quo*;[1] others have insisted on the *status quo* requirement[2] or the preliminary adversary hearing.[3] The position thus remains in practice somewhat unsettled.

Three other possible forms of motion picture restraint remain for consideration: zoning regulations, censorship boards, and declaratory judgements. As far as the first is concerned, the decision in *Erznoznik v City of Jacksonville*[4] is in point: any municipal regulation by content of protected speech is unconstitutional. Zoning in terms of obscenity would therefore be constitutional, but any other standard would apparently be suspect. An initial question which arises in relation to zoning is whether it constitutes a prior restraint at all. It certainly has effect prior to publication, and provided that one is prepared to accept a restriction rather than a prohibition as a restraint in this context, it may arguably be seen as a potential prior restraint. The point is of course, that were zoning regulations to be implemented in this area, they would, practically speaking, be couched, unless the state had abolished its obscenity statute, in terms of some standard other than obscenity. Unless the Court was prepared to discuss those policy issues such as the protection of children and offensiveness implicit in *Erznoznik*, the only choice apparently open to it was to find any such zoning unconstitutional. Predictions were therefore made[5] prior to

---

1 See the authorities cited in Schauer op.cit. at 238, footnote 56.

2 Ibid., footnote 57.

3 Ibid., footnotes 58 and 59.

4 422 US 205 (1975).

5 See Schauer *The Law of Obscenity* at 92–5.

the hearing of *Young v American Mini Theaters*[1] by the Court that the 'adult' standard employed by Detroit in zoning would be struck down as unconstitutional. The Court in the event displayed greater ingenuity than had been anticipated. The Detroit zoning ordinance in question regulated the location of adult motion picture theatres. Such a theatre is defined[2] as 'An enclosed building ... used for ... presenting material distinguished or characterised by an emphasis on matter depicting, describing or relating to "Specified Sexual Activities" or "Specified Anatomical Areas" for observation by patrons within'. 'Specified Sexual Activities' are defined as:

1. Human genitals in a state of sexual stimulation or arousal;
2. Acts of human masturbation, sexual intercourse or sodomy;
3. Fondling or other erotic touching of human genitals, pubic region, buttock or female breast.

'Specified Anatomical Areas' are defined as:

1. Less than completely and opaquely covered:
   (a) human genitals, pubic regions;
   (b) buttock, and
   (c) female breast below a point immediately above the top of the areola; and
2. Human male genitals in a discernible turgid state, even if completely and opaquely covered.[3]

The Court clearly did not wish to find these regulations unconstitutional; rather than find them overbroad or an impermissible regulation by content, they were apparently faced with upholding a prior restraint on speech in terms basically of offensiveness, for it was the latter with which the regulations were concerned. This appraisal of policy objectives the Court wished to avoid: the plurality therefore opted for the alternative, if it may legitimately be called such, of regarding the speech involved as having a second-class status, in relation to which the governmental aim of town planning, together with the fact that a restriction rather than a prohibition was involved, easily justified constitutionality.[4] Justice Powell (concurring) preferred to skirt the First Amendment, regarding the regulations not as a

---

1   427 US 50 (1976).

2   For details of the regulations, see ibid. at 52, footnote 3.

3   Ibid. at 53—4, footnote 4.

4   Ibid. at 70—1.

censorship measure at all, but as something aimed at the legitimate governmental aim of town planning;[1] in the latter terms the question of what was required procedurally in terms of the First Amendment did not arise, nor did the question of First Amendment overbreadth in relation to the standard employed. One was concerned with a restriction rather than a prohibition; the restriction on speech was indirect rather than direct (as in *Erznoznik*); finally, the restrictions did not offend the least restrictive alternative doctrine, which requires that where a restriction impinges on some fundamental right, the restriction must be such as to further the governmental interest involved in the least restrictive manner (in relation to that fundamental right) possible: state regulation of speech is justified in these terms if '... it furthers an important or substantial governmental interest, if the governmental interest is unrelated to the suppression of free expression, and if the incidental restriction on alleged First Amendment freedom is no greater than is essential to the furtherance of that interest'.[2]

The plurality approach appears to regard the prior restraint involved as justified, but justified in terms of second-class speech. The balancing process in these terms probably demands no more than a due process rational connection, which in effect means a virtual skirting of the First Amendment, opening an avenue for the restriction of speech in terms of potentially overbroad standards; it might have been far better to take the First Amendment head-on, and fashion an acceptable offensiveness and/or protection of children doctrine in terms acceptable under it. Under the present regime the definition of 'adult' is a broad one, and therefore unless all cinemas showing films at all sexually explicit are to be relocated,[3] some further judicial construction is required. Under *Young* an exhibitor only occasionally showing material that is fairly explicit sexually (and which may therefore be classified as adult) has three choices: either he can impose self-censorship, and cease any such occasional screenings; or he can apply to the zoning commission for waiver of the zoning restrictions; or he can relocate his cinema to comply with zoning regulations. As the definition of 'adult' is not particularly definite, predictions as to whether a film would be regarded as 'adult' by the zoning commission would be hazardous to make; the result may well be the imposition of self-censorship, and the reduction of 'the adult population ... to

---

1 Ibid. at 84.

2 *United States* v *O'Brien* 391 US 367 (1968) at 377.

3 See e.g. J. Friedman 'Zoning "Adult" Movies: The Potential Impact of Young's American Mini Theaters' 28 (1977) *Hastings LJ* 1293; Schauer 'The Return of Variable Obscenity' 28 (1977) *Hastings LJ* 1275.

viewing only what is fit for children'.[1] The dangers inherent in the *Young* approach were neatly illustrated in *Schad* v *Borough of Mount Ephraim*.[2] Here the borough operated an ordinance in terms of which all live entertainment was prohibited in the jurisdiction. The appellants had been convicted under the ordinance for introducing into their adult bookstore, in addition to coin-operated adult movie shows, a similar device, whereby a client could insert his coin and watch a live dancer, usually nude, performing behind a glass panel. Both the Camden County Court and the Appellate Division of the Superior Court of New Jersey relied in affirming appellants' convictions, on *Young*.[3] On appeal, the Supreme Court plurality distinguished *Young*, emphasising that the borough had not demonstrated sufficient justification for its direct prohibition (within its jurisdiction) on a broad body of First Amendment protected speech; the least restrictive alternative doctrine had clearly not been satisfied. The Court it is true, struck the ordinance in *Schad* down; had the ordinance been rather more narrowly drawn, distinguishing *Young* might well have been more elusive, whilst it is noteworthy that the New Jersey Supreme Court viewed the *Young* approach as sufficiently wide to cover the *Schad* ordinance. The approach in *Young* will be considered in relation to such policy questions as offensiveness and the protection of children, and in terms of constitutional alternatives, in the next chapter.

Private or non-legal censorship — as imposed by censorship boards for example — would not appear *prima facie* to raise First Amendment problems, in view of the fact that their operation does not involve the state, and therefore falls beyond the scope of the amendment. This is to disregard the question of access to the media;[4] even more relevant for our purposes here, it is to assume that the line between state and private action is always an immediately apparent one. The problems involved here have been discussed at length earlier.[5] A final form of prior restraint in this area is the declaratory judgement. Many states provide legislatively for such judgements (which, depending on the statute, may be requested by prosecutor, and/or vendor or exhibitor), thereby obviating the need for any criminal proceedings. Does such a

---

1   *Butler* v *Michigan* 352 US 380 (1957) at 383.

2   US 68 LEd 2d 671, 101 S.Ct (1981).

3   Ibid. at 678; the Supreme Court of New Jersey refused further review.

4   See for example Barron 'Access to the Press — A New First Amendment Right' 80 (1967) *Harv L Rev* 1641.

5   See non-legal prior restraints, chapter 7.

procedure involve a prior restraint? Although a declaratory judgement is not necessarily determinative of future proceedings, and there can be no question of its issue on the basis of past conduct as with nuisance-type injunctions, a declaration may nonetheless constitute a prior restraint in view of the civil burden of proof imposed in its hearing. In these terms one clearly has a more onerous burden than that imposed by the criminal law, and provided that one accepts the chilling effect a declaration might have on speech, full *Freedman* guarantees should be applicable, at least as far as prompt hearings, decisions, and burden of proof are concerned.

IV)   Live shows

Although all of the prior restraints mentioned above in relation to films are potentially relevant to live shows, probably the most significant restraint in this respect is licensing. A foretaste of the Court's attitude to such expression was given in *Adams Newark Theater Co v City of Newark*:[1] here the Supreme Court (*per curiam*) upheld the constitutionality of a city licensing scheme which allowed the prohibition (by refusal of licence) of 'lewd, obscene or indecent' shows. Such a standard in relation to films for example, would very probably have been found overbroad; the constitutional status of live shows remained as a result rather murky. There was an obvious problem in this respect: the First Amendment quite clearly does not in the Court's view extend to all forms of expression. The amendment is couched in terms of 'speech', and this the Court has interpreted as excluding conduct. The type of expression at issue here potentially straddles the distinction between speech and conduct. Just where is the line to be drawn, for any expression falling outside the First Amendment may be subject to prepublication restriction without raising questions of prior restraint, whilst the standard employed in such regulation is not itself subject to First Amendment limitation?

No single philosophical rationale seems adequate in relation to the First Amendment;[2] perhaps the best that can be said from a philosophical and constitutional viewpoint is that the Amendment is concerned with the communication of mental stimulus. Conduct may be argued to provide just this; how is any distinction to be drawn between speech and conduct? In line with the position with privacy, the answer, short of a novel or more satisfying philosophical basis for the Amendment,

---

1   354 US 931 (1957).

2   See chapter 14.

would appear to be to limit speech to its usual meaning — verbal speech, writing, film, etc., and conduct to physical action. Even this is not adequate, as extensions of speech into the *prima facie* conduct area may be felt necessary. Also, even in these fairly literal terms, it is not always easy to distinguish speech from conduct: expression may comprise both, in varying mixes. The Supreme Court appears to have operated a literal speech/conduct distinction in the live show area. Shows of this sort, as pointed out by the Williams Committee,[1] potentially raise questions of public order; restrictions on conduct not protected as speech may then be justified in terms of public order considerations. Where such performances take place on premises licensed to sell alcohol, the public order aspect becomes even weightier; it may be felt to be such as to justify the regulation of shows even though they fall into the speech area. This describes the approach apparently followed by the Court in *California v La Rue*:[2] at issue here was California's power to make the grant of a liquor licence dependent on the type of entertainment offered in bars and night clubs. The state's particular target was to put an end to 'bottomless' dancing in such pleasure resorts. State power, in the liquor regulation context, was upheld on the basis of a factual distinction between 'speech' and 'conduct' or 'action'. Insofar as some at least of the performances concerned fell within the limits of constitutionally protected speech, the Court was clearly balancing considerations of public order against freedom of speech. It was loath to admit this, the liquor licence situation apparently being regarded as an exception: if the show in question, even though *prima facie* speech, may be termed 'gross sexuality', then *La Rue* permits regulation. It has been emphasised however that nudity is not *per se* decisive,[3] nor is nude dancing necessarily without First Amendment protection.[4] The Court has added a third alternative to the two approaches of distinguishing conduct and speech, and (in essence) balancing public order threats against freedom of speech: that is, the approach espoused by Justice Powell in *Young* in relation to zoning. Where the restriction can be said to be aimed at a legitimate governmental objective and not at censorship, and is the least restrictive alternative — in relation to the latter — available, it may

---

1   See live shows, chapter 6.

2   409 US 109 (1972).

3   See *Jenkins v Georgia* 418 US 153 (1974); *Southeastern Promotions v Conrad* 420 US 456 (1975); *Erznoznik v City of Jacksonville* 422 US 205 (1975) at 211–12, 213.

4   See *Doran v Salem Inn, Inc.* 422 US 922 (1975); *Schad v Borough of Mount Ephraim* 68L Ed 2d 671, 101 S.Ct (1981).

be permissible.[1] The Court in *Miller* espoused the conduct or speech and the latter approach without apparently distinguishing them:

> Although we are not presented here with the problem of regulating lewd public conduct itself, the states have greater power to regulate non-verbal, physical conduct than to suppress depictions or descriptions of the same behaviour. In *United States* v *O'Brien*, 391 US 367, 377 (1968), a case not dealing with obscenity, the Court held a state regulation of conduct which itself embodied both speech and non-speech elements to be 'sufficiently justified if ... it furthers an important or substantial governmental interest; if the governmental interest is unrelated to the suppression of free expression; and if the incidental restriction on alleged First Amendment freedoms is no greater than is essential to the furtherance of that interest.[2]

The *Young*-type approach is open to criticism in that although it avoids the necessity of discussing fully policy questions, it makes possible the restriction of speech in terms of overbroad standards. The basic distinction appears to be in terms of speech as opposed to conduct. This is a distinction which has been followed throughout this essay, but it is not always an easy one to make: cases involving indecent exposure and massage parlours for example clearly involve conduct; theatre[3] or ballet on the other hand are likely to be regarded as speech. Much that falls in between would have to be decided *ad hoc* on the basis of which predominates: speech or conduct. As a result of the uncertainties involved, some lower courts have applied strict obscenity standards;[4] others have held all live shows to be 'conduct', and thus outside First Amendment protection.[5] This is quite clearly unjustifiable. The trend apparent in *Newark Theaters* has been continued in that even with theatre for example, the standard of obscenity applied may not be the same as for other media;[6] full procedural safeguards are, however, applicable. The approach suggested by the Williams Committee in regard to the speech/conduct distinction

---

1 For interpretation of *Young* in this respect, see *Schad* v *Borough of Mount Ephraim* 68L Ed 2d 671, 101 S.Ct (1981); see motion picture censorship, *supra*.

2 413 US 15 (1973) at 26, footnote 8.

3 See e.g. *South Eastern Promotions Ltd.* v *Conrad* 420 US 546 (1975).

4 See Schauer op.cit. at 202, footnote 51.

5 Ibid. footnote 52.

6 *South Eastern Promotions* v *Conrad* 420 US 546 (1975).

with live shows was that it be based on an actual sexual conduct/ simulation distinction; this appears to be a clearer distinction than that operated by the Supreme Court. Were it desired to extend prohibition to shows constituting speech in these terms, it would be preferable to do so in terms of the First Amendment and public order justifications, rather than a virtual skirting of the First Amendment as in *Young*.

V) Books

Most of the more recent cases in the prior restraint area have concerned films, or have at any rate not involved book censorship. The principal guidelines in the area were laid down in *Freedman*, a case concerning film licensing, and their viability with book censorship is not clear. Indeed, it is not very clear whether the Supreme Court would sanction prior restraints as to books at all. *Near v Minnesota*[1] would seem to indicate their broad acceptability; on the other hand *Kingsley Books* v *Brown*,[2] the principal book censorship case to reach the Court, did not regard the procedures concerned as involving a prior restraint at all. Take also the remarks of the Court in *Bantam Books* v *Sullivan*:[3]

> Nothing in the Court's opinion in *Times Film Corp* v *Chicago*, 365 US 43, 5 L Ed 2d 403, 81 S Ct 391, is inconsistent with the Court's traditional attitude of disfavour toward prior restraints of expression. The only question to the Court in that case was whether a prior restraint was necessarily unconstitutional *under all circumstances*. In declining to *hold* prior restraints unconstitutional *per se*, the Court did not uphold the constitutionality of any specific such restraint. Furthermore, the holding was expressly confined to motion pictures.

It may be that certain restraints permissible with films, are impermissible with books, particularly licensing schemes. The operation of injunctions may be regarded by the Court as something less than a prior restraint whilst seizures would, in the light of *Marcus* and *Quantity*, appear to be permissible. Were any restraints to operate, *Freedman* guarantees would be essential. With municipal regulations such as zoning, censorship boards and declaratory judgements also — were these to operate with regard to books — considerations applicable to

---

1   283 US 697 (1931).

2   354 US 436 (1957).

3   372 US 58 (1963) at 70, footnote 10, emphasis in original.

films would similarly be of relevance.

VI) Broadcasting

The only other civil agency of obscenity control exists in the Federal Communications Commission's power over licensing and licence renewals. There is in existence a criminal statute prohibiting the broadcasting of 'any obscene, indecent, or profane language by means of radio communication'.[1] The statute's main use is against 'ham' radio operators, and has been construed as following the constitutional definition of obscenity; it is thus of very limited application.[2] The commission is also empowered to impose a fine of up to $1,000 for the use of improper language over the air;[3] this also applies to citizens' band radio only, and has rarely been used. It is thus the licensing power (for radio and television) which is of primary importance.

Judicial control over the exercise of this power has been much looser than has been the case with other media. The argument appears to be that such media as radio and television are both intrusive and of limited access, and that an analysis akin to the fairness doctrine is therefore apposite in dealing with the exercise of licensing powers which enable the authority to determine whether, in view of the use of offensive language or 'immoral programming', any particular operation is in the public interest. It is not proposed to explore this issue any further here, but it should be noted that one has here a power over two potentially powerful media that may be exercised in much wider terms than the exclusion of the legally obscene, extending rather to the vulgar, profane or sexually explicit, even if not obscene.[4] Although broadcasting has not been examined in any detail in either jurisdiction in this essay, it is noteworthy that in *FCC* v *Pacifica Foundation*[5] the Supreme Court upheld the restriction of George Carlin's 'Seven Dirty Words' monologue as broadcast over the radio. In so doing the Court

---

1   18 USC Sect 1464.

2   *United States* v *Gagliardo* 336 F 2d 720 (9th Cir 1966); scienter is required; *Tallman* v *United States* 465 F 2d 282 (7th Cir 1972). *Miller* v *California* 413 US 15 (1973) required that 'hard-core' sexual conduct be described (see pp.446ff.) and in terms of radio, this severely limits the statute.

3   Under 47 USC Sect 503(b)(1)(13) and 47 USC Sect 510.

4   See generally note 'Morality and the Broadcast Media: A Constitutional Analysis of FCC Regulatory Standards' 84 (1971) *Harvard L Rev* 664; note 'Offensive Speech and the FCC' 79 (1970) *Yale L J* 1343; also 78 (1978) *Col L Rev* 164.

5   428 US 726 (1978); see alternative approaches, pp.468ff.

did not even mention the scarcity rationale, but relied rather on the gratuitous offence occasioned by the language to unwilling listeners. The Court in fact used the term 'patently offensive' in the latter respect, a term clearly borrowed from obscenity jurisprudence. To this extent *Pacifica* may well be relevant to First Amendment jurisprudence quite aside from the question of broadcast regulation.

VII)   Procedural problems not involving prior restraints[1]

With procedures that do not essentially involve prior restraint, the question remains whether normal Fourth Amendment considerations apply, or whether something more is required. This problem has arisen principally with regard to search and seizure: where *all* the copies of a publication are removed and destroyed, one is probably concerned with a prior restraint, and the requirements mentioned above will apply. Authorities may well wish to seize only for evidential purposes; with such *bona fide* evidential seizures one is not dealing essentially with prior restraint, although this might be an incidental result, as where there is only one copy of a film and this is taken, or where there is a multiple seizure of copies. What rules apply? Material might be seized pursuant to a warrant, or incidentally to an arrest. With regard to warrants, *Marcus* has laid down that there should be 'a procedure designed to focus searchingly on the question of obscenity',[2] and that this procedure should operate prior to seizure in the form of an adversary hearing. *Marcus* was clearly applied in *Lee Art Theatre* v *Virginia*,[3] where films were seized under warrant in connection with a criminal prosecution; the warrant had been issued on the basis of a police officer's conclusory affidavit, and was therefore defective. A prescription of the constitutionally correct procedure with seizures not involving a prior restraint was not, however, given.[4] In the absence of Supreme Court guidance, most lower courts differentiated between film seizures and book and magazine seizures: with the former (the reasoning ran), one was concerned with something that could be seen by a large number of people; the seizure of a single copy of a film was thus equivalent to a massive seizure of books; *Marcus* and

---

1   It is not proposed to deal with the problem of *res iudicata* and collateral estoppel; for these, see Schauer op.cit. at 219–22.

2   367 US 717 (1961) at 732.

3   392 US 636 (1968).

4   The issue had arisen, and was similarly deferred in *Mishkin* v *New York* 383 US 502 (1966).

Quantity therefore applied in full, and a preliminary adversary hearing was necessary.[1] Conversely, no adversary hearing was required with seizures of books or magazines for use in evidence.

The issue was finally reached in 1973 in *Heller* v *New York*:[2] the court was here faced with the seizure of a film for use in evidence in a subsequent prosecution. The judge issuing the warrant had actually seen the film, and the approach taken by the Court in *Lee Art Theatre* was thus not available. On the question of seizures under warrant for evidential purposes, the majority provided an emphatic statement of procedural requirements:

> This Court has never held, or even implied, that there is an absolute First or Fourteenth Amendment right to a prior adversary hearing applicable to all cases where allegedly obscene material is seized ... In particular, there is no such absolute right where allegedly obscene material is seized, pursuant to a warrant, to preserve the material as evidence in a criminal prosecution.[3]

A prior adversary hearing was not therefore required. The Court did not leave the matter there, but laid down some specific and positive guidelines:

> (a) The seizure should be 'pursuant to a warrant, issued after a determination of probable cause by a neutral magistrate';[4]
> (b) If the defendant so requests, an adversary hearing should be held promptly after the seizure;[5] and
> (c) If no other copies of a film are available, the court must allow a copy to be made of the film seized. Anything seized in any other manner was to be returned.

In this way, prior restraint of speech is as far as possible avoided: copying and showing of the copy could presumably take place up to and after the adversary hearing, other[6] than in the cases of a determination of obscenity (at such hearings) under a statute authorising

---

1 See e.g. *Bethview Amusement Cop* v *Cahn* 416 F 2d 410 (2d Cir 1969) at 412.

2 413 US 483 (1973).

3 Ibid. at 488–9.

4 Ibid. at 492–3.

5 With regard to the evidential problems raised in this context, see Schauer op.cit. at 214–5.

6 Under a solely criminal statute, even were there a determination of obscenity at the adversary hearing, the mechanism for final restraint would not be present.

seizure and destruction. In these circumstances, *Freedman* requirements for a *final* restraint would have been satisfied, and one could thence forward be imposed, irrespective of the prospective criminal trial. The purpose of the adversary hearing in this context is presumably primarily to cover the situation where the seizures, although principally for evidentiary purposes, have an incidental prior restraint effect. This could arise with a multiple seizure of copies of a film for use in evidence;[1] under *Heller* this is permissible, even though it may have a censorship effect. The adversary hearing provides a safeguard against the prolongation of this incidental prior restraint.

Something more then than Fourth Amendment protection is required with warrants: although the Court has never held that the judicial officer concerned must see the film, something more than a conclusory affidavit is required. Each item to be seized must be specified so as not to delegate the initial determination of obscenity to the police officer.[2] The requirement of a warrant issued by a neutral magistrate has been strictly upheld: in *Roaden v Kentucky* the Court faced a search and seizure of a film subsequent to an arrest without warrant. The Sheriff of Pulaski County, Kentucky, after sitting through a showing of the film *Cindy and Dorma*, and having determined its obscenity, arrested the cinema manager and removed the film. Such seizure would normally have been valid.[3] The Court perceived a prior restraint in the seizure: where no initial judicial examination has taken place, non-obscene material (whose evidential value is thus nil) may perhaps more readily or more often be seized.[4] A search without warrant is thus impermissible, although the Court did remark that it may be permitted in a genuine 'now or never' situation.[5] The requirement of a specific search warrant authority has been upheld in the recent case of *Walter v United States*:[6] here a consignment of films depicting homosexual activities were shipped interstate to the wrong consignee. After being examined but not projected by the private parties to whom they had been delivered, they were projected without warrant by FBI agents. Despite the earlier private examinations, the

---

1   The issue of multiple seizures of the same film for use in evidence was before the court in *Hicks v Miranda* 422 US 332 (1975); the Court did not reach the merits.

2   *Marcus v Search Warrant* 367 US 717 (1961).

3   See *Chimel v California* 395 US 752 (1969).

4   *Roaden v Kentucky* 413 US 496 (1973) at 504.

5   Ibid. at 505.

6   65L Ed 2d 410 (1980).

official screening constituted, without a warrant and in the absence of exigent circumstances, an unconstitutional invasion of Fourth Amendment privacy.

13 *Miller* and the Burger Court

I   The obscenity test

The *Stanley* promise of minimal restriction was not to be fulfilled; not at least by the Supreme Court. Substantial changes in the personnel of the Court were imminent by the late 1960s, with the impending replacement of Chief Justice Warren and Justice Fortas. It was not long before these changes made themselves felt: in *United States* v *Reidel*[1] the real significance of *Stanley* was abruptly curtailed: the *Stanley* principles were to apply to possession *in the home*, and nothing else: commercial distribution (via the mails in this case) remained unaffected. This despite the fact that the Court felt that

> ... There is developing sentiment that adults should have complete freedom to produce, deal in, possess and consume whatever communicative materials may appeal to them and that the law's involvement with obscenity should be limited to those situations where children are involved or where it is necessary to prevent imposition on unwilling recipients of whatever age. The concepts involved are so elusive and the laws so inherently unenforceable without extravagant expenditures of time and effort by enforcement officers and the courts that basic reassessment is not

---

1   402 US 351 (1971).

only wise but essential.[1]

Such restructuring was for the legislature, and not the Court. Arguments as to the invalidity of the federal customs law were equally summarily dismissed: consent by adults as to receipt was not relevant to prohibition.[2] The position was held to be the same with regard to transportation across state lines.[3] The rejection of *Stanley* received final confirmation in *Paris Adult Theatre I v Slaton*,[4] one of the eight obscenity decisions handed down by the Court in June 1973. Aside from pronouncements on minors, pandering and procedural issues, the approach of the Court since 1966 had been a fragmented one. Nonetheless, a basic trend towards minimal regulation was discernible, culminating in *Stanley*. Warren Burger was now Chief Justice and Justices Blackman, Powell and Rehnquist had replaced Justices Black, Fortas and Harlan. The Court had undoubtedly shifted to the right: it remained to be seen whether the apparent rejection of *Stanley* in cases such as *Reidel* would be confirmed, and if so, what direction obscenity was now to take: some firm direction was clearly necessary.

In *Paris* the court clearly rejected the *Stanley* approach, whose rationale was confirmed as being applicable only to the private home. This the court managed to do by stressing the privacy aspect of *Stanley*, rather than the latter's primary emphasis: the justifications for obscenity controls. As far as privacy was concerned, its relevance was strictly curtailed: 'The idea of a privacy right and a place of public accommodation are, in this context, mutually exclusive'.[5] The emphasis on privacy was then only to mean its broad rejection in this context. The *Roth* exception approach was in effect reinstated, whilst privacy was seen as an individual right applicable only in terms of the private home.[6] All the state need do was to show a rational connection between restriction and state objective, and this Chief Justice Burger felt had been done by showing, even if it were an 'unprovable assumption', such connection between obscenity and

---

1 402 US 351 (1971) at 357.

2 *United States v Thirty-Seven Photographs* 402 US 363 (1971); see also *United States v 12 200ft Reels of Film* 413 US 123 (1973).

3 See *United States v B & H Dist Corp* 403 US 927 (1971) and 413 US 909 (1973); also *United States v Orito* 413 US 139 (1973).

4 413 US 49 (1973).

5 Ibid. at 66—7.

6 See note 'Roe and Paris: Does Privacy Have a Principle?' 26 (1974) *Stan L Rev* 1161; see privacy, pp.159—66 *supra*.

crime.[1] Of the eight 1973 decisions the most significant, in that it focused on the definition of obscenity, was undoubtedly *Miller* v *California*.[2] The fact situation in *Miller* would have permitted a decision on *Stanley* terms: it concerned a California conviction for the sending of sexually explicit advertising brochures, the presumption being that the recipients were non-consenting:

> This case involves the application of a State criminal obscenity statute to a situation in which sexually explicit materials have been thrust by aggressive sales action upon unwilling recipients who had in no way indicated any desire to receive such materials.[3]

The Court chose rather — in the first majority opinion in this area since *Roth*, sixteen years earlier — to reaffirm the *Roth* exception approach: the only justification necessary for the Court (or state) to adduce was that required in terms of the Fourteenth Amendment rational basis test. Such rational basis the Court held in *Paris*[4] to exist. The Court then went on to examine the *Roth* definition (as further elaborated) of obscenity.

II Applicability

1) *Intention*

The position in regard to a publisher's intention remains unchanged. Insofar as intention is not required as to the material's obscenity, there would seem to be an implicit admission by the Court of the vagueness of obscenity as a standard of proscription. This would appear to have been acknowledged to an extent by the Court in *Miller*, with the requirement that the sexual conduct in question be specified. Intention

---

1   413 US 49 (1973) at 57–62; the Court here admitted that the effects of pornography amounted (in terms of social and moral ills) to 'no more than an unprovable assumption'; such assumption is apparently to be regarded as rationally acceptable.

2   413 US 15 (1973); the others, besides *Paris*, were: *Kaplan* v *California* 413 US 115 (1973) (relevant to the *Miller* hard-core requirement); *United States* v *12 200ft Reels of Film* 413 US 123 (1973) (relevant to customs restrictions and prior restraint: see chapters 7 and 13); *United States* v *Orito* 413 US 139 (1973) (relevant to federal controls over transportation over state lines: chapter 11); *Heller* v *New York* 413 US 483 (1973) (relevant to prior restraint issues: chapters 7 and 13); *Roaden* v *Kentucky* 413 US 497 (1973) (relevant to prior restraint: chapters 7 and 13); *Alexander* v *Virginia* 413 US 836 (1973) (relevant to prior restraints: chapters 7 and 13).

3   Ibid. at 18.

4   Ibid. at 21; *Paris Adult Theatre I* v *Slaton* 413 US 49 (1973) at 57–62.

in this form, however, is still not required, something which, in view of the vagueness still inherent in the standards, is scarcely surprising. The position in relation to pandering also remains unchanged. If prurient appeal operates as more or less a constant with patently offensive material, a 'close' case will presumably be one in which the 'seriousness' of the merit factor is arguable. Pandering is in fact nothing more than a means of penalising the commercial exploitation of pornography. Certainly the majority[1] of the Court has heavily emphasised the commercial exploitation aspect. This emphasis has been the subject of considerable criticism;[2] it does seem strange that in a capitalist economy the commercial aspect of pornography rather than its inherent nature should receive such clear emphasis, if not in the obscenity test itself, at least in terms of the majority of the Court's motivation in sustaining proscription? This emphasis does not accord with a recent shift in constitutional ruling in relation to commercial speech. This had by means of the exception or definitional approach, been regarded as being outside First Amendment protection;[3] this approach has, at the risk of oversimplification, since been abandoned, the state now having rather to justify suppression.[4] This would seem to be based on a shift in the Court's attitude to the exception approach: proscription should rather, on balance, be justified. It is also difficult to see why (particularly if one takes prurient appeal as a near constant) commercial speech, itself protected, should by its very nature serve to place other expression beyond the scope of protection. Mr Justice Stevens strongly emphasised this in his dissent in *Splawn*, arguing that in the light of *Virginia Pharmacy Board*,[5] the pandering doctrine cannot survive:

> The Statements [advertising the films] make it clear that the films were 'sexually provocative', but that is hardly a confession that they were obscene. And, if they were not otherwise obscene, I cannot understand how these films lost their protected status by being truthfully

---

1 See e.g. *Miller v California* 413 US 15 (1973) at 35: *Paris Adult Theatre I v Slaton* 413 US 49 (1973) at 57: *Jenkins v Georgia* 418 US 153 (1974) at 161: *Splawn v California* 431 US 595 (1977) at 598.

2 See e.g. Magrath op.cit. at 60—2.

3 *Valentine v Chrestensen* 316 US 52 (1942); *Pittsburgh Press Co v Human Relations Commission* 413 US 376 (1973).

4 *Virginia State Bd of Pharmacy v Virginia Citizens Consumer Council, Inc.* 425 US 748 (1976); *Bigelow v Virginia* 421 US 809 (1975).

5 *Splawn v California* 431 US 595 (1977) at 603, footnote 2.

described.[1]

2 *Forms of speech*

One further uncertainty that was clearly resolved by the 1973 opinions was the applicability of obscenity regulation to material in written form, and containing no illustrations or pictures. As Chief Justice Burger pointed out in *Kaplan v California*,[2] the Court had held books as such obscene in only one case, and there most of the materials were illustrated.[3] He then went on to rule, however, that 'When the Court declared that obscenity is not a form of expression protected by the First Amendment, no distinction was made as to the medium of expression ... obscenity is not protected by the Constitution'.[4]

3 *Publication/possession*

Possession of obscene materials is protected only in the home.

III The standard applicable

The Court in *Miller* in fact laid down a definition of obscenity: material is obscene if

- (a) 'The average person, applying contemporary community standards', would find that the work, taken as a whole, appeals to the prurient interest ... and if it
- (b) depicts or describes, in a patently offensive way, sexual conduct specifically defined by the applicable state law; and if
- (c) the work, taken as a whole, lacks serious literary, artistic, political, or scientific value.[5]

1) *Effect*

(i) *Its nature.* Thought arousal remains a sufficient effect. The

---

1 431 US 595 (1971) at 603. See R. Shiro 'Commercial Speech: The Demise of a Chimera' (1976) *Supr Crt Rev* 45.

2 413 US 115 (1973) at 118, footnote 3.

3 *Mishkin v New York* 383 US 502 (1966) at 514–5.

4 413 US 115 (1973) at 119–20.

5 *Miller v California* 413 US 15 (1973) at 24.

continued relevance of this factor, as the emphasis in the obscenity debate shifts more to hard-core pornography, is open to doubt. It is not unreasonable to assume that material both written and bought principally for its effect, will normally have just that result: an effect. This factor may well with hard-core pornography be in practice very close to a constant. This is not to say that the effect factor is irrelevant: the law's outside perimeter is set in terms of the arousal of thoughts of a sexual kind; it is not sufficient that the material is merely offensive. This corresponds to the strictures of the aversion defence in English law. Pandering still remains relevant in terms, in theory at any rate, of prurient appeal.[1]

(ii)   *Distribution.* The standard in terms of which effect is to be assessed remains the average person. As far as the exceptions to this in terms of minors and deviants are concerned, the problems engendered in relation to the former because of assessment in terms of patent offensiveness or hard-core pornography, were highlighted in *Miller*: the *Miller* majority saw the first clear adoption by the Court of a hard-core pornography approach, which is apparently irreconcilable[2] with the variability of the obscenity of materials when distributed to minors. If only hard-core material is to be suppressed, is any additional protection of minors possible? Mr Justice Stewart did not have an answer in *Jacobellis*. The Court in *Miller* did not appear disposed to adopt that offered by Professors Lockhart and McClure: that where material is treated (by its disseminators) as hard-core pornography, this evaluation should be accepted. In relation to Mr Justice Brennan's dissent in *Paris* advocating a consenting adult approach, Chief Justice Burger remarked: 'Nor does Mr Justice Brennan indicate where in the Constitution he finds the authority to distinguish between a willing "adult" one month past the state law age of majority and a willing "juvenile" one month younger'.[3] The uncertainty in this regard was underlined in *Erznoznik* v *City of Jacksonville*[4] where Mr Justice Powell, delivering the opinion of the majority, remarked: 'We have not yet had occasion to decide what effect *Miller* will have on the

---

1   *Hamling* v *United States* 410 US 87 (1974) at 130. See also *Splawn* v *California* 431 US 595 (1977) at 598; the Court here also accepted the estoppel approach: that is, that pandering may affect the assessment of material's social value, in that a presentation solely in terms of its erotic appeal may be taken at face value; any attempt to assert such social value may therefore be estopped.

2   See Schauer *The Law of Obscenity* at 167–8.

3   *Miller* v *California* 413 US 15 (1973) at 27.

4   422 US 205 (1974).

Ginsberg formulation'.

The same problems were not raised with regard to distribution to deviants: no clash with the 'hard-core' formulation arises; *Mishkin* was specifically reaffirmed on this point in *Paris*.[1] The nature of the average person standard in general distribution has been clarified: in *Pinkus* v *United States*[2] it was made clear that the average person standard is a composite of the community; no section is to be emphasised, whilst the composite, although permissibly taking cognisance of the range of adult variation in the community, is not to include children.

National standards, even though widely accepted in regard to community standards, had never commanded a majority on the Court. The majority were then free, without disturbing precedent, to declare it an 'exercise in futility' to require a state 'to structure obscenity proceedings around evidence of a national "community standard"', which it felt was 'hypothetical and unascertainable'.[3] A further factor cited by the Court was the fact that although local standards may inhibit national distributors (in the sense of being regionally stricter perhaps), it equally operates in the opposite direction in those areas more permissive than the national average.[4] However, under a national standard, more permissive areas need not enforce the law, whilst local standards pose in practice a serious First Amendment threat to the national distributor.[5] The Court left undefined just what the relevant area was to be: just how small (or large) geographically[6] should the 'community' be to remain (in this sense) constitutional. The Supreme Court in *Miller* approved the instructions to the jury in the court below that they were to apply statewide (California, in this instance) standards;[7] beyond clearly intimating the inapplicability of national

---

1   413 US 49 (1973).

2   436 US 293 (1978).

3   *Miller* v *California* 413 US 15 (1973) at 30–1. The Chief Justice's opinion is based (in this regard) essentially on that of his predecessor, in *Jacobellis* v *Ohio* 378 US 184 (1964).

4   Ibid. at 32, footnote 13.

5   See Lockhart 'Escape from the Chill of Uncertainty: Explicit Sex and The First Amendment' 9 (1975) *Georgia L Rev* 533 at 549; Schauer op.cit. at 121.

6   The geographical size of the community is not the only problem to arise in this context: where an offence involves more than one state, for example, a conflict of laws problem arises as to which community is (in this sense) the relevant one. It is not proposed to deal here with this specialised problem. See Schauer op.cit. at 127–30 and Schauer 'Obscenity and the Conflict of Law' 77 (1975) *W V L Rev* 377.

7   413 US 15 (1973) at 30.

standards, the Court took the matter no further than this. A second question to be left unanswered was the applicability of the local standards rule to federal prosecutions. Following *Manual Enterprises* v *Day*[1] and *Jacobellis* v *Ohio*,[2] it had become generally accepted that the rule in federal cases was the application of a national standard. This question was settled in two of the companion cases to *Miller*, *United States* v *12 200ft Reels of Film*[3] and *United States* v *Orito*,[4] where the Court ruled that the *Miller* standards were equally applicable both to state and federal prosecutions. Potential problems exist as a result with regard to the latter: by 1974, six states had repealed their obscenity statutes, and were left without obscenity laws at all, or had enacted child obscenity statutes.[5] This they are quite at liberty to do.[6] What is the situation were a federal prosecution to take place within such a jurisdiction? Just this situation arose in *Smith* v *United States*.[7] Smith had been convicted under 18 USC 1461 in the United States District Court for the Southern District of Iowa. Iowa did not at the relevant times have on the statute book an adult obscenity statute.[8] The local community standards concept was equally applicable in federal as in state prosecutions.[9] The Supreme Court had to determine whether

> ... the jury is entitled to rely on its own knowledge of community standards, or whether a state legislature (or a smaller legislative body) may declare what the community standards shall be, and, if such a declaration has been made, whether it is binding in a federal prosecution under S1416.[10]

---

1   370 US 478 (1962) at 488.

2   378 US 184 (1964).

3   413 US 123 (1973) at 130.

4   413 US 139 (1973) at 195.

5   Lockhart op.cit. at 535.

6   See Schauer 'Reflections on "Contemporary Community Standards": The perpetuation of an Irrelevant Concept in the Law of Obscenity' 56 (1978) *N Car L Rev* 1 at 18.

7   431 US 291 (1977).

8   The relevant Iowa law had been found unconstitutionally overbroad in *State* v *Wedelstredt* 213 NW 2d 652 (1973); thereafter, the Iowa legislature had decided against amending the adult statute, enacting at that stage only a child obscenity statute. See Lockhart op.cit. at 535, footnote 13.

9   *Hamling* v *United States* 418 US 87 (1974) at 105.

10 *Smith* v *United States* 431 US 291 (1977).

The Court here had no choice: to rule other than against the Iowa legislation being conclusive in relation to contemporary community standards, would have meant a potentially ragged application of the federal prohibition. It may be true that community standards and legislation are not necessarily 'congruent';[1] it would be odd to suppose that they very often are not. The Court in *Smith* did not, perhaps understandably, go on to define 'local' standards in more specific terms geographically. There remains then not only the basic uncertainty as to the standard to be applied, but problems may also arise with respect to federal prosecutions. However, as the focus has shifted to pornography, the effect factor has probably become, irrespective of local standards, virtually a constant. This was probably why the Court dropped the community standards reference in *Memoirs* in relation to prurient appeal; it is doubtful whether its reassertion in *Miller* will make much difference to this aspect of the test.

2)   *The nature of the material*

(i)   *Work as a whole.* The phrase used in *Roth* in this regard was that obscenity existed if 'the dominant theme of the material taken as a whole'[2] would appeal to the prurient interest. *Miller* omits the phrase 'dominant theme', thus clearly widening the scope of the test:[3] a work might, for example, have a dominantly political theme, and yet might appeal, taken as a whole, to the prurient interest. Under the old formula, this would not have been enough; under the new it would. This leaves unchanged the Court's approach to magazines consisting (for example) of a number of articles.

(ii)   *Literary or other merit.* The third aspect of the *Miller* test introduced substantial changes to the *Roth—Memoirs* formulation: in relation to the *Memoirs* test that material should be 'utterly without redeeming social value',[4] Chief Justice Burger remarked:

> We do not adopt as a constitutional standard the 'utterly without redeeming social value' test of *Memoirs* v *Massachusetts*, 383 US, at 419; that concept has never commanded adherence of more than three Justices at one time.[5]

---

1   Schauer 'Reflections' op.cit. at 25.

2   354 US 476 (1957) at 489.

3   *Contra* Schauer op.cit. at 105—7.

4   *Memoirs* v *Massachusetts* 383 US 413 (1966) at 418.

5   *Miller* v *California* 413 US 15 (1973) at 24—5.

In place of the social value formulation the Court substituted the requirement that the material should lack 'any serious literary, artistic, political or scientific value'.[1] The import of this was to settle the question of just what was or was not relevant to establish a work's merit: social value could have encompassed virtually anything, but in particular opened the way for the plea of the psychotherapeutic value of pornographic material. The uncertainty in this area now appears to have been resolved.[2] Equally significant was the abandonment in this regard of the phrase 'utterly without'. Any value at all, no matter how slight, is now no longer sufficient: it has rather to be 'serious'. The weighing-up of the value required has significant First Amendment implications; the utterly without value approach had in fact done no more than mirror the basic First Amendment exception approach adopted in *Roth*: obscenity, because it lacks any social value, is outside First Amendment protection. Now material with some, but less than 'serious' merit may be proscribed. It may be true that the utterly without value approach of *Memoirs* did create 'a burden virtually impossible to discharge under our criminal standards of proof';[3] the difficulties attendant on the new formulation raise doubts as to future viability of the 'exception' approach.

A question which was apparently still open was the explicit relevance of contemporary community standards to the assessment of First Amendment values, particularly as such standards were now to be assessed locally. The Court appeared in *Miller* to baulk at the application of local standards in such an assessment. Such application would the Court felt, leave First Amendment value undesirably subject to geographical variations. In view of the Court's widening the proscriptive net in relation to literary and other values by dropping the 'utterly without' requirement, to have had these values judged by local standards would have compromised the First Amendment 'exception' approach too far. This view has been subsequently endorsed in *Smith v United States*.[4]

(iii) *Author's intention.* The author's intention remains relevant in

---

1   For a full discussion of what might or might not constitute such values, see Schauer op.cit. at 143–7.

2   In *United States* v *One Reel of Film* 481 F 2d 206 (1st Cir 1973) for example, it was argued (in relation to the film *Deep Throat*) that the film has a sexually liberating impact; this interpretation of 'literary, artistic, political, or scientific value' was not accepted by the court.

3   *Miller* v *California* 413 US 15 (1973) at 24.

4   431 US 291 (1977).

relation to the material's merit; in fact, in view of the serious value formulation it probably has added importance, in the sense that a serious intention on the author's part is clearly helpful in establishing such serious value. It may also be relevant in relation to difficult decisions as to whether text is separable from the accompanying graphics, and as to whether separate articles are judged individually or collectively.

(iv) *Patent offensiveness*. The second aspect of the *Miller* test is a restatement of the requirement of patent offensiveness. Such offensiveness is to be judged in terms of contemporary community standards, the latter being assessed locally:

> Under a national Constitution, fundamental First Amendment limitations on the States do not vary from community to community, but this does not mean that there are, or should or can be, fixed uniform national standards of precisely what appeals to the 'prurient interest' or is 'patently offensive'.[1]

Offensiveness is not judged in terms of an effect on a particular audience, but rather in terms of affront to positive morality; in this sense it appears akin in application to the standard of indecency in English law. Indecency is however used in relation to restrictions, and not prohibitions; context then remains relevant. Patent offensiveness, although the more tightly drawn of the two standards — in terms of its reference to sexuality only, if for no other reason — is used in relation to a prohibition: aside from possession in the home, context is generally irrelevant. The standard is in these terms very broad, as one is concerned only with an affront to contemporary community standards or positive morality; it is in fact so broad that it runs the risk of becoming inoperable: although there may be a positive moral consensus in relation to offensiveness, it may relate to a particular context only, and not be apposite to a prohibition. The Court in introducing patent offensiveness in order to allow the jury to move with shifts in positive morality, may have added a requirement that was itself being left stranded by shifting community standards, whilst at the same time, particularly in view of the *Miller* application of local standards, laying the test open to charges of overbreadth.

If the potential overbreadth of patent offensiveness was not to be limited by the application of a national standard, the Court had only two alternatives: the one was to define the term more specifically; the other was to provide a list of examples of what might or might not

---

1   413 US 15 (1973) at 30.

legitimately be found patently offensive. The Court opted for the latter: it equated patent offensiveness with hard-core pornography — to be obscene, material must 'depict or describe patently offensive "hard-core" sexual conduct'.[1] A further indication of what the Court had in mind emerges from the examples it gave of subjects that might be regulated by obscenity laws:

> (a) Patently offensive representations or descriptions of ultimate sex acts, normal or perverted, actual or simulated.
>
> (b) Patently offensive representations or descriptions of masturbation, excretory functions and lewd exhibition of the genitals.[2]

The narrowing effect probably intended in the limitation to depictions of sexual conduct only, was confirmed a year later in *Jenkins* v *Georgia*:[3] in relation to the film *Carnal Knowledge*, Mr Justice Rehnquist remarked for a unanimous Court:

> While ... there are scenes in which sexual conduct including 'ultimate sexual acts' is to be understood to be taking place, the camera does not focus on the bodies of the actors at such times. There is no exhibition whether of the actors' genitals, lewd or otherwise, during these scenes. There are occasional scenes of nudity, but nudity alone is not enough to make material legally obscene under the *Miller* standards.[4]

So far legislatures had been limited in terms of overbreadth and vagueness in their use of terminology in this area; provided they stuck to legal obscenity they were safe. Now obscenity statutes themselves are limited to the control of sexual conduct, whilst in this regard 'That sexual conduct must be specifically defined by the applicable state law, as written or authoritatively construed'.[5] Implicit in this is an apparent acceptance by the Court of the argument, raised time and again over the years in relation to obscenity regulation, that the word 'obscene' was itself overbroad and/or vague. *Miller* itself gave examples

---

1   413 US 15 (1973) at 27.

2   Ibid. at 25.

3   418 US 153 (1974); see also *South Eastern Promotions* v *Conrad* 420 US 546 (1975); *Erznoznik* v *City of Jacksonville* 422 US 205 (1975); *Schad* v *Borough of Mount Ephraim* US 68L Ed 2d 671, 101 S.Ct (1981).

4   Ibid. at 161.

5   *Miller* v *California* 413 US 15 (1973) at 23.

of such conduct: 'ultimate sexual acts, normal or perverted, actual or simulated ... masturbation, excretory functions, and lewd exhibition of the genitals'.[1] Clearly if the statute parrots these examples — and many now do[2] — it will not be overbroad or vague; to hold otherwise would require an exhaustive list of every form of sexual conduct sought to be proscribed, a task probably beyond any legislature's reasonable competence. This was clearly affirmed in *Ward* v *Illinois*[3] where it was argued that because the *Miller* examples did not include sado/masochistic materials, that these were outside constitutionally 'approved' hard-core pornography. The Court's answer was that the former were merely examples: not an exclusive list. What is required is something more than legislative description in terms of obscenity, hard-core pornography or the like: the actual varieties of sexual conduct in question must be specified. Alternatively, such examples have been included by judicial construction: in *United States* v *12 200ft Reels of Film*,[4] a companion case to *Miller*, the Court indicated it was prepared to define 'obscene', 'lewd', 'lascivious', 'filthy', 'indecent', and 'immoral' as incorporating the *Miller* examples, and has since in these terms specifically reaffirmed 18 USC 1461 against a vagueness challenge.[5]

The *Miller* ruling on patent offensiveness in fact pulls in two directions: although subjectivity is increased in terms of applying local standards, what may be found patently offensive has been subject to some specification, thus in turn apparently narrowing such subjectivity. The specificity requirement has been rendered virtually toothless, however, by the *Ward* ruling, leaving the standard even more subject to a charge of overbreadth than it was in pre-*Miller* days.

IV   Jury decision

1)   *Expert evidence*

Such evidence, particularly when given in terms of external or national standards, is presumably an agency for constant obscenity. If the

---

1   413 US 15 (1973) at 25.

2   Lockhart op.cit. at 548.

3   431 US 767 (1977).

4   413 US 123 (1973) at 130, footnote 7.

5   *Hamling* v *United States* 418 US 87 (1974) at 110–6. 18 USC 1462, 19 USC 1305(a) and other federal statutes would thus similarly not be overbroad or vague. See also *Ward* v *Illinois* 431 US 767 (1977).

application of local standards represented an attempt by the Court to escape from the trend towards constant, and in practice, minimal obscenity restriction, the admissibility of expert testimony was an obvious target. In *Paris Adult Theater I* v *Slaton*[1] the Court remarked:

> This is not a subject that lends itself to the traditional use of expert testimony. Such testimony is usually admitted for the purpose of explaining to lay jurors what they otherwise could not understand ... No such assistance is needed by jurors in obscenity cases; indeed, the 'expert witness' practices employed in these cases have often made a mockery of the otherwise sound concept of expert testimony ... Simply stated, hard-core pornography ... can and does speak for itself.

The majority did not rule expert evidence inadmissible: they would have it admissible, however, only where strictly necessary, and overruled Justice Frankfurter's view that such evidence should be a requirement of due process in obscenity prosecution.[2]

2) *Jury discretion*

Obscenity remains a matter for the jury. Jury discretion has increased in certain regards, both prurient appeal and patent offensiveness lying for assessment in terms of local standards. The difference with respect to the former may well be more illusory than real: to begin with statewide standards appear quite acceptable, and these may often be as nearly external to the jury as national ones. Prurient appeal moreover, with the type of material envisaged by the test, will often in average person terms be more or less constant both in terms of the community involved,[3] and in terms of distribution within it. Distribution remains largely irrelevant: with general distribution, prurient appeal is judged in terms of the average person, and therefore probably remains more or less constant. Some variability is possible in distribution particular to deviants: the standard here should be the 'average deviant'. Similar variability accepted by the Court in the case of minors has not been excluded, but in view of the hard-core pornography formulation, remains doubtful.

The patent offensiveness factor gives the greatest scope for subjectivity, and this is increased by the application of local standards.

---

1   413 US 49 (1973) at 56, footnote 6 (citations omitted); also *Kaplan* v *California* 413 US 115 (1973) at 115.

2   *Smith* v *California* 361 US 147 (1959).

3   Schauer 'Reflections' op.cit. at 16.

This may also, if statewide standards are applied, be judged externally however, whilst in addition the Court has placed some limitations on what is, or is not, relevant in terms of patent offensiveness; *Ward* on the other hand has rendered such limitations virtually toothless. The change from utterly without redeeming social value to the serious value test certainly did increase subjectivity: it probably involves a greater exercise of discretion to decide whether something has 'serious' value, as opposed to its being utterly without any value whatever. It must be remembered, however, that serious value, as representing First Amendment values, is judged by national, and not by local community standards; also, only hard-core pornography may be suppressed (assuming that the latter phrase means anything very definite).

Such increase in subjectivity as there has been, stems largely from the affirmation of local standards, coupled with a tightening-up in relation to the admissibility of expert evidence. It must be remembered however that a finding of obscenity, although affirmed in *Miller* as a matter for the jury, is subject to independent Supreme Court review.[1] In *Jenkins* v *Georgia* for example, Mr Justice Rehnquist noted that:

> even though questions of appeal to the prurient interest or of patent offensiveness are essentially questions of fact, it would be a serious mis-reading of *Miller* to conclude that juries have unbridled discretion in determining what is 'patently offensive' ... it would be wholly at odds with this aspect of *Miller* to uphold an obscenity conviction based upon a defendant's depiction of a woman with a bare midriff, even though a properly charged jury unanimously agreed on a verdict of guilty.[2]

Although the Court had gone some way in adjusting some of the mechanisms pointing the test in the direction of constancy, it had not reinstated variability in a pronounced way. On the other hand, the standard of patent offensiveness, employed in relation to a prohibition, and locally assessed in terms of affront to community standards, is — after *Ward* — particularly susceptible to charges of overbreadth.

A critical point of compromise

Supreme Court obscenity jurisprudence was clearly in one sense in

---

1   *Miller* v *California* 413 US 15 (1973) at 24.

2   418 US 153 (1974) at 160–1.

better shape by the late 1970s than it had been a decade earlier: *Miller* was a majority opinion, whilst *Jenkins* v *Georgia* for example, was decided by a unanimous Court. Although the earlier fragmentation was avoided, this was probably the result of changes in the Court's personnel, rather than a reappraisal of the *Roth* approach. In this respect Mr Justice Brennan, the author of the *Roth* and *Memoirs* opinions, remarked (dissenting) in *Paris*

> I am convinced that the approach initiated 16 years ago in Roth ... and culminating in the Court's decision today, cannot bring stability to this area of law without jeopardising fundamental First Amendment values, and I have concluded that the time has come to make a significant departure from that approach.[1]

The exception approach to the First Amendment was certainly badly flawed: the anomalous position of this approach in terms of Mr Justice Marshall's judgement in *Stanley* remained unexplained. Although the *Miller* hard-core ruling had made the survival of the *Ginsberg* exception to the average person test in favour of minors doubtful, the latter has not as yet been rejected by the Court; the difficulties it creates for the exception approach, in terms of protected material becoming liable to proscription because of distribution, remain. The utterly without redeeming social value test has now given way to serious value in specified regards. The selection of these values appears arbitrary in terms of the exception rationale: it may well be, in terms of individual development, that psychotherapeutic value is a matter of social concern and value. Such selection appears to offend one of the possible rationales of the First Amendment: it constitutes an assumption of infallibility and an arbitrary interference in the market place of ideas. Not only this, but the *Miller* serious value formulation permits some balancing by a jury of First Amendment values against prurient appeal and patent offensiveness: despite the entire exercise being based on an approach that denies protection only to material utterly without social value, one now has material with some but not 'serious' value open to proscription. As Mr Justice Brennan remarked in *Paris Adult Theater I* v *Slaton*: 'The modification of the *Memoirs* test may prove sufficient to jeopardise the analytic underpinnings of the entire *Roth* scheme'.[2]

Perhaps the most telling criticism of the exception approach lies in the requirement of patent offensiveness. Under the *Roth* approach

---

1   *Paris Adult Theater I* v *Slaton* 413 US 49 (1973) at 84.

2   Ibid. at 96.

material may be suppressed if it does not deal in ideas,[1] if it utterly lacks any redeeming social value,[2] or if it lacks any serious literary, political, artistic or scientific value.[3] Patent offensiveness is clearly incompatible with this basic approach, in that it extends First Amendment protection beyond that which propagates ideas, or has any social value. The cutting-edge of the First Amendment has in the obscenity area in fact been set in terms of Learned Hand's 'present critical point of compromise', which has been defined in terms of patent offensiveness or hard-core pornography. In an attempt apparently to answer this criticism it has been argued that the Court in *Miller* is guilty of perpetuating a number of irrelevant concepts, one of them being patent offensiveness. It is specifically argued[4] that in applying the average person standard for prurient appeal to much material (particularly pornography) very little variation from community to community is likely to be encountered in that appeal; that prurient appeal is, in other words, a virtual constant. This is very probably correct. It is also asserted that (local) contemporary community standards can have no place in the assessment of the First Amendment value factor; again this would seem correct. The only other factor of relevance for community standards is patent offensiveness; the assertion here is not so much that contemporary community standards are inapplicable to patent offensiveness,[5] but that the entire patent offensiveness standard is 'mere surplusage'.[6] It is pointed out that the policy consideration underlying the patent offensiveness concept is almost certainly the same as that which prompted Learned Hand to ask '... should not the word obscene be allowed to indicate the present critical point in the compromise between candor and shame at which the community may have arrived here and now?'[7]

Literary or other value was not in 1913 relevant to an assessment of obscenity, the arousal of lustful thoughts being sufficient. Over time this became unacceptable; hence Learned Hand's plea that the

---

1   *Chaplinsky* v *New Hampshire* 315 US 568 (1942).

2   *Roth* v *United States* 354 US 476 (1957).

3   *Miller* v *California* 413 US 15 (1973).

4   See Schauer 'Reflections on "Contemporary Community Standards" ' 57 (1978) *N Car L Rev* 1.

5   If one accepts patent offensiveness as a valid standard, they almost certainly would be: views on patent offensiveness would surely vary from community to community?

6   Schauer 'Reflections' op.cit. at 18.

7   *United States* v *Kennerley* 209 F 119 (SD NY 1913) at 121.

tolerance level of the community be taken into account in this respect. Mr Justice Harlan was probably motivated in precisely the same way in *Manual* in introducing the concept of patent offensiveness: to ensure that material generally acceptable could not, despite its possible prurient appeal, be proscribed. As the value factor had in *Jacobellis* become an absolute, it is argued that patent offensiveness was at this stage irrelevant, and should have been dropped.[1] Account of literary value sought in terms of community standards by Learned Hand in *Kennerley* was, however, clearly — if implicitly — operative at the time of *Manual* in terms of the *Roth* test. Society's tolerance levels with respect to sexually-orientated material are by no means constant: as there had earlier been a willingness to compromise over the arousal of lustful thoughts approach in the interests of literature, so there was by the 1960s an apparent willingness to compromise even further, in the sense that some material, without merit and with a prurient appeal, might be acceptable. It is almost certainly with this that the requirement of patent offensiveness is and was concerned: material had not only to be utterly without social value, but had *also* to be patently offensive. First Amendment protection extended beyond material with such value, to include the valueless, but non-patently offensive, or as is now clear from *Miller*, the non-hard-core pornographic. Patent offensiveness is therefore anything but surplusage.

The surplusage argument relies on the ideas/non-ideas distinction in relation to speech. This apparently is not felt sufficient however, and an allied but distinguishable argument is advanced: that is, that material without value and with prurient appeal is so closely allied to sexual conduct as to be virtually indistinguishable from it; it therefore, as conduct, falls outside First Amendment 'speech'. This will be discussed later.[2] Professor Schauer, whilst advancing the irrelevance of the patent offensiveness requirement, at the same time concedes it is useful in protecting material with such value from the chilling effect of the overbreadth inherent in *Miller*; that the requirement in other words constitutes a buffer zone between clearly protected speech and regulation.[3] This is an ingenious attempt at having one's cake and eating it: if regulation is permissible in relation to material without value, any extension in terms of patent offensiveness, or 'buffer zones', consti-

---

1   Schauer op.cit.

2   See chapter 14.

3   See Schauer 'Speech and "Speech" — Obscenity and "Obscenity": An exercise in the interpretation of Constitutional Language' 67 (1979) *Georgetown LJ* 899 at 931; also 'Fear, Risk and the First Amendment: Unravelling the "Chilling Effect" ' 58 (1978) *Boston U L Rev* 685 at 714ff.

tutes a fatal flaw in the logic.

The exception approach has led the Court in the direction of other anomalies: it seems absurd, for example, to assert local standards as to patent offensiveness, in practice the determinative element of the obscenity test, whilst at the same time reiterating the propriety of the Court's reviewing *de novo* obscenity findings. The exception approach, in terms of which the obscenity definition has acquired a constitutional status, probably left the Court little choice. Nor does the *Roth* approach achieve its apparent goal: if it is designed to avoid discussion of policy factors and balancing, it does not achieve the latter, in that the Court now has to balance First Amendment value against prurient appeal and patent offensiveness in each and every case. In its desire both to avoid discussing policy issues, and to achieve some First Amendment reconciliation, the Court has moreover achieved a formulation which threatens to ignore two basic and rationally assessable harms in this area: the protection of children and the prevention of gratuitous offence. Both these were raised in *Redrup*, and more substantially in *Stanley*; Justice Marshall's discussion and rejection in *Stanley* of the justifications in First Amendment terms for the suppression of non-commercial speech also remain unanswered. Instead, the court continues to sustain, without discussing the policy issues involved, the constitutionality of a prohibition designed to enforce, and applied in terms of positive morality, asserting rather brusquely in the process the necessary rational connection between the relevant governmental aim and the prohibition in question. The appropriateness of the application of strict liability in the speech area remains largely undiscussed, whilst obscenity decision essentially in terms of affront to local community standards is not calculated to assuage overbreadth criticisms.

The Court, moreover, in introducing patent offensiveness, and subsequently in *Miller*, in asserting local standards, was probably aiming at a loosening of the trend towards constancy in obscenity adjudication. Patent offensiveness allowed juries greater discretion, and in the process probably allowed them more accurately to reflect community standards. It may be, though, that community standards have in the interim between *Manual* and *Miller* shifted even further: the main concern of the community today may be the protection of children and the prevention of gratuitous offence. Restriction in other words, rather than prohibition, may be more appropriate in terms of positive morality. If this is so, obscenity law becomes something which juries will find it increasingly difficult to assess and assert. The Court itself in its trend towards minimal restriction in the late 1960s appeared to find just this; it was presumably in the process attempting to reflect community standards. Even the Burger Court appears to have acknowledged this possibility; the passage quoted at the beginning of this chapter from *Reidel* is probably worth rehearsing here:

> ... There is developing sentiment that adults should have complete freedom to produce, deal in, possess and consume whatever communicative materials may appeal to them and that the law's involvement with obscenity should be limited to those situations where children are involved or where it is necessary to prevent imposition on unwilling recipients of whatever age. The concepts involved are so elusive and the laws so inherently unenforceable without extravagant expenditures of time and effort by enforcement officers and the courts that basic reassessment is not only wise but essential.[1]

Many state legislatures have repealed their adult obscenity statutes: although legislative decision may not be — in the Court's terms, is not — decisive of community standards, it does appear possible that the Court has attempted in *Miller* to resurrect a system the basis of which no longer corresponds sufficiently closely to the needs and views of society to be viable. It might be answered that the trend towards the repeal of adult obscenity statutes could be followed in more states; this however leaves one with potential problems in terms of federal regulation, whilst what may be seen as more pressing concerns — the protection of children and the prevention of gratuitous offence — remain in effect unaccommodated. Offence has to some extent been accommodated in terms of zoning regulations:[2] although the Court resolutely eschewed the constitutional accommodation of the regulations in *Erznoznik* v *City of Jacksonville*,[3] the zoning provisions — operated in terms of an 'adult' standard — at issue in *Young*[4] were found permissible. This the Court managed by in effect skirting the First Amendment, in part by regarding zoning provisions as aimed at town planning and not speech regulation; as they had the minimum of impact on speech, all was well. Although regulations essentially aimed at the prevention of offence are then within this narrow ambit constitutional, this does not constitute a satisfactory appraisal of the policy issues involved, whilst the avoidance of such discussion in First Amendment terms has meant the sanctioning of a grossly overbroad

---

1 *United States* v *Reidel* 412 US 351 (1971) at 357.

2 See zoning, chapter 12.

3 422 US 205 (1975).

4 427 US 50 (1976). For a fuller discussion of *Young* see motion picture censorship, chapter 12; alternative approaches, chapter 14.

standard.

All this surely points in one direction, and that is the abandonment of the exception approach, coupled with a reappraisal in First Amendment terms of the policy issues involved and their possible accommodation in terms of First Amendment theory. One has so far been talking solely in terms of the First Amendment; the clear relevance of privacy in this area was asserted in *Stanley*; this relevance has not been adequately explored and synthetised with privacy guarantees as effective in other areas of law. Such policy questions and their possible constitutional accommodation will be considered over the course of the next two chapters.

14 Obscenity and the First Amendment

I) The *Roth* approach

It has been argued that the flaws in the exception approach detailed above are in no way fatal to the *Roth* approach to the First Amendment:[1] one should look, it is suggested, not at the Supreme Court's definition of obscenity, but rather at the philosophical basis of the First Amendment, and in turn, the exception approach. If the latter is sustainable in these terms, its rehabilitation amounts to no more than a reshaping of the obscenity definition. The First Amendment it is argued, is concerned with the communication of ideas, and not more loosely with freedom of expression. Its most likely philosophical basis is the market place of ideas formulation, and not a general theory of liberty, which would potentially provide protection for an enormous range of activities. The word 'speech' in the First Amendment is, in other words, to be interpreted to reflect this narrower philosophical base: it is to be seen as excluding that which does not communicate ideas, and more particularly, that which is not designed 'to appeal to the intellectual process'. In these terms

... the refusal to treat pornography as speech is grounded

---

1 See especially F. Schauer 'Speech and "Speech" — Obscenity and "Obscenity": An Exercise in the Interpretation of Constitutional Language' 67 (1979) *Georgetown LJ* 899; Schauer 'Response: Pornography and the First Amendment' 4 (1979) *U Pitts L Rev* 605.

> in the assumption that the prototypical pornographic
> item on closer analysis shares more of the characteristics
> of sexual activity than of the communicative process. The
> pornographic item is in a real sense a sexual surrogate. It
> takes pictorial or linguistic form only because some
> individuals achieve sexual gratification by those means.[1]

Pornography is thus to be assimilated to many varieties of conduct, and to be excluded from the category of constitutionally protected speech. The reformulation of the definition follows close on the heels of all this: as the exception is in terms of the cognitive communication of ideas, the *Memoirs* formulation in terms of social value is overbroad. One is concerned rather with the *Miller* variety of values, and these should be seen in assessment terms as absolute, and not merely 'serious'.

The outstanding criticism of the present formulation relates to patent offensiveness and the fact that it extends protection beyond that which has any merit. The answer here is that with an absolute value factor, this requirement is unnecessary, and may therefore be scrapped, the formulation operating in terms of prurient appeal and First Amendment value:

> If the prurient interest test isolates material that has
> physical as opposed to mental effect, and if the 'value'
> test restricts regulation to material that is *solely* physical
> in nature, what is left is not speech in the constitutional
> sense, regardless of whether anyone is offended, and
> regardless of whether any community's standards are
> affronted.[2]

Is this restatement any more viable than the *Roth* prototype? It appears to rest on two separable propositions: the first is that pornography can be assimilated to conduct, and may therefore be seen as outside the speech area; second, that such material is additionally, and in any case, outside the speech area because of its lack of cognitive or communicative function. These two propositions are run together, in the sense that material is non-cognitive because of its physical effect: it is seen as 'sex'. Equally, they may be dealt with separately in the sense that a speech/conduct distinction does not necessarily correspond to a speech/value distinction. Taking the speech/conduct distinction first: does this rest on either philosophical or constitutional foundations? Certainly those theories

---

1   Schauer 'Speech and "Speech" ' op.cit. at 922.

2   Ibid. at 929; emphasis in the original; citations omitted.

rehearsed earlier[1] of liberty in terms of self-development, self-expression, liberty as a good in itself, or individual rights, are so broad as to cover expression in any form at all; on the other hand most theorists would appear willing to accord freedom of speech a pre-eminent position in their formulations on the basis of its constituting, either in terms of rights or individual liberties, a fundamental aspect of any libertarian philosophy. This distinction between speech in the sense of one or other material of communication, as opposed to conduct, has been recognised by the Supreme Court as fundamentally relevant to the First Amendment in relation, for example, to live shows.[2] The distinction has been endorsed by commentators who favour an absolutist approach to the Amendment: Professor Emerson (for example) proposes a differentiation between speech and action.[3] This is a distinction which has been followed throughout this essay: to attempt to examine the philosophical and/or constitutional implications of freedom of expression in the broad sense would be unmanageable. The Court clearly felt that the constitutional reference to speech had to be limited in the same way.

What one is in fact doing here is according, in First Amendment terms, a fairly literal meaning to 'speech': it comprises writing, illustration, film, record, etc.; in other words communication in a literal sense, as opposed to conduct. Such distinction is not always easy to draw: what of art forms such as ballet? The Court has recognised this underinclusivity by permitting the extension of First Amendment protection on the basis of the predominance of speech over conduct. In other words, where the activity in question involves more conduct than speech, and provided the effect on protected speech is as small as possible, regulation may be permissible.[4] This is a question of fact, and often not an easy matter to decide; take the case that the Supreme Court faced in *Spence* v *Washington*:[5] was the display, upside down and and with peace symbols affixed to both sides, of the national flag, speech within the First Amendment or not? The Court answered (*per curiam*) in the affirmative. A suggestion made by the Williams Committee as to such decisions in the live show area, was that distinction be made in terms of actual sexual conduct and mere simulation

---

1   See pp.121ff. *supra*.

2   See chapters 7 and 12.

3   See T. Emerson *The System of Freedom of Expression* (New York 1970).

4   See live shows, chapters 7 and 12.

5   418 US 405 (1974).

thereof.[1] This suggestion might well serve to reduce the subjectivity inherent in any attempt to define the word 'speech' in the above terms.

Our immediate concern here is whether the latter term is overinclusive in the sense of including, as commonly or literally defined, speech which clearly should be excluded from the First Amendment; the basis of such exclusion is that certain varieties of speech may be assimilated to conduct, thus removing them from the speech area. All must depend here on whether one accepts that pornography 'is sex': 'The mere fact that in pornography the stimulating experience is initiated by visual rather than tactile means is irrelevant if every other aspect of the experience is the same.'[2] This is unconvincing: reading pornographic material may produce a physical reaction; this can take place only as the result of a cognitive process. The reader or viewer is in mental receipt of the portrayals in question; the physical reaction concerned follows from this. Pornography is thus not only speech in the colloquial or usual sense; it also involves communication. Although one may argue that all action is communicative,[3] 'Implicit in any meaningful constitutional definition of speech as communication is the idea that one can separate advocacy of an act from the act itself, even though the act contains an element of the advocacy'.[4] Pornography is advocacy and not action, and is distinguishable from sexual conduct.

This leaves one in the position of apparently regarding all communication effected by means other than conduct as speech; speech in other words, is given its usual meaning of covering verbal communication, writing, film, etc. There is a difficulty with this, in that it does not explain why ballet for example, which is *prima facie* conduct in the above terms, should be regarded as speech. This brings one to the second, and related leg, of the proposition that obscenity is not speech. It is argued that the form which speech takes is not decisive; what is decisive is the rationale of the First Amendment. Because general theories of liberty do not explain the pre-eminence of freedom of speech, it is argued[5] that the central or core rationale of the Amendment is Mill's market place of ideas formulation. In these terms, ballet may be included within speech as communicating ideas, whilst obscenity may be excluded on the basis that it does not so communicate.

---

1 See live shows, chapter 7.

2 Schauer 'Speech and "Speech" ' op.cit. at 923.

3 See J. Lyons *Chomsky* (2d edn 1977); quoted ibid. at 925.

4 Schauer 'Speech and "Speech" ' op.cit. at 925.

5 Ibid. 914–8.

Although it may be argued that obscenity is 'thematic' — that in other words it argues for an alternative lifestyle, etc. — this is not particularly convincing; the Williams Committee for example, accepted that pornography cannot generally be said to be concerned with the purveying of ideas. There is nonetheless a difficulty with this reasoning: the Court's jurisprudence does not reflect only the communication of ideas formulation:

> To use language to arouse feelings or emotions, to induce someone to take action, to create a sense of beauty, to shock, to offend, or to ask a question is in each instance a use of language for some purpose other than the exposition of ideas.[1]

In order to escape this difficulty, Professor Schauer proposes that the philosophical ideas formulation and the Court's apparent use of it, is concerned with or aimed at the protection of the communication of mental stimulus; because obscenity 'is sex', it does not do the latter, and may therefore be regarded as non-speech. This brings one back to the rejection of obscenity as non-cognitive, and the proposition falls.

The idea that because obscenity is not concerned with ideas, it falls outside speech is not a novel one: besides its judicial enunciation, the pre-eminent statement of its relevance in this respect was advanced in an article in 1967: obscenity

> ... is regarded by Mr Justice Brennan as devoid of relevant or 'redeeming' social utility precisely because it pertains, not to the realm of ideas, reason, intellectual content and truth-seeking, but to the realm of passion, desires, cravings, and titillation. As such, obscenity belongs to a realm outside first amendment protection. The two constitutional levels of speech, in effect, are defined in terms of the two realms of the human mind.[2]

The Court's application of this formulation with the obscenity formulation has not been consistent: the Court in *Roth* spoke of obscenity not having any 'social importance',[3] and in *Memoirs* of it lacking 'social value'.[4] This indicates a much broader rationale than one in

---

1 Schauer, 'Speech and "Speech" ' op.cit. at 921; see e.g. *Cohen* v *California* 403 US 15 (1971) at 16.

2 Finnis ' "Reason and Passion": The Constitutional Dialectic of Free Speech and Obscenity' 116 (1967) *U Pa L Rev* 222 at 227; see also T.J. Murphy *Censorship: Government and Obscenity* (1963) at 29.

3 354 US 476 (1957) at 484.

4 383 US 413 (1966) at 418–9.

terms of ideas; although these formulations were narrowed in *Miller* v *California*,[1] the varied usage hardly indicates a sustained adherence by the Court to a clearly articulated and pre-eminent First Amendment rationale, particularly in view of the Court's extension of protection to material not concerned with ideas, but not patently offensive. The First Amendment does not in fact appear to have a clearly articulated and core meaning, or rationale. The closest one comes to such meaning is the protection of political debate.[2] This could be said to be based on the ideas formulation; it could equally be based on the closely allied but — according to its author — otherwise based, Meiklejohn democratic theory model. This argues that the American people granted only certain powers to federal and state governments, reserving in the process significant governing powers to themselves. 'This was because their basic decision was to govern themselves rather than be governed by others.'[3] These powers of governing importance are embodied in the First Amendment: in order to govern rather than be governed, information[4] on public issues is essential. These reserved powers in turn find ultimate expression in the voting power of the people in elections: 'The revolutionary intent of the First Amendment is, then, to deny all subordinate agencies authority to abridge the freedom of the electoral power of the people'.[5] Speech which has no relation to the business of governing would not be protected.

Dr Meiklejohn's theory appears to attempt a First Amendment accommodation of a central aspect of Mill's views on freedom of speech: in order for a democratic society to operate, men must be sufficiently informed on anything pertinent to the society and its operation. With this as its central object, it attempts the accommodation via an amalgam of the essence of two older First Amendment theories: it affects the approach of the absolute theory with respect to public speech whilst at the same time drawing a distinction between public and private speech; such distinction is the essence of the exception or two-tier approach: such private speech is then beyond First

---

1   413 US 15 (1973): the control of obscenity is distinct from (for example) 'a control of reason and the intellect'; at 27.

2   See H. Kalven 'A Note on the "Central Meaning of the First Amendment"' 1964 *Supr Crt Rev* 191.

3   W. Brennan 'The Supreme Court and the Meiklejohn Interpretation of the First Amendment' 79 (1965) *Harv L Rev* 1 at 11; see also Meiklejohn 'The First Amendment is an Absolute' 1961 *Supr Crt Rev* 245.

4   With information on public issues, is included science, literature and the arts: in fact everything that equips a citizen responsibly to exercise his vote.

5   Meiklejohn op.cit. at 254.

Amendment protection. The theory made its debut in *New York Times v Sullivan*:[1] the central question here was whether First Amendment protection covered (to the extent of displacing the traditional libel laws) statements made criticising the official conduct of a public servant. The case, in the sense of involving an activity of governing importance, was virtually tailor-made. The Court, in deciding that such protection was available, '... examined history to discern the central meaning of the first amendment, and concluded that that meaning was revealed in Madison's statement "that the censorial power is in the people over the Government, and not in the Government over the people" '.[2] The ruling has been followed in a number of subsequent cases,[3] all of which fell within the area of damage to reputation;[4] it does not appear to have been more extensively applied. Is a more extensive application (to the area of obscenity for example) likely? Certainly the Court would appear to have taken up the invitation identified by Professor Kalven after the *New York Times* case: '... to follow a dialectic progression from public official to government policy to public policy to matters in the public domain, like art, ...'.[5]

The *Hill* decision for example, involved the definition of constitutional concern in terms of 'newsworthiness': that is, what is of public interest. This seems very close to Professor Kalven's classification of the public domain above. The extension of this doctrine into other areas of constitutional concern must seem very doubtful however: the distinction between public and private speech is at least ill-defined,[6] whilst exceptions to the guarantee of public speech go largely unelaborated:

> Once you push punishment beyond action into the
> realm of language, then you have to say pretty plainly
> how far back the law should go. You must enable
> future judges and jurymen to know where to stop. That

---

1   376 US 254 (1964).

2   Brennan op.cit. at 15, quoting 4 Annals of Congress 934 (1794).

3   *Rosenblatt v Baur* 383 US 75 (1966); *Time, Inc v Hill* 385 US 374 (1967); *Pickering v Board of Education* 391 US 563 (1968).

4   Some may for example have involved essentially invasion of privacy: see e.g. *Time, Inc v Hill* 385 US 374 (1967).

5   H. Kalven op.cit. at 221.

6   For a strong criticism of the Meiklejohn approach, see Zachariah Chafee's review of Meiklejohn's *Free Speech and its Relation to Self-Government*, 62 (1948–9) Harv L Rev 891.

is just what Holmes did when he drew his line at clear and present danger, and [Dr Meiklejohn] ... gives us no substitute test for distinguishing between good public speech and bad public speech.[1]

As regards obscenity, the doctrine would be unlikely to add anything to the present approach: Dr Meiklejohn equated 'governing importance' with 'social importance',[2] and although he then (perhaps inconsistently?) goes on to reject any suggestion that those works without such social importance be singled out, it would seem probable, were the Court to apply his approach more generally, that obscenity would merely continue to be regarded as speech without social value, and therefore an exception.

The distinction then between the ideas formulation and the social value formulation is probably not preserved in Meiklejohn's terms, whilst his theory has not commanded a general First Amendment application. If the ideas formulation is not pre-eminent in First Amendment jurisprudence and its philosophical basis, what is? There are two difficulties here: the first is that philosophical formulations of the importance of individual liberty are not generally specifically related to the question of constitutional guarantees; second, there is the related aspect that most philosophical formulations of this sort, although they may recognise the importance of freedom of speech in particular, are not necessarily so specific as to help one define 'speech' in a constitutional context. Professor Dworkin, for example, appears to find essentially the same basis for freedom of speech as he does for a variety of other conduct,[3] whilst Mill, although he bases the importance of freedom of speech on the market place of ideas, did caution against any assumption of infallibility; what has no value in terms of ideas should be assessed as such in the market place, and not beforehand. It may be then that not only is there no exclusive rationale[4] for the First Amendment, but that those rationales that are on offer are not sufficiently specific to found a particular interpretation of the term 'speech'. Even though most theorists accord freedom of speech some pre-eminence, their basis for doing so does not always permit a

---

1   Chafee op.cit. at 898.

2   For an apparent application of the governing importance/social value equation, see *Garrision* v *Louisiana* 379 US 64 (1964) at 75, where the ruling that false criticism of a public official (if made in the knowledge of its falsity) was not protected under the *New York Times* rule, was justified by the classification of such criticism as being without social value.

3   R. Dworkin *Taking Rights Seriously* (London 1977) at 275—6.

4   See e.g. L. Tribe *American Constitutional Law: Cases and Materials* (9th edn 1975) at 899—990.

ready distinction between speech and conduct. The theory probably providing the clearest basis of distinction in this respect is the market place of ideas formulation: even if the latter does not allow one to predetermine what conveys ideas and what does not,[1] one is clearly concerned with that which communicates mental stimulus; an idea could scarcely be communicated in any other way. This theory does not necessarily hold exclusive sway however; aside from it, philosophical rationales take one little further in assigning a particular meaning to speech. Any attempt to classify obscenity as non-speech on the basis of First Amendment rationales is thus unlikely to succeed. Even if one adopts the rationale of the market place of ideas, interpreted in the sense of broadening concern to the communication of mental stimulus, to claim that pornography does not so communicate is quite simply, in physiological and psychological terms, wrong.

As was pointed out earlier,[2] the distinction between speech and expression may seem, in philosophical terms, an arbitrary one. The market place of ideas formulation provides some help in narrowing concern to the communication of mental stimulation. Alexander Meiklejohn's democratic theory model, although it limits the functions of the market place in terms of the requirement of social value in relation to that which is protected, is clearly similarly concerned: the proper exercise of democratic functions, and more particularly one's vote, is essentially dependent on the extent to which one is open to the communication of mental stimulus. If one looks beyond the philosophical sphere, the importance of the latter may be argued to have clear constitutional significance in that the very development of philosophical formulations itself requires a context in which the communication of mental stimulus is guaranteed.[3] What one looks for then is not to weed out *a priori* what one feels does not convey ideas, but rather to look, with speech, for that which is aimed at conveying mental stimulus. This would comprise all forms of speech, taking the latter in its usual sense of comprising one or other form of communication, together with those varieties of conduct which fairly clearly fall within the definition. The boundaries will not always be easy to draw: there might be disagreement about actual sexual conduct in a live show for example, although it could be argued, as does Williams, that such conduct cannot be said primarily to be aimed at communi-

---

1   The court has long since refused to draw the line between entertainment and ideas: *Winters v New York* 333 US 507 (1925).

2   See substantive common law offences, chapter 3.

3   See R. McKeon, R. Merton, W. Gelhorn *The Freedom to Read* (New York 1957) chapter 1.

cation; it may be said to be an act, as opposed to advocacy thereof.

If the aforementioned proposition is felt to be philosophically deficient, this is not the place to attempt a remedy. The philosophical basis of freedom of speech is more developed, but reminiscent in this sense, of that in relation to privacy: formulations in respect of the latter are again not sufficiently specific as to predetermine the meaning to be assigned in a constitutional context (say) to the term 'privacy'.[1] In respect of speech, one's concern here is to assess the attempt at refurbishment of the exception approach to the First Amendment, and to determine whether it holds any more water than its discredited prototype; it clearly does not, for it is even less credible in terms of more general formulations of individual liberty than it is in terms of the market place or Meiklejohn approaches. To the extent that the above represents a more neutral approach to the First Amendment and its application it is in line with the so-called equality principle argued to underlie the Amendment.[2] This proclaims that all speech should be treated as being equal; although this could be argued to be relevant only once a determination of what is or is not speech has been made, there would seem no reason to exclude its application as an agent of neutrality in relation to the latter crucial decision? This neutral approach to the Amendment and its application may have underlain the recent abandonment of the exception approach in relation to commercial speech.[3] Quite aside from neutrality however, is there any other basis than mental stimulation or its absence which may possibly ground a viable obscenity exception? The only apparent possibility here is offensiveness to community standards. Such exception would not square with any First Amendment rationale; its acceptance by the Court is so remote that it may be discounted. Whether, once obscenity is admitted as protected speech, a restriction (rather than prohibition) is viable in terms of offensiveness, will be discussed later.

Even if one were to accept that obscenity is not speech in mental stimulus terms, one would still be faced with those potential avenues of constitutional attack rehearsed in earlier chapters: the standard to be applied would almost certainly be overbroad, for although it has been argued that patent offensiveness is unnecessary, it would be

---

1   See privacy, pp.159–66.

2   See Karst 'Equality as a Central Principle in the First Amendment' 43 (1975) *U Chi L Rev* 20.

3   *Virginia St. Bd. of Pharmacy* v *Virginia Citizens Consumer Council, Inc.* 425 US 748 (1976).

desirable to limit the test to hard-core pornography; a requirement such as patent offensiveness would thus still be necessary, a requirement which must needs be reconciled with the argued rationale of absence of mental stimulation. Such reconciliation has been rather unconvincingly attempted by arguing that although soft-core pornography does not stimulate mentally, it is protected via a patent offensiveness requirement, the latter acting as a buffer zone to protect First Amendment speech.[1] One would have also the question of Fourteenth Amendment due process requirements: if, for argument's sake, one accepts obscenity as non-protected conduct, one would still be required to establish a viable governmental aim, and a rational connection between regulation and that aim. The aim in terms of the present formulation is undoubtedly the prevention of affront, irrespective of context, to positive sexual morality. The permissibility of this then lies for assessment both constitutionally and philosophically: it has been argued that the only permissible governmental aim in these terms is the regulation of rationally assessable harms.[2] Even were this not accepted, one is, assuming a close connection between perusal of pornography and physical stimulation, primarily concerned, presumably, with masturbatory conduct; is such conduct regarded today as immoral? The question remains also whether legal enforcement is effective in sustaining morality. Such issues have been only cursorily examined by the Court.[3] One has also problems in terms of privacy. The holding in *Stanley* that the possession of obscenity in the home is protected, has been confirmed; the case's implications in privacy terms in relation (for example) to customs controls, have however been abruptly curtailed.[4] Although the scope and basis of privacy protection has not been clearly defined, if the concept has a core meaning of protecting the basic privacy of the home, there would not seem to be any reason in principle why this protection should not extend to one's private possessions whilst in transit through customs, or to private possessions in the mails, say.

II) Alternative approaches

The First Amendment is on the face of it, an absolute: '... Congress

---

[1] See Schauer 'Speech and "Speech" ' op.cit. at 931.

[2] L. Henkin 'Morals and the Constitution: The Sin of Obscenity' 63 (1963) *Col L Rev* 391.

[3] As in *Miller v California* 413 US 15 (1973) for example.

[4] See privacy, pp.159–66 *supra*.

shall make no law ...'. If one accepts that obscenity or pornography is speech, does this, in view of the apparently absolute nature of the Amendment, end matters as far as regulation is concerned? An absolute approach was for many years espoused on the Court by Justices Black and Douglas.[1] The approach, as with its recent jurisprudential rights theory counterparts, is not literally an absolute: none of its advocates has suggested that *all* speech is at all times and in all circumstances protected from governmental restraint. As Mr Justice Black, probably its best known proponent, remarked:

> The First and Fourteenth Amendments, I think, take away from government, state and federal, all power to restrict freedom of speech, press and assembly *where people have a right to be for such purposes*. This does not mean, however, that these amendments also grant a constitutional right to engage in the conduct of picketing or patrolling, whether on publicly owned streets or on privately owned property ... Were the law otherwise, people on the streets, in their houses and anywhere else could be compelled to listen against their will to speakers they did not want to hear.[2]

It would follow from this that *all* forms of speech are protected, but the manner of exercise of this freedom may fall beyond the Amendment's protection. The extent of permissible restriction has never been formulated with any precision however, probably because the test has never commanded a majority on the Court; proponents of the test differ in their conclusions. Because all speech is regarded (initially at any rate) as being protected, this test does not involve any balancing of values as do its rivals;[3] one is rather concerned here with the definition of words in the Amendment such as 'abridges', and phrases such as 'no law' and 'the freedom of speech'. This can perhaps be over-emphasised, as such definitions in themselves involve a weighing-up process, but it is probably a test that lends itself more easily to the judicial process than a *de novo* balancing in each case. Certainly it

---

1 See the dissenting opinions of Mr Justice Black in *Barenblatt* v *United States* 360 US 109 (1959), *Konigsberg* v *State Bar* 386 US 36 (1961), *Communist Party* v *Subversive Activities Control Board* 367 US 1 (1961), and *Braden* v *United States* 365 US 431 (1961); the concurring opinion of Mr Justice Douglas in *Speiser* v *Randell* 357 US 513 (1958) and his dissenting opinions in *Times Film Corp* v *City of Chicago* 365 US 43 (1961) and *Scales* v *United States* 367 US 203 (1961). See also Meiklejohn 'The First Amendment is an Absolute' 1961 *Supr Crt Rev* 245; Reich 'Mr. Justice Black and the Living Constitution' 76 (1963) *Harvard L Rev* 673.

2 *Cox* v *Louisiana* 379 US 559 (1964) at 578 (dissenting opinion); emphasis in original.

3 On this see Paul G. Kauper *Civil Liberties and the Constitution* (1962) at 114; Alexander Bickel *The Least Dangerous Branch* (1962) at 93.

emphasises the positive aspect of the constitutional guarantee, and not its limitations. Not only does this approach lack essential elaboration however: it is also apparently out of step with interpretation and attitudes towards freedom of speech, both philosophical, judicial and political. Mill for example, was quite clear that certain forms of speech which cause harm to individuals or society may be suppressed.[1] Jefferson, in his second inaugural address in 1805 remarked:

> No inference is here intended that the laws provided by the State against false and defamatory publications should not be enforced ... the press, confined to truth, needs no other restraint ...: and no other definite line can be drawn between the inestimable liberty of the press and demoralising licentiousness. If there still be improprieties which this rule would not restrain, its supplement must be sought in the censorship of public opinion.[2]

The absolute approach has never commanded a majority on the court; in view of the fact that it compromises its own supposed absoluteness without adequately articulating such compromise, it is perhaps justifiable to look elsewhere in terms of First Amendment approaches. The Court has admitted a number of contexts in which government may curb speech; even the most fervent of libertarians would be unlikely to reject all of these. Aside from the Meiklejohn approach, these contexts have broadly taken three forms: the bad tendency test, the balancing test, and the clear and present danger test. The first of these provided that speech which had a tendency (or which the legislature reasonably assessed to have a tendency) to lead to substantial evil could be prohibited. The Court in *Gitlow* v *New York*[3] stated the doctrine broadly:

> That a state in the exercise of its police power may punish those who abuse this freedom of speech by utterances inimical to the public welfare, tending to corrupt public morals, incite to crime, or disturb the public peace, is not open to question.

The test offers virtually no protection to freedom of expression, and was soon supplanted[4] by the clear and present danger test. This

---

1 See pp.107ff. *supra*.

2 Paul K. Padover, *The Complete Jefferson* (New York 1943) at 109.

3 268 US 652 (1927) at 667.

4 The test was finally rejected in *Dennis* v *United States* 341 US 494 (1951) at 507.

was first enunciated by Mr Justice Holmes in *Shenck* v *United States*[1] a case concerning speech affecting national security: 'The question in every case is whether the words are used in such circumstances and are of such a nature as to create a clear and present danger that will bring about the substantive evil that Congress has a right to prevent'. Mr Justice Brandeis in *Whitney* v *California* added: '... no danger flowing from speech can be deemed clear and present, unless the incidence of the evil apprehended is so imminent that it may befall before there is an opportunity for full discussion.[2] Three conditions are apparently inherent in the test:[3]

(i) There must be in view a substantive evil that the legislature has a right to prevent from materialising. Both Justice Holmes and Justice Brandeis saw the evil in question as something 'with which the law might deal'.[4] An obvious example would be incitement to crime or violence.[5]

(ii) The danger of the materialisation of the evil has to be imminent: as a result any statutory or judicially approved test defining the effect of the expression concerned in terms of mere tendency was clearly unconstitutional.[6]

(iii) There had to be a clear causal link between the prohibited speech and the evil sought to be prevented. In assessing the imminence of the danger and the presence of the causal link, reasonable grounds for holding such a belief were necessary.

---

1 249 US 47 (1918) at 52; with respect to the test in this area see also *Debs* v *United States* 249 US 24 (1919); *Abrams* v *United States* 250 US 616 (1919); *Herndon* v *Lowry* 301 US 242 (1931). The test also found application in areas of religious expression (*Cantwell* v *Connecticut* 310 US 296 (1940)) and the improper influencing of the administration of justice (*Bridges* v *California* 314 US 252 (1941); *Pennekamp* v *Florida* 328 US 331 (1946); *Craig* v *Harney* 331 US 367 (1947); *Wood* v *Georgia* 370 US 375 (1962)).

2 274 US 357 at 366 (1927).

3 To examine 'clear and present danger' in detail is beyond the scope of this analysis. See Autiean ' "Clear and Present Danger" — Its Meaning and Significance' 25 (1950) *Notre Dame Law* 325; Gorfinkel and Mack 'Dennis v United States and the Clear and Present Danger Rule' 39 (1951) *California L Rev* 475; Mendelson 'Clear and Present Danger — From Schenck to Dennis' 52 (1952) *Colorado L Rev* 313; Richardson 'Freedom of Expression and the Function of the Courts' 65 (1951) *Harvard L Rev* 1; note 'Clear and Present Danger Re-examined' 51 (1951) *Colorado L Rev* 98; Lockhart and McClure op.cit. 295 at 363—8.

4 *Gitlow* v *New York* 268 US 652 (1925).

5 *De Jonge* v *Oregon* 299 US 353 at 338 (1937); see also e.g. *Musser* v *Utah* 333 US 95 at 114 (1948).

6 *Bridges* v *California* 314 US 252 (1945) at 273.

The standard is a very much more stringent one than demanding merely a due process rational connection between the remedy provided and the evil proscribed.[1] 'The rational connection between the remedy provided and the evil to be curbed, which in other contexts might support legislation against attack on due process grounds, will not suffice. The [First Amendment] rights rest on firmer foundations.'[2] This test represented a substantial advance on the bad tendency test, as it in theory protects speech that interferes with legitimate governmental objectives unless the danger to those interests is clear and immediate. The doctrine was extensively used by the Court in First Amendment cases until the early 1950s when it was clearly rejected in *American Communications* v *Douds*[3] and *Dennis* v *United States*.[4] This rejection was probably the result of political pressures on the Court. Certainly in purporting to lay down an absolute guarantee of free speech in circumstances other than those involving a clear and present danger, the test was for some too rigid; on the other hand there were those who argued that in view of judicial discretion[5] as to what was or was not such a danger, it gave little clarity in advance of a judicial decision. The test was as a result expanded to include other factors such

> 'as the nature and gravity of the evil sought to be prevented, the alternatives open to the government,

---

1   The standard normally employed when reviewing state legislation on due process grounds.

2   *Thomas* v *Collins* 323 US 516 at 530 (1945).

3   339 US 382 (1950); for an account of the history of the clear and present danger test (together with references to previous material discussing it) see McKay 'The Preference for Freedom' 34 (1959) *NYU L Rev* 1182.

4   341 US 494 (1951).

5   This was by no means a settled point in clear and present danger cases: 'In the *Schenck* case, and in his dissents in *Abrams* and *Gitlow*, Mr. Justice Holmes although never explicit about the point, seemed to be making up his own mind as to whether, under the circumstances, there was a clear and present danger in the speech. Schenck v United States, 249 US 47 (1919): Abrams v United States, 250 US 616, 624 (1919): Gitlow v New York, 268 US 652, 672 (1925). In *Gitlow* the majority opinion appeared to hold that the judgement of the danger can be made conclusively by the legislature. In *Dennis* the confusion on the point is further confounded: the majority accepted the trial judge's finding that there was a sufficient danger; Mr. Justice Douglas argued that the danger must be found by the jury; Mr. Justice Frankfurter deferred to the legislative judgement; Mr. Justice Jackson argued that the test is unworkable when the Communist conspiracy is involved, since no one would be in a position to evaluate rationally when so complex a danger becomes "clear and present". Dennis v United States, 3412 US 494 (1951)'. Kalven op.cit. at 20, footnote 66. To the extent that the legislative judgement prevailed, the clear and present danger test is open to the same criticisms made of the balancing test in this respect: the criticism must carry less weight however, as the room for discretion with the former test must certainly be considerably less than with the latter?

477

and the value of the expression in relation to the harm feared ... when this is done, however, the clear and present danger test becomes indistinguishable from its [successor][1] the ad hoc balancing test ...[2]

According to the latter doctrine, the gravity of the evil, discounted by its improbability is to be weighed against freedom of speech values. The principal difficulty here, however, is that the rule — if it can be called such — is so vague as to afford little protection *per se* to freedom of speech: much hinges on the exercise of judicial discretion:[3]

it is true that the test does not necessarily compel this excessive deference to the legislature. But the operation of the test tends strongly towards that result. For a court must rest its decision on the broadest considerations of policy, which are normally the grist of legislative determination. A court is therefore in the difficult or impossible position of having either to acquiesce in the legislative judgement or to overrule the legislature on the latter's own ground.[4]

The test therefore amounts to little more than a restatement of the bad tendency test: the court will overrule the legislature only when legislative judgement is unreasonable. This in turn may well amount to no more than the protection afforded by the due process clause.[5] The First Amendment may as a result become virtually superfluous. The history of balancing with the First Amendment has perhaps not been an altogether happy one, and there has recently been in advocacy cases an apparent shift by the Court back to the clear and present danger

---

1   The clear and present danger doctrine continued to be used in certain circumstances: for example to invalidate a conviction for contempt of court based on utterances alleged to interfere with a grand jury: e.g. *Wood* v *Georgia* 370 US 375 (1962).

2   T.I. Emerson 'Towards a General Theory of the First Amendment' 73 (1963) *Yale LJ* 377 at 911. In addition the requirement of 'presence' or 'imminence' with regard to the danger was dropped; thus although *Dennis* purported to apply the clear and present danger test, the opinion in practice amounted to its clear rejection.

3   For a critical appraisal of balancing see L. Frantz 'The First Amendment in the Balance' 71 (1962) *Yale LJ* 1424, 'Is the First Amendment Law? — A Reply to Professor Mendelson' 51 (1963) *Calif L Rev* 729; *contra* W. Mendelson 'On the Meaning of the First Amendment: Absolutes in the Balance' 50 (1962) *Calif L Rev* 821, and 'The First Amendment and the Judicial Process: A Reply to Mr. Frantz' 17 (1964) *Vand L Rev* 479.

4   Emerson op.cit. at 913.

5   Reasonableness is probably however a more rigid standard where the First Amendment is involved: see Fried 76 (1963) *Harv L Rev* 735.

test.[1] With the *Dennis* balancing approach action (for example) did not have to be imminent; in fact no matter how far in the future it might be, it was potentially the subject of consideration. As a result the test could not be said to exclude (for example) advocacy of belief in the principle of violent overthrow. This the Supreme Court found difficult to sustain, retreating to some extent in *Yates* v *United States*[2] to a definition in terms of incitement. This approach also involved serious difficulties: the distinctions involved are difficult to grasp, whilst as there is no insistence on the action being imminent, such a test '... might lead to conviction on the basis of choice of words alone, without an independent requirement that the state show an objective likelihood of imminent lawless action as a result of the speech'.[3] As a result *Brandenburg* v *Ohio* introduced the following formulation: that advocacy of lawlessness cannot be proscribed unless such advocacy is '... directed to inciting or producing imminent lawless action and is likely to incite or produce such action'.[4] This amounts to an apparent reaffirmation of the clear and present danger test in this area at least.

The application of the clear and present danger or the balancing tests would not necessarily mean the linking of obscenity regulation to the control of subsequent action. Although Justices Holmes and Brandeis may well have had such action in mind when the formulation was originally floated, its application would not appear to be clearly limited in this way: the evil the government seeks to suppress must merely be 'serious'. Are the legitimate governmental aims involved necessarily rationally assessed? Professor Henkin has argued strongly that any governmental aim is required merely in terms Fourteenth Amendment due process so to be assessed.[5] There does not appear to be any clear constitutional or judicial limitation of this sort; although due process requires a rational connection between governmental aims and regulation, a requirement clearly acknowledged judicially, the aims in question are not apparently so restricted. It has been argued that there is no constitutionally imposed limitation of any sort that restricts governmental concerns to harms at all, whether rationally assessed or not.[6]

---

1   See comment 'Brandenburg v Ohio: A Speech Test for All Seasons?' 43 (1975–76) *U Chi L Rev* 151 at 158.

2   354 US 298 (1957) at 324–5.

3   Comment *U Chi L Rev* op.cit. at 158, footnote 36.

4   395 US 444 (1969) at 447–8; followed in e.g. *Hess* v *Indiana* 414 US 105 (1973).

5   Henkin op.cit.

6   Schauer 'Response: Pornography and the First Amendment' 4 (1979) *U Pitts L Rev* 605 at 613.

Although the philosophical basis of the First Amendment for example may not be a clear one, to separate constitutional government from the mainstream of political philosophy is questionable. This again is something that cannot be explored here; what general public policy the Court should pursue, and indeed, whether it should involve itself very obviously in such questions at all, is beyond the ambit of this investigation. What is clear is that the governmental aim involved with respect to obscenity controls at present is the protection of public morality; this is both constitutionally and judicially sanctioned. Even if one were prepared to avoid harm requirements, the enforcement of morality in this way presumably requires at least something approaching a moral consensus in the community? Far less questionable would be to assume a harms framework, even if a non-rational one, and to assess governmental aims of protecting morality within it, in terms of balancing or clear and present danger. The same could be said of any other governmental aims which might found a prohibition of this sort. It might be argued that balancing has not had either a sustained or conspicuously successful First Amendment career, and that a clear and present danger approach is preferable both on the basis of past application and on the basis of the clearer recognition it accords the preferred position of free speech. This is however to assume that a clear and present danger approach does not involve balancing; in fact, it clearly does. The Court has not been explicit about the governmental objectives permissible in clear and present danger terms: Justices Holmes and Brandeis required in this respect a serious harm, such harm being both clear and present. The test is more specific in other words, in relation to the link required between harm and regulation, than in relation to the harm itself. Inevitably then, balancing is required: the difference is that clear and present danger excludes all other than the most immediate of harms; balancing may include the most remote of harms. It may be moreover that although the most remote of harms should necessarily be excluded, harms that are not immediate, but very likely or even certain to eventuate, should be taken into account. This may not be the case with political speech for example, where one is concerned essentially with public order; the obscenity area may well include harms, which although not immediate in the clear and present danger sense, are appropriate considerations in relation to regulation. Although balancing is apparently sufficient to satisfy most non-rights theory libertarians,[1] it may be that constitutional considerations demand a higher standard. What would seem appropriate is a balancing standard in terms of which the harms in question need be serious; a possibility of such harm eventuating should not be sufficient, the

---

1   See the enforcement of morality, chapter 4.

standard being a compromise between immediacy and likelihood, perhaps a real probability sufficing? Such a standard would clearly satisfy Fourteenth Amendment rational due process. In balancing in this manner, privacy may be relevant as a constitutional and philosophical factor militating against prohibitions on the dissemination of obscene materials. Such relevance must depend on how far one wishes to extend the meaning of privacy in terms of individual self-fulfilment and development. The question of obscenity prohibition in these terms will be pursued in the next chapter.

The only other avenue possibly open to the Court in assessing obscenity as speech would be that adopted in *Young* v *American Mini Theaters:*[1] in upholding the constitutionality of zoning restrictions in terms of an 'adult' standard, the Court took the view that the town planning restrictions — as opposed to prohibitions — affected only second-class speech. Mr Justice Powell in his concurrence emphasised that the restrictions were legitimately aimed at town planning, and not censorship, and impinged on freedom of speech as little as possible. In view of *Schad* v *Borough of Mount Ephraim,*[2] in which the plurality in striking the ordinance down, emphasised (*inter alia*) the prohibitive as opposed to restrictive operation of the borough's zoning ordinance, this approach would not appear to be open in relation to obscenity prohibitions in the general sense.

To summarise: in constitutional terms, four possible approaches may arguably be open in assessing obscenity prohibitions:

(i) That obscenity, as non-speech, falls outside the First Amendment. Even were one to take this view, there must in due process terms be a permissible governmental aim involved, and there must be established a rational connection between such aim and the regulation in question. Whether the governmental aim need itself be rationally assessable appears a moot point. Privacy would be relevant in relation to the home, private possessions, and perhaps individual self-development, in the sense of limiting the regulation of obscenity distribution. As has been argued earlier however, this approach does not square with the First Amendment, or its possible rationales, and should be rejected.

(ii) That obscenity is speech in First Amendment terms, but that the American constitution does not necessarily

---

1   427 US 50 (1976) at 84.

2   68L Ed 2d 671, 101 S.Ct (1981). See motion picture censorship, chapter 12, for a fuller discussion of this decision.

observe a utilitarian harm rationale. Even if this questionable proposition is correct, one would still require some governmental objective; it would be necessary to demonstrate by balancing in terms of a real probability the necessary relationship between objective and regulation. Balancing in this form would require more than is necessary in due process terms, and would appear to accord the height of hurdle that seems appropriate in relation to speech. Privacy would be potentially relevant as above.

(iii) Obscenity as speech can be restricted only on a utilitarian, but non-rational basis. One would in these terms require a harm, and a clear and a real probability of its fulfilment, whilst privacy would potentially play the same role once again.

(iv) Obscenity is speech, and a real probability of a rationally assessable harm is required for its restriction; privacy is potentially relevant here also.

III) The constitutionality of restrictions, as opposed to general prohibitions, on speech dealing with human sexuality

One is concerned here with the constitutional position of restrictions on speech in terms of protecting the young, and preventing gratuitous offence to adults, together with limited prohibitions on the production of pornography and live shows. If one accepts that rationally assessable harms are involved in all three of these areas,[1] one's concern here resolves itself into whether such harms could be accommodated to First Amendment jurisprudence, and whether the Court is at all likely to accept suggested accommodations.

Although the earlier and looser style of balancing employed by the Court following *Dennis* may not have proven particularly durable, it has probably become clear that the clear and present danger approach is not one that lends itself to universal First Amendment application;[2] insofar as it would in any event probably itself involve an element of balancing, the approach recommended above in relation to the assessment of obscenity prohibitions appears to be a viable compromise. Were a prohibition to be found constitutional in these terms, it would

---

1   See the protection of children, chapter 5; displays, chapter 6; production of pornography, chapter 7.

2   See A. Cox 'Foreword: Freedom of Expression in the Burger Court' 94 (1980) *Harvard L Rev* 1 at 5.

involve regulation on the basis of content. Such regulation by content is argued to offend the equality principle. One answer may be that equality in relation to speech is best effected by rejecting the type of contrived exclusion perpetuated by the Court in relation to obscenity, and is best not seen as aimed at reasoned and justifiable restrictions on what is acknowledged as speech. Even if one accepts regulation by content as offending equality, such regulation may be constitutionally permissible: as in relation, for example, to the protection of security in wartime. The Court has moreover made it clear that equality was never an absolute, and should not be seen as such.[1] Because one is dealing with a prohibition rather than a restriction, the burden of justification is greater.

The Burger Court in particular has espoused the equality principle with respect to regulation on a time, manner or place basis; with respect in other words, to restriction, if not to prohibition. An example of this approach is the result in *Erznoznik v City of Jacksonville*:[2] although alternative constitutional approaches such as overbreadth were available, the Court chose to invalidate the regulation essentially in terms of equality and the invalidity of regulation by content. This approach has not been consistently followed, however: the Court in *Young* very clearly permitted regulation 'keyed to content'.[3] The rationales for this were varied. Mr Justice Powell in his concurrence advocated an approach that amounted to a skirting of the First Amendment. The regulation was not a censorious one, being aimed at town planning, and constituted the least restrictive alternative.[4] The second approach was presaged in *Virginia State Board of Pharmacy v Virginia Citizens' Consumer Council, Inc*:[5] here the Court, in placing commercial advertising within the First Amendment as speech, cautioned that 'We have not held that it is undifferentiable from other forms of speech. There are commonsense differences ...'.[6] Such speech may in other words have only a second-class status; its restriction, as opposed to prohibition, may therefore be more easily justifiable. Just how easily justifiable was made clear in the plurality opinion in *Young*: Mr Justice Stevens in delivering the opinion made mention of the fact

---

1   *Young v American Mini Theaters* 427 US 50 (1976) at 66.

2   422 US 205 (1975).

3   Cox op.cit. at 43.

4   427 US 50 (1976) at 84.

5   425 US 748 (1976).

6   Ibid. at 771, footnote 24.

that the regulation imposed a restriction and not prohibition, and that it involved a valid governmental aim of town planning. Of the essence, however, was the second-class status of the speech involved. Although this approach does not apparently skirt the First Amendment, it in effect does so by according a status to certain varieties of speech such that the legislature need apparently merely demonstrate a due process rationale connection between restriction and governmental aim for First Amendment constitutionality to be assured.[1]

This approach was followed yet again in the plurality opinion in *FCC* v *Pacifica Foundation*:[2] here Justice Stevens, joined by Chief Justice Burger and Justice Rehnquist, although emphasising the intrusive offensiveness involved, particularly as regards minors, preferred apparently to rely on the second-class status of the speech involved. This approach has never apparently commanded a majority on the Court: Justices Powell and Blackmun, although concurring in *Pacifica*, rejected the categorisation of speech in this way, preferring to stress the offensiveness of the broadcast and the necessity of protecting children. The plurality in *Young* and *Pacifica* were clearly engaged in balancing, but the terms in which they did so seem unsustainable. There does not appear to be any support, doctrinal or philosophical, for the categorisation of speech in this manner. If equality is of relevance, then such categorisation surely offends it in a fundamental way? The second-class status assigned to speech in these cases appears to be an overhang from the exception approach to the First Amendment, without even the justification advanced in respect of the latter, and allows the constitutionality of potentially overbroad standards. Would it not be far preferable for the Court in such cases to balance the interests involved, stressing the fact that it is concerned with restriction and not prohibition, and stressing the necessity for a clear governmental aim in the sense of a substantial harm and a real probability of its occurrence? The restrictions recommended earlier in relation to the protection of children and the prevention of gratuitous offence would arguably pass muster in these terms. Both are essentially concerned with the time, manner and place of communication. Regulation is keyed to content, but that does not necessarily mean invalidation in equality terms. To begin with, equality is not an absolute rule. Second, such regulations are arguably neutral in the sense that one is concerned with a rationally assessable harm; the fact that one chooses to regulate, or that the harm is occasioned by, a particular variety of speech categorised essentially in terms of positive sexual

---

1   Cox op.cit. at 29–30.

2   438 US 726 (1978).

morality, does not necessarily overturn this initial and basic neutrality. The argument here is reminiscent of that advanced in relation to privacy: that if certain invasions of privacy of the home are selected for regulation, that such regulation *a priori* has as a result nothing whatever to do with privacy.[1] Such regulation would, moreover not offend basic First Amendment rationales by imposing a particular variety of moral orthodoxy: one is not concerned with prohibition, but merely restriction in tightly drawn terms. The threat to the growth of ideas or individual development for example, is therefore limited. We turn now to examine the proposed restrictions in more detail.

(i) *The protection of children*

One is concerned here in philosophical terms with paternalism: the young are to be protected in view of their immaturity, from influences with which adults might be expected quite readily to cope; this is the essence of the harm posed here. The protection of children is a factor whose relevance has been clearly recognised by the Supreme Court in this area: although the Court couched such relevance in *Ginsberg* in terms of the obscenity exception to the First Amendment, the court was clearly in effect weighing harm to minors against First Amendment values. To view the exception created in favour of minors in any other light is to make a nonsense of the exception approach, for it is very difficult to see how material which has First Amendment value in adult terms, is suddenly stripped of the latter when distributed to minors. The Court then would probably be prepared to countenance restrictions on sales particular to minors. The restriction proposed earlier[2] in this respect is arguably sufficiently tightly drawn to satisfy First Amendment demands, in the sense of a real probability of harm resulting. The fact that the present obscenity formulation probably makes the protection of minors in this sense unconstitutional must be an added factor in favour of this approach.

As far as restrictions on general distribution in favour of children are concerned, they would not seem unconstitutional at present, aside from the difficulties created by the *Miller* hard-core formulation. Although the licensing scheme in *Interstate Circuit Inc v Dallas*[3] was found unconstitutional, this was arguably on the basis of the overbreadth of the standard employed, and not on the basis of the constitutional impermissibility of restrictions on general distribution in

---

1 See privacy, pp.159–66.

2 See protection of children, chapter 5.

3 390 US 676 (1968).

favour of minors. The reasoning in *Butler* v *Michigan*[1] would surely be satisfied by any regulation in favour of the young, provided that it did not restrict the availability of the material in question to adults. In these terms the standard proposed earlier would probably pass constitutional muster if applied not only to sale to minors but also to the exclusion of minors from premises selling material suitable only for adults. The type of application of this standard which is likely to cause constitutional problems is in relation to public displays: here one is restricting the access not only of minors, but also of adults, thus contravening *Butler* due process strictures. On the other hand, the protection of children has been stressed in a general way on a number of occasions by members of the Court, leading examples being the *per curiam* decision in *Redrup* v *New York*,[2] Mr Justice Marshall's opinion in *Stanley* v *Georgia*,[3] Mr Justice Brennan's dissent in *Paris Adult Theater* v *Slaton I*,[4] and the Court in *United States* v *Reidel*.[5] Equally, were the prevention of gratuitous offence to be accepted by the Court as a legitimate First Amendment rationale, this could be added as a back-up rationale here, as could privacy, were the latter to be regarded as extending to invididual development, rather than more literally, the home or personal possessions. Much must depend on the narrowness in the Court's view of the standard applied, and the weight of a real probability of the basic harm (to children) eventuating. The combination of the protection of children and offensiveness should arguably be sufficient in relation to a restriction rather than prohibition, to tip the scales in favour of constitutionality. As far as equality is concerned, it is surely not argued that the only regulation of speech permissible in favour of minors is one which restricts all speech harmful to minors? There would be a clear conflict here between the reasonable claims of harm to the young as a justification, and problems of overbreadth. In short, a restriction in favour of minors on speech dealing with sexuality would surely be upheld despite its constituting a restriction on the basis of content?

A second potential difficulty lies in the possible conflict that might arise between regulations of this sort and parental choice in relation to children. The Court's attitude on this question is not absolutely clear: it would appear that parental choice as far as one's children are

1   352 US 380 (1957).

2   386 US 767 (1967).

3   394 US 557 (1969).

4   413 US 49 (1973).

5   402 US 351 (1971).

concerned will be accorded considerable weight, unless the children would otherwise be exposed to influences which are 'clearly', 'demonstrably' or 'inherently' harmful to the child.[1] The Court stressed in *Ginsberg* however that 'the prohibition against sales to minors did not bar parents who so desire from purchasing the magazines for their children'.[2] It may be therefore that in the event of a clash, parental rather than state authority would prevail; this of course depends on the Court's view of the potential harm involved. The likelihood of this constituting a real constitutional problem, in the sense of state and parental authority frequently coming into conflict, is probably remote; it constitutes a potential rather than probable constitutional problem.

Finally, it might be argued that the constitutionality of regulations aimed at the protection of the young might in this area be upheld in terms of Justice Powell's approach in *Young*: that the governmental aim is not a censorious one, and that it constitutes, in relation to the speech in question, the least restrictive alternative. The difficulty with this approach is that by avoiding the First Amendment, it courts in the standards it sustains, difficulties of overbreadth; if pursued to extremes, it constitutes a considerable threat to the effectiveness of the Amendment.[3] It would be far better, even though articulation is not by any means easy, to take on the Amendment squarely and justify what regulation may be accommodated in terms of it.

(ii) *Offensiveness*

The Court upheld the constitutionality of what is essentially an offensiveness regulation in *Young* v *American Mini Theaters*,[4] essentially by skirting the First Amendment, arguing the constitutionality of the regulation as a restriction (rather than a prohibition) not aimed at censorship, and constituting the least restrictive alternative in relation to speech; or additionally, the second-class status of the speech involved. This constitutes at least oblique recognition by the Court of offensiveness as a justification for regulation. The court also, despite its rejection of the standard at issue in *Erznoznik* v *City of Jacksonville*,[5]

---

1 See *Pierce* v *Society of Sisters* 268 US 510 (1925); *Prince* v *Massachusetts* 321 US 158 (1944); *Wisconsin* v *Yoder* 406 US 1205 (1972).

2 390 US 629 (1968) at 639.

3 See the breadth of the zoning ordinance found unconstitutional in *Schad* v *Borough of Mount Ephraim* 68L Ed 2d 671, 101 S.Ct (1981); see motion picture censorship, chapter 12.

4 427 US 50 (1975).

5 422 US 205 (1975).

after remarking that anyone in a public place can readily 'avert his eyes' and thus avoid exposure to objectionable material, did grudgingly admit that if such escape is virtually impossible — that is, if 'the degree of captivity makes it impractical for the unwilling viewer or auditor to avoid exposure'[1] — then some regulation (this would particularly apply to public advertisements, for example) may be permissible. As argued in relation to regulation in favour of the young, the content rule is not and cannot be regarded as an absolute: where the public cannot avoid exposure to objectionable material, regulation by content may be permissible.[2]

A telling recognition of offensiveness as a viable policy factor in this area has come in the elaboration of the *Roth* test itself. The cutting-edge of this test is now clearly set in terms of patent offensiveness: for prohibition, material must not only appeal to the prurient interest and be without serious First Amendment value; it must also be patently offensive. Insofar as the latter is determined in relation to contemporary community standards, and insofar as obscenity law generally is concerned with public sexual morality, the offensiveness requirement here is concerned with an affront to positive morality. In an attempt to accommodate shifts in community standards, the court has then already allowed assessment in terms of offensiveness, and insofar as such offensiveness is assessed in relation to the question of serious value, has allowed the former to be balanced against First Amendment values. It is perhaps significant that without any reference to the rationale of the shortage of airwaves, the Court recently in *FCC v Pacifica Foundation*[3] upheld the restriction of George Carlin's 'Seven Dirty Words' monologue as broadcast over the radio, partly in terms of offence caused to unwilling listeners. It is significant that the court in *Pacifica* employed the familiar — in the obscenity context — phrase 'patent offensiveness'; if *Pacifica* has significance beyond the context of broadcasting, and this would appear to be the case, that significance lies in the at last overt recognition, by at least the concurring justices, of the role of offensiveness as a properly drawn policy factor in relation to speech. Its relevance in this respect has, together with the protection of children, been asserted in a general sense *per curiam* in *Redrup*, by Justice Marshall in *Stanley*, by Mr Justice Brennan in *Paris*, and the Court in *Reidel*.

It may be argued that offensiveness is not a suitable policy factor in First Amendment terms: that to allow regulation in terms of offensive-

---

1 422 US 205 (1975) at 206–7.

2 See Cox op.cit. at 44.

3 438 US 726 (1978).

ness, in other words, is to limit commentary to polite debate. The right to be informed need not necessarily include the right to be insulted; it may be no bad thing that excesses in the latter respect are to some extent curbed.[1] It must be remembered also that one is concerned solely with gratuitous offence here; with a restriction in other words, rather than a prohibition. In terms of freedom of speech this is a crucial distinction: there does not seem any reason why the freedom to communicate mental stimulus should extend to the occasioning of harm to others or of the infringement of the rights of others, depending on one's philosophical viewpoint: the fact that speech is restricted in the sense that the unwilling may evade it should they so wish, does not do violence to those rationales rehearsed earlier as possible rationales for the First Amendment; prohibition might. The operation of such restrictions in imposing politeness on debate and commentary would depend very much on the breadth of standard involved; that recommended earlier[2] in relation to offence caused to adults employs what appears to have come close to being a generally constitutionally recognised standard in this respect: patent offensiveness. If the standard is sufficiently tightly drawn, only the most abrasive intrusions would be subsumed in terms of the restriction. A further fear raised here is that were a narrowly based restriction in relation to sexual materials to be recognised, this would open the way for a proliferation, with disparate bases, of such measures. One cannot assert that no other regulations would pass muster in these terms; on the other hand, it is open to the Court to assert a rationally assessable harm as necessary, and demand, in relation to any proposed restriction, a real probability of that harm eventuating. A proliferation of restrictions must in these terms seem most unlikely.[3] One would be working in terms of what the majority of the community rather than the susceptible few found offensive. There would be no difficulty in sustaining restrictions aimed at suppressing the type of language which was offensive to the extent of rendering public disturbance a clear and present danger. Because sexual representation is generally unlikely (outside of the live show area) to have the same result, does not necessarily mean that unwilling viewers of such representation suffer no appreciable harm, and should be without protection. Affront to positive morality very often depends on context: it may be that positive morality has in both jurisdictions moved so far as to regard

---

1   See Cox *loc.cit.*

2   See displays, chapter 6.

3   See displays, chapter 6.

varieties of public display as an affront to morality, but to exhibit a general lack of concern were the same material found in private. If one is to allow community standards any play here at all, it may be that the restriction of offence is the only relevant forum.

A final consideration in favour of constitutionality is the interrelated (to offensiveness) question of harm to minors. Restrictions on public displays would be couched primarily in terms of the latter, and offensiveness to adults would feature as one's primary rationale only in terms of the restriction of patently offensive materials to restricted shops. Alternatively, were the harm to children standard felt to be too onerous in relation to public displays, offensiveness to adults might be employed primarily in both contexts, with the protection of minors as a back-up. One might add privacy to the latter, depending on one's view of its appropriate definition.

(iii) *Live shows*

The Court apparently countenances the regulation of such shows on three bases; the factual distinction between speech and physical conduct, the relevance of public order considerations in the context of liquor licensing and the provision of such entertainment, and finally on the *Young* basis of motivated regulation not aimed at censorship and constituting, as a restriction and not a prohibition, the least restrictive alternative in relation to speech. The latter approach, by bypassing the First Amendment in terms of prior restraint procedural requirements and the standard applied, allows restriction on the basis of potentially overbroad standards. The type of regulation recommended in terms of English law[1] would almost certainly be constitutionally permissible in the United States: regulation would be in relation to public order considerations, and in terms of a conduct/speech distinction that would be perhaps clearer in operation than the approach the court follows at present. Were it desired to prohibit live shows within the speech area on a public order basis, it would seem preferable to do this straightforwardly in First Amendment terms, as opposed to a least restrictive alternative or second-class speech approach.

(iv) *The production of pornography*

The First Amendment does not generally extend to physical conduct; there would not appear to be any question in these terms of the constitutional validity of statutes prohibiting sexual interference with minors, for example. If such prohibitions are generally constitutionally

---

1   See live shows, chapter 6.

sustainable in terms of their policy aims, may not the photographing of such behaviour be viewed in the same light?[1] This would be to adopt Justice Powell's approach in *Young*: in other words, to regard the prohibition as being aimed at a legitimate governmental objective, and not at censorship, the regulation constituting the least restrictive alternative in relation to speech. Although this approach may be open to criticism when employed elsewhere, the governmental aim here genuinely is the suppression of the conduct in question, and the photography of it appears to form no more than an adjunct in this respect. If the prohibition is closely linked in this way to the primary conduct involved, one may legitimately skirt the First Amendment, and in turn evade difficulties of justifying a prior restraint. What may give rise to greater difficulty in First Amendment terms is a prohibition on the products of such photographic sessions. One might here argue that the prohibition is not aimed at censorship, but at the suppression of the primary conduct involved; this may be convincing to the extent to which such distribution could be argued to constitute complicity in the latter respect. It may be to stretch this line of reasoning however; possibly better would be to justify the prohibition in First Amendment terms, the justification depending on the establishment of a real probability that such distribution would promote the primary conduct involved. This approach may in fact provide a convenient method for dealing with the hardest of hard-core pornography, quite apart from censorship-based regulation: were the prohibition on production and distribution to be extended to other sexual conduct independently assessed as meriting criminal penalties, then a body of pornography that may give rise to the most concern in society could be regulated largely independently of First Amendment and prior restraint inhibitions.

(v) *Prior restraint*

The development of prior restraint doctrine in this area has been based on the exception approach to the First Amendment: in other words, provided material is determined to be obscene, it falls outside the Amendment; 'prior restraint' of it does not in turn raise First Amendment problems. Attention has therefore focused on just how and by whom a determination of obscenity is made; provided procedural safeguards aimed at a speedy judicial hearing are followed, one has quick determination of obscenity, and prior restraint inhibitions fall away. This to an extent obscures an important question in this area: are prior restraints necessarily and invariably much more burdensome

---

[1] See production of pornography, chapter 7.

in relation to speech than subsequent sanction? In other words, can prior restraints be justified in their own right? The area in which this has arisen principally is in relation to injunctions: it has apparently been resolved in respect of injunctions aimed at specific materials; the future of the nuisance-type injunction, although probably susceptible in terms of *Near* v *Minnesota*, is not absolutely clear. Although prior restraints may require special justification, it may be that in certain areas they constitute the most convenient, effective, and least burdensome regulation available. Two recommendations in this respect are in relation to the cinema, and to restrictions in favour of the young, and to prevent offence to adults.[1] Whether the court would be prepared to uphold schemes of this sort which, practically speaking, probably could not be tailored to satisfy *Freedman* requirements, must seem very doubtful. To this extent the exception approach to obscenity and the First Amendment may have rendered free speech jurisprudence a disservice.

We turn now to the final chapter in this essay: an assessment of the possible justifications for an obscenity prohibition, as opposed to the restrictions immediately considered.

---

[1] See licensing of books, films, chapter 7.

15 Policy and prohibition

English law in this area is apparently concerned with the enforcement of positive morality in two related ways: first by imposing prohibitions on material which is corruptive of such morality; second by imposing restrictions on material which is felt, in certain contexts, to affront community standards. There may originally have been an appreciable distinction between these two standards in the sense that the former was concerned with something more harmful than offensiveness, whilst the latter, although clearly concerned with offensiveness, was generally concerned with it only in a public context, or in other words, with gratuitous offence. This distinction has been eroded over time: indecency restrictions can no longer be described as being generally aimed at preventing gratuitous offence; offence has as a result been applied as a standard of restriction in contexts which might originally have been thought the preserve of corruption prohibitions only. The application of the offence (or affront to positive morality) standard can no longer be said to be concerned, in other words, with gratuitous offence, arguably a rationally assessable harm; its concern is rather simply the prevention of affront to positive morality in the broad sense, without the necessary exclusion of those contexts not involving gratuitous offence. Prohibitions on the corruption of public or positive morality have also been subject to some pressure: with obscenity, for example, a jury need not demand consequential conduct when looking for a sufficiently immoral effect with material to justify a finding of obscenity. They may not be happy with a finding that thought arousal constitutes such an effect; as a result, despite the aversion defence strictures that obscenity is not, as a prohibition, concerned with offensiveness, they may feel constrained, in the absence of any other obvious effects on which to fasten, either to acquit, or, strictly impermissibly, to reach a finding in terms of offensiveness. The latter in this context clearly does not necessarily have anything to do with gratuitous offence. The development of American obscenity jurisprudence has been similar, to the extent that the original — albeit piecemeal — application of a corruption standard has given way to a test which operates, practically, in terms of offensiveness. Such offensiveness does not necessarily involve a gratuitous element; the law's concern with obscenity prohibition is merely affront to positive morality in the broad sense.

The question of restrictions based more narrowly on gratuitous offence and the protection of children, and limited prohibitions based on public order and primary conduct considerations, have already been discussed in relation to both jurisdictions.[1] Our concern here is whether prohibitions, or in turn more widely based restrictions, are any longer sustainable in terms of enforcing positive morality or any other possible justifications. These questions will be considered within a broad utilitarian harm framework. It may be argued that the United States Constitution is not wedded to the enforcement of a particular libertarian philosophy, and that such analysis is therefore, in the American context at any rate, not apposite. The prevailing Anglo/American philosophical framework for the assessment of governmental aims is a utilitarian one; if the Supreme Court is a policy-making body, a harms formulation should have first claim as its policy *modus operandi*. One is talking of a Constitution, however: such interpretation is not prescribed, although it is, in terms of presently accepted theory, both advisable and probable.[2] To urge, without offering a clear alternative, that a harms formulation is to be avoided, takes matters very little further; one is then asking the Supreme Court to assess legitimate policy aims without taking into account prevailing philosophy with regard to the latter. That one is asking the Court to assess policy aims is clear: although the maintenance of public morality is constitutionally (whatever its philosophical basis) within the ambit of state power, the First Amendment makes no concessions as to its permissibility as an aim in the speech context. Whether such policy assessment is jurisprudentially best seen as within the legislature's functions,

---

1   See chapters 5, 6 and 14.

2   The philosophical and policy aims and practice of the Supreme Court cannot be analysed here: in this respect, see for example J. Spaeth *Supreme Court Policy Making: Explanation and Prediction*, (San Francisco 1979).

is hardly a question upon which to embark here. It seems legitimate to proceed then in relation to both jurisdictions in terms of a harms framework. The Court has not, in First Amendment terms at any rate, been particularly explicit on this policy issue. Certain aims, such as the preservation of public order, lie more for consideration in terms of the reality or otherwise of the threat to such order necessary for proscription, rather than in terms of analysis of the legitimacy of the preservation of basic public order. With something such as the preservation of public morality, some analysis of the basic aims seems necessary, and this will be essayed in utilitarian terms.

This is not to say that the question of the connection between the harm in question and the regulation involved is not very relevant in this area: besides an identification of the harm involved, the policy-maker, be it the Supreme Court, or (particularly in the English context) the legislature, must determine the link between harm and regulation regarded as necessary in free speech terms. The Williams Committee espoused the clear and present danger approach in this regard, translating the latter into a requirement of the likelihood of the relevant harms being established beyond reasonable doubt: '... the causation of the harm should lie "beyond a reasonable doubt" '.[1] Yet, as was argued earlier,[2] there are a number of difficulties in the application of a clear and present danger approach in this area. The first is that the clear and present danger formulation is concerned principally with the immediacy or otherwise of the alleged harm: although this is obviously related to the question of likelihood of occurrence, this is not necessarily the case, as a harm may be certain to eventuate, even if not immediately. Although immediacy may be of the essence in relation to political speech, the same is not necessarily true here, where the time-scale may be somewhat more protracted. The second problem is that clear and present danger gives one no clear guarantees in relation to the harm in question: the Supreme Court has not been specific in relation to the question of permissible governmental aims with clear and present danger. Although this difficulty probably does not arise with harms such as public disorder, is a clear and present danger of (for example) an isolated instance of sex crime resulting from the distribution of pornography sufficient, or is something more than this required? Common sense would seem to dictate more: as the Williams Committee point out: 'It may well be that reading the Bible, for instance, has harmed someone. The question is, whether pornography

---

[1] Report of the Committee on Obscenity and Film Censorship (Cmnd 7772 1979) para 5.31; hereafter referred to as *Williams*.

[2] See alternative approaches, chapter 14.

constitutes a class of publication to which, as such, there belongs a tendency to cause harms'.[1] In order to effect the latter form of narrowing, one would in essence be engaged in balancing.

Even if one accepts that balancing in this area is necessary, and even if one accepts that the likelihood of the harm eventuating rather than its immediacy is of the essence, one is still faced with the choice of specifying or leaving open the likelihood requirement. This may after all range from the remotest possibility to certainty. One of the major criticisms of balancing as espoused by the Supreme Court was the looseness of definition in this respect: no matter how remote an alleged harm, account could still be taken of it. This aspect of balancing clearly needs tightening. On the other hand, to require too high a burden of proof may be to render behavioural science with regard to the instigation of criminal behaviour as a result of reading pornography (for example) virtually irrelevant. Behavioural science does not generally, in terms of statistical analysis, operate on the basis of certainty. Experimental results tend rather to exclude chance, and operate within and indicate, ranges of, or specific, probabilities. The selection by Williams of 'beyond a reasonable doubt' as the prescribed test of likelihood appears to set the standard perhaps too high. The optimum approach is possibly rather to balance, prescribing in the process a high level of likelihood, in the sense of a real probability of the harm's eventuating.

Harms would appear, from a philosophical point of view,[2] to lie potentially for assessment in three respects: in relation to individuals, in terms of paternalism, and in relation to society as a whole. Those harms possibly relevant here will be examined in these terms.

I) Harm to individuals

That harm which may be occasioned by adult consumers of pornography to others, is a principal, and potentially a rationally assessable harm:

> The arguments here are that certain kinds of behaviour, particularly in the form of criminal offences of violence and of a sexual nature, are either directly provoked by exposure to particular stimuli — such as the reading of a sex magazine producing a state of arousal which is manifested in rape or sexual assault, or the viewing of a film producing imitative violence — or are at least more likely

---

1 *Williams* para 5.34.

2 See chapter 4.

to occur in an atmosphere created by pornography and violent material.[1]

There has been a vast amount of experimental work and investigation undertaken in this area; to attempt any detailed evaluation of this material is not only beyond the scope of this essay, but also beyond both the inclination and/or qualifications of its author. Fortunately, two major governmental investigations have been undertaken over the past decade into such material and its effects, one American and one English: the earlier was the American Presidential Commission on Pornography, which reported in September 1970; the second, the Williams Committee, which reported in December 1979. In view of the chronology, the principal emphasis here will be on the Williams findings, although reference will be made to the earlier American inquiry. Because the findings of both these committees are in accord, and because their examination of the sources cannot be verified here, it is proposed to accept their broad conclusions in relation to such material, unless their interpretation or examination of such material has been subject to specific methodological criticism. The latter, as opposed to disagreement with the broad approach of Williams, for example, in excluding the enforcement of morality as a non-rational harm, has been raised specifically in relation to the committee's approach to the work of Dr John Court. This issue deserves, then, special consideration.

Williams divided the evidence submitted to it into three broad categories: anecdotal evidence, research studies, and analysis of crime statistics. What is at issue here is not so much the question of whether the criminal activity alleged to result is a rationally assessable harm, but rather whether the necessary causal connection between pornography and such conduct can be established.

(i) *Anecdotal evidence*

An example of this is the allegation by the defence in criminal trials that the criminal conduct in question could be ascribed to the influence of pornography. Perhaps the best known of such trial allegations were made in the cases of the Moors murderers and the Cambridge rapist. The committee concluded that 'both these cases seem to be more consistent with pre-existing traits being reflected both in a choice of reading matter and in acts committed against others'.[2] The committee records that no psychiatric or psychological witness was able to tell

---

1   *Williams* para 6.2.

2   *Williams* para 6.7.

them of a case of which they had experience, where the necessary causal link between pornography and criminal conduct could be established. Many of their witnesses, such as Dr Gallwey of the Portman Clinic, Professor Eysenck of the Institute of Psychiatry, and Dr Hyatt Williams of the Tavistock Clinic in fact took the view that pornography might actually in such cases provide an outlet, and lessen the likelihood of the commission of an offence.[1] The committee make the point that one is not in any case concerned here with isolated instances: even if a particular crime could be ascribed to the influence of pornography, the same might be found of a great variety of literature or other material freely available. Such anecdotal evidence does little to establish the type of influence which would be likely to satisfy philosophical and constitutional demands. It is noteworthy in this regard, however, that although the committee reached this conclusion in relation both to material dealing with sexuality and that dealing with violence, expert opinion had reservations in relation to the latter; this is a point to which we shall return later.

(ii)   *Research studies*[2]

None of these studies represents the real world, in the sense that 'criminal and anti-social behaviour cannot itself, for both practical and ethical reasons, be experimentally produced or controlled ...'.[3] Any results must then be potentially subject to the criticism that in attempting to investigate the relationship between fantasy and reality, the latter is an ingredient the investigator can only simulate or estimate. Many of these surveys were undertaken for the United States Commission on Obscenity and Pornography[4] amongst groups such as young male offenders, sexual offenders, and various other population groups. They take three broad forms: retrospective studies of personal exposure to such material, self-reports before and after experimental exposure, and 'physiological and biochemical measures of change in

---

1   *Williams* para 6.8.

2   In this regard the committee had reference, aside from evidence submitted to them, to the following in particular: a review of the relevant literature on the effects of obscene material by M. Yaffé *Pornography: The Longford Report* (London 1972) Appendix V, as updated: *Williams* Appendix 5; S. Brody *Screen Violence and Film Censorship*, Home Office Research Study No. 41 (HMSO 1977); H.J. Eysenck and D.K.B. Nias *Sex, Violence and the Media* (London 1978); D. Howitt and G. Cumberbatch *Mass Media Violence and Society* (London 1975). See also B. Kutchinsky 'Pornography in Denmark' in R. Dhavan and C. Davies (eds) *Censorship and Obscenity* (London 1978).

3   *Williams* para 6.14.

4   *The Report of the Commission on Obscenity and Pornography* (Bantam Books 1970) at 169–308; hereafter referred to as *Report*.

response to experimental exposure'. The commission concluded in the light of all the studies undertaken for it that 'empirical research has found no evidence to date that exposure to explicit sexual materials plays a significant role in the causation of delinquent or criminal behaviour among youth or adults'.[1] The methodology employed by the commission has been subject to considerable criticism, much of which the commission acknowledged.[2] Such criticisms include the fact that the time available for conducting research was so short that no proper longitudinal studies could be carried out; that the self-report methods of data collection are open to all sorts of distortion; and that there had been problems in obtaining adequately matched control groups for comparison. It was pointed out to Williams by Maurice Yaffe, however, that in terms of updating the commission's investigations, there is no strong evidence to contradict the commission's conclusions.[3] One should not presume, moreover, that the commission's conclusions were necessarily what its members wished to see: a minority statement to the *Report* by Doctors Morris A. Lipton and Edward D. Greenwood in this respect provides strong support for the majority conclusion:

> We would have welcomed evidence relating exposure to erotica to delinquency, crime and anti-social behaviour ... However, the work of the Commission has failed to uncover such evidence. Although the many and varied studies contracted for by the Commission may have flaws, they are remarkably uniform in the direction to which they point. This direction fails to establish a meaningful causal relationship or even significant correlation between exposure to erotica, and ... antisocial behaviour among adults.[4]

It must be remembered that American obscenity law does not extend to violent material, and although there may be some overlap the commission's investigations were therefore limited to erotica. It was principally in relation to material dealing with violence that

---

1   *Report* at 32; see also Lockhart 'The Findings and Recommendations of the Commission on Obscenity and Pornography: A Case Study of the Role of Social Science in Formulating Policy' 24 (1971) *Oklahoma L Rev* 209 at 216ff; *contra* Cairns, Paul and Wishner 'Sex Censorship: The Assumptions of Anti-Obscenity Laws and the Empirical Evidence' 46 (1962) *Minn L Rev* 1009, at 1035, whose conclusion is that although the evidence does not establish a causal link, it does not disprove one either.

2   Ibid. at 170.

3   *Williams* para 6.16.

4   *Report* at 452.

Williams encountered real disagreement amongst behavioural scientists. Although much of the work in this regard has been undertaken with respect to television, it was felt that the results could equally be true of films. Mr Stephen Brody's work in this area led him to conclude in his review of literature[1] that

> The most reasonable interpretation of the considerable quantity of research results so far available would suggest that some people — particularly young people — may be inclined both to actual aggressiveness (however this is manifested, and not necessarily in criminal behaviour) and to a preference for entertainment dealing with aggressive themes, for reasons which probably originate with the development of personality and character; but that watching violent action on the screen is unlikely in itself to impel ordinary viewers to behave in ways they would otherwise not have done. Research into the causes of crime has repeatedly indicated the enormous variety of possibly contributory factors, all of which overlap in complex ways and are quite unpredictable for any one individual; in all these studies, incidentally, the mass media have warranted scarcely a mention. That potentially violent or anti-social persons may find their own sentiments and dispositions confirmed and perhaps reinforced by television and films is not a consideration to be ignored, but it is in the amplification of existing tendencies that the main influence is likely to lie, not in the moulding of social behaviour.[2]

Howitt and Cumberbatch were more positive: their research had shown, they felt, that 'the mass media — as far as it is possible to tell using social scientific methodologies — do not serve to amplify the level of violence in society'.[3] Eysenck and Nias disagree completely with this, concluding that 'the evidence is fairly unanimous that aggressive acts new to the subject's repertoire of responses, as well as well established acts, can be evoked by the viewing of violent scenes portrayed on television'.[4] These conclusions have been criticised as relying on investigations based on a stimulus—response approach that

---

1   S. Brody op.cit.

2   Ibid.

3   *Williams* para 6.18.

4   Eysenck and Nias op.cit.

cannot accurately reflect the real world.[1] Williams cites as an example of the fallibility of such investigations, the use of a so-called Bobo doll to provide an aggression model for children, that group of children which had watched an adult assaulting the doll being more inclined to violence than groups provided with non-violent models. As the committee point out, such results must be interpreted in the light of many possibly vitiating factors: the doll may be taken to be intended as a punch-bag or it may be a novel toy to the subjects. Eysenck and Nias, the committee felt, do 'not so much dismiss these objections, as ignore them'. They then themselves in effect apparently dismiss Eysenck and Nias' findings, the latter being dispatched with the devastating indictment that 'their book is indeed aimed more at the popular market, drawing on press reports to illustrate the alleged effects of media violence ...'.[2]

Such discrepancy in expert opinion must nonetheless give rise to concern: it may be that to concentrate on Eysenck and Nias' deficiencies in methodology is to lose 'sight of a charging elephant while chasing a butterfly'.[3] Many experiments in other words '... on the effects of television violence retain the "artificiality" unavoidable in studies of this kind, and yet have nothing to do with the ding-dong stimulus—response theory. Together with many of the more "realistic" studies, they provide an impressive array of evidence of a link between watching violence on television and engaging in violence when away from the box'.[4] Some of the better evidence available draws essentially on three basic theories[5] as to why television violence may affect behaviour: it could be by imitation or behaviour modelled on what has been seen; by desensitisation, or the lowering of viewers' thresholds in relation to violence: or by disinhibition, in terms of which guilt or embarrassment normally felt in relation to certain conduct is eroded. The Williams Committee are possibly a little disingenuous in their rejection of findings in relation to violent materials: when they arrive at the point of considering films specifically, they recommend, in addition to the application of general restrictions[6] aimed at protecting

---

1   See e.g. Laurie Taylor's review of *Sex, Violence and the Media* (London 1978): *The Times*, 24 August 1978; *Williams* paras 6.19–6.21.

2   *Williams* para 6.21.

3   Letter from Professor H. Tajfel, *The Times* 30 August 1978.

4   Ibid.

5   See Elaine Potter in 'Spectrum', *The Sunday Times*, 6 August 1978.

6   See films, chapter 7.

children and preventing offence, a prohibition peculiar to the cinema. According to this a film may be declared unfit for public exhibition if, in addition to constituting material whose production is prohibited,[1] it is 'unacceptable because of the manner in which it depicts violence, sexual activity or crime ... having regard to the importance of allowing the development of artistic expression and not suppressing truth or reality'.[2] The rationale for this distinction seems to be the empirically unsubstantiated assertion that the impact of film is considerably greater than printed material.[3] This may be a factor, amongst others, which may influence one in favour of prior restraint rather than subsequent restraint in relation to cinema restriction; to assert it as essentially *the* basis for regulation as such, after a carefully rational approach hithertofore, seems both inconsistent and disingenuous. As *The Times* remarked in a leader column on the report: 'The Committee is sailing along in rational detachment towards the farther shore where it will deliver its message of Not Proven. No evidence of harm such as to justify suppression, when it is hit by a sudden squall ... these thirteen calmly rational men and women jump in the air like Mrs. Whitehouse and upset their own applecart'.[4] The squall in question was some film the committee had been shown:

> It is not simply the extremity of the violence which concerns us: we found it extremely disturbing that highly explicit depictions of mutilation, savagery, menace and humiliation should be presented for the entertainment of an audience in a way that appeared to emphasise the pleasures of sadism ... It may be that this very graphically presented sadistic material serves only as a vivid object of fantasy, and does no harm at all. There is certainly no conclusive evidence to the contrary. But ... in this connexion it seems entirely sensible to be cautious ... We are more impressed by the consideration that the extreme vividness and immediacy of film may make it harder rather than easier for some who are attracted to sadistic material to tell the difference between fantasy and reality.[5]

The committee, as *The Times* notes, is here proceeding intuitively;

---

1 See production of pornography, chapter 7.

2 *Williams* para 12.45.

3 Ibid. paras 10.10 and 12.7.

4 *The Times*, 29 November 1979.

5 *Williams* para 12.10.

it as a result opens itself and its recommendations to criticism on the basis of inconsistency. A possible further example of such inconsistency occurs with the committee's recommendation in respect of controlling the production of pornography: after recommending a prohibition on the production of pornography involving physical harm to the participants or the sexual exploitation of minors, the committee goes on to argue that such prohibition should extend to films where there is reason to believe that the person(s) filmed was/were under age, or was/were physically harmed.[1] It is argued that to require these considerations to be established in the normal way would be to impose an unrealistic burden on the prosecution, particularly in the case of foreign films. The prohibition in question is, however, aimed at the production of films involving particular conduct; as soon as one compromises in the way the committee suggest, the prohibition becomes one that is arguably more concerned with the *effect* such simulated conduct has on prospective audiences, and not with primary conduct at all. This impression is to some extent confirmed by the committee's conclusion that '... we regard the case of actual physical harm being inflicted as more hypothetical'.[2] What Williams appears to be doing is to justify prohibitions on film production and distribution where such films involve particularly graphic depictions of violence; this they attempt via the backdoor, rather than as an integral part of their investigation of the effect of material on prospective readers or viewers. On the basic concern of this essay, material dealing with sexuality, research studies would not appear to establish any real probability of criminal conduct resulting from the perusal of erotica; Williams and the United States commission are at one here, and it is proposed to accept these conclusions. Material dealing with violence overlaps with erotica, and has been judicially included within the ambit of English obscenity law; it is perhaps nonetheless something which may best be dealt with quite apart from sexual pornography as such. Expert evidence does not display anything like the same unanimity, whilst society at large may well be far more concerned with violence in this context than sexuality. Because no prohibitions are proposed here in relation to violent material does not mean that the experts are at one, whilst such material occasioned the outstanding flaw in the Williams Committee report; this is a question which is best dealt with on its own, and it must seem doubtful whether Williams, in the light of the above, in any way seriously pre-empts such an inquiry.

    Aside from a causation role in relation to crime, it has been argued

---

1   *Williams* para 10.7; see production of pornography, chapter 7.

2   Ibid.

that pornography leads consumers to alter their sexual habits, an alteration that may in turn affect others, as for example, between partners in marriage. It is alleged that pornography 'sometimes implanted in husbands the desire to engage in sexual experimentation which their wives found abhorrent, and which therefore introduced tensions into the marriage'.[1] Mrs Whitehouse told Williams that she had received a large number of letters in this vein, but could not produce them for the committee to see. Besides such very limited evidence, submissions were received that pornography actually helped flagging marital relations.[2] These latter claims may be supported by the fact that such material is used to 'alleviate the problems of those whose relationship is suffering through impotence or frigidity';[3] such material may also be used to treat sexual deviations. In the latter respect the treatment may proceed by aversion, in the sense of a paedophiliac (for example) being given shocks whilst viewing slides of children. Reorientation of patients may also be attempted by fantasy substitution based on the use of erotica. Although problems still remain with respect to both forms of treatment, studies appear to indicate considerable success.[4] Much the same can be said of the use of erotica in treating sexual dysfunction, where although it cannot be claimed to constitute a cure, it would appear to 'enhance sexual pleasure and performance and helps patients to function again'.[5] Against these results in relation to deviants or those with sexual dysfunctions, may be set the research conducted for the American Presidential Commission in this respect, which broadly concluded that established patterns of sexual behaviour and fantasy are stable and are not appreciably altered by exposure to pornography.[6] Such research findings have been subject to criticism on the grounds that under-representative sampling was employed; that the exposure time to stimuli was very short; that behaviour before

---

1 *Williams* para 6.63.

2 Ibid.

3 Ibid.; see also P. Gillan 'Therapeutic Uses of Obscenity' in Dhavan and Davies op.cit. at 127.

4 P. Gillan op.cit. at 132–3.

5 Ibid. at 144.

6 *Report* at 197 *et sequor*; see S.P. Jones 'The Underlying Assumptions of Pornography Legislation: A Critical Appraisal, with Special Reference to Psychological Effects', unpublished thesis submitted in partial fulfilment of the requirements for the Diploma in Criminology in the University of Cambridge, 1974, Section II. See also H.J. Eysenck 'Psychology and Obscenity: A Factual Look at Some of the Problems' Dhavan and Davies op.cit. 148 at 161.

and after was investigated only for a very short period; and that self-report investigations are liable to particular distortions.[1] Although Maurice Yaffé pointed out[2] the desirability of repeating such investigation in the light of criticisms such as these, he states in his updated review of literature for Williams[3] that individual behaviour, even amongst adolescents, appears to relate to previously established sexual identity rather than the potential influence of pornography.

Even were one to accept that pornography does predispose individuals to sexual experimentation, assuming that this is not essayed with unwilling partners, this may not be a bad thing. Disapproval hinges essentially on the view that such activities, although legal, are immoral. Aside from a bald assertion that a particular brand of sexual morality is to be upheld, immorality as a harm is generally and most cogently argued as a harm to society, and will be considered later in this respect. The only other harm advanced here is that pornography affects for example the attitudinal responses of consumers to sexual affairs.[4] A particular example of this is that the degradation of women allegedly involved in much pornography results in sex-calloused male attitudes towards women. As with conduct, studies in this regard indicate that pornography has little or no impact on established attitudes to sexuality or sexual morality. Even were one to accept that it does have such an effect, provided the attitudes are not directly associated with crime, disapproval of such effects would seem to be based essentially on a view of their immorality. The same may be said of an engendering in men of a callous sexual attitude towards women: incitement to misogyny is perhaps, together with incitement to racial hatred, for example, best seen as a moral harm to society?

(iii) *Analysis of crime statistics*

A number of difficulties[5] beset attempts at assessing possible correlations here: a major one is the fact that official crime statistics do not reflect unreported crime; there is no way of knowing whether the latter remains in constant proportion to reported crime or not. In international comparisons such difficulties are compounded in the sense that what constitutes a particular criminal offence may vary from

---

1   Jones op.cit.

2   *The Longford Report* op.cit. at 472.

3   *Williams* Appendix 5.

4   Jones op.cit., Section III.

5   *Williams* paras 6.23–6.29.

system to system. A further difficulty concerns information about the availability of pornography: this concerns not only the volume of pornography, but the kind as well; there may for example be an increase over time in the availability of soft-core pornography, but not hard-core material. How can and should this be taken into account? A final problem here is perhaps the most difficult of all: even if the two variables, crime and pornography, can satisfactorily be isolated statistically, does this necessarily establish a causal nexus? There are many factors that may contribute to crime, and even where a correlation is established, it cannot be taken as proof of a connection, nor, if crime statistics are rising generally, may it be enough to satisfy those concerned with probabilities. As far as the incidence of crime is concerned, Williams considered first the position in England and Wales. Figure 15.1 shows the indictable sexual offences, together with those against the person, recorded by the police during the period 1946—78.[1] It indicates that sexual offences began increasing long before the 1960s; if the years 1964—70 are isolated, there is an increase, but it is less marked than that between 1946—59. Between 1973 and 1977 there was a sharp decline, this being reversed in 1977. This forms a sharp contrast with the sharp and continuing rise in offences against the person. Any correlation between pornography and crime must be seen then against a general background of sharply rising crime statistics. Indictable offences over the period have increased fivefold, whilst sexual offences have doubled in number. In 1946 sexual offences formed 2 per cent of all indictable crimes recorded by the police; this rose to 4 per cent in 1955, but has fallen to 1 per cent by 1977 and 1978.[2] There have of course been changes in the law on sexual offences over this period: two such offences which may be taken as constants, and particularly relevant potentially to pornography, are rape and indecent assault. Rape has increased faster than sexual offences have as a whole, but at the same rate as for indictable offences as a whole, and at a much slower rate than offences against the person, which have increased twentyfold over the postwar period. Indecent assault on a female has increased at roughly the same rate as have sexual offences generally.[3] It should be pointed out in relation to the increase in reported cases of rape, that the changes effected by the Sexual Offences (Amendment) Act 1976, which provides for anonymity for complainants and imposes certain restrictions on their cross-examination, may well have made victims more willing to go to the

---

1 *Williams* p.73.

2 Ibid. para 6.35.

3 Ibid. para 6.36; figure 3, page 77.

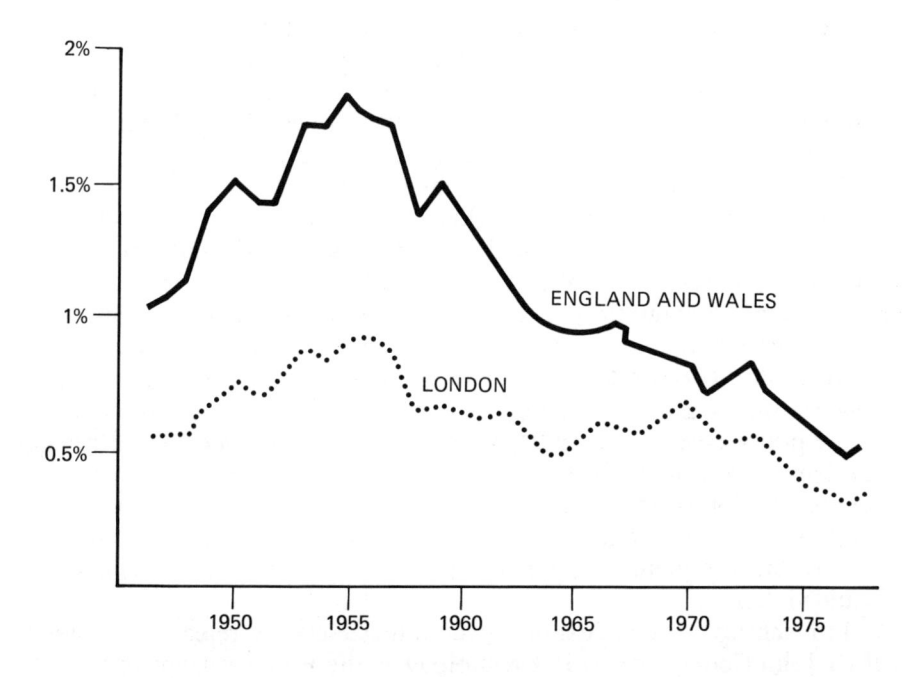

Fig. 15.1 Indictable offences recorded by the police (England and Wales) 1946–78

police, and therefore have contributed to the increase in rape statistics.

Although there has broadly been a trend over the last twenty years towards a greater tolerance of material dealing with sexuality, in respect both of quantity and kind, evidence on the availability of pornography is often conflicting. Over the period 1972—78, for example, the Metropolitan Police informed Williams that there had been a considerable reduction in the availability of hard-core pornography from overseas; equally, between 1975 and 1977 British magazines had become considerably less restrained. In addition, police action against publishers and retailers increased from 1977, with a corresponding reduction in sales from early 1977 onwards. There are too many variables, in other words, for firm information about the type and quantity of pornography available, although circulation figures for British sex magazines would appear to have reached a peak in 1976, and to have declined after that.[1]

Any correlation that may be alleged with respect to these two variables has to be measured, moreover, against soaring crime figures, particularly in relation to crimes against the person, the increase in sexual offences generally being significantly slower. The difference with rape alone has been less significant in this respect, and where rape figures for London alone are taken, they are consistent with other forms of crime. To be set against this, is the fact that the increase in reported cases of rape in England and Wales, and particularly in London, occurred principally in the period 1977 onwards: this corresponds to the introduction of the change in law as to rape hearings, and to an apparent *decrease*, particularly in London, in the availability of pornography. If one adds to this the fact that rape and sexual assault have declined steadily as a proportion of indictable offences recorded by the police (see Figure 15.2), the committee concluded that although not denying the possibility that pornography might be associated with the commission of sexual offences, '... we unhesitatingly reject the suggestion that the available statistical information lends any support at all to the argument that pornography acts as a stimulus to crimes of sexual violence'.[2]

In reaching this conclusion, the committee clearly rejected the views of Dr John Court, Reader in Psychology at the Flinders University of South Australia. As far as the availability of pornography is concerned, Dr Court submitted to the committee that there were two periods at which the availability of pornography in Britain increased significantly: 1964 and 1970. These periods both correspond to upturns in rape

---

1   *Williams* para 4.26.

2   Ibid. para 6.43.

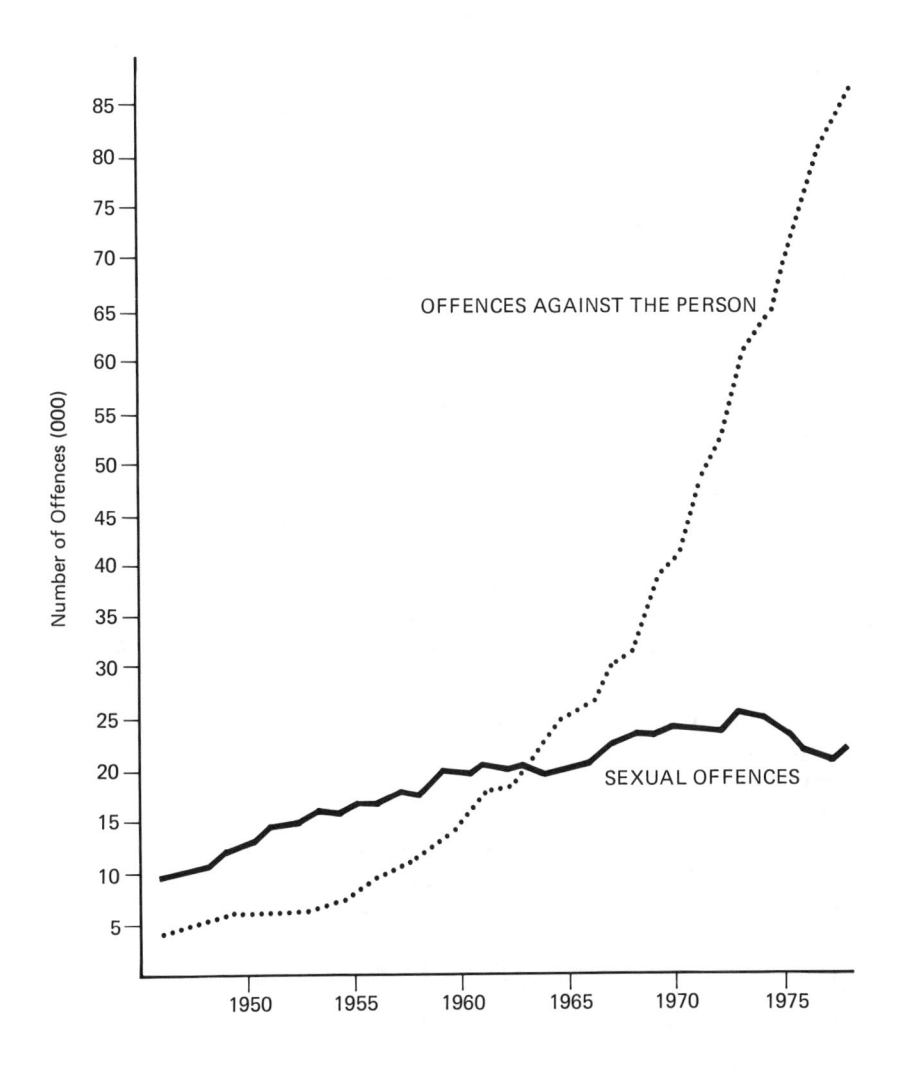

Fig. 15.2   Rape and sexual assault as a proportion of indictable offences recorded by the police

statistics. His reasoning as to these two dates is that the first saw the 1964 Obscene Publications Act, and the second the publication of the Report of the American Commission on Obscenity and Pornography; he cites in support of the earlier date an article by Mr Ronald Butt in *The Times* on 5 February 1976, which attacked the ineffectiveness in practice (in Mr Butt's view) of the 1959 and 1964 Acts. Williams points out that the selection of these two dates is apparently unsubstantiated, and 'less than convincing'.[2] Because of the selection of 1964 as the base date, Dr Court did not furnish the committee with crime statistics for the earlier period from 1946—64; these, as the committee point out, show a rising trend in sexual offences long before pornography is alleged to have become widely available. Not only this, but Dr Court relies particularly on rape statistics, and especially rape figures for London: this he justifies on the ground that there is a greater concentration of pornography in some parts of London than in the provinces. Finally, in relation to the rise in crime generally over this period, especially crimes against the person, Dr Court has proposed that the rise in sexual crime in the United States of America and Australia has been greater than the general rise in crime, but that this has in Britain been 'masked in recent years by the upsurge of violent offences associated with the Irish problem'.[3] The committee concludes in this regard that given '... the fact that the trend in violent crime ... goes back at least a quarter of a century, and given the scale of that increase, we doubt whether Dr. Court would wish to stand by that statement'. They conclude that 'the case put to us by Dr. Court, and by other witnesses who have looked to Dr. Court's work for support, cannot on the basis of the situation in England and Wales, we believe, survive even as a plausible hypothesis'.[4]

This rejection of Dr Court's findings extended to the committee's examination of the Danish experience also. Prohibitions on written obscenity were abolished in Denmark in 1967, and on pictorial matter in 1969; the situation has therefore lent itself to 'before and after' studies. A problem in relation to Denmark was the abolition of a number of sexual offences, a factor which will clearly influence statistics. Dr Berl Kutchinsky of the Institute of Criminal Science at the University of Copenhagen, who undertook work for the American Commission and subsequently submitted evidence to Williams, assured

---

1   *Williams*, figure 4, p.79.

2   Ibid. para 6.31.

3   *The Times*, 7 August 1976; *Williams* para 6.34.

4   *Williams* para 6.42.

the committee that despite suggestions by Mrs Whitehouse and Dr Court to the contrary, he had excluded from his figures any offence in relation to which the law had been liberalised.[1] Another potential difficulty pointed out in relation to the Danish situation was that liberalisation in this area meant that certain more minor sexual offences were more frequently left unreported by the public. Dr Kutchinsky, both the committee and Dr Court felt, had made a 'commendable' effort to allow for this potentiality. According to Dr Kutchinsky,[2] sex offences had remained steady at 85 cases *per annum* per 100,000 of population. In 1967 this dropped to 67, and then fell to 40; such decrease took place in urban rather than rural areas. Heterosexual crimes dropped after 1966 from 100 per 100,000 to less than 30 in 1973, and then levelled off. As far as rape alone is concerned, the rate seems to have remained fairly steady at around 30 per 100,000.[3] On the other hand, Dr Kutchinsky confirmed to the committee a dramatic reduction (taking into account reluctance to report offences) of two-thirds in the number of sex offences against children between 1967 and 1969; this he concluded was difficult to explain other than in terms of the availability of pornography. Williams adopted a cautious attitude to the latter correlation, but in view of its likelihood, found it at least plausible. Dr Court, the committee concludes, has attempted in an unsubstantiated manner, to discredit Dr Kutchinsky's findings as 'counter-intuitive'. Even if one were not to accept the latter's suggested correlation in respect of sexual offences against children, there is nothing, they felt, in the Danish experience to substantiate Dr Court's conclusions that it supports his hypothesis.[4]

Such conclusions in relation to crime statistics have led to a counter-blast: Mrs Whitehouse described the committee's conclusions as 'intelligentsia gone off the rails', adding in relation to their broader recommendations against general prohibitions that 'It strikes me that we are going from a quicksand into a quagmire and it is a very mucky quagmire'.[5] Her support for Dr Court remained undiminished: although acknowledging that the committee spent nineteen pages in 'attacking' Dr Court's work, Mrs Whitehouse then accuses them of ignoring his claim of an 'irrefutable' link between pornography and rape and

---

1   *Williams* para 6.46.

2   Ibid. para 6.49.

3   Ibid., figure 5, p.82.

4   Ibid. para 6.56.

5   *The Sunday Times*, 25 November 1979.

attempted rape, as illustrated by 'evidence from police authorities all over the free world'.[1] Dr Court flew into London for a publicity campaign aimed at refuting Williams on this issue, including an interview with the Home Secretary. He has apparently three principal points of disagreement with Williams:[2] first, that the evidence as to harms should be evaluated as a body, and not assessed piecemeal; we will return to this point at the end of this chapter. Second, Dr Court states that the trend for rape and attempted rape in Copenhagen is in fact a rising one, and has been steadily rising since 1972.[3] This is in direct contradiction of the trend as represented by Williams, which they show as declining sharply since 1972. Both representations are alleged to be based on Copenhagen police figures; insofar as they contradict one another, Dr Court implies that Williams has put forward an untruthful and distorted representation of official figures. Even were these figures to be considered conclusive, for present purposes Williams is to be preferred: it is difficult to see that a committee of this type consisting of thirteen members would collectively lend themselves to such clear sharp practice. Third, Dr Court argues, and here he has been enthusiastically supported by Mr Ronald Butt,[4] that Williams should have considered not all offences against the person in England and Wales, but more serious offences of this type, when looking for a point of comparison for rape. Such offences, it is argued, rose by 31 per cent between 1969 and 1978, whilst rape rose by 43 per cent. As Professor Bernard Williams points out,[5] however, if one takes 1969 as the base line instead of 1970, the figure for serious violent crime is 36.8 per cent and not 31 per cent. If, moreover, one takes the period 1969—77, the relevant figures for serious violent crime and rape are 37.5 per cent and 16.8 per cent. From 1977 to 1978 there was a rise in reported cases of rape of 22.5 per cent, an increase which the official *Handbook of Criminal Statistics*[6] itself says may have been contributed to by 'a growing willingness of victims to report offences of rape now that, because of the Sexual Offences (Amendment) Act 1976, they can remain anonymous in court'. It seems reasonable to assume in the

---

1   *Bristol Evening Post*, 28 July 1980.

2   See J.H. Court 'Pornography, Harm and Williams', a lecture given in London, 3 July 1980; text obtained from Dr Court.

3   Ibid. at 10, figure 6.

4   See *The Times*, 3 July 1980; 26 July 1980.

5   In a letter to *The Times*, 8 July 1980; see also *The Times*, 1 July 1980.

6   Cmnd 7670, at 52.

light of all this that a real probability of crime resulting from pornography has not been established, particularly if violent material is excluded from these calculations.

II) Paternalism

The arguments here reflect the broad divisions between resultant conduct and resultant attitudes discussed heretofore in relation to research studies into the effects of pornography. To deal with conduct first: one's concern here is not with other individuals, but with inducement of conduct changes which affect the consumer of pornography; with patterns essentially of masturbation, in other words. Experiments undertaken for the American Commission show that as with sexual conduct in general, masturbatory patterns are related generally to past conduct and development, and not to exposure to pornography.[1] As far as character is concerned, studies have not been able to say that moral character is in any way related to exposure to pornography, but was rather associated with deviant home backgrounds and deviant peer influences.[2]

Two further and allied arguments here are that pornography leads to dependence or addiction on the part of consumers, and that its distribution constitutes exploitation of that dependence. As far as dependence is concerned, research has tended to establish a pattern of satiation with pornographic materials;[3] these conclusions, together with those as to conduct inducement and character, have been subject to the same methodological criticisms made of many of the research studies quoted by the commission.[4] The essence of both the addiction and exploitation arguments is, however, that the material harms its consumers. Commercial exploitation is apparently an acceptable part of capitalist or mixed economies; the only reason to single out the inducement of masturbation, or the exploitation allegedly involved in pornography distribution, is presumably on the basis of the harm this does consumers. Masturbation in particular was viewed as satisfying just such harm requirements:

> ... obscenity law, then, must be understood as a political expression of broader popular moral attitudes toward

---

1   *Report* at 222.

2   *Technical Reports*, vol.7, at 202; quoted in Jones op.cit., Section III.

3   *Report* at 214.

4   Jones op.cit., Section III.

the putative proper use, and improper abuse, of the body. It is no accident that such laws have been used to forbid the transport of abortifacient and contraceptive information and dissemination of sex manuals and to prosecute advocacy of contraception and population control. The moral attitudes behind such laws, directed against a supposed 'abuse' of the body, were founded on a compound of religious, psychological, and medical beliefs basic to which was a deep fear of masturbation. Masturbation it was believed, led directly to physical debility and even death, as well as crime, and civil disorder.[1]

It is trite to say that such dire consequences are no longer attributed by either medical or psychological opinion to masturbation. In the absence of the demonstration of a rationally assessable harm in this sense, one is left solely with the question of morality and society's dependence on it.

III) Society

Obscenity was introduced into the common law in the teeth of judicial argument that the law should in such matters concern itself only with threats to the peace.[2] This was and has been a common requirement with respect to blasphemy, seditious libel and criminal libel.[3] It was rejected in *Curl*, however, and has not since been a consideration in this area of law. This was probably only realistic: to assert that obscenity is likely to lead to a breach of the peace seems, other than in exceptional circumstances such as live entertainment for example, to be very probably unsustainable. Obscenity prohibition had early associations with blasphemy and seditious libel: it was in other words concerned with the enforcement of political/religious orthodoxy as evidenced in a particular brand of sexual morality. Not surprisingly, insofar as its basic rationale has remained unaltered, this early association has never been lost, even if a trifle obscured in the course of the tortuous legislative and judicial development of the obscenity theme. This political/religious basis has, however, occasionally broken through the legal morass with startling clarity: the *Oz* trial in the early 1970s

---

1   D.A.J. Richards 'Free Speech and Obscenity Law: Toward a Moral Theory of the First Amendment' 123 (1974) *U Pa L Rev* 45 at 72–3.

2   Mr Justice Fortesque in *R* v *Curl* (1727) 2 Strange 788.

3   See pp.89ff, *supra*.

in England is an excellent example of this. As has been succinctly remarked in this regard: 'The issue in the *Oz* trial was less concerned with the song than with the singer'.[1]

In the absence of demonstrable harms of a rational character to individuals as consumers, or as caused by consumers of pornography to others, the rationalist should at this stage conclude that obscenity prohibition cannot be supported. It is worth asking, however, in view of its clear role, and the apparent ambivalence of some of its opponents when this so suits, whether public morality may serve to justify prohibitions of the sort with which we are concerned here. This is to depart from the rationalist approach, but such departure, if it may serve to settle the moralism point, may be justified. The argument as to the sustenance of morality in this area as being necessary to prevent harm has been most cogently argued by Lord Devlin; the harm in question is argued to be either the disintegration or at least dramatic deterioration of society. One has in this respect to accept (amongst others) a number of propositions:[2]

(i) That pornography affects the sexual morality of those individuals who consume it. As has been pointed out, however, what evidence there is here, even if open to methodological criticism, tends to refute this.[3]

(ii) That pornography not only affects sexual morality and attitudes, but that this in turn affects the morality of consumers generally: that morality is in other words indivisible. Again, research results would tend to disprove this, leading to the conclusion that moral character is essentially dependent on deviant background influences, and not exposure to pornography.

(iii) Lord Devlin argues that such enforcement is necessary to sustain the established code of morality in society; that pornography breaks down sexual morality; that this in turn leads to a breakdown of morality as a whole, with dire consequences for the society in question. Even if one accepts the first two propositions, Lord Devlin concedes that this sequence presupposes and logically requires a prevalent code of morality. Although he argues that morality is best assessed by a jury, this is open to criticism on the grounds of legality. If uncertainty or fragmentation is alleged in relation to positive sexual

---

1 Michael Beloff in *Encounter* 38, p.48, quoted in Jones op.cit., Section V.

2 See pp.105ff, *supra*.

3 Jones op.cit.

morality, it seems both equitable and practicable in a democratic society to consult public opinion in this regard.

In the United States a number of states have repealed their adult obscenity laws, presumably on the basis of public opinion in regard to them. The Presidential Commission reported that 60 per cent of those surveyed favoured a removal of controls on the sale of sexually explicit material to adults (twenty-one years of age and over).[1] In England the General Synod of the Church of England recently found itself debating such subjects as masturbation, homosexuality, chastity, intercourse between engaged couples; the Catholic Church appears to be in a similar state of ferment. The circulation figures for British sex magazines as supplied to Williams are probably, to the uninitiated, quite staggering: the total market every month appears to be of the order of three million copies. Extrapolating these results, the committee suggest that 'the gross audience for magazines of this kind is about 8 million adults in Britain, but this does not mean that 8 million adults in Britain read these magazines, because some read more than one. However, the indications are that about 4 million people have read one or more of these magazines during the preceding month'.[2] Approximately 90 per cent of this readership is male, the bulk of readers being under the age of 45.[3] This means that a considerable proportion of the adult male population would presumably not, unless quite hypocritical, regard such magazines, many of which have become increasingly explicit, as flagrantly immoral. For confirmation of this, one need only turn to opinion poll results in this respect: an Opinion Research Centre poll[4] conducted for *The Sunday Times* in 1973 indicated that 56 per cent of the representative national sample selected (1,014 adults over 15 years of age) thought pornographic literature should be available to those who want it provided it is not publicly displayed. A second survey based on a representative sample of 900 adults (aged 15 years or over) showed that 74 per cent thought adults should be allowed to buy what pornography they pleased, only 18 per cent dissenting. A Gallup Poll conducted in Denmark in June 1970 asked its subjects whether it was right or wrong to repeal the ban on pornography; 57 per cent considered it was right, 25 per cent wrong, and 18 per cent were uncertain.[5]

---

1 Lockhart op.cit. at 218.

2 *Williams* paras 4.26 and 4.27.

3 Ibid., Appendix 6.

4 *The Sunday Times*, 25 February 1973.

5 Jones op.cit., Section IV.

In a recent survey[1] conducted by Market and Opinion Research International of a representative sample of 1,930 people (aged 15 years or over), 50 per cent thought soft-core pornographic magazines morally acceptable, only 29 per cent dissenting. The dissenters included only 16 per cent of those between 15 and 24 years of age and 59 per cent of those over 65 years of age. Of those surveyed 69 per cent thought it morally acceptable that unmarried couples live together, only 7 per cent of those between 15 and 24 years of age dissenting, as opposed to 50 per cent of those over 65 years of age. Findings such as these serve only to confirm the fragmentation, particularly in age terms, of sexual morality in English society. Lord Devlin argued that the legal enforcement of morality should not be relaxed until that morality was shown to be clearly fragmented; such fragmentation is fairly clearly in the area of positive sexual morality a *fait accompli*. Moral pluralism in sexual matters is the reality today; to continue to provide legal prohibitions on pornography would appear to be to attempt to enforce one strand of such pluralism. To do so through jury decision would be to invite fluctuating results in criminal trials, and stands condemned in terms of legality if nothing else; to do so through legislative enshrinement is not only to perpetuate legislative fossilisation, but similarly to invite fluctuating jury decisions, for juries at odds with the legislative option before them might well feel impelled to acquit. The result would be patchily enforced law and confusion amongst the general public as to just what is unlawful, together with a corresponding decline in public regard for the law, in this area at any rate.

If one accepts the arguments advanced above, no demonstrable or sustainable harms appear to underlie pornography prohibitions, unless one is prepared to accept as such what has been termed cultural pollution. It was strongly argued in submission to Williams that there is today — aided by pornography — 'a widespread mental obsession with sexuality, a considerable degree of commercialisation of sex, a growing egotistical nihilism, a preoccupation with satiation and a corruption of culture'.[2] The committee did not appear inclined to disagree with all of this, but pointed out that pornography as a part of cultural development, should be seen as a symptom of a general malaise (if there is such), rather than a cause of it. Much the same can probably be said of the role played by pornography in evoking sex-calloused masculine attitudes towards women: unless one wishes to employ this as an enforcement-of-morality type of justification, the point is possibly

---

1 *The Sunday Times*, 2 March 1980

2 *Williams* para 6.74; this seems to be the principal potential effect Professor Eysenck assigns to sexual materials: Dhavan and Davies op.cit. at 167–8.

best answered in the same terms as might allegations of cultural pollution: where such attitudes to women are represented in pornography, they are probably more symptomatic than causative.

The answer would appear to be, then, the abolition of pornography prohibitions in favour of those restrictions and limited prohibitions with respect in particular to children and gratuitous offence, suggested earlier. It has been suggested by Dr Court that this is not the case, in that those concerned with evaluating harms in this area have done so piecemeal, and have not added alleged harms one to another before effecting balancing. Although this latter approach may to some extent be characteristic of the assessment of alleged harms occasioned by such material in relation to minors, it would seem appropriate to recall that one is concerned here not with the freedom of speech and individual liberties of children, but with those of adults. The harm side of the scale is inevitably more easily satisfied with the young than with adults, in view of an understandable reluctance to take risks with those not sufficiently mature to cope with the potentially harmful. The standard of a real probability of harm in relation to adults is one which should be applied rigorously: such application would not appear to involve a single instance of a harm approaching what might satisfy such a standard.

It must be remembered also that these recommendations relate only to material dealing with sexuality. This essay's concern is censorship on the basis of public sexual morality. There is clearly an overlap between such censorship and that based on the effect of violent material; the two areas would appear, despite their apparent juncture in English law under the heading of obscenity, to be nonetheless susceptible of separate treatment. The restrictions recommended earlier as to gratuitous offence and the protection of children include violence; these restrictions would appear rationally sustainable. As far as a prohibition on violent material is concerned, this is something which appears susceptible of further investigation, and must be left to another day. Any harms alleged to result from the distribution of sexually orientated material must to some extent, moreover, be devalued insofar as privacy is apparently regarded in both jurisdictions as a sufficiently cogent philosophical/constitutional consideration to outweigh potential harms, in the United States in relation to possession in the home, in England and Wales in relation to possession *per se*. Were it felt that pornography involved pressing harms, then as was suggested in *Stanley* v *Georgia*,[1] privacy would not — as with the possession of firearms for example — be sufficient to guarantee individual freedom from regulation. Not only this, but depending on one's view of the

---

1   394 US 557 (1968); see privacy, pp.159–65 *supra*.

proper philosophical and/or constitutional meaning to be assigned to privacy, the latter may well be a further factor to be entered on the freedom side of the balance. In these terms, prohibition in relation to sexually-orientated material does not appear, in philosophical or constitutional terms, to be appropriate.

Bibliography

English law

Official publications – HM Stationery Office, London

'Conspiracies relating to morals and decency' *Law Commission Working Paper* No. 57 (1974)
'Conspiracies to effect a public mischief and to commit a civil wrong' *Law Commission Working Paper* No. 63 (1975)
'Inchoate Offences' *Law Commission Working Paper* No. 50 (1973)
Law Commission Report on Conspiracy and Criminal Law Reform (1976)
Minutes of Evidence taken before the Select Committee on the Obscene Publications Bill HC 122 (1958)
Report from the Select Committee on Obscene Publications HC 123 – I (1958)
Report of the Committee on Obscenity and Film Censorship Cmnd 7772 (1979)
The Report of the Committee on Privacy Cmnd 5012 (1972)
'Working Party on Vagrancy and Street Offences' *Home Office Working Paper* (1974)
'Working Party on Vagrancy and Street Offences' *Home Office Report* (1976)

Articles

Bates, F.: 'Pornography and the Expert Witness' (1977–78) *Criminal Law Quarterly* 250

Clark, C.: 'Obscenity, the Law and Lady Chatterley' (1961) *Criminal Law Review* 156 and 224.

Dybikowski, J.C.: 'Law, Liberty and Obscenity' (1972) 7 *University of British Columbia Law Review* 33

Feldman, D.: 'Declarations and the Control of Prosecutions' (1981) *The Criminal Law Review* 25

Grey, A.: 'Sexual Law Reform Society – Working Party Report' (1975) *Criminal Law Review* 323

Hall Williams, J.E.: 'Obscenity in Modern English Law' 20 (1955) *Law and Contemporary Problems* 630

Leigh, L.H.: 'Vagrancy, Morality and Decency' (1975) *Criminal Law Review* 381

Leigh, L.H.: 'Indecency and Obscenity. Indecent Exposure' (1975) *Criminal Law Review* 413

Lynch, A.C.E.: 'Counselling and Assisting Homosexuals' (1979) *Criminal Law Review* 630

Miller, C.J.: 'Recent Developments in the Law of Obscenity' (1973) *Criminal Law Review*

Price, D.G.: 'The Role of Choice in a Definition of Obscenity' 62 (1979) *Canadian Bar Review* 301

St. John Stevas, N.: 'Obscenity and the Law' (1954) *Criminal Law Review* 819

Wilkinson, H.: 'Planning Law and Undesirable Activities' 30 (1979) *New Law Journal* 1099

Williams, D.G.T.: 'The Control of Obscenity' (1965) *Criminal Law Review* 471 and 524

Williams, D.G.T.: 'Sex and Morals 1954–1963' (1964) *Criminal Law Review*

Williams, D.G.T.: 'Racial Incitement and Public Order' (1966) *Criminal Law Review* 320

Williams Glanville: 'Law and Fact' (1976) *Criminal Law Review* 472 and 532

Zellick, G.: 'Violence as Pornography' (1970) *Criminal Law Review*

Zellick, G.: 'Offensive Advertisement in the Mail' (1972) *Criminal Law Review* 724

Zellick, G.: 'Films and the Law of Obscenity' (1971) *Criminal Law Review* 126

Zellick, G.: 'Two Comments on Search and Seizure under the Obscene Publications Act' (1971) *Criminal Law Review* 504

Zellick, G.: 'Obscene or Pornographic? Obscenity and the Public Good' (1972) 27 *Cambridge Law Journal*

Books

Arts Council: *The Obscenity Laws* (A Report by the Working Party, London 1969)

Brownlie, I.: *The Law Relating to Public Order* (London 1968)

Chandos, J.: 'To Deprave and Corrupt ...' Original studies in the nature and definition of 'obscenity'. (London 1962)

Chesney, K.: *Victorian Underworld* (London 1970)

Cornish, W.R.: *The Jury* (London 1968)

Craig, A.: *Suppressed Books* (London 1963)

De Smith, S.A.: *Judicial Review of Administrative Action* (4th Edn, London 1980)

Devlin, P.: *Trial by Jury* (London 1956)

Findlater, A.: *Banned! A Review of Theatrical Censorship in Britain* (London 1967)

Hazell, R.: *Conspiracy and Civil Liberties* (A Cobden Trust Memorandum, 1974)

Hyde Montgomery, H.: *A History of Pornography* (London 1954)

Leigh, L.H.: *Police Powers in England and Wales* (London 1974)

Munro, C.: *Censorship, Television and the Law* (Farnborough 1979)

O'Higgins, P.: *Censorship in Britain* (London 1972)

Robertson, G.: *Obscenity* (London 1979)

Rolph, C.H.: *The Trial of Lady Chatterley* (London 1961)

Smith, J. and Hogan, B.: *Criminal Law* (3rd Edn, London 1973)

Stephen, J.H.: 'History of the Criminal Law of England' (3 Vols, London 1883)

St. John Stevas, N.: *Obscenity and the Law* (London 1956)

Street, H.: *Freedom, the Individual and the Law* (Harmondsworth 1972)

Thomas, D.: *A Long Time Burning* (London 1969)

Tribe, D.: *Questions of Censorship* (London 1973)

Williams, D.G.T.: 'Prosecution, Discretion and the Accountability of the Police' in *Crime, Criminology and Public Policy*, Ed. R. Hood (London 1974)

Williams Glanville: *Textbook of Criminal Law* (London 1978)

Williams Glanville: *Criminal Law: The General Part* (London 1962)

Zellick, G.: *Against Censorship* (NCCL Pamphlet, 1973)

American Law

Articles

Alpert, G.M.: 'Judicial Censorship of Obscene Literature' 52 (1938) *Harvard Law Review* 40

Abse, D.: 'Psychodynamic Aspects of the Problem of Definition of Obscenity' 20 (1955) *Law and Contemporary Problems* 572

Brennan, W.J.: 'The Supreme Court and the Meiklejohn Interpretation of the First Amendment' 79 (1965) *Harvard Law Review* 1

Bogen, D.S.: 'The Supreme Court's Interpretation of the Guarantee of Freedom of Speech' 35 (1976) *Maryland Law Review* 555

Berbysse, E.: 'Conflict in the Courts: Obscenity Control and First Amendment Freedoms' 20 (1974) *Catholic Lawyer* 1

Chafee, Z.: Review: Free Speech and its Relation to Self-Government (Meiklejohn, A.S.) 62 (1948–1949) *Harvard Law Review* 891

Cairns, Paul and Wishner: 'Sex Censorship: The Assumption of Anti-Obscenity Laws and the Empirical Evidence' 46 (1962) *Minnesota Law Review* 1009

Clor, H.: 'Obscenity and the First Amendment: Round Three' 7 (1974) *Loyola University Law Review* 207

Clor, H.: 'Public Morality and Free Expression: The Judicial Search for Principles of Reconciliation' 28 (1977) *Hastings Law Journal* 1305

De Grazia: 'Obscenity and the Mail: A Study of Administrative Restraint' 20 (1955) *Law and Contemporary Problems* 608

Dyson: 'Looking-Glass Law: An Analysis of the Ginzburg Case' 80 (1966) *Harvard Law Review* 189

Davidow, R.P. and O'Boyle, M.: 'Obscenity Laws in England and the United States: A Comparative Analysis' 56 (1977) *Nebraska Law Review* 249

Emerson, T.: 'Toward a General Theory of the First Amendment' 72 (1963) *Yale Law Journal* 877

Emerson, T.: 'The Doctrine of Prior Restraint' 20 (1955) *Law and Contemporary Problems* 648

Fairman: 'Does the Fourteenth Amendment Incorporate the Bill of Rights?' 2 (1949) *Stanford Law Review* 5

Feinberg, J.: 'Pornography and the Criminal Law' 40 (1979) *University of Pittsburgh Law Review*

Frankel, C.: 'The Moral Environment of the Law' 61 *Minnesota Law Review* 921

Finnis: ' "Reason and Passion": The Constitutional Dialectic of Free Speech and Obscenity' 116 (1967) *University of Pennsylvania Law Review* 222

Frantz, L.B.: 'The First Amendment in the Balance' 71 (1962) *Yale*

Law Journal 1424

Frantz, L.B.: 'Is the First Amendment Law? A Reply to Professor Mendelson' 57 (1963) *California Law Review* 729

Friedman: 'The Motion Picture Rating System of 1968: A Constitutional Analysis of Self-Regulation by the Film Industry' 73 (1973) *Columbia Law Review* 185

Friendly, H.: 'The Bill of Rights as a Code of Criminal Practice' 53 (1965) *California Law Review* 929

Gardiner, H.: 'Moral Principles Towards Definition of the Obscene' 20 (1955) *Law and Contemporary Problems* 560

Grant and Anghoff: 'Massachusetts and Censorship' 10 (1930) *Boston University Law Review* 36

Green: 'The Bill of Rights and the Fourteenth Amendment' 46 (1947) *Michigan Law Review* 869

Harrington: 'The Evolution of Obscenity Control Statutes' 3 (1962) *William and Mary Law Review* 302

Henkin: 'Morals and the Constitution: The Sin of Obscenity' 63 (1963) *Columbia Law Review* 391

Hunsaker, D.M.: 'The 1973 Obscenity—Pornography Decisions: Analysis, Impact and Legislative Alternatives' 11 (1974) *San Diego Law Review* 906

Hunter, I.A.: 'Obscenity, Pornography and Law Reform' (1977) *Dalhousie Law Journal* 483

Kalven, H.: 'The Metaphysics of the Law of Obscenity' (1960) *Supreme Court Review* 1

Kalven, H.: 'Reading Mr. Justice Black on the First Amendment' 14 (1967) *University of California Los Angeles Law Review* 428

Kaplan, A.: 'Obscenity as an Esthetic Category' 20 (1955) *Law and Contemporary Problems* 544

Karst: 'Equality as a Central Principle in the First Amendment' 43 (1976) *University of Chicago Law Review* 20

Katz, A.: 'Privacy and Pornography' (1969) *Supreme Court Review* 203

Krislov: 'From Ginzburg to Ginsberg: The Unhurried Children's Hour in Obscenity Legislation' (1968) *Supreme Court Review* 153

Larrabee, E.: 'The Cultural Content of Sex Censorship' 20 (1955) *Law and Contemporary Problems* 672

Le Barre, W.: 'Obscenity: An Anthropological Appraisal' 20 (1955) *Law and Contemporary Problems* 533

Leventhal: '1973 Round of Obscenity—Pornography Decisions' 59 (1973) *American Bar Association Journal* 1261

Lockhart, W. and McClure, R.: 'Censorship of Obscenity' 45 (1960) *Minnesota Law Review* 1

Lockhart, W. and McClure, R.: 'Literature, The Law of Obscenity and the Constitution' 38 (1954) *Minnesota Law Review* 295

Lockhart, W. and McClure, R.: 'Obscenity in the Courts' 20 (1955) *Law and Contemporary Problems* 587

Lockhart, W.: 'Escape from the Chill of Uncertainty: Explicit Sex and the First Amendment' 9 (1975) *Georgia Law Review* 533

Lockhart, W.: 'The Findings and Recommendations of the Commission on Obscenity and Pornography: A Case Study of the Role of Social Service in Formulating Public Policy' 24 (1971) *Oklahoma Law Review* 209

Magrath: 'The Obscenity Cases: Grapes of Roth' (1966) *Supreme Court Review* 7

Managhan: 'The Marriage of Obscenity Per Se and Obscenity Per Quod' 76 (1966) *Yale Law Journal* 127

Managhan: 'First Amendment "Due Process" ' 83 (1970) *Harvard Law Review* 578

McKay: 'The Preference for Freedom' 34 (1959) *New York University Law Review* 1182

Meiklejohn: 'The First Amendment is an Absolute' (1961) *Supreme Court Review* 245

Mendelson, W.: 'On the Meaning of the First Amendment: Absolutes in the Balance' 50 (1962) *California Law Review* 821

Morrison: 'Does the Fourteenth Amendment Incorporate the Bill of Rights?' 2 (1949) *Stanford Law Review* 140

Nathansan, N.: 'The Communist Trial and the Clear-and-Present Danger Test' 63 (1950) *Harvard Law Review* 1167

Note: 'Obscenity: Construction and Constitutionality of Statutes Regulating Obscene Literature' 28 (1953) *New York University Law Review* 875

Note: 'Obscenity — Test of Obscene Literature' 48 (1934) *Harvard Law Review* 579

Note: 'Obscenity and the Post Office: Removal from the Mail under Section 1461' 27 (1960) *University of Chicago Law Review* 354

Note: 'Obscenity in the Mail: Post Office Department Procedures and the First Amendment' 58 (1963) *New York University Law Review* 664

Note: 'The Supreme Court 1969 Term' 84 (1970) *Harvard Law Review* 177

Note: 'Morality and the Broadcast Media: A Constitutional Analysis of FCC Regulatory Standards' 84 (1971) *Harvard Law Review* 664

Note: 'Legal Responsibility for Extra-Legal Censure' 62 (1962) *Columbia Law Review* 475

Note: 'Extra-Legal Censorship of Literature' 33 (1958) *New York University Law Review* 989

Note: 'Prior Adversary Hearings on the Question of Obscenity' 70

(1970) *Columbia Law Review* 1403

Note: 'The Prior Adversary Hearing: Solution to Procedural Due Process Problems in Obscenity Seizures?' 46 (1971) *New York University Law Review* 80

Note: 'The Scienter Requirement in Criminal Obscenity Prosecutions' 41 (1960) *New York University Law Review* 791

Note: 'The Chilling Effect in Constitutional Law' 69 (1969) *Columbia Law Review* 808

Note: 'The First Amendment Overbreadth Doctrine' 83 (1970) *Harvard Law Review* 844

Note: 'The Void-for-Vagueness Doctrine in the Supreme Court' 109 (1960) *University of Pennsylvania Law Review* 67

Note: 'More Ado About Dirty Books' 75 (1966) *Yale Law Journal* 1364

Note: 'Fifty Years of 'Clear-and-Present-Danger': From Schenck to Brandenberg — and Beyond' (1969) *Supreme Court Review* 41

Note: 'Still More Ado About Dirty Books' 81 (1971) *Yale Law Journal* 309

Note: 'Roe and Paris: Does Privacy Have a Principle?' 26 (1974) *Stanford Law Review* 1161

Paul: 'The Post Office and Non-Mailability of Obscenity: An Historical Note' 8 (1961) *University of California Los Angeles Law Review* 44

Paul and Schwartz: 'Obscenity in the Mail: A Comment on some Problems of Federal Censorship' 106 (1957) *University of Pennsylvania Law Review* 214

Review: 'The System of Freedom of Expression' 46 (1971) *New York University Law Review* 429

Review: 'The First Amendment in Theory and Practice' 80 (1970) *Yale Law Journal* 1070

Reynolds: 'Our Misplaced Reliance on Early Obscenity Cases' 61 (1975) *American Bar Association Journal* 220

Richards, D.A.J.: 'Free Speech and Obscenity Law: Toward a Moral Theory of the First Amendment' 123 (1974) *University of Pennsylvania Law Review* 45

Schauer, F.: 'The Return of Variable Obscenity' 28 (1977) *Hastings Law Journal* 1275

Schauer, F.: 'Reflections on "Contemporary Community Standards": the Perpetuation of an Irrelevant Concept in the Law of Obscenity' 56 (1978) *North Carolina Law Review* 1

Schauer, F.: 'Hudgens v NLRB and the Problem of State Action in First Amendment Adjudication' 61 (1977) *Minnesota Law Review* 433

Schauer, F.: 'Response: Pornography and the First Amendment' 40 (1979) *University of Pittsburgh Law Review* 605

Schauer, F.: 'Speech and "Speech" — Obscenity and "Obscenity": An Exercise in the Interpretation of Constitutional Language' 67 (1979) *Georgetown Law Journal* 899

Schauer, F.: 'Fear, Risk and the First Amendment: Unravelling the "Chilling Effect" ' 58 (1978) *Boston University Law Review* 685

Schwartz and Paul: 'Foreign Communist Propaganda in the Mail: A Report on Some Problems of Federal Censorship' 107 (1959) *University of Pennsylvania Law Review* 621

Slough and McAnany: 'Obscenity and Constitutional Freedom' 8 (1964) *St. Louis University Law Journal* 279

Twomey, J.: 'The Citizens' Committee and Comic-Book Control: A Study of Extra-Governmental Restraint' 20 (1955) *Law and Contemporary Problems* 621

Zuckman: 'Obscenity in the Mail' 33 (1960) *Southern California Law Review* 480

Books

Bickel, A.M.: *The Least Dangerous Branch* (1962)
Boyer, P.S.: *The Vice Societies in the Nineteenth Century* (New York 1968)
Chafee, Z.: *Free Speech in the United States* (2nd Edn, 1941)
Clor, H. (Ed.): *Censorship and Freedom: Essays on Obscenity and the Law* (1971)
Clor, H.: *Obscenity and Public Morality: Censorship in a Liberal Society* (1969)
Craig, A.: *Suppressed Books, A History of the Conception of Literary Obscenity* (1963)
De Grazia: *Censorship Landmarks* (1969)
Emerson, T.J.: *The System of Freedom of Expression* (New York 1970)
Ernst, M. and Schwartz, A.U.: *Federal Censorship: The Search for the Obscene* (1964)
Ernst, M.L. and Seagle, W.L.: *To the Pure — A Study of Obscenity and the Censor* (1928)
Gellhorn: *Individual Freedom and Governmental Restraints* (1956)
Gerber, A.: *Sex, Pornography and Justice* (1965)
Haskins, G.L.: *Law and Authority in Early Massachusetts* (1960)
Kauper, P.G.: *Civil Liberties and the Constitution* (1962)
Kilpatrick, T.: *The Smut Peddlers* (1960)
Kuh, R.H.: *Foolish Figleaves* (New York 1967)
Lockhart, W., Kamisar, Y. and Choper, J.: *Cases and Materials on Constitutional Rights and Liberties* (3rd Edn, 1970)
Murphy, T.: *Censorship, Government and Obscenity* (Baltimore 1963)
Padover, S.K.: *The Complete Jefferson* (1943)

Paul, J. and Schwartz, M.: *Federal Censorship: Obscenity in the Mail* (1961)
Rembar, C.: *The End of Obscenity* (1969)
Rembar, C.: 'The Outrageously Immoral Fact' in *Censorship and Freedom of Expression: Essays on Obscenity and the Law* (1971)
Rollins and Perkins: *Criminal Law* (3rd Edn)
Rolph, C.: *Books in the Dock* (1969)
Schauer, F.F.: *The Law of Obscenity* (1976)
Schroeder, T.: *'Obscene' Literature and Constitutional Law* (1972)
Smith, J.H. and Barnes, T.G.: *The English Legal System: Carryover to the Colonies* (1975)
Tribe, D.: *Questions of Obscenity* (1973)

Comparative law and other material

Official Publications

Brody, S.: 'Screen Violence and Film Censorship, A Review of Research' *Home Office Research Unit* Research Study Number 40 (1977)
The Report of the Commission on Obscenity and Pornography (New York 1970)
Report of the Committee on Obscenity and Film Censorship (Cmnd 7772, 1979)

Articles

Barnett, W.: 'Corruption of Morals — The Underlying Issue of the Pornography Report' (1971) *Law and Social Order* 189
Davidson, R.P. and O'Boyle, M.: 'Obscenity Laws in England and the United States: A Comparative Analysis' 56 (1977) *Nebraska Law Review* 249
Frenkel, C.: 'The Moral Environment of the Law' 61 (1977) *Minnesota Law Review* 921
Hart, H.L.A.: 'Social Solidarity and The Enforcement of Morality' 35 (1967) *University of Chicago Law Review* 1
Hart, H.L.A.: 'Rawls on Liberty and its Priority' 40 (1973) *University of Chicago Law Review* 534
Hart, H.L.A.: 'Between Utility and Rights' 79 (1979) *Columbia Law Review* 828

Books

Blom-Cooper, L. and Drewry, G. (Eds.): *Law and Morality* (London 1976)

Comstock, G. and Fisher, M.: *Television and Human Behaviour: a Guide to Scientific Literature* (New York 1976)
Devlin, P.: *The Enforcement of Morals* (London 1965)
Dhavan, R. and Davies, C. (Eds.): *Censorship and Obscenity* (London 1978)
Dugard, J.: *Human Rights and the South African Legal Order* (Princeton 1978)
Eysenck, H.J.: *Sex, Violence and the Media* (London 1978)
Fawcett, J.E.S.: *The Application of the European Convention on Human Rights* (1975)
Fitzgerald, P.J.: *Criminal Law and Punishment* (London 1962)
Gellhorn, W.: *Individual Freedom and Governmental Restraint* (Baton Rouge 1956)
Glazebrook, P.R. (Ed.): *Reshaping the Criminal Law* (London 1978)
Hart, H.L.A.: *Law, Liberty and Morality* (Oxford 1963)
Kronhausen, E. and P.: *Pornography and the Law* (New York 1959)
McKeon, R., Merton, R.K., Gellhorn, W.: *The Freedom to Read* (New York 1957)
McQuoid-Mason, D.: *The Law of Privacy in South Africa* (Cape Town 1978)
Mitchell, B.: *Law, Morality and Religion in a Secular Society* (Oxford 1967)
Morawetz, T.: *The Philosophy of Law* (New York 1980)
Morris, N. and Howard, C.: *Studies in Criminal Law* (London 1964)
Pornography, The Longford Report (London 1972)
Spaeth, J.: *Supreme Court Policy Making: Explanation and Prediction* (San Francisco 1979)

Index

Advertising,
 children in, 224
Alberts, David and Violet,
 obscenity case concerning,
  373–4, 376
 US Supreme Court judgment on, 374–5
American Law Institute, 106
 Model Penal Code, 400
 view on obscenity, 379, 385
American Library Association,
 307
Anderton, James, 24
Annan Report on Broadcasting,
 300–1, 303
Attempt, 77
Attorney-General, 313, 314,
 315, 319

Bail Act 1976, 255
Besant, Annie, 8
Black, Mr Justice, 378, 399,
 406, 442, 474
Black, Sir Cyril, 321

Blackburn, Raymond, 227,
 258, 260, 285, 286, 301,
 321, 323
 attacks police procedure,
  317, 318
 film prosecutions, 277–8,
  283, 319
Blackman, Mr Justice, 442,
 484
Blackstone, W.,
 on freedom of press, 215
Bok, Mr Justice, 354, 359
Books, magazine, photographs,
 licensing of publications,
  262–6
 in NSW, 263–5
 in South Africa, 265–6
Books, magazines, photographs,
 prior restraints concerning,
  238–72
 administrative restraints,
  262–6
 arrest, 255–7
 declarations, 257–8

531

injunctions, 258—62
non-legal, 303
search and seizure,
 238—55, 437
US restraints, 435—6
zoning, 266—72
Bradlaugh, Charles, 8
Brandeis, Mr Justice, 476, 479, 480
on pornography and the mails, 230—1
Brennan, Mr Justice, 381, 385, 391, 395, 400, 403, 415, 418, 446, 456, 467, 486, 488
defines social value of article, 399
on children and adult material, 392
on *Fanny Hill*, 398—9
on literary or other merit of work, 397
on obscenity in Alberts' case, 374—5
on pandering in *Ginzburg* case, 387, 388—9
on *Roth* test and First Amendment, 456
Bridge, Lord Justice, 48, 61
on indecency in photographs, 222—3
on jury problem in obscenity case, 39—40
rules on indecency of imported book, 154
British Adult Publications Association, 310
guidelines of, 193—4
British Board of Film Censors, 274, 277, 278, 280, 284, 308, 321
categories of certificates, 281—2, 293
standards of, 281, 282

British Broadcasting Corporation, 155, 301
administrative regulation of, 298—9
consensus views reflected by, 299
personality of Director-General strong determinant of views of, 299—300
British Film Fund Levy, 309—10
grants for 'soft-porn' films, 310
British Youth Council, 143
Brody, Stephen,
on research into pornography, 500
Broadcasting and TV,
excluded from 1959 and 1964 Acts, 75, 78, 297
law reform and, 302—3
prior restraints on, 298—302
administrative regulation, 298—301
declarations, 301—2
injunctions, 302
US restraints, 436—7
subsequent restraints, 297—8
Burger, Chief Justice Warren, 165, 442, 446, 449, 484
on obscenity and the First Amendment, 445
Bush, Mr Justice,
on 'indecency' at film club, 63, 85
Butt, Ronald, 510, 512
Byrne, Mr Justice,
on question of literary merit, 33—4
quotes Lord Devlin, 49

Campbell, Lord Chief
    Justice, 5, 127, 167
Canadian Supreme Court, 56
Cane, Judge,
    on seditious libel, 101
Censorship,
    as including prior and subsequent restraint, 215—16
Chesser, Dr Eustace, 9—10
Children and Young Persons
    (Harmful Publications) Act
    1955, 129—32, 136, 173,
    217—18, 224, 236, 314
    defines harmful publications,
    130
Cinematograph Acts,
    1909 — 273, 275, 276, 280,
    286, 287, 288, 292
    1952 — 280, 284, 285, 287,
    292
    1977 Amendment — 287
Clark, Mr Justice, 387, 399, 408
Cockburn, Lord Chief Justice,
    21, 101, 147, 351
    his definition of obscenity
    analysed, 6—8
    on meaning of obscenity, 6
Coleridge, Mr Justice, 101
Common Informers Act 1951,
    86
Comstock Act of 1873, US,
    167, 230, 233, 347, 348,
    363, 364—5, 420, 421
    passing of, 347
Comstock, Anthony,
    as anti-vice campaigner,
    347, 348, 363—4
Conspiracy, 51—77
    attempt to conspire, 77
    prosecution and law reform,
    67—77
    some forms of, 66—7
    to corrupt public morals,
    52—9

compared with publishing
    obscene article, 57—9
definition of corruption,
    52—3
definition of public
    morals, 54—6
fluctuations in prosecution policy, 71—2
to outrage public decency,
    59—66, 148
    cases of, 60, 61—2
    defining indecency, 60,
        61, 62
    defining outrage, 65—6
    defining public, 64
    fluctuations in prosecution policy, 71—2
    penalties for, 66
Constitutional dimension,
    commitments to international law, 328—33
    freedom of speech, 325
    privacy, 325—6
    question of British Bill of
        Rights, 333—43
Court, Dr John, 497, 511, 518
    connects pornography with
    increase in sexual crime,
    508, 510, 512
Court of Appeal, 84, 85, 154,
    168, 218, 219, 222, 240,
    242, 275, 277, 286, 301,
    302, 317, 318, 332
    defines disorderly house, 83
    Last Tango in Paris judgment, 279—80
    on expert evidence and the
        law, 32
    on indecency, 60
    Practice Direction in
        conspiracy cases, 69
    upholds *Gay News* conviction, 95, 96
Criminal Law Acts,

533

1967 – 321
1977 – 71, 73, 77, 85, 283, 288, 289, 297, 314
  method of dealing with conspiracy, 76–7
Criminal Law Revision Committee, 269
Criminal libel, 102
Cross, Lord, of Cheltenham, 24
  on depravity and corruption, 22
Curl, Edmund, 2
Customs and Excise Management Act 1979, 152–7, 331, 332
  Customs embarrassments under, 155
  prior restraint on pornography under, 236–8
  search and seizure under, 252–3
Customs Consolidation Act 1876, 152, 331
  applicability to films, 280
Cutler, Sir Horace,
  threat to remove GLC grant to National Theatre, 308–9

Denmark,
  acceptance of pornography in, 516
  analysis of sexual crime and pornography in, 510–11, 512
Denning, Lord, MR, 45, 46, 277, 286, 301
  on blasphemy, 95
  on indecency, 61
  on seizure of property, 241–2
Devlin, Lord,
  belief in positive morality, 106, 110–11, 112, 114, 117, 120, 121, 517
  on freedom, 122
  on morality and pornography, 515–16
  on self-expression and morality, 49
Dicey, Prof. A.V., 97, 214
Dilhorne, Lord, 45, 103
  on insulting behaviour, 92
Diplock, Lord, 56–7, 98
Director of Public Prosecutions, 313–14, 315, 316, 318, 319, 323
  grading of obscene publications, 324
  uncertain about obscenity law, 321
Dishonesty, 96
Disorderly Houses Act 1781, 85–86
Displays, 179–201
Douglas, Mr Justice, 378, 393, 406, 407, 408, 474
  comment on pandering concept, 389
  disquiet at mail blocks, 421
  on free speech and its exercise, 474
Dworkin, Prof. R., 470
  on basic liberties, 124, 125

Eastman Kodak,
  problem of pornography with slides, 25–6
Emerson, Prof. T., 465
Ernst, Morris and Seagal, William, 3
European Communities Act 1972, 331, 332
European Convention on Human Rights and Fundamental Freedoms, 121, 328–30, 333
  on freedom of expression, 328
European Court of Human

Rights, 328–9
appeals in obscenity cases to, 329
on national laws on obscenity, 329
rules on conflict between British Customs and Treaty of Rome on obscene importations, 332–3
Eysenck, Dr H.J., 498
and Nias, D.K.B., 500, 501

Fanny Hill, John Cleland's, 4, 251
considered by US Supreme Court, 398–9
Federal Anti-Pandering Act, 151
Federal Communications Commission,
licensing power, 436
Films, 272–96
children in, 224
early safety legislation, 273
First Amendment protection for, 416, 426
first censorship, 273
historical background, 272–80
prior restraint 272–4
subsequent restraints, 274–80
law covering indecency with children, 78
law reform, 289–96
local authority censorship, 274, 282–5
prior restraint currently applicable, 281–7
prosecutions for obscenity, 71, 73, 85, 394
protection of children, 225–7
question of protection of adults, 227–30
search and seizure provisions, 287
in USA, 427, 437, 438, 439
self-censorship by industry, 274, 278
subsequent restraints currently applicable, 287–9
US censorship, 424–32
boards of, 431
declaratory judgments, 431–2
licensing, 425–7
use of injunctions against, 286
in USA, 427–8
zoning and, 286–7, 294
in USA, 428–31
Foot, Sir Dingle, 155
Fortas, Mr Justice, 387, 398, 441, 442
Frankfurter, Mr Justice, 259, 415, 427
on expert evidence in obscenity cases, 404, 454
on Michigan obscenity law, 372
Fuller, Prof. L.,
on link between law and morality, 98

Gallup Poll,
on acceptance of pornography in Denmark, 516
Gallwey, Dr, 135, 498
Gardiner, Lord, 224
Gay News, 95
Ginsberg, Sam, 392
points raised by case of, 392–5, 407, 408, 446–7, 485

535

Ginzburg, Ralph, 386, 387
  points rising from obscenity
    case, 387, 388–9, 397,
    402
Goddard, Lord, 248
Goldberg, Mr Justice, 399
Greater London Council, 212,
    227
  film censorship role, 278,
    283, 285–6
Greene, Sir Hugh, 299
Greenwood, Dr Edward D.,
    499

Hall, Radclyffe,
  Well of Loneliness, The, 9
Hall, Sir Peter, 309
Hand, Judge Learned, 386, 457
  on changing community
    standards, 396, 457–8
  on obscenity rules, 367–8,
    369
Harlan, Mr Justice, 375, 389,
    393, 401, 403, 409, 442,
    458
  dissent in *Roth* case, 375–6,
    378, 385
  on patent offensiveness, 400,
    403
  on role of US Supreme Court
    in obscenity cases, 405–6
Hart, Prof. H.L.A.,
  view of law and morality,
    106, 107, 109, 110, 111,
    114, 115, 118, 119, 121,
    123, 124, 126
Henkin, Prof. L., 293, 479
Holmes, Mr Justice, 327, 476,
    479, 480
Home Office Working Party on
  Vagrancy and Street
  Offences, 74, 78, 140
Horror comics, 130
House of Lords, 32, 45, 51, 90,
    92, 241, 331
  differentiates between
    publication and con-
    spiracy to publish, 51–2
  on blasphemous libel, 101
  on conspiracy to outrage
    public decency, 65
  on courts as *custos morum*,
    326, 327
  ruling on depravity and
    corruption, 21
  ruling on *res iudicata*, 44
  upholds *Gay News* con-
    viction, 95
Howitt, D. and Cumberbatch,
  G., 500

Incitement, 77
Indecent Displays (Control)
  Act 1981, 78, 143, 148,
    204, 238, 239, 254, 298,
    319
  Acts replaced by, 179
  cinema clubs and, 288
  power of arrest under,
    256–7
  provisions of, 180–1
  replaces 'obscene' by
    'indecent', 179–80, 181,
    182
  seizure under, 239, 244–5
Indecency,
  Parliamentary difficulty in
    defining, 191–2
  problem of standards, 190,
    192–4
  public opinion poll on,
    190–1, 195
  question of expert evidence
    and, 196–7
Indecency with Children Act
  1960, 218
  loopholes, 218
Independent Broadcasting

Authority Act 1973, 300
Independent Broadcasting
  Authority (IBA),
  duty of censorship, 300, 301
Inside Linda Lovelace case,
  30–1, 37, 156, 320
Inskip, Sir Thomas, 9
Insulting behaviour, 90, 92, 93
International Agreement for
  the Suppression of Obscene
  Publications, 330
International Convention for
  the Suppression of the
  Circulation and Traffic in
  Obscene Publications, 8–9,
  330–1, 332
International Covenant on Civil
  and Political Rights, 330

James Committee on Distribution of Criminal Business,
  147
Jefferson, Pres. Thomas,
  on liberty of press, 475
Jenkins, Roy, 102
Joint Committee on Theatre
  Censorship, 202
  recommendations, 202–4
Joyce, James,
  Ulysses case, 9, 368, 374,
  390
Judicial Proceedings (Regulation of Reports) Act 1926,
  157–9, 314
  positive morality provision
    in, 174
  protection of privacy under,
    167
Jury,
  admissibility of expert
    evidence to help, 34–5,
    339, 404–5, 453–4
  discretion in obscenity cases,
    US, 405–6, 454–5
  in obscenity cases, 34–45,
    48, 339–41, 404–9,
    453–5
  questions to be answered by,
    89–94

Kalven, Prof. H., 406, 469
Kilbrandon, Lord, 92
Kinsey, Dr Alfred, 390
Kutchinsky, Dr Berl,
  on relation of sexual crime
  and pornography in
  Denmark, 510–11

Lambard, William, 263
Lane, Lord, 46
Last Tango in Paris case,
  279–80, 319
Law Commission, 78, 82, 88,
  218
  definition of ballet, 205
  on film shows at home, 289
  on theatrical performances
    at home, 165, 207, 268
  recommendations con-
    cerning live shows,
    207–8
  recommendations on film
    shows and obscenity, 82,
    83
  report on conspiracy and
    law reform, 218, 219
  reviews conspiracy offences,
    72–3, 74, 75, 76
Law enforcement, 313–24
  by individuals, 318–19
  by police, 315–18
    discretion of, 316–17
    procedures, 315–16
  law officers, 313–15
    statutes authorising,
      314–15
  practice, policy and censor-
    ship, 319–24

Lawrence, D.H.,
  Lady Chatterley's Lover
    cases, 16, 17, 62, 358
    416–17
Lawton, Lord Justice, 15
Lindsay, John,
  victim of double jeopardy,
    46–7
Lipton, Dr Morris A., 499
Live shows, 201–12, 296–7
  censorship, 201–2
  constitutionality of US
    restrictions, 490
  licensing, 296–7
  prior restraint in USA,
    432–5
  zoning, 297
Lockhart, W. and McClure, R.,
    392, 394, 395
  advocate proscription of
    hard-core pornography,
    406–7, 446
  on concept of pandering,
    387–8
  on distribution of
    pornography, 391, 407
Lord Chamberlain,
  censorship of theatre, 201,
    202
  rules for stage dress, 201

MacCormack, Prof. D.N., 160,
    162
McWhirter, Ross, 300
Magazines, *see* Books, maga-
  zines, photographs
Market and Opinion Research
  International (MORI),
  poll showing general
    acceptance of
    pornography, 517
Marshall, Mr Justice, 408, 456,
    459, 486, 488
  on freedom of speech and
    privacy, 163–4, 166
  on obscene matter in
    private possession,
    383–4
Maryland State Board of
  Censors,
  procedures ruled uncon-
    stitutional, 418–19
Massachusetts, 346
  development of obscenity
    laws, 345, 350
  obscenity rulings in, 351,
    359, 361, 384
Megarry, Sir Robert
  condemns courts acting as
    legislators, 327
Meiklejohn, Dr Alexander,
  democratic theory model,
    468–9, 470, 471, 472,
    475
Metropolitan Police, 241, 315,
    320, 508
  'disclaimer' procedure,
    246–7
  on question of bail, 256
  question of corruption in,
    322–3
Mill, John Stuart, 468, 470,
    475
  on importance of freedom,
    121
  On Liberty, 107
  on paternalism, 109
  view on rightful exercise of
    power, 107–8, 121, 164
Miller test of obscenity, 485
  applicability, 443–5
    forms of speech, 445
    intention, 443–5
    publication/possession,
      445
  critical point of com-
    promise, 455–61
  jury decision, 453–5

expert evidence and,
    453–4
  jury discretion, 454–5
  standard applicable, 445–53
    effect, 445–6
    nature of material,
      449–53
Missouri,
  prior restraint in, 418
Morality,
  conflict with legality, 97
  enforcement by law,
    105–26
    positions for and against,
      106–7, 113, 117–18
    question of inability to
      enforce, 113
    question of paternalism
      or harm prevention,
      107–9, 110, 119, 120,
      123, 124, 513–14
  freedom and, 107, 121, 122,
    123
  moral codes and circum-
    stances, 115–16
  moral pluralism, 113, 115,
    116, 119, 123
  offences against in law,
    89–100
  positive, 109, 110, 112, 113,
    118–21 passim, 189, 493
  and privacy, 160–1, 162
  public, 119, 120, 121
  rights and restrictions, 124–6
  theory of society's need for,
    111–13
Morris, Lord, 46, 92, 98
  on corruption, 54
Motion Picture Association of
  America, 289, 306
Motion pictures, see Films

National Theatre, 308, 309
National Viewers' and
  Listeners' Association, 299
National Vigilance Association,
  8
Nationwide Festival of Light,
  15
  action against *Last Tango
    in Paris*, 279–80
New England Watch and Ward
  Society, 347
New York Board of Regents,
  416
New York Society for the
  Suppression of Vice, 347
New York state, 349, 359
  court ruling on obscenity,
    356–7
  introduces *Hicklin* test, 348
  obscenity statutes, 357, 393
Nixon, Pres. Richard M., 114
Nozick, Robert,
  on promotion of basic
    rights, 124, 125

Obscene Publications Act
  1857, 5, 127, 167, 246,
  250
Obscene Publications Acts
  1959 and 1964, 11, 51, 52,
  53, 57, 66, 69, 99, 127,
  129, 131, 132, 142, 146,
  147, 149, 150, 152, 155,
  165, 203, 208, 276, 297,
  301, 314, 315, 317, 319,
  329, 335, 368, 369, 510
  amended by Criminal Law
    Act 1977, 71, 73
  amendment of, 1964, 14
  application of, 14–17
    publication/possession,
      14–16, 275
    question of intention,
      16–17
  attempts to supersede
    common law, 51, 78

539

compared with Theatres
  Act 1968, 205–7
concern with children, 217
defines obscene article, 13,
  14, 274–5
disposition of seized
  articles under, 246
forfeiture proceedings under,
  247–51
incitement under, 77
jury and cases under, 34–45,
  48
  double jeopardy, 44–7
  expert evidence
    admissible, 34–5
  jury challenges, 36–8
  process of decision,
    38–44
loopholes in, 70, 71, 73–4
patchy enforcement, 319–21
rationale of offence under,
  47–50
relation to films, 275–6,
  277–80 *passim*, 283, 285,
  288
search and seizure under,
  238–9, 240–3, 251–2,
  287
standard applied, 17–34
  effect, 17–28
  nature of the work, 28–34
TV and broadcasting excluded
  from, 75
Obscene Publications Bill 1580,
  262–3
Obscenity,
  concept of patent offensive-
    ness, 23–4, 42, 105,
    188–9, 393–4, 399–404,
    405, 451–3, 454–5, 464,
    473, 487–90
  emergence of concept in
    English law, 1–12
  early prosecutions, 2–3

Hicklin test, 5–12, 17,
  24, 39, 129
nineteenth- and
  twentieth-century
  prosecutions, 8–12
obscene libel, 3, 51, 52,
  67, 68, 129
extended to cover drug-
  taking, 1964, 29
pandering concept, 387–90
protection of children from,
  see Pornography
publication/distribution of,
  14–16, 145–78, 382–5,
  390–6
  author's intentions in
    respect of, 380–3
  demarcation in shops,
    198–9, 200–1
  depraving and corrupting
    by, 17–23, 40, 47,
    91–2
  written word and, 197
  form of prosecution of,
    321–4
  literary or other merit
    and, 30–4, 397–9,
    449–51
expert evidence and, 34–5
strict liability and,
  100–4
work as a whole, 29–30,
  396–7, 449
zoning and, 199, 200,
  268, 270, 271
society and, 514–19
  polls expressing accept-
    ance of, 516–17
  question of morality and
    pornography, 514–16
  sales of sexually explicit
    material, 516
vulgar language, 80
Opinion Research Centre, 516

Parker, Lord Chief Justice, 19, 146
  on expert evidence, 35
  on forfeiture proceedings, 249
  on indecency, 60
  on inherent obscenity, 25
Payne, Mrs Cynthia, disorderly house case, 84–5
Pearson, Lord, 41
Pennsylvania, 346, 359
  court ruling on state regulation on obscenity, 354
Philadelphia
  obscenity prosecution, 1815, 346
Photographs, see Books, magazines, photographs
Pornography
  change of standards regarding, 39, 40–1
  constitutionality of US restrictions on production, 490–1
  defined, 40
  exposure of children to, 132–3
  hard-core, US, 401–2
  Geneva Convention for suppression of Traffic in, 8–9, 330–1, 332
  import control of material, 5, 73–4. See also Customs Acts 1876 and 1979
  law and distribution of, 24–8
  protection of children from, 28, 136–42, 143–4, 186, 211, 217–27, 392, 485–7
  question of harms to individuals, 496–512, 517, 518
  analysis of crime statistics, 505–13
  anecdotal evidence, 497–8
  research studies into, 498–505
  video cassettes and, 14–15
  See also Films and various Acts
Post Office Act 1953, 145–9, 150, 154, 156, 179, 223, 319, 329
  indecency under, 62, 148
  prior restraint role of, 230–3
  prohibits obscene matter on packets, 171
  protection of Post Office staff under, 167–8
  provisions, 145–6, 167–8, 230, 231
  question of justifiability of Post Office powers, 234
  reasons for restriction on indecency, 168–9
  relation to films, 280
Post Office (Protection) Act 1884, 167
Postal Statute 1865, US, 420
Powell, Mr Justice, 187, 429, 442, 446, 487, 491
  approach to zoning, 433–4, 481, 483
Prior restraint, 213–17, 411–19
  censorship as, 215–16
  constitutionality of US, 491–2
  Customs control, 236–8. See also Customs Acts 1976 and 1979 and United States Customs
  licensing, 411
  non-legal, 303–10
  on books, magazines and photographs, 238–72,

541

435–6
  on films, 272–96, 424–32.
    See also Films
  on live shows, 296–7,
    432–5
  on production, 217–30
  on TV and sound broad-
    casting, 297–303, 436–7.
    See also Broadcasting and
    TV
  Post Office regulation,
    230–6, 419–23. *See also*
    Post Office Act 1953 and
    United States Post Office
    Department
  seizures for evidentiary
    purposes and, 235,
    310–11
  US procedural problems not
    involving, 437–40
Privacy, 159–66, 518
  defined, 160
  importance of, 159
  invasion of, 162
  inviolability of property
    and, 325–6
  positive morality and,
    160–1, 162
  possession of obscene
    materials and, 163–4,
    165, 166
  question of controls to
    protect, 161, 162, 163
  rules and Acts protecting,
    167
  unsolicited mail and, 151–2,
    163, 171
Prosecution of Offenders Regulations
  1946 – 315–16
  1978 – 316
Prosser, W.L., 160
Prostitution,
  and obscenity, 18
  control of prostitutes'
    advertisements, 75
  nuisance remedies, 271
  zoning of, 268–9, 270
Protection of Children Act
  1978, 74, 132, 136, 177,
  227, 289, 314, 315
  provisions concerning
    indecent photographs,
    219–24
  search and seizure under,
    252
Protestant Electoral Union, 5
Public Order Act 1936, 90,
  102, 103
  definition of public place,
    203

Race Relations Act 1965,
  102, 120
Rawlinson, Sir Peter, 70
Rehnquist, Mr Justice, 414,
  442, 452, 484
  on jury discretion, 455
Reid, Lord, 70
  defines limits of speech, 93
  on corruption, 53, 54, 56
  on indecency, 60
  on insulting behaviour, 90,
    92
Rival assemblies, 103–4
Roskill, Lord Justice, 317
Roth, Samuel, 373
Roth test of obscenity, 23, 33,
  41, 105, 134, 142, 195,
  338, 341, 342, 380–409,
  443, 456, 463–73
  applicability, 380–5
    forms of speech, 380
    intention, 380–1, 404
    publication/possession,
      382–5
  jury decision, 404–9
  expert evidence, 404–5

jury discretion, 405–9
standard applied, 385–404
  effect, 385–96
  nature of material, 396–404
dissenting approach in Supreme Court, 375–7
majority approach in Supreme Court, 377–9
New York case previous to appeal, 373
Royal Commission on Press, 324
Royal Shakespeare Company, attack on censorship, 201

Salmon, Lord Justice, 19, 24
  on freedom of press, 214–15
  on jury's duty in obscenity case, 38–9
Salvation Army, 104
Sankey, Mr Justice, 274
Scarman, Lord,
  on 'legitimate reason' defence against indecency, 221–2, 223
Schauer, F., 458, 467
Sedition, 94–5
Seditious libel, 101
Sedley, Sir Charles, 2
Segal, Dr Hanna, 135
Select Committee on Obscene Publications, 322
Sex shops,
  injunction against, 261–2
  nuisance remedies, 262, 271
  zoning of, 268, 270, 271
Shackleton, Edward, 279, 319
Simon, Lord, of Glaisdale, 53, 54
  on conspiracy to outrage public decency, 59–60, 64, 65
  on morality and law, 98–9

Simonds, Viscount,
  on conspiracy to corrupt public morals, 68–9
  on incitement to homosexuality, 68
  on law-making authority of courts, 327
Society of Authors, 11, 129
Society for the Suppression of Vice, 4–6, 8
South Africa,
  licensing of books and entertainment, 265–6
Speech,
  distinction between speech and conduct, 78–80, 209–10, 211, 434–5, 465–6
Stable, Mr Justice,
  application of *Hicklin* test, 1974, 10–11
Stephen, James Fitzjames, 107
Stevens, Mr Justice, 483, 484
  on pandering doctrine, 444–5
Stewart, Mr Justice, 389, 394, 395, 402, 446
  on patent offensiveness, 402
Street Offences Act 1959, 184
Substantive common law offences, 77–88
  blasphemous libel, 87–8, 95–6, 101
    Gay News case, 95
  corruption of public morals, 83, 91
    question of strict liability, 100–5
  indecent exposure, 78, 80
  keeping disorderly house, 81, 82, 83–6
    disorderly house defined, 83, 84
  mounting indecent

exhibition, 81, 82, 86–7
outraging public decency, 83
Sunday Observance Act 1780, 86
Sunday Times,
poll to define indecency, 190–1, 195
polls on acceptance of pornography, 516

Theatres Act 1843, 201, 202, 204
Theatres Act 1968, 69, 81, 82, 99, 176, 177, 201–7, 289, 314
defines stage 'plays', 204–5
distinctions from Obscene Publications Act 1959, 205–7, 208
loopholes in, 73, 74–5
obscenity sole control under, 204
Theatres, *see* Live shows
Theft Act 1968, 96
Times, The, 37, 510
on 'expert' evidence, 31
on Williams Committee, 502–3
Trades Descriptions Act 1968, 172, 225
Treaty of Rome, 331–3
legislative conflict with British Customs on import of obscene material, 331–3
Trevelyan, John, 308

United Kingdom,
basis of government, 214
fundamentals of constitution, 326
private censorship in, 307–10
effect of Bill of Rights in, 333–43
free speech in, 213, 262
United Nations Organisation, human rights conventions, 330
United States Commission on Obscenity and Pornography, 114, 497, 503, 510
some conclusions of, 132–3, 516
studies undertaken by, 498–9, 504–5, 513
United States Constitution,
First Amendment, 303–4
and prior restraint, 216, 217, 412
limitations imposed by, 304–6, 307, 310
question of obscenity and, 11, 42, 43, 78, 82, 109, 126, 134, 136, 145, 149, 151, 157, 164, 175, 185–8 *passim*, 200, 210, 212, 227, 254, 289, 302–3, 334–5, 336, 338, 355, 356, 357, 361, 369, 372–9 *passim*, 383, 390, 393, 394, 395, 404, 407, 408, 429, 431–8 *passim*, 444, 447, 450, 456–61 *passim*, 463–92, 494, 495
Fourth Amendment,
and obscenity, 437, 439, 440
Fifth Amendment, 233, 420
Ninth Amendment, 373
Tenth Amendment, 373
Fourteenth Amendment, 352, 355, 356, 372, 376, 379, 438, 443, 473, 474,

479, 481
United States Customs,
423–4
  controls on import of
    pornography, 157,
    236–7
United States of America,
  approach to displays, 187–8
  average person approach to
    obscenity, 28, 36, 134,
    194–5
  constitutionality of obscenity
    restrictions, 482–92
    live shows, 490
    offensiveness, 487–90
    prior restraint, 491–2
    production of pornography,
      490–1
    protection of children,
      485–7
  courts' approach to
    pornography by mail,
    233–4
  evidence in assessing obscenity,
    196
  federal obscenity controls,
    362–70
    court decisions, 366–70
    with regard to mails,
      362–5
  freedom of speech in, 213
  film censorship, 289, 306–7.
    See also Films
  Hicklin test in, 348,
    349–52, 358, 359, 366,
    374
  indecency cases, 62, 131
  jury challenges, 36
  library censorship, 307
  obscenity as exception to
    First Amendment, 11,
    335, 341–2, 343, 353,
    355, 366, 398, 413, 445
  privacy in, 161, 163, 172
  some approaches to
    obscenity restriction,
    473–82
  state obscenity controls,
    345–62
    constitutionality,
      352–62
    developments in,
      358–61
    effect of Civil War, 347
    Hicklin test and, 350–2
  test of obscenity, 336–41
    passim
  thrust of law on obscenity,
    494
  use of injunctions in, 261
United States Post Office
  Department,
  prior restraints operated by,
    419–23
    addressee permitted to
      refuse mail, 422–3
    censorship of mail,
      421–2
    mail block, 421–2
    refusal of second class
      mailing privileges, 422
United States Supreme Court,
    11, 56, 99, 109, 118,
    131, 142, 143, 145, 187,
    188, 194, 195, 200, 216,
    227, 233, 253, 259, 341,
    355, 356, 361, 366, 368,
    369, 424, 496
  cases concerning prior con-
    straint, 412–19
  clear and present danger
    test and free speech,
    475–81
  difficulties with obscenity
    cases, 26–7, 41, 42,
    133–4, 406–9
  lists obscene acts, 193
  move towards proscription

545

    of hard-core pornography, 406
obscenity definition, 445
obscenity test, 441–3
    on broadcasting restrictions, 302–3, 436–7
    on disposition of seized articles, 245–6
    on line between speech and conduct, 78–9, 80, 209, 210, 434–5
    on privacy, 161, 163, 166
    on zoning, 272, 428–31, 460
    position on book censorship, 309
    position on book obscenity, 197–8, 435
    position on seizure of obscene articles, 239–40, 243–4, 287, 437, 438–9
    position on unsolicited mail, 151–2, 235
    question of policy-making in obscenity area, 494–5
    restraint in obscenity area, 326–7
    rulings on live shows, 432–5
    rulings on Post Office restraints, 421, 422–3
    views on film censorship, 293, 294
    See also *Miller* test and *Roth* test
Universal Declaration of Human Rights, 330
Universal Postal Convention 1974, 170, 331, 332
Unsolicited Goods and Services Act 1971, 149–52, 163, 314, 319
    coverage, 150

Vermont,
    first state obscenity law, 346

Warren, Chief Justice, 17, 41, 387, 398, 441
    on intention in *Roth* case, 380, 387
White, Mr Justice, 387, 399, 414
Whitehouse, Mrs Mary, 299, 504, 511, 512
Wilberforce, Lord, 34, 48
    on freedom of press, 214
    on injunctions, 259
Wilkes, John, 4
Williams Committee, 49, 76, 78, 123, 132, 157, 190, 191, 192, 207, 208, 232, 251, 253, 263, 264, 320, 323, 471, 495, 496
    analysis of crime statistics on pornography, 505–13
    anecdotal evidence on pornography, 497–8
    endorsement of Customs control on pornography, 237
    findings on pornography, 134–5, 467
    on blasphemy, 87–8
    on control of films and pictures, 174–8, 197, 272, 282, 290, 291–2, 294, 295–6
    on distinction between speech and conduct, 79, 465–6
    on Judicial Proceedings (Regulation of Reports) Act, 174
    on jury challenges, 36–7
    on obscenity law, 23, 43, 48

on offensiveness of pornography, 182–5
on power of arrest, 256
on search and seizure, 254, 255
on setting standards of indecency, 192–3, 194, 198
on sex shops, 271
opposed to private prosecutions, 321–2
recommendations on mailing of indecent material, 169–71, 234, 235
recommendations on pornography and children, 136–42, 143–4, 186
recommendations on obscenity, 82, 83
recommended restriction on unsolicited mail, 171–2
rejects pornography as stimulus to sexual crime, 508
research studies consulted, 498–505
view of live shows, 209, 210, 211, 433
Williams, Dr Hyatt, 498
Williams, Prof. Bernard, 512
Williams, Prof. Glanville, classification of jury questions, 89–90
defines civil 'liberty', 213
Wireless Telegraphy Act 1949, 298
Wistrich, Mrs Enid, 278
Wolfenden Report on homosexuality and prostitution, 18, 68, 184, 200
recommends de-criminalisation, 105–6
Woolsey, Judge, 390

Yaffe, Maurice, 499, 505
Younger Committee on Privacy,
on advertisements for indecent material, 172–3
on unsolicited circulars, 151, 163